HAGGAI, ZECHARIAH 1-8

VOLUME 25B

THE ANCHOR BIBLE is a fresh approach to the world's greatest classic. Its object is to make the Bible accessible to the modern reader; its method is to arrive at the meaning of biblical literature through exact translation and extended exposition, and to reconstruct the ancient setting of the biblical story, as well as the circumstances of its transcription and the characteristics of its transcribers.

THE ANCHOR BIBLE is a project of international and interfaith scope. Protestant, Catholic, and Jewish scholars from many countries contribute individual volumes. The project is not sponsored by any ecclesiastical organization and is not intended to reflect any particular theological doctrine. Prepared under our joint supervision, THE ANCHOR BIBLE is an effort to make available all the significant historical and linguistic knowledge which bears on the interpretation of the biblical record.

THE ANCHOR BIBLE is aimed at the general reader with no special formal training in biblical studies; yet, it is written with the most exacting standards of scholarship, reflecting the highest technical accomplishment.

This project marks the beginning of a new era of cooperation among scholars in biblical research, thus forming a common body of knowledge to be shared by all.

William Foxwell Albright
David Noel Freedman
GENERAL EDITORS

THE ANCHOR BIBLE

HAGGAI, ZECHARIAH
1-8

A New Translation with Introduction
and Commentary

by

CAROL L. MEYERS

and

ERIC M. MEYERS

DOUBLEDAY & COMPANY, INC.
GARDEN CITY, NEW YORK
1987

Maps by Rafael Palacios

Library of Congress Cataloging-in-Publication Data
Bible. O.T. Haggai. English. Meyers. 1987.
Haggai; Zechariah 1–8.
(The Anchor Bible; v. 25B)
Bibliography: p. lxxi
Includes index.
1. Bible. O.T. Haggai—Commentaries. 2. Bible.
O.T. Zechariah I–VIII—Commentaries. I. Meyers,
Carol L. II. Meyers, Eric M. III. Bible. O.T.
Zechariah I–VIII. English. Meyers. 1987. IV. Title.
V. Title: Zechariah 1–8. VI. Series: Bible. English.
Anchor Bible. 1964; v. 25B.
BS192.2.A1   1964   .G3 vol. 25B   220.7'7 s   85-20924
[BS1663]   [224'.97077]
ISBN 0-385-14482-2

For Julie and Dina.
For five years
they have lived with
two parents and two prophets.

PREFACE

This work originally began as a commentary on Haggai, all of Zechariah, and Malachi. As our work progressed it became clear that a single volume dealing with those three biblical books was not feasible. Our work on the late sixth-century prophetic books, Haggai and the first eight chapters of Zechariah, had become far more lengthy than in our original conception. The related treatment of Zechariah 9–14 and Malachi will appear in a subsequent volume, and it is our present contention that those two works emanate from the latter part of the first half of the fifth century. So it is both practical considerations and those regarding the social and historical setting that have ultimately led us and the editor to the decision to separate three canonical books into two separate volumes of this Anchor Bible series.

Many people have assisted in the enormously complex task of preparing this manuscript, and many have helped us set aside time in which to do it. The bulk of this manuscript was prepared while the authors were on leave from Duke at Oxford University, where both were fellows of the Oxford Centre for Post-Graduate Hebrew Studies, with associations also at Wolfson College. We would especially like to thank Professor David Patterson, President of the Oxford Centre, for his gracious assistance at every level and for our very fine accommodation in Noel Cottage at Yarnton Manor. To colleagues at the Oxford Old Testament Seminar, Professors James Barr, Ernest Nicholson, Rex Mason, and others, we are especially grateful for warm colleagueship. At Duke our chairman, Professor Kalman P. Bland, has been unfailingly helpful in so many matters both personal and professional.

Mrs. C. McPherson of Yarnton typed virtually the entire first draft of this manuscript. The chore of converting the long European pages to American-size paper with many editorial revisions fell to Gay Trotter, secretary of the Graduate Program in Religion at Duke. She has been helpful, patient, and good-natured throughout this endeavor. Karen Hoglund, above and beyond her duties as assistant editor of *Biblical Archaeologist,* converted all of this to word processor for final submission. She has been a constant source of technical advice and support. Among many graduate students who merit mention and a word of appreciation for their efforts as research assistants are Ken Hoglund, Ben Shaw, Tony Cartledge, and Gary Anderson. All of them are preparing for careers in Old Testament research, and we wish them every success.

At Doubleday, Eve Roshevsky was a continuing voice of encouragement and assistance, and Theresa D'Orsogna has been extremely helpful throughout the production process. But there can be no editor for a biblical commentary like David Noel Freedman. This book is more than a statement of our research on two books of the Bible; it is also the product of a scholarly dialogue that has enriched our professional lives in the most fruitful way imaginable. At first his comments came, ream after ream, and we felt overwhelmed; then they came and we were exhilarated. For us, the greatest joy of the Anchor Bible has been to work with Freedman the editor. Any shortcomings of this work, however, are the sole responsibility of the authors.

Finally, scholarship involves families; and our daughters, Julie and Dina, have been hearing about Haggai or Zechariah over breakfast or dinner too many years now. For their good humor, support, and understanding we dedicate this book to them as they enter the years of their life when scholarship and study of Hebrew Scripture will, we hope, mean more and more.

CAROL L. MEYERS

ERIC M. MEYERS

Thanksgiving 1984
Duke University
Durham, North Carolina

CONTENTS

Preface   IX
List of Illustrations   XV
Abbreviations and Signs   XVII
Glossary of Terms   XXI
Note on the Translation   XXV

INTRODUCTION   XXVII

THE HISTORICAL CONTEXT   XXIX
    Persian Imperial Policy   XXIX
    The Edict of Cyrus and the Two Returns   XXXI
    The Restoration in Yehud   XXXVII

PROPHETIC RESPONSE   XL

LITERARY CONSIDERATIONS   XLIV
    The Structure of the Composite Work   XLIV
    Haggai   XLVIII
    First Zechariah   L
        Part One (1:1–6)   LII
        Part Two (1:7–6:15)   LIII
        Part Three (7:1–8:23)   LX
    Form: Prose or Poetry   LXIII

TEXT   LXVII
    Haggai   LXVII
    Zechariah 1–8   LXVIII

RECENT STUDY OF HAGGAI AND ZECHARIAH 1–8   LXVIII
  Haggai   LXVIII
  Zechariah 1–8   LXX

BIBLIOGRAPHY   LXXIII

THE BOOK OF HAGGAI   1

  1. Restoration of the Temple (1:1–15)   3
  2. Oracles of Encouragement (2:1–23)   47

THE BOOK OF FIRST ZECHARIAH   85

Part One. Zech 1:1–6. Oracular Introduction   87
  1. Call for Obedience with Retrospection (Zech 1:1–6)   89
Part Two. Zech 1:7–6:15. The Visions with Oracular
          Supplements   105
  2. First Vision: Horses Patrolling the Earth (1:7–17)   107
  3. Second Vision: The Four Horns and the Four
     Smiths (2:1–4; RSV 1:18–21)   135
  4. Third Vision: The Man with the Measuring-Cord
     (2:5–9; RSV 2:1–5)   149
  5. Expansion on the Themes of the First Three
     Visions (2:10–17; RSV 2:6–13)   161
  6. Joshua and the Priestly Vestments: A Prophetic
     Vision (3:1–10)   178
  7. Fourth Vision: The Lampstand and the Two Olive
     Trees (4:1–6a, 6b–10a insert, 10b–14)   227
  8. Fifth Vision: The Flying Scroll (5:1–4)   277
  9. Sixth Vision: The Ephah (5:5–11)   293
  10. Seventh Vision: The Four Chariots (6:1–8)   316
  11. The Crowning (6:9–15)   336
Part Three. Zech 7–8. Address to the Delegation from Bethel,
            and Concluding Oracles   377
  12. Introduction (7:1–6)   379

13. Address to the Delegation from Bethel: Further
    Retrospection on Divine Justice (7:7–14)   395
14. Zion and Judah Restored: Seven Oracles (8:1–17)   408
15. Judah and the Nations: Three Oracles (8:18–23)   432

Indexes   447

LIST OF ILLUSTRATIONS

MAPS

1. Map of Satrapy of Beyond the River (Eber Nahara), *page* XXXIII.
2. Map of Satrapy of Libya-Egypt, *page* XXXV.
3. Map of Yehud and other Persian provinces in the Satrapy of Beyond the River, *page* XXXVI.

CHARTS

1. Chronological data relevant to Haggai-Zechariah 1–8, *page* XXXI.
2. Chronological data in Haggai-Zechariah 1–8, *page* XLVI.
3. Correspondences between Haggai and First Zechariah Part III (7–8), *page* XLIX.
4. Location of prophetic "genres" in First Zechariah, *page* LI.
5. Correspondences between First Zechariah Parts I (1:1–6) and III (7–8), *page* LII.
6. Correspondences between First Zechariah Parts II (1:7–6:15) and III (7–8), *page* LIII.
7. Correspondences between Haggai and First Zechariah Part I (1:1–6), *page* LIV.
8. Purview of the visions, *page* LVI.
9. Formulaic language of the visions, *page* LVII.
10. Percentage distribution of prose particles in Haggai, *page* LXV.
11. Percentage distribution of prose particles in First Zechariah, *page* LXVI.
12. Governors, Davidides, and High Priests of Yehud in the Persian period (538–433), *page 14.*
13. Reconstruction of the Tobiad line, *page 342.*

PHOTOGRAPHS

following page 98

1. Darius I's monument at Behistun.
2. Cylinder seal of Darius I.
3. Drawing of head of Darius I from relief at Behistun.
4. The Shelomith seal. Reading: "Belonging to Shelomith, maidservant of Elnathan the governor."
5. Seal impression on a store-jar handle. Reading: "Yehud/Yeho'ezer/the governor." Early fourth century B.C.E. from Ramat Raḥel.
6. Aramaic inscription on store-jar handle. Reading: "Yehud." Early fourth century B.C.E. from Ramat Raḥal.
7. Bulla of Elnathan the governor. Reading: "Belonging to Elnathan the governor."
8. A hoard of bullae and seals from a postexilic Judean archive.

following page 290

9. Attic silver tetradrachm of late sixth century B.C.E. struck at Athens and found in Jerusalem.
10. Fourth-century hemiobol struck in Jerusalem ca. 340 B.C.E. as an autonomous Jewish coin.
11. Fourth-century silver hemiobol struck in Jerusalem between 350 and 333 B.C.E.
12. Seven-spouted lamp from Tell Dothan, Late Bronze-Iron I.
13. Persian (?) period multispouted lamp from ancient Palestine.
14. Illustration of Zech 4 from Cervera Bible, Cervera, Spain, 1300 C.E.
15. Horses in the Persian Empire, drawing from two bronzes at Persepolis.
16. Discovery of foundation deposit from Persepolis.
17. Foundation deposit of the main hall at Persepolis laid by Darius I.

ABBREVIATIONS AND SIGNS

ABR	*Australian Biblical Review*
AH	*Akkadische Handwörterbuch*, W. von Soden. Wiesbaden: Harrassowitz, 1965–81
AJSLL	*American Journal of Semitic Languages and Literatures*
AKK	Akkadian—the language of ancient Mesopotamia
ANEP	*The Ancient Near East in Pictures Relating to the Old Testament*, ed. J. Pritchard. Princeton: Princeton University Press, 1954, 1969
ANET	*Ancient Near Eastern Texts Relating to the Old Testament*, ed. J. Pritchard. Princeton: Princeton University Press, 1955, 1969
AO	*Archiv für Orientforschung*
AV	Authorized Version (=King James Version). *The Holy Bible containing the Old and New Testaments.* New York, American Bible Society, n.d.
BA	*Biblical Archaeologist*
BANE	*The Bible and the Ancient Near East*
BAR	*Biblical Archaeology Review*
BASOR	*Bulletin of the American Schools of Oriental Research*
B.C.E.	Before the Common Era
BDB	F. Brown, S. Driver, and C. Briggs, *Hebrew and English Lexicon of the Old Testament.* Oxford University Press, 1907, 1955
BH³	*Biblia Hebraica*, 3rd ed., ed. R. Kittel, Stuttgart, 1937
BHS	*Biblia Hebraica Stuttgartensia*, Stuttgart, 1977
BJRL	*Bulletin of the John Rylands Library*
BZAW	*Beihefte zur Zeitschrift für die Alttestamentliche Wissenschaft*
CAD	*Chicago Assyrian Dictionary*, ed. L. Oppenheim, University of Chicago Press, 1956–
CBQ	*Catholic Biblical Quarterly*
C.E.	Common Era
CTM	*Concordia Theological Monthly*

EAEHL   *Encyclopedia of Archaeological Excavations in the Holy Land.* Jerusalem: Massada Press

EI   *Eretz Israel*

EJ   *Encyclopaedia Judaica*

GKC   *Gesenius' Hebrew Grammar,* ed. E. Kautzsch, trans. A. E. Cowley. Oxford: Clarendon Press, 1910 (2nd ed.)

HAT   *Handbuch zum Alten Testament*

HTR   *Harvard Theological Review*

HUCA   *Hebrew Union College Annual*

IB   *Interpreter's Bible.* Nashville: Abingdon Press, 1951–57

IDB   *Interpreter's Dictionary of the Bible.* Nashville: Abingdon Press, 1962

IDBS   *Interpreter's Dictionary of the Bible Supplement.* Nashville: Abingdon Press, 1976

IEJ   *Israel Exploration Journal*

JAOS   *Journal of the American Oriental Society*

JBL   *Journal of Biblical Literature*

JJS   *Journal of Jewish Studies*

JNES   *Journal of Near Eastern Studies*

JQR   *Jewish Quarterly Review*

JSOT   *Journal for the Study of the Old Testament*

JSS   *Journal of Semitic Studies*

JTS   *Journal of Theological Studies*

KAT   *Kommentar zum Alten Testament,* ed. E. Sellin, continued by J. Herrmann

LXX   Septuagint

MT   Masoretic Text

MQR   *Michigan Quarterly Review*

NEB   *New English Bible.* Oxford and Cambridge, 1970

NJPS   The New Jewish Publication Society of America Translations of the Holy Scriptures:
The Torah, 2nd ed., Philadelphia, 1967;
The Prophets: Nevi'im, Philadelphia, 1978;
The Writings: Kethubim, Philadelphia, 1978

NT   *New Testament*

OA   *Oriens Antiquus*

OTS   *Oudtestamentische Studien*

PEQ   *Palestine Exploration Quarterly*

QM   *The War Scroll*

RHPR   *Revue d'histoire et de philosophie religieuse*

RSV   *The Holy Bible, Revised Standard Version,* New York: Nelson, 1952

RTR   *Reformed Theological Review*

SBL   Society of Biblical Literature

Taan	Ta'anith
T.B.	Babylonian Talmud
TDOT	*Theological Dictionary of the Old Testament*, 4 vols. Eds. G. J. Botterweck and H. Ringgren. Grand Rapids: Eerdmans, 1974–80
THAT	*Theologisches Handwörterbuch zum Alten Testament*, 4 vols. Eds. G. J. Botterweck, H. Ringgren, and H.-J. Fabry. Stuttgart: Kohlhammer, 1970–84
ThZ	*Theologische Zeitschrift*
UT	*Ugaritic Textbook*, C. H. Gordon. Rome, 1965. Supplement, 1967
VT	*Vetus Testamentum*
ZAW	*Zeitschrift für die Alttestamentliche Wissenschaft*
ZDPV	*Zeitschrift des Deutschen Palästinas Vereins*
1QM	The "War Scroll" from Qumran
*	Unattested form

GLOSSARY OF TERMS

Achaemenid   term commonly used to refer to the Persian Empire established by Cyrus, a descendant of Achaemenes, in the sixth century B.C.E.

anthropopathic   having human feelings.

apodosis   the part of a conditional sentence which states the expected or logical result of the condition.

aposiopesis   rhetorical device of breaking off or interrupting a sentence for literary effect.

archaizing   the technique of making something appear to be ancient.

astragal   architectural term for a rounded molding near the top of a column.

athnach   Hebrew accent mark which serves as the principal divider within a verse.

bicolon   a line (usually poetic) containing two parts, each of which is called a "colon."

bulla(e)   seal(s) appended to a document.

chiasm   the literary device of reversing the order in the second of a pair of otherwise syntactically parallel phrases or clauses, resulting in an "X" pattern.

cohortative   a lengthened Hebrew verb form, usually in the first person, used to express a wish, command, or exhortation.

conversive perfect   use of the Hebrew conjunction *waw* with the perfect tense to indicate present or future situations.

Davidide   a descendant of David. The term is commonly used in reference to a king.

defective   a type of Hebrew spelling in which no vowel letters are used.

Deuteronomic history   the history of Israel as told from the point of view of a late seventh- and sixth-century Judean school called the "Deuteronomists." Often used to refer to the books from Deuteronomy through 2 Kings.

dittography   accidental repetition of a letter, word, or larger unit of a text during the process of copying.

dyarchy   a government in which power is vested in two rulers or authorities.

elliptical   literary manner of expression in which one or more parts are omitted but understood. Usually done for rhetorical effect.

forma mixta   "mixed form" which supposedly mixes the character and meaning of two different tenses, genders, or conjugations.

gloss   a scribal or editorial correction, addition, or explanation usually introduced to the text to clarify or expand an obscure or important point.

gnomic   a proverbial expression dealing with some general truth.

Halakah   the body of Jewish oral laws which supplement the written law.

hapax legomenon   a word or form that occurs only once in a given document or text.

haplography   the accidental omission in copying of adjacent and similar letters, words, or lines.

hendiadys   the use of two nouns connected by a conjunction to express what normally would be expressed by a noun and an adjective.

Hiphil   Hebrew verb form which usually carries a causative force.

Hithpael   Hebrew verb form which usually denotes a reflexive sense.

homoearcton   an occurrence in writing of two words or lines that have similar beginnings; a frequent cause of scribal omissions in copying.

homoeoteleuton   an occurrence in writing of two similar endings of words or phrases in close proximity; a cause of many scribal omissions.

Hophal   Hebrew verb form which usually carries a causative-passive form.

hypocoristicon   shortened or abbreviated form, usually of a personal name.

inclusio   a literary structure marked at the beginning and end by identical words or phrases. Also called an "envelope construction."

ipsissima verba   "the very words"—usually in reference to a divine utterance.

jussive   a shortened Hebrew verb form, in the third person, used to express a wish, command, or exhortation.

kernos   a circular, tubelike vessel perforated on its upper side with holes or receptacles for the receiving or pouring out of liquids.

kethib   "what is written." A term used to indicate what is written in the received Hebrew text, especially when it differs from the word presupposed by the Masoretic vocalization; see *qere.*

Masoretic   pertaining to the Masoretes, a group of medieval Jewish scribes whose primary function was the preservation of the Hebrew text.

menorah   a candelabrum or lampstand usually containing seven branches; an important cultic object in Judaism.

merism   a figure of speech in which a totality is expressed by the use of two contrasting parts.

Niphal   Hebrew verb form used in the simple stem; usually indicating a passive or reflexive meaning.

onomasticon   a collection or listing of the names of persons and/or places, as well as specialized words, often with etymologies.

oracle   a divine revelation usually expressed through a priest or prophet.

papponymy the practice of naming a child for its grandfather.

pars pro toto expression referring to an instance in which a part stands for the whole.

patronymic occurrence in which the writing of a name includes references to one's father, father's father, or other paternal ancestors.

pentacontad a type of calendar in which the basic unit of time reckoning was the seven-day week and the secondary unit was a period of fifty days, consisting of seven weeks plus an additional day. Thus a year consisted of seven pentacontads plus two festival periods of seven days each and one additional day of highly sacred character.

Pharisees a party within Judaism that sought to keep both the oral and written law; became the dominant group in Judaism by the end of the first century C.E.

Piel Hebrew verb form, commonly called the "intensive" stem, but also having other nuances of meaning.

plene manner of spelling Hebrew words which includes all of the vowel letters.

Primary History an authoritative, quasi-canonical work published and promulgated ca. 560 B.C.E. in the Babylonian exile, consisting of the Pentateuch and Former Prophets (Josh–2 Kgs).

protasis in a conditional sentence, the clause that states the condition.

Qal the simple form of the Hebrew verb.

qere term used to indicate that the Masoretic vocalization is at variance with the consonants of the received text; see *kethib*.

quoin a large or specially shaped stone in the exterior corner of a building.

redaction the revision or adaptation of one or more sources to form a single text.

satrapy a large administrative territory governed by an official called a "satrap" during the time of the Persian Empire.

Shephelah a lowland area of foothills between the coastal plain and the central highlands of Palestine.

stratigraphic a type of archaeological excavation in which the time sequence of cultures and habitations is determined by studying the relative locations of layers of material uncovered by careful digging.

synecdoche use of a word designating a part or quality of a thing to refer to the whole.

Targum Aramaic translation of scriptural books originally delivered orally in the Second Temple period, usually in accordance with a generally accepted tradition of interpretation.

theophanic relating to a theophany, a personal manifestation of the deity to an individual.

theophoric derived from or bearing the name of a god; many personal names are theophoric—e.g., Elnathan, Jehozadak.

tradent   one who passes along traditional materials, written or oral.

Vulgate   Jerome's Latin translation of the Bible.

Yehud   subunit of the Persian satrapy of "Beyond the River," a smaller approximation of the preexilic kingdom of Judah.

Yehudite   a resident of Yehud.

NOTE ON THE TRANSLATION

Every work of translation must repeatedly come to grips with the necessity of making a decision between a smooth and artful style in the language to which the text is being translated and a translation which may appear awkward or stilted but which remains as faithful as possible to the original. The variations in convention, syntax, and structure between any two languages render this task formidable if not insurmountable at times. Furthermore, the vocabulary of one language rarely admits of a one-to-one correspondence with words of another. Nuanced terms have no close parallels, and some words have not even a remote equivalent. Idiomatic expressions are notoriously difficult to render into another language in a way that provides their meaning and also gives a sense of how that idiomatic language has been used in the original.

In the face of such problems, our guiding principle has been to remain as faithful as possible to the Hebrew syntax, to provide to the best of our ability an arrangement of words and a rhythm of language that characterizes the Hebrew original. To do so has meant, more often than we had anticipated, that the English does not read smoothly. The artistry of the Hebrew in such cases can only be recovered for the non-Hebrew reader by reference to the NOTES, where the reasons for the apparently awkward English renderings are laid forth.

Much of our analysis of these two prophetic works involves awareness of literary features such as the repetition of key words and phrases, envelope constructions, chiasms, and the use of formulaic or stereotyped expressions. Transferring these features into English often produces a repetitious or stilted text, which would be unacceptable in a language such as English which has a rich vocabulary and in which the conscious varying of words and phrases is as much a stylistic feature as is the repetition of words and phrases in Hebrew. To provide a varied diction in English would be to misrepresent the artful arrangement of words in the Hebrew text. To create a smooth word order in English would be to destroy the conscious balancing of terms and parts of speech in the Hebrew.

The places in the translation that appear flawed are for the most part the result of our attempts to be consistent in rendering a given Hebrew root by the same English word, at least where the context is approximately the same, and by our efforts to respect the structure and integrity of the Hebrew sentence, whether it be poetic, prosaic, or somewhere in between. Since the vague last-mentioned category is a prominent feature of these prophetic books, we have deemed it especially important to refrain as much as possible from tampering with the Hebrew word order and from using more or fewer words for a given Hebrew word or phrase than appear in the original. It has not been possible in every case to follow these self-imposed guidelines, but the effort has been made.

The reader should also note that in several situations we have resorted to the use of punctuation to convey the meaning of a Hebrew word or the arrangement of a passage. The Hebrew authors wrote without such conventions. Yet we sensed occasionally that a word was being employed in Hebrew in much the same way that a writer in English would insert a form of punctuation. In such cases we have supplied what appears to be the appropriate equivalent punctuation mark. Another feature of this translation is the precision in the English spelling of Hebrew proper names. For example, seeking to be precise, we have endeavored to imitate as appropriate the exact spelling of the Hebrew original (compare our "Shealtiel" of Hag 1:1 and "Shaltiel" of Hag 1:12 with other English translations, such as the King James version and the New Jerusalem Bible, which level through this variant) where a difference in pronunciation probably underlies the difference in spelling.

Our arrangement of quoted speech, and of quotes within quotes, was achieved with considerable difficulty. English simply does not have sufficient conventions to deal with the multiple layering of quoted material that appears in these prophetic works. As many as six layers of quotations (as in Zechariah Part One) appear in a single unit of prophecy. Hebrew has no quotation marks at all, and our rendering of the dialogic passages and the segments of reported speech rests, in the last analysis, upon our understanding of the verbs indicating speech and the antecedents of those verbs within the context of the particular passage.

Finally, the reader should realize that the arrangement of some lines of Hebrew text into poetic form is the result of our analysis of the structure of the Hebrew line, the relative paucity of particles associated with prose, and the presence of parallelism (see below, our discussion of "Prose or Poetry"). Many lines were borderline, or rather could be said to partake of both prose and poetry. In such cases our decision to arrange some of these lines as poetry and others as prose was meant to create a variation, and so to indicate that Haggai-Zechariah 1–8 contains a fair amount of such language, which can be termed oracular or elevated prose.

INTRODUCTION

THE HISTORICAL CONTEXT:

Persian Imperial Policy

No period in the history of Israel so definitively shaped the destiny of the Jewish people as did the exilic age and its aftermath, the period of the return from Babylon to Yehud, once called Judah. When the neo-Babylonian armies of Nebuchadnezzar wrought havoc upon Jerusalem in 587 or 586 B.C.E. and thousands of Judeans were taken captive and marched to Babylon, the story of Israel could well have ended. Instead, a uniquely creative epoch in Judean history began, ironically, in the diaspora and in exile, as the survivors of the Babylonian conquest sought to examine the causes of the calamity that had destroyed their holy city and the Jerusalem temple and had made so many homeless and impoverished. With Judeans dispersed into many new lands besides Babylon—into trans-Jordan, Egypt, and Syro-Phoenicia—the familiar sociohistoric framework of Israel, which had been limited to the southern tip of the Syro-Palestinian corridor from the thirteenth century B.C.E. until the Exile, was shattered once and for all.

However, a burst of classical prophecy (Ezekiel and Second Isaiah) enabled the exiled people to comprehend their suffering. From a similar prophetic perspective, a determination to collect their common past manifested itself in the form of the Primary History (Gen–Kgs), which provided the means for reviewing events in the more distant past; and the Pentateuch, actually part of the Primary History, now promulgated in its earliest form, provided the motivation for national life and the authoritative guide to Law in society. It is in this period that we may first refer to the people of Israel as Jews. Composed of the former residents of the Kingdom of Judah and their descendants, who are normally referred to as Judahites or Judeans, Jews were to be known as those who adhered to the religion of Yahweh as understood in the Primary History. Such adherents included those scattered in exile and also those who stayed behind in Palestine clinging to their ethnic and religious legacy as well as to the hope for a restoration of national life.

It was mainly the aristocracy, the leadership of Judah, that was deported to Babylon; the vast majority of the people either fled to neighboring lands or stayed behind in Palestine. There is no evidence to suggest that the neo-Babylonians introduced foreign elements into the local population, into Judah, as the Assyrians had done when they conquered the northern kingdom of Israel in the eighth century. Still, the presence of unfriendly neighbors, such as the Edomites in northern Judah or the Samaritans who laid claim to deserted

Judahite estates, meant that certain areas of Palestine were pressured from without. The basic Judahite heartland, however, reclaimed in the restoration period as Yehud, remained virtually free of foreigners throughout the years between the Destruction in 586 and the First Return in 538. Even the cult in Jerusalem seems to have persisted at the site of the ruined temple (Jer 41:4–8).

The condition of the exiles in Babylon is not known, but we may infer from Ezra (2:59; 3:15) that they were kept together in discrete units and settled on deserted agricultural sites. At some point prior to the Persian overthrow of neo-Babylonian rule, the detained exiles were released into society at large. From later reports of Second Isaiah, we know they willingly entered the world of their conquerors and achieved a high degree of assimilation into Babylonian culture and society. It was in Babylon's imperial interests to have subjugated peoples become active and useful members of the realm.

But if Babylon's inviting new culture infringed upon the exiles' hallowed past, the activities of the Judahite leadership in exile demonstrated that they were ready to meet this challenge. Certainly some form of worship was carried out, and generations of scholars have attributed the origin of the synagogue to the exilic age when collective prayer assemblies must have arisen to meet the spiritual needs of the people now deprived of a temple as focus or symbol of its relationship to God. Common to such worship no doubt were prayer and song, and probably some sort of scriptural reading. It is our belief that it was in such a setting that Jehozadak, father of the high priest Joshua, who figures prominently in the Books of Haggai and Zechariah 1–8, achieved the first compilation of the Primary History sometime before 560 B.C.E. Within approximately a single generation, the Judahites had succeeded in rallying their energies in a new land, under adverse conditions, and had edited the traditions and stories from their common past which they wanted to carry into the present and which in turn would sustain them in the future.

Two eloquent prophetic voices of the exilic age spoke out in response to these new conditions, Ezekiel at the beginning and Second Isaiah at the end of that period. Each in his own way and with his distinctive language and style sought to help the community deal with the epochal impact of the dispersion on Jewish history. Ezekiel emphasized the ceremonial aspect of Jewish life and encased it in a visionary mode that was to influence Zechariah. His view of the restored temple in particular no doubt found a sympathetic audience among those who were to build the Second Temple. Second Isaiah gave new meaning to the experience of suffering and offered comfort in a time when it was sorely needed; he aroused the exiles to the fact that the world was about to change and that a new Exodus was to begin. Upon such a stage entered one Cyrus of Anshan, a prince of the Medes, to assume the mantle of Persian authority in 559 B.C.E. and to conquer Babylon in 539 (see Chart 1). Not only does Second Isaiah herald the era of Persian dominion about to begin, but also he assigns to

Cyrus the ultimate sign of approval, referring to him as "shepherd" and "messiah," Yahweh's special instrument of deliverance (Isa 44:28; 45:1).

Chart 1
Chronological Data Relevant
to Haggai-Zechariah 1–8

587/6	Destruction of Jerusalem and the temple; mass deportation of Judeans to Babylon
585	Assassination of Gedaliah
561–60	Release of exiled king Jehoiachin and the first edition of Primary History
559	Cyrus the Great (559–30) comes to the Persian throne
539	Cyrus conquers Babylon
538	Edict of Cyrus; First Return under Sheshbazzar
530	Cambyses (530–22) succeeds Cyrus, unexpectedly dies ca. July 1, 522
522	Revolt of Gaumata (Bardiya or Smerdis) and problems of accession (March 11–October 5); Darius takes office (October 5), organizes satrapies
522–21	Darius consolidates his empire; Zerubbabel appointed governor in Yehud
520	Work begins (again?) on the rebuilding of the Jerusalem temple; temple refoundation ceremony (December 18)
518	Darius decrees codification and authority of Egyptian laws
515	Temple rededication (possibly 516)

The Edict of Cyrus and the Two Returns

The occasion for such unbridled optimism was the Edict of Cyrus in 538 B.C.E., attested in a clay cylinder and echoed in two similar versions in the Bible, one in Hebrew (Ezra 1:1–4; cf. 2 Chron 36:22–23), the other in Aramaic (Ezra 6:1–5). From the Judahite perspective preserved in the former, it is clear that the decree which permitted the return and rebuilding of the temple was viewed as a sign of Yahweh's favor. From the more neutral latter source we gain a sense that Persian imperial policy was very much committed to the building and resettlement project, which was but one expression of a much broader policy of restoring conquered subjects when politically and physically feasible in the hope of installing loyal colonies in critical geopolitical areas. Although the Cyrus cylinder does not directly mention the Jerusalem temple and its cult, lines 30–32 of the cylinder specifically mention that Cyrus restored cults and returned exiled peoples to their homes. It is this section which provides the background for interpreting the biblical tradition as we have done

(Kuhrt 1983:83–84). Persian policy toward its conquered territories contrasted strongly with that of preceding empires, such as Assyria, which often oppressed the local populations to the point that the subject peoples hated their overlords and were always ready to rebel. Persian policy after Cyrus, however, was designed to ingratiate the conquered peoples and to encourage them to be cooperative members of the larger configuration. Such a policy of deliberate noninterference in local affairs and customs and of encouraging peoples to cultivate their own national traditions helped to secure for Persia the loyalty of many of the newly conquered nations. Under this "patrimonial" system, the existing cultural and social patterns of conquered peoples, especially local legal systems, were largely retained and used as the basis for the order and well-being of the empire.

Persia is treated well in the Hebrew Bible as a result of these policies, but it is still true that despite all its apparent largesse toward Israel, Persia was still a world military power that could also destroy other nations at will. It was in short an ancient superpower, and the double-edged nature of Persian imperial power is perhaps best reflected in the Second Vision of Zechariah (2:1–4; RSV 1:18–21), the Four Horns and the Four Smiths (see NOTES and COMMENT below).

Darius I, like Cyrus the Great before him, adhered to the policy of imperial rule which involved only a minimum of disruption in the conditions of local governance. Because of this, the transition to the satrapal or provincial organization of territories which he initiated was relatively smooth. The largest units of administrative rule of Persia were the satrapies or "protectorates," which included within them smaller units or subunits known as provinces. Judah (yĕhûdâ), now called Yehud (yĕhûd) in Aramaic, was one such smaller unit within the larger satrapy of Eber Nahara, Beyond the River (see Maps 1 and 3). In the reorganization process that reached its peak under the leadership of Darius I, many locals were installed in key leadership positions. In Sardis, Cyrus installed a Lydian to run the treasury; he similarly installed a Judahite, Sheshbazzar, as the first governor of Yehud to lead the First Return, during which the gold and silver vessels once removed by Nebuchadnezzar would be brought back and the plan to rebuild the destroyed Jerusalem temple would be implemented (Ezra 1:8–11). By the time of Darius, Cyrus's predisposition to favor local leadership groups and institutions such as priesthoods and temples, which could contribute to the stability of local communities and hence of the empire, was entrenched policy, with only Cambyses displaying a brief period of intolerance in his short and erratic tenure as king. In Egypt (see Map 2) under the dynamic priestly leadership of Ujahorresne, the priest of Neith at Sais, Persian imperial aims were furthered by Darius's policies. Ujahorresne not only reconstituted the colleges attached to major temples but also served as a loyal representative of the king. So too in Yehud, by the time of the Second Return under the civil governor Zerubbabel, the high priest Joshua

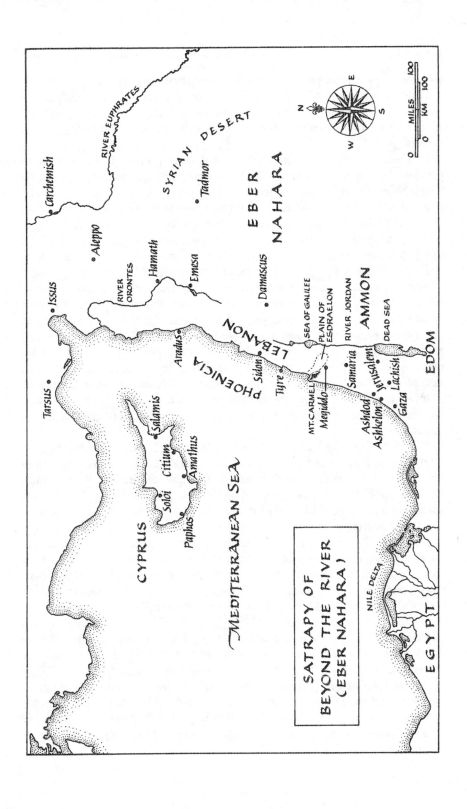

SATRAPY OF
BEYOND THE RIVER
(EBER NAHARA)

RIVER EUPHRATES

Carchemish

SYRIAN DESERT

Tadmor

EBER NAHARA

Aleppo

Hamath

RIVER ORONTES

Emesa

Damascus

Issus

Tarsus

LEBANON

SEA OF GALILEE

PLAIN OF ESDRAELON

RIVER JORDAN

AMMON

DEAD SEA

EDOM

Aradus

PHOENICIA

Sidon

Tyre

MT. CARMEL

Megiddo

Samaria

Jerusalem

Lachish

Ashdod

Ashkelon

Gaza

Salamis

Cittium

Amathus

Soloi

Paphos

CYPRUS

MEDITERRANEAN SEA

NILE DELTA

EGYPT

N

E

S

W

MILES 100

KM 100

0

was given new and important administrative powers within the larger framework of Achaemenid administration in order to assure cordial relations between Persia and Yehud. In both the First and Second Returns, the rebuilding of the temple was encouraged, for that would strengthen the authority of local powers.

It is not entirely clear from the biblical record whether Yehud enjoyed provincial status from the time of the first governors, Sheshbazzar and Zerubbabel. New archaeological discoveries in the Jerusalem area, however, suggest that Yehud was in fact granted full provincial status in this period and was not part of the more northerly province of Samaria, as has been alleged by many scholars (for a full discussion see NOTE to "governor" in Hag 1:1). Indeed, we can now fill in the "governor gap" (see Chart 12, p. 14) for the period prior to Ezra and Nehemiah, by which time Yehud possessed full provincial status. The so-called meddling of Samaritan authorities (Ezra 4:17) in the enterprise of the temple's rebuilding is the subject of much scholarly debate. Were the Samaritans exercising fundamental and legitimate rights in their capacity as supervising provincial authority, or were they simply exercising whatever leverage they may have had, while at the same time expressing a jealous concern over the matter of future influence within the Persian administration? The visit of Tattenai, administrator of the province of Beyond the River (Ezra 5:1), is surely a reflection of the Samaritans' concern about their favored position within the empire, a privilege they had enjoyed since the fall of the kingdom of Israel.

It is clear from the biblical record that the First Return encountered such political difficulties, and also that it failed to restore the temple. The mission of Sheshbazzar did not succeed, possibly because as the "first" governor, Sheshbazzar did not possess the same power as did Zerubbabel and his successors. The mission could have failed also because it took place so long before the reorganization of the provinces by Darius. Before Darius's implementation of the satrapal system, sufficient financial support for such an enterprise may have been impossible. A lack of tax revenues in an impoverished Palestine would have greatly altered the effects of Sheshbazzar's visit. In any case, Persia might well have anticipated some Palestinian resistance to its policies by installing strong and well-trained leaders with excellent pedigrees like that of Sheshbazzar, who was presumably a Davidide if he is to be equated with Shenazzar, who was one of the sons of Jehoiachin (1 Chron 3:17–18). Zerubbabel after him (see 1 Chron 3:19 and NOTE to "Zerubbabel" in Hag 1:1 below) was not only a Davidide but also was heir apparent to the Judahite throne as Jehoiachin's grandson. Accordingly he was one who aroused great hopes among the people that they would be politically independent at some time in the future (Hag 2:20–23). In this respect it is interesting to observe that, although Zerubbabel is always called "governor" in Haggai, he is never so described in Zechariah.

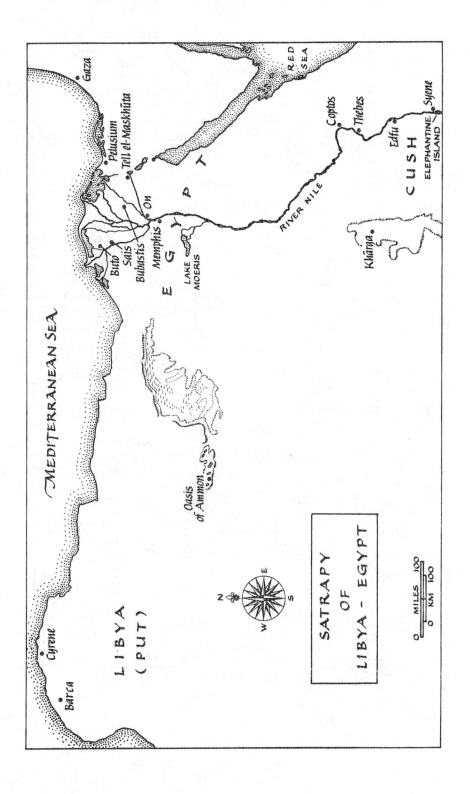

MEDITERRANEAN SEA

RED SEA

Gaza

Pelusium
Tell el-Maskhūta

On

E G Y P T

RIVER NILE

Coptos

Thebes

Edfu

C U S H

Elephantine
Island

Syene

Memphis

Buto
Sais
Bubastis

LAKE
MOERIS

Khārga

Oasis
of Ammon

LIBYA
(PUT)

Cyrene

Barca

N
E
W
S

SATRAPY
OF
LIBYA – EGYPT

0   MILES   100
0   KM   100

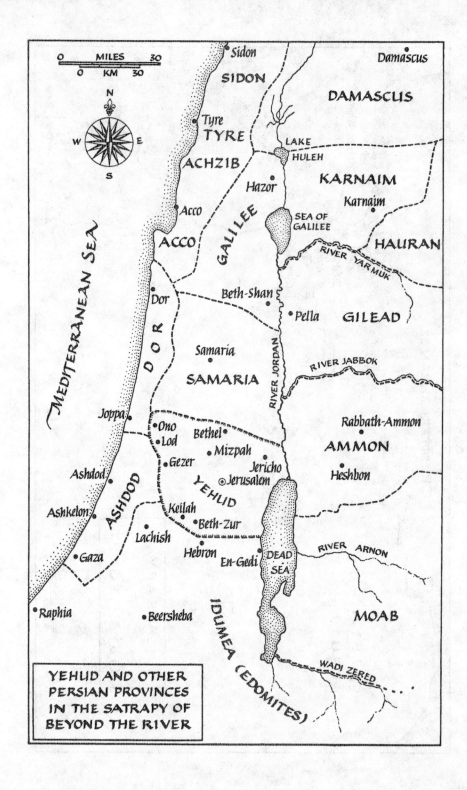

YEHUD AND OTHER
PERSIAN PROVINCES
IN THE SATRAPY OF
BEYOND THE RIVER

Any number of reasons might explain why many Judahites would not be eager to return home to Palestine. First and perhaps foremost, some of them had achieved a good measure of success in Babylon and could not face the uncertainty of returning to an area devastated by earlier wars. In addition, the local Palestinian forms of Yahwistic tradition which they would encounter upon their return would not necessarily be compatible with an openness to the adjusted Babylonian forms. The Samaritans could well have been merely protecting their particular brand of Yahwism, which they believed to be authentic. Futhermore, in the absence of a completely reorganized Persian empire, which was achieved only under Darius I (ca. 520 B.C.E.), the Judahites in Babylon and in Palestine could count on only minimal support from their overlords who were engrossed in state projects from Egypt to India.

The scene which greeted the first group of returnees would have been much like that depicted in Haggai 1:3–11: a depressed economy with little motivation for the people to go about the challenging task of rebuilding the temple. A new consensus had to be forged. Palestinians and returnees had to be reacquainted with and reassured by one another; and the common good had to be desired and established by both. Our prophetic sources of Haggai-Zechariah 1–8 deal only with the period of the Second Return. At this time a second wave of immigration together with an inspired leadership enabled Yehud to establish a new national spirit as a positive response to the prophecies of Haggai and Zechariah, who in Ezra (5:1 and 6:14) are rightly credited with a high degree of success.

The Restoration in Yehud

Whatever prevented the success of Sheshbazzar's first mission to Palestine (Ezra 5:15), Zerubbabel's mission in 520 B.C.E. in the second year of King Darius I (Hag 1:1) came at a time when a modicum of stability had returned to the Persian Empire. Such stability had been attained only after the unexpected death of Cyrus in 530 and after the challenge in 522 to the leadership of Cambyses, who succeeded him, had been successfully resolved in the accession of Darius I to the Persian throne.

Cambyses' eight-year reign was marked by internal as well as external conflict. Only in 525, after years of struggle, did he become king of Upper and Lower Egypt. He discontinued the practice of large revenues going to the priesthood in Egypt, and as a result engendered much hostility. Darius later restored this practice. In Persia too Cambyses was regarded unfavorably and was referred to as a "despot" (Herodotus III.89) because he was harsh-natured and contemptuous. The circumstances of his sudden death in 522 are not clear from the sources. The difficulties which attended Darius's accession to the throne may be reconstructed from Herodotus (Bk. III) and the Behistun inscription. The most serious problem facing Darius was the revolt beginning in March 522 under the leadership of a Magus called Gaumata, claiming to be Bardiya (Smerdis). Bardiya seized the kingship by July, and Cambyses died shortly after. Gaumata was killed by Darius on September 29, after which Darius became king.

Darius was quick to assert himself and to reactivate the liberal policies that Cyrus had begun. With a commitment to responsible government, he undertook efforts to codify local laws and worked effectively through local officials such as Ujahorresne and Zerubbabel. Darius achieved what Cyrus had not really attempted. He organized the empire into satrapies—twenty, according to Herodotus (III.89)—over which he appointed rulers; and he fixed the amount of annual tribute to be paid by each. To these satrapies he attached various groups of people. Yehud, according to Herodotus, was incorporated into the satrapy of Phoenicia but is referred to in Semitic sources as Beyond the River (Eber Nahara; see NOTE to "governor" in Hag 1:1) and achieved a measure of autonomy early in Darius's reign.

The appointment of Zerubbabel, Davidic scion and grandson of King Jehoiachin, thus must be viewed as an integral part of Persia's overall policy of installing loyal representatives in critically important areas. Clearly Darius was not investing power in someone he believed would foment a rebellion to reestablish an independent monarchy. Some of the details of the events associated with the power struggle just prior to the ascendancy of Darius are recounted in the Behistun inscription (see illustration 5), where it is clear that Darius's seizure of the throne was followed by uprisings in Mesopotamia, Armenia, and the Iranian lands (Herodotus III.76,126–27, I.130). However, the outlying satrapies in Asia Minor and Egypt apparently were not much affected by Darius's coming to power. In any event, by 520 things were relatively quiet in Beyond the River and its subprovince Yehud. Zerubbabel the governor had been sent by Darius by that year to take charge once and for all of affairs in Yehud, Zerubbabel's authority and the status of Yehud being legitimized once again by appeal to Cyrus's decree authorizing work on the temple. In this endeavor Zerubbabel was joined by Joshua, the high priest and the son of Jehozadak, probably the one who had figured prominently in the promulgation of the Primary History some forty years before. The high priesthood under Jehozadak had probably achieved some of its renewed importance and authority during the exile because of the imprisonment or restraint of the exiled king, Jehoiachin.

Aside from the dynamic leadership of the prophets Haggai and Zechariah, both of whom advocated support for the Persian appointees (Haggai apparently to a greater degree than Zechariah, judging from his final oracle, 2:20–23), it was Darius's singular efforts at general satrapal reorganization in his entire realm which influenced Yehudite actions more than anything else. As we have already pointed out, the Persians had a positive attitude toward indigenous leaders in the conquered territories. It is likely that the Edict of Cyrus in 538, permitting the first wave of returnees and the commencement of work on the Jerusalem temple, allowed the temple itself to be exempted from forms of taxation that were usually in force in the whole of the Empire. The people of Yehud, however, were still liable for taxes and subject to the corvée (Ezra 4:12–16). Because the Persian policy, tolerant and supportive of local governance, had been hailed in Judahite circles since the days of Cyrus, it doubtless came as no surprise that Darius would continue those policies, at least by 520, when he was fully in control of his empire. Darius's confirmation of Cyrus's policy to assist financially in the temple reconstruction process is borne out in Ezra's reference (6:8) to a system of tax redistribution. In addition, Darius ordered that once the temple was completed, a daily offering and prayer were to be made for the welfare of the king (Ezra 6:10). Zerubbabel as governor was responsible to the king for returning tribute and tax payments from the province, and at the same time he served as official agent of imperial policy. Joshua, on the other hand, exercised expanded or new powers in managing the fiscal resources brought in by the priesthood to the temple, as well as in acting as chief legal and religious authority of the land (see NOTE to "the high priest" in Zech 3:1).

We know that Darius took special interest in what went on in the provinces, to such an extent that in Egypt he ordered Aryandes to set up a commission to collect and codify Egyptian laws such as they were at the end of the reign of Cyrus. Within sixteen years those laws were codified on papyrus and published in Egyptian demotic and Aramaic. No doubt the authority of the Primary History (in particular its legal portions), as it had existed since the days of Jehozadak, was considerably strengthened by Darius's activities as "lawgiver" and as a ruler who desired to organize the affairs of state in a way that was acceptable and meaningful to both the conquerors and the conquered. Darius aimed to uphold if not strengthen traditional legal frameworks, rather than develop a new and overarching legal system for all components of his realm.

The remainder of the time period with which we are concerned extends to the ceremony of refoundation, alluded to in both Haggai and Zechariah, which took place on December 18, 520 (see below and NOTES to chronological headings), and ultimately to the rededication of this Jerusalem temple in 516 or 515 B.C.E., an event mentioned in the Bible only in Ezra (6:14). For the details of these years we are largely dependent upon Haggai and First Zechariah, whose prophetic works both reflected the unique circumstances of these years and shaped the developments that characterized this very brief time span. No evidence exists in these prophetic works for a revolt or rebellion led by Zerubbabel or any other member of the Jewish or Yehudite community. That Zerubbabel disappears from the literary sources after 518 is testimony to the growing power of the high priesthood in civil and religious affairs, and to the centrality of the temple. The fact is that the governor was still in residence in the period after 518. The restoration of the Davidic house, however, is relegated to an eschatological future despite the fact that Zerubbabel the governor was apparently around for some time after the temple's rededication. That his successor as governor, Elnathan, is closely associated with a Davidic descendant, Shelomith, indicates that the Yehudite populace demanded leaders connected with the royal line even into the next century.

A high point of achievement for Yehud in the restoration was the publication of the composite work, Haggai-Zechariah 1–8, in anticipation of the ceremony of rededication and for presentation at that event. The prophets had exhorted their fellow countrymen to heed God's word and to restore God's earthly dwelling place, the temple. The fact that nowhere in either prophetic work is the rededication of the temple mentioned surely means that their combined literary work was completed prior to that event.

PROPHETIC RESPONSE

It is amid the new and unfamiliar circumstances of the beginning of Darius I's rule that Haggai and Zechariah join the ranks of Israelite prophecy. More than any other factor, the absence of any realistic opportunity to restore the monarchy influenced the content of their utterances. The hegemony of Persia in all local affairs is presupposed by both prophets. Moreover, a dyarchic pattern of home rule consisting of governor and high priest is never questioned. The preexilic prophets had little use for Assyria and Babylonia except as instruments of divine punishment, but Persia was a different matter altogether for the postexilic prophets. Both Haggai and Zechariah placed their prophetic office in support of the reestablished province of Yehud. Zechariah in particular viewed Persia as an instrument of divine will. A kind of realistic, pragmatic viewpoint therefore is assumed by each prophet as he tried to assist his fellow Yehudites in the difficult transition back to "normalcy."

But the normalcy of the Second Temple was not to be that of the First Temple, and the premonarchic pattern of dual leadership in civil and religious affairs gained new meaning and cogency. It was an enormous challenge for the two prophets to sensitize their audience to the traditional authority and the feasibility of the new pattern of leadership. At the same time, the temple still lay in ruins. The prophets provided that crucial measure of support for the enterprise of rebuilding that tipped the balance in favor of the temple's restoration being achieved. Haggai in particular is almost singlehandedly responsible for inspiring his countrymen to get about the task of actual labor on the temple. More than the accounts in Ezra (5:1 and 6:14) of those days, the Book of Haggai provides vivid testimony of the effect his words had on the people (Hag 1:12–13): the people heeded the words of Haggai and set about their task of rebuilding the temple. Since the two prophets Haggai and Zechariah overlap in their ministries, and since Zechariah presupposes that temple work had already recommenced, we can assume that the building efforts had been brought about by Haggai's exhortations. Whereas Haggai is largely concerned with the reluctance of the Yehudites to respond to the Persian mandate, and with their preoccupation with personal over national affairs, Zechariah is more concerned with the meaning and symbolism of the temple as a legitimate and legitimizing expression of the new pattern of dyarchic leadership that went along with it. There is a clear progression in these two prophetic sources regarding the pattern of work on the temple and the social and political concerns which Haggai encountered and Zechariah faced.

There are other differences in outlook in the two books that also seem to reflect changes in the international context. Haggai's brief ministry falls closer to the beginning of Darius's reign (520) than does that of Zechariah, who prophesied from 520 until 518 and possibly remained active in public life as he and his disciple(s) prepared a compendious work (Hag-Zech 1–8) for final publication in advance of the rededication of the temple in 516 or 515. It is possible that the uncertainty which surrounded the beginning of Darius's rule in 522, when rebellions and problems of succession plagued him, underlies the final utterance of Haggai in 2:20–23. But our exegesis of that oracle confirms that Haggai has projected his hopes for a monarchic kingdom into a time in the future. Nonetheless, Zerubbabel's name is repeatedly mentioned in Haggai; in Zechariah, Zerubbabel is explicitly mentioned only in the oracular Insertion to the Fourth Vision (Zech 4:6b–10a). Zechariah even omits any reference to Zerubbabel's secular office of governor.

Haggai thus seems to reflect a more heightened eschatology than Zechariah, one in which the hope of future monarchic restoration was nevertheless "realistic." By postponing the fulfillment of the expectation until the end time, Haggai was steering clear of those of his countrymen who expected that with the rebuilding of the temple the monarchy would also be restored. However, there is no hint even in the final oracle that he envisions a breakdown of the present social order in which priest, prophet, and governor work hand in hand to bolster the common welfare. Haggai's concerns are extended beyond temple work and ideology to include a prophetic interpretation of a priestly ruling (2:10–14). In so doing, he establishes a new role for the prophetic figure in the absence of prophecy's traditional association with monarchy and kingship.

Critics have claimed that the value of the Book of Haggai is to be discerned merely in the modest amount of historical detail preserved in the text. They claim either that the book is devoid of spiritual content and religious significance or that Haggai fostered a narrow and rigid exclusiveness that signaled the decline of Judaism in the Second Commonwealth period. We, however, have found Haggai to stand squarely in the tradition of his prophetic forebears in language, idiom, and point of view. At the same time Haggai clearly points toward a future that was at first uncertain. He eases his countrymen over the trauma of return and succeeds in rousing them to work on the temple. This he does with rhetorical ingenuity and skill and with a sophisticated, elevated prose style.

Haggai speaks to a people who are about to be revitalized and who are clearly invigorated by the prophetic word. He has set the stage for a changing world order that is ultimately, with the help of Zechariah, to be accepted by the Yehudites despite their initial misgivings. That new world was further presented and expounded by Zechariah, but the new order to come was to be fully achieved only in the mid-fifth century, in the time of Ezra and Nehemiah. Second Temple Judaism was to survive largely because of the success of the careers of Haggai and Zechariah; and Haggai, despite the fact that he was on the scene for so short a time, must be credited with steering Israel over the most delicate stage in this critical transition period.

For Zechariah the national focus of Yehud has already been transformed, or revitalized. The work on the temple was in progress, and Zechariah makes clear the object lessons of the past that were evident in the destruction and exile of Judah. Part One (Zech 1:1–6), which overlaps in time with Haggai, expresses Zechariah's only reservations about his fellow men and women. For the rest of the work his main business is to clarify in visions and oracles the world about him and to articulate a hopeful vision of the future. That world is painted with literary artistry and prophetic authority, and the reader of his words or a listener is transported into a symbolic world in which the temple and its chief appurtenances come to signify and legitimize aspects of the contemporary world order. This prophet, like so many of his predecessors, is clearly an individual of great political acumen and a man who has correctly perceived the stability and staying power of Persian dominion. Only the Second Vision reflects his concern for the potentially negative manifestations of Persian rule. It is the progress on the rebuilding of the temple, however, that inspires Zechariah to reflect on the world around him and to advise people how to operate within it.

The restoration of the sacred temple in Jerusalem is the key to the establishment of the new, largely ecclesiastical system of community autonomy under Persian rule. The construction of a temple in the absence of a dynastic power in Yehud ran counter to the pattern of the centuries of the Davidic monarchy in Judah and to the general integration of temple and palace in the political states of the ancient world. Could Yehud countenance a temple without a king? Could internal rule be legitimate, resting on the temple and its leadership alone, without the historically predominant monarchic component of national life? Zechariah provides an affirmative answer to both these questions. Chapter 3 offers divine sanction for the expanded powers of the high priest, and chapter 4 and the final oracular scene of Part Two, The Crowning (6:9–15), justify the presence of a civil leader who is of the royal line and at the same time interpret how the monarchic kingdom is to be realized only at some eschatological moment. Part Three of Zechariah (cc 7–8), which bears the latest chronological marker of the entire Haggai-Zechariah 1–8 corpus, presupposes a Jerusalem ecclesiastical power in full control (7:3), despite the fact, which we know from internal biblical as well as from external archaeological sources, that civil governors continued to function throughout the restoration period.

In terms of religious affairs, Zechariah exhibits a sense of concern over the presence of foreign cults or influence (Sixth Vision); Persian hegemony must not threaten Yahweh's supremacy. But in articulating his eschatological expectations, he is simultaneously broadminded in his view of the role of the gentile nations (8:23). As in Haggai, Zechariah's ground of theological retrospection is the authoritative Law of the Covenant (Fifth Vision) and the influential words of the earlier prophets to whom he repeatedly refers (e.g., 7:7,12). Persian efforts to organize the provinces and to encourage local religious leaders to collect and codify their laws, especially during the reign of Darius, clearly had a great effect on Zechariah and his contemporaries. Zechariah's persistent reference to what appears to be a written corpus suggests that the Primary History together with a prophetic corpus already constituted a body of sacred writings.

Indeed, the impetus to combine Zechariah 1–8 with Haggai could well have arisen in part from Darius's policies in this regard. The composite work, if it was intended to be presented to the people in time for the rededication ceremony, would thus stand as the repository of words which expressed the ideological basis for the Second Commonwealth. How appropriate it would have been to have had it recited at the dedication of the Second Temple, the institutional center of developing Jewish life!

Haggai and Zechariah, two Yehudites who had survived the exile and the uncertain period of the early years of the restoration, must be given enormous credit for using their prophetic ministries to foster the transition of a people from national autonomy to an existence which transcended political definition and which centered upon a view of God and his moral demands. Some may find it difficult to comprehend how a prophet could serve the authorities without losing the true spirit of what a prophet should be. We can only say that the unique circumstances of the restoration period and Persian governance represent a situation that differed fundamentally from the monarchic world in which classical prophecy had emerged. Insofar as the two prophets saw that this was the case, they both endeavored to express their own comprehension of past events and contemporary affairs. Both prophets succeeded in an unprecedented way in helping to reconcile the present circumstances with sacred traditions. If they seem to point in a new direction, it is because there was no turning back. If they seem too committed to supporting the powers that be, it is because the alternative was to oppose the mightiest power of the day, which probably would have led to the destruction of much that was valuable in their national heritage. As transmitters of Yahweh's word in a period where it might not have been otherwise heard, they serve as spokesmen for Yahweh and also as tradents of the past. With society lacking a king and a palace, there was no course but to develop another society with different emphases. All this was accomplished by Haggai and First Zechariah who, according to the wisdom of later rabbinic tradition, were among the last of the prophets and were among those who were responsible for assuring Judaism of its passage to the sages of the Great Assembly. For us it is enough to say that they enabled exilic Judaism to be transformed in such a way as to secure its survival far into the future.

LITERARY CONSIDERATIONS

The Structure of the Composite Work

Haggai and the first eight chapters of the canonical book of Zechariah belong together as a composite work. Justification for this statement can be found on thematic grounds alone. Both prophets deal with the reorganization of national life and institutions in the restoration period. The dated prophecies of both Haggai and Zechariah 1–8 take place within a very close time frame (August 29, 520, to December 7, 518 B.C.E.). The cast of characters in the two works is virtually the same: the high priest Joshua, the governor Zerubbabel, priests, the citizenry or representatives thereof. While they diverge to a certain extent in the specifics of their words, the two prophets complement each other, as one might indeed expect of two men of God who are responding to virtually the same questions and the same quandaries. Together they provide a pragmatic program as well as a worldview which looks to the future in the process of dealing with the challenges and opportunities their people confronted at the outset of the reign of Darius I.

Aside from these obvious congruencies of content and context, various features of their literary structure indicate that Haggai and Zechariah 1–8 can be viewed as a combined work. Furthermore, the individual utterances of these two prophetic leaders of the restoration were apparently delivered and then collected and organized into their present arrangement all within a relatively few years. Haggai's words serve to initiate, or reinitiate, work on the temple in 520 and then to draw attention to the significance of the actual ceremony of refoundation. Zechariah is similarly moved to experience and describe his visions and utter his oracles in connection with that event. His last group of oracles comes less than ten months after the refoundation ceremony. The chronological headings (see Chart 2) provide a span of less than two and a half years for the material in Haggai and Zechariah 1–8 and indicate that the two works could not have been put together as they stand any earlier than the last date given, December 7, 518. In other words, the latest date in Zechariah 1–8 serves as a *terminus post quem* for the compilation of the whole work.

The date for the completion or publication of the composite work is more difficult to ascertain. However, two considerations lead us to believe that the process of completing the work took place within a very short time after the last date given. The first consideration comes in response to the question of what might have led to the act of compilation. If the temple work and refoundation ceremony were the events that elicited the prophecies of Haggai and Zechariah 1–8, then it seems likely that the temple rededication itself in 516 or 515 B.C.E. would have had an equally great impact upon the prophets of the restoration. Yet that momentous event of the postexilic period (cf. Ezra 6:14) is not once mentioned in the Haggai-Zechariah 1–8 corpus. Its absence can only be understood as a consequence of the fact that this prophetic work was completed *before* the rededication took place. That is, the ceremony of 515 is the *terminus a quo* of the Haggai-Zechariah 1–8 composite. While the dedication itself is not mentioned, the imminence of that event must have been a significant factor for increasing the esteem in which those prophecies dealing with the rebuilding of the temple would have been held. The anticipation of the rededication of the temple would have provided the motivation for the organization and promulgation of these two prophetic works. We might even posit a functional relationship between publication of Haggai-Zechariah 1–8 and the rededication ceremony. The former may have helped to ensure that the latter took place.

The second consideration bearing upon our understanding of the completion of Haggai-Zechariah 1–8 is the relationship of the authorship of all the parts of this work with the final redaction. Our detailed examination of all the sections of these two prophets reveals two important kinds of unity. The varied literary genres within each prophetic work are interwoven into a coherent whole, and there is no evidence to suggest that the distinct kinds of material would have existed as separate collections of prophetic utterances. This is particularly true of Zechariah 1–8, in which oracular material is juxtaposed with visionary units. Not only have we found no cause to recognize an independent context for each, but also we have found good reason to view the visions and the oracles as integral parts of a whole. The mixing of genres is a sign of artistry rather than of differentiation of authorship or setting. In several places, internal cross-references mandate that the materials were integrated at a time very close to the time of their original utterance. In short, each prophetic work is composed of materials that can legitimately be assigned to the chronological framework the books themselves establish.

The other kind of unity involves the connection of Haggai with Zechariah 1–8. In addition to the interlocking chronological headings, there are several stylistic and thematic features, which we shall present below, that demonstrate conclusively an overall scheme meant to unite the two chapters of Haggai with

Chart 2
Chronological data in Hag-Zech 1-8

Passage No.	Passage	Year of Darius	Month	Day	Date of New Moon	Equivalent Date B.C.E.	Date No.
1	Hag 1:1	2nd	6th	1st	Aug. 29	Aug. 29, 520	1
2	Hag 1:15	2nd	6th	24th	Aug. 29	Sept. 21, 520	2
3	Hag 2:1	2nd[a]	7th	21st	Sept. 27	Oct. 17, 520	3
4	Hag 2:10[b]	2nd	9th	24th	Nov. 25	Dec. 18, 520	4
5	Hag 2:20	2nd	9th	24th	Nov. 25	Dec. 18, 520	4
6	Zech 1:1[c]	2nd	8th	—[d]	Oct. 27	Oct. (Nov.), 520	5
7	Zech 1:7	2nd	11th	24th	Jan. 23	Feb. 15, 519	6
8	Zech 7:1	4th	9th	4th	Dec. 4	Dec. 7, 518	7

[a]The year appears at the end of the preceding date, Hag 1:15.
[b]This date is repeated, without the year, in 2:18 as a summary of the 2:10-18 section.
[c]This date breaks the sequence, being earlier than the previous two dates in Haggai.
[d]The formula omits the day.

the eight chapters of Zechariah. The latter are called First Zechariah, to distinguish them from the six additional chapters, Zechariah 9–14 or Deutero-Zechariah, of the canonical Book of Zechariah.

Recognizing that Haggai-Zechariah 1–8 is a single compendious work, published in anticipation of the auspicious event of the temple's rededication, does not resolve the issues of who edited the work or how much independent input into its final shape the editor may have provided. Such questions cannot be resolved, given the lack of direct information about the process of redaction. However, it is not impossible that the prophets themselves, or more likely (First) Zechariah, since he comes second, were responsible for putting the material together. Indeed, the first-person references in Zechariah 7:4 and 8:1 (see NOTES) suggest the distinct possibility of Zechariah's direct involvement. Alternatively, the third-person references to Haggai and to Zechariah might constitute a narrative framing provided by a follower of one or the other of these prophets. Yet it is not inconceivable that the prophets themselves, in shaping their words and in knowledge of their prophetic heritage, introduced their own work with such language. Nothing that we have discovered in the two prophets has proved definitive in arguing against the assumption that Haggai and Zechariah were the authors of virtually all that is attributed to them and that Zechariah himself, since his concluding words echo some of Haggai's themes, had a composite work in mind. Zechariah or a close disciple would have united the two small prophetic collections into the form in which they now appear.

The many chronological markers found within the text of Haggai and First Zechariah provide the overall structure for the combined work. They are also important for dating the materials to which they are attached, for presumably the prophet or editor would not otherwise have bothered with them. The arrangement of the dates in and of itself is of interest. Although there are eight headings, five in Haggai and three in First Zechariah, there are only seven dates (see Chart 2) in all. Number 4 and 5 signify the same day. Not only is December 18, 520 B.C.E., mentioned twice, but it also occupies positions 4 and 5, in the center of the sequence of eight listings. That is, there are three dates given, all in Haggai, before the December 18, 520, date; and there are three dates provided, all in Zechariah, following that date. This arrangement creates a focus on the central date. The chronological climax of Haggai-Zechariah 1–8 is clearly the event of December 18, 520, the refoundation ceremony. All the chronological markers thus have been carefully set into place in Haggai-Zechariah 1–8 to draw attention to a momentous event and also to provide a structure for the work as a whole.

With respect to the latter observation, that the dates create a structure for the composite work, the total number of dates (8), or more properly their arrangement into a 7 + 1 pattern, is also to be noted. The final editor, be it Zechariah or his disciple, has a distinct interest in maintaining the combination 7 + 1. Seven is the most obvious symbolic and sacred number in the Hebrew Bible and in the Semitic world in general. Therefore 7 + 1 represents an adherence to seven's symbolic value, with an extra thrust. The most obvious way in which the author/editor of the final work demonstrates his consciousness of this is in the arrangement of the visions, as we shall explain below, into 7 + 1 separate visionary units. In the chronological headings we see other examples of this: 1) seven have the month/day/year, and an eighth (Zech 1:1) omits it; 2) seven separate dates are given, and an eighth (Hag 2:20) repeats one; 3) seven dates are in the second year of Darius's reign, and an eighth (Zech 7:1) is in the fourth year; 4) seven dates include the year, and in one the year appears at the end of the preceding date, where it does double duty for both (Hag 1:15, 2:1); 5) seven dates precede the unit for which they provide the chronological information, and one date (Hag 1:15) concludes the unit. This list shows five different ways in which the combination of 7 + 1 is maintained when the works of Haggai and First Zechariah are taken as a composite work. Such structural unity, along with the identity of thematic interests, marks the combined prophecies. Yet this is not to suggest an identity, from either an ideological or a literary perspective, in the way in which each prophet responds to the issues of his day.

Haggai

This commentary divides the Book of Haggai into two parts, or two chapters, according to the two canonical chapters. However, this short prophetic work actually is composed of five units, which correspond to the five subunits in our arrangement of the material. *Restoration of the Temple* (1:1–15) consists of two subunits: "Prophetic call to work on the temple" (1:1–11) and "Response of leaders and people" (1:12–15). *Oracles of Encouragement* (2:1–23) is divided into three subunits: "Assurance of God's presence" (2:1–9), "Priestly ruling with prophetic interpretation" (2:10–19), and "Future hope" (2:20–23).

The creation of five subunits is dictated by the five chronological headings in Haggai. These headings set off prophetic materials which evidently emerged at separate, consecutive moments in the second year of Darius's reign. Each subunit has its own integrity with respect to content, although there is a development from first to last and a building upon themes which give an overall unity to this book.

The "Prophetic call to work on the temple" is introduced by a full date formula in which the regnal year of the Persian king is the first item presented. Only the last date in the Haggai-Zechariah 1–8 composite (Zech 7:1) has the same sequence of components; the arrangement of the first and last dates thus frames the entire work. The material in 1:1–10 is varied, containing the narrative description of Yahweh's call to Haggai and five separate oracular statements: 1) a brief retrospective description explaining the situation in which the people have put off work on the temple; 2) an initial call, couched as a rhetorical question, for the people to begin work on the temple; 3) a reflection upon the present state of hardship; 4) an exhortation to take the initial steps for temple construction; 5) an explicit causal connection between the economic difficulties and the ruined temple. Two of these messages are quasi-poetic in form (1:6; 1:8–9), as our arrangement of the translation suggests. Even the last oracle (1:9b–11), which contains several intricately ordered sets of items, exhibits prose artistry verging on the poetic. The themes and terms of the last three oracles all can be related to the language and content of chapters 7–8 of Zechariah (see Chart 3 and our discussion below of those chapters).

Chart 3
Correspondences Between Haggai and First Zechariah
Part Three 7–8

Feature	Haggai	Zechariah
date formula	1:1,15; 2:1,10,18,20	7:1
oracular question	2:11ff.	7:3ff.
"House of Yahweh of Hosts"	1:14	7:3; 8:9
"people of the land"	2:4	7:5
devastation of land	1:6	7:14
"remnant" of the people	1:12,14; 2:2	8:6,11,12
be strong	2:4(3×)	8:9–10
refound/rebuild temple	1:2; 2:18	8:9
House = temple	1:2; 2:3,7,15,18	8:9; 7:3
earnings	1:6	8:10
man/beast	1:11	8:10
prosperous sowing/temple building	1:6–11; 2:18–19	8:12
land/produce; heavens/dew	1:10	8:12
blessing	2:19	8:13
"do not fear"	2:5	8:13
"nations"	2:7,22	8:13,22,23
hem/garment	2:12	8:23
Elohim	1:12(2×),14	8:8,23

The second section of Haggai consists of a narrative describing the "Response of the leaders and people" to the prophet's call. It concludes with the date formula. One brief oracular statement, "I am with you," appears in the center of this short subunit and signifies God's support for a people who will attend to what is demanded of them.

The next three subunits, contained in Haggai 2, offer various forms of encouragement for the task the people have undertaken. In "Assurance of God's presence," the "I am with you" message of the previous subunit is expanded. The present enterprise, under way a month after the last oracle, is related to both past conditions and future expectations. The heightened prose, particularly when the future is contemplated, can be compared with that of the oracles at the end of Haggai-Zechariah 1–8. The "Priestly ruling with prophetic interpretation" provides another, and quite distinct, form of encouragement. This subunit is set off not only by its unique dialogic format but also by its being framed by dates—that is, by a repetition of the December 18 date in the summation of vv 18–19. Again a chronological awareness involving past, present, and future is evident in the prophetic language. Finally, the "Future hope" section concludes Haggai's brief ministry. A second oracle in that momentous day, December 18, 520, is directed toward the future, but a future connected with the present.

First Zechariah

The division of First Zechariah into three major sections is determined in the first place by the threefold appearance of the date formula in Zechariah 1–8. The sections marked by that formula are hardly equal in size. The division in that sense seems awkward, with Part One consisting of only six verses (1:1–6), Part Two containing over five chapters (1:7–6:15), and Part Three comprising two chapters. However, a number of features make such a subdivision compelling.

To begin with, the nature of the material in each of the three parts, despite the interconnections that can be demonstrated in style and subject matter, is quite distinct. The first part, with its brief narrative and its retrospection, serves as an introduction to the whole. The second part is marked primarily by the presentation of a sequence of visionary experiences for which First Zechariah is perhaps best known. The third section is largely oracular in nature. Furthermore, the literary style in each section has unique qualities. This aspect of their differentiation is a function of the use of three distinct genres: narration, vision, oracle. In addition to these differences in the genre and style of prophetic utterances, the internal content of each section fits the chronological information provided at the outset of each. Although the total time frame is not great, there are evidently important developments in what is happening within the prophet's community which evoke his response at intervals. The responses which constitute the three parts stand respectively in relationship to the particular conditions of October (November) 520 (Part One), February 15, 519 (Part Two), and December 7, 518 (Part Three).

Chart 4
Location of Prophetic Genres in First Zechariah

Genre	Part One	Part Two	Part Three
narration with retrospection	X		y
visions		X	
oracles	y^a	y	X

X = dominant type   y = type also present

^{a} appears within the retrospection

Although the organization of the material into three sections is quite clear, the overall unity of the whole is equally compelling on literary grounds alone for two reasons. First, while each section is dominated by one genre, each section also contains material which can be identified with a genre that dominates another section. Chart 4 shows this arrangement: the narration/retrospection of Part One contains oracular statements; visions dominate Part Two but oracles are only somewhat less prominent and probably are equally important as vehicles for the prophetic message; and the oracles that characterize Part Three are set within a context introduced by a narration/retrospection. Chart 4 shows also that the prophetic visions constitute the centerpiece of the book of First Zechariah. They appear only in the second section, whereas the other two forms appear in other sections. More specifically, the narration with retrospection that characterizes Part One is echoed in Part Three, creating an envelope that links these two parts as do many other aspects of those two sections (cf. Chart 5). The third type—oracular material—although dominating the third section is found in all three parts. This is not surprising, since the oracle is the *sine qua non* of prophecy.

Second, certain examples of the phraseology and vocabulary of each section are repeated in the other sections. Charts 5 and 6 contain listings of the major correspondences among the three parts of First Zechariah. Although the charts do not indicate it, the correspondences involve the several genres within each section—and there is crossing of genres. For example, the theme of scattering or strewing as an image of exile appears in the Second Vision (2:2,4) and in an oracular insertion (2:14) in the narration of Part Three. Or, "decided to" appears in the narrative (1:6) of Part One and in an oracle (8:14,15)

Chart 5
Correspondences Between First Zechariah Parts One
(1:1–6) and Three (7–8)

Feature	Zech 1:1–6	Zech 7–8
"word of Yahweh came to"†	1:1	7:1,4; 8:1,8
"earlier prophets"	1:4,5,6	7:7,12 (8:9)
"proclaim"†	1:4	7:7,13
ancestors	1:4–6	7:11–12
divine anger/wrath†	1:2	7:12
"Thus spoke Yahweh of Hosts"†	1:3,4	7:9; 8:2,3,4,6,7,9, 14,19,20,23
"decided to"	1:6	8:14,15

† also appears in First Zechariah Part Two (1:7–6:15)

of Part Three. Then it becomes very difficult if not impossible to argue that the language of one genre or part influenced that of another. The interconnections transcend the differentiation of the prophetic genres. In sum, the material as a whole cannot be adequately represented by simply pointing to correspondences of language and repetitions of genre. The disparate types of material have been interwoven into a single fabric. Such intermingling points to a unity of authorship or a common origin for the bulk of the material in First Zechariah, and is matched by the intermingling of prose and poetry, a feature of Haggai-Zechariah 1–8 that we treat separately below.

Part One (1:1–6)

This small unit stands as a discrete section of First Zechariah alongside the much longer sections of Parts Two and Three. Those other two parts are themselves divided into subunits, whereas this first part is not. Hence we can direct the reader to our COMMENT to 1:1–6, *Call for Obedience with Retrospection,* for a discussion of the salient features of that unit and of its meaning as the introduction to the prophecies of First Zechariah.

When seen as a part of the compendious work Haggai-Zechariah 1–8, these six verses emerge as a transitional piece connecting the two sections of Haggai with the two subsequent sections of Zechariah. Zechariah 1:1–6 exhibits awareness of Haggai's ministry by echoing some of his language (see Chart 7) and by referring to Haggai's effectiveness in bringing about a change in the stance of the community with respect to temple building. The mixture of genres in Part One—narration with retrospection along with oracular material —accords with the style of Haggai.

The insertion of oracular statements into 1:1–6 has the same general charac-

Chart 6
Correspondences Between First Zechariah Parts Two
(1:7–6:15) and Three (7–8)

Feature	Zech 1:7–6:15	Zech 7–8
"word of Yahweh came to"†	1:7 (cf. 4:6)	7:1,4; 8:1,8
"seventy years"	1:12	7:5,(3)
"proclaim"†	1:17	7:7,13
Jerusalem inhabited	2:8	7:7
Jerusalem protected/secure	2:9	7:7
divine anger/wrath†	2:15	7:12
strewn/scattered = exile	2:2,4	7:14
"Thus spoke Yahweh of	1:14,17; 2:12; 3:7;	7:9; 8:2,3,4,6,7,9,
Hosts"†	6:12	14,19,20,23
"Thus spoke Yahweh"	1:16	8:3
holy mountain	2:17	8:3
return to Zion/Jerusalem	1:16	8:3
"They will be my people"	2:15	8:8
nations will go to Jerusalem	2:15	8:22
Yehud as holy land	2:16	8:22–23

† also appears in First Zechariah Part One (1:1–7)

ter as the use of oracles elsewhere in Haggai-Zechariah 1–8. However, in this section the layering of oracles is particularly dense, with an intricate series of quotes within quotes contained within these few verses. No fewer than five, and perhaps six, quotations appear, and they are layered as well as consecutive. This complex arrangement represents several converging influences: Zechariah's sensitivity to previous prophetic activity; the nature of prophecy as the mediated word of God; the growing authority of traditional materials; and perhaps also the highly developed epistolary style of the Persian Empire, with its reports of conversations held by government officials.

Part Two (1:7–6:15)

The prophetic reputation of First Zechariah rests largely on the unique set of visions, which predominate in the second section of Zechariah 1–8. The use of the prophetic or symbolic vision is hardly new to Zechariah. Classical Hebrew prophecy was interspersed with visionary materials from its inception. The prophet "sees" in the objects or persons around him meanings that transcend the normal qualities of those figures. The prophet's perception of reality is extraordinary. The conventional properties of realia are transformed. The physical, spatial details that the prophet confronts leap out at him and

Chart 7
Correspondences[a] Between Haggai and
First Zechariah Part One (1:1–6)

Feature	Haggai	Zech 1:1–6
your "ways" (and "deeds")	1:5,7	1:4,6
"heed"	1:12	1:5
covenant "word"	2:5	1:6
"proclaim"	1:4	1:4

[a] exclusive of formulaic language introducing oracles

take on temporal significance. They can recall to the prophet past events, or they can signify future occurrences, or they can do both. Objects become symbols in the prophetic vision as their three-dimensionality is infused with the heightened sense of time, past through present to future, that is a feature of Hebrew prophecy.

Zechariah's visions exhibit these characteristics and so stand in the line of classical prophecy. Yet they take the prophetic vision in new directions, which can be evaluated both as the culmination of the visionary mode as it exists in the Hebrew Bible and also as the harbinger of the visionary cycles that characterize apocalyptic literature, particularly in its floruit of 200 B.C.E. to 100 C.E. Two features of Zechariah's visions, which we shall discuss in full, emerge as determinative in this evaluation: the organization of the visions into a structured set so that there is meaning to each vision on its own and also as part of a larger whole; and the role of angelic beings in the auditory component of the prophet's visionary experience.

First Zechariah offers his audience a carefully arranged sequence of eight visions which exhibits a number of important characteristics. First, the visions are organized into three subsets. There are three visions in front (nos. 1–3), three visions at the end (nos. 5–7), and two visions in the middle (prophetic vision plus Vision 4):

Vision 1: Horses Patrolling the Earth
Vision 2: The Four Horns and the Four Smiths
Vision 3: The Man with the Measuring-Cord
     Prophetic vision: Joshua and the Priestly
     Vestments
Vision 4: The Lampstand and the Two Olive Trees
Vision 5: The Flying Scroll
Vision 6: The Ephah
Vision 7: The Four Chariots

Second, this sequence is justified by the fact that there are correspondences and correlations between the first three visions and the last three. These connections, which are presented in detail in our COMMENT on each of those visions, include subject matter (e.g., the horses of Visions 1 and 7), internal structure (e.g., two parts each to Visions 2 and 6 and direct inclusion of oracular material in Visions 3 and 5), and language. These general correspondences are accompanied by other specific ones, found in each pair of visions though different for each.

Third, the correspondences between the individual units of the first and third subsets are organized in inverse order, with the first and last visions complementing each other, the same for the second and sixth, and also for the third and fifth. The correlations can be established on stylistic grounds for the first three and last three visions. This has the effect of establishing the central pair as a complementary set, although the stylistic correspondences between those two are absent; stylistic contrast (see below) in fact characterizes the relationship of the central two visions to each other.

Fourth, the stylistic correlations between the first and third subsets are accompanied by thematic relationships. In particular, the scope of one member of the paired visions is comparable to that of the other member. Chart 8 shows in two ways the purview of the visions. The outer two have a universal dimension, dealing as they do with Yahweh's worldwide scrutiny (Vision 1) and power (Vision 7). The middle two (nos. 2 and 6) are international in scope in that they are concerned with Judah/Yehud and the imperial powers (Assyria, Babylon, and/or Persia) that determined Yehud's destiny in the seventh and sixth centuries. The inner two narrow to a national focus, examining Jerusalem's territory (Vision 3) and self-rule (Vision 5). As a result of this progressively smaller field of interest, the central subset emerges with the temple in Jerusalem as the center of the prophet's universe. The overall structure, in spatial terms, can be conceived of as a series of superimposed circles as shown on Chart 8, with Yahweh and the whole world as the largest circle and the temple and the leadership of Yehud at the center. Such an arrangement is meant to show that the smaller circles are inseparable from the larger ones, which contain them. Jerusalem at the center is part of Yehud, of the international community of nations, and of the cosmos as ordered by Yahweh.

Fifth, all of the above points relate in some fashion to the existence of a centerpiece. The intricate structure of the sequence of eight visions has the effect of drawing the attention of the audience to the central subset, the prophetic vision and the Fourth, or Lampstand, Vision. The prophet's ultimate concern, we learn from this arrangement, lies with the temple and the leadership in Jerusalem. In this sense, the full visionary set can properly be called Zechariah's Temple Visions. Although only the central two visions deal explicitly with the temple, the fact that the center is an integral part of a carefully constructed whole indicates that the entire sequence emerges from the

Chart 8: Purview of the Visions

A. 1. UNIVERSAL: God's omniscience   7. UNIVERSAL: God's omnipotence

    2. INTERNATIONAL: Judah, the empires   6. INTERNATIONAL: Yehud, Persia

      3. NATIONAL: Jerusalem's territory   5. NATIONAL: self-rule of Yehud

    Prophetic Vision + 4. JERUSALEM: leadership, temple.

B.

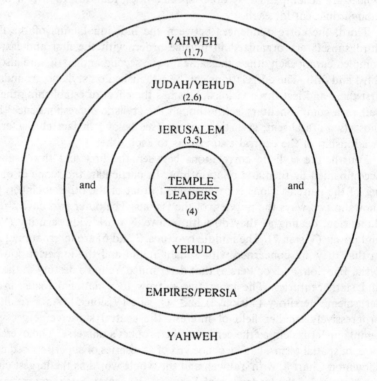

prophet's acute awareness of the conceptual and political problems surrounding the reorganization of the postexilic community and the reconstruction of that community's institutional core.

All of these characteristics of the eight visions have been presented using a system of numbering whereby the first three are called Visions 1, 2, and 3 and the last three are designated Visions 5, 6, and 7. In the center are the Fourth Vision and an unnumbered one. In a sense this enumeration is arbitrary, since the prophet himself did not number his visions. However, our analysis of 3:1–7 has revealed enough (five) distinct characteristics of that passage to warrant its being excluded from the numbered sequence. We have discussed these five separate features in our COMMENT to the *Heavenly Court and Investiture* (3:1–7), which is a subsection of chapter 6, "Joshua and the Priestly

Vestments: A Prophetic Vision." In addition to those features, which deal with the content and structure of the vision, the matter of stylized language must be considered.

Chart 9
Formulaic Language of the Visions

	1	2	3	Investiture Scene	4	5	6	7
"I raised my eyes"		X	X				X^b	X
"I looked/see" (Qal)	X	X	X	(X)^d	X	X	X^c	X
"(and) behold"	X	X	X^a		X	X	X^a	X
"again"					X	X		X
Zechariah asks "what/ where/whither"	X	X^a	X		X^a		X^a	X
Angel asks "what"					X^a	X		

^{a} appears twice
^{b} appears twice, first in imperative, then in declarative
^{c} imperative
^{d} "He showed me" (Hiphil)

The seven numbered visions are characterized by formulaic language, which recurs more or less throughout those seven units. Chart 9 shows the location of the major formulas that recur in the visions and that frame the specific contents of the individual visions. It is to be noted that none of the words or phrases found in the seven numbered visions appears in the Investiture Scene. Even the ubiquitous "I looked/see," which one would expect to characterize a prophet's reporting of any visionary experience, does not occur in the Investiture Scene in a way that would constitute a meaningful correspondence with the numbered visions. Zechariah 3:1 reads "He showed me" (Hiphil) rather than the expected "I looked" or "I see" (Qal).

One further consideration affecting our decision to omit the prophetic visions of chapter 3 from the numbered sequence is the recurrence of a 7 + 1 pattern in various aspects of the Haggai-Zechariah 1–8 work. The arrangement of the chronological markers, as discussed above, shows the repeated use of 7 + 1 combinations. The author exhibits an interest in maintaining a 7 + 1 structure, and to number the visions consecutively from 1 to 8 would in our opinion detract from one's consciousness of the 7 + 1 organization which recurs in Haggai-Zechariah 1–8. Since the prophetic vision of chapter 3 diverges in so many ways from the other visions, it seemed essential to us to have it stand alone, as the "one," the differing element in a 7 + 1 scheme.

Nonetheless, the investiture of chapter 3 must be designated a prophetic vision and must still be listed among Zechariah's Temple Visions. It is essential in form and in meaning to the sequence, and its resemblances to the seven numbered visions are as important as its differences. As part of the central set, its presence is vital to the understanding of the Fourth Vision, the other member of that set. In the symmetry of the whole sequence, those two become a matched pair, like the other three pairs. The messages of the two central visions are likewise complementary, with the meaning of the one being incomplete and incomprehensible without the meaning of the other.

All told, the complex organization of the visions stands out as a unique contribution of Zechariah to the Hebraic tradition of the prophetic vision. Symbolic visions are only sporadically interspersed in earlier prophecy, notably in Amos, Jeremiah, and Ezekiel. It is difficult to understand why they emerge as the dominant literary mode of First Zechariah's prophetic ministry. The reasons for this are undoubtedly complex but may result in part from the same influences and developments that gave rise to the simultaneous expansion of the role of mediating or angelic beings in the prophetic consciousness (see below). The more transcendent view of God in the late sixth century is accompanied by more indirect channels of communication: angels as well as prophets, symbols as well as words. In addition, the visions may have become central in Zechariah because of the way they relate to temple-building typology. Throughout the ancient Near East, and in Israel, the construction or restoration of temples was consequent upon a revelation to the king in which the deity gave instructions or approval for the ruler's plans to build or restore a temple, the earthly dwelling for that god. God's revelation to Moses (Exod 25:8–9) with respect to the tabernacle, and Solomon's dream at Gibeon (1 Kgs 3:5–14) participate in that typology. What would be the equivalent for the postexilic temple, built without the supervision of a royal leader? Perhaps Zechariah's visions constitute the functional equivalent of the divine revelation to the king. Like so much else in the postexilic period, premonarchic patterns are reawakened. The sanction for the tabernacle via Moses as prophet may find its counterpart in the dreamlike visions of the major prophet of the restoration. The Temple Visions of First Zechariah legitimize, according to the ancient typology, the rebuilt temple.

Just as the visionary mode characterizes Zechariah's special place in prophetic tradition, the role of heavenly beings within the visions marks Zechariah's special position in the ongoing history of the visionary mode in Hebraic literature. Angelic beings that share some of Yahweh's characteristics and serve as divine messengers are hardly new in Zechariah. The Hebrew Bible contains a plentitude of references to such figures. However, the combination of prophetic vision with one or more angelic mediators for the auditory component or exposition of the vision is distinctive in First Zechariah. We suggest (in our NOTES to 1:9) that the expanded world of Yehud with respect to divine sovereignty in the sixth century may be responsible to some extent for this innovation. Yahweh is more emphatically than ever the universal deity; and Yehud has been reduced to less than independent status. Communication with sovereign power, in the human plane, must take place through bureaucratic channels through emissaries and representatives. Insofar as political models consistently colored Israel's ideology, it should come as no surprise to have the prophetic communication of Yahweh's will become mediated by Yahweh's bureaucrats, the heavenly host, at just that time when Yehud's populace became one step more removed from ultimate political authority. The veritable explosion of angelic personalities in late biblical and in postbiblical apocalyptic literature stands to some extent in relationship to the increasingly severe problems of national autonomy and identity in the Hellenistic-Roman period.

The foregoing discussion of the prophetic visions, extensive as it has been, does not complete this treatment of Part Two. The visions are not the only prophetic material that appears in Part Two. A substantial number of oracles are interspersed with the visions. Although it would be convenient to separate the oracles and consider them as a distinct component of Part Two of First Zechariah, their integral relationship with the visionary units invalidates such a separation.

The oracles are incorporated into the visions in several ways. In some cases they have been worked into the very fabric of a vision, as in the First, Third, and Fifth Visions. In other places they appear to be more self-contained units, as in Expansion of the first three visions (2:10–17 [RSV 2:6–13]), the Supplementary Oracle of Chapter 3 (3:8–10), the Zerubbabel insertion of the Fourth Vision (4:6b–10a), and the oracular portion of the final crowning scene (6:9–15) of Part Two. However, in these latter instances the words "expansion," "supplement," and "insertion" are to be understood appropriately. In no way are these terms meant to indicate a separate origin or identity for the material so designated. In reality, all of these oracular sections not already incorporated into the actual visions are nonetheless integral to the visions. The ideas contained within the oracles amplify themes found in the visions and at the same time are based upon features of these associated visions. In other words, vision and oracle complement and supplement each other. They are alternative modes of prophetic communication, employed in tandem by the prophet. Each is peculiarly suited to an aspect of his message, and so the message is communicated in the two modes. But the message is incomplete without the mutuality of these two forms of prophetic language.

The convergence, or more accurately the merger, of vision and oracle in First Zechariah is analogous to, and perhaps also functionally related to, the close relationship of poetry and prose in Haggai-Zechariah 1–8 (see below). The language for conveying a visionary experience is normally the prose of narration, whereas the language for communicating an oracle is often poetry. The former describes an indirect communication of the divine will, through the symbolic meaning of objects or people; the latter communicates, as only poetry can, the prophet's direct experience of God's word. If Zechariah's prophetic activity involves both visions and direct "auditions" of Yahweh's word, then we should not be surprised to find vision and oracle, narrative and poetic language. They are intermingled because of the rich and varied expressions of First Zechariah's prophetic consciousness. The presentation of the visions takes on its characteristic dialogic character because of the role of the Interpreting Angel, but that feature should not deflect us from perceiving the basic narrative structure of those visions.

Part Three (7:1–8:23)

Chapters 7 and 8 of the Book of Zechariah play a special role in the organization of Zechariah alone and also in the relationship between the Books of Haggai and Zechariah. These two chapters constitute a distinct literary unit. Although itself composed of four subunits, it has an overall integrity as one of the major sections of First Zechariah. Furthermore, its clear relationship to the material in Haggai, as shown in Chart 9, creates a framework for Haggai-Zechariah 1–8 and indicates that Zechariah 1–8 forms a composite work with the two chapters of Haggai. These two important observations about Zechariah 7–8 are suggested sporadically throughout our NOTES to that section, as one or other of the features that have made us aware of them has been encountered in the text.

The independence of chapters 7 and 8 as a literary whole within Zechariah is apparent first and foremost from an examination of several of its stylistic qualities. The use of formulaic clauses or phrases at the outset of this section sets it apart as a unit with respect to the rest of Zechariah 1–8. The chief and most obvious example of this is the use of the date formula, introducing the time of the ensuing prophetic materials in relationship to the regnal year of the Persian emperor. The dated formulas create three sections, of which this is the third. While this feature in and of itself might not be sufficient to justify such a division, it is accompanied by an oracular formula ("The word of Yahweh came . . .") which likewise is found in Zechariah 1:1 and 1:7. This formula is rather awkward in its present position within the chronological heading, a fact which suggests that it has been inserted there in order to reinforce the impression, already created by the date formula, that Zechariah 7–8 stands as a section distinct from 1:1–6 and 1:7–6:15. Furthermore, Part Three contains no visions and in that way is distinct from Part Two; and it does contain extensive oracular passages and so differs from the terse narration with retrospective that dominates Part One (cf. Chart 4).

The two chapters contain diverse kinds of prophetic and oracular materials. They have been shaped into a unit by the event that, according to the information supplied at the beginning of chapter 7, occasioned the prophetic utterance in the first place. A delegation arrives at the temple with a question about fasting, which provokes a series of retrospectives and oracles. These culminate in an eschatological vision that transforms the original question about fasting into an opportunity to depict the future of Israel and of all the nations. Yet it is the delegation's arrival and query that frame and underlie the prophetic words. The internally stated stimulus for the prophetic activity recorded in Part Three is accompanied by external conditions implied by the date of this section. All the other dates given in Haggai and Zechariah are in the second year of Darius's reign. Part Three is attributed to the fourth year (cf. Chart 2). The temple building project was the stimulus for the prophecies of Haggai and Zechariah 1–6. It was another development in Yehud within the Persian Empire, two years later, that provoked Zechariah's final prophetic outburst.

The ways in which the form and content of Part Three make it a discrete part of Zechariah should not obscure the fact that at the same time it is an integral part of Zechariah 1 through 8. It shares with Part One a strong and direct retrospective interest. The prophet in both sections is acutely aware of the events leading up to and coming after the destruction of 587; and in both parts he proclaims the authority of Yahweh's words, which come to Israel both in the covenant and through prophecy. Not surprisingly, some of the vocabulary with which Zechariah treats his retrospective concern in Part One ("ancestors," "earlier prophets," "words") is found again in Part Three. See Chart 5 for a listing of correspondences between Zechariah 7–8 and Zechariah 1:1–6.

Similar observations can be made about connections between Parts Two and Three. Very few direct stylistic contacts exist between the material in chapters 7 and 8 and the visions, but the visions are a category unto themselves and we should not expect correspondences. Furthermore, the visions deal directly with the initiation of the temple project which, two years later, is no longer of immediate concern to Zechariah. However, the visions of 1:7–6:15 are interspersed with oracular passages. In these sections we see many themes and much language encountered again in Part Three. Our NOTES specify those shared features (see, e.g., NOTES to 7:7 or 8:2). In particular, we would point to the seventy-year consciousness of 1:12 and 7:5 and the important concept of prophetic "proclaiming" of 1:17 and 7:7,13. Consult Chart 6 for these shared features.

Finally, the links between Haggai and Zechariah that we have described above are particularly evident in Part Three of Zechariah, despite the fact that Zechariah 7–8 comes two years later than Haggai and does not deal directly with the building activity of such central concern to Haggai. The cross-references between Haggai and Zechariah 7–8 are more numerous than those between Haggai and Zechariah 1–6; indeed, the latter are virtually nonexistent except for the chronological headings. Again we refer the reader to our NOTES to chapters 7–8, where each instance of correspondence with Haggai is recorded, and to Chart 3. In particular, the oracular language of 8:9–12 and of 8:22–23 contains many themes, words, and phrases clearly dependent upon

Haggai's work. But perhaps most striking is the structure of the date formula of 7:1 in relation to that of Haggai 1:1. Both begin, unlike all the other chronological headings, with the regnal year; and the month-day sequence of the two verses is chiastically arranged. The temple terminology used in Part Three of Zechariah is also significant for thematic as well as for stylistic reasons. The words for "build" and "found" appear separately in Haggai (and also in Zechariah Part Two). Only at the end of Zechariah 1–8, in 8:9, are the two terms found together. In addition, in that same verse, Haggai's alternate terms for the Jerusalem sanctuary ("House of God" and "Temple," *hêkāl)* are brought together. Zechariah, in the concluding section of the Haggai-Zechariah 1–8 corpus, recognizing the temple focus of the entire work, unites the most important words used by Haggai in reference to the construction of Yahweh's earthly abode in Jerusalem.

Such features taken together provide two important insights. First, Zechariah Part Three, even more than Parts One and Two, shows strong awareness of prophetic tradition. This emerges not only from the forthright mention of "earlier prophets" but also from the direct utilization of the language appearing in earlier prophets. Zechariah in Part Three draws to a remarkable degree upon the material recorded *(sic;* perhaps already in written form) by his close colleague, Haggai. Haggai's prophetic authenticity was obviously accepted at once, and his words were known at least in the Jerusalem area. Second, the correspondences between Haggai and Zechariah 7–8 are so clear and apparently deliberate that their function as framing devices to create a single continuous prophetic work must be acknowledged.

Recognition of the overall unity of Haggai and Zechariah 1–8 raises questions about the circumstances of its organization into that form and about the role, which might be termed redactional activity, of either of the two prophets in that process. These questions have been explored above, and we need only reiterate here our conviction that either Zechariah himself or else someone close to him in time and in worldview was responsible for the shaping of the corpus, and that this redactional activity occurred very close in time to, if not at the very time of, the prophetic utterances of Part Three at the end of 518 B.C.E. Furthermore, the existence of connections between the Part Three oracles and those of Part Two does not necessarily imply that all the oracles were inserted simultaneously. We hold to the view that most if not all of the Part Two oracles are integral to the visions and that the material of Part Two as a whole could have taken shape before Zechariah produced the core prophecies of Part Three, in which he echoes some of that oracular language.

Part Three itself can be divided, as our chapter titles (12, 13, 14, 15) signify, into four segments or subunits. This division is based on both content and stylistic features. By the latter we mean, first, the use of an introductory statement indicating the transmission of a divine message. The formula "The word of Yahweh came (to Zechariah)" occurs as such or with minor variations four times in chapters 7–8. Each of those occurrences serves to mark a new unit of material. Second, several features within the units so formed further suggest the integrity of those units. For example, the second unit *(Further Retrospection on Divine Justice)* begins in 7:7 with a question containing the word "proclaim"; it draws to a close in 7:13 with a sentence featuring "Thus . . . proclaimed." The response to the initial question has been brought to its conclusion, and an appended oracle (verses 12b–14) develops from the second part of the "Thus . . . proclaimed" statement and serves as a coda to the second subunit. For the third and fourth subunits, the separate oracles within each are distinguished by the use of another formula (in addition to the initial transmission formula noted above) marking the actual delivery of the divine message. "Thus spoke Yahweh of Hosts" introduces the ten (seven in 8:1–17, three in 8:18–23) oracular pronouncements of these units in every case except one (8:3), which lacks only "of Hosts."

These literary features which separate Zechariah 7–8 into four subunits are accompanied by differences in content. The *Introduction* (7:1–6), as our subtitle suggests, provides the setting of time and place, the people involved, and the situation ostensibly responsible for evoking the subsequent collection of prophetic utterances. The next three subunits follow a time sequence. *Further Retrospection on Divine Justice* (7:7–14) takes us backward from the prophet's day to the preexilic period and then to the trauma of destruction and dispersion. *Zion and Judah Restored* (8:1–17) moves the chronological orientation into the prophet's immediate past, his present, and the imminent future. An eschatological perspective perhaps also colors some of the seven oracles, but they can for the most part be seen as referring primarily to the prophet's own historical period. Finally, *Judah and the Nations* (8:18–23) takes us fully into the eschatological future. Furthermore, building upon the situation described in the Introduction, the prophet expands the demographic focus of interest from Jerusalem to all of Yehud, to the neighboring Palestinian peoples, and by way of simultaneous climax to Zechariah 7–8, to Zechariah 1–8, and to Haggai-Zechariah 1–8, to all the nations of the world. Zechariah's message ends on a resoundingly universalistic note.

Form: Prose or Poetry

The literary texture of Haggai and Zechariah 1–8 is difficult to characterize. A simple glance at *BH³* and *BHS* reveals how varied opinion is on the matter. The Kittel edition of the MT prints Haggai entirely as a prose work. The Stuttgart edition interprets much of Haggai as poetry by setting out the following sections as poetry: 1:3–11; 1:15b; 2:3–9; 2:14–19; 2:20–23. Similarly, for First Zechariah the Kittel edition prints all of Zechariah 1–8 as prose whereas the Stuttgart edition construes the following sections as poetry and sets them off accordingly: 1:3b,5–6;14b–17; 2:8b–14; 3:7–10; 4:6b–10a; 5:4;

6:12b–13; 7:5,9–10; 8:2–13,20–22. This tremendous variation between the Kittel and Stuttgart editions reflects the enormity of the problem.

Many scholars have argued that Haggai's oracles were originally uttered in poetic form and that the term "poetic prose" best describes the language of Haggai (Ackroyd 1950–51:165–66). However, by applying the Andersen-Freedman method of statistical analysis of the prose particles *ʾšr*, *ʾt*, and *h* (1980:60ff.), we have found that both Haggai and Zechariah fall well within the percentages of what they call "oracular prose" (1980:57–66, 313). A cautionary word has been raised on this technique by Hoftijzer (1965:50), who has expressed serious doubts about techniques of prose-poetry discrimination. Nonetheless, on the basis of his study of *ʾt syntagmemes* (the particle *ʾt* and the word or group of words following it), he has concluded that the language of Haggai, as well as Zechariah 1–8, 10–14, and of Malachi, with regard to density of *ʾt syntagmemes,* is comparable to that in the prose narratives. Hill (1981:5; 1982) has come to similar conclusions in his usage of the Andersen-Freedman scheme of particle counting. Hill describes all of Haggai, Zechariah (except chapter 9), and Malachi as "simple prose." In our view, the designation "simple prose" does not adequately signify the complex nature of the literary style of either Haggai or Zechariah 1–8.

The data for the entire book of Haggai and Zechariah 1–8 may be summarized in the following tables (Charts 10 and 11). Haggai is organized according to the headings, or units of material, adopted in our translation; Zechariah is organized by chapter only.

Normally it is unwise to apply the prose-particle count method to very small units as we have done in Haggai. The frequency percentages, however, do not vary significantly. The average percentages of 18.7 percent (Hag) and 15.8 percent (Zech 1–8) fall squarely within the range of standard Hebrew prose, and both are certainly among the highest of the prophets. Although the definite article is the most common of the three particles, it is probably the least reliable indicator since it is so frequent in poetry. The other particles, *ʾšr* and *ʾt,* are less frequent in prose but occur often enough to serve as markers. They are exceedingly rare in poetry, so much so that their absence is almost always characteristic.

The basic conclusion to be drawn from these statistics is that Haggai-Zechariah 1–8 must be formally characterized as prose or "oracular prose." A sample of 5,000 prose words from the Pentateuch and Former Prophets runs about 17 percent. At the same time a 2,500 poetic word sample from the same corpus runs about 2 percent, which provides striking evidence for the difference between true poetry and standard prose. Although it is tempting to break up chapters into smaller units in an attempt to recover earlier poetic or oracular units, anything less than a chapter can be misleading because it is quite possible to construct prose sentences without using any of the particles. Even the final oracle of Haggai (2:20–23), which exhibits the lowest percentage of

Chart 10
Percentage Distribution of Prose Particles in Haggai

Haggai	Words	ʾšr	ʾt	h	Totals	Percent
1:1–11	162	2	0	23	25	15.4
1:12–15a	72	1	3	8	12	16.7
1:15b–2:9	148	2	9	28	39	26.4
2:10–19	160	2	4	24	30	18.8
2:20–23	58	0	2	4	6	10.3
Book	600	7	18	87	112	18.7*

*average percent

Chart 11

Percentage Distribution of Prose Particles in Haggai

Zechariah	Words	'šr	't	h	Totals	Percent
1:1-17	273	7	6	25	38	13.9
2:1-17	220	2	11	16	29	13.2
3:1-10	164	1	7	21	29	17.7
4:1-14	187	3	2	25	30	16.0
5:1-8	155	0	6	25	31	20.0
6:1-15	203	2	4	23	29	14.3
7:1-14	187	6	4	18	28	15.0
8:1-23	356	7	16	38	61	17.1
Book	1745	28	56	191	275	15.8*

*average percent

particle frequency along with 1:5–10 and which is generally regarded as original to the prophet, falls within the normal range of oracular prose.

Nonetheless, whether in Haggai or Zechariah, the sensitive reader is sure to come up with smaller units that are clearly "poetic" in their structure (e.g., Hag 1:5–10; Zech 2:14–17), as the Stuttgart edition of the Hebrew text indicates. Clearly the language of our books by any statistical reckoning is prosaic in character, but it is difficult to deny the flair of the prophetic writer or editor when he breaks out in, or perhaps imitates, a poetic style. In such places it is probably best to use the term "oracular prose" or even more simply "elevated prose" to characterize the nature of these works.

The existence of sections similar to poetry next to sections more prosaic does not, in any case, have to indicate separate authorship or separate times of composition. Hebrew literature as well as Western literature, it is now recognized, is replete with the commingling of such forms, although traditional biblical scholarship has rather erroneously held to an arbitrary principle that the mixing of forms can only be the result of independent origins for the different forms. We see no reason to sustain such an evaluation, at least with respect to the well-integrated oracular prose of Haggai and First Zechariah.

TEXT

Haggai

The Hebrew Masoretic text of Haggai is in an excellent state of preservation. Only in several places has it been necessary to revocalize (1:2,9; 2:7,16,19). In no single instance have we rearranged the consonantal text. Parts of Haggai (1:12–2:10; 2:12–23) are to be found in the scroll of the Minor Prophets that was discovered in Wadi Murabba'ât and dates to the second century C.E. Although those passages contain no readings considered superior to the MT, some commentators prefer to read with the Murabba'ât text at 2:1, substituting *ʾl* for the rather unusual *byd* of the MT. Both the MT and Murabba'ât preserve texts that differ significantly from the LXX. The LXX of Haggai is marked by expansions (2:9,14) and tends to harmonize difficult readings (2:17,21). In two instances (2:7,16a), however, the LXX has provided a helpful corrective to a problematic MT by suggesting a revocalization that resolves the textual difficulty.

Our translation of Haggai therefore is based on the MT, which has proved superior to all the other versions. In view of such a reliable tradition we have also avoided rearranging the order of the text, especially in 2:10–19, where many scholars have resorted to reordering (see NOTES). In the main, justification for such reordering has derived from redactio-critical concerns which have focused upon separating the original utterances of the prophet from the editorial framework in which they are preserved. The results of our analysis have shown an integrity to all the sections represented in Haggai, a situation which makes rearrangement unwarranted.

Zechariah 1–8

The Hebrew text of First Zechariah is also in a remarkably fine state of preservation. In two instances the medieval qere tradition has proved superior to the MT (1:16 and 4:2) and is supported by the LXX in the first instance (1:16) and several versions in the second instance (4:2). At 2:12 we have restored what we believe to be the original Hebrew ("my eye"). In 4:9 we have corrected a singular verb to a plural with considerable versional and manuscript support. The most obvious change in the text occurs at 6:14 where we have read singular "crown" with the LXX and Peshitta. This problematic reading is supported also by the Hebrew syntax and by an old Phoenician · singular which permits retention of the consonantal text. For an extensive discussion of this question the reader is referred to the NOTES at 6:11 ("crowns") and 6:14 ("crown") and COMMENT for that section.

RECENT STUDY OF HAGGAI AND ZECHARIAH 1–8

Haggai

Much of the earlier work on Haggai concentrated on efforts to understand the editorial framework, which is identified by the many third-person references in the text (1:1,12,13a,14,15; 2:1,10,13a,14a,20). Indeed, it is generally agreed that an editorial framework has been superimposed upon a core of original material. The result is a prophetic discourse that was prepared, in our opinion, for presentation at the ceremony of the rededication of the temple in 515 B.C.E. as part of a composite work with Zechariah 1–8. The thirty-eight verses of Haggai that survive comprise only six hundred words in all. This fact alone should serve as a warning to the higher critic that too detailed a dissection of the whole work may not be justified. Eissfeldt has been alone among the critics in suggesting that the third-person form may be a literary device of the prophet himself, utilized to enhance the objectivity of his reporting and to bring his prophecies in line with the formulaic introductions to earlier prophetic books. Most scholarly discussion of the matter is concerned with the degree to which the editor or compiler, or the circle in which the prophet's words were preserved and finally promulgated, was influenced by the nature of the events that occurred after the termination of Haggai's prophetic activity.

Numerous commentators have been impressed by what they believe to be similarities between the editorial framework and the point of view of the

Chronicler. Chief among them is W. Beuken, who has inspired much of the discussion, and R. Mason. Beuken has been careful to avoid identifying the redactor or compiler with the Chronicler, but nonetheless has opted for a redactional setting for both Haggai and Zechariah in a "chronistic milieu"— that is, a setting allied with or akin to that of the Chronicler. Chief among the similarities between the Chronicler and the compiler of Haggai, for Beuken, are the following: ritual concerns, the presence of God mediated through the temple cult, the view of prophets as messengers, the covenantal language associated with the rebuilding, and God's stirring up the spirit of the leaders and the people. According to Beuken, the redactor(s) must have added the introductory formulas such as 1:1 or 2:1–2 in order to impose a narrative continuity upon what had been earlier, isolated, prophetic materials. In this view the redactor(s) also would have added some words on the impact of the prophet (e.g., 1:12–14). Beuken consequently identifies Haggai 1:3–11 as part of the original, preliminary collection and Haggai himself as a rural Judahite who had not been exiled to Babylon but who remained faithful to Yahwism.

Mason has incorporated much of Beuken in his treatment of the problem. He has steered clear of taking any extreme position that would bring the date of the final redaction down to the period of Ezra and Nehemiah, and suggests a time shortly after 515 B.C.E. Mason attributes these passages to the editorial framework: 1:1,3,12,13a,14,15; 2:2 (probably), 10,20, and possibly 1:4, and characterizes them as Deuteronomistic. He has correctly attributed to the original oracles eschatological elements he sees as central to Haggai's preaching and has criticized Hanson for making these elements "peripheral" to Haggai's more pragmatic and hierocratic interests, though Hanson does not assign these elements to a secondary status in any editorial sense. For Mason the following distinguishing features of the editorial framework may be observed: the expression "the word of Yahweh through the prophet" (1:1,3, and 2:1; but cf. 2:10,20) as an indication of the fulfillment of the prophetic word and/or linking of the establishment of the First Temple with the Second Temple; a concentration and emphasis of the word as spoken to leaders (1:1,12,14, and possibly 2:4); a concern for the "remnant" (1:12,14; 2:2); God's working through the spirit to rouse Zerubbabel and Joshua as well as the people (1:14); and finally the use of the term "work" as reminiscent of earlier temple building accounts. By suggesting a relatively early date, Mason has removed the possibility of any direct influence or connection with the Chronicler. He concludes, however, that the compiler(s) could well represent the viewpoint of those who later produced the Chronicler's work.

Pioneering work on this subject that predates both Beuken and Mason has been contributed by P. Ackroyd. In his several works dealing with the restoration, Ackroyd tried to recover two layers within the editorial framework. Only one of those layers, however, does he regard as truly independent of the original oracular material and capable of being interpreted apart from it. Those passages he views as secondary and thus not to be adjudged as integral to the prophetic oracles are: 2:1–2,10(the gloss in 18),20–21a. Those secondary passages that are too much a part of the original oracular material to be understood independently are: 1:12–14; 2:3–5; 2:11–14a. The editorial work, in Ackroyd's opinion, cannot be considered to have been added less than one hundred years after Haggai's activity, or ca. 420 B.C.E., and possibly can be dated to as much as two hundred years later, or ca. 320 B.C.E.

Although we have been unable to utilize D. L. Petersen's Westminster commentary, since it appeared only in December of 1984, it should be noted that Petersen argues that Haggai is a "brief apologetic historical narrative" *(historische Kurzgeschichte)* akin to Jeremiah 26 and 36, Jeremiah 37–41, and 2 Kings 22–23. Although he agrees with the efforts of scholars to identify the setting of the redaction of the work, he finds the contemporary setting of the restoration most appropriate for understanding both the editorial framework and the few identifiable units which constitute the original, preliminary stage in the creation of the canonical book.

As we have indicated above, under the heading "Literary Considerations," the conclusions arrived at in this commentary differ considerably from those described above. We have observed literary continuity between the oracles and the so-called narrative portions of Haggai. We would agree with Petersen that since there is such a short time between original utterance and redaction, there is little hope or even purpose in separating out all of the individual units. Haggai, as it appears in the MT, was meant to be considered not only as an independent prophetic work but also as a part of the larger composite work of Haggai-Zechariah 1–8. If Haggai's present form of composition has been difficult for critics to untangle, then it is a great tribute to both prophet and redactor(s) who have transmitted a polished and self-contained literary work.

Zechariah 1–8

New studies of First Zechariah, and in particular of the visions, have come forth in the last decades at a prodigious rate. Those studies have in the main been brought about by the fresh discussions of apocalyptic literature, of the phenomenon of prophecy and of temple ideology in the ancient Near East, and by an increasing interest in postexilic Judaism. To the best of our knowledge none of the older or more recent studies has attempted, as does this commentary, to be sensitive to these issues and at the same time to integrate the plethora of relevant archaeological materials into the setting of either Haggai or Zechariah 1–8 and to bring social-scientific method to bear on special points and on the restoration period in general.

Hanson attempted to demonstrate in his several studies of apocalyptic materials that the postexilic period was one fraught with dissension and social conflict. In promulgating his engaging view of the emergence of apocalyptic visions, he portrays the followers of the so-called Third Isaiah as visionaries and the audience and followers of Haggai and Zechariah 1–8 as pragmatists dedicated to stabilizing the *status quo* and selling out to the Achaemenids. Such an accommodation, he avers, represents a reversal of the fundamental course of classical prophecy. Hanson's "restoration" is not the one we have found to be represented in either Haggai or First Zechariah, and the reader is referred to his essays or major work, *The Dawn of Apocalyptic,* for a presentation of a view entirely different from that which unfolds here.

Seybold presents Zechariah's visions as a sacred document that legitimizes the Second Temple, analogous to Jacob's dream (Gen 28). He focuses entirely on the significance for postexilic Yehud of the reconstruction of the temple. Similarly, Halpern in a lengthy essay also concentrates on the centrality of temple reconstruction and demonstrates how the visionary material elaborates on this theme, the visions taking the reconstruction event and elevating it to a cosmic framework. He also discerns a divine warrior pattern in the visions in which Israel is saved by a cosmic figure. Halpern's dependency on the combat myth to explain the visions is the weakest element in an otherwise entirely praiseworthy effort. Ackroyd to a lesser extent has also taken the rebuilding of the temple as the key to understanding Zechariah.

Other scholars such as Rignell and Rudolph, to name only two, interpret Zechariah on a much broader level and relate the visions in particular to events at the end of time and to the concept of salvation. Such an attempt to broaden the scope of the visions does not do justice to the object that has inspired them, namely the temple. In general, one could argue that the oracles, and especially Part Three of First Zechariah, succeed in doing just this by elaborating and interpreting themes of the visions in a more universalistic language.

Beuken and Petitjean have argued that the visions and the oracles of Zechariah must be treated separately. Both studies are magisterial in scope but leave the student of First Zechariah and, in the case of Beuken, Haggai also, wondering about the overly complex redactional process presupposed in either treatment. Both studies are to be commended for reference, but in our opinion the relationship between oracles and visions in Zechariah is far more direct, and attributable to the times of the prophet, than either of those works would allow.

Uffenheimer's Hebrew commentary takes to task much of modern Bible scholarship and argues that the visions do not reflect a single experience, but rather a series of experiences that occurred over a considerable period of time. He sees the order of the visions as being arranged by subject matter and literary associations. He has attempted to demonstrate how Zechariah 1–8 constitutes a transitional stage in prophecy that forms a bridge to the world of later apocalyptic literature. In this last respect, Uffenheimer is very similar to Hanson.

D. Petersen's work on Zechariah points in another direction in the study of Zechariah. A summary of his views may be found in his 1984 essay "Zechariah's Visions: A Theological Perspective," available to the authors and published prior to his commentary. Petersen charts a middle course between the extremes of much of the existing scholarly literature. He portrays Zechariah as a prophet who speaks to the central issue of the renewal of Judean life in the postexilic period. He sees the temple reconstruction as a major part of Zechariah's utopian focus which is balanced by many mundane concerns also. Petersen speaks of Zechariah's visions as "the doing of theology." They constitute an experiential response to the problems of a community attempting to reorganize itself. He contrasts Zechariah's program of renewal with that of Ezekiel 40–48 and that of Second Isaiah. In all, Petersen offers a sensitive alternative that is not far removed from the approach adopted in this commentary, which also sees Zechariah as providing the theological perspective needed in the new situation in which Israel found itself in the restoration period—namely, that of a Yahwism without an independent territorial state.

The world of secondary literature, especially commentaries, is a special one, one that is filled with generation upon generation of reflection upon the canonical books of Scripture. It is simply not feasible or helpful to summarize that vast literature. The bibliography at the end of this Introduction reflects the works and studies we have consulted in order to do our work. This brief review is intended to encourage serious readers to consult some of the many giants who have worked before us on these prophetic books and to refer everyone to the Bibliography for general reference to the existing scholarship.

BIBLIOGRAPHY

Abel, F.-M.
1936   Aṣal in Zechariah 14:5. *RB* 45: 385–400.
Ackroyd, P. R.
1950–51   Studies in the Book of Haggai. *JJS* 2: 1–13, 163–76.
1958   Two Old Testament Historical Problems of the Early
              Persian Period. *JNES* 17: 13–27.
1962   Zechariah. Pp. 646–55 in *Peake's Commentary on the
              Bible,* ed. M. Black. London: Nelson.
1968   *Exile and Restoration.* Old Testament Library. Lon-
              don: SCM.
1970   *Israel under Babylon and Persia.* Oxford: Oxford.
Aharoni, Y.
1979   *Land of the Bible* (2nd ed.). Philadelphia: Westmin-
              ster.
————— and M. Avi-Yonah
1968   *The Macmillan Bible Atlas.* New York: Macmillan.
Ahlström, G. W.
1982   *Royal Administration and National Religion in An-
              cient Palestine.* Studies in the History of the Ancient
              Near East 1. Leiden: Brill.

Albright, W. F.
1921   The Date and Personality of the Chronicler. *JBL* 40:
              104–24.
1941   *From Stone Age to Christianity: Monotheism and the
              Historical Process.* Baltimore: Johns Hopkins.
1945   The List of Levitic Cities. *Louis Ginsberg Jubilee Vol-
              ume* I: 49–73 (English section). New York: American
              Academy for Jewish Research.
1950   The Judicial Reform of Jehoshaphat. Pp. 61–82 in
              Alexander Marx Jubilee Volume, ed. S. Lieberman.
              New York: Jewish Theological Seminary.

1954   *The Archaeology of Palestine*. 3rd revised printing. Harmondsworth: Penguin.

1963   *The Biblical Period from Abraham to Ezra*. New York: Harper Torchbooks.

1968   *Yahweh and the Gods of Canaan*. School of Oriental and African Studies. University of London. Winona Lake, Ind: Eisenbrauns.

Alt, A.

1934   Die Rolle Samarias bei der Entstehung des Judentum. Pp. 5–28 in *Festschrift Otto Procksch*. Leipzig: Deichert-Hinrichs.

1953–59   *Kleine Schriften zur Geschichte des Volkes Israel 1–3*. Munich: Beck.

Alter, R.

1981   *The Art of Biblical Narrative*. New York: Basic Books.

Amiran, D. H. K.

1964   Land Use in Israel. Pp. 101–12 in *Land Use in Semi-Arid Mediterranean Climates*. UNESCO/International Geographic Union. Paris: Unesco.

Amsler, S.

1981   *Aggée, Zacharie 1–8*. Commentaire de l'Ancien Testament XIc: 11–126. Neuchâtel-Paris: Delachaux & Niestlé.

Andersen, F.

1958   Who Built the Second Temple? *ABR* 6: 1–35.

——— and D. N. Freedman

1980   *Hosea*. Anchor Bible 24. Garden City, N.Y.: Doubleday.

Anderson, B. W.

1962   Host of Heaven. *IDB* 2: 654–56.

Ap-Thomas, D. R.

1956   Notes on Some Terms Relating to Prayer. *VT* 6: 225–41.

Avigad, N.

1953   The Epitaph of a Royal Steward from Siloam Village. *IEJ* 3: 137–52.

1957   A New Class of *Yehud* Stamps. *IEJ* 7: 146–53.

1976a   *Bullae and Seals from a Post-exilic Judean Archive*. Qedem 4. Monographs of the Hebrew University Institute of Archaeology, Jerusalem.

1976b   New Light on the *Na'ar* Seals. Pp. 294–300 in *The Mighty Acts of God, G. E. Wright Festschrift*. Eds.

F. M. Cross, Jr., *et al.* Garden City, N.Y.: Double-day.

1986   *Hebrew Bullae From the Time of Jeremiah.* Jerusa-lem: Israel Exploration Society.

Baldwin, J.
1972   *Haggai, Zechariah, Malachi.* Tyndale Old Testament Commentaries. Downers Grove, Ill.: Inter-Varsity.

Barker, M.
1977   The Two Figures in Zechariah. *Heythrop Journal* 18: 33–46.
1978   The Evil in Zechariah. *Heythrop Journal* 19: 12–27.

Barrick, W. B.
1982   The Meaning and Use of *RKB* in Biblical Hebrew. *JBL* 101: 481–503.

Baumann, A.
1978   *"deleth." TDOT* 3: 230–33.

Becker, J.
1980   *Messianic Expectation in the Old Testament.* Tr. David E. Green. Philadelphia: Fortress.

Begrich, J.
1936   Die priestliche Thora. *BZAW* 66. Pp. 63–88 in *Wei-den und Wesen des Alten Testament,* eds. P. Volz, F. Stummels, and J. Hempel. Berlin: Topelman.

Bentzen, A.
1930   Quelques remarques sur le monument messianique parmi les Juifs aux environs de l'an 520 avant Jésus-Christ. *RHPR* 9: 493–503.

Bertman, S.
1961   Tassled Garments in the Ancient East Mediterra-nean. *BA* 24: 119–28.

Beuken, W. A. M.
1967   *Haggai-Sacharja 1–8.* Assen: Van Gorcum.

Bewer, J. A.
1919   Ancient Babylonian Parallels to the Prophecies of Haggai. *AJSLL* 35: 128–33.

Blenkinsopp, J.
1983   *A History of Prophecy in Israel from the Settlement in the Land to the Hellenistic Period.* Philadelphia: West-minster.

Bodenheimer, F. S.
1962   Fauna. *IDB* 2: 246–56.

Boer, P. A. H. de
    1948   An Inquiry into the Meaning of the Term Missa. *OTS*
                      5: 212–13.

Braun, R.
    1977   Malachi—A Catechism for Times of Disappointment.
                      CTM 4/5: 297–303.

Bratsiotis, N. P.
    1975   *"bāśār." TDOT* 2: 317–32.

Brenner, A.
    1982   *Colour Terms in the Old Testament.* JSOT Supple-
                      ment Series, 21. Sheffield: JSOT.

Brichto, H. C.
    1968   *The Problem of "Curse" in the Hebrew Bible.* SBL
                      Monograph Series 13. Philadelphia: Society of Bibli-
                      cal Literature.

Bright, J.
    1965   *Jeremiah.* Anchor Bible 21. Garden City, N.Y.: Dou-
                      bleday.
    1981   *A History of Israel* (3rd ed.) Philadelphia: Westmin-
                      ster.

Brockington, L. H.
    1969   *Ezra, Nehemiah and Esther.* Century Bible, New Se-
                      ries. London: Nelson.

Broshi, M.
    1978   Estimating the Population of Ancient Jerusalem.
                      BAR 4: 10–15.

Camp, C.
    1985   *Wisdom and the Feminine in the Book of Proverbs.*
                      Bible and Literature Series, 11. Sheffield, Eng.: Al-
                      mond.

Campbell, E. F.
    1975   *Ruth.* Anchor Bible 7. Garden City, N.Y.: Double-
                      day.

Cansdale, G. S.
    1970   *All the Animals of the Bible Lands.* Grand Rapids:
                      Zondervan.

Caquot, A.
    1978   *"gāʿar." TDOT* 3: 49–53.

Carroll, R. P.
    1979a   Twilight or Prophecy or Dawn of Apocalyptic? *JSOT*
                      14: 3–35.
    1979b   *When Prophecy Failed.* London: SCM.

Cazelles, H.
1964   Fille de Sion et Théologie Mariale dans la Bible.
              *Mariologie et Oecuménisme (Recherches catholiques
              Théologie et Pastorale)* 3: 51–71.
1967   Histoire et Géographie en Michée IV, 6–13. *Fourth
              World Congress of Jewish Studies* 1: 87–89. Jerusalem:
              World Union of Jewish Studies.

Ceresko, A. R.
1980   *Job 29–31 in the Light of Northwest Semitic.* Biblica et
              Orientalia 36. Rome: Biblical Institute.

Chary, T.
1969   *Aggée—Zacharie—Malachie.* Paris: Gabalda.

Chiat, M. J.
1982   *Handbook of Synagogue Architecture.* Brown Judaic
              Studies 29. Chico, Calif.: Scholars.

Childs, B. S.
1959   The Enemy from the North and the Chaos Tradition.
              JBL 78: 187–98.

Christensen, D. L.
1984   Review of T. Mettinger, *The Dethronement of Saba-
              oth. CBQ* 46: 124–26.

Clements, R. E.
1975   *"gôy." TDOT* 2: 426–32.

Clifford, R. J.
1966   The Use of *Hôy* in the Prophets. *CBQ* 28: 458–64.
1972   *The Cosmic Mountain in Canaan and the Old Testa-
              ment.* Harvard Semitic Monographs 4. Cambridge:
              Harvard.

Cohen, G.
1961   Zion in Rabbinic Literature. Pp. 39–43 in *Zion in
              Jewish Literature.* New York: Herzl.

Coogan, M. D.
1976   *West Semitic Personal Names in the Murašû Docu-
              ments.* Harvard Semitic Monographs 7. Missoula:
              Scholars.

Cook, J. M.
1983   *The Persian Empire.* London: Dent. New York:
              Schocken.

Cook, S. A.
1950   The Age of Zerubbabel. Pp. 19–36 in *Studies in Old
              Testament Prophecy* presented to Theodore H. Robin-
              son, ed. H. H. Rowley. Edinburgh: Clark.

Cooke, G.

1964   Sons of (the) God(s). *ZAW* 76: 22–47.

Cowley, A. E., ed.

1923   *Aramaic Papyri of the Fifth Century B.C.* Oxford: Clarendon.

Cross, F. M., Jr.

1953   The Council of Yahweh in Second Isaiah. *JNES* 12: 274–77.

1966   Aspects of Samaritan and Jewish History in Late Persian and Hellenistic Times. *HTR* 59: 201–11.

1969   Judean Stamps. *EI* 9: 20–27.

1973   *Canaanite Myth and Hebrew Epic.* Cambridge: Harvard.

1975   A Reconstruction of the Judean Restoration. *JBL* 94: 4–18.

1981   The Priestly Tabernacle in the Light of Recent Research. Pp. 169–80 in *Temples and High Places in Biblical Times,* ed. A. Biran. Jerusalem: Hebrew Union.

———— and D. N. Freedman

1950   *Studies in Ancient Yahwistic Poetry.* Ph.D. thesis, Johns Hopkins; later published as SBL Monograph 21.

1952   *Early Hebrew Orthography.* New Haven: American Oriental Society.

1953   A Royal Song of Thanksgiving. *JBL* 72: 15–34.

———— and R. J. Saley

1970   Phoenician Incantations on a Plaque of the Seventh Century B.C. from Arslan Tash in Upper Syria. *BASOR* 197: 42–49.

Curtis, J. B.

1957   An Investigation of the Mount of Olives in Judaeo-Christian Tradition. *HUCA* 29: 137–80. Cincinnati: Hebrew Union-Jewish Institute.

Dahood, M.

1965, 1968, 1970 *Psalms* I, II, III. Anchor Bible 16, 17, 17A. Garden City, N.Y.: Doubleday.

Davies, W. D.

1974   *Gospel and the Land; Early Christianity and Jewish Territorial Doctrine.* Berkeley: University of California.

———— and L. Finkelstein, eds.
1984   *The Cambridge History of Judaism: Vol. One, Intro-
               duction; The Persian Period.* Cambridge: Cambridge.
Demsky, A.
1981   The Temple Steward Josiah ben Zephaniah. *IEJ* 31:
               100–3.
Dever, W.
1984   Asherah, Consort of Yahweh? New Evidence from
               Kuntillet ʿAjrud. *BASOR* 255: 21–37.
Donner, H. R., and W. Röllig
1964–68   *Kanaanäische und Aramäische Inschriften.* Wiesba-
               den: Otto Harrassowitz.
Driver, G. R.
1940   Hebrew Notes on Prophets and Proverbs. *JTS* 41:
               162–75.
1976   *Semitic Writing from Pictograph to Alphabet.*
               Schweich Lectures, 1944. London: Oxford.
Driver, S. R.
1906   *The Century Bible. The Minor Prophets II.* Edin-
               burgh: T. C. & E. C. Jack.
Dumbrell, W. J.
1983   No King in Israel. *JSOT* 25: 23–33.
Edelstein, G.
1982   Agricultural Terraces in the Judean Mountains. Pp.
               211–12 in *AAR/SBL Abstracts* (Annual Meeting).
               Chico, Calif.: Scholars.
Eichrodt, W.
1967   *Theology of the Old Testament.* Tr. J. Baker. Old Tes-
               tament Library. Philadelphia: Westminster.
Eisenstadt, S. N.
1979   Observations and Queries about Sociological Aspects
               of Imperialism in the Ancient World. Pp. 21–33 in
               *Power and Propaganda; A Symposium on Ancient Em-
               pires, Mesopotamia 7.* Copenhagen: Akademisk
               Forlag.
Eising, H.
1980   *"zākhar." TDOT* 4: 64–82.
Eissfeldt, O.
1974   *"ʾadhôn." TDOT* 1: 59–72.
Eitan, I.
1924   *A Contribution to Biblical Lexicography.* New York:
               Columbia.

Elliger, K.
1975   *Das Buch der zwölf Kleinen Propheten.* Vol. 2. Das Alte Testament Deutsch, 25. Göttingen: Vandenhoeck & Ruprecht.

Ellis, R.
1968   *Foundation Deposits in Ancient Mesopotamia.* New Haven: Yale.

Fabry, H.-J.
1980   *"ḥbl." TDOT* 4: 172–79.

Falkenstein, A. and W. von Soden
1953   *Sumerische und Akkadische Hymnen und Gebete.* Bibliothek der alten Welt. Zurich: Artemis.

Farbridge, M.
1970   *Studies in Biblical and Semitic Symbolism.* New York: KTAV.

Feliks, J.
1971   Stork. *EJ* 14: 416.
1981   *Nature and Man in the Bible: Chapters in Biblical Ecology.* London: Soncino.

Fensham, F. C.
1977   The Numeral Seventy in the Old Testament and the Family of Jerubbaal, Ahab, Panammuwa and Athirat. *PEQ* 113–15.

Fishbane, M.
1980   Revelation and Tradition: Aspects of Inner-Biblical Exegesis. *JBL* 99: 343–61.

Fisher, L. R.
1963   The Temple Quarter. *JSS* 8: 34–41.

Forbes, R. J.
1950   *Metallurgy in Antiquity.* Leiden: Brill.

Freedman, D. N.
1955   God Compassionate and Gracious. *Western Watch* 6: 7–24.
1961   The Chronicler's Purpose. *CBQ* 23: 436–42.
1963   The Law and the Prophets. *Supplements to Vetus Testamentum* 9. Leiden: Brill.
1964   Divine Commitment and Human Obligation. *Interpretation* 419–31.
1974   Strophe and Meter in Exodus 15. Pp. 163–203 in *A Light Unto My Path,* eds. H. N. Bream, R. D. Heim, and C. A. Moore. Philadelphia: Temple.
1975   Early Israelite History in the Light of Early Israelite Poetry. Pp. 3–35 in *Unity and Diversity,* eds.

H. Goedicke and J. J. M. Roberts. Baltimore: Johns Hopkins.

1976   Canon of the Old Testament. *IDBS* 130–36.

1977   Pottery, Poetry, and Prophecy: An Essay on Biblical Poetry. *JBL* 96: 5–26.

1980   *Pottery, Poetry and Prophecy.* Winona Lake, Ind.: Eisenbrauns.

1981   Temple Without Hands. Pp. 21–30 in *Temples and High Places in Biblical Time,* ed. A. Biran. Jerusalem: Hebrew Union College.

1983   The Earliest Bible. *MQR* 22: 167–75.

——— and F. M. Cross

1955   The Song of Miriam. *JNES* 14: 237–50.

See also Cross, F. M., Jr.

Freedman, D. N. and M. P. O'Connor

1984   *"kĕrûb."* Theologisches Handwörterbuch zum Alten Testament IV: 322–34. Eds. G. J. Botterweck, H. Ringgren, and H.-J. Fabry. Stuttgart: Kohlhammer.

Frick, F.

1977   *The City in Ancient Israel.* SBL Dissertation Series 36. Missoula: Scholars.

Friedman, R. E.

1983   The Prophet and the Historian: The Acquisition of Historical Information from Literary Sources. Pp. 1–12 in *The Poet and the Historian,* ed. R. E. Friedman. Harvard Semitic Series, 26. Chico, Calif.: Scholars.

Frymer-Kensky, T.

1984   The Strange Case of the Suspected Sotah (Numbers v 11–31). *VT* 34: 11–26.

Gadd, C. J.

1953   Inscribed Barrel Cylinder of Marduk-Apla-Iddina II. *Iraq* 5: 123–34.

Gaster, T. H.

1962   Satan. *IDB* 4: 224–28.

Gelston, A.

1966   The Foundation of the Second Temple. *VT* 16: 232–35.

Gerber, P. L.

1962   Silver. *IDB* 4: 355–56.

Gerstenberger, G.

1962   The Woe-Oracles of the Prophets. *JBL* 81: 249–63.

Gese, H.

1973   Anfang und Ende der Apocalyptik, dargestellt am

Sacharjahrbuch. *Zeitschrift für Theologie und Kirche* 70: 20–49.

Goodenough, E. R.

1954   *Jewish Symbols in the Greco-Roman Period.* Vol. 4. Bollingen Series. New York: Pantheon.

1965   *Jewish Symbols in the Greco-Roman Period.* Vol. 12. Bollingen Series. New York: Pantheon.

Gooding, D. W.

1959   *The Account of the Tabernacle.* Cambridge: Cambridge.

Gordon, C.

1943   *The Loves and Wars of Baal and Anat.* Princeton: Princeton.

1965   *Ugaritic Textbook.* Rome: Pontifical Biblical Institute.

Gottwald, N. K.

1979   *The Tribes of Yahweh.* Maryknoll: Orbis.

Gradwohl, R.

1963   *Die Farben im Alten Testament. Eine terminologische Studie. BZAW* 83. Berlin: De Gruyter.

Gutmann, J., ed.

1975   The Origin of the Synagogue: The Current State of Research. Pp. 72–76 in *The Synagogue: Studies in Origins, Archaeology, and Architecture.* New York: KTAV.

Haag, H.

1975   *"bath." TDOT* 2: 332–37.

Halpern, B.

1978   The Ritual Background of Zechariah's Temple Song. *CBQ* 40: 167–90.

1981   *The Constitution of the Monarchy in Israel.* Harvard Semitic Monographs 25. Chico, Calif.: Scholars.

Hamp, V.

1975   *"bākhāh." TDOT* 2: 116–20.

Hanson, P. D.

1975   *The Dawn of Apocalyptic.* Philadelphia: Fortress.

Haran, M.

1960   The "ʾOHEL MOʿED" in the Pentateuchal Sources. *JSS* 5: 50–65.

1961   The Complex of Ritual Acts Performed inside the Tabernacle. *Scripta Hierosolymitana* 8: 272–302.

1963   The Disappearance of the Ark. *IEJ* 13: 46–58.

1980   *Temple and Temple Service.* Oxford: Oxford.

Hareuveni, N.
1980   *Nature in Our Biblical Heritage.* Tr. Helen Frenkley. Kiryat Ono, Israel: Neot Kedumim.

Harrelson, W.
1962   Torah. *IDB* 4: 673.
1982   The Trial of the High Priest Joshua: Zechariah 3. *EI* 16: 116–24.

Hensley, L. V.
1977   *The Official Persian Documents in the Book of Ezra.* Doctoral dissertation, University of Liverpool.

Hill, A.
1981   *The Book of Malachi: Its Place in Post-Exilic Chronology Linguistically Reconsidered.* Unpublished dissertation, University of Michigan.

Hoffner, H.
1974   *"ʾalmānāh." TDOT* 1: 287–91.

Hoftijzer, J.
1965   Remarks Concerning the Use of the Particle ʾt in Classical Hebrew. *Oudtestamentische Studien* XIV:1–99.

Huffmon, H.
1983   Priestly Divination in Israel. Pp. 355–59 in *The Word of the Lord Shall Go Forth,* eds. C. L. Meyers and M. O'Connor. Winona Lake, Ind.: Eisenbrauns/The American Schools of Oriental Research.

Hurowitz, A.
1983   *Temple Building in the Bible in Light of Mesopotamia and North-West Semitic Writings.* Ph.D. thesis. Jerusalem: Hebrew University.

Hurvitz, A.
1974   The Data of the Prose-Tale or Job Linguistically Reconsidered. *HTR* 67: 17–34.
1982   *A Linguistic Study of the Relationship between the Priestly Source and the Book of Ezekiel: A New Approach to an Old Problem.* Cahiers de la Revue Biblique 20. Paris: Gabalda.

Hyatt, J. P.
1937   A Neo-Babylonian Parallel to *Bethel-sar-eser,* Zech. 7:2. *JBL* 56: 387–94.

Ishida, T.
1977   *The Royal Dynasties in Ancient Israel: A Study on the Formation and Development of Royal-Dynastic Ideology.* BZAW 142. Berlin: De Gruyter.

James, F.
1934   Thoughts on Haggai and Zechariah. *JBL* 53: 229–35.

Janzen, W.
1972   *Mourning Cry and Woe Oracle. BZAW* 125. New York/Berlin: De Gruyter.

Japhet, S.
1982   Sheshbazar and Zerubbabel. *ZAW* 94: 66–99.

Jepsen, A.
1945–48   Kleine Beitrage zum Zwölfprophetenbuch III. *ZAW* 61: 95–114.

Junker, H.
1938   *Die Zwölf kleinen Propheten.* Die Heilige Schrift des Alten Testaments. Bonn: P. Hanstein.

Kallai, Z.
1960   *The Northern Boundaries of Judah from the Settlement of the Tribes until the Beginning of the Hasmonaean Period.* Jerusalem: Magnes Press (Hebrew).

Kapelrud, A. S.
1963   Temple-Building, a Task for Gods and Kings. *Orientalia* 32: 52–62.
1974   "'ebhen." *TDOT* 1: 48–51.

Kaufmann, Y.
1961   The Messianic Idea. *El Ha'Ayin* No. 5. Jerusalem.
1977   *History of the Religion of Israel IV: From the Babylonian Captivity to the End of Prophecy.* New York: KTAV (for Institute of Jewish Studies, Dallas).

Kaupel, H.
1930   *Die Dämonen im Alten Testament.* Augsburg: Benno Filser.

Kedar-Kopfstein, B.
1980   "zāhābh." *TDOT* 4: 32–40.

Keel, O.
1974   *Wirkmächtige Siegeszeichen im Alten Testament.* Göttingen: Vandenhoeck & Ruprecht.

Kellermann, D.
1975   "gûr." *TDOT* 2: 439–50.

Kingsbury, E. C.
1964   The Prophets and the Council of Yahweh. *JBL* 83: 279–87.

Koch, K.
1967   Haggais unreines Volk. *ZAW* 79: 52–66.
1978   "derekh." *TDOT* 3: 270–93.

Köhler, A.
1860   *Die nachexilischen Propheten.* Erlangen: Deichert.

Kuhrt, A.
1983   The Cyrus Cylinder and Achaemenid Imperial Policy. *JSOT* 25: 83–97.

Kutsch, E.
1963   *Salbung als Rechtsakt im A.T. und im Alten Orient.* BZAW 87: Berlin: De Gruyter.

Lacocque, A.
1981   *Zacharie 9–14.* Commentaire de l'Ancien Testament XIc: 127–215. Neuchâtel-Paris: Delachaux & Niestlé.

Lane, E.
1863–   *Arabic-English Lexicon.* London: Williams & Norgate.

Lapp, P. W.
1976   Iraq el-Emir. *EAEHL* 2: 527–31.

Le Bas, E. E.
1950   Zechariah's Enigmatical Contribution to the Corner-Stone. *PEQ* 102–22.

1951   Zechariah's Climax to the Career of the Corner-Stone. *PEQ* 139–55.

Levine, B.
1965   The Descriptive Tabernacle Texts of the Pentateuch. *JAOS* 85: 307–18.

1968   On the Presence of God in Biblical Religion. Pp. 71–87 in *Religions in Antiquity.* Studies in the History of Religions (Supplements to Numen) 14. Leiden: Brill.

1974   *In the Presence of the Lord.* Studies in Judaism in Late Antiquity 5. Leiden: Brill.

Liedke, G.
1971   "*dīn.*" *THAT* I: 446–47.

Lindblom, J.
1962   *Prophecy in Ancient Israel.* Philadelphia: Fortress.

Lipiński, E.
1965   *La Royauté de Yahwé dans la poésie et le culte de l'ancien Israël.* Brussels: Palais der Academiën.

1970   Recherches sur le livre de Zacharie. *VT* 20: 22–55.

Liver, J.
1967   Book of the Acts of Solomon. *Biblica* 48: 75–101.

Loud, G.
1939   *The Megiddo Ivories.* Chicago: University of Chicago.

Luciani, F.
1972   Il verbo šākar in Aggeo 1,6. *Aveum* 46: 498–501.

Lundquist, J. M.
1982   *The Legitimizing Role of the Temple in the Origin of
                the State.* SBL Seminar Papers 21, ed. K. M. Rich-
                ards. Chico, Calif.: Scholars.
1983   What Is a Temple? A Preliminary Typology. Pp. 205–
                19 in *The Quest for the Kingdom of God: Studies in
                Honor of George E. Mendenhall,* eds. H. B. Huffmon,
                F. A. Spina, and A. R. W. Green. Winona Lake, Ind.:
                Eisenbrauns.
1984   The Common Temple Ideology of the Ancient Near
                East. Pp. 53–76 in *The Temple in Antiquity,* ed. T. G.
                Madsen. Religious Monograph Series 9. Provo: Brig-
                ham Young.

McCarter, P.
1980   *I Samuel.* Anchor Bible 8. Garden City, N.Y.: Dou-
                bleday.

McConville, G.
1979   God's 'Name' and God's 'Glory.' *Tyndale Bulletin*
                30: 149–63.

McCown, C. C.
1957   The 'Araq el-Emir and the Tobiads. *BA* 20: 63–76.

McEvenue, S. E.
1981   The Political Structure in Judah from Cyrus to Nehe-
                miah. *CBQ* 43: 353–64.

McHardy, W.
1968   The Horses in Zechariah. *ZAW* 103: 174–79.

Malamat, A.
1982   Longevity: Biblical Concepts and Some Near Eastern
                Parallels. *AO* Beiheft 19: 215–24.

Marenof, S.
1931–32   Note Concerning the Meaning of the Word "Ephah,"
                Zechariah 5:5–11. *AJSLL* 48: 264–67.

Marti, K.
1904   *Das Dodekapropheton.* Kurzer Handkommentar zum
                Alten Testament. Tübingen: Mohr.

Mason, R.
1977a   The Purpose of the "Editorial Framework" of the
                Book of Haggai. *VT* 27: 413–21.
1977b   *The Books of Haggai, Zechariah and Malachi.* Cam-
                bridge Commentary on the NEB. Cambridge: Cam-
                bridge.
1982   The Prophets of the Restoration. Pp. 137–54 in *Is-*

rael's Prophetic Tradition, eds. R. Coggins, A. Phillips, and M. Knibb. Cambridge: Cambridge.

Mastin, B. A.
1976   A Note on Zechariah VI 13. *VT* 26: 113–16.

May, H. G.
1938   "This People" and "This Nation" in Haggai. *VT* 18: 190–97.

Mazar, B.
1957   The Tobiads. *IEJ* 7: 137–45, 229–38.

Mettinger, T. N. D.
1982   *The Dethronement of Sabaoth.* Coniectanea Biblica, Old Testament Series 18. Lund: Gleerup.

Meyers, C.
1976   *The Tabernacle Menorah.* American Schools of Oriental Research Dissertation Series 2. Missoula: Scholars.

1979   Was There a Seven-Branched Menorah in Solomon's Temple? *BAR* 5: 46–57.

1981   The Elusive Temple. *BA* 45: 33–41.

1983   Jachin and Boaz in Religious and Political Perspective. *CBQ* 45: 167–78.

1985   Temples. Pp. 1030–32 in *Harper's Bible Dictionary.* New York: Harper.

Meyers, E. M.
1971   The Theological Implications of an Ancient Jewish Burial Custom. *JQR* 62: 95–119.

1983   The Use of *Tora* in Haggai 2:11 and the Role of the Prophet in the Restoration Community. Pp. 69–76 in *The Word of the Lord Shall Go Forth: Essays in Honor of David Noel Freedman in Celebration of His Sixtieth Birthday,* eds. C. L. Meyers and M. O'Connor. Winona Lake, Ind.: Eisenbrauns/The American Schools of Oriental Research.

1985   The Shelomith Seal and Aspects of the Judean Restoration: Some Additional Reconsiderations. *EI* 17: 33–38.

———— and J. Strange
1981   *Archaeology, the Rabbis, and Early Christianity.* Nashville: Abingdon Press.

Milgrom, J.
1972   The Alleged Wave-offering in Israel and the Ancient Near East. *IEJ* 22: 33–38.

1976   Sacrifices and Offerings, OT. *IDBS* 763–71.

Miller, P. D., Jr.
1967   El the Warrior. *HTR* 60: 411–31.
1971   Animal Names as Designations in Ugaritic and He-
                brew. *Ugarit-Forschungen* 2: 177–86.

Mitchell, H.
1912   *A Critical and Exegetical Commentary on Haggai,
                Zechariah, Malachi, and Jonah.* International Critical
                Commentary. Edinburgh: Clark.

Möhlenbrink, K.
1929   Der Leuchter im fünften Nachtgesicht des propheten
                Sacharja: eine archäologische Untersuchung. *ZDPV*
                52: 257–86.

Moldenke, A. L. and H. N.
1952   *Plants of the Bible.* New York: Ronald.

Mowinckel, S.
1956   *He That Cometh: The Messiah Concept in the Old
                Testament and Later Judaism.* New York: Abingdon.

Mullen, E. T.
1980   The Assembly of the Gods. *The Divine Council in
                Canaanite and Early Hebrew Literature.* Harvard Se-
                mitic Monographs 24. Chico, Calif.: Scholars.

Muraoka, T.
1983–84   The Tell-Fekherye Bilingual Inscriptions and Early
                Aramaic. *Abr-Nahrain* 22: 79–117.

Myers, J.
1965   *Ezra. Nehemiah.* Anchor Bible 14. Garden City,
                N.Y.: Doubleday.

Neusner, J.
1973   *Idea of Purity in Ancient Judaism.* Studies in Judaism
                in Late Antiquity 1. Leiden: Brill.

Niditch, S.
1983   *The Symbolic Vision in Biblical Tradition.* Harvard
                Semitic Monographs 30. Chico, Calif.: Scholars.

North, R.
1970   Zechariah's Seven-Spout Lampstand. *Biblica* 51: 183–
                206.

Noth, M.
1953   Das altestamentliche Bundschliessen im Lichte eines
                Mari-Textes. Pp. 433–44 in *Mélanges Isidore Lévy.*
                Annuaire de l'Institut de Philologie et d'Histoire
                Orientales et Slaves 13. Brussels.
1966   *The Laws in the Pentateuch and other Studies.* Tr.
                P. R. Ap-Thomas. London: Oliver & Boyd.

Nowack, W.
1894   *Lehrbuch der Hebräischen Archäologie.* Leipzig: Mohr.
1903   *Die Kleinen Propheten.* 2 aufl. HAT. Göttingen: Vandenhoeck & Ruprecht.

Oded, B.
1979   *Mass Deportation and Deportees in the Neo-Assyrian Empire.* Wiesbaden: Dr. Ludwig Reichert Verlag.

Olmstead, A. T.
1948   *History of the Persian Empire.* Chicago: University of Chicago.

Oppenheim, A. L.
1949   The Golden Garments of the Gods. *JNES* 8: 172–93.
1968   "The Eyes of the Lord." *JAOS* 88: 173–80.

Oppenheimer, A.
1977   *The ʿam Ha-Aretz: A Study in the Social History of the Jewish People in the Hellenistic-Roman Period.* Tr. I. H. Levine. Arbeiten zur Literatur und Geschichte des Hellenistichen Judentum 8. Leiden: Brill.

Orlinsky, H. M.
1965   The Seer in Ancient Israel. *OA* 4: 153–74.

Ostborn, G.
1945   *Tora in the Old Testament. A Semantic Study.* Lund: Gleerup.

Ottosson, M.
1974   "ʾerets." *TDOT* 1: 390–405.
1978   "hêkhāl." *TDOT* 3: 382–88.

Parker, R. A., and W. A. Dubberstein
1956   *Babylonian Chronology 626 B.C.–A.D. 45.* Chicago: University of Chicago.

Peter, F.
1951   Zu Haggai 1, 9. *ThZ* 7: 150–51.

Petersen, D. L.
1974   Zerubbabel and Jerusalem Temple Reconstruction. *CBQ* 36: 366–72.
1977   *Late Israelite Prophecy: Studies in Deutero-Prophetic Literature and in Chronicles.* SBL Monograph Series 23. Missoula: Scholars.
1984   Zechariah's Visions: A Theological Perspective. *VT* 34: 195–206.

Peterson, J. L.
1977   *A Topographical Surface Survey of the Levitical "Cities" of Joshua 21 and 1 Chronicles 6.* Dissertation,

Chicago Institute of Advanced Theological Studies and Seabury-Western Theological Seminary.

Petitjean, A.

1966   La Mission de Zorobabel et la Reconstruction du Temple. *Ephemerides Theologicae Lovanienses* 42: 40–71.

1969   *Les Oracles du Proto-Zacharie*. Paris: Gabalda. Louvain: Editions Imprimerie Orientaliste.

Plöger, J. G.

1974   *"'adhāmāh." TDOT* 1: 88–98.

Polzin, R.

1976   *Late Biblical Hebrew: Toward an Historical Typology of Biblical Hebrew Prose*. Harvard Semitic Monographs 12. Missoula: Scholars.

Pope, M.

1962   Number, Numbering, Numbers. *IDB* 3: 561–67.

1973   *Job*. Anchor Bible 15. Garden City, N.Y.: Doubleday.

Porten, B.

1967   Structure and Theme of the Solomon Narrative. *HUCA* 38: 93–128.

Porter, P.

1983   *Metaphors and Monsters: A Literary-Critical Study of Daniel 7 and 8*. Coniectanea Biblica, Old Testament Series 20. Lund: Gleerup.

Preuss, H. D.

1975   *"bô." TDOT* 2: 20–49.

Rad, G. von

1953   *Studies in Deuteronomy*. Tr. D. Stalker. Studies in Biblical Theology 9. London: SCM.

Radday, Y.

1973   *An Analytical Linguistic Key-Word-in-Context Concordance to the Books of Haggai, Zechariah and Malachi*. The Computer Bible Vol. IV. Wooster, OH: Biblical Research Associates, Inc.

———— and M. A. Pollatschek

1980   Vocabulary Richness in Post-Exilic Prophetic Books. *ZAW* 92/3: 333–45.

Rainey, A.

1969   The Satrapy "Beyond the River." *Australian Journal of Biblical Archaeology* 1: 51–78.

Rignell, L.

1950   *Die Nachtgesichte des Sacharja*. Lund: Gleerup.

Ringgren, H.
1974   *"ʾelōhîm."* *TDOT* 1: 267–84.
Roberts, J. J. M.
1973   The Davidic Origin of the Zion Tradition. *JBL* 92:
               329–44.
Robinson, H. W.
1944   The Council of Yahweh. *JTS* 45: 131–57.
Rothstein, J. W.
1910   *Die Nachtgesichte des Sacharja. Studien zur Sacharja-
               prophetie und zur jüdischen geschichte im ersten nach-
               exilischen Jahrhundert. Beiträge zur Wissenschaft von
               Alten Testament* 8. Leipzig.
Rudolph, W.
1955   *Chronikbucher.* HAT. Tübingen: J. C. B. Mohr.
1976   *Haggai; Sacharja 1–8; Sacharja 9–14; Maleachai.*
               KAT 13, 4. Gütersloh: Gütersloher Verlagshaus Gerd
               Mohn.
Sarna, N.
1967   Psalm XIX and the Near Eastern Sun-God Literature
               in *Papers, Fourth World Jewish Congress.* Jerusalem:
               World Union of Jewish Studies.
Sasson, J.
1968   Bovine Symbolism in the Exodus Narrative. *VT* 18:
               380–87.
Scharbert, J.
1958   "Fluchen" und "Segnen" im Alten Testament. *Bib-
               lica* 39: 1–26.
1974   *"ʾālāh."* *TDOT* 1: 261–66.
Schmidt, W. H.
1978   *"dābhar."* *TDOT* 3: 94–125.
Schneider, D. A.
1979   *The Unity of the Book of the Twelve.* Ph.D. disserta-
               tion, Yale University.
Scott, R. B. Y.
1949   Secondary Meanings of *ʾaḥar,* after, behind. *JTS* 50:
               178–79.
1959   Weights and Measures of the Bible. *BA* 22: 22–39.
1962a   Mildew. *IDB* 3: 378.
1962b   East Wind. *IDB* 2: 4.
Seebass, H.
1975   *"bāchar."* *TDOT* 2: 74–87.
Sellers, O.
1962   Weights and Measures. *IDB* 4: 828–39.

Sellin, E.
1930   *Das Zwölfprophetenbuch übersetzt und erklärt. KAT* 12,2. 2nd-3rd ed. Leipzig: Scholl.

Seybold, K.
1971–72   Die Königsberwatung bei den Propheten Haggai and Sacharja. *Judaica* 27–28: 69–78.
1980   *"chālāh." TDOT* 4: 399–409.

Smith, M.
1957–58   The Image of God. *BJRL* 40: 473–512.
1971   *Palestinian Parties and Politics that Shaped the Old Testament.* New York: Columbia University.

Smith, R. H.
1964   The Household Lamps of Palestine in Old Testament Times. *BA* 27: 1–31.

Smitten, W. T. in der
1980   *"chămôr." TDOT* 4: 465–70.

Speiser, E. A.
1964   *Genesis.* Anchor Bible 1. Garden City, N.Y.: Doubleday.

Sperber, D.
1965   History of the Menorah. *JJS* 16: 135–49.

Steck, O. H.
1971   Zu Haggai 1 2–11. *ZAW* 83: 355–79.

Stern, E.
1982   *Material Culture of the Land of the Bible in the Persian Period, 538–332 B.C.* Warminster, England: Aris & Phillips.
1984a   The archaeology of Persian Palestine. Pp. 88–114 in Davies and Finkelstein 1984.
1984b   The Persian empire and the political and social history of Palestine in the Persian period. Pp. 70–87 in Davies and Finkelstein 1984.

Stuhlmueller, C.
1970   *Creative Redemption in Deutero-Isaiah.* Analecta Biblica 43. Rome: Biblical Institute Press.

Tadmor, H., et al.
1984   *The World History of the Jewish People: The Restoration—the Persian Period.* Jerusalem: 'Am Oved (Hebrew).

Talmon, S.
1961   Synonymous Readings in the Textual Traditions of the Old Testament. *Scripta Hierosolymitana* 8: 335–83.

1971	The Biblical Concept of Jerusalem. *Journal of Ecumenical Studies* 8: 300–16.
1976	Ezra and Nehemiah (Books and Men). *IDBS:* 317–28.
1978	"*har.*" *TDOT* 3: 427–47.

Thomas, D. W.

1931–32	A Note on *mḥlṣwt* in Zechariah 3:4. *JTS* 33: 279–80.
1933	A Note on *ḥlyṣwtm* in Judges 14:19. *JTS* 34: 165.
1956	The Book of Haggai (intro, exegesis), 1037–52. The Book of Zechariah (intro, exegesis), 1053–1114. *Interpreter's Bible* 6. Nashville: Abingdon.

Thompson, J. A.

1962	Horse. *IDB* 2: 646–48.

Tidwell, N. L. A.

1975	Wā'ōmar (Zech. 3:5) and the Genre of Zechariah's Fourth Vision. *JBL* 94: 343–55.

Toombs, L.

1962	Signet. *IDB* 4: 347–48.

Townsend, T. N.

1968	Additional Comments on Haggai II 10–19. *VT* 18: 559–60.

Tufnell, O.

1962	Seals and Scarabs. *IDB* 4: 254–59.

Uffenheimer, B.

1961	*The Visions of Zechariah: From Prophecy to Apocalyptic.* Jerusalem: Kiryat Sepher (Hebrew).
1964	Serubbabel und die messianischen Hoffnungen der Rueckkehrer aus dem babylonischen Exil. *El Ha'Ayin* 34, Jerusalem.

Van der Woude, A. S.

1980	Be not like your fathers. Pp. 167–73 in *Prophecy. Essays presented to Georg Fohrer on his sixty-fifth birthday, Sept 6, 1980. BZAW* 150.

Vaux, R. de

1961	*Ancient Israel.* Tr. John McHugh. London: Darton, Longman, & Todd.
1971	The Decrees of Cyrus and Darius on the Rebuilding of the Temple. Pp. 63–96 in *BANE.* Garden City, N.Y.: Doubleday.
1972	The King of Israel, Vassal of Yahweh. Pp. 152–66 in *BANE.* Tr. D. McHugh. London: Darton, Longman, & Todd.

Wagner, N. E.

1960	"*rinna*" in the Psalter. *VT* 10: 435–41.

Wagner, S.
1975   *"biqqēsh."* *TDOT* 2: 229–41.
Warmuth, G.
1978   *"hôdh."* *TDOT* 3: 352–56.
Weiser, A.
1962   *The Psalms: A Commentary.* Tr. H. Hartwell. Old
                Testament Library. Philadelphia: Westminster.
Weiss, M.
1966   The Origin of the "Day of the Lord"—Reconsidered.
                HUCA 37: 29–60.
Wellhausen, J.
1898   *Die kleinen Propheten.* Berlin.
Wevers, J. W.
1962   Chariot. *IDB* 1: 552–54.
Whitelam, K.
1979   *The Just King: Monarchical Judicial Authority in An-
                cient Israel.* JSOT Supplement Series, 12. Sheffield:
                JSOT.
Whitley, C. F.
1954   The Term Seventy Years' Captivity. *VT* 4: 60–72.
Widengren, G.
1977   The Persian Period. Pp. 489–538 in *Israelite and Ju-
                dean History,* eds. J. H. Hayes and J. M. Miller. Phil-
                adelphia: Westminster.
Wiklander, B.
1980   *"zāʿam."* TDOT 4: 106–11.
Williams, R. J.
1962   Writing and Writing Materials. *IDB* 4: 909–21.
Wilson, R. R.
1980   *Prophecy and Society in Ancient Israel.* Philadelphia:
                Fortress.
Wolf, C. U.
1962   Archives, House of the. *IDB* 1: 215–16.
Wolfe, R. E.
1935   Editing of the Book of the Twelve. *ZAW* 53: 90–129.
Wright, G. E.
1950   *The Old Testament Against Its Environment.* Studies
                in Biblical Theology 2. London: SCM.
1961   The Temple in Palestine-Syria. Pp. 169–84 in *Biblical
                Archaeologist Reader* 1, eds. D. N. Freedman and
                G. E. Wright. Garden City, N.Y.: Doubleday.
1962   The Lawsuit of God. A Form-Critical Study of Deu-
                teronomy 32. Pp. 26–67 in *Israel's Prophetic Heritage,*

eds. B. Anderson and W. Harrelson. New York: Harper.

Yadin, Y.
1963   *The Art of Warfare in Biblical Lands.* 2 vols. New York: McGraw-Hill.

Zadok, R.
1979   *The Jews in Babylonia During the Chaldean and Achaemenian Period According to the Babylonian Sources.* Haifa: University of Haifa.

Zobel, H.-J.
1978   *"hôy." TDOT* 3: 359–63.

Zohary, M.
1982   *Plants of the Bible.* Cambridge: Cambridge.

THE BOOK
OF HAGGAI

1. RESTORATION OF THE TEMPLE
(1:1–15)

Prophetic call to work on the temple

1 ¹ In the second year of King Darius, in the sixth month, on the first day of the month, the word of Yahweh came through the prophet Haggai to Zerubbabel ben-Shealtiel, the governor of Judah, and to Joshua ben-Jehozadak, the high priest: ² Thus spoke Yahweh of Hosts: "This people has said the time has not come[a]—the time for the House of Yahweh to be built."

³ Thereupon the word of Yahweh came through the prophet Haggai: ⁴ "Is it time for you yourselves to dwell in your finished houses while this House lies desolate?"

⁵ Thereafter thus spoke Yahweh of Hosts, "Reflect upon your ways—

> ⁶ You have sown much but have brought in little;
> you keep eating but there is never enough
>> to fill up,
> you keep drinking but there is never enough
>> to be drunk,
> you keep putting on clothes but there is no
>> warmth for anyone;
> As for the hired hand, he works for a bag full of
>> holes."

⁷ Thus spoke Yahweh of Hosts, "Reflect upon your ways—
⁸ Go up in the hills so that you may bring in wood,
And build the House so that I may be pleased with it,
That I may be glorified," said Yahweh.
⁹ You have looked for much but there is[b] little;
What you have brought to the House I have blown away.

"Why is this?"—Oracle of Yahweh of Hosts. "Because my House lies desolate while you run about, each man to his own house. ¹⁰ There-

---

[a] Reading either the infinitive absolute as written or emending to perfect *bāʾ*.

[b] Reading with LXX, Syriac, and Targum which read verb "to be," reconstructed as infinitive absolute *hāyōh*.

fore, because of you, the heavens have withheld the dew in part and the earth has withheld some of its yield. ¹¹ Thus I have proclaimed a desolation affecting the land and the hills; the grain, the new wine, the fresh oil, and whateverᶜ the ground brings forth; mankind and beast and all products of human toil."

Response of leaders and people

¹² Then Zerubbabel ben-Shaltiel along with Joshua ben-Jehozadak, the high priest, and all the rest of the people gave heed to the voice of Yahweh their God, even to the words of the prophet Haggai when Yahweh their God sent him to themᵈ; thus the people revered Yahweh. ¹³ Then Haggai, Yahweh's messenger, spoke to the people with the message of Yahweh: "I am with you!"—Oracle of Yahweh. ¹⁴ Thus Yahweh roused the spirit of Zerubbabel ben-Shaltiel, the governor of Judah, and the spirit of Joshua ben-Jehozadak, the high priest, and the spirit of all the rest of the people so that they came to do the work on the House of Yahweh of Hosts their God¹⁵ on the twenty-fourth day of the sixth month in the second year of Darius.

NOTES

1:1. *second year of King Darius, in the sixth month, on the first day of the month.* The chronological headings for Haggai, as well as for Zechariah, are reckoned in relationship to the Persian emperor Darius I, who became king about October 5, 522 B.C.E., and ruled until his death in November 486 B.C.E. (Cook 1983:55). The second year of his reign would thus be 520 B.C.E. The sixth month would be the month of Elul (August/September), when late summer and early fall harvesting would have begun. See our Introduction, pp. xlii–l, for remarks on the chronological framework of Haggai and Zechariah 1–8 and for a summary chart (p. xliv). A detailed and helpful discussion of chronological equivalencies appears in Ackroyd 1958:15ff.; cf. Parker and Dubberstein 1956 for a full and technical listing of these equivalencies.

The reference here to Darius's regnal year is the first of six chronological indicators in the Book of Haggai (cf. 1:15 and 2:1,10,18,20). While only two of the other five repeat the phrase "second year of King Darius," that information is clearly implicit in all the date formulas. The beginning of chapter 2, for example, omits the reference to the king's regnal year, since that datum is supplied by the immediately preceding verse (1:15), which does double duty in providing the exact year for the material before it and also after it. Similarly, both 2:18 and 2:20 are abbreviated versions of the full date

---

ᶜ Read *ʾl kl* instead of *ʾl*; loss of *kl* due to haplography.
ᵈ Restoring *ʾălēhem* with most of the versions; absence in MT due to haplography.

insignia of 2:10. In short, the brief time span represented by Haggai's prophecies has been carefully tagged with absolute chronological markers, all of which directly or indirectly are derived from the Persian monarchic reckoning.

Haggai and his colleague Zechariah (or their editor) are exceptional among the biblical prophets in providing this kind of full chronological information, with specific designation of the day and month as well as year of a foreign ruler. The Book of Daniel designates Babylonian rulers, but since that work is a retrospective account from centuries after the rulers who are mentioned, it cannot be classified as serving the same kind of chronological purpose as do the "days"—i.e., the era (Andersen and Freedman 1980:153)—of the Judean and/or Israelite kings during whose reign(s) the prophet has delivered his oracles from Yahweh. For the exilic prophets, especially Jeremiah and Ezekiel, the date formulas are much more akin to those of Haggai and Zechariah. Jeremiah's prophecies are labeled with the consciousness that they come to an end at a specific time, and an actual month appears: "in the era of Josiah ben-Amon, King of Judah, in the thirteenth year of his reign . . . until the end of the eleventh year of Zedekiah ben-Josiah, King of Judah, until the captivity of Jerusalem *in the fifth month"* (Jer 1:2–3; italics ours). In actuality, the last date in Jeremiah is not the day of captivity (the tenth day of the fifth month of Jehoiachin's eleventh year; Jer 52:12) but rather the day in which the exiled King Jehoiachin is released from prison by Evil-Merodach, King of Babylon.

That the chronological information in Jeremiah is keyed to the fact of the exile becomes especially evident in two further features of the dates that are given. (1) Beginning with the date of the destruction and exile of Jerusalem, a synchronism with the Babylonian king is offered (e.g., Jer 52:12). (2) The calculation of a time span dealing with an event after 538 B.C.E. is made for the first time in reference to the exile: "the thirty-seventh year of the captivity of Jehoiachin King of Judah, in the twelfth month on the twenty-fifth day of the month" (Jer 52:31). The captivity as the frame of chronological reference thereafter characterizes the date formulas in Ezekiel (e.g., Ezek 1:1–2; 8:1; 24:1; 40:1). All of Ezekiel's dates, whether they refer to the beginning of the exile or to the destruction of Jerusalem, specify day of the month as well as the month in addition to the year: e.g., "in the sixth year, in the sixth month, on the fifth day of the month . . ." (Ezek 8:1).

The information in Haggai, in light of these developments in the chronological specificity of biblical prophecy, reveals two features of the time orientation of the late sixth century. Although the dates mention Haggai by name and are probably the work of a hand other than the prophet's, the works of both Haggai and Zechariah show evidence of a very short time lapse between composition and compilation so that the influence and interest of these prophets are apparent in all the material in the works bearing their names (cf. NOTES and COMMENT to Zech 1–8). First, a non-Judean monarch (Darius) is the royal figure whose reign provides the framework for the prophecies of Haggai and Zechariah 1–8. Although Jeremiah anticipates this, he nonetheless provides the dates of Babylonian kings as synchronisms with those of the Judean kings. Haggai's work, well beyond the termination of Judean independence, acknowledges Persian domination. Jeremiah's persistence in reckoning time with respect to the time of a Davidide in captivity has not been retained. This aspect of the Haggai and First Zechariah dating reflects an acceptance, in our opinion, of the legitimacy of the Persian rule over Yehud, an acceptance which might not have been forthcoming for the destructive Babylonians but which was tolerated for the Persians, who appeared to be doing the will of Yahweh in their policy toward the exiled Judeans and the province of Yehud (cf. NOTES to Zech 4:6b–10a).

Second, the dates in Haggai and First Zechariah (except Zech 1:1; cf. NOTE) are uniform in noting not only the month within Darius's reign but also the day of the month. They share this attention to specificity with Ezekiel, who does so with the duration of exile in mind. Why do Haggai and Zechariah provide such exact dates? The listing of day, month, and year probably can be linked to the similar phenomenon in Ezekiel, who exemplifies the sensitivity of the prophets of the exile and later to the passage of time since the destruction of Jerusalem. These prophets are acutely aware of the exile as a disruption in the relationship of Yahweh to his people. They simultaneously anticipate a termination to that disruption, a future date certain to have been conditioned by Jeremiah's seventy-year projection, Jer 25:11–12; 29:10 (cf. our discussion in NOTES to Zech 1:12 and 7:5). As that span nears its conclusion, the consciousness of the passage of the smallest units of time—a countdown situation—would have become particularly sharp. The sequence of events in both Haggai and Zechariah are linked to the expected termination of the disruption. The restoration of Yahweh's home, they believe, will mark the full return of Yahweh to his people. Hence the close chronological notation in both these prophets reflects their assiduous scrutiny of events relating to the long-anticipated reunion of God, people, and territory.

One other point about prophets and chronological data: the two prophetic works that follow Haggai and First Zechariah show no tendencies whatsoever to relate the prophecies to the course of historical events. Not a single date appears in Deutero-Zechariah (Zech 9–14) or in Malachi. One might argue that this absence of reckoning stems from the difficulty in using a foreign (Persian) regnal system when Yahweh's renewed presence as sovereign in Jerusalem was not accompanied by an indigenous dynastic structure against which to mark the passage of time. But Ezra and Nehemiah show no reluctance to utilize the Persian regnal dates (e.g., Ezra 7:7; Neh 2:1). After the temple was restored, the intense awareness of the ongoing hiatus in God's symbolic presence in Jerusalem and in Israel's existence in Zion would have dissipated. The exact counting of years, months, and days makes most sense when it is done in relation to concrete and momentous events, those of the past and/or those anticipated. With the temple of Yahweh standing once again, Second Zechariah and Malachi do not dwell on this type of event and mention no specific dates; at the same time their prophecies have a stronger eschatological cast than do those of their closest predecessors.

The specific arrangement of year, month, and day is noteworthy. Only the last chronological heading of the Haggai-Zechariah 1–8 composite work, Zech 7:1 (see first NOTE to that verse) also begins with the year, if we omit from consideration the Hag 1:15–2:1 date, in which the year does double duty and so must come first in the second heading (see NOTE to 1:15). The sequence in Zech 7:1 has the regnal year first, but the day is second, followed by the month. The correspondence in the position of the year and the chiastic relationship of the day and month along with other stylistic features of Haggai and of Zechariah 7–8 create a link between the beginning and the conclusion of Haggai-Zechariah 1–8.

the word of Yahweh. As a noun meaning "word" the root *dbr* ("to speak") together with "Yahweh" is a technical term for prophetic revelation. The "word" characterizes the prophet, just as "counsel" is associated with the sage and "torah" with the priest (Jer 18:18). With "came" (see next NOTE), this phrase constitutes a standard announcement of the transmission of a message from Yahweh to his intermediary, the prophet. The final stage in the delivery of God's word to the public usually is signified by the additional phrase "thus spoke Yahweh" (see first NOTE to 1:2). These stereotyped expressions originate, according to Mullen's analysis (1980:220–25), in the language of royal courts. Messages that were delivered orally were introduced in standard ways that helped to confirm the authenticity of the words. When Yahweh is the ultimate source of a message, the Divine Council is the setting from which the oracular imperatives are issued. Drawing upon mythological or royal language, Israelite literature envisions Yahweh as a king or judge who sits in council and proclaims his orders. In this conception, prophets are members of the council who act as couriers to deliver God's judgment to the people. The prophets utter the appropriate formulas to clarify the source of the message, the fact of its being transmitted, and the authority of its contents. The oracle itself, according to such a paradigm, has the force of a decree of judgment, emanating as it does from the Council of Yahweh.

The formulaic introductions to oracles are not the only features in Haggai and Zechariah that show the influence of the Divine Council on postexilic prophecy. The Investiture Scene of Zech 3 (see NOTES) is structured as a session of the Heavenly Court, and the angelic beings in Zechariah emerge as members of Yahweh's assembly who take on functions of Yahweh himself and begin to develop individuality.

came through. Literally "was by the hand of." Most usages of *bĕyad* ("by the hand of") in the Hebrew Bible occur in relationship to an active verb. Two main categories are formed, one indicating authority (usually with the verb *ntn:* "into the power, custody of") and the other denoting instrumentality. In the latter case the verb *dbr* ("to speak") occurs most frequently (e.g., Exod 9:35; Jer 37:2), although *ṣwh* ("to command") and others are found. The rendering in Haggai is significant in its expression of prophetic instrumentality without the use of an active verb. Instead, *hāyâ* ("came") expresses the verbal idea in keeping with traditional formulaic introduction to prophecy, "the word of Yahweh (which) came to X" (cf. Hos 1:1; Jer 1:1–2; Zeph 1:1; etc.) Haggai uses *bĕyad* ("by the hand of") in place of the expected "to" (*ʾel*), a shift which has the effect of emphasizing the instrumentality of the prophet. In Malachi this change is carried one step further and no verb at all appears: "The word of Yahweh to Israel through Malachi" (Mal 1:1). The use of *bĕyad* also heightens the authority of the prophet as Yahweh's spokesman.

Although the translation of *hāyâ bĕyad* as "came through" implies movement, the actual conveying of God's word to the prophet should not be understood to involve motion (Andersen and Freedman 1980:151). The prophet by his vocation hears directly what Yahweh has to say. If any movement is intended, it is that which transmits Yahweh's word from the prophet to his audience. Because of this, *hāyâ bĕyad* ("came through") is something of an improvement over *hāyâ ʾel* ("came to"), in that it reveals that the transmission of God's word involves its communication to those addressed by the prophet and not to the prophet himself in the first place.

The formula is repeated in Hag 1:3 and 2:1 and 10, indicating that its usage here serves as a heading for the first oracle and not as a general introduction to all of Haggai's prophecies. In this respect Haggai exhibits the pattern found frequently in Jeremiah and Ezekiel, and also in Zechariah, where this idiomatic phrase (albeit with *'el*, "to") begins oracular units. The Book of Hosea, in contrast, inserts an explanation of the prophet's personal situation after the appearance of the formula.

Haggai. This prophet is the only biblical personage bearing this name, which is derived from *ḥag* ("feast, holiday"), although several other names formed from this noun can be cited (e.g., Haggi, son of Gad, Gen 46:16; and Haggith, wife of David, 2 Sam 3:4). Haggai himself also appears in Ezra (5:1; 6:14), in addition to the nine places in which he is mentioned in the book bearing his name. Another possible source of the name "Haggai" is the root *ḥgg*, which may underlie an Aramaism (*ḥāggā*, "reeling") of Isa 19:17. But that root itself is ultimately related to *ḥag* (BDB:290–01). Mitchell (1912:42) suggests that the name may simply be a mutilated form of *ḥgyh* (1 Chron 6:15, [RSV 6:30]); but that too is related to *ḥag* or *ḥgg*.

The question as to whether the prophet's name was meant to contain symbolic significance is one which cannot be easily answered, but it arises nonetheless because no patronymic or city or region of origin is given for him. In the case of Malachi, for whom there is a similar lack of such information, the name "Malachi" is suspected by many to be an appellation meaning "my messenger." Can "Haggai" likewise be an appellation, "festal," relating somehow to the celebrations attendant upon the temple work which he has been instrumental in effecting? Haggai is not the only writing prophet, in addition to Malachi, lacking identifying material; Habakkuk is not identified either, nor are those anonymous writers whose works have been included in the Book of Isaiah—i.e., Second and Third Isaiah. Unlike Malachi, however, Haggai at least is given a title, "the prophet," a feature he shares with Habakkuk as well as with several other prophets, notably Nathan, Gad, Jeremiah, and Zechariah.

The name Haggai is found in the onomasticon of Babylonian Jews only in sources which postdate the exile. There the suffix *-ai*, which is common in Aramaic and late Akkadian, has probably been attached to *ḥag*, forming an Aramaic counterpart of the Hebrew name Haggi (Zadok 1979:23–24). This information shows Haggai to be a perfectly common name in the postexilic period and decreases the likelihood that the prophet's name is an appellative. We also note that, in contrast with other non-Yahwistic Jewish names occurring in Babylonian sources (e.g., *šabbātay*), Haggai cannot be shown to be exclusively a Jewish name. None of the persons by the name *Ḥaggay* in the Murashu archive has a Yahwistic genealogy, and Zadok (1979:24) suggests that the ancestors of one Haggai, who was the father of a Jewish Shabbatai, may have been Babylonians. If this is so, we may have a reason for the omission of a patronymic and the town of origin for the prophet Haggai. Haggai perhaps was a returned exile, as the Aramaic form of his name along with the indirect evidence of Ezra suggests. Surely a book emphasizing the responsibilities of returned exiles would not want to cite a Babylonian town in order to identify Haggai. Similarly, his pedigree may also have been inappropriate for a Hebrew prophet. While all this may seem a bit remote and hypothetical, it does at least offer some explanation for the strange lack of identifying material, especially since a lineage is provided for his colleague Zechariah, with whom he is closely linked in the canon and in history.

Further evidence that Haggai is a name rather than an appellative comes from seals and from bullae of the time of Jeremiah. Bulla #55 in Avigad's publication (1986) reads "belonging to (or of) Haggai son of Hodoyahu." Avigad (1976b) reports that the name Haggai also is common on many seals of the late Iron Age, including one that refers to a man named Benyahu as an "official (*na'ar*) of Haggai"; cf. below, NOTE to "official," Zech 2:8. The occurrence of the name Haggai on artifacts from Judaea from the time of Jeremiah does not, however, mean that the prophet Haggai several generations later could not have been a returned exile.

Zerubbabel ben-Shealtiel. Because of the complexity of the issues involved and the length of our discussion of the problems surrounding Zerubbabel's identity and role, we begin by providing for the general reader an introductory statement highlighting the salient points. Zerubbabel is the Davidic descendant of King Jehoiachin who is appointed governor by the Persians of the province of Yehud in the period of the restoration of the temple. He returned to the holy land from Babylon after the Persian authorities had authorized rebuilding the temple of Yahweh in Jerusalem. As work on the temple progressed in the days of Haggai, many people were hopeful that Zerubbabel would also become king of Israel. The Book of Zechariah, especially chapter 4, deals with the limited powers of the governor under Persian rule. Zerubbabel shared the duties of administering the affairs of Yehud with Joshua the high priest and had a special role to play as secular liaison with the governing Persian authority and as tax collector. He is the last male Davidic descendant to hold significant power in postexilic Yehud and is succeeded by a series of governors who have little or no dynastic connections to Israel's past. The fact that Zerubbabel figures so prominently in Haggai and is so downplayed in Zechariah has led many scholars to speculate on his fate. Recent archaeological discoveries, however, strongly suggest that he held his post as governor for at least five years or so after the rededication of the temple in 515 B.C.E.

The Zerubbabel in question is presumably the grandson of the exiled King Jehoiachin. He is designated here as the son of Shealtiel, who is elder brother or uncle of one Sheshbazzar (see below) according to 1 Chron 3:17 (Talmon 1976:319; cf. Freedman 1961:439–41; Bright 1981:366–67; and Brockington 1969:53). The spelling of his patronymic, *še'alti'ēl,* is curiously plene, with an *aleph* appearing after the initial *šin,* in contrast with the defective spelling below in verses 12 and 14 and also in 2:2. However, the final mention in Haggai of Zerubbabel, in 2:23, resumes the plene rendering, thus forming a pair of full spellings, which appear at the beginning and the end of the book and serve as a framing device. Ezra 3:2,8 and Neh 12:1 also preserve the plene, which may represent the formal spelling of the name, with the defective reflecting its actual pronunciation.

The name Zerubbabel, a fairly common Babylonian name, is attested in inscriptions of the early Achaemenid period (Mitchell 1912:43; Talmon 1976:391) and is usually understood to mean "offspring of Babylon" or "seed of Babylon" (originally *zēr-bābili?).* It occurs frequently elsewhere in the Hebrew Bible without any patronymic (Zech 4:6,7,9,10; Ezra 2:2; 4:2,3; Neh 7:7; 12:47; and 1 Chron 3:19). In addition, it occurs twice without "ben-Shealtiel/Shaltiel") in Haggai, making a total of seven occurrences of the name Zerubbabel in this prophetic book.

The form *zeru* is East Semitic and equivalent to West Semitic *zera';* but the Masoretic vocalization is difficult and the double *b* is probably a back formation to protect the shortened *u* vowel before it. Junker (1938:95) would understand the name as pure

Hebrew, derived from *zerū'ăbĕbābel*, and would explain the doubling as the result of the loss of the first *b*. At one time, *bbl* may have stood as a surrogate for some god of that city, perhaps the chief god of Babylon; or, as suggested by others, it may have designated a long-standing citizen of Babel. It is curious, to say the least, that a member of the royal house of Judah possesses a Babylonian name, whereas many others in exile retained good Yahwistic names (Zadok 1979:7–21).

One wonders whether, had he ever become king, Zerubbabel would have forsaken his birth name for a more appropriate—i.e., Yahwistic—throne name. There is some evidence for the practice in Judah of the king's taking a new name (e.g., Eliakim/ Jehoiakim, 2 Kgs 23:34 and Mattaniah/Zedekiah, 2 Kgs 24:17; see the discussion in de Vaux 1961:107–8 of these and other examples) upon accession to office; and Zerubbabel would surely have been likely to have availed himself of such a custom.

The use of the name Zerubbabel perhaps can be better understood by a closer look at his patronymic. Shealtiel is West Semitic, a fact which suggests that the father of Zerubbabel had already been born before Jehoiachin was exiled from Jerusalem. Shealtiel, according to contemporary practice, undoubtedly had married and had fathered children at an early age, possibly at eighteen. The adoption of an East Semitic name for Zerubbabel suggests either a) that the royal family then in exile was assimilationist by the time of his birth or b) that the name represents the exiles' hope for an imminent return from Babylon. Shealtiel himself bore an interesting name. Its etymology may be the same as the one proposed for Samuel in 1 Sam 1:20, where Hannah proclaims that she "called his name Samuel because from Yahweh have I asked him *(mê YHWH šĕʾiltîw),*" although "Shealtiel" does not preserve the "from" *(min)* before "God" *(ʾēl).* The name Saul, for which the Bible does not record an etymology, may have a similar origin, since "Saul" is probably a passive participial form of *šʾl,* "to ask."

The problems with Zerubbabel's lineage do not end with the question of the etymology of Shealtiel. In the genealogical list of 1 Chron 3:19, Zerubbabel's father is listed as Pedaiah. The apparent discrepancy cannot be easily resolved by assuming that there were two men by the name Zerubbabel who were both involved in the enterprise of rebuilding the destroyed temple (Talmon 1976:391). Similarly, the suggestion that Pedaiah fathered a son by the widow of his deceased brother Shealtiel in accordance with the laws of Levirate marriage (Deut 25:5ff.) is unconvincing. This ingenious solution first offered by Köhler (1860) has more recently been proposed by Rudolph (1955:29) and has been accepted by Brockington (1969:53) and Bright (1981:366 n.60) among others. Such attempts to harmonize the sources, however, have not been successful. The proposal of Mitchell (1912:43) to substitute Shealtiel for Pedaiah in 1 Chron 3:19 on the basis of the LXX would resolve all difficulties with respect to Zerubbabel's lineage and make the Chronicler consistent without resorting to unproven theories; yet the LXX itself may have inserted Shealtiel in the 1 Chronicles passage in order to resolve the same difficulties. Another possibility is that if Judean kings were assigned throne names even before their accession, the two names Pedaiah and Shealtiel could represent the same individual. The New Testament also reflects the confusion in identifying Zerubbabel's parentage. Both Matt 1:12 and Luke 3:27 list Zerubbabel as the son of Shealtiel, but while Matthew follows the Chronicler's genealogy, Luke takes Shealtiel as the son of Neri of the house of David rather than as Jeconiah (= Jehoiachin).

Since the confusion over Shealtiel's lineage cannot be satisfactorily resolved, we merely reiterate the position of Haggai, that Zerubbabel is the proper heir of Shealtiel. Assuming that Zerubbabel's lineage is proper does not remove the problem of his brother (or uncle) Sheshbazzar, who was apparently appointed governor in 538 B.C.E. Presumably Shealtiel had already died when Cyrus issued his edict allowing the exiles to return and so could not assume a leadership role. Yet Zerubbabel may have been still too young to have assumed the office of governor at that time. Sheshbazzar, presumably the fourth son of Jehoiachin, could then have been appointed to serve on his behalf. An analogy is suggested by the case of Zedekiah, who became king when his nephew Jehoiachin was taken into exile. Jehoiachin was very young at the time—only eighteen—and his children, if any, would hardly have been competent to rule (2 Kgs 24:8,15–17). If this analogy is valid, it would help to explain why Sheshbazzar's children, if there were any, were not in line to succeed him. Surely the Persians would have been sensitive to the political expediency, for securing provincial support, of continuing the royal line. The Persian authorities who selected the civil officer or *peḥâ* for Yehud would in that case have tried to accommodate the wishes of the royal house in their efforts to appoint an administrator whose official status would best capitalize upon indigenous authority. However Sheshbazzar came to serve as governor, the fact remains that there is considerable confusion in the sources regarding the relationship between Sheshbazzar's governorship and that of Zerubbabel.

The Babylonian origin of the name Zerubbabel and also Sheshbazzar apparently indicates the accommodation of the royal house to a foreign (Babylonian) court. Such accommodation would have aided the next foreign court (the Persians) in its presumed attention to the Judean lineage. The name Sheshbazzar may be understood as a corruption of Sin-ab-uzur and preserved as "Shenazzar" in the Davidic genealogy of 1 Chron 3:18 (Albright 1921:108–10; 1941:16ff.; Bright 1981:362; Freedman 1961:439; and Talmon 1976:319). Listed in the Aramaic of Ezra (5:14) as the first governor appointed by Cyrus, he is called "prince" of Judah in the Hebrew (Ezra 1:8), where he is also said to have received the holy vessels of the temple from the Persians (Ezra 1:7–8). It is not entirely clear from that text (Ezra 1:11) whether he actually took them up to Jerusalem himself, as is indicated elsewhere (Ezra 5:15–16), or whether he was merely responsible for having them transported there (the second occurrence of the Hiphil of *ʿlh*, "to bring up," not being translated by the LXX). While Sheshbazzar's activities surely occurred in the reign of Cyrus the Great, it remains difficult a) to resolve whether Sheshbazzar went to Jerusalem at all with the vessels (Hebrew source, 1:7–8) and b) to identify the nature of his work on the Temple of Yahweh (Aramaic source, 5:16).

Zerubbabel's role in the work on the temple is more easily discerned because of the material in Haggai and Zechariah, but even this information is confused in Ezra and Nehemiah. Ezra 2:2 (= Neh 7:7) and Neh 12:1 assert that Zerubbabel headed a group of returning exiles, but it is not clear in which period that event happened—in the reign of Cyrus or in that of Darius I. The traditional manner of resolving this difficulty appears valid to us. It assumes that there were two waves of emigration back to Jerusalem, one in the time of Cyrus under the leadership of Sheshbazzar and another in the time of Darius I under Zerubbabel's leadership (assumed by Haggai and Zechariah). The latter is possible because Zerubbabel would by then have been old enough to assume such a position.

The absence of any further information regarding the nature of Sheshbazzar's work on the initial rebuilding effort in 538 B.C.E. other than "laying the foundations" (Ezra 5:16), a task which in Haggai and Zechariah as well as in Ezra 3–5 (except for 5:16) is attributed to Joshua and Zerubbabel alone, supports such an understanding of events, yet we still cannot be sure why the initial efforts did not succeed. The Chronicler has confused the careers of Zerubbabel and Sheshbazzar and has made matters worse by giving Zerubbabel's lineage through Shealtiel in 1 Chron 3:19. If Zerubbabel had come of age in the reign of Darius I, or possibly slightly earlier, we could understand why Sheshbazzar suddenly receded into the background. The confusion in the sources is ameliorated by assuming that Sheshbazzar was surrogate governor, either because a) the Persians preferred to have a son rather than a grandson of the exiled king begin the process of return and the reestablishment of sacrifice at the altar of the ruined temple (Ezra 3:3), or b) Zerubbabel was too young in 538 B.C.E. to be an active official. In either case, by 520 B.C.E. Zerubbabel is in full charge. Since he was in some way associated with the activities of Sheshbazzar from the start, the sources tend to credit him with the whole undertaking and confuse his actual work with that of his elder brother or uncle, Sheshbazzar.

New information on the history of the Davidic line has appeared recently with the publication by Avigad (1976a) of a corpus of some 65 bullae and two seals of the early Persian period. In a seal of Shelomith, the 'amah of one Elnathan the governor (see NOTE below on "governor of Judah"), may be discerned a significant postscript to the story of the fate of the family of Zerubbabel (E. Meyers 1985). Avigad has been hesitant to equate the Shelomith of the seal with the Shelomith mentioned as a daughter of Zerubbabel in 1 Chron 3:19. However, his reconstruction of the list of governors of Yehud and the internal biblical evidence does allow for such an identification. Elnathan, as successor to Zerubbabel, apparently married into the royal house of David; alternatively, at the very least, he elevated Shelomith to a position of great responsibility (Avigad 1976a:30ff.) in order to maintain the close association between the office of civil authority—i.e., the governor—and the royal line as had evidently been the case with the previous two incumbents, Sheshbazzar and Zerubbabel.

Shelomith is one of very few women mentioned in the list of the Davidic line in Chronicles. The list, however, is unusual in that it explicitly singles out Shelomith as the sister of Meshullam and Hananiah, sons of Zerubbabel. The specific mention of Shelomith as their sister seems to indicate that she played a significant role in the matter of dynastic succession. It was not uncommon either in the ancient world or in more recent times for political ambitions and matters of bloodline to be made complicated by marital plans. Indeed, the very founder of the royal dynasty in question, King David, was the son-in-law of the king he succeeded (1 Sam 18:17). Moreover, it was common practice in Solomon's days for the prefects who administered the provinces to marry the king's daughters (1 Kgs 4:7ff.). One is reminded also of Herod the Great's marriage to a Hasmonaean princess in order to strengthen his blood ties to the royal line of the Maccabees. Yet none of these analogies explains the basic problem of how Elnathan, rather than Zerubbabel's male heirs, acquired the position of governor.

What emerges from all this is that Elnathan, as successor to Zerubbabel, for unknown reasons married into or attached himself to the Davidic line, an act which would have strengthened his position as governor in the province of Yehud. Although there is no absolute proof, it seems highly unlikely that there would have been two women named Shelomith at this time, one the daughter of one governor, Zerubbabel, and another the 'amah of another governor, Elnathan. At the very least, even if 'amah corresponds to the term 'ebed and as such only connotes a woman of very high standing rather than a relative, a suggestion initially made by Albright (1954:134) and accepted by Avigad (1976a:13) and Stern (1982:207), Shelomith would still have been a functionary of the governor, presumably the one who succeeded Zerubbabel.

Professor Avigad is inclined to attach a matrimonial connotation to 'amah in his publication of the seal. He noted that in the Bible 'amah may have the meaning of secondary wife (as in the case of Hagar and Abraham, Gen 16:3; but for use of term see Gen 21:10,12,13). Also, he long ago observed that the term is associated with a high-ranking official who was buried in Jerusalem with his 'amah, presumably a concubine (1953:145–46). Finally, accepting a suggestion put forth by Professor Yadin, he writes "where royal officials bear the title 'ebed, 'servant,' or any such title, their wives bear the appellation 'amah as an honorific title" (1976a:12–13). We would agree with his suggestion that Shelomith's exceptional administrative responsibilities, as implied by the designation 'amah, resulted from her marital connections to the office of governor. That these responsibilities derive also from the fact that she is a descendant of the Davidic line indicates that, at least through her generation, consciousness of royal succession played a part in the Persian appointment of governors in Jerusalem.

Zerubbabel ben-Shealtiel hence would not have been the last of the Davidides to have achieved high office in ancient Palestine. It may be that Shelomith's position represents only the aftermath of a period that witnessed one of the most difficult transitions in the history of Israel—namely, the emergence of national consciousness without full political independence. Nonetheless, her presence brings to an end a significant, albeit unusual, aspect of the history of the Davidic line in the postexilic era. The continuing fortunes of the Davidic house remain conjectural, for after Shelomith the convergence between governorship and Davidides ceases.

In sum, Chart 12 presents our understanding of the principals involved in the leadership of Yehud from Cyrus to Nehemiah—i.e., 538–445 B.C.E. (cf. the charts in Avigad 1976a:35; Cross 1975:17; and Talmon 1976:327).

governor of Judah. The term *peḥâ,* "governor" (cf. Akkadian *paḥatu),* is derived from the administrative structure of the Persian empire and is used for both Persian satrap and provincial governor. It is employed for Zerubbabel, whose name occurs a total of seven times in Haggai, in his role as the civil administrator. The term itself appears four times in Haggai, here and in 1:14; 2:2,21. In contrast, the title *peḥâ* is never used in the Book of Zechariah, where Zerubbabel's name appears four times, all without his patronymic and without his title of office, and all within the Zerubbabel Insertion to the Fourth Vision (Zech 4:6b–10a). The title in Haggai reflects the Persian practice of appointing governors to either great satrapies or small provinces (Widengren 1977:510–11) and is also used for Nehemiah (Neh 12:26) and for the governors who preceded him (Neh 5:15; see Chart 12).

The Hebrew text designates the territory of which Zerubbabel is governor by the word Judah, *"yĕhûdâ,"* which is the same term used for the preexilic Davidic kingdom. However, the Aramaic sources such as Ezra 7:14 and the bullae and seals mentioned in the previous NOTE use "Yehud" *(yhd),* which apparently was the imperial designation

Chart 12.
Governors, Davidides, and High Priests of Yehud
in the Persian Period (538–433 B.C.E.)

Dates	Governors	Davidides	High Priests
538	Sheshbazzar *(phh,* Ezra 5:14; "prince," Ezra 1:8)	Sheshbazzar b. before 592 (uncle of)	Jehozadak before 587 (father of)
520–510?	Zerubbabel *(pht yhwdh,* Hag 1:1,14)	Zerubbabel b. 558–556 (?) (father of)	Joshua b. ca. 570
510–490?	Elnathan *(phw',* bulla and seal)	Shelomith (*amah of Elnathan) b. ca. 545 Hananiah b. ca. 545	Joiakim b. ca. 545 (brother of)
490–470?	Yeho'ezer *(phw',* jar impression)	Shecaniah b. ca. 520 (father of)	Eliashib I b. ca. 545 Johanan I b. ca. 520 (father of)
470–	Ahzai *(phw',* jar impression)	Hattush b. ca. 495	Eliashib II b. ca. 495 (father of)
445–433	Nehemiah *(hphh,* Neh 5:14; 12:26)	'Elioenai b. ca. 470	Joiada I b. ca. 470

for this province. Our discussion, in NOTES and in COMMENT, uses the Aramaic term so that we can distinguish the Persian province from the preexilic monarchic state (cf. Introduction, pp. xxvii–xxxviii).

Determining the precise status of Yehud within the Persian Empire presents some difficulties. Opinions differ on this matter because of the discrepancy between the list of satrapies in Herodotus and the inscriptional evidence (Rainey 1969:51–57; Cook 1983:58–66). Rainey, for example, is of the opinion that Yehud was a "sub-province" of the larger satrapy of Beyond the River (Eber Nahara), which was established at the beginning of the reign of Darius I. The older view of Alt (1934:5–28) maintains that the Kingdom of Judah was annexed to Samaria after the Babylonian conquest and that it enjoyed a separate status, with limited autonomy, only after the visitation of Nehemiah who, according to Alt, would have been its first governor. Prior to that time (445 B.C.E.), Yehud would have been ruled by a governor appointed by the Neo-Babylonian government over the larger unit, Eber Nahara. Alt argues, moreover, that the governor of Samaria would therefore have felt entitled to interfere with the affairs of Yehud and Jerusalem. Such might have been the background, in his view, of the hostility and interruption of the temple rebuilding efforts reported in Ezra 3:3. Alt's views have won recent support in Stern (1982:213) and McEvenue (1981:353–64), but the critiques of Smith (1971:193–201), Avigad (1976a:33) and Widengren (1977:509–11) show problems in Alt's reconstruction.

Indeed, there are compelling reasons today for abandoning Alt's reconstruction. First and foremost, it seems to us, is the archaeological evidence of the Yehud jar impressions, bullae, and seals that have been convincingly dated by Avigad to the late sixth and early fifth centuries B.C.E. This view, although it has been criticized, has gained acceptance (compare Talmon 1976:321 with Stern 1982:239, 245ff.; see also Cross 1969). Avigad's dating of the pertinent materials is based both on paleographical and archaeological—that is, stratigraphic—considerations. His reconstruction of the so-called "governor gap" first accepted by Talmon (1976) has been incorporated into Chart 12 above, p. 14. His argument, on nonarchaeological grounds, is based on the text in Neh 5:15 which presupposes that the governors who preceded Nehemiah himself exacted heavy taxes from the people of Yehud (Avigad 1976a:34). We agree with Avigad that there is no compelling reason to suppose that Nehemiah is referring specifically either to Sheshbazzar or Zerubbabel, the only governors specifically mentioned in the biblical record prior to Nehemiah.

Second, despite the absence of *peḥâ* in association with Zerubbabel in Ezra, Nehemiah, and also Zechariah, its consistent and explicit usage in Haggai cannot be dismissed. The absence of the term in Zechariah may be explained in terms of the prophet's strategy *vis-à-vis* the Yehudite community: he sought to deflate the monarchic expectations that might have arisen because of Zerubbabel's Davidic ancestry (see below, NOTES and COMMENT to Zech 4:6b–10a and 6:9–15); and he simultaneously endeavored to gain acceptance for the new community structure that was emerging under Persian domination. The apparent silence of Ezra and Nehemiah on the subject of Zerubbabel's governorship has led some scholars (cited by Japhet 1982:68, n. 8) to understand Zerubbabel as the intended referent in Ezra 2:63 or 6:7. Japhet concludes that the silence of Ezra and Nehemiah with respect to the use of the title *peḥâ* is "not a reflection of historical fact" but rather is a deliberate omission that serves their own purposes (1982:82). In other words, it is possible to assume that Yehud did possess limited autonomy within the larger framework of Achaemenid controls, which is reflected both in the biblical source and in the substantial corpus of archaeological data.

An acceptance of limited autonomy for Yehud under Persian auspices underlies the political philosophy of both Haggai and especially First Zechariah. To the extent that the use of *peḥâ* in Haggai contrasts with its non-use in Zechariah, we may conclude that Haggai was more active in his sponsorship of the Davidic line than was Zechariah. Haggai's support of the Davidic dynasty is reflected in the final oracle of the book, 2:20–23, especially in verse 23 which constitutes the only case in the Hebrew Bible in which an eschatological prophecy is focused upon a known historical figure. Many of the differences in tone occurring in Haggai and Zechariah 1–8 have perhaps become muted in the redaction process (see Introduction and Japhet 1982:76–80), but the disparate use of the term *peḥâ* has survived the editorial process.

A further consideration in the confusing use of *peḥâ* is the ambiguity that exists in

Persian sources which mention titles of the administrators of the various divisions and subdivisions of the empire. The duties of the officers of state were not sharply defined, and it is often difficult to determine the scope of their powers or the specific territorial districts for which they were responsible. Persons of different rank could be and apparently were designated by the same title (Hensley 1977:197–99).

Joshua ben-Jehozadak. The chief priestly leader of the early postexilic period, Joshua ben-Jehozadak, is mentioned together with Zerubbabel several times in Ezra (e.g., 3:2,8; 5:2) and appears as an important figure in the Book of Zechariah, where an entire chapter (3:1–10) covers his role in the restoration community (see also Zech 6:11–13). The name Joshua without the patronymic also appears in various listings of priestly families (as in Ezra 2:36 and Neh 7:7,39) and presumably refers to the contemporary of Zerubbabel.

In Ezra and Nehemiah the spelling yēšuâ; rather than the yĕhôšûaʿ which means "Yahweh saves" of Haggai and Zechariah, is consistently found. The RSV, following a long tradition, renders "Yehoshua" as "Joshua," dispensing with the full theophoric element. Our rendering of yĕhôšûaʿ remains in that tradition; but we note that Joshua's patronymic is not similarly altered, and our spelling Jehozadak preserves the theophoric component of yĕhôṣādāq, which means "Yahweh is just." Unlike the governors of Yehud (Sheshbazzar and Zerubbabel) in the sixth century, the chief priests of the restoration period retain Yahwistic names untainted by Babylonian influence.

The Chronicler (1 Chron 5:40–41 [RSV 6:14–15]) reports that Joshua was of the lineage of Seraiah, who was chief priest in Jerusalem at the time of the destruction. Seraiah was put to death by Nebuchadnezzar at Riblah, and his son Jehozadak was carried off to Babylon where Joshua (Jeshua in Ezra and Nehemiah) appears to have been born. The earliest possible birthdate for Jehozadak can be reckoned at 595 B.C.E. (see 1 Chron 5:41 [RSV 6:15]; cf. 1 Esdr 5:5). Joshua's birth is estimated on the basis of that datum, so that when he returned with Zerubbabel (1 Esdr 5:5–6) in the second year of Darius I—i.e., 520 B.C.E.—he would have been a man of about fifty. In order to explain the involvement of Sheshbazzar in the first return (538), we have conjectured (see above, NOTE to "Zerubbabel ben-Shealtiel") that Zerubbabel was somewhat younger than Joshua. Consequently he would have been about thirty-five in 520. Cross (1975:17) prefers to make the two leaders exact contemporaries.

Joshua's pedigree may be of the utmost importance for understanding the role that he and the priesthood came to play in the postexilic period. Jehozadak, according to Freedman (1983), was the individual in exile responsible for overseeing the editing and preparation of the Pentateuch (Torah) and Former Prophets (Joshua through 2 Kings), a combined work which Freedman calls the Primary History. This interpretation is based on the date of the latest event mentioned (2 Kgs 25:27–30) in that work—viz., the release of Jehoiachin from prison by Evil-merodach (Amel-marduk, 562–50 B.C.E.; see Bright 1981:352–53). Freedman proposes that Jehozadak, as incumbent chief priest in the mid-sixth century, undertook the process of promulgating, or publishing, an authoritative body of literature as a guide for the exiles; the motivation for this project may have been the hopes aroused by the turn in the fortunes of the royal house. If Jehozadak was in fact instrumental in compiling a Primary History—and Freedman's thesis to that effect has great merit in our opinion—Joshua's childhood experiences and family heritage would have prepared him in a unique and valuable way for the role he was ultimately to play as high priest in the reestablishment and reorganization of community life in the semiautonomous province of Yehud.

The fact that Joshua and the civil leader Zerubbabel are the intended recipients of Haggai's prophecies in itself indicates a restructuring of the governance of the restoration community in comparison with that of the preexilic monarchy. Before the exile, the dynastic figure was the head of state and wielded ultimate power. No matter how important the chief priest or any other of the royal officials might have been, the king stood alone at the helm of the administrative structure; the chief priests did the bidding of the king (e.g., Jer 21:1, where Pashhur is a messenger for King Zedekiah, and 2 Kgs 22:12, where Josiah issues orders to Hilkiah and company). The kings' regnal years provide the chronological frame of reference for various preexilic prophetic books (cf. our first NOTE to Hag 1:1). Furthermore, the preexilic prophets choose to address kings alone (e.g., Jer 22:1–2), unless they are speaking to a wider audience. Never do we have a case similar to this one, with a prophet speaking to two men together, with one being a priestly official. But then, before the exile the king was the locus of power and the one the prophet felt was responsible for the social and religious ills in the land and also the one able to rectify them.

Haggai, of course, had no king to address. That he does not speak to the governor, or *pehâ,* alone indicates that that official was not the absolute authority within the community. The addition of Joshua as "high priest" (see following NOTE) to Haggai's immediate audience (here and in 1:12,14; 2:2,4) provides additional information about the organization of Yehud—namely, that a priest is now on a par with a civil figure as the highest authority in the land. This duality of leadership may not be so much a result of the elevation of the priesthood as of the removal of the monarch, who had exercised a combined religio-political authority. The *pehâ* lacks that dimension, and the priestly ruler must fill that gap both conceptually and pragmatically. The prophecies of Zechariah, especially the Vestment Scene of chapter 3, deal directly with the shift in the balance of leadership; and we refer the reader to our NOTES and COMMENT on that section and also to the discussion of the Fourth Vision of Zechariah with its "two olive trees."

One final point about Haggai's persistence in directing his prophecies to both *pehâ* and priest concerns the omission of the priest from his final oracle (2:20–23). The eschatological context there allows for the resumption of monarchic authority, with a king as Yahweh's viceroy. The priest at that time would recede in relative power, and hence Joshua's name does not appear. Haggai clearly has a different perspective than does Zechariah, who retains a vision of dyarchy (4:14 and 6:11–14).

high priest. This designation, *hakkōhēn hagādôl* in the Hebrew, is found in Haggai (1:12,14; 2:2,4) and Zechariah (3:1,8; 6:11), and represents a departure from the prevalent preexilic phrase *hakkōhēn hārōʾš,* "chief priest." Apparently a new usage of the sixth century, which is also reflected in Chronicles as well as in Ezra and Nehemiah, the title "high priest" suggests a significant broadening of the scope of priestly responsibility in the restoration era. This is borne out in Zechariah in any number of instances but especially in 3:7 (see NOTES). For an extensive discussion of the question of the new terminology and expanded priestly powers see our NOTE to "high priest" in Zech 3:1.

2. *Thus spoke Yahweh.* This formula, *koh ʾāmar YHWH,* introduces the actual

words of Yahweh. Like the first prophetic formula in verse 1, "the word of Yahweh came" (see NOTE), the stereotyped language used to announce a message from God is derived from the context of the Divine Council. The prophet is a courier who authenticates his oral delivery of a message by citing its source. In this case, the expression is often expanded by the addition of divine epithets to the name Yahweh. In Haggai-Zechariah 1–8, the embellishment nearly always takes the form of "of Hosts"; see following NOTE.

of Hosts. The epithet ṣĕbāʾôt occupies a unique position in the prophecies of Haggai and Zechariah. Like all divine titles, it demands careful attention in any attempt to understand biblical conceptions of God. The distribution of the designation "Yahweh of Hosts" in the Hebrew Bible (see table in Mettinger 1982:12) reveals a surprising pattern. Although the title is presumably a major expression of temple and ark tradition during the monarchy, it is absent from Deuteronomy (where "name," šēm, designates God's presence) and is relatively rare in 1 and 2 Samuel (eleven times), 1 and 2 Kings (only four times), and the Psalter (fifteen times, mainly in Zion or royal psalms). Its most frequent usage is in Isaiah 1–39 (fifty-six times, as opposed to only six times in Isaiah 40–55) and Jeremiah (eighty-two times, though only ten times in the LXX of Jeremiah); but it is completely absent from Ezekiel, where the "glory" (kābôd) of God represents the divine presence in the temple.

The occurrences of Yahweh of Hosts in Haggai and Zechariah, when measured against the above information, are disproportionately frequent. Haggai constitutes only about .2 percent of the Hebrew Bible, yet it contains 5 percent of the number of appearances of the title—namely, fourteen occurrences. Similarly, Zechariah 1–8, which represents about .6 percent of the Hebrew Bible, includes forty-four occurrences of the title, or 15 percent of the total. Malachi and Zechariah 9–14 also favor the expression, but the Chronicler virtually omits it (only three times in Chronicles, with no mention in Ezra-Nehemiah). Together, Haggai, Malachi, and Zechariah account for over one third of the biblical occurrences (ninety-one of 284 in all).

What can one make of this configuration, in which the absence of the term in Ezekiel seems anomalous as does its infrequency in the Primary History (Joshua through 2 Kings)? Mettinger's recent work (1982) reviews the extensive literature on the meaning of the designation as well as on the curious pattern of its biblical occurrences. He sees the term as an indication of theological shifts associated with stages in the institutional history of ancient Israel, in which "Yahweh of Hosts," "glory," and "name" play distinct roles. We would not argue with such an assessment, and Mettinger's analysis provides many important insights (although it also exhibits certain weaknesses—e.g., see Christiansen's review, 1984:124–26). For example, the theophanic tradition of the God enthroned in the temple can surely be associated with the "Yahweh of Hosts" designation. The image of God in his chariot with his armies or "Hosts" is related to the cherubim throne in the temple. If the heavenly King is present in his earthly abode, he is there with his retinue. Outside the monarchy—i.e., in tabernacle traditions preceding the construction of the temple—God's presence is depicted as his "glory," a somewhat more temporary conceptualization than the permanent enthronement of Yahweh of Hosts in the Jerusalem temple. The exile and destruction, accordingly, meant a radical disruption in the perception of the enthroned God. God's presence had been removed; God had been "dethroned."

Postexilic prophecy marked the restoration of the temple and the return of Yahweh to his people and to his holy mountain (see Hag 1:13; 2:5; Zech 1:6,16; 2:14 [RSV 2:10]; 8:3). Prophetic language in Haggai through Malachi revitalizes the language, which is prominent in First Isaiah and Jeremiah, of divine presence in the sanctuary. By referring to "Yahweh of Hosts," it asserts the fact of Yahweh's return to Zion and the reestablishment of his mighty power. The recurrent usage of the expression is a case of archaizing, to a certain extent. But it also takes on new meaning under the changed circumstances of the postexilic period and so transcends its ancient origins in mythic tradition. During the monarchy, the enthronement of Yahweh in Jerusalem was linked to the royal ideology of the Davidic dynasty. In the restoration era, the reenthronement of Yahweh of Hosts is not accompanied by the coronation of a human king. Yahweh's universal sovereignty, though grounded in his presence in Jerusalem, is set free of the political and military considerations of a monarchy. "Yahweh of Hosts" for Haggai and his colleagues reestablishes the preexilic conception of divine presence and expresses the ultimate authority of Yahweh, even over the Persian emperor or any other human ruler.

This people. The identity of the group about whom Yahweh is speaking here is determined by the fact that the oracle is directed toward the governor and the high priest. Yahweh, through his prophet, is providing information about attitudes which those two leaders should theoretically be able to alter. While priestly authority might conceivably extend to Yahwists outside Yehud, the *peḥâ*'s authority would not have extended beyond this provincial division. The following oracle, addressed to those who live in "finished houses," appears to limit the range of local inhabitants to returned exiles; however, that designation for dwellings (see NOTE, v 4) may reflect the quality of the buildings and not the process of construction. Compare Haggai's other references to the local population: "the rest of the people" (1:12,14; 2:2), "people of the land" (2:4), and "this nation" (2:14). This variation in terminology, which has confounded commentators who have tried to link each term with a segment of the population or otherwise to delineate a political or ethnic group, does not easily lend itself to such refinement. Probably there is considerable overlap in these phrases, a situation which would in fact suit the restoration period with its significant demographic and political changes. As the postexilic community was in the process of being defined according to a new interplay of religio-political forces, the terms used to designate the community and its inhabitants were necessarily in flux.

the time has not come—the time. The repetition of *'et* in the MT has caused much confusion in the versions and disagreement among modern commentators and translators (e.g., Mitchell 1912:51; Rudolph 1976:29; Ackroyd 1968:155; Baldwin 1972:39–40), most of whom emend the phrase, rendering it "the time has not yet [now, *'attā*] come." However, the rhetorical context may support our following the MT, as does Amsler 1981:2, and retaining the repetition of "time"; cf. also Steck 1971:361–62, especially n. 21. Yet there are a number of difficulties which need clarification. Since the word "time" (*'et*) is normally feminine, one would expect *bā'â* ("has come") instead of the preserved masculine form *bā',* which can be read as either a perfect or participial form. Another possibility would be to read the verb as an infinitive absolute, no doubt the same form as the ordinary infinitive, thus obviating the need for agreement between noun and verb. The use of the infinitive absolute is very common in Haggai, especially in 1:6. *GKC* § 113.ff(ε) cites a number of instances in which the infinitive absolute substitutes for the finite verb and where the subject is sometimes added. The infinitive absolute of *bw'* occurs in Lev 14:48, 1 Sam 9:6; Jer 36:29; Ps 126:6; Dan 11:10 and 11:13; and probably 2 Chron 25:8, where it seems to be used in the place of an imperative. Consequently it is reasonable to suppose that *bā'* here is an infinitive absolute, thus solving the first of several grammatical problems in this verse.

The absence of the definite article in the first *'et* is also problematical, since it appears to be definite when read with the second *'et*. An adverbial short form is preserved in Ezek 23:43 and Ps 74:6 with the qere in both places suggesting the fuller spelling, which is also attested in preexilic inscriptions. Even if one were to read a simple perfect instead of the infinitive absolute, the attestation of the masculine in late Hebrew (*BDB* 773) eliminates the issue of gender agreement. A further problem concerns the repetition of *'et*. The second usage, although it also lacks the definite article, is qualified by the clause following and is undoubtedly connected with the repetition of the word at the conclusion of the oracle in verse 4. The threefold repetition of "time" in two verses is a rhetorical device which calls attention to the passage of time in relationship to the temple.

Haggai's desire to stress the time factor, we believe, derives from the imminence of the termination of the seventy-year period referred to in the prophecies of Jeremiah (25:11–12 and 29:10). Consciousness of that time span was surely sustained throughout the exile and into the postexilic era, as witness its role in Zechariah's prophecies (1:12 and 7:5; see NOTES to those verses). While the exact reckoning of the seventy years may be uncertain because of Jeremiah's Babylonian frame of reference, it is clear that during the exile the starting point for the seventy years was understood to be the destruction of Judah, Jerusalem, and the temple in 586 B.C.E. By 520, the date of Haggai's prophecies, the end point was obviously approaching. Insofar as the prophetic heritage of Israel was held sacred, Jeremiah's words were taken seriously and, at least for Haggai and no doubt for many of his countrymen, caused considerable anxiety. If Israel's subjugation was about to come to an end, were the land and people in proper condition to resume their independence? For Haggai, the answer was assuredly no. A people could not resume self-rule, which was really rule under divine sovereignty, without also restoring the home—the temple—in which that sovereign's presence might reside and give sanction and guidance to his revitalized earthly territory (see following NOTE).

In urging the people to restore the temple as the end of the seventy-year period approached, Haggai was conscious of an expected compliance with the seventy-year tradition. But he was also going against the timetable of previous prophecy. According to Jeremiah, the destruction of the nations will precede, or at least accompany, the restoration. Haggai's words invoke the seventy-year concept but allow for the temple to be rebuilt without a cataclysmic overthrow of Judah's enemies.

Haggai was convinced of the urgency for rebuilding the temple, probably for reasons of contemporary political development—that is, in response to the directives and organizational changes put forth by the new Persian regime of Darius I (see Cook [1983:72], who points out Darius's efforts to organize codification of laws in the provinces, and our first NOTE to Zech 7:1), and also because of his sensitivity to prophetic tradition. Yet he met with reluctance, which may have been the result of skepticism or ignorance concerning the seventy years concept. In addition, the shaky state of the economy in Yehud would have made people unwilling to commit their scanty resources. Furthermore, the specific period of August–September 520 during which this prophecy is given was harvest time. Early fall was a labor-intensive season in which human resources, to say nothing of material ones, would have been at a minimum. The people may have meant quite literally that it was not the ideal time to add to their burden of labor.

House of Yahweh. Hebrew *bêt* for "house," in construct with God's name, is the normal designation in Hebrew for the Yahwistic temple buildings of ancient Israel. In preexilic times, or at least prior to Josiah's reform, a number of sanctuaries throughout Judah would have been designated by the term "House of Yahweh" (see Haran 1978:26–40). For the people of Haggai's day, however, there can be no doubt that Jerusalem was the only place for the temple.

The term "House of Yahweh" is first and foremost the designation of an architectural entity of a special kind. A temple in the ancient world was conceived of as a residence, a house or palace, for the deity; it was not a house of worship for the general public. As befits a dwelling place, a temple in Israel, as in the rest of the ancient Near East, contained all the furnishing that a royal resident might require. As the abode of a god, a temple had to be constructed of materials suitable to its divine inhabitant. Furthermore, the needs of the resident deity had to be met. Temple sacrifice and other cultic acts in Near Eastern religions can be explained in part as the ritual provision for all the needs of the god. Israel's elaborate sacrificial system is rooted in such a conceptualization, but is not bound by the archaic anthropomorphic view of divine beings that gave rise to the system long before Israel existed.

The origins and essence of the temple as a divine dwelling place and, for Israel, the symbolic locus of God's presence are contained in the term "House of Yahweh." But it would be a mistake to assume that the temple's role was confined to its function as a cultic institution carrying out fossilized rituals to provide for the comforts of a deity who in reality transcends physical form and material needs. The temple, in Israel and in the ancient Near East, was inextricably related to the formation and administration of the state. Western language has so strongly associated "temple" with purely sacral concerns that it is difficult to grasp the centrality of temples for the existence and vitality of the political states in the ancient world. Temples were intimately bound up with the founding or legitimizing of nations. No human king could claim the authority to execute justice, levy taxes, and conscript armies without the approval of the stronger forces of the cosmos—i.e., the deity or deities. Building a temple in which the god took up residence was a powerful symbolic statement meaning that the god sanctioned the dynastic power. The citizenry could not oppose the dictates of rulers who had the approval of the resident deity. The construction of a temple by Solomon, as recorded in 1 Kings, exemplifies such a mind-set. The description of the temple itself and of the process leading to its construction provides evidence of Israelite adherence to the common temple ideology of the day (cf. C. Meyers 1983; Lundquist 1983, 1984; Hurowitz 1983).

Once erected on its specially prepared spot in the capital city, the temple became part of the economic, political, and legal life of the nation and of the dynasty that was responsible for its existence. While the king was the chief officer of state, the officials of the temple were also important administrators. Palace and temple together constituted the administrative core of the realm. Each polity in the ancient world surely had its own bureaucratic adaptations, yet adhered to the underlying principle that the temple was a quintessential part of the political and economic structure of the state. Israel was no exception. Hence the restoration of the temple under Persian rule had implications that transcended the architectural and cultic aspects of a temple. It raised questions of authority and/or royal involvement. If a monarchical nation-state could not exist without a temple, could a temple exist without dynastic rule? Both Haggai and Zechariah were motivated by the fact of temple building to work out an understanding of a legitimate temple for Yahweh's presence apart from an autonomous state. In the next NOTE and many times elsewhere in our NOTES and COMMENT to both Haggai and First Zechariah, we will elaborate upon or refer to the temple so conceived: a residence for Yahweh as well as the administrative center of a semiautonomous state.

The designation "House of Yahweh" or "House" appears five times in the first section of Haggai, and the houses of the Yehudites are mentioned twice. Elsewhere Haggai uses the term another four times, and also employs a nearly synonymous expression in 2:15 and 18 (see NOTE to "Temple" at 2:15). Zechariah also uses both terms, and in one climactic verse (8:9) the two words for temple appear together along with the two verbs ("build," *bnh;* "found," *ysd*) that are used separately by both prophets in reference to the temple construction project.

to be built. The Niphal of *bnh,* "to build," represents the passive and does not specify that the construction work is a "rebuilding," as many translations (e.g., RSV, NJPS, NEB) would have it. Although *bnh* can refer to any amount of building work and does not exclude the notion of a partial or rebuilding enterprise, the ideological context of the erection of a temple demands that this project promulgated by Haggai be considered a new building in its own right. Its connection with the former preexilic temple was of critical importance: Haggai himself demonstrates a sensitivity to the relationship between old and new temples (2:3,9), and Zechariah provides technical language derived from the material and ceremonial linkage of the postexilic building with its predestruction antecedent (see Zech 4:7–10 and NOTES to those verses, especially "platform" and "bring forth the premier stone" of v 7). However, at the same time each reconstruction of a sanctuary on the site of a previously existing holy building was nonetheless considered a new building in its own right. While our Western minds may find this notion confusing, the Semitic mind saw no difficulty in the overlap. The sanctity of a site persisted from one building to the next, but each construction of a temple on that site was of necessity a new building.

The latter feature is the result of the fact that temples were not simply religious institutions in the ancient world but rather were components of a religio-political entity. Erecting a temple in an administrative center was an integral part of the process of establishing the authority of the political regime (see preceding NOTE and also Ahlström 1982; Lundquist 1982). In light of this pattern, the temple alterations or repairs made by many of the Judean kings might be seen as efforts to reinvoke divine legitimization of their regimes and thereby to strengthen their regnal authority. For the period of the restoration, there was obviously no monarchic government to be supported by a rebuilt temple, a problem which Zechariah addresses. Yet the political dimension of temple building cannot be dismissed for that reason. The temple was an important administrative tool, and the postexilic House of Yahweh was to partake no less of that function because the administrative structure it facilitated and legitimized was, for the first time in hundreds of years, nondynastic.

The House of Yahweh for Haggai was to be a new building on an old and sacred site, even as the construction process utilized, as much as possible, the surviving materials and foundations of the previous temple (cf. Hag 1:8, NOTE to "wood," and also 2:15). A similar concept underlies his usage of the word *ysd* ("to found") in 2:18, where the founding of the new temple represents an ideological rather than a physical process. Zechariah also reveals this ideology in his eschatological prophecy of the Crowning Scene (6:9–15), where the future verbal idea of "he will build" does not conflict with the fact that a temple will presumably already exist in Jerusalem (see NOTE on "to build the temple of Yahweh," Zech 6:12). The urgency for the temple project in Haggai's time surely derives from the confluence of two factors: 1. administrative innovations originating in Darius's bureaucratic organization of the Persian Empire, which relied heavily on the strength of local centers of administration; 2. the impending termination of the seventy years of desolation (see above NOTE in this verse to "time . . ." and also the NOTES to "seventy years" in Zech 1:12 and 7:5).

Not until the conclusion of the Haggai-Zechariah 1–8 corpus does *bnh* in the Niphal reappear. There, in 8:9, it is accompanied by "refounded" *(ysd;* cf. NOTE at 8:9).

3. *Thereupon the word of Yahweh came through the prophet Haggai:.* This formulaic introduction is the same as that of 1:1 (see above) and also 2:1 and 10. It signals the transmission of a message from God to a prophetic courier and is used here to herald a separate oracular section. The following section itself contains additional oracular formulas, as in verses 5, 7, 9.

4. *you yourselves.* The Hebrew syntax of *lākem 'atem,* with two pronouns, is unusual and shows how much the prophet stresses the involvement and responsibility of his audience. Taken with the second-person masculine plural pronominal suffix on "houses" ("your finished houses"), there is a threefold emphasis upon the people whom Haggai is addressing that serves to heighten the contrast between the condition of Yahweh's house and the houses of these people.

to dwell. Literally, "to sit." The image of nonactivity contrasts with the use of "run" below in verse 9 and contributes towards a merism. This link between the language and meaning of verses 4 and 9 is just one in a complex interweaving of the two verses (see NOTES to vv. 4 and 9, especially to "My House lies desolate" of v. 9).

finished. The word *sĕpûnîm* is rendered "paneled" by some (e.g., NJPS; Ackroyd 1968:155; RSV; Elliger 1975:85) and "ceiled" or "roofed" by others (NEB; Mitchell 1912:45). The architectural meaning has been colored by its usage in the descriptions of the construction of the Solomonic temple and palace in Jerusalem, where cedar beams or paneling is indicated. However, the word does not need to imply richness. It can denote the final stage of construction work when the wooden finishing, whether laid across stone or wooden walls, has been completed; cf. 1 Kgs 6:9, where completion of work on the temple is specified as the setting of the wooden elements in place.

The contrast in this verse (*contra* Ackroyd 1968:155) is between the unfinished and thus unusable House of Yahweh and the complete and functional homes of the Yehudites rather than between ornamental or elaborate homes of the people and a ruined temple. The Greek Esdras, it is to be noted, specifically mentions (6:4) that the work completed on the temple during the reign of Darius was the roofing. See our discussion, following, of *ḥārēb,* "desolate."

desolate. i.e., uninhabited or unfinished. The root *ḥrb,* the basic meaning of which is "dryness," can mean "laid waste" or "made uninhabitable" (by virtue of being laid waste by war or climatic conditions). Andersen (1958:22–27) demonstrates that the usage here, akin to Jer 26:9 and 33:10,12 which refer to the uninhabited temple or "place" *(māqôm),* can signify an uninhabited or unused facility. The physical condition of the building is not unrelated to this, since an unused building is likely to be in disrepair. However, this verse alone does not offer conclusive information about the condition of the building. It does not preclude the possibility that the temple was not totally in ruins at this time. Thus NJPS, RSV, NEB, *KAT* "in ruins" is to be rejected (cf. Hag 1:9). Furthermore, as we have indicted above in our discussion of Zerubbabel, the fact that the temple itself was not functional does not mean that the entire temple complex was in disuse. Evidently the altar had been rebuilt earlier and sacrifices were being made there, according to Ezra 3:2–3, which refers to the pilgrim Feast of Tabernacles or Succoth. Yet a functioning altar in the temple court is not the same as a restored temple building.

The intent of the word *ḥārēb* in reference to the House of Yahweh can be considered as twofold. First, it offers a contrast between the inhabited dwellings of the human population and the uninhabitable residence of God. That contrast is furthered and augmented below in verse 9 (see NOTE to "because my house lies desolate . . ."), where the personal interests of the people have apparently taken precedence over their attention to the public concern—i.e., God's earthly shrine. Second, it anticipates the description of the food shortages in verse 11, in which God has created a "desolation" *(ḥōreb),* a drying up, which has greatly diminished (according to v 6) the productivity of the land (see second NOTE to v 11). Together, these factors reflect Israelite temple ideology, wherein a completed house would provide the requisite setting for the ongoing presence of Yahweh and the blessings attendant thereupon.

5. *Reflect.* Literally, "set one's heart toward." This idiom appears again in verse 7, where "your ways" is also the object as it is here. Haggai calls upon his countrymen to think about their activities: what they have done, agriculturally, with such unsatisfactory results, and, by implication, what they have not done—that is, their inattention to Yahweh's ruined dwelling. The same idiom appears three more times in Haggai, once in 2:15 and twice in 2:18 (see NOTES), where it is accompanied by a complex sequence of chronological markers that focus on the significance of the day (December 18, 520) of a temple refoundation ceremony. As in this passage, "reflect" draws attention to the relationship between the behavior of the people and their welfare. "Reflect" also serves as a key word, coming near the beginning of Hag (1:5–7) and again near the end (2:15–18), thereby framing the intervening materials.

your ways. Literally, "your paths," Hebrew *darkêkem* refers to what the people have been doing and also not doing. The prophet obviously wants them to become conscious of their behavior. At the same time, *derek* can have a more figurative meaning, indicating "course of life" or "welfare," which may not be so differentiated from its literal meaning as it might seem. Koch suspects (1978:271) that "the distinction between a literal and figurative use of *drk* is due to a prior judgment based on modern Western language in which we do not view life as a coherent movement (toward a conscious goal)." English "welfare," derived from Old English *fare*, "to go," would convey the notion of ongoing activity underlying the human condition. In light of this figurative nuance of *derek*, we suggest that "your ways" includes also the idea of "your welfare," in which case the prophet would be referring to the economic difficulties and deprivations specified in the next verse.

The prophet's call to reflect upon ways and welfare contains an implicit admonition: the people are *not* faring well and the cause must be sought in their own improper behavior. They have obviously (v 6) been dutiful in their agricultural chores, but those efforts have not been rewarded. What is missing from their "ways"? Haggai supplies the answer following the repetition, in verse 7, of the clause "reflect upon your ways."

6. *You have sown much but have brought in little.* Hebrew *zrˁ*, "to sow," usually refers specifically to the planting of seeds for field crops. However, the following three clauses refer to food, drink, and clothing, the three basic subsistence commodities of an agrarian economy in addition to shelter, concerning which there was clearly no problem for Haggai's audience. The introductory clause mentioning sowing must therefore have a more extended meaning, with the basic agrarian chore of seeding a field representing all tasks undertaken to secure a food supply. The addition of "much" *(harbê)* adds the connotation of industriousness, so that the consequence, "[you] have brought in little," stands out as a signal of some flaw in the effort expended.

This clause introduces an oracle of five units, the overall poetic structure of which suggests an affinity with proverbial or gnomic material. The language is terse and elliptical, but the meaning is nonetheless clear. The opening bicolon of 5 + 5 syllables seems intended to balance the closing one (v 6e), but in its present form that is not the case (cf. NOTE below to "hired hand").

The concept of sowing but not reaping the full benefits of that effort is reiterated in Hag 2:16, where the discrepancy between expectation and reality is specified. The rectification of that system is linked in 2:19, with God's blessing. Consequently the existence of severe shortages can be seen in contrast as God's curse. Similar language about a diminished food supply occurs in the recently discovered Tell-Fekherye texts. A basalt statue from this site in northeast Syria is inscribed with a bilingual (Aramaic and Akkadian) document which probably dates to the ninth century B.C.E. The inscription concludes with a group of curses that Hadad-yisi, the dedicator of the statue, invokes upon anyone who, in a later period, might remove his name. These curses include the following: "And even if he sows [seeds], may he not harvest. Even if he should sow a thousand measures, may he get half [as much] therefrom" (Aramaic text, 1. 19; translation is that of Muraoka 1983–84). The first part of this line is similar to this verse in Haggai; the second part of the line, with its specification of a fractional yield, can be compared with Hag 2:16 and also Isa 5:10. For these two prophets, the dearth of a food supply is understood to be Yahweh's doing in response to the misbehavior of the people. The language in which they express this idea echoes the curse of the Aramaic inscription from Tell-Fekherye.

you keep eating . . . drinking . . . putting on clothes . . . These three units constitute a triad of seven-syllable bicola, each divided 2 + 5. The three verbs used in the three clauses describing the difficulties in Yehud are infinitive absolutes. The subject "you" (pl) is understood on the basis of the "you have sown" of the introduction to this sequence, where the verb is second person plural. The use of the infinitive absolute emphasizes the contrast between the action represented by the verbal form and the results, which do not fulfill the expectations that would have accompanied the actions. This description of shortages, it should be noted, does not indicate total disaster. Commodities evidently were available to a certain extent (cf. 2:16, which suggests that production was off by 50 to 60 percent), but not enough to allow people ever to feel sated. The second condition, *wĕ'ēn—lĕšākrâ*, "there is never enough to be drunk," conveys the idea that one ought to be able to drink enough wine once in a while in order to become cheerful; i.e., "to become drunk." Jotham's parable (Judg 9:13), for example, comments on the ability of wine to gladden men just as it comments on the value of oil for its fatness or the fig for its sweetness. Although the word "drunk" has negative connotations in English, it probably would have been neutral for the biblical mind. Its usage here implies that some wine is available but not as much as would be desirable. Similarly, a bare minimum of food is available, and there is clothing such that people are not naked yet are not warm either. The striking imagery expressing partial subsistence in this triplet accords with the information provided in verse 10 about God's partial withholding of the natural conditions required for a full harvest.

The second half of each of these bicola uses the ethical dative to denote the shortage or problem at issue. The Hebrew is very terse, but it suits the abstraction of the infinitive absolutes that begin each clause. This triad, literally, reads:

> To eat, but there is no satiety
> To drink, but there is no drunkenness
> To dress, but there is no warmth in it.

the hired hand, he works. Literally, "the hired hand hires himself out." The Hithpael participle of *mištakkêr* appears twice in succession, the first time with the definite article. The second usage is not necessary and does not accord well with the terse style of the previous bicola of this verse. As we suggested in our first NOTE to verse 6, the opening bicolon of 5 + 5 syllables, with an intervening triad of 2 + 5 syllable bicola, should be matched with a 5 + 5 pattern in this concluding clause. Eliminating the second *mištakkêr* as an example of dittography would achieve that result. Either way, the participle is an impersonal mode and represents the final stage in a verbal shift in this verse from the clear 2nd m. pl. of "you have sown" through the intervening infinitive absolute to this third person form. Perhaps the infinitive absolutes facilitate the shift.

Whereas the preceding clauses depict the economic difficulties of an independent farmer, the term *mištakkêr*, "hired hand" or "wage earner," denotes those individuals who worked for others in order to earn a living. The use of the Hithpael is interesting and might also mean one who employs himself—i.e., a self-employed individual— rather than a participant in free-market labor. In either case, this is one of the few words in Haggai that appear to belong exclusively to the vocabulary of the postexilic period (Hill 1981:140); cf. the excellent word study of Luciani (1972:498–501).

For a bag full of holes. Literally, "to a pierced bag"—i.e., it is as if one's earnings are put in a purse with holes so that a portion of the wages is immediately lost. In antiquity it would have been quite usual for someone to carry his wages in a small pouch that was attached to his waist cord. This image of a holey bag is one which has left its mark on the contemporary idiom, "to be left holding an empty bag."

The use of "bag full of holes" continues the imagery of the previous triplet of clauses in suggesting that virtually nothing is left for a laborer after he procures the barest of necessities. It is difficult to determine what sort of economic conditions would have had such an effect. Inflation is a possibility, with wages not keeping up with costs. A more specific form of inflation might appear as temporary shortages of basic products, so that the prices are driven way up and the worker must spend far more than he is accustomed to in order to feed and clothe his family. The image does not suggest an inadequate income so much as an extraordinary drain on existing income. The general implication, that there is a disequilibrium between wages and prices, seems clear even if the specific conditions causing that discrepancy cannot be enumerated.

7. *Thus spoke Yahweh of Hosts, "Reflect upon your ways—."* While lacking an initial "Thereafter," this verse is an exact repetition of verse 5. The information in verse 6 provides the details of the condition upon which the people are urged to reflect. The oracle introduced here is directly related to that information, in that the steps outlined in it are meant to rectify the economic difficulties and hardships that have resulted. Repeating the introductory formula along with the exhortation to "reflect" connects the content of the two oracles and also anticipates a further stage in the prophet's cause-and-effect thinking found in 2:15–19, where "reflect" appears three more times (2:15,18; see NOTE to "reflect" in 2:15).

8. *go up in the hills; bring in wood.* It would seem that this directive concerns the procurement of materials for refurbishing the temple. However, the fact that this verse urges the people to "go up" into the hills to secure wood casts some doubt upon the idea that actual building materials are to be sought. The only local tree growing in Yehud that could have provided timber suitable for building would have been the sycamore. This tree, *Ficus sycomorus* (spelled "sycamore" in the RSV) is a species of fig tree common in Syria-Palestine, Egypt, and other Near Eastern countries and valued for its wood and also, though less so, for its nutritious edible fruits. The sycamore of the Bible is not to be confused with two other trees: the European sycamore, which is actually a maple, *Acer pseudo-platanus,* and is planted largely as a shade tree; and the North American sycamore, also called the buttonwood or plane tree, of the genus *Platanus.*

When rafters for the superstructure of houses were needed, the sycamore—if carefully tended and lopped—normally provided such beams, sycamore timber being fairly strong and light. Indeed, the fast-growing sycamore tree appears to have been cultivated for such purposes. In 1 Chron 27:28, David is said to have appointed a supervisor over the stands of olive and sycamore trees. Yet, two facts would prevent this verse from having sycamore as its point of reference. First, the sycamore, while an indigenous Palestinian tree, at least in historical times, originated in Africa (Feliks 1981:58; but cf. Zohary 1982:68) and was acclimatized only to the lowlands, where it flourished. In 1 Chron (27:28) and 1 Kgs (10:27) its habitat is specified as the Shephelah. Thus a prophetic directive to go up to procure wood could hardly indicate that sycamore was the desired material. Second, while the sycamore is eminently suitable for the construction of roofs in ordinary houses, it cannot be used for larger buildings, which require longer and stronger beams. Sycamore, in addition, cannot be polished; on this account, too, it is not the premier choice of wood for a building such as a palace or temple. Only the cedar, which had to be imported from Lebanon, could have provided suitable timber.

In Cyrus's day, when the idea of restoration was first conceived, cedar was procured from Sidon and Tyre (Ezra 3:7). While building stones could have been reclaimed from the rubble, the timber would need to be ordered anew. The difficult Aramaic of Ezra 6:4 apparently refers to "new wood" which was acquired then for the temple (although a case could be made for "one course of timber" as in NEB, RSV). Perhaps the wood ordered in Cyrus's day was still stockpiled in Jerusalem. Even if that was not so, it would be strange to have wood alone mentioned as a material to be procured, since other temple-building passages always refer to a range of materials (wood, stone, metal, etc.). If this verse does not allow for sycomore to be fetched, it hardly could refer to cedar either, which does not grow at all in southern Palestine. What then does this command mean? It would appear *not* to refer to actual building materials. Rather, the local stands of trees in the Jerusalem hills would have provided wood for the construction equipment—that is, for the scaffolding, ramps, ladders, and other devices necessary for work on the superstructure of any building. For a large building in particular, a considerable amount of time and effort would be required for preparatory tasks. Since no mention is made concerning the procurement of the actual materials, we must assume that the efforts made eighteen years earlier to amass the required items could sustain the renewed building project.

build. See NOTE on 1:2.

House. Normal designation, often with "of Yahweh" or "of God" for the temple as God's earthly residence. See our discussion above in NOTE to "House of Yahweh," 1:2.

I may be glorified. The Niphal imperfect of the verb *kbd* is unusual in that it preserves an old subjunctive ending in *wĕʾekkābĕdâ* understood by the qere to be a cohortative; it has been corrected accordingly as many commentators have done. The rare subjunctive incorporates the meaning of the cohortative and is obscured somewhat by the preceding verb *wĕʾerṣeh* ("so that I may be pleased"), which would remain the same whether it is indicative or subjunctive. Alternatively, it is possible to read the indicative, *wĕʾekkābēd*, which has some justification. In any case the MT needs no correction.

God's presence is reestablished through the powerful symbolic means of his dwelling made habitable (cf. NOTE to "glory," 2:7). The concept of God's glory in relation to the temple draws upon the ancient belief that God's presence was made manifest in his "glory." In fact, God's "glory," as distinct from his "name," appears to represent an extraordinary and dramatic manifestation of God's presence and power (McConville 1979), a condition which Haggai could rightly anticipate following the long period of exile and the desolation of the temple.

9. *You have looked.* Heb. *pānōh.* The infinitive absolute instead of the finite verb reflects the hurried style here (cf. *GKC* § 113Y), where verses 9–10 are a reiteration and summation of the message of verses 4–6. Verses 9–11 have been understood by Steck (1971: op. cit.) to refer to those who have returned from the Babylonian exile as compared with verses 4–8, which he suggests refer only to the Judeans who had remained in the land. We find no justification for this distinction and take the whole, verses 4–11, as referring equally to both groups. The phrase "You have looked for much" may appear on the surface to be more pertinent to Yehudites who had returned

from Babylonia than to those who had remained in the land. That is, the Palestinian peasant would have been accustomed to the agricultural conditions of the Judean hills and would have understood the periodic droughts that beset the mountainous regions. Unfortunately, the semiarid climate of the hill country meant that every farmer in the region would have experienced recurrent years of subnormal rainfall, each with a negative deviation of 30 percent or more from the average (Amiran 1964), with a deviation of 50 percent coming as often as once every nine or ten years. The high degree of variability in rainfall caused considerable agricultural risk, but the emergence of traditional strategies for dealing with those risks were part of Israel's rise to statehood in the early first millennium. Local farmers would have had recourse to these strategies for coping with such exigencies, except that the termination of statehood, with its centralized markets and exchange mechanisms, would have brought an end to the strategies as developed by the monarchy. The people who had grown up or lived in an area of irrigation agriculture such as the Tigris-Euphrates Valley would have had higher expectations for regular annual crop yields than those who lived in Palestine and practiced rainfall agriculture, which was characterized by uncertainties. A season of drought, therefore, would also have been viewed by the returnees from Babylon as disastrous. No doubt many of the people who returned might have overestimated the anticipated returns from their planting, making their disappointment that much greater even in a year of normal precipitation than if their initial expectations had been more circumscribed.

but there is little. The reading of the versions (see Text Note b) is to be preferred, and we read the infinitive absolute *hāyōh* for *hnh.* The *l* before *m't* is correct and is confirmed by the *l* before *hrbh* in the first colon. The similarity between this verse (9a) and verse 6a is striking and indicates that they belong together. Although the order is reversed, verse 6 beginning with a 2nd m. pl. perfect verb followed by an infinitive absolute and verse 9 beginning with an infinitive also and followed by a 2nd m. pl. perfect, the repetition of *hrbh* and *m't* clearly binds them together.

What you have brought. I.e., sacrifice. The sacrificial altar was in the temple courtyard and was part of a sphere of cultic life distinct from the structural House of Yahweh (Haran 1980:15–16). That the altar was functional at this time, as this verse implies, does not refer to the condition of the House itself (cf. NOTE to "desolate," 1:4). Ezra 3:2–6 reports explicitly that the altar was rebuilt and set to use at once following the return in the time of Cyrus.

"Why is this?" This rhetorical question, *ya'an meh* (literally, "on account of what?"), is unique to Haggai. As an inquiry into the reasons for the difficult condition in Yehud, it is a further indication of the causality in human events which the prophet perceives and strives to impress upon his audience. The prophet proceeds to give an answer to his query and, appropriately, introduces the answer with the same word, *ya'an,* as in the question. Its first usage is as a preposition, its second as a conjunction.

Because my House lies desolate. The language of this clause, *y'n byty 'šr-hw' hrb,* presents a striking relationship with the language of verse 4b, which has *hbyt hzh hrb,* "this House lies desolate." In addition to the repetition of the key words *byt* ("house") and *hrb* ("desolate"), the intermediate words in each case, *hzh* and *hû'* balance each other. Furthermore, the formula "Yahweh of Hosts" precedes the clause in verse 9 and follows it in verses 4–5. Finally, verse 4a emphasizes the 2nd m. pl. pronoun and so does the last colon of verse 9. All these features are part of an envelope construction that links verses 4 and 9 and suggests that verses 4 through 9 are a unit, with verses 10 and 11 constituting a conclusion to the entire section, verses 2–11.

The use of "House" in this clause also relates to "house" in the second part of the verse. The twofold appearance of *byt* helps to establish a contrast between God's dwelling and the homes of the people. A similar contrast exists in verse 4, where *byt* also occurs twice, once in reference to Yahweh's house and once referring to the people's homes. The contrasts of verses 4 and 9 are parallel, and the inclusio formed by those two verses is thereby strengthened.

while you run about. Because verses 4 and 9 (see previous NOTE) are parallel in depicting the contrast between the desolate House of Yahweh and the inhabited private dwellings of the Yehudites, this term can be related to "dwell" of verse 4. "Dwell," or literally "sit," poses its own contrast with the intense activity conveyed here by the participial form of the verb *rṣ,* "to run." The contrast between the two verbs forms a merism: *all* the activity of the people, in or out of their homes, sitting or moving, is undertaken for the sake of those homes—that is, for their private lives and personal benefit. The ultimate contrast is with the neglect of their public obligations as represented by the temple, which symbolized the traditional ties among all the people and which housed at least part of the administrative structure dealing with the community as a whole (cf. NOTE to "House of Yahweh," 1:2).

each man to his own house. This phrase forms the final element in the series of contrasts within this clause and also within the contrasts and parallels that link this whole verse with verse 4. The private dwelling of an individual is parallel to the collective "your houses" of verse 4; together they represent all private homes as opposed to the public structure, Yahweh's house, which is being ignored amidst the plethora of activities (cf. previous NOTE) that characterize daily life. The word "house" in Hebrew represents more than a physical building. It can mean "household" and encompass the economic and social activities of the persons living together as a family unit. As such, the "house" is the basic unit of society. In this verse, the extended meaning of "household" is particularly apt because of the running about that takes place there: "run about" denotes activity, and activity characterizes "house" as a productive unit. The oracle chastises the Yehudites for attending to individual ("each man . . . own") productivity to the exclusion of communal concerns—i.e., the temple as a religious and administrative institution.

10. *Therefore.* The participle *ʿal-kēn* introduces a new section which is the conclusion to this first section of Haggai's first chapter. The language of the preceding verse, as it echoes that of verse 4, served to close the internal unit of oracles in this section; and now a final oracle reiterates and emphasizes the content of that unit.

because of you. The Hebrew preposition *ʿl* has a variety of usages, and this translation reflects the causative effect of the people's behavior upon the economy, which is in a sorry state because of the lack of sufficient moisture. However, *ʿl* can also mean "against" and point directly to the negative effect of the diminished supply of dew on the people themselves. The difference in the two is not great, and the meaning is not radically altered by preferring one translation over the other. Indeed, the Hebrew may allow for both.

The heavens have withheld the dew in part and the earth has withheld some of its yield. The lack of rainfall, or moisture, and the devastating results of such water shortages in an agrarian society dependent upon dry-farming techniques, had long been linked with divine punishment for sin. 1 Kgs 8:35 is particularly relevant: "When the heavens have shut up and there is no rain because the people have sinned against you, if they pray toward this place . . . ." Accordingly, the remedy for drought is prayer toward "this place"—i.e., the Jerusalem temple, and the concomitant acknowledgment of Yahweh and obedience to his word.

However, the drought described in this passage is not a total one. The use of *min* before "dew" *(miṭṭāl)* is partitive, a standard use for that preposition (cf. Gen 27:39 and Deut 33:13). Its partitive force also governs "yield" in the next clause ("the earth withheld its yield"), which is bound together with the first clause ("the heavens withheld their dew in part") by the chiasm in Hebrew of the subject and verb of each (*kl'w šmym,* "the heavens withheld," and *wh'rṣ kl'h,* "the earth withheld"). Just as there has been a loss of moisture, so too has there been a diminution in the earth's produce; both of these conditions are understood to be a warning rather than a full-fledged punishment. The partial hardship implicit in this situation corresponds exceedingly well to the picture presented in verse 6 above, in which there may be hunger and thirst and cold but not utter starvation and nakedness. Similarly, 2:16 below depicts partial rather than complete crop failure.

The use of the word "dew" and the presentation of the conditions associated with an insufficient supply of it are particularly appropriate to the season of the year at which this oracle was uttered, according to the chronological formula of 1:1, which gives a date of late August (520 B.C.E.). The presence of sufficient dew during the period just before the fall harvest is a particularly critical factor in dry farming. At the height of summer, the "cloud of dew" (Isa 18:4) was especially beneficial for increasing the yield of certain crops (Feliks 1981:152–55).

While the overall meaning of this verse is quite specific and clear, it does contain one technical difficulty which does not affect the meaning but which is not easy to resolve. There is a discrepancy between the use of the definite article before *'rṣ,* "earth," and its omission before *šmym,* "heaven," even though the intent is for the latter to be definite along with the former. Some manuscripts have added the article before "heaven" in order to remove the inconsistency, but that is so obviously an improved reading that the more difficult reading of the MT probably should be retained. Such omissions do sometimes occur for definite rather than accidental reasons, which may be difficult to ferret out but which nonetheless make sense while scribal carelessness does not.

In this particular instance, we can note two features which possibly have caused "heavens" to be recorded without the definite article. "Heavens" precedes "earth," which itself precedes a repetition of "earth" in the next verse (v 11) along with an associated series of substantives, all of which elaborate upon the notion that the earth is less productive than it should be. All those subsequent substantives (except the last one) occur with the definite article, so that all the effects of the dew shortage are thereby linked together. The reason for the crop shortages—the "heavens," which have withheld some of the expected dew—lacks the definite article and so stands apart from the result. The omission of the *heh* has the force of distinguishing, therefore, between cause and effect. Haggai's attention to causality in human affairs is served by the contrast.

The situation here (in vv 10–11) is made more complex by a second feature notice-able in the arrangement of definite articles. The very last substantive in verse 11 ("products of human toil," *ygyʿ kpym*) also lacks the definite article even though the meaning is quite definite. This last item is a summation of all the preceding entities of verse 11 and perhaps lacks the article in order to make it stand out as a summary item rather than as a part of an enumerated listing. If this be the case, then our very first noun ("heavens") in the longer series in verses 10 and 11 together may have been written, or spoken, without the article in order to achieve a balance with the last item in the series. The other feature discussed above may have been the reason for the last noun to be presented without the article. Although one cannot establish the priority of either of these explanations, there is no reason not to admit that both of them may be present and contribute together to the rhetorical finesse of the prophet.

The language of this verse is very similar to that of Zech 8:12 (see NOTES to that verse). The correspondences are part of a set of connections (see Introduction) between Haggai and Zechariah 7–8 that frame a combined Haggai-Zechariah 1–8. Zechariah's use of Haggai's description of poor yield reverses the situation: heaven and earth will indeed provide what they should. Zechariah's optimism fits the situation in 518 B.C.E. The temple is nearly complete. The people have obeyed Yahweh and Yahweh will treat them accordingly. Haggai's own account (2:19) of the results of the beginning of the temple work also depicts economic security.

11. *Thus I have proclaimed*. A new oracular unit is begun appropriately with *wᵊqrʾ*, a formulaic introduction relatively rare in biblical prophecy (see our discussion of "Pro-claim!" in Zech 1:14). Although its use in Zechariah seems to be more technical, it is employed here to highlight the pronouncement of a "desolation" or drought which is a divine warning and which concludes the first section of chapter 1.

desolation. Literally a "drying up," the Hebrew *ḥōreb* is clearly a play upon the word *ḥārēb*, "desolate," used to describe the ruined and uninhabited temple in verses 4 and 9 above. We have translated *ḥōreb* as "desolation" in order to emphasize, as does the Hebrew, the thematic connection between the people's inattention to Yahweh and the insufficiency of the land's productivity. The root *ḥrb* describes a condition of dryness or absence of dew, as in Judg 6:37,39,40 (cf. NOTE to "desolate," v 4).

affecting. Hebrew *ʿl*, "on, upon, concerning, against," is used before "land" at the outset of this verse and again in the Hebrew before all the succeeding items. When used with "ground" it occurs before the conjunction and verb of the relative clause in which "ground" appears. Although *ʿl* is not rendered each time in our translation, its first usage is intended to govern all the subsequent nouns in the series.

the land and the hills. As the first of the three sets of entities which constitute verse 11, this pair denotes the territory affected by the "desolation." The word for "land" is *ʾereṣ*, the same as in verse 10, where it is a comprehensive term contrasted with "heav-ens" and rendered "earth." Here it is paired with "hills" and seems to be part of a description of the arable land available in Yehud. Much of the province was hill coun-try, with little of the adjacent plains or Shephelah comprising Yehudite territory. "Hills" defines "land" in this verse, indicating that not much flat terrain was available to the Yehudite farmers. As in much of preexilic Judean history, the intensive agricul-tural base was concentrated in the hill country. Note Ezekiel's repeated (sixteen times) reference to the land as "the mountains of Israel." After the destruction, Ezekiel envisages that Israel will be restored, like sheep, to their accustomed locale: "the mountain of Israel" (Ezek 34:1-14; cf. Feliks 1981:144-47 for a discussion of Ezekiel's usage of this terminology). In this mountainous territory the growing of sufficient grain, a field crop, would have been especially difficult.

the grain, the new wine, the fresh oil. This triad of commodities is the second of three sets of entities which form verse 11. The first (see previous NOTE) is the natural setting in which agriculture was carried out, and this second group is composed of the products of its cultivation. The three products enumerated reflect the basic tripartite economy of Palestine. The listing of these three items is, as one might expect, found sporadically in the Hebrew Bible. It is particularly characteristic of Deuteronomistic language, yet is hardly an exclusively Deuteronomistic formula. The term for "oil" in this triad is usually *yiṣhār* ("new oil," "fresh oil"; cf. NOTE to "sons of oil," Zech 4:14) rather than the more general word *šemen*. Similarly, wine is denoted by *tîrôš*, "new wine," rather than the broader *yayin*. In both cases the connotation of harvest is present, as suits this passage. The three basic foodstuffs are appropriate here in a passage depicting shortages; compare the expanded list of products in Hag 2:19, where plenitude is described.

whatever the ground brings forth. This phrase is complementary to the preceding group of three. It is introduced by the conjunction *ʾšr*, which is incomplete without a preceding *kl*. Following most Greek and Syriac manuscripts (cf. Text Note c), we read the conjunction as if *kl* were present. The elusive *kl* appears in the last colon ("*all* products of human hands") and may do double duty for this phrase, or else its absence here may be a simple haplography after *ʾl*, owing to homoeoteleuton.

The various commodities that supplement the basic subsistence economy, of which grain, wine, and oil are the major components, may be the intended referents of this collective phrase; alternatively, the phrase may simply summarize the three main items of agricultural productivity.

mankind and beast and all products of human toil. These three items constitute the third set of entities enumerated in verse 11. The natural setting and then its products having been designated, the instrumentality which procures subsistence from soil is now specified. "Mankind and beast" is often a pair in itself (cf. Zech 2:8 [RSV 2:4] and 8:10). It is supplemented here by "all products of human toil" perhaps in the same way stylistically, so that the previous set of three has a complementary phrase. Yet it seems rather extraneous as part of this set in terms of its meaning, since man and animals would seem to constitute a complete set. The addition of "all products of human toil" (cf. 2:14, "work of their hands") perhaps takes into account nonagrarian labors, which also will show diminished productivity according to the meaning of this passage. However, stylistic considerations may provide another explanation. The absence of an expected definite article before *ygyʿ kpym*, literally, "the products of the hands," has already been discussed (see above third NOTE to v 10). We have suggested that its omission may be part of a literary arrangement which sets apart this last item of the series and balances the *šmym* of the previous verse which also lacks the expected definite article. If such be the case, then this final phrase may have a meaning which extends beyond its group and in a general way summarizes all the specific items listed in the foregoing units, both the efforts of human activity ("hands," *kpym*) and also the results ("products").

We should also point out that the definite article, and also sometimes a qualifying suffix, is occasionally omitted (cf. Isa 49:16; Mic 7:3) before the dual forms that express parts of the body, as in the present "hands" *(kpym)*. It is possible that the article has been left out for this simple reason. However, in light of all our remarks above about the sequence of prepositional phrases and the framing of the series in verses 10 and 11, it seems that the article was deliberately omitted as a deviation from the norm so that it could function in these other ways. Its omission is the last device in an intricately arranged series of interlocking sets of items. Taken as a whole, they demonstrate the interrelatedness of human behavior and well-being.

12. *Then Zerubbabel . . . Joshua.* The names of the two main community leaders are repeated here, having been mentioned for the first time in 1:1. See our discussion above of both these men. Note that Zerubbabel's patronymic in this verse has the shortened form—Shaltiel rather than Shealtiel—and that his title is omitted whereas Joshua's title is included (cf. NOTE to 2:4, "O High Priest").

rest of the people. Coming within the editorial framework, the phrase, Hebrew *šĕ'ērît hā'ām*, is taken by some to mean "remnant" and to refer to a faithful nucleus of the people (e.g., Mason 1977a:17 and 1982:142–85). However, the compiler stands so close to the prophet (see Kaufmann 1977:253), who simply refers to the community as "this people" (1:2, 2:14) or "all the people of the land" (2:4), that it may be unwarranted to accept a specialized theological intent of the compiler. Ackroyd (1968:162–63) suggests that interpretation of this verse has been determined by the more explicit designations in Zechariah. Indeed, it is extremely difficult to judge whether or not the word *šĕ'ērît* ("rest of" or "remnant") possesses any special significance in its position within the editorial framework. It could well be a simple designation of the prophet's audience, which did in fact come to heed the word of Yahweh in time. It is also possible that the term preserves a distinction between those who returned from Babylon and those who did not, however impossible that may seem to us. The use of a loaded word such as "remnant," which is clearly intentional, perhaps does reveal something about the point of view of Haggai's compiler, for its three occurrences in Haggai (here and 1:14; 2:2) are in the editorial framework. It also is found three times in Zechariah, all in the oracles of chapter 8 (8:6,11,12; see NOTES) which were uttered over two years later, closer to the time of the final editing of Haggai-Zechariah 1–8. Zechariah's usage may well have influenced the compiler's terminology in Haggai. Haggai himself does not appear to distinguish between segments of the Yehudite population (cf. NOTE to "this people," 1:2).

gave heed . . . voice. The verb "to hear" *(šm')* followed by the preposition *b* and "voice," meaning the voice of Yahweh, is a combination found frequently in the Hebrew Bible. It has a Deuteronomistic cast, occurring frequently in the Book of Deuteronomy and being a favorite phrase of Jeremiah. Haggai's efforts to arouse his audience to action in accord with God's word was evidently successful, and this report on the response to the oracles transmitted by Haggai is couched in standard biblical language denoting obedience to God's word.

voice of . . . words of the prophet Haggai. These two phrases, one after the other, have the effect of emphasizing that God communicates to the people through his prophetic messenger (cf. NOTE following).

Yahweh their God. The name Yahweh with the appellative and pronominal suffix ("their") occurs twice in this verse and once below in verse 14. A discussion of this striking repetition is offered in our COMMENT to 1:12–15.

sent. Like "messenger" (cf. following NOTE), the verb "to send" *(šlk)* is part of the vocabulary of apostolic prophecy and is derived from the concept of the Heavenly Council (cf. NOTE to "the word of Yahweh," 1:1). Zechariah (2:12,13 [RSV 2:8,9]), Isaiah (6:8), and Moses (Exod 3:13–15) are other examples of Israelite prophets given Yahweh's charge to carry his word to the people.

13. *messenger.* Divine will is transmitted to the people through prophetic emissaries, and this designation (Heb. *mal'ak*) is applied specifically also to Malachi (1:1), whose name may actually be an appellative meaning "my messenger." Imagery is drawn from the Divine Council scene as well as from the means for transmitting God's judgments, once they are made in the Council, to the people (see NOTE to "the word of Yahweh," 1:1). In Zechariah's visionary sequence, angelic messengers figure prominently (cf. 1:9, NOTE to "angel-who-speaks-with-me" and 3:1, NOTE to "angel of Yahweh").

message. The noun *malā'kût* appears only here in the Hebrew Bible. LXX renders "messenger." The similarity in Hebrew to the word "work" *(mĕlā'ka)* in verse 14 has perhaps influenced this choice of word.

with you! This phrase denotes divine presence with its attendant power. Levine (1968) has pointed out the two major beneficial components of God's presence: protection from enemies or illness, and provision of food and water. For example when Moses warns the Israelites not to challenge the Amalekites and Canaanites, he asserts that they will fail because "Yahweh will not be with you" (Num 14:42–44). Perhaps the best example of God's presence providing military power is the story of Gideon (Judg 6–8), in which it is repeatedly stated that God is with Gideon (Judg 6:12,13,16,17). The twenty-third Psalm shows both benefits of being near God: the psalmist is provided with food while his enemies stand by, unable to harm him. Although the language is not necessarily the same as the phrase in this verse, the idea of divine presence is nonetheless clearly present in these and other biblical examples (cf. 2:7).

14. *roused the spirit.* The verb (*ʿwr,* "to arouse") is the same as that used several times in Zechariah (2:17 = RSV 2:13; 4:1), especially to indicate his entering a state of great receptivity for a visionary experience. Used with "spirit" *(rûaḥ),* it expresses arousal to action. In all such cases there is a political context for the activity in question: Jer 51:11 refers to the anticipated Medean conquest of Babylon (cf. 51:1); 1 Chron 5:26 describes the Assyrian kings and their treatment of several Israelite tribes; 2 Chron 21:16 relates the combined Philistine-Arab advance against Jehoram and Judah; and 2 Chron 36:22, and Ezra 1:1 deal with Cyrus's proclamation regarding the rebuilding of the Jerusalem temple. Without *rûaḥ* *ʿwr* is used in the same way, and the absence of *rûaḥ* is probably elliptical (e.g., Isa 13:17). Only here and in the related passage in Ezra 1:5 does "raise the spirit" refer to Israelite action. Since the other usages are so patently political, the appearance of the phrase in Haggai suggests the possibility that the action initiated by the rousing of the people's spirit was not devoid of political significance. The construction of a temple was an act intimately associated with the administration and control of a political unit (cf. NOTE to "House of Yahweh," 1:2), and the Persian policy allowing Yehud to proceed with temple work cannot be separated from the semi-autonomy and internal self-rule represented and

facilitated by a functional national shrine (see NOTES to "flying scroll," Zech 5:1; to "high priest," Zech 3:1; and to the date heading of Zech 7:1).

came to do. Literally, "they came and did." The verb "to come" *(bw')* is used as an auxiliary in this instance (cf. Josh 11:5).

House of Yahweh of Hosts their God. This is the last mention of the temple in Haggai; it is also the fullest, with "of Hosts their God" added to the usual "House of Yahweh" (cf. NOTE to "of Hosts" in 1:1). It repeats for the third time in 1:12–15, the appellative "their God" (cf. 1:12 and COMMENT to 1:12–15a). In addition, it is the eighth and climactic appearance of the word "house" in the first chapter of Haggai. Its use here, with the elaborate designation of its divine owner, is a fitting conclusion to the section of Haggai which has been so concerned with the idea of having the temple restoration undertaken.

15. *on the twenty-fourth day of the sixth month in the second year of Darius.* Most commentators take this to be a misplaced introduction to the oracle in 2:15–19 (e.g., Mason 1977a:44; Amsler 1981:28–30); or they understand the last part of the verse ("in the second year of Darius") to belong with the date formula immediately follow- ing in Hag 2:1, where the king's regnal year is lacking. Alternatively, and more proba- bly, it is in its proper place here at the end of chapter 1, where it indicates a passage of several weeks between the initial prophetic call and the beginning of the temple recon- struction work. This lapse is perhaps the result of time being required for preparatory tasks before the actual rebuilding project could begin; see NOTE to "go up in the hills . . . bring in wood," verse 8. The fact that work began so soon after intention was established would seem to support our suggestion regarding verse 8, that only building equipment had to be procured and that the materials themselves, which had been ordered in Cyrus's day, were still available. Ordering essential cedarwood from Phoeni- cia would not have been accomplished in less than a month.

Verse 15 is exceptional in its offering a date formula at the end of a unit rather than at the beginning, a fact that has influenced the exegetes who would move it. It brings to a conclusion the unit, 1:12–15, which begins with the editorial description of how the leaders and people were obeying Yahweh. This unusual placement can be explained as a device to form an envelope with the date formula at the beginning of the book (1:1). The ordering of the chronological information in 1:15 repeats, in reverse order, the information provided at the beginning of the chapter: 1:1 gives year, month, day; and 1:15 has day, month, year. Verse 15 is slightly abbreviated (reading "twenty-fourth day of the sixth month," whereas a fuller form with the word "month" repeated appears in verse 1, "in the sixth month, on the first day of the month"), as it also does in 2:10; the fuller formula in 1:1 probably is a function of its initial position. This variation does not detract from the fact that verse 15 corresponds so well with verse 1, and that the two formulas mark the beginning and end of a section of Haggai's prophecy. Zech 7:1, which provides the last date in Haggai-Zechariah 1–8, also gives the chronological information in an order which is the reverse of that of Hag 1:1. The correspondence between Hag 1:1 and Zech 7:1 likewise marks the beginning and end of something— namely, the Haggai-Zechariah 1–8 composite work.

Although all of verse 15 is perfectly and properly positioned at the end of the first chapter, the regnal information may at the same time be read in relation to the second chapter. More specifically, verse 15b would surely supply 2:1 with the missing year.

Consequently, "in the second year of Darius" may have been intended to do double duty. Another possibility is that haplography may have caused the loss of one year phrase, if two year phrases had originally stood back to back in 1:15 and 2:1.

COMMENT

Prophetic call to work on the temple, 1:1–11.

The ministry of the prophet Haggai is brief; three and a half months elapse between his first prophecy and his last. The Book of Haggai is also short; only Obadiah is shorter. Yet the chronological and historical information provided in the opening verse of Haggai is full and detailed. Haggai is concerned with the reckoning of calendar time in a way that appears in no other prophetic work except for First Zechariah. Dates are given twice in the first chapter and four times in the second chapter. This extraordinary concern, as we have explained in our NOTES, arises from the particular confluence of external imperial policy and internal historical consciousness in the province of Yehud early in the reign of Darius Hystaspis.

By the time Haggai began to prophesy, Darius I had dealt with the unrest and rebellion that had accompanied his accession to the throne. He had begun the enterprise of organizing his vast empire in a way that his predecessors had not (see Introduction). Although Cyrus had been brilliant in his military conquests, he had not really followed up his dramatic successes on the battlefield with a program of civil administration. As conqueror, he could exact tribute and establish certain policies by the sheer force of his martial reputation. But his successors could not sustain that pattern, and Darius at last set about to establish satrapies, or units, under the unified direction of crown-appointed officials. The results may not have been as systematic as our Western standards may expect, but they nonetheless imposed order and control over the vast territories of the Persian Empire. By the second year of his reign, Darius's imperial reorganization was well under way.

A hallmark of Darius's policies was the semiautonomy he granted, wherever possible, to provincial units or subunits. Documentation of such a policy, to establish Persian control of Egypt and various other provinces (see Cook 1983:71–72), exists in imperial records or correspondence. For Israel, or Yehud as the political unit was called by the Persians, documentation appears only in biblical sources. The apparently magnanimous gesture of Darius in allowing the ancient Judean temple to be rebuilt was in Persian eyes part of the overarching plan to restore local governance in provincial territories. The temple in Jerusalem was, like all temples in the ancient world, an administrative institution. It functioned in political, economic, and judicial matters as well as in strictly cultic or religious ones. Consequently, the restoration of a temple was a means of fostering local self-rule in a subunit of the Persian

Empire. From the Yehudite perspective, for which the biblical record is our source, permission for and encouragement of temple building were viewed as nothing other than the abatement at last of Yahweh's divine anger and a sign of God's renewed attention to his people.

The internal, or Yehudite, perspective was determined by a strong historical consciousness which went hand in hand with the role of authoritative written traditions. Ancient covenantal concepts of blessings and curses, meted out according to the behavior of the people, helped explain the devastation of conquest and exiles and also provided hope for the end of that state. Prophetic oracles of the preexilic or exilic period echoed the covenantal ideas and gave them specificity. Jeremiah in particular proclaimed that God's wrath would come to an end in seventy years (Jer 25:11–12; 29:10). That time period is probably a symbolic one, and its onset and termination would be calculated in various ways by later generations. For Haggai's generation there could be no doubt that the seventy years' span was imminent; the chronological headings of Haggai and of Zechariah constitute a prophetic countdown to the anticipated rededication of the temple, which would mark God's return to Zion and to his people in fulfillment of what was stated in sacred tradition.

The date formula of Haggai 1 represents an awareness of Persian policy, for it was keyed to the regnal years of Darius. The date simultaneously records the imminence of the conclusion of the seventy-year period. Our discussion thus far has addressed itself to issues that explain the appearance of the regnal year (520 B.C.E.). But the date is more specific than that; it gives month and day of the month. Is such additional information essential to the international and nationalist perspectives? It probably adds nothing at that level, and another reason must be considered. The day and month of Haggai 1:1 appear, as do the similar headings further on in Haggai and in Zechariah even to the exclusion of the emperor's regnal year, to mark internal developments. The efforts required to rebuild the temple must have been considerable, given the economic situation in Yehud in the late sixth century. Prophetic encouragement in the face of hardship, a theme which pervades Haggai and to which we shall return below, is enormously strengthened by Haggai's ability to point to an improvement in the economy and to link it with Yahweh's returning to the land of his people. The close reckoning of dates, when related to the progress of the agricultural calendar, allows the prophet to make his point about God's intervention in history.

The chronological information is part of a narrative introduction to Haggai, and as such may not be from the hand of the prophet himself. However, all the headings of Haggai and Zechariah 1–8 precede the 515 B.C.E. date of temple rededication (see Chart 2, p. xliv), an event which surely would have been noted by these prophets had it occurred during their ministries. Even if Haggai himself did not utter the date formulas, they were supplied by someone within a few short years of the delivery of Haggai's oracles. Perhaps Haggai himself provided the third-person framework. Traditional scholarly theories of redactional activity must be reconsidered in light of the short time frame which can be posited between oracles and final written form. The date formula not only is related to the political situation of the restoration and to an important theological point that the prophet wishes to make, it also is one of several features which, from a stylistic perspective, signify the overall unity of Haggai with Zechariah 1–8. As we have described in our Introduction, Haggai and First Zechariah share many themes. Their prophecies overlap, as the chronological sequence contained in the date headings is careful to indicate. More important, literary correspondences among the oracular materials of the two prophets suggest cross-influence. In particular, the last of Zechariah's oracles (Zech 7–8) develops themes found in Haggai. Finally, the date formulas, in conjunction with other phrases and key words, are repeated in certain patterns that reflect an overall literary framework of Haggai and Zechariah 1–8 together. Since the last two chapters of Zechariah balance the two chapters of Haggai in this scheme, the contacts between those two units are particularly strong. The mirroring of the date formulas, with both Haggai and Zechariah 7–8 beginning with the year and with the day-month chiastically arranged, is a case in point.

In addition to providing a date, the opening of Haggai informs us that his utterances were directed toward the two leaders of the people at that time, Zerubbabel the Davidic governor and Joshua the high priest. Both leaders are named, along with their patronymics and titles. Although the close relationship between the phenomenon of classical prophecy and the religio-political leadership of Israel (Petersen 1977) is maintained, the principal leadership of Israel (Yehud) has now dramatically shifted. The king has been replaced by a Davidic scion who is a political appointee of the Persian authorities and whose responsibilities lie in matters of liaison with the Persian government. The office of high priest, which in compensation has been upgraded in importance in the postexilic period (cf. NOTE to "high priest" in Zech 3:1), also operated because of the beneficence of the Persian government and in consort with the governor; but it takes over much of the internal administration that previously resided with the royal house. The priesthood had always been important during the monarchy, even though the king had to be supreme, because the temple itself was an administrative institution along with the palace. The apparent expansion of priestly powers may to a certain extent have been the result of the removal of royal powers so that the priesthood, no longer sharing power, loomed larger. This dyarchic structure of Yehudite leadership is presupposed in Haggai but intermittently gives way to eschatological outbursts focused upon the Davidic scion in Haggai 2:21–23 and Zechariah 4:6b–10a, suggesting that the dyarchic pattern was considered temporary and that eventual revival of monarchic leadership was expected. The consistent listing of Zerubbabel before Joshua, even with the latter possessing considerable power, is interesting. It may be a reflex action of a monarchic mind-set in which the king, to whom Zerubbabel was the equivalent, would have to be named first. Or it may show a sequence keyed to the ultimate responsibility for Yehud in the imperial structure, in which the civil leader answerable to the Persians, no matter how circumscribed his authority, was the ranking official.

The Persians were well aware that they had appointed a governor who was in direct line to the Davidic throne and a high priest who was the offspring of a major priestly leader of the Exile. The lineage of these two individuals is provided because their pedigrees were critical components of the appointments. The Persians must have been well aware of the qualifications of Zerubbabel and Joshua. Indeed, it was Persian sagacity rather than naïveté which produced the dynamic leadership of this period and which succeeded in turning a situation of economic and national despair into one of relative prosperity and renewal of national identity. Both Yehud and the Persian Empire were to benefit from these developments, and the full form of address to Zerubbabel and Joshua through the prophet reflects an awareness of the contemporary situation.

The high priest would have been working with the priestly establishment that had survived the disruption of the Babylonian exile. Revenues in the form of tithes and sacrifices provided support for the high priest and the lower ranks of temple officials. Hence, for the project of temple work with which the Book of Haggai is concerned, priestly cooperation with the office of governor was essential. The financial procedures by which the workmen and materials were secured no doubt rested upon a complex voucher system in the taxation process. Since, according to Ezra 6:8, the provincial revenues could be diverted for the temple work, Zerubbabel as chief tax officer would have had to work with Joshua as chief temple officer. The latter's role in the collection and disbursal of funds was one aspect of the expansion of his traditional duties; we learn about other aspects in First Zechariah.

The people are not mentioned in verse 1, as they are in the parallel verse in 1:12 that introduces the second section of this chapter. This is somewhat surprising, because they are ultimately the audience for the prophetic message. What they are called upon to accomplish cannot be done without administrative action; hence the dual leadership of priest and governor constitutes the immediate audience of the prophet in this introductory heading. The people are, however, included in verse 2 as the opening of the book continues, for they are the ones who for a variety of reasons have been reluctant to agree that the present time is the right and propitious moment for recommencing work on the temple. The formulaic language of prophecy introducing verses 2 and 3 sets the stage for the presentation of Haggai's call to work which begins in verse 4 and continues until verse 11. Haggai's oracles are delivered in his role as a messenger from Yahweh. He receives God's words and transmits them to the leaders and to the people.

All of the exhortations of this section of Haggai's prophecies are rooted in his appraisal of the state of the economy in Yehud and his connection of present conditions with divine disfavor. His evaluation anticipates the central oracle of chapter 2, which takes the shape of a prophetic interpretation of a priestly ruling (2:10–19) and is also the longest of the oracles among those delivered by his colleague Zechariah two years later (Zech 8:9–13). Much scholarly work has been directed toward understanding the economy of Yehud in 520 B.C.E. Short of the information that careful archaeological work of sixth-century sites in Yehud may be able to provide, fresh insights about the economy remain theoretical.

Several well-established features of the economy of the restoration period can be reviewed. First, the Babylonian conquest of 587 probably had, as the biblical sources assert, a depressing effect on the economy. In addition to actual physical destruction of fruit trees and vines, of terraces and enclosing walls, the decimation of the population would have impeded efforts to restore agricultural activity and would have limited productivity. Although the Babylonian conquerors allowed at least part of the population to remain in the land "to be vine dressers and plowmen" (2 Kgs 25:12), it is unlikely that all the fields, orchards, vineyards, and gardens that had supplied the preexilic state would have been maintained for a reduced population. Second, natural forces acting upon the ruined fields and terraces would have, over the course of time, further impaired their productivity. As time went by, the amount of work required to restore the land to its preexilic potential would have increased. Third, the gradual demographic recovery of Palestine during Babylonian and subsequently during Persian rule would have been augmented by the return of Judeans (perhaps accompanied by some northerners) to their homeland (see Ezra 2:1–58). The population growth would have taxed resources and required that the wasted fields, vineyards, and orchards be revitalized, a task which would have required an increased output of human energy over a number of years. Such a need could not have been met instantly.

In addition to these factors, the variations in climate that characterize Palestine must be taken into account. Periodic droughts were endemic, with a mean annual rainfall deviating negatively from the norm every few years. In fact, several (up to three, usually) consecutive dry years together could be expected once in a decade. Farmers in semiarid areas such as Palestine developed storage and exchange mechanisms to cope with the food shortages posed by recurrent droughts, and the incorporation of animal husbandry into land-use strategies likewise helped to compensate for diminished yields. However, when the population of such regions reached a certain point, the risks inherent in the agrarian basis for the economy could no longer be handled on the local level. Farmers or groups of farmers by themselves could not accrue sufficient surpluses to provide for drought-caused emergencies. At this point, centralized agencies for collection and redistribution of resources became essential.

The very emergence of the Israelite monarchy at the beginning of the Iron Age can be related in part to the growth of population in Palestine in the period of the Judges and the associated need for a political force that could extract local surpluses and use them over a wider geographical territory as needed. The situation in 520 B.C.E. parallels the condition of the early monarchy in that respect. The local population had recovered decades after the exile and had been augmented by returnees from Babylon. Yet the climate did not change in its age-old pattern of considerable annual fluctuations. Could the apparently unstructured local governance of the early Persian period cope with the shortages that resulted? It would not have been necessary for a drought to be severe for a situation of scarcity to have developed, and Haggai informs us that only a partial decrease in expected moisture had occurred. Yet with a population increase even relatively minor negative variations in rainfall and dew would have caused severe hardship.

Haggai's call to work on the temple, as he himself proclaims, is rooted in economic considerations. The text seems to imply that if the people rebuild God's temple, he will reward them with economic prosperity. We would not argue with that implication, which is firmly rooted in Near Eastern temple typology, in which the building of the temple brings about fertility. However, in our opinion the prophet is elliptical in proclaiming the way in which prosperity will accompany the rebuilding of the temple. The temple was an administrative institution, and the restoration of the physical building signified a corresponding recognition of God's presence and of divine sanction for its priestly administrators. In other words, the establishment or reestablishment of traditional mechanisms of internal governance under the priesthood alone, without the monarchy, would have provided the authority for bringing about communal strategies of resource management. That is, priestly revenues in kind (agricultural products) replaced royal revenues in providing national stockpiles. With the burden of foreign tribute also to be met, the raising of such revenues would not have been easy. Perhaps the additional sanction of divine will made the difference. Haggai urged the people to refound the temple because, in this analysis, he understood that Yehud could not survive economically without the centralized management that only the temple could offer.

The imagery of verse 9 is instructive. The people of Yehud have already been contributing to the temple, in the form of sacrificial offerings resumed long before the temple structure itself was restored. But what happened to the offerings? They were dissipated, "blown away" or consumed as by fire, so that whatever the populace hoped for from the temple was not forthcoming. Could this mean that, in addition to conditions of drought, the economic problems that beset the people as a community were exacerbated because help did not come from its expected quarter, the temple as communal storehouse or clearinghouse? The economic hardships that Haggai reflects are apparently largely agricultural ones. Scarcity of subsistence commodities was not necessarily accompanied by lack of other resources. Many returnees would have been able to contribute in silver and gold to temple work costs, but could not have converted such assets into foodstuffs if local supplies were depleted and if the imperial government controlled trade between its territories.

Although we have cast this analysis in terms of economic management and political strategies, our assessment should not obscure the fact that Haggai's language, rooted as it may have been in his astute grasp of worldly realities, appealed to the people in traditional terms. While Haggai may have known full well that the Persians would not interfere and would even support work on a Yehudite temple, and while he may well have understood the importance of centralized control of economic affairs, he addresses the people with the religious belief that the will of God was directly involved in the reconstruction of the temple. His tactics in arousing the people to work depended greatly upon fundamental convictions about the relationship between God and his people. And Haggai experienced revelations from God which in the last analysis drew him into prophetic activity. For him, prophetic activity involved a mandate to bring about the activity of the people.

Haggai approaches his task of mustering cooperation, but whether in the form of funds or labor or both is not specified except for the information contained in verse 8, through skillful literary techniques. His use of a rhetorical question in verse 4, which plays upon the use of the word "time" in the reported speech to the people, is an example of the way he directs the people's self-stated interests into the scope of national interests. His repeated use of the word "house" for God's dwelling in verses 2, 4, 8, and 9 (twice), and for individual households in verses 4 and 9, also helps establish the contrast between personal well-being, or lack of it, and the national welfare. A similar contrast is accomplished by the parallel "much . . . little" opposition in verses 6 and 9; personal expectations are not distinct from communal ones. He also employs wordplay to suggest connections, as in the relationship between the "desolate" (vv 4,9) House of Yahweh and the "drying up" or desolation (v 11) of all productivity. And he echoes just enough covenantal language, as in verses 10 and 11, so that the causality he sees between the people's behavior and God's blessings cannot be ignored.

Response of leaders and people. 1:12–15a

The response of all sectors of the community to Haggai's plea is immediate and unanimous. If there was a dissenting opinion about whether or not to proceed with the temple project, we do not hear about it. Indeed, the citation of the two leaders and of "all the rest of the people" is repeated in full at the beginning (v 12) and at the end (v 14) of this brief unit. Yehudite unity, in spirit and in deed, is an important theme.

The absence of any reference to Persia or Persian policy is also noteworthy. In our NOTES to Haggai 1:1 and COMMENT above, we have explained the role that contemporary developments in the reign of Darius I played in the local decision in Yehud to restore the temple. Yet the arguments Haggai addresses to the people were not based on any appeal to external political power. He never says that his countrymen should build their temple because the Persians explicitly say they should or otherwise encourage them to do so. Were it not for the information preserved in Ezra 5–6, we would not know that the temple work in Jerusalem received close scrutiny in Ecbatana. Ezra records a sequence that accords well with Haggai, that the initiative in 520 to comply with Cyrus's original edict of 538 for temple work lay with the Yehudites and then was approved by the Persians.

Haggai's argument was powerful, judging from the full compliance it received. He had observed the physical suffering and mental anguish of the people, who had tried hard to support themselves and could not understand why misfortunes had befallen them. The prophet traced the problem to their neglect of the temple building and insisted that the only escape from their predicament lay in the rebuilding of God's house. Only then could appropriate blessings flow and the just rewards of human labor be realized, according to the promise of the covenant.

The narrative of 1:12–15a names Haggai in the third person. Except for the oracular quotation in verse 13, the rest of this section could well be the contribution of the redactor of Haggai-Zechariah 1–8. That individual was surely a disciple of Zechariah and/or Haggai and could have been Zechariah himself. Even Haggai himself conceivably could have reported how the Yehudites reacted to his words. Although the author of this section cannot be identified, he must have formulated it prior to 515, since all of Haggai-Zechariah 1–8 was completed by that date. In other words, the report of Yehudite compliance is in all likelihood an eyewitness account.

The remarkable agreement of all the Yehudites to do what Haggai had asserted needed to be done demonstrates the power of the prophet's words and the appeal that he makes. Haggai had invoked the concept that God wanted them to carry out the restoration of the temple, and the leaders and people were evidently in full accord with that belief. The validity of a message from Yahweh through his prophet is fully accepted. The language of verses 12–15 communicates the acknowledgment of Yahweh's supremacy, and it also provides evidence of the authoritative role of the prophet in transmitting Yahweh's will.

Yahweh's sovereignty is emphasized by the repetition of the divine name. In no other section of either Haggai or Zechariah does "Yahweh" appear so frequently in so few verses. Eight times "Yahweh" is mentioned, and at least several of those occurrences are redundant. In verse 13, for example, Haggai is named as "Yahweh's messenger" and then is said to have delivered a "message of Yahweh." The audience hardly needs to be reminded, within the space of the same Hebrew sentence, that the source of the message is Yahweh.

In addition to the striking recurrence of the divine name, the appellative "their God" appears three times in this section. The threefold repetition, twice in verse 12 and once in verse 14, is unparalleled in Haggai-Zechariah 1–8, for the expression does not appear elsewhere in Haggai. Its sole use in Zechariah (6:15), although with "your" rather than "their," is in a context reminiscent of Haggai. It comes in a passage describing the eschatological temple building, when people "listen to [give heed to] the voice of Yahweh your God" and recognize prophetic authority ("Yahweh of Hosts has sent me"). Ringgren (1974:277–78) has suggested that the appellative "God" with the pronominal suffix has an implicit covenant connection. The phrase derives from the concept of the ancient allotment of Israel to Yahweh (Deut 32:8–9). The consequence of this special relationship is the covenant, which is epitomized in the statement "I will be your God, and you will be my people" (simply in Exod 6:7; Lev 26:12; in expanded form in Deut 26:17ff.; etc.; for about twenty-five passages; and Zech 8:8). In Haggai, the oracular quotation "I am with you!" of verse 13 perhaps echoes, elliptically, the covenant idea in addition to denoting God's presence. This section of Haggai otherwise reflects Deuteronomic language, such as the idea of giving heed to Yahweh's voice. The repetition of "their God" is similarly Deuteronomic. The stereotyped formula consisting of the name of God plus a pronominal suffix appears 285 times in the Book of Deuteronomy. The phrase "Yahweh your God" is a standard expression that, in Ringgren's opinion, represents the Deuteronomic concept of God, with the pronominal suffix providing a strong relational dimension to Yahweh's supremacy. Although the suffix here is "their" rather than the typical "your" or "my," the narrative context demands it; and we note that Zechariah 6:15, influenced by this passage, does have "your God."

The repetition of "their God" in Haggai emphasizes the relationship of Yahweh to his people. God's word is heeded precisely because he is connected to Israel in the covenant tradition. Because of its strong Deuteronomic connection the use of this appellative implies, in addition to God's role in calling for temple work, the validity of the covenant or of pentateuchal materials in the restoration period. Haggai explicitly allows us to observe postexilic reliance on traditional materials in the "priestly ruling" section of the next chapter (especially 2:10–14), and we refer the reader to our COMMENT on that section.

Not only does Haggai 1:12–15a herald Yahweh's authority, but also it delineates the role of prophets in delivering the word of God to the people. The direct response of the people is to the prophet who stands before them. That Haggai can elicit an immediate response is testimony to the fact that he had been accepted as a prophet of Yahweh. But that acceptance is further acknowledgment of God's authority rather than a statement of any independent prophetic authority as such. The words "message" and "messengers" as well as the verb "sent" capture the essence of the prophetic role. The words the prophet speaks are not his own; he transmits God's judgments as a courier from the Divine Court (see NOTE to "the word of Yahweh," 1:1). The people are responding to the message of the prophet in the first place and only secondarily to the person of the prophet. The first verb in verse 14 testifies to the authority of the message over the messenger. Yahweh himself is said to have brought about the activity of the people: he "roused" the leaders and the people so that they proceeded to work on his House.

Haggai's authority is only a function of his special relationship to God. Yet the prophet is accorded a prominent place in Israelite tradition so that his status does have independent value. Certainly the prophet in pre-monarchic Israel was a major leadership figure, if one thinks of Moses and of Samuel. The enormous emphasis on Moses in both Deuteronomic and priestly traditions, which were known and authoritative in Yehud as we have already suggested, surely prepared the way for the effect that Haggai and Zechariah had in the postexilic community. Without the political authority of a king whose ultimate jurisdiction could countermand the words of Yahweh even though delivered by the most eloquent or outspoken of his prophets, the unquestioned status of the prophet as God's spokesman could reemerge. The postexilic prophets recaptured the pre-monarchic situation by virtue of their ability to deliver Yahweh's commands directly to the people as well as to the leaders. They could exact ready compliance because the leadership provided by governor and priest did not possess the same kind of absolute authority that the royal figures of the monarchy had exerted, despite the warning of Samuel and the strictures of Deuteronomic law.

The description of the Yehudite response ends with a date formula, giving the day and month (September 21) of the year 520 B.C.E. The date is completed with the addition of Darius's second regnal year in verse 15b, which also initiates the next unit of Haggai, 1:15b–2:23. Less than a month has elapsed since Haggai's initial address on August 29 to Zerubbabel and Joshua and to all the people who heard the actual words of the oracles. The Yehudites had wasted no time in beginning the temple project. The several weeks involved may have been the time required for community deliberation. Or that deliberation may have taken place at once. The decision was made and the preliminary work on the temple site began immediately. The next date, about a month later (October 17) reports significant progress on the temple; people already can compare it to the preexilic building.

2. ORACLES OF ENCOURAGEMENT
(2:1–23)

Assurance of God's presence

2 ¹ In the seventh month, on the twenty-first of the month, the word of Yahweh came through the prophet Haggai: "Speak to Zerubbabel ben-Shaltiel, the governor of Judah, and to Joshua ben-Jehozadak, the high priest, and ² to allᵃ the rest of the people: ³ 'Who is left among you who has seen this House with its former glory? How do you see it now? Does it not seem like nothing in your eyes? ⁴ Now be strong, O Zerubbabel'—Oracle of Yahweh. 'And be strong, O Joshua ben-Jehozadak, O High Priest, and be strong, all you people of the land.'—Oracle of Yahweh. 'Indeed I will be with you.'—Oracle of Yahweh of Hosts. ⁵ 'Do the Word which I covenanted with you when you went forth from Egypt. My spirit is standing in your midst; do not fear.' "

⁶ For thus spoke Yahweh of Hosts: "In only a moment I will shake the heavens and the earth and the sea and the dry land; ⁷ I will shake all the nations so that all the nations will arrive with richesᵇ and thus will I fill this House with glory," spoke Yahweh of Hosts. ⁸ "The silver is mine and the gold is mine"—Oracle of Yahweh of Hosts. ⁹ "The glory of this latter House will be greater than that of the former," spoke Yahweh of Hosts; "and in this place I will grant well-being"—Oracle of Yahweh of Hosts.

Priestly ruling with prophetic interpretation

¹⁰ On the twenty-fourth of the ninth [month], in the second year of Darius, the word of Yahweh came to the prophet Haggai:

¹¹ "Thus spoke Yahweh of Hosts, 'Ask the priests for a ruling: ¹² "If someone carries sacred meat in the corner of his garment and with his corner he touches bread, pottage, wine, oil, or any foodstuff, will any of these be sanctified?" ' "

ᵃ Reading with LXX; loss of *kl* in MT due to haplography.
ᵇ Read *ḥămūdōt* for MT singular construct *ḥemdat*.

The priests replied and said, "No."

¹³ Then Haggai said, "If a person defiled by contact with a corpse touches any of these, will it be defiled?"

The priests replied and said, "It will be defiled."

¹⁴ Then Haggai replied and said, "So is this people and so is this nation before me"—Oracle of Yahweh—"and so is all the work of their hands; whatever they offer there is defiled."

¹⁵ "Now reflect back from this day. Before you set stone to stone in the Temple of Yahweh, ¹⁶ how were you?ᶜ

"Whenever one came to the grain-heapsᵈ for twenty [heaps], there were only ten; whenever one came to the wine vat to draw off fifty measures, there were only twenty. ¹⁷ I smote you, with scorching and green-mold, and with hail, and all the work of your hands, but nothing [brought] you to me."—Oracle of Yahweh. ¹⁸ "Reflect from this day forward, from the twenty-fourth of the ninth [month]. From the time when the Temple of Yahweh was founded reflect [also]. ¹⁹ Is there still seed in the storehouse? Have not evenᵉ the vine, the fig tree, the pomegranate tree, and the olive tree borne fruit? From this day I will bless you."

Future hope

²⁰ Then the word of Yahweh came a second time to Haggai on the twenty-fourth of the month: ²¹ "Speak to Zerubbabel, governor of Judah: 'I am about to shake the heavens and the earth, ²² and I am going to overthrow the throne of kingdoms and destroy the power of foreign kingdoms; and I will overturn the chariotry and its charioteers so that horses and their riders will fall, each by the sword of his brother. ²³ On that day'—Oracle of Yahweh of Hosts—'I will take you, O Zerubbabel ben-Shealtiel, as my servant'—Oracle of Yahweh—'and I will set you as my signet. For you have I chosen'—Oracle of Yahweh of Hosts."

ᶜ Reading with LXX over MT; Hebrew should read *ma-hĕyîtem*.
ᵈ Emending MT to *ʿărēmōt*, fem. pl.
ᵉ Read *ʿōd* for *ʿad*.

NOTES

2:1. *on the twenty-first of the month.* This date is toward the end of Tishri—that is, on October 17, 520 B.C.E. If this editorial dating is correct, as its specificity would indicate, nearly a month would have passed since the people responded to Haggai's initial call to work. We have argued above that the regnal date of 1:15b ("in the second year of Darius"; cf. NOTE to 1:15b) forms an envelope with the regnal year of 1:1 and thus properly belongs at the conclusion of the first chapter. Note also that the day citation of 2:1 is abbreviated. It does not include the word "day," whereas "day" does appear in the month/day information in 1:15. Perhaps this signifies that the chronological formulas ending the first chapter are intended to be fuller, making it more appropriate for the year to be part of the end of chapter 1 than the beginning of chapter 2.

Many commentators (e.g., Ackroyd 1950–51:170–71) and *BHS* have placed 1:15b at the beginning of the second chapter. While we do not accept such an arrangement, we do recognize that "in the second year of Darius," even in its placement as 1:15b, does double duty: it provides the regnal year for both the sixth month date of 1:15a and the seventh month date of 2:1.

Zerubbabel . . . Joshua. Zerubbabel's patronymic again appears in its shortened form, but his title is given along with that of Joshua. A full discussion of these leaders appears in the NOTES to 1:1.

2. *to all the rest.* The restoration of *kl* ("all") is justified not only by its attestation in the LXX but also because of a probable haplography: the scribe could well have skipped from the *l* at the end of *ʾl* ("to") to the *l* at the end of *kl.* The loss is thus caused by homoeoteleuton. The use of *šʾryt* ("rest") with "all" also occurs in 1:14. For the possible significance of this phrase, see the NOTE to "rest of the people," 1:14.

3. *Who is left among you . . . ?* That is, who is old enough to have seen the temple of Jerusalem prior to its destruction by the Babylonians in 586? This query and the two following ones imply a comparison between the preexilic temple and its present state. Individuals in their late sixties could have seen the Jerusalem temple, since about sixty-seven years would have elapsed since its destruction. However, people who could recall the temple well enough to make a comparative judgment would have to be well into their seventies. Some scholars infer from this statement that Haggai himself was an old man who had in fact seen the preexilic temple. But it is difficult to see how verse 3 provides sufficient evidence for such a supposition, while also accounting for his prophetic silence until this advanced stage of his life.

Another instance of comparison between the temples of the monarchy and of the restoration appears in Ezra 3:12–13, which refers to the emotional reaction of individuals, members of priestly families, who had been alive while the preexilic temple was still operational. Myers (1965:26) believes that the Ezra passage stems from a first movement toward reestablishing the temple—i.e., in 538 B.C.E. after the Edict of Cyrus. Such an interpretation would not accord with our argument below (see NOTES to Zech 3:8–10 and 4:6b–10a) that the Ezra passage refers to a ceremony of refoundation. Whatever the date of the event in Ezra, the tendency to relate the postexilic sanctuary to its preexilic counterpart is noteworthy for Ezra as it is for Haggai. The very fact that

Haggai raises the issue and poses it in the form of three successive questions indicates that he and, later, Ezra were part of a postexilic community keenly aware of its links with the monarchic period; Zechariah too shows strong consciousness of his preexilic cultural heritage. The set of three queries in verse 3 functions as a rhetorical device for involving all of Haggai's audience in the continuity-discontinuity tension that characterized the restoration period.

glory. Hebrew kābôd here designates splendor and perhaps also a term which can be related to God's presence as bestowing glory (see below, NOTE to v 7).

like nothing in your eyes. In Hebrew, a double usage of the comparative prefix k ("like") serves to intensify the comparison being made; cf. Gen 44:18b and Judg 8:18b. The phrase contrasts the present desolate condition of the temple with its previous glorious state, when Yahweh dwelt there and when it was also still in good repair, having been refurbished during Josiah's reign toward the end of the seventh century. However, even the preexilic temple was somewhat diminished in its physical glory at the time of the 597 deportation, in which the major golden appurtenances of the temple's interior were broken up and carried away along with the "treasures of the house of Yahweh" (2 Kgs 24:13). Because the temple's glory had already suffered at that early point, a date which would have made eyewitnesses to its post-Josianic condition well into their eighties, the rhetorical rather than literal nature of the appeal to survivors becomes somewhat more compelling.

4. be strong. Three repetitions of the verb ḥzq, "be strong," along with three subjects in the vocative case, heighten Haggai's call for action. Compare Zechariah's use of this verb in 8:9 and 13 in a more extended meaning, in a call to fearlessness, denoting emotional rather than physical strength. Haggai concludes this oracle calling for strength with the admonition not to be afraid (v 5). The obvious meaning of physical strength to effect the temple project takes on for Haggai too the extended sense of spiritual courage; with Yahweh's spirit now in Yehud, the spirit of the people receives the support it had lacked.

The root ḥzq ("to be strong") appears also, in the Hiphil, twice more in Zechariah (8:22–23). The vocabulary of Zechariah 7–8 in this and other instances has affinities with that of Haggai and helps to create an envelope forming Haggai and Zechariah 1–8 into a composite work (see Introduction, Chart 2; also see COMMENT to Zech 7–8).

O High Priest. Haggai three times (1:1,14; 2:2) gives titles to both Zerubbabel and Joshua when he mentions both of them. However, in this verse and 1:12 the high priest designation appears for Joshua but Zerubbabel's title is absent. Can this be a sign of the ascendency of the high priest over the governor from the perspective of the internal organization of the postexilic community? Surely Zechariah's visions give that impression. We refer the reader to our discussion in both NOTES and COMMENT to the prophetic vision of Zech 3:1–10 and The Crowning of 6:9–15.

all you people of the land. It is difficult to determine what is the precise political meaning of the phrase ʿam hāʾāreṣ. Although by rabbinic times it denotes a rural, unlettered populace (see Oppenheimer 1977 and literature cited therein), it exhibits a varying range of meaning in biblical times. Haggai addresses, in his oracles, only the two leaders plus "the people." Thus his usage seems to be a generalized one, indicating the general populace and not any one segment of it. That is to say, Haggai seems to include in this designation all legitimate elements of Yehudite society, landowners and citizens with full rights, whom he holds responsible for the temple rebuilding efforts. This view in Haggai comports well with the preexilic usage of ʿam hāʾāreṣ where a concept of citizenry appears (cf. 2 Kgs 14:21, which has ʿm yhwdh with 21:24) and contrasts strongly with the negative picture presented in the Chronicler (e.g., Ezra 4:4 and Neh 9:10). Halpern has recently explored the dimensions of the term "people of the land" in relationship to the Israelite monarchy (1981:190–96) and has concluded that the designation is not a technical expression for any fixed group or subgroup of the people or the tribe of the kingdom of Judah. Rather it represents the broad base of citizenry who, through both direct voice and representative assembly, played an important role in establishing and limiting royal power.

Because the decision to rebuild the temple is of momentous national importance and was previously a monarchic prerogative, Haggai's appeal to the "people of the land" or citizenry, in the same meaning as its preexilic connotation of "assembly of people," makes sense. He is hoping to legitimize an action that concerns all the people formerly subject to the Judean monarchy and therefore responsible for dealing with the monarch's programs of office. Moreover, because Haggai's usage of the phrase as a continuation of preexilic patterns is particularly appropriate to the expectations of monarchic restoration that would accompany temple reconstruction, the attempts to find in the appeal to the ʿam hāʾāreṣ some evidence of a power struggle between factions of the postexilic community seem unfounded. Hanson (1975:245–46) suggests that Haggai's address to the "people of the land" is part of a confrontation between his own hierocratic faction and a visionary group. Haggai must then appeal to the "people of the land" in order "to overpower the rival claims of opponents." While the notion of appeal to a constitutive assembly is clearly a factor in Haggai's language, that appeal, which aims to promote the ascendancy of one leadership group over another, finds no support in this text nor does it fit the ideological context.

In addition to the literature cited by Halpern, see also Andersen (1958:27–33) for a discussion of the social structure of postexilic Judah and the place of "the people of the land" in it. Ackroyd (1968:150, n. 50), in addition, provides a convenient summary and critique of some of the extensive literature on the subject.

I will be with you. Cf. NOTE to 1:13, which is echoed here.

5. *Do the Word which I covenanted with you . . .* This is a complicated sentence in Hebrew. The LXX omits it, and many commentators regard it as an editorial gloss. NEB for one excludes it from its translation; and others—NJPS, AV, RSV—translate it as part of verse 4. The problem of the location of this clause arises from the fact that in the MT the word "do," ʿāśū, actually occurs in verse 4 before " 'Indeed I will be with you'—Oracle of Yahweh of Hosts." We have translated ʿāśū with its proper object, "Word," in verse 5. The distance between verb and object does not necessarily imply a secondary insertion of a phrase but rather can be an intentional displacement of the object to heighten the authority of the command and to include citation of Yahweh's involvement. A similar situation occurs in Amos 6:14, where Yahweh's authority is cited between a verb and its direct object. While English syntax could not allow such displacement, its occasional use in Hebrew cannot be discounted. Certainly the linkage between "do" and "word" *(dābār)* is well established. The imperative ʿāśū frequently does take "word" or "words" as the direct object (see Gen 22:16; 2 Sam 17:6; Ps 33:6; 103:20; 148:8; Joel 2:11).

The covenant context of the clause as a whole is established by the relative clause "which I covenanted [= cut, made] with you when you went forth from Egypt." This clause amplifies "Word" and is very close to 1 Kgs 8:9—"which Yahweh covenanted [= cut, made] with the children of Israel when they went forth from the land of Egypt." The latter example refers to the two tablets of stone, and like the present verse it signifies the mosaic covenant at Sinai. Haggai is using somewhat elliptical language in referring, literally, to the doing of "the Word [of the covenant] which I cut with you . . ." "Word" or "words" are closely enough associated with covenant in biblical language (e.g., Exod 34:28) for *bryt* ("covenant") to be understood in instances such as this. "Word" here no doubt stands for the "words of the covenant," which in the postexilic period could well refer to the stipulations and requirements of the Pentateuch (cf. NOTES to "words and statues," Zech 1:6; "words," Zech 7:7; "the Torah . . . words," Zech 7:12).

my spirit. Although Hebrew *"rûaḥ"* usually means "breath" or "wind," it can also refer to God's presence or a manifestation thereof; cf. 1 Kgs 22:21ff. In this instance it stands for Yahweh's potent presence, which provides protection and indeed allows human fear to be removed. The associated verb, "is standing," has the effect of personifying "spirit" and making this a powerful expression of divine presence. Compare the use of God's "spirit," as the divine power to do what humans cannot do, in Zech 4:6.

do not fear. This prophetic exhortation as a negative imperative for bravery complements the threefold positive command "be strong" of the preceding verse (see NOTE). A similar combination appears in Zech 8:13 (cf. NOTES there) and serves to connect Haggai with Zech 7-8.

6. *In only a moment.* (Lit. "once again, in a little while.") Some see this as a gloss. Carroll (1979b:157, 161), for example, takes it as a prophetic response to the "cognitive dissonance created by unfulfilled prophecy" whereby the expected event is pushed into the future. However, this strikes us as quite unnecessary on semantic (see below) as well as contextual grounds; rather, it can just as well indicate the sense of urgency or immediacy perceived by the prophet in the portentous events connected with the temple rebuilding and the leadership associated with it (cf. Ackroyd 1968:153–54, especially n. 3). The prophet was sure that Yahweh would carry out great deeds; he just did not know precisely when they would occur.

The grammar of the expression is complex and requires some elucidation. The last element in the Hebrew, the fem. sing. pronoun, is presumably the copula, agreeing in gender with *ʾht.* The interesting feature is that *ʾht* intrudes into the familiar idiom *ʿôd mēʿat* ("very soon"), apparently to emphasize the imminence of the time specified; see *GKC* § 141 l; 142 f,g. The uniqueness and strangeness of the term argue in favor of its originality and make it unlikely that it was added later in an attempt to bring prophecy into line with what was predicted at an earlier date. On the contrary, the expression seems to have been coined specifically to convey a sense of the nearness of the eschatological events depicted in the rest of verse 7 and in verses 8–9.

I will shake. This is the first of three times that the Hiphil of *rʿš* ("to shake") is used for the eschatological events associated with God's entry into the sphere of human history (cf. 2:7 and 2:21 and NOTES). In verse 2:21b, exactly as in the present instance, the object of the shaking is "the heavens and the earth." This verse also includes "the sea and dry land," an addition that stresses the totality of the impact of God's action. Childs (1959:197) has convincingly demonstrated the eschatological context of the root *rʿš* in postexilic literature. Cf. the following NOTE to "riches" and the NOTE to "north-land" in Zech 6:8.

The imagery of an earthquake (= "shaking") here and in the final oracle possibly reflects the residue of political instability that accompanied Darius's accession to power in 522 B.C.E. after the death of Cambyses. However, Zechariah at about the same time shows virtually no awareness of Persian weakness (except, perhaps, in the Second Vision, 2:1–4 [RSV 1:18–21]; but see COMMENT and NOTES). And indeed, Haggai's words depict a universal world upheaval and not an insurrection in Yehud. Therefore the eschatological earthquake language appears to be rooted in old preexilic ideas and not tied to current political expectations. Similarly, the political consequences of the upheaval—Yahweh ruling the world from Jerusalem—are well established in older prophetic works (cf. Isa 2:1–4; Mic 4:1–4). In his last oracle, Haggai becomes even more political in his specification of a Davidide to be Yahweh's instrument of universal rule.

7. *all the nations . . . all the nations.* This phrase provides a universalistic dimension to Haggai's eschatological vision. The arrival in Jerusalem of all foreign political entities or their emissaries, in recognition of Yahweh's supremacy, is a theme with which the composite Haggai-Zechariah 1–8 concludes, see Zech 8:22–23 and NOTES; see also introductory COMMENT to Zech 7:1–6. The oracle of Zech 2:15 (RSV 2:11) also presents an eschatological vision of "many nations" coming to Yahweh; see NOTES to 2:15–16 (RSV 2:11–12).

riches. The simple plural *ḥămūdōt* is to be understood as the object of a preposition, "with," which does not appear and is not required in this oracular context. "Riches" also has no pronominal suffix (possessive pronoun in English), but the context makes it clear that "their" could be supplied: "all the nations will arrive with (their) riches"— i.e., they will send tribute through their ambassadors and emissaries. The pronominal suffix is under the force of the plural nominal and verbal forms. The elimination of the suffix is an important rhetorical device that appears in poetry and is quite suitable for oracular utterances, which share certain features of poetry. Note the quasi-poetic parallelistic character of the second part of verse 7, with "glory" in the second clause lacking, as is "riches," both a preposition and a pronominal suffix. Both clauses ("all nations will arrive with riches" and "thus will I fill this House with glory") inform us of the positive consequences of God's "shaking" the world. Contrast the eschatological "shaking" of verse 21 below, in which the result is calamitous for the other nations. Presumably the downfall of nations of verse 21 would then lead to their acknowledgment, as in this passage, of Yahweh's universal rule.

"Riches," along with the "silver and gold" of verse 8 (see NOTE) is part of the vocabulary of political tribute, not a simple designation of items freely sent. These words imply the deference involved when vassal nations send costly items to a foreign capital whose regime dominated theirs. The capital's symbolic role as the center of a far-flung empire was enhanced by the incorporation of items from the farthest parts of its dominion into its buildings and treasuries. The eschatological vision has Yahweh rather than any human ruler as the cosmic emperor.

glory. Like "riches" mentioned above (cf. NOTE) in this verse, "glory" *(kābôd)* also lacks both preposition and pronominal suffix. But the Hebrew syntax provides no problem, and the word can easily be translated "with my glory."

"Glory" here directly signifies the resplendent presence of God and, in particular, his presence in the sanctuary. Haggai here and in verse 9 below, and Zech in 2:9 and 12 (RSV 2:5 and 8), share with Ezekiel (e.g., 1:28; 8:4; 9:3; 10:4,18,19; 11:22,23; 43:2,4,5; 44:4) this designation of divine immanence. Rooted in royal terminology associated with the kingship of the enthroned God, "glory" in these postexilic prophets continues to associate "glory" with God's presence as the medium of divine revelation in the tabernacle or on Sinai, as found in priestly texts (Exod 24:16,17; 29:43; 40:34,35; Lev 9:6,23). This connection of glory with the tabernacle does not appear in pentateuchal texts dealing with the tent of meeting. Presumably, the royal connotation of *kābôd* could not have entered the priestly terminology until Israel itself had a monarch and a conceptual framework that would have made royal terminology meaningful (see Ps 24:8–10; 26:8; 102:15–16 [RSV 16–17]), although ancient mythological patterns could alternatively have provided such a framework. In either case, the use of royal terminology for God enhances the theocratic stance of postexilic prophecy: God's kingship becomes more prominent than ever in the absence of a human monarch. The appearance of *kābôd,* a term from the royal Zion tradition, is probably related to the many occurrences of "Yahweh of Hosts" in Haggai and Zech 1–8 (but not in Ezekiel; cf. NOTE to "Yahweh of Hosts," Hag 1:2; see also the extensive discussion of these terms in Mettinger 1982).

8. *silver . . . gold.* The designation of temple treasures as "riches" in the previous verse here receives some specificity—i.e., precious metals or, we assume, items made of precious metals. As these commodities pour into Jerusalem and to Yahweh's house, the ideas of plunder and looting associated with destruction are reversed (as Hos 13:15; Dan 11:8; 2 Chron 36:10; and especially Nah 2:10 [RSV 2:9], which mentions "silver," "gold," and "riches"). Full national treasures in the temple (cf. Ezra 1:5–11) represent the return of Yahweh's rule, exercised once more from his House in Jerusalem and now with universal acknowledgment of his sovereignty. The flow of material goods from outlying areas to a religio-political center marks the acceptance of its dominion by those outside that center.

The listing of "silver" before "gold" is probably significant with respect to the economic standards of the early restoration period. This order apparently reflects the old economy of Palestine, in which the market value of silver exceeded that of gold. A reversal of that situation occurred sometime during the Persian period, with gold replacing silver as the more valuable trade commodity. See our discussion in the NOTE to "silver and gold" of Zech 6:11.

9. *glory will be greater.* The apparent model for the present comparison is Isa 6:2–4. It is the reflected glory, *kābôd,* of the temple as perceived by the onlookers that can increase and decrease. Haggai says clearly here that the new temple will end up more glorious than the previous one. This statement would seem to contradict the fact that the first phase of the rebuilt Second Temple dedicated in 515 B.C.E. was of a very modest nature and lacked the resplendent nature of the Solomonic temple. However, this is an eschatological prophecy, when Jerusalem becomes the capital of more than Yehud, then the nations' treasures and "riches" (see NOTE to v 7) will fill the House, making its glory greater than it ever was.

place. Heb. *māqôm* can signify "holy place" or shrine; see de Vaux 1961:289, 291. However, it can also mean a wider "place," the temple section of the city or the whole city itself as the estate of God, as shown by Fisher (1963:34–41); cf. Zech 8:3. Here the temple, or Jerusalem as a whole (see Talmon 1971), becomes the locus from which God extends *šālôm,* the "peace" or "well-being" which will characterize the life of the people when God dwells in their midst.

10. *twenty-fourth.* The day of the month is given but the actual word "day" is omitted, as it is in 2:1 above and in 2:18 and 20 below as well as in Zech 7:1.

the ninth [month] in the second year of Darius. This means the month of Kislev or December 18, 520 B.C.E. According to the editorial framework, two months have passed since the first oracle of encouragement. This date, the latest in Haggai, is almost exactly two years before the latest in Zechariah (cf. first NOTE to Zech 7:1). The regnal year is supplied for the last time in Haggai.

11. *ruling.* The use of Heb. *tôrâ* here, without the definite article, is part of a new idiom that emerges from the legal texts of the Pentateuch—e.g., Exod 12:49; Lev 7:7; Num 15:16,29, etc. The closest parallel is provided by Mal 2:7, where instead of the accompanying verb *š*l we find *bqš tôrâ.* The idiom has been called "proto-rabbinic" (E. Meyers 1983) because of its similarity to later Jewish forms of *midrash halakah* (on the teaching role of the priests see the essay of Begrich 1936:63–88). It is also related to the position of the prophet in the restoration community; see COMMENT on 2:10ff. The issue addressed in this context is ritual fitness–defilement is not a matter of idolatry or of sin. Haggai refers the people to a priestly court and conveys the results to the people, utilizing this priestly teaching as a vehicle for his prophetic message. The priests' decision takes the form of a "ruling" or *tôrâ,* which might also be considered a "judgment" in the sense of a legal decision.

The phenomenon of consulting the priesthood on a matter for which only a yes or no answer is required can perhaps also be related on formal grounds to the practice of dealing with oracular questions. Both priests and prophets dealt with such inquiries in the ancient world, including Israel. We discuss this manifestation of priestly prophetic function below in relationship to the oracular question brought to Jerusalem two years later by the delegation from Bethel (see NOTES to Zech 7:3). The present query is of such a technical cultic nature, however, that it is difficult to know whether its correspondence to the oracular question of Zech 7 is more than formal. In both cases, the query about a problem is met by a prophetic utterance which goes well beyond the kind of response the situation requires, although the questions in Haggai do also offer the requisite simple "yes" and "no" answers.

12. *someone.* Heb. *?îš.* Since a priest is not specified, the person carrying meat here must be a non-priest. Thus the sacrifice would be a *šĕlāmîm* offering, the only kind of which the offerer himself can partake. Cf. Lev 7:15–16 and Milgrom 1976:766.

sacred meat. Holy meat or animal flesh, offered as sacrifice as indicated here; if, as supposed above, the *šĕlāmîm* offering is involved here, then the context of the sacred meat offering can be adduced. These offerings were brought as special sacrifice for thanksgiving, fulfillment of vows, or freewill offerings. The motivating factor would have been to secure Yahweh's blessing on the produce of the land, the flocks and herds, and the people—i.e., to encourage fertility (so Milgrom 1976:764). The other possible objectives—military victory or forgiveness of sin and impurity—can be excluded here;

the former because Yehud as a dependent polity was denied the right of having a standing army, and the latter because only a priest would have carried the sacral meat of sin or guilt offerings. Furthermore, if this verse refers to less sacred altar offerings such as tithe or festival sacrifice, then the considerations advanced above do not apply. Nevertheless, in view of the context and contents of the oracle, we believe that only the *šĕlāmîm* sacrifice could be involved in this case.

corner of his garment. On the significance of the four corners of the garment as symbols of status in the ancient world, see Bertman 1961:119–28. Cf. Deut 22:12, where the four ritual tassels are attached to the corners, or wings, of the outer garments, and 1 Sam 24:6,7,12 (RSV 24:4,5,11), where David cuts Saul's robe. The corner *(knp)* figures again in the Haggai-Zechariah 7–8 corpus in Zech 8:23 (see NOTE to "hem"), where foreigners hold on to the hem of the garment of a Yehudite in recognition of his knowledge of Yahweh.

will any of these be sanctified? That is, will the contact of an object (garment) with holy material (meat) allow that object to impart holiness to other materials (other foodstuffs)? The question here deals with indirect contact. It is doubtful that this issue would have arisen as a theoretical question; rather, it implies that sacrifices at this point were being offered, irrespective of the state of the temple building itself.

"No." The priestly answer is clear. Sanctity is apparently not communicable indirectly. Several practical considerations probably underlie the case mentioned. How did one handle such meat and what did one do with items with which such meat came indirectly into contact? The people would surely have been relieved to know that they did not have to worry about possible contamination. If holiness were contagious, then other rites would be necessary in dealing with the newly sanctified food. Thus the ruling here presented is eminently practical.

But surely it is not the pragmatic issue that Haggai wishes to bring to the attention of his audience. For the subsequent question in verse 13 about defilement, Haggai explicitly takes the priestly ruling and uses it as an analogy for the behavior of the people, thus illustrating a lesson. Haggai's interpretive expansion of the case of defilement carries with it an implicit explanation of this first-mentioned case of holiness transmission. Although defilement is contagious (the answer to the second question being affirmative), holiness in contrast is not (the answer to the first question being negative). Sanctity is much more difficult to acquire and must be generated by direct involvement or behavior. Each individual becomes responsible for adherence to standards that lead toward holiness. This lesson greatly influenced the development of classical Judaism in which adherence to the *halakah,* standards or law, became the only vehicle for achieving "godlike" status—i.e., holiness. The principle established in Haggai's implied interpretation of the first question, along with his direct treatment of the next one, became determinative for mainstream Judaism until liberal Judaism emerged in the eighteenth century and altered the *halakhic* (legal) framework that had been dominant for over two millennia. See also our NOTES to verses 13 and 14.

13. *contact with a corpse.* The negative aspect of holiness, defilement, is here at issue. Again the matter of indirect contact is posed. For the pentateuchal laws on corpse defilement, see Num 19:11–13. As in the previous question to the priests, the pentateuchal texts seem to provide straightforward answers. The authoritative status of

pentateuchal law can hence be presupposed (cf. Freedman 1963:250–65 and 1976:130–32).

replied. As in verse 12 above and verse 13 below, the word *'nh*, "reply, answer" along with "said" creates a dialogic situation which resembles the characteristic mode by which the visions of Zechariah unfold. Both prophets exemplify in this regard the propensity of the ancient Hebrew writers to communicate profound ideas through direct language. Articulated speech, that uniquely human ability, provides a ubiquitous means in the Bible for defining alternatives and expressing realities (see the discussion of dialogue-bound narration in Alter 1981:63–87).

It will be defiled. There is no clear-cut word in biblical Hebrew for "yes." One way to indicate an affirmative answer is to repeat the question as a declarative statement (cf. Gen 18:15; 29:5; and Speiser's [1964] NOTES to these verses), which is the case here: just as the priests said "no" to the first question, now they are saying "yes" to the second question. The affirmative response causes the situation considered in this question to function as the obverse of the first. Holiness cannot be communicated indirectly, but defilement can. The strong contrast between the answer to the two questions allows for the lesson of analogy drawn for the second question in verse 14 below to impart an unstated analogy with the first question. We have explored that lesson briefly in our NOTE to "No" in verse 12.

14. *this people . . . this nation.* Both these terms are applied directly here to the Yehudites. We accept the parallelism of these terms, as do May 1968:190–97, Townsend 1968:559–60, Ackroyd 1968:167–70 and n. 71, Kaufmann 1977:258–59, and others, rather than the suggestion that "nation" refers to the Samaritan or other non-Yehudites (so Rudolph 1976:49–50; Baldwin 1972:51; and Thomas 1956:1046). Talmon (1961:343, n. 24), while endorsing a similar position—i.e., that the expressions refer only to one subject (the returned exiles)—demurs by suggesting that it also might refer to adversaries (n. 24). The demurrer is unjustified. Koch (1967:52–66), in a searching form-critical analysis, has refuted the Samaritan thesis. He has also argued convincingly, through an examination of concepts regarding uncleanness, that verses 10–14 cannot be separated from their continuation in verses 15–19. Koch's position has been followed here. Haggai therefore regards the people as "unclean" or "defiled" because the temple is not yet completed and because the uncleanness that abounds cannot yet be restrained.

Zechariah in his last set of oracles uses "people" and "nations" in a rather different way, to articulate his universalistic vision. See our discussion of that section (8:18–23) and in particular the NOTES to "people" and "nations."

whatever they offer. On the meaning of sacrificial offerings as representative of all the products of human labor, see de Vaux 1961:451–52. This would be specifically appropriate to the function of the *šĕlāmîm* offering, which is implied by verse 12, rather than to sin or guilt offerings. Included among *šĕlāmîm* offerings are thanksgiving, voluntary, and votive sacrifices (Milgrom 1976:769–70).

work of their hands. While *ma'ăśēh yĕdêhem* has a variety of usages and can indicate all manner of things produced by human hands (e.g., idols, 2 Kgs 19:18; transgression, Jer 32:30; crafts, Cant 7:2 [RSV 7:1]), there is a consistent set of occurrences in Deuteronomy which have a clear agricultural intent. Deut 14:29, 16:15, 24:19, 28:12, and 30:9 all equate "work of the hands" with harvest bounty, part of which is to be returned to

Yahweh in the form of offerings (see below, 2:17). Mason (1982:144) has stressed the eschatological nature of the entire oracle (vv 10–14) and has construed "work of their hands" in general as a preparatory stage for God's work or making his presence known (cf. 1:8; 2:9) and in particular as referring to the rebuilding of the temple. Although we understand the phrase to refer to the results of manual labor, we agree with his general observation on the relation between human activity and divine action. Ackroyd (1968:166ff.) has also stressed that temple rebuilding or human activity in and of itself confers no guarantee of holiness on the community. These approaches contrast strongly with the ideas of those who would regard the prophet as a cultic prophet only and who showed little concern for ethical conduct. For a discussion of these views see Mason (1982:138–42), especially his criticism of Hanson (1975), whom he takes to task for understanding the purpose of postexilic prophecy too narrowly, as primarily historical and theocratic, and of Petersen (1977), who he believes places too much emphasis on the relationship between the fall of the monarchy and the decline of prophecy.

they offer there. Again (cf. NOTES to v 12), the functioning of the sacrificial cult is indicated by this technical term *qrb* in the Hiphil, which is found mainly in the priestly texts of Leviticus and Numbers.

is defiled. The contagion of defilement in a literal and cultic sense has its clear counterpart, in Haggai's analogy, in the larger social sphere. By drawing on a text (Leviticus) and a case that are familiar to his audience, the prophet makes his point forcefully and effectively. Failure to act in accordance with God's will in one area constitutes disobedience, or defilement, which contaminates all other activities in which the people engage. It is no wonder that their hard work has not enabled them to reap benefits, and that is exactly the situation to which Haggai next turns as he elaborates further on the principle of general contamination because of a particular act of disobedience. The belief that defilement is contagious also has moral implications that contrast with the idea of the incommunicability of holiness. It is a difficult and individual task to follow God and seek holiness, whereas the antithesis of holiness, defilement, spreads all too easily.

15. *reflect.* The effect of the threefold repetition of this phrase, once here and twice in verse 18, is exactly the same as in 1:5 and 7. All are linked by the occurrence of the verb *sîmû* which, with its object "heart," means "think about, reflect," literally "set one's heart onward." The use of "reflect" in verse 15 here anticipates its twofold use in verse 18, and the addition of several time indicators establishes the proper sequence of the events that are to be considered. In this verse "back from this day" (see following NOTE) uses *wāmāʿĕlâ* in a retrospective sense; "from this day forward" in verse 18 employs *wāmāʿĕlâ* in a future sense. A similar progression in time, using "reflect," is achieved in 1:5 and 7, by the change in verbal tense (v 6 "you have sown"; v 8 "go up in the hills"). The *miṭṭerem* ("before") in 2:15 further clarifies the retrospective context of the information provided in verses 16 and 17. The date in verse 18, the same in 2:10 and 20 (December 18, 520) specifies the present moment signified by "this day" in both verses 15 and 18. To reiterate, both 1:5–9 and 2:15–19 have chronological movement from past to future marked by "reflect"; only in the second passage is the present also marked.

The twofold repetition of the phrase "reflect from this time" in verse 18 also serves to emphasize the prophet's overall appeal to his people to attend to matters of great importance. Haggai's exhortations began in 1:5 and 7 with the same words. Their striking reappearance in this penultimate section of Haggai connects the two units (1:5–9; 2:15–19) in an envelope construction that frames all of Haggai's prophecies. Only 1:1–4, an introduction, and 2:20–23, an eschatological epilogue, stand outside the collection created by these correspondences in language.

back from this day. (Heb. *min-hayyôm hazzeh wāmā̔ĕlâ.*) This phrase, repeated at the beginning of verse 18, may be somewhat ambiguous here. However, while literally meaning "to think of the future," that thinking is to include first of all a recollection of the immediate past. Certainly original (cf. following NOTE and also NJPS and NEB), the repetition of this phrase below, along with the call to reflect on past events, effectively calls attention to the change in the people's fortunes (see v 19) since work on the temple was resumed. Alternatively, the first use of the phrase may be secondary, influenced by verse 18. Note the inconclusive treatment of *wāmā̔ĕlâ* by *BDB* (751, 1125), which reads it as either "upwards," and "back" or "onwards." LXX supports the former, reading "from this day and beforetime" for verse 15 and "from this day and upward" for verse 18. However, we prefer the first explanation because the accompanying sequence using "reflect" moves from past to future in analogous fashion with the usage found in the similar repetition of "reflect" in 1:5 and 7.

Before. Heb. *miṭṭerem,* the sole use of *min* with the preposition "before" in the Hebrew Bible. This unique construction perhaps is an indicator of the direction which the ambiguous phrase that precedes it implies—i.e., *wāmā̔ĕlâ,* meaning "before." See above NOTE to "reflect."

stone to stone. This phrase apparently refers to the masonry work which would have been a major component of the temple restoration project. It may also or alternatively denote the refoundation ceremony which involved setting forth a symbolic stone (cf. especially our NOTES to "this stone," Zech 3:9; "premier stone," Zech 4:7, "tin-stone," Zech 4:10) at the auspicious moment when work on the temple recommenced. In the overall structure of this section (2:15–19), verse 15 is closely related to verse 18 because of the repetition of "reflect" and the use of a time indicator. Since verse 18 then refers to temple refoundation, its parallelism with verse 15 may well serve to establish that "stone to stone" does indeed signify the ceremony of refoundation. We discuss this ceremony in considerable detail below in our NOTES and COMMENT to Zech 3:8–10 and 4:6b–10. If the "stone to stone" terminology is a literal reflection of the fact of the temple's being reestablished as indicated below in verse 18, then the twenty-fourth day of the ninth month may be the actual refoundation date (cf. Petersen 1974:369). That date recurs three trees in Haggai (2:10,18,20). No other date is so prominently featured. Perhaps it has earned that prominence by denoting a pivotal event in the history of the postexilic period: the refoundation of Yahweh's House. Through such action, Zerubbabel and Joshua would have established continuity with earlier building efforts in the days of Cyrus as well as with the preexilic temple itself.

Temple. Hebrew *hêkāl* is translated "temple" when it is combined with Yahweh. However, the Hebrew word like its Canaanite and Ugaritic cognates (from Akkadian *êkallu* and originally Sumerian *é-gal,* "big house") actually means "palace." Its cultic usage is derived from the royal vocabulary of the ancient Near East, and it can designate any large, luxurious dwelling (e.g., 1 Kgs 21:1; Isa 13:22). Like "House of God" (cf. 1:2,4,9; 2:7,9), it too expresses the concept of a temple as the dwelling place for a deity (cf. C. Meyers 1985). In the Bible, when it appears with the definite article, *hêkāl* sometimes is used for the large main room or outer sanctum, between the "porch" or forecourt and the holy of holies, or inner sanctum, of the Jerusalem temple (as in 1 Kgs 6:5,17; Ezek 41:1, etc.). Haggai apparently uses this term interchangeably with "House of Yahweh," although the latter appears somewhat more frequently, with *hêkāl* used only here and in verse 18 below, which parallels this verse in its use of "reflect" plus its reference to the temple foundation. Zechariah too uses both terms, and in one climactic passage (8:9; see NOTES to that verse) the two designations for temple are used together, along with two expressions for the building/founding of Yahweh's earthly dwelling.

16. *how were you?* Literally, "how was it for you?" Our translation uses the LXX over the difficult MT *mihyôtām;* see Text Note c. Confusion probably arose when the scribe wrote two words as one: *ma* ("what" or "how") and *hĕyîtem* ("were," second m. pl.).

Whenever . . . whenever. Verse 16 is difficult because of its elliptical, semipoetic character; but MT in its present form can be understood without resorting to emendation. The problems arise from the absence in verse 16a of a word that parallels *yeqeb* ("wine vat") in 16b and from the absence of a word for measure (which we have supplied as ["heaps"]) in 16a parallel to that of *pûrâ* for "measure" in 16b. In addition, the first line has no infinitive corresponding to "to draw off" *(laḥśôp)* of the second line. The versions and commentaries all reflect the confusion caused by these omissions as well as the further complication arising from the fact that, on analogy with Isa 63:3, *pûrâ* ("measure") can also mean "winepress." *BDB* (807) explains *pûrâ* as a "measure of juice from one filling" of the wine press; and that comprehensive definition, involving both container and the measure it contains, is the one preferred by Mitchell (1912:69, 74).

The following organization shows the quasi-symmetry of these two lines:

	syllables
bā' 'el 'ărēmōt 'eśrîm	7
wĕhāyĕtâ 'ăśārâ	7
bā' 'el hayyeqeb laḥśôp hamiššîm pûrâ	11
wĕhāyĕtâ 'eśrîm	6

The first clause of the second line is obviously longer than its parallel clause because of the presence of the verb ("to draw off," *laḥśôp*) and the unit of measure, *pûrâ*. The omission of the verb in the first line is not unusual, considering the poetic nature of the two lines; and the use of a unit of measure would be redundant in Hebrew. The second clauses or cola are closer, with "twenty" in the second forming a six-syllable unit because the word "twenty" has two syllables as opposed to the three that "ten" has.

The difficulty with *pûrâ* in the second line is not unlike that of *'ărēmā,* of the first line. This term can be translated either "heap" or "grain-heap," the former probably signifying a unit measure and the latter the place where piles of grain were stored or heaped up (so Jer 50:26; Ruth 3:7; Cant 7:3 [RSV 7:2]). In 2 Chron 31:6–9, the plural "grain-heaps" designates piles of tithes—i.e., "the tithes of cattle and sheep" and "the tithes of dedicated things." Therefore we have accepted an emendation of MT feminine singular construct to read *ʿărēmōt*, a feminine plural (see Text Note d). This alteration requires no change in the consonantal MT if we adopt a defective spelling. The overall meaning of the verse is clear, the problems of text and ellipsis notwithstanding. The yields of grain and wine were 50 percent or 60 percent less than expected. As in 1:6 and 9, total deprivation is not the issue; rather, only partial realization of the desired situation of plenty has been achieved. As in 1:6–11, Haggai emphasizes the less than satisfactory returns on the agrarian efforts of his countryman in order to relate such conditions to the status of Yahweh's House. The retrospective depicting a less than flourishing economy is used here, however, and a prelude to the prophet's assertion of what the reestablishment of the temple has achieved. This verse provides effective contrast with the amplitude of harvest, following temple refoundation, depicted in verse 19 below. The harvest will be a sign of divine blessing (2:19), and the shortages described in this verse are an indication of God's displeasure (cf. first NOTE to 1:6).

17. *scorching and green-mold, and with hail.* These three disasters are listed as part of the careful structure of the whole verse; see following NOTE.

Agricultural products (cf. 2:14) are failing because of natural disasters. All three of these disasters are associated in particular with either of the two transitional periods, April/May or October/November, falling between the dry season and the rainy season in the Palestinian calendar. "Scorching" refers to the destruction of standing crops by the sirocco or east wind (Scott 1962b:4); and hail damages plants during the unstable weather of the transitional season. Since this prophecy refers back to a time before temple work had begun—i.e., before the sixth month—the crucial spring shift from winter to summer must be involved. The fall harvest, which is the setting for this prophet's activity, would have been severely limited because of damage to crops when buds were forming in the spring (see Hareuveni 1980:35–37, 59–60). Compare the language of Deut 28:22 (Amos 4:9; but see following NOTE), which omits "hail" but which describes God's response to the people's disobedience: "Yahweh will smite you with . . . heat and drought, blight, and mildew."

but nothing [brought] you to me. This phrase is among the most difficult in Haggai and is usually taken to be a corrupt quotation of Amos 4:9 (Mitchell 1912:70). The beginning of verse 17 does indeed contain language similar to that of Amos ("I smote you with blight and with mildew"); and this line apparently echoes the familiar refrain found in Amos (4:6,9,10,11), "and yet you did not [re]turn to me." The LXX reads Haggai exactly like Amos; *BHS* adopts that reading. However, the required emendation would not resolve all the problems in the MT. It would produce the following translation: "Yet you did not return to me" (RSV, *et al.*). As it stands, MT literally reads: "And not (or nothing) you unto me." The verb is missing in the Hebrew. As vocalized, *ʾetkem* ("you") has the sign of the definite direct object but has no verb to govern it.

A somewhat analogous situation is found in Hos 3:3, where the omission of the verb *bwʾ* is purposeful, probably because the idiom *bwʾ ʾl* is often associated with sexual union. The usage in Hosea, though it has a sexual connotation, transcends sexuality and hence omits the verb (Andersen and Freedman 1980:305). Here in Hag 2:17, however, there is no hint of avoidance due to sexual overtones, although the missing verb could well be *bwʾ*. The Hiphil of that verb, "to bring," is nearly always associated with the objects, offerings, and gifts that people are required to bring to Yahweh (*BDB*:99). The Hiphil also occurs frequently with *'l;* and *'tkm* plus *'l,* like the "you to me" of this verse, occurs three times in the Hebrew Bible with the verb *šlḥ* (2 Kgs 22:15; Jer 37:7; 2 Chron 34:23). The elimination of the verb here would seem to be intentional, as the following considerations also indicate.

This line comes directly after an excellent example of chiasm which is not present in Amos 4:9 and hence suggests that Haggai's citation of natural disasters is original and not derivative. The chiasm in the first clause of verse 17 involves two sets of nouns and pronouns which follow the archaic verb "I smote," which has the troublesome lack of a parallel in the second line ("nothing [brought] you to me"). The following arrangement of the line beginning "I smote" reveals the chiasm:

17aA *hikētî 'etkem bašidāpôn ūbayyērāqôn*   I smote you with scorching and green-mold;
17aB *ūbabārād 'ēt kōl ma'ăśê yĕdêkem*   and with hail all the works of your hands.

	verb	pronoun	noun	noun
		noun	noun (+ noun)	pronoun

17bA *wĕ'ēn 'etkem [hēbi'] 'ēlay*   and [nothing] brought you to me—
17bB *nĕ'ūm–yhwh*   Oracle of Yahweh.

The definite direct object "you," *'etkem* in 17aA, is followed by three nouns expressing means or agency, all of which occupy the center of the line and which express three different kinds of disaster. At the end of 17aB a repetition of the definite direct object sign *'t* is followed by a noun and then another noun that ends with the second m. pl. suffix (*yĕdêkem*, "your hands"). We have divided the line after "green-mold" around the middle; the single-word indirect object ("you") is followed by two nouns expressing the means of the blight. "With hail" begins the second colon; it is a third agent of destruction, followed by a longer description of the indirect object ("all the work of your hands"), which ends in Hebrew with the pronominal suffix "your." This arrangement brings balance, with the short indirect object and the two means of disaster ("scorching," "green-mold") occupying one colon, and the third means of disaster ("hail") alone accompanying the longer indirect object of the second colon.

This elegant structure has the effect, in addition to creating cola of proportionate components, of having the direct and indirect combinations begin and conclude with prepositions in Hebrew ("you," "your"). The emphasis on prepositions anticipates the succeeding line (17bA), which also has two pronouns ("you," "me") in just one colon. The omission of the verb in that colon, the problem discussed at the beginning of this NOTE, may perhaps be understood also as a further way to emphasize the pronouns, complementary to the use of the pronouns in the previous line. Finally we note that 2:17b, without a verb, forms a neat chiastic contrast with Hag 1:13, which reads *'ani 'ittĕkem nĕ'ūm–yhwh:* " *'I* am with *you!'*—Oracle of Yahweh." Here we have: " 'nothing [brought] *you* to *me'*—Oracle of Yahweh."

Because of all these subtleties, the verb's absence, though unusual, seems more logical than if it were present. The point is, verb or no verb, that "nothing" brought man to God, not even scorching, green-mold, and hail. Man brings many things to God: cereal offerings, animals, etc., but the reverse of that does not necessarily follow; that is the emphasis of the present enigmatic phrase.

18. *Reflect from this day forward.* See first two NOTES to verse 15. The repetition of these words, referring to the past in verse 15 and to the future here, allows the prophet to create a sense of the causal relationship comparing two things, the present event of temple work (or lack of it) and the past, and the present event and the future.

twenty-fourth of the ninth [month]. This is the same date as verse 10—i.e., December 18, 520 B.C.E.—and thus is thought to be an editorial insertion, so *BHS,* Ackroyd 1950–51:166–67, and Amsler 1981:28. Rudolph (1976:44,46,51–52) retains the phrase, changing "ninth" to "sixth," taking the date in Hag 1:15 as the one that refers to the commencement of work. The threefold repetition of this date, however, in 2:10,18, and 20 is intended to emphasize the significance of the major event, a temple refoundation ceremony, of December 520, approximately a month after Zechariah began to prophesy (Zech 1:1) in anticipation of that event and three months after the preliminary labors, probably of clearing the rubble and accumulation supplies, had begun. The repetition of the date also accentuates the link between the two units of chapter 2 (2:1–19 and 2:20–23) and heightens the intensity of the final oracle. To be sure, the date in 1:15 of September 21, 520, when temple work was initiated, represents a critical turning point in Haggai's prophetic mission; but so does this date. In the absence of compelling versional or contextual support, there seems to be no reason to alter or delete the existing chronological information on the sequence of times referred to in chapter 2. See NOTE above to "reflect" in 2:15; on the general chronological framework see first NOTE to 1:1.

reflect. Repeated for the third time in this section, it here refers to the immediate past. In the first instance (v 15, see NOTE) it referred to the most distant past. The second usage, at the beginning of this verse, points to the future. The prophet seems to be stressing the conditionality of events, using the near-and-far-past sequence as evidence that human behavior has its consequences.

from the time when. Literally, "since the day when."

founded. That is "re-founded." The Hebrew root is *ysd,* "to establish, found." Many translators and commentators take this to mean that "the foundation was/are/hath been laid" (e.g., RSV, NJPS, NEB, *KAT ad loc*). If these translations and analyses understand this as a literal or structural laying of the foundation, then we would reject such a notion. First, some preliminary temple work may already have taken place shortly after Cyrus's edict in 538 B.C.E., in which case Haggai's countrymen would probably not have been laying foundations (cf. first NOTE to 1:8). Second, the verb *ysd* is not necessarily limited to the matter of setting foundation stones, as Andersen (1958:13–22) and Gelston (1966:232–35) have both argued convincingly. Perhaps the biblical passage most relevant to this second consideration is the account in 2 Chron 24:27 of Joash's accomplishments. In that verse he is said to have "restored the house of God." The nature of his restoration work is indicated in 2 Chron 24:12–15, which records his arrangement for having artisans (masons, carpenters, metalworkers) hired to repair, strengthen, and renew the temple. The collective results of this activity are indicated in verse 27 by *wîsôd bêt hā'ĕlōhîm* ("and the founding [= restoring] of the House of God"). Third, archaeological evidence in general shows that the destruction of buildings or cities through warfare rarely if ever involved total razing. Indeed, archaeological stratigraphy is continually frustrated by the repeated use of the same materials from not only foundations but also much of the superstructure of walls in successive strata. Destruction levels are marked by burn layers, representing the conflagration of wooden parts of buildings and sometimes also by the decay of mud brick. The foundation courses are below level and these cannot be destroyed without being dug up, an extremely unlikely action for a conquering army to take. Thus, not even the beginning of restoration work can be construed as the literal laying of foundation stones.

While the notion of laying an actual foundation must be rejected, the use of *ysd* ("to found") surely indicates a symbolic founding. The decision to build, or rebuild, a house for a deity was one of the most important decisions that a community could make in the ancient Near East. The very fact that two canonical prophets, Haggai and First Zechariah, are concerned almost solely with such a decision reflects the significance of temple building. Temple projects, whether the erection of new buildings or the reestablishment of older ones, evidently conformed to a typological sequence of ceremonial events (Hurowitz 1983) which brought divine sanction and public support to the enterprise. The founding or refounding ceremony was an integral part of that sequence. Our NOTES to Zech 4:7–10, to Hag 1:2, "to be built," and elsewhere provide extensive discussion of the temple as a religio-political institution and of the dynamics of the actual temple refoundation ceremony as well. See the report in Ezra 3:6–11. As we have also pointed out in our various NOTES to this passage (2:15–19), the repetition of the date formula and the emphasis on "this day" point to the significance of the moment of temple refoundation, the ceremony which marked simultaneously its origin in 520 and its contact with the old temple in Jerusalem.

19. *still seed.* The summer wheat harvest must provide not only grain for consumption but also seed for planting. Since wheat *(Triticum durum L)* is sown with the first winter rains (mid October-November), this query is appropriate to a date late in the ninth month, December. Seed would have been sown, and grain still remains for sustenance. To avert famine conditions, household granaries must contain enough to meet household food needs until the next harvest, and they must also contain sufficient grain to be used for planting, lest there be no succeeding harvests. The question of "seed in the storehouse" epitomizes the fragile dividing line in Palestine between need and plenty.

The *ʿôd* ("still") with which verse 19 opens in Hebrew is probably intended to govern both rhetorical questions, although it is repeated in the second question (see next NOTE).

even. This second *ʿd* (see previous NOTE) is probably a defective spelling of the same word, and its appearance may be intended to provide continuity between the two rhetorical questions. The defective spelling is the usual northern spelling but may not be intentional here; the *waw* could easily have fallen out in transmission (cf. Job 1:16,17,18).

vine . . . fig . . . pomegranate . . . olive. All the designated species involve a late summer harvest and may represent an actual agricultural sequence, terminating with the late olive harvest. These trees and vines have all survived whatever natural disasters could have impeded their productivity at the time of the formation of their fruits in the spring. The vine and the olive, along with the grain (cf. "seed" above), constitute the three basic food crops of Palestine (cf. Hag 1:11); and the fig and pomegranate were part of the "seven species" which, along with "honey" and the three basic foodstuffs, characterize the hill country in Deut 8:8. The pomegranate, however, differs from the fig in that it was not a staple (Zohary 1982:62). Its inclusion in this list therefore provides an image of abundance, and not mere subsistence. The association of abundance with temple building, or rebuilding, is a recurring concern of Haggai's in his statements about the temple project. The construction of a sacred building, according to Near Eastern typology, should be the cause of prosperity (cf. last NOTE to this verse). Haggai's imagery reflects that typology.

from this day. This is the third repetition of this phrase within verses 15–19. Like the threefold repetition of "reflect" (see NOTES to that word in 2:15,18), it is interspersed throughout this unit and helps focus on the significance of the "day" to which it refers, probably the occasion of the temple refoundation ceremony (as explained in our NOTE to "found" in 2:18). "From this day" occurs near the outset of 2:15–19 and again here, almost at its conclusion; its usage thus constitutes an envelope which organizes the intervening material into a unit.

I will bless you. The agricultural bounty specified in the two preceding rhetorical questions is the material expression of God's blessing, just as the covenant blessings of Leviticus 26 and Deuteronomy 28 are enumerated in terms of agrarian as well as human fertility. (Cf. NOTE to "blessing" in Zech 8:13.) The Israelite belief that the temple was the source of agricultural plenty and fertility as a consequence of God's presence there is to be found in Canaanite mythology (Cross 1973) as well as in Mesopotamian temple texts (Bewer 1919; Lundquist 1983). Such a belief was an integral part of the ancient Near Eastern worldview in which temple ideology played an essential if not determinative role in the organization of society. In the context of developing a temple typology which identifies common Near Eastern ideologies surrounding temple building, Lundquist reviews Mesopotamian texts that associate the construction of a temple with "abundance and prosperity" (1982:2,6). Fertility is only one of many items associated with temple building that place the prophecies of Haggai and Zechariah within the general ideological framework surrounding temple building in Israel and the ancient Near East. Throughout Haggai-Zechariah 1–8 the administrative restructuring of Yehud, a kind of state formation in itself, is linked with the construction of God's house in Jerusalem (cf. above, NOTE to 1:2, "to be built," and *passim* in Zech).

Although Lundquist has provided extensive evidence for a common Near Eastern temple typology, Julius Bewer (1919) was the first modern scholar to note the similarity between Haggai's notion of blessing and the idea of abundance recorded in the cylinder inscriptions of the neo-Sumerian temple hymns of Gudea of Lagash. Bewer translated a particularly apt portion of Gudea cylinder A as follows:

> When the foundations of my temple will be laid, abundance shall come. The great fields shall bring forth for thee (fruit), (the waters of) the ditches and channels shall rise out of the fissures of the ground, whence the water no longer sprang forth, water shall spring forth. In Shumer oil shall be poured forth in abundance, wool shall be weighed in abundance (1919:129).

More recently Petersen (1974:369) has identified the Mesopotamian *kalû* ritual as lying behind Haggai's idea of connecting a period of bounty and blessing with the program of temple building (cf. NOTES to Hag 2:15 and Zech 4:7ff.). The day on which such benefits would accrue to the people would be the day of ritual dedication, "the day when the continuity between the old and new temple would be ritually declared" (ibid.). At Ugarit fertility would usually follow the enthronement of the god in the temple.

For Hanson, however, the persistence in Haggai of such a view is perceived as something entirely negative (1975:249): "It is this resurgent mythical equation of temple structure and prosperity, and this inability to conceive of the presence of Yahweh apart from the temple edifice, which sets Haggai apart from the preexilic prophets and explains the bitter opposition which his message met from groups regarding themselves as carriers of the prophetic tradition." However, the recognition that Haggai is expressing a common Near Eastern temple theme need not involve so narrow an understanding of the biblical metaphor. Rather, the fact that Haggai draws upon such a typology implies that he sees it in its entirety: semiautonomy is restored to Yehud, and social harmony is reestablished. These are hardly issues of limited cultic import. Yahweh's favor as represented in the abundance or blessing of the land need not be construed to mean that rebuilding of the temple brought about any guarantees of divine favor. Similarly, Haggai hardly suggests that Yahweh could be worshipped or approached only in his Jerusalem temple. Perhaps because of the brevity of his utterances, Haggai has been misunderstood on this critical point. By expressing his words in the vocabulary of a common Near Eastern language and metaphor, however, the prophet has rendered his oracles more vivid and immediate and hence more effective (on this point see Ackroyd 1968:169–70) to his own audience. We moderns fail to grasp this unless we properly appreciate the pivotal role of the temple in ancient society.

20. *second time.* That two divine revelations take place on this auspicious day, the "twenty-fourth of the month" or December 18, 520, further underscores that day's significance. Compare the repetition of terminology in the preceding unit (such as "reflect," "from this day," "forward/backward"), which also emphasizes the importance of that day, probably the occasion of the temple's refoundation ceremony (so in our NOTES to "founded," 2:18, "stone to stone," 2:15, and elsewhere).

21. *governor of Judah.* See NOTES and COMMENT to 1:1. Zerubbabel is addressed as governor, not as Davidide; his patronymic, which connotes lineage, is omitted.

I am about to shake. This Hiphil verb from the root *rʿš* has a distinct eschatological dimension which is present here and which is sustained in the following verse by the verb "I am going to overthrow." The Hiphil of *rʿš* is used above in verses 6 and 7, where it also has distinct political and future overtones (cf. NOTES to "riches" and "shakes" in 2:7, to "northland" in Zech 6:8, and also to the following NOTES).

22. *overthrow.* The verb *hpk* is used for divine intervention in human affairs. Such action could involve the overthrow of political entities, such as Sodom and Gomorrah (Gen 19:21ff.; Deut 29:22 [RSV 29:23]; Amos 4:11) and Nineveh (Jonah 3:4). In the former case, a violent natural catastrophe is involved. In the latter, it is not clear how Nineveh will be overthrown, although the military language of Haggai ("chariotry," "charioteers," "horses," "riders," "sword") features prominently in Nahum's invectives against that city (Nah 3:1ff.).

As indicated in the preceding NOTE, the orientation here, as above in 2:6–7, is eschatological. That future context, however, does not in any way diminish the import for the prophet's own day of this final oracle, which anticipates the end of any foreign domination, no matter how benign or minimal, over Yehud. God assuredly and in due course will reestablish his world sovereignty by dramatic means. Haggai's language is more vivid in this respect than anything in Zechariah 1–8 and suggests that hopes for full political independence, which would be the ultimate consequence of Yahweh's return to his residence in Jerusalem, were stronger for him than for Zechariah.

throne of kingdoms. Perhaps this is an oblique reference to the Persian dynasty, the rulers of an empire composed of many political entities, and the sovereign power in the ancient world at this time. "Throne" refers to the locus of authoritative rule; cf. the two uses of this term in Zechariah 6:13, where it refers to the reign of the future king and of the ruling high priest (see NOTES there to "sit upon his throne" and "on his throne").

destroy . . . overturn. These words are reflective of military terminology expressing Yahweh's power to affect the course of human events. Cf. Exod 15:1ff.; Hab 3:3ff.; Zech 9:10–14, and preceding NOTES. "Overturn" is an alternative translation of the same verb *hpk*, "overthrow," that expresses the action of the first part of the first clause in this verse. The repetition of the identical Hiphil of the verb continues to maintain the imagery of the reversal that will take place in human affairs and prepares the audience for the next event in the sequence—i.e., the replacement for foreign imperialism. The replacement appears in the climax to this section, and to all of Haggai, in verse 23.

foreign kingdoms. The repetition of "kingdoms" *(mmlkwt)* in the second part of the first clause appears awkward. The editor of *BHS* proposes to delete it as a dittography. However, a subtle difference may exist between the two usages so that they complement each other. "Throne of kingdoms" may refer to the ruler or dynast controlling all the kingdoms composing the empire, with "foreign kingdoms" (literally, "kingdoms of nations") representing the constituent polities. Compare the use of "nations" above in 2:7.

chariotry . . . charioteer. "Chariots" *(merkābôt)* figure prominently in Zechariah's Seventh Vision (6:1), and "riders" *(rōkbîm)* appear in his First Vision (1:8); see NOTES to those verses. Although only the singular form of "rider" is used in Zech 1:8 it is quite clear from the context that there are several "riders." The singular form *merkābâ* ("chariotry") is used here. Both terms are associated with military prowess, since chariotry in antiquity—from the end of the second millennium and thereafter—was the key to military dominance. The utilization of this imagery in the final oracle of Haggai is an expression of the prophet's awareness that great power will be required, for the present worldwide regime will give way to Yahweh's global sovereignty.

23. *On that day.* Standard prophetic language for future, eschatological time, as in Amos 9:11; Hos 2:18; Jer 25:33; Zech 13:2, 14:4ff. The day anticipated by Haggai is the day in which the Yehudites will once again achieve political independence and self-rule under the Davidide Zerubbabel, Yahweh's representative.

O Zerubbabel ben-Shealtiel. This is the seventh and final occurrence of the name of Zerubbabel in the Book of Haggai. His patronymic is spelled in the full or plene formal style as in 1:1 and thus forms an envelope construction with the opening. In Zechariah, Zerubbabel's name occurs only four times, all in the Oracular Insertion of chapter 4, where no patronymic is included. In Haggai, a work which bears the signs of being deliberately crafted, these subtle differences are hardly accidental. The placement of Zerubbabel's name between two verbs at either end forms a chiasm, emphasizing his unique role in God's plan. The seven occurrences of Zerubbabel's name further symbolize the important role that Haggai sees for him, insofar as seven is a sacred number in the Semitic world.

The naming of a historical personage to figure in God's eschatological purpose is unique in Hebrew prophecy. In this respect Haggai differs from his fellow prophet Zechariah, who nowhere employs Zerubbabel's name in an eschatological context. Consequently Haggai has been labeled narrow, particularistic, nationalistic, and even overly historical (e.g., James 1934:233–35; Hanson 1975:176–77). However, this final oracle expresses the prophetic hope for the reestablishment of a Davidic scion solely as an instrument of Yahweh's universal sovereignty. Perhaps the universal dimension of his last oracle is not so pronounced as that of Zechariah's concluding oracles (Zech 8:18–23), but it would be unfair to see in Haggai merely an expression of political chauvinism. Haggai uses Zerubbabel's name because he was profoundly aware, in light of his political and cultural heritage, of the implications of temple building. The potential for Yahweh's rule from his dwelling in Jerusalem would begin at once, with the restoration of the temple; and so it was only logical for Haggai to cite Zerubbabel as the Davidide at hand.

For Haggai, the eschatological establishment of Yahweh's cosmic sovereignty is discernible in the present situation of temple construction with which he has been so involved. Whether he expected also to witness the transformation of Yehud into a fully independent nation-state in the near future is difficult to say, for the very nature of eschatology entails a willingness to move that time progressively forward. Zerubbabel's role in Yehudite governance, however, has stimulated the prophet to place "that day" in a time frame which, while in the future, could well be at hand. Haggai's words do not at all suggest that Zerubbabel himself sought to achieve, in reality, regnal powers. In the prophet's eschatological language, he is the passive designee of Yahweh's plan for sovereignty. The two words, "servant" and "signet," with which Haggai characterizes Zerubbabel's role (see following NOTES) are both terms of instrumentality and hence do not suggest direct monarchic powers.

my servant. Used to describe Zerubbabel's place in the future organization of the world, "servant" is an ancient biblical term used to describe the ideal role of the Israelite ruler in intimate relationship to Yahweh's supremacy. De Vaux (1972:154) points out that this title is reserved for David (e.g., 2 Sam 3:18; Ps 78:70; Ezek 34:23ff.; 37:24). It is not used for Solomon (except in prayers that the Deuteronomic editor ascribes to him) or for any other king (except once for Hezekiah, by the Chronicler in 2 Chron 32:16). Clearly "servant" was not a normal designation for an incumbent king of Israel or Judah. Haggai's use of the term for a Davidide surely places him in the tradition of earlier prophets, such as Isaiah and Jeremiah, who used the "servant" terminology in their prophecies of the future. The term places Zerubbabel, or anyone else so designated, in a subservient relationship to Yahweh, who emerges as the sovereign ruler. Zerubbabel's role, therefore, as a ruler in and of himself is not indicated in this oracle. Both "servant" and "signet" (see below) emphasize his instrumentality and not his independence.

The contrast between Haggai's use of "my servant" and Zechariah's in 3:8 reveals the rather striking difference in perspective that each held. In the Supplementary Oracle of Zechariah 3:8 Zerubbabel's name is never mentioned, though his participation in a temple ceremony of refoundation is assumed. Moreover, Zech 3 as a whole is focused primarily upon Joshua; and the term which accompanies "my servant" there is "the Shoot." The presence of a Davidic scion has not only been fully eschatologized in Zechariah, but it has also been deemphasized as is evident in Zech 4:6b (see NOTES and COMMENT to Zech 3:8–10 and 4:6b–10a). Haggai's expectations emerged from the historical present, which involved the rebuilding of the temple and the immediate potential for a monarchic state under the rule of a Davidide who in all likelihood would be Zerubbabel. That Zechariah was far less specific on this matter was probably a function of his much greater concern for the mechanics of day-to-day administration of Yehud, in which the priesthood was ascendant. Yet he sought to convince his audience that Zerubbabel's limited authority as Persian appointee did not preclude the future restoration of an independent Davidic state. For Zechariah, unlike Haggai, the present restoration era with its new internal organization was one that would surely endure for some time to come.

my signet. The two verbs in this verse, "take" and "set," are used in parallel, with Zerubbabel and "you" (referring to Zerubbabel) as direct objects. Therefore the two nouns designating him also have a parallel status. "Servant" has a first-person singular suffix: "my." "Signet" does not, but it appears with the definite article. Literally, it reads "I set you as the signet" and is probably elliptical for "I set you as the signet on my finger/hand" (as in Jer 22:24). For these reasons, we have translated it as *"my signet"* rather than *"the signet."*

A signet *(ḥôtām)* or seal, usually on a ring or otherwise attached to a chain or thong so that it could be worn on one's person, was an individual's official signature in the ancient world (see Tufnell 1962:254–59 and Toombs 1962). In particular, royal or official acts were authorized through the use of a monarch's seal (so 1 Kgs 21:8; cf. Seybold 1971–72:69–78 and our NOTE to "stone" in Zech 3:9). Archaeological excavations have produced quantities of seals and seal impressions that can be categorized as signets. Some of them are inscribed with artistic motifs, ranging from mythological scenes to geometric designs, divine emblems, assorted animals and plants, and stylized human figures. Others included a person's name or feature it alone without an accompanying design. These seals with names, particularly in the Persian period (cf. NOTE to "engraved" in Zech 3:9), designated high officials. The use of such a seal was the way of carrying out the authority of the person to whom the seal belonged. "My signet" in Haggai means Yahweh's signet, through which his sovereignty will be exercised.

"Signet" is therefore a marvelous metaphor for the concept of Yahweh's cosmic and supreme rule being effected on earth through a designated "servant" who would be his signet, assigned to carry out the divine will. The imagery dramatically reverses that found in Jeremiah: " 'As I live'—Oracle of Yahweh—'even if Coniah ben Jehoiakim, King of Judah, were the signet of my right hand, even from there would I tear you off and give you into the hand of those who seek your life . . .' " (Jer 22:23–25). Coniah (= Jehoiachin, the grandfather of Zerubbabel according to 1 Chron 3:17–19), even if he were God's signet—which he isn't—would still be wrenched away for not having heeded God's word. Judean kings, in other words, should be carrying out Yahweh's will as his signet; but none of them were doing so. In Haggai's words, only the eschatological ruler will have that intimate and trusted relationship with Yahweh. Only Zerub-babel will be God's signet.

Like "servant," the term "signet" places Zerubbabel in a subservient relationship to Yahweh. He may exercise great authority, but that royal power would come to him in his role as a vice-regent. Haggai uses no language that refers directly to Zerubbabel as king, and the eschatological orientation thus remains constant. The authenticity of this oracle, it should be noted, is evident in that Zerubbabel, as far as we know, never did become more than a Persian governor. The oracle was never fulfilled, yet it remained part of Haggai's prophecies.

For you have I chosen. The oracle closes with the verb *bḥr,* "to choose," a verb directly associated with the dynastic hope of the house of David in Ps 78:70: "He chose David his servant, and took him from the sheepfolds . . . [71] to be the shepherd of Jacob his people, of Israel his inheritance" (RSV). Zerubbabel as future Davidic scion is singled out through the use of this verb. "Choose" is an ancient term used, with God as the subject, to describe God's choice of a king (cf. the use of *bḥr* in God's choosing of Jerusalem in NOTES to Zech 1:17; 2:16 [RSV 2:12]; 3:2). The element of scrutiny in the root *bḥr* is appropriate to the idea that, for so important an office, Yahweh looks carefully at qualifications before making his appointment. As with "servant," the notion of God's choosing a king does not appear for any king after David (although it is used once in 2 Sam 16:18 for Absalom, who never in fact became king). David, like Saul before him, receives his designation for the kingship through the use of *bḥr* (1 Sam 10:24; 2 Sam 6:21); no subsequent ruler is so described. While this may have something to do with the military factors present in the original establishment of a monarchy and no longer present after that event (Seebass 1975:77), it is clear that dynastic succession in itself would have precluded the exercise of Yahweh's choice. The resurgence in prophecy of the word "choose" implies a break in dynastic succession and anticipates the eschatological rule of a righteous and just king after the model of an idealized David. Such is the case in Isa 42:1, where "choose" appears together with "servant," as well as in this verse. The last verse of Haggai provides a powerful conclusion to the prophet's message: the future is in Yahweh's hands and will unfold according to his discerning plan.

COMMENT

Assurance of God's presence, 1:15b–2:9

After less than a month, Haggai once more speaks in the name of Yahweh. As in the previous section, he addresses the civil leader Zerubbabel, the priestly leader Joshua, and the people. These three components of his audience are named first in God's call to the prophet in verse 2. They appear a second time, although the terminology used for the third group is altered, in the oracle of verses 3–5, in the course of a direct command to each of them to show strength in the task at hand. The full listing of the prophet's audience twice in this section emphasizes once more the prophetic role as mediary between God and God's people.

The Yehudites, according to the information contained in 1:12–15a, had rallied to Haggai's exhortations to rebuild Yahweh's house. Now he is offering further support to the efforts required for that task. Had the willingness of the people to heed God's word, which is reported in 1:12 and 14, flagged during the several weeks that passed between the oracle of September 21 and the present oracles of October 17? It is possible that the economic difficulties and the general inertia that had inhibited building activity in the first place were still in effect (see below). However, the content of Haggai's oracles in this section is not concerned, at least not explicitly, with economic factors. As progress on the building site has become evident to any observer, other questions about the validity of the enterprises have been raised. Haggai hopes to allay these fears and to reassert, in terms other than the economic ones of his initial call to work, the importance for continuing to work on the temple. This section of chapter 2 and the two succeeding ones are full of encouraging words. The prophet offers support through his ability to see in present accomplishments the unfolding of Yahweh's eschatological purposes, to view immediate tasks in the context of ultimate goals that have worldwide scope.

What were the factors, other than the economic ones, which appear to have disheartened the leaders and the people and to have stimulated further words from the prophet? Verse 3 provides a clue. It reveals that people are comparing the condition of the temple at the beginning of restoration work with the remembrance of the magnificence it had before the Babylonians burned it. The preexilic temple had belonged to the sacral-royal complex that had dominated Jerusalem and Judah (and also, initially, the northern tribes of Israel as well as conquered foreign nations) in all aspects of national life—social, economic, political, and cultic—for the hundreds of years of the Davidic monarchy. Those few elders who were still alive at the time of the restoration effort, and who had seen the temple in its last days of existence, must have been discouraged at the prospects for rebuilding it. The statement about the "former glory" of the temple on the surface refers to its physical attributes. But it would be a mistake to think that the comparison was limited to those qualities. The preexilic temple had served national interests, and the comparison could be extended to the way it had served the kingdom of Judah before 587 and how it might serve Yehud after 520. Could Yehud be held up against Judah and not suffer in comparison? In other words, the dimness of the prospects for re-creating an independent state in Yehud could have accounted for the discouragement reflected in this section.

To examine this possibility, let us first consider the physical aspect of the temple that was being restored. The postexilic temple could hardly duplicate the ancient Solomonic structure, which itself had undergone numerous changes in the centuries after its erection. Some kings had to surrender its treasures and ornamental fittings; others had sought to restore its pristine splendor (see C. Meyers 1981). The rebuilt temple of Haggai's day would in important respects have closely resembled its preexilic prototype. It would have used the same floor plan because its foundation would have been visible, because it could reuse major walls that were surely still standing, and because its builders would have had access to the verbal blueprint of 1 Kings 5–7. In addition, Ezra reports that quantities of silver and gold vessels (5,469 of them!) and other material resources along with contributions of Persian darics of gold and minas of silver (see Ezra 1:4–11; 2:68–69; and comments by Myers 1965:8–9, 14, 21, 147–48) had been brought to Jerusalem in Cyrus's time. While the accuracy of the figures has been questioned, and while they may well have been exaggerated, there can be no question that considerable support was given to the project by the Persian authorities. Similarly, the workmen and artisans employed on the project were paid out of imperial revenues (Ezra 6:8). Darius evidently took great interest in the temples of at least some of the administered provinces (Cook 1983:71, 149, 157).

For these reasons, we suspect that the comparison between preexilic and postexilic temples suggested by verse 3 does not refer to purely material matters. Additional hesitancy to see a physical comparison as the key issue stems from the fact that none of the surviving eyewitnesses to the temple of King Zedekiah's day, which had already been robbed of its treasures and golden vessels (2 Kgs 24:13), would have seen the interior of the former temple. The inside of the House of Yahweh was virtually off limits to all but the chief priest, at least in terms of the ritual schedule. Seraiah (probably the grandfather of Joshua ben-Jehozadak; cf. last NOTE to Hag 1:1) would have been the only one to have been intimately familiar with its interior splendor (or "glory"), and he was certainly not among the survivors of the Babylonian period. The exterior of the temple was relatively simple, consisting as it did of massive stone masonry virtually uninterrupted by windows or architectural embellishment. Elaborate carvings and costly appurtenances, except for Jachin and Boaz (see C. Meyers 1983), were confined to the interior of the building. All who had access to the written descriptions of 1 Kings and probably also to the tabernacle texts of Exodus to some extent (cf. Ezek 43:11) knew what the temple was supposed to have looked like inside. But no survivor would have seen that interior; and even if one had, the glory and gilt had already been removed before the final destruction of 587.

The difference between the former and the latter temples lay not in the material splendor they exhibited but rather in the political role each played. The restoration of the temple, as a locus of national identity and self-rule, would give a measure of autonomy to the postexilic community. But the tiny province of Yehud could not compare with the Judean kingdom of the seventh–sixth centuries, and it was certainly at opposite ends of the political spectrum from the empire of David and Solomon, under whose auspices the First Temple was established. The temple, instead of signifying the seat of an Israelite empire, apparently could represent only the smallest component of a foreign empire. But perhaps that wasn't really so. The content of Haggai's prophecy in verses 6–9, as we shall explain below, affirms that even a Yehudite temple is not a small, negligible structure in Yahweh's scheme of things. Its very existence initiates its ultimate role as the center of more than an empire: it is an international community under Yahweh's sovereignty.

The notion of the "glory" (v 3) of the former temple is not limited to physical splendor, which was only one component of that glory. The religious and political status of the temple, which had always stood within the palace complex of Jerusalem and was part of the administration of the kingdom, is a central concern for Haggai's audience. "Glory" represented not only the splendor of the building itself but also the wealth of its treasuries. Those riches would not be forthcoming, no matter how resplendent the postexilic temple would be, for two reasons. First, the local economy, which, had Yehud been independent, would have used some of its surpluses for gifts to the temple treasuries (cf. 2 Kgs 12:5 [RSV 12:4]), was not able to supply anything. Yehud was a province of the Persian Empire, and Darius was rigorous in his extraction of gifts and tributes from the satrapies. Second, the vassal status of Yehud meant that no foreign gifts would flow into the capital and its official buildings as they had in the days when the Solomonic temple had been constructed. The phrase "former glory" incorporates the place of honor and status accorded to an institution which was an integral part of national life. The temple in the ancient Near East, as we have already described in our NOTES and COMMENT to chapter 1 of Haggai, was an essential component of the administration of a political state (see Lundquist 1982, 1983, and 1984). The qualms of the prophet's audience could be rephrased: How can we have a temple without the associated monarchy that draws to it the riches and honor it deserves as Yahweh's House?

That "glory" has such political overtones is further demonstrated in the shift in the way the prophet's audience is named between verses 2 and 4. In both places the designation of the leaders is the same. But the wider audience is called "rest of the people" in verse 2 and "all you people of the land" in verse 4. The latter group was, during the monarchy, associated with dynastic succession and the sacral anointing of the new king. The use of the phrase "people of the land" in replacement of "rest of the people" reflects monarchist concerns of the Yehudites that were aroused by the rebuilding of the temple. What does a rebuilt temple signify for a community in the absence of the monarchic political structure that had historically accompanied a temple? Or, is the temple a legitimate House of Yahweh when it doesn't legitimize dynastic power? Such questions represent the magnitude of the transition made during the Second Temple period: national identity and governance without a king now exist, but with a temple and priestly establishment.

The priestly establishment did have its civil counterpart in the restoration period. And the civilian leader Zerubbabel was a scion of the House of David.

As the chief political officer of the province and as a surrogate for an appointed king, his role is not to be minimized. Zerubbabel may have ruled side by side with Joshua, but in the last analysis he did not have the powers that the Davidides had exerted. Zerubbabel was a Persian civil servant, answerable to Darius and not to Yahweh. Therein lies a significant difference. The dyarchic arrangement of Joshua and Zerubbabel may have symbolized the historic priest-king relationship and in that way aroused expectations that Zerubbabel might become king. But in reality Zerubbabel's power was less than that of a dynastic ruler; in compensation, the balance of power shifted to Joshua. Haggai does not tell us this directly, especially because he focuses, in his last oracle, on Zerubbabel. But this oracle indirectly shows concern for the lack of a monarch. In addition, Haggai is coupled with Zechariah 1–8, whose focus upon Joshua, especially in the Investiture Scene of chapter 3, indicates that the civilian leadership of the governor was hardly the same as that provided by the preexilic king.

The model of earliest Israel, when Moses as civilian leader worked in tandem with his brother Aaron the high priest, no doubt lent support to the postexilic pattern of dyarchic leadership. The situation during the period of the Judges, when Israel existed without a king, would have provided an additional and important example of theocratic rule. Dumbrell (1983) goes so far as to suggest that the Book of Judges, with its emphasis on the rule of charismatic leaders empowered by the "spirit of Yahweh," was not an apology for the monarchy but rather a recommendation to postexilic Israel for national existence without monarchic rule. To be sure, the Persian-appointed governor (pehâ) did not have the charismatic qualities of the premonarchic models, but the enduring traditions of those times must surely have figured in Yehudite acceptance of the dyarchy. The Primary History of Israel, Pentateuch through 2 Kings, recently promulgated during the exile, would have made the premonarchic past a vivid ideal, with the intervening monarchy for the most part a disaster not to be emulated. And the great prophet of the exile, Ezekiel, also deemphasized monarchy in his graphic portrayal of restored Israel.

Economic factors have been put aside in our examination of the chief reasons for Haggai's further support of the people in chapter 2. But the state of the economy may have continued to be a factor. Consider the date again. In the middle of October the harvest season was not yet over. The vintage was in its final stages, and the olive harvest was just under way. The anxiety about insufficient productivity that Haggai had addressed in chapter 1 could not yet have been fully alleviated. Persisting perhaps in their despair of ever achieving adequate subsistence, the people again request words of encouragement which speak to their economic as well as their political misgivings. The contents of verse 5 in fact would answer an ongoing uncertainty about food supplies. The prophet assures the people that Yahweh's presence among them has been secured. After only a month or so of work on his House, God's spirit is present in Jerusalem. That presence, according to covenantal traditions the prophet cites as proof for his point, will bring God's blessings, the increased yield of flocks and fields.

Haggai implores the people to be strong and not afraid; that language speaks to the present situation, both economic and political. But another oracle follows and the chronological perspective expands to include the future which, for Haggai, is contained in and initiated by the actions of the present. Haggai invokes a universalistic vision of the future. In so doing, he deals with the problems raised by the comparison of preexilic temple with postexilic temple. The latter may not now have an associated monarchy, but it is the building to which, eventually, riches will flow. As soon as God tumbles the world order, as only he can do, the glory that had previously characterized the temple when it was associated with the royal palace will once again come to Jerusalem. The twofold repetition of the word "glory," and the use of the terms "riches," "silver," and "gold" provide the imagery of royal dominion. We are not told whether or not, or how, a Davidic dynast will be part of that eventuality. The tribute coming to Jerusalem will belong to Yahweh (verse 8). It is only in the final eschatological vision that the participation of a Davidide is specified.

The origins of the universal vision of 2:6-9 (and 2:21-23 below) are rooted in the imperial context that was in effect when the temple was first built, in the days of Solomon. It received not only national support but also external acknowledgment. It legitimized the monarchy in the eyes of the Israelites and of the subjugated nations which sent tribute (C. Meyers 1983). Exotic materials from throughout the empire were used in its construction and furnishings, and tribute from subject peoples poured into the capital. The ancient tradition of the imperial authority of Jerusalem and the riches it brought lay behind the vision of the future ascendancy of Jerusalem: the present restoration of God's house will produce a center not only of a national life but also, in the future, of an international community. That condition will come about not through the ordinary course of events, nor through military campaigns or political maneuvers, which historically had created imperial capitals that drew the riches of conquered peoples. Rather, God's powerful and miraculous intervention will bring about the universal recognition of a single sovereign, Yahweh reigning from his Jerusalem abode.

The dual concerns of this oracle of reassurance, economic well-being, and political structure come together in its final statement: "I will grant well-being through this place" (1:9). The well-being for which the Yehudites yearn will become available to them, but not only to them. In the future time, when other nations recognize Yahweh's universal rule, those nations too will achieve well-being. The power of Yahweh as universal ruler will not be exploitative. In contrast to human emperors, Yahweh will establish universal plenty. This eschatological vision accords Yahweh the position of king. It is his House that is to be exalted with treasures, and Yahweh will give his blessings from there. The temple is a symbol of divine kingship, and no political king shares Yahweh's rule. The eschatological imagery of this passage, like that of Isaiah 2:2, is surely derived from the political experience, from the short-lived zenith of the Israelite empire, when glory and wealth filled Jerusalem (1 Kgs 4 and 10). But even that empire was a God-given structure in its Deuteronomic formulation, and so its ideal future replication shifted the focus to God's kingship.

Priestly ruling with prophetic interpretation, 2:10–19

Perhaps this is the most difficult of Haggai's oracles for the modern reader to comprehend. The prophet uses a rather arcane priestly question as a vehicle for his message, and the message itself is expressed in agricultural terminology which is not readily familiar to the non-Palestinian and the non-farmer. In short, the language is dependent, institutionally and environmentally, upon features largely limited to the prophet's own world and not easily translated into universal terms. Furthermore, the phraseology which provides the time indicators in this passage is perhaps awkward for the English reader and even ambiguous in the Hebrew and has been persistently troublesome for translators and interpreters (see our NOTES to vv 15 and 18 in particular).

This prophetic unit, like most of the sections of Haggai and Zechariah, is introduced with a chronological formula coupled with a standard expression recording the transmission of a message from Yahweh to the prophet who will then deliver it to the intended audience. Two months have gone by since Haggai's last utterances, on October 17 (520). In the interim his colleague Zechariah has begun his mission as a spokesman for Yahweh. Zechariah's first, brief, oracular statement, with its strong consciousness of history and of the role of prophecy, was delivered several weeks before the date given in 2:10. Only the month and year (November/December, 520) are given for Zechariah's opening message (Zech 1:1–6), and we can't be sure about the interval between it and Haggai 2:10ff., since the former occurred in the eighth month and the latter in the ninth, but we do know that Haggai's last prophetic utterances followed Zechariah's first ones.

The two-month interval between the words of encouragement of 2:1–9 and the present unit means, in terms of the agricultural calendar of southern Palestine, that the harvest season has been completed. Economic problems had beset the Yehudites, had provided the impetus for Haggai to urge his countrymen to rebuild Yahweh's temple, and had at the same time made them reluctant to take on the extra burden of that enterprise. Now the temple work was well under way and the yields of the year's planting had been gathered and stored. The intense labor of the summer and fall months had abated. There were both time and cause for reflection.

Haggai uses a complex priestly ruling as a vehicle for conveying his message that the work on the temple can be related to the fortunes of the people. We can make several observations about the nature of this technique. First, the request for a priestly ruling is cast in the form of a dialogue between Haggai and the priests. The situation portrayed in this dialogue may be staged, in the way that prophetic actions in general are contrived for symbolic purposes (cf. Zech 6:9–15 and NOTES to that scene). Yet any artificiality that may adhere to a staged scene is offset to a degree by the dialogic mode. The direct speech of the human characters creates for the audience a sense of the reality of the issues that are being examined. It also exemplifies the human situation, the individual confronted with uncertainty and attempting to understand the world. The prophet represents all of us; he has a question about a situation and about its meaning within the scheme of God's design. Zechariah too uses this characteristic Hebraic technique of presenting scenes through discourse as well as through narration.

Second, the dialogic form consists of two queries put to the priests. The responses in both cases are simple "yes" or "no" answers, although the former consists of a restatement of the question rather than the utterance of a simple "yes," since such an affirmative would not be possible in Hebrew. This particular kind of question-answer format, which appears again though in a somewhat different situation in Zechariah 7:3, may be reminiscent of ancient oracular techniques. Certain questions put to priestly figures called for answers that could be provided by mechanical devices. In this instance, however, the kind of question diverges from the queries involved in such oracular situations (see NOTES to Zech 7:3). This poses an interpretative question about a state of existence and not an objective question about a course of action.

Third, the fact that Haggai utilizes the priests' ruling to make his point reveals something of the authoritative position that the priesthood held even in this period preceding the completion of the temple. The functioning of the priesthood was evidently not dependent upon the existence of the temple building, just as the bringing of sacrifices was not contingent upon whether or not God's House loomed above the courtyard and temple precincts which were the setting for the sacrificial cult. The priests respond immediately to Haggai's question, and their ruling is fully acceptable to the prophet, so much so that he extrapolates from it a principle applicable to his beliefs about the relationship between the deeds and the well-being of the people. The insight this passage gives us into the function of the priesthood in the early postexilic period is both helpful and also unfortunate. It allows us to perceive a functioning priesthood able to give authoritative responses, but it does not provide an appreciation of the full power of the priesthood. The more comprehensive role of priests during the restoration surfaces only in Zechariah and Malachi, and we touch upon that role in the fourth point, following:

Fourth, the clarity of the priestly response is based upon pentateuchal texts (see NOTES to vv 12 and 13). Haggai's audience must appreciate the logic of the priestly answers in order for the prophetic message to have its intended impact. In other words, Haggai's use of a priestly ruling based on cases found in Leviticus and Numbers presupposes an awareness on the part of his audience of the existence of those texts and their validity for the community, if not a familiarity with the actual content of those texts. Pentateuchal law was obviously a factor in the community life of the early restoration period with respect to priestly responsibilities.

The passage in Leviticus (10:10–20) describing priestly functions is particularly instructive in this regard. It relates two facets of priestly responsibility, matters of holiness and of communication: the priests are enjoined "to distinguish between the holy and the common, and between the impure and the pure [v 10]," and "to teach *[lĕhôrōt]* the children of Israel all the statutes which Yahweh spoke to them through Moses *[bĕyad-mōšeh]*" (v 11). The two commands should not be separated from each other. If the first command has a somewhat restricted cultic dimension, it is nonetheless part of a broader function of the priesthood. Yet even that command implies wide responsibilities, for matters of holiness and purity are not to be construed as strictly cultic or ritual concepts (see below). The Leviticus text appears to have direct relevance to this passage in Haggai. In verse 10, where a chiasm links the nouns, "holy" and "pure" are related and "common," or "profane," and "impure" are equated. This relationship will help us in our discussion of the content of Haggai's priestly example. The companion verse (Lev 10:11) has the priests "teaching" the Israelites, and the verb "to teach" comes from the same root as the noun "Torah" or "ruling," as in Haggai 2:11 (E. Meyers 1983). Note too that the phrase "through Moses," literally "by the hand of Moses," employs the same terminology for prophetic instrumentality that appears in Haggai 1:1 and 2:1 as well as in the introduction to this section, in 2:10.

A priestly role that reaches beyond ritual and cult is further suggested by the Chronicler's report of one aspect of King Jehoshaphat's reform, the teaching role of the priesthood (2 Chron 17:9). The reform included a correction of cultic abuses, but the emphasis or focus on the priests lay in a description of their teaching and also (2 Chron 19:8–11) their judicial functions. Admittedly, some of the Chronicles passages are of questionable authenticity. However, the historicity of at least some of Jehoshaphat's measures appears certain (Bright 1981:251; Albright 1950:61–82), and a precedent of the ninth century could well have been appealed to by the Chronicler in establishing support for a comparable system in the postexilic community. Even if the Jehoshaphat information does not allow for a precedent during the monarchy, it would surely reflect the interests and observations of the Chronicler's own day (de Vaux 1961:344).

To summarize this point, the priestly ruling gives evidence that an authoritative legal system, probably some form of the Pentateuch, existed. That system provided sacrificial regulations which were being followed. It also would have supported a priestly role with powers in the judicial and teaching spheres, as reflected too in the Chronicler's report of Jehoshaphat's reform. Zechariah's attention to the priesthood and its powers during the restoration, since he obviously focuses in Zechariah 3 on Joshua (the high priest), has long been recognized. But Haggai too, in this passage, offers a similar conceptualization of priestly responsibilities.

Our fifth observation deriving from the matter of the priestly ruling concerns the heart of the issue, the concepts of sanctity and defilement. Haggai is asserting that sanctity is nontransferable but that defilement is. Or rather, sanctity can be transmitted only through direct contact with a sacred substance or person and not via a third party or object, whereas contamination can be transmitted both directly and indirectly. This provides an interesting distinction that says something about holiness, which is closely related to the concept of purity, and its opposite—defilement and the related state of impurity. That these categories have contrasting properties means that sanctity, which surrounds God, is much more difficult to contract than is uncleanness, which is apparently very contagious.

Why should this contrast exist? Perhaps the answer lies in the nature of sanctity or purity as a negative state. It represents the absence of any quality of behavior or physical condition that would impair the condition of absolute holiness, which only God can possess. All contact that an individual has, through the very condition of living in the real world, with other persons or with objects, has the unavoidable potential for creating impurity. And by impurity we mean more than "ritual impurity," a term to be avoided (Neusner 1973:1–3) beause it implies an antonymic term "moral purity." Biblical Israel had no such distinction, and therefore purity entailed the avoidance of all acts that contravened godlike behavior as well as physical contact with imperfect, impure, or otherwise unacceptable entities. The absence of what we would, for want of more appropriate language, call the moral dimension of sanctity may explain why it was so difficult to attain sanctity. Only God is truly pure, unadulterated by any misdeed. Yet the human approximation of divine sanctity constitutes a major theme of biblical religion: to be holy "because Yahweh your God is holy" (e.g. Lev 19:2; cf. Exod 19:6). Impurity results from sin, which is caused in the Israelite view by the working of destructive forces outside the will of God; as such, impurity was not simply a cultic status although it was most obvious or dangerous there because God's own dwelling was affected (see Levine 1974:55–112).

This brief exploration of a complicated subject, the biblical concept of sanctity and defilement, indicates that there would have been nothing casual in the concern about the transmission of these states. Ezekiel, for example, says that the uncleanness in Israel had caused Yahweh to punish Israel and to absent himself—literally, to hide his face (Ezek 39:28–29). The hiding of the divine face has its opposite—the presence of God, or God's spirit in the midst of the people. Haggai has just asserted, in 2:5, that Yahweh's spirit has returned. The sinfulness that had caused his withdrawal has abated. The Yehudites had thought that their behavior in the restoration period was not particularly disobedient. Yet God's absence was manifest in the lack of blessings, in the low productivity. The failure of the Yehudites in just one aspect of obedience, the building of the temple, was "unholy" behavior and had its unavoidable consequences. It pervaded all areas of life; it prevented prosperity despite the hard work of the Yehudites.

Haggai's audience was evidently fully aware of this conceptualization, which was common to all ancient societies as well as to some modern primitive ones, but is less obvious to the Western mind. Verse 14, containing the prophetic lesson to be learned from the priests' ruling, tersely applies the meaning of the principle of contagion. The rationale behind his application needed no further elaboration, although the next subsection (2:15–19) of this unit (2:10–19) constitutes the example *par excellence* which verifies the priestly principle and Haggai's prophetic declaration based on the principle.

The sequence of conditions set forth in 2:15–19 amplifies Haggai's assertion of 2:14, that the sacrifices offered by the people before God's House was restored were not acceptable. God's favor was not forthcoming because the people were tainted by some aspect of their behavior which was sinful and had caused the inevitable pervasive impurity. Before temple restoration began, the people were experiencing economic deprivation. The prophet recounts this graphically in his use of statistics in verse 16: grain stores were 50 percent under the norm and the wine supply was 60 percent below expectation. The harvest had been severely limited by natural disasters (2:17) that took place during the critical transition period in the agrarian calendar, between summer and winter.

When work on the temple began, the fortunes of the people were turned around. The conclusion of the harvest season, between the seventh and ninth months if not already in the sixth month, provided storerooms with ample provisions (2:19). That there was still seed in December, after the sowing of the winter wheat which would have taken place with the first winter rains (in October, about the time of the previous oracle), signifies that bread would be available until the spring harvest provided replenishment of grain supplies. The ripening crops had been virtually destroyed two months earlier, and now a condition of relative bounty obtains. What can have caused this miraculous reversal? God's presence and blessing are responsible, and God is present because the people have dealt with their defilement by responding at last to God's will by agreeing that his house should be restored.

God has turned his face back to his people by offering them material blessings (v 19). His power to do so is implicit in the dramatic change of fortunes. Haggai draws attention to God's power being used in the present time for economic purposes. In so doing he opens the way for the message of the final section of his prophetic work, which portrays Yahweh's exercise of power in the future and in the political realm.

The prophetic utilization of the priestly ruling or *tôrâ* is dependent, as we have suggested, on the audience's recognition of authoritative texts and officials as well as its understanding of contamination. It is also dependent, we reiterate, on a grasp on the part of Haggai's listeners of the sequential nature of developments in the economy. That sequence is provided by the threefold repetition (once in v 15 and twice in v 18) of the word "reflect," which literally means "set your hearts upon"—that is, take to heart or take very seriously what the prophet is saying about a) conditions before temple work, b) conditions now that temple work has begun and Yahweh's place in the community has been accorded its proper attention, and c) conditions that will prevail in the future.

The threefold use of "reflect" has its counterpart in the repeated references to the date on which this prophetic statement is made. In 2:10 we learn that the prophet seeks the priestly ruling on the twenty-fourth day of the ninth month, and verse 15 refers again to "this day," as does verse 18, which also cites the day and month once more. Verse 19 too mentions "that day." We note that the final revelation to Haggai, the last section of the Book of Haggai (2:20–23), is also attributed to this date and constitutes a second revelation on that very day. Six notations of this day or date occur in 2:10–19, and one more comes in 2:20. The day must have held unusual significance, to have been noted so often in Haggai's words or in those of the redactor's and to have been the occasion for two distinct experiences of divine revelation to Haggai.

Because the twenty-fourth day of the ninth month of the second year in Darius's reign receives such unusual attention, the event recorded for that date in 2:18, the founding of the Temple of Yahweh, must have been a pivotal event in the history of the postexilic period. The reader should refer to our NOTE above to "founded" (2:18) and also to our NOTES to Zechariah 4:7–10 and to Haggai 1:2. The significance of the day of a temple foundation or refoundation ceremony underlies the emphasis on December 18, 520.

Jewish tradition has focused upon the matter of temple rededication in Hanukkah, its festal celebration of the recovery from the Seleucid desecration of the temple in the second century B.C.E. And biblical tradition dwells upon Solomon's great feast of dedication (1 Kgs 8) when the original temple was completed and upon dedication offerings of the tabernacle (Num 7) when it was first established. These emphases have obscured the role of temple foundation in the biblical world. Throughout the ancient Near East the day of laying the foundations, or of the symbolic relaying of foundations in the case of a temple restoration, was a moment of particular importance. In Mesopotamia the foundation rituals were the ones most often mentioned in the ancient building inscriptions (Ellis 1968:31). Royal officials participated, prayers were offered, and the god's presence and sanction were invoked. Similarly for post-

exilic Israel, the time of refoundation was imbued with cosmic meaning. The
real beginning of the Second Temple was the day of its refoundation ceremonies in December 520, five years before its actual dedication.

Future hope, 2:20–23

The momentous day of temple refoundation had elicited from Haggai the
complicated prophecy of encouragement (2:10–19) which used the vehicle of a
priestly ruling. But that day was not yet over for the prophet. He had spoken
to the people and had allayed their anxieties about present conditions. However, the present was part of the future that he had already envisaged in 1:6–9,
and it is to that future that he turns once more. The oracle of future hope is
separated from the recapitulation of the past and present condition, since it is
recorded as a discrete unit of revelation with its own formulaic introduction.
This separation seems natural in that the lessons of the past and present were
derived from the shared experiences and concerns of community life. Although the reality of future events was no less vivid to the prophetic mentality,
nonetheless those events had not yet been actualized in time. What will take
place in the future constitutes an inevitable conclusion to the prophetic summation in 2:15–19; yet the future is treated in a separate oracle. Therefore the
future stands apart from the present. Inextricably linked with the present, it
nonetheless is set forth separately, perhaps reflecting prophetic awareness that
a gap exists between the ongoing course of history and the ultimate and universal intervention of Yahweh in human events.

In this second oracle of the twenty-fourth day of the ninth month, Haggai's
audience consists of a single individual, Zerubbabel. Although Zerubbabel is a
Davidic figure, as the final verse of the oracle makes clear, he is addressed as
governor. Moreover, Zerubbabel's lineage is downplayed by virtue of the
omission of his patronymic. The man to whom this private oracle is addressed
is therefore a civil leader who has shared with the high priest the ceremonial
aspects of temple refoundation. That event had marked a restoration of the
high priestly role that accompanied traditional depictions of temple and tabernacle, in the Pentateuch and in Ezekiel's visions. What did this mean for
monarchic expectations? The rebuilding of the temple meant the reestablishing of the kingship of God and not of man.

The eschatological end brought into Yehudite sight by temple restoration
was viewed in terms of political imagery, which meant that a political ruler
such as had existed in the days of Israel's greatest grandeur, the Davidic
empire, should once more appear on the world scene. Yet there is a difference.
David as royal prototype had conquered many lands and had then established
imperial domination. In contrast, the universality of Jerusalem's future role in
this oracle will be created by God's first overthrowing foreign kingdoms
(2:22). Yahweh has taken on the military tasks essential to the overthrow of
lands that do not acknowledge his sovereignty. The Davidic model of a war-

rior king is absent. Only suprahuman intervention can bring about the universal kingdom. Because Yahweh himself will one day bring an end to the powers that dominate the world, it is Yahweh whose sovereignty is to be established. The role of a Davidide cannot be the same as it was in the past. Once God has overturned the world order, then he will reign with the Davidide as his "servant" and his "signet." These two terms (see NOTES) relegate the Davidide to a vice-regency, a participant in God's administration of the nations of the world but not the initiator or leader in that task. The overwhelming imagery of the oracle is not only eschatological, it is also theocratic. The monarchic potential contained in the figure of a Davidide has been made a component of theocratic rule; he is a device or implement of Yahweh's dominion and not a political monarch of an independent kingdom. The accession of a Davidide to a special relationship with Yahweh in the future signifies the centrality of Jerusalem but not of a monarchy. Rather than being a messianic figure, an active participant in the struggle to bring about the new age, he will be a passive earthly symbol of divine sovereignty.

The mention of Zerubbabel by name has occasioned all manner of speculation about political developments in Yehud. Did the Yehudites perhaps expect Zerubbabel's status to change abruptly from governor to king? Does this oracle reveal a stirring of nationalism, about to erupt as rebellion against Persian rule? The answer to these questions, in the light of the preceding discussion, is negative. Zerubbabel is governor now; his future role could only be a subsidiary one in a theocratic scheme. The naming of Zerubbabel is the choosing of Zion, which is the place where Zerubbabel governs, where the temple is being restored, and where the locus of universal well-being will be established. That Zerubbabel's name appears in this eschatological vision testifies to Haggai's intense awareness of the Yehudite uncertainty about rebuilding a temple without restoring the palace, not to an expectation of some alteration in Yehud's provincial status. The Jerusalem temple and priestly establishment had always accompanied, and indeed had legitimized, a royal house. That royal house is not absent, in Haggai's words, from this period of rebuilding. The prophet deeply believed that the temple project brought Yahweh's power back into the world as an active presence. Could the overthrow of nations and the rule of Yahweh with his Davidic assistant be far behind? It is no wonder that with such a view of the temple, Haggai's words display a sense of imminence.

The eschatological force of this last oracle has perhaps been weakened for subsequent generations by the specificity given to it by the mention of the name of a particular Davidic descendant. At the same time, pinpointing Haggai's utterance to this crucial transition period in Yehudite history, in which a social and religious community emerges with a strong sense of national identity and purpose, yet without full political autonomy, has merit of another kind. It links the present moment, concretized by Zerubbabel's name, with the future. It inserts a contemporary figure into the age when God's benign and universal rule will prevail. Haggai, by using a living individual in his future vision, bridges the gap between present and future. It's not that he makes the future imminent; rather, he presents a view of time in which eschatology is not distinguished from history—the two belong together for him. That his prophecy was not fulfilled historically only serves to confirm its authenticity. Although it was not fulfilled, it nevertheless accomplished a great deal: it helped to get the temple rebuilt on its ancient foundations and to revive and transform the mechanism of national life.

THE BOOK
OF FIRST ZECHARIAH

Part One

Zech 1:1–6

ORACULAR INTRODUCTION

1. CALL FOR OBEDIENCE WITH RETROSPECTION
(1:1–6)

1 ¹ In the eighth month of the second year of Darius, the word of Yahweh came to the prophet Zechariah ben-Berechiah ben-Iddo: ² "Yahweh was very angry with your ancestors. ³ Therefore speak to them,"

> Thus spoke Yahweh of Hosts, "Return to me"—Oracle of Yahweh of Hosts—"and I will return to you," spoke Yahweh of Hosts. ⁴ "Don't be like your ancestors, to whom the earlier prophets proclaimed: 'Thus spoke Yahweh of Hosts, "Turn away from your evil ways and from your evil deeds." ' But they did not listen or heed me"—Oracle of Yahweh. ⁵ "Your ancestors, where are they? And the prophets, do they live forever? ⁶ But didn't my words and my statutes, which I commanded my servants the prophets, overtake your ancestors?"

So they returned and said, "Whenever Yahweh of Hosts decided to deal with us according to our ways and our deeds, he has done so with us."

NOTES

1:1. *eighth month of the second year of Darius.* Zechariah's prophetic activity begins in the month of Heshvan, which could be either in November or December since the day of the month is not supplied. All the other chronological headings in Haggai and Zechariah contain both month and day, although not always the year (as Hag 2:18,20); and the Peshitta supplies a day, "the first day," evidently taking ḥōdeš ("month") to mean the new moon or the first day of the month.

This chronological heading is the first of three such headings (1:1; 1:7; 7:1) in Zechariah. It serves, along with a formula indicating the transmission of a divine message (cf. following NOTE), to indicate a major unit of Zechariah's prophecies. Accordingly, we have divided Zechariah 1–8 into three sections: Part One, 1:1–6; Part Two, 1:7–6:15; Part Three, 7:1–8:23.

Our NOTE to the date formula of Hag 1:1 contains an extensive discussion of the appearance of Haggai and Zechariah as prophets of Yahweh at this particular point in the postexilic period. Even without the day of the month specified, the present heading reveals that Zechariah's ministry began two months after Haggai's did and that this first evidence of Zechariah's activity preceded by a month the last recorded material produced by Haggai (2:10–20; December 18, 520). Zechariah's visions then begin two months after Haggai's last oracles; 1:7 gives a date of February 15, 520. The prophets overlapped in their ministries, and could well have been influenced by each other's words. Indeed, Zechariah, especially 8:9–12, contains clear evidence of an awareness of Haggai's words. Both prophets were obviously concerned with the same community and with developments in that community, although their emphases were rather different. Or perhaps it is more judicious to say that they were interested in similar issues and their individual treatments of those issues were complementary.

The interlocking nature of the chronological headings has the effect of making the prophecies of Haggai and Zechariah 1–8 form a composite work, which we call Haggai-Zechariah 1–8 (see Introduction). The relative uniformity of the headings is just one of several literary features that suggest a common editor or redactor. This hypothetical editor must have been a contemporary of the two prophets, perhaps a disciple or supporter of one or both of them; it may even have been Zechariah himself, pulling Haggai's words into the framework of his own at some point prior to the rededication of the temple, in or before 515 B.C.E., an event not mentioned in Haggai-Zechariah 1–8 (see Introduction and a similar view presented in Schneider 1979:124–30). The combination of the works of the two prophets not only achieves a literary unity but also, in our opinion, is evidence of the basic ideological agreement between the two prophets and the interdependence of what each stresses apart from the other.

An actual written document need not be posited in order to account for the mutual awareness by these prophets of the other's words. Given the small size of Yehud at this time, each prophet was undoubtedly fully cognizant of the activities of the other. However, the existence of a written form of the oracles coinciding closely with the time of their oral delivery cannot be ruled out. Our NOTE to "these words" in 8:9 examines such a possibility. Surely the availability of a written text of Haggai and Zechariah's words of the year 520, the year to which eight of the ten canonical chapters are attributed, would have facilitated the rapid formation of a composite work sometime between 518, the date of the last two canonical chapters of Zechariah, and the apparent *terminus a quo* of 515.

Nothing in the foregoing discussion offers a direct explanation for the curious absence of a day of the month in the date formula with which the Book of Zechariah begins. However, this heading is the only one that gives a date prior to the end of Haggai's ministry. In view of the way this first part of Zechariah interlocks with the end of Haggai, we might suppose that the omission of the day is somehow related to that arrangement. The visions, according to 1:7, come after Haggai's mission ended. But since the close relationship of the two prophets is of concern to whoever organized the composite work, a vision of Zechariah's that preceded Haggai's last oracles would serve to intertwine their missions. The combined prophecies of Haggai and Zechariah may originally have been arranged chronologically; and when they were organized into units according to each prophet, the date in Part One (1:1) contained a day which then interrupted the chronological sequence. Perhaps the full chronological heading was omitted as a way to ameliorate the blatant departure from an overall chronological arrangement. The specific reasons or literary procedures behind the day's omission, if we assume it to be intentional, cannot be more than speculative. But its absence is surely a sign of the overriding concern to link the prophecies of Haggai and Zechariah so that their messages become complementary parts of one larger whole.

We also point out that November/December 520 is the fourth, or central, date in the total series of seven dates provided by all the headings in Haggai-Zechariah 1–8 (see Chart 10 in Introduction). Its central position may likewise have something to do with its divergent form.

the word of Yahweh came to. This phrase signaling prophetic material is integrated into the narrative introduction to Zechariah. Identical formulas in Zech 1:7 and 7:1, along with chronological headings, mark the three major parts of Zechariah 1–8. A variant of the formula also occurs internally in Zechariah, in 6:9 and 7:4; and its several other occurrences in Part Three (7:8; 8:1; 8:18) serve to create subunits of that section (see NOTES to those verses). The Book of Zechariah is hardly alone among the biblical prophets in using this formula; the headings of several other prophetic books contain exactly the same words or a minor variation of them: Hos 1:1; Joel 1:1; Jonah 1:1; 3:1; Mic 1:1; and Zeph 1:1. The formula recurs frequently in Jeremiah (thirty times) and in Ezekiel (fifty times). In Haggai, a slight variation appears: "The word of Yahweh came through . . ."

The formula děbar-yhwh hāyâ ʾel, "the word of Yahweh came to," represents a significant change from the familiar "Yahweh spoke," which is slightly more anthropomorphic. It serves to separate the word from the speaker somewhat and renders it "a quasi-independent entity befitting its divine status" (Andersen-Freedman 1980:149). The prophet is thus seen to be less important as an individual and more able to transmit God's word verbatim, though in another sense the prophet is regarded as someone more exalted and important because he alone can pronounce the word of Yahweh (ibid. 140). It often precedes the usage of another, shorter formula, "thus spoke Yahweh," which marks the actual oracular content. The longer formula thus signifies the transmission of the message, a prior stage in the process of the prophetic mediation of God's word. These stages probably derive from the royal language used in the Divine Council, which can be discerned in Canaanite mythology as well as in the Bible, for the publication of decisions or judgments reached in heaven (see Mullen 1980:220–25, and NOTES to the prophetic formulas in Hag 1:1 and 1:2).

The noun děbar ("word") appears in construct before individuals' names normally with the meaning of "matter, affair" (e.g., 1 Kgs 15:5). It can sometimes refer to the utterances of humans (1 Sam 4:1; 1 Kgs 17:1; 2 Sam 14:17), but by far the most common usage of the noun with the meaning "word" is as a construct with "Yahweh," referring to divine utterance. As such it is a typical and specific, if not also a technical term for prophecy. The term dābār ("word") characterizes prophecy just as "torah" relates to a priest and "counsel" relates to the sage (Schmidt 1978).

the prophet Zechariah ben-Berechiah ben-Iddo. Zechariah, meaning "Yahweh has remembered," is a rather common biblical name. It appears here in its shortened form, zěkaryâ; some other individuals bearing this name use the full theophoric designation, zěkaryāhû. The name occurs more than forty times in the Hebrew Bible, in reference to twenty-nine different individuals, thus making it one of the most popular of all biblical names. The frequency with which it is found perhaps underlies some of the confusion which exists concerning the lineage given for the prophet. At least two of the other Zechariahs appear to have been postexilic figures (so Neh 8:4; 12:35). Perhaps for this reason, the compiler of Zechariah has deemed it necessary to give Zechariah's lineage. Note that for Haggai, no such lineage appears. In addition, the title "prophet" is found for Zechariah, further identifying him and also setting him apart from the priestly aspect of his family background, information the patronymics provide.

The name of Zechariah's father may serve a useful purpose in identifying the bearer of a common name. But it is not clear why Zechariah's lineage for two generations back is included. Possibly there was another Zechariah with the same immediate patronymic, since Berechiah was also a very common name, in which case the addition of Zechariah's grandfather's name would serve to resolve any confusion about which Zechariah ben-Berechiah was the prophet. A more likely solution, however, lies in the fact that in Ezra 5:1 and 6:14 and in Neh 12:16, Zechariah is listed as Iddo's son, not his grandson: "Zechariah bar-Iddo." Iddo himself is listed in Neh 12:4 as part of a priestly family that returned from exile with Zerubbabel, presumably in 538 B.C.E. Perhaps Iddo was so important a figure in his own right that he was naturally retained in the citation of Zechariah's lineage.

While that explanation may deal with the inclusion of a second generation of Zechariah's ancestry, it leaves open the question of why Ezra would have omitted the first generation. The confusion cannot easily be resolved, though four possibilities can be offered: 1) Zechariah's father died when the prophet was very young and the grandfather Iddo raised him as his own son; 2) the Chronicler has strong priestly considerations and chose to emphasize the priestly lineage of Zechariah in the Ezra-Nehemiah references (at least in the final edition of Ezra-Nehemiah; see Cross 1975:11ff.); 3) the "ben-Berechiah" designation is not a lineal one but rather indicates his family or his ancestry several generations back (Mitchell 1912:82); and 4) Iddo really was Zechariah's father, and the compiler of Haggai-Zechariah 1–8 has been influenced by Isa 8:2, which refers to one Zechariah, son of Jeberechiah, an associate of Uriah the priest in the eighth century, and has inserted part of that name before Iddo.

While the Iddo/Berechiah problems cannot be sorted out on the basis of existing information, it is important to realize that Zechariah's priestly background would have been conveyed to his contemporaries by the use of the name Iddo, evidently a man of special prominence. Thus Berechiah cannot simply be discarded (so *BHS*) from this verse. There are ample reasons for Iddo to have been added here and for Berechiah to have been omitted by the Chronicler.

2. *your ancestors.* '*ăbôtêkem* here and in verses 4, 5, 6, and 8:14 refers to those preexilic Judeans who were subjected to the Babylonian destruction and/or exile. The prophet thus understands those events as punishments that were expressions of divine anger. The concept of divine anger reappears in Parts Two (1:15) and Three (7:12) of Zechariah. In all three cases, God's wrath is linked with the destruction and exile.

Zechariah here begins a retrospective passage, a feature which recurs in a much expanded form in Part Three of Zechariah 1–8. The repetition of the recital of past events as well as some of the language with which that rehearsal is effected creates a literary connection between Parts One and Three of Zechariah 1–8. The retrospectives frame the central section, dominated by the visions, and bring all of Zechariah 1–8 together into a unified work. See our Introduction and also various NOTES to Part Three.

3. *to them.* There is no antecedent for this phrase, but the prophet is undoubtedly

addressing Yehudites of his own day (cf. Mason 1977b:32). In the oracle which follows (vv 4 and 5), Zechariah exhorts his audience to recall their forebears of preexilic times.

Thus spoke Yahweh of Hosts. This is a standard prophetic formula (see Hag 1:2), often followed by the infinitive *lē'mōr* as in verse 4 below; here it occurs without the infinitive. It appears in numerous oracular insertions in the visions (1:14,17; 2:12 [RSV 2:8]; 3:7; 6:12; cf. NOTE to 6:12) to introduce the actual words of a divine oracle. Note too its frequent use in Part Three of Zechariah (7:9; 8:2,3,4,6,9,14,19,20,23).

Return to me . . . and I will return to you. The return from exile has evidently not brought about a full return to Yahweh. The decision to rebuild the temple has already been made, and so Yahweh's "return" to Zion would seem to have been mandated. What can be lacking? The clue lies, rather obliquely, in the language of this oracle and, more directly, in the information provided by the analogous retrospective in Part Three. Zechariah here refers to "words and statutes" (v 6), which the inhabitants of the preexilic state did not "listen" to or "heed" (v 4); similarly, 7:7–14, and verses 9–12 in particular, describe the defiance of those who lived in Judah in the early sixth century. Both these passages deal with the failure of the community to obey God's word, presumably in the form of the covenant, a collective of proto-canonical pentateuchal law, as well as the prophetic oracles already in fixed form. Zechariah in Part Three urges his countrymen to acknowledge the authority of such traditional materials despite the absence of the normal monarchic administration of justice; in 518 B.C.E. the matter is fairly urgent (see first NOTE to 7:1). Here the prophet apparently anticipates this aspect of providing community stability that must accompany the temple project and the establishment of the priesthood as the internal administrative body of Yehud (cf. NOTE to "high priest," 3:1, and NOTES to 3:7).

The issue of the people's return to obeying God's word is coupled with Yahweh's "return." The latter is indicated below in 8:3 in more explicit language, which involves God's restored presence among the people with all the blessings that ensue and where God's return to Zion is expressed in terms evocative of God's dwelling in his holy habitation. Zechariah and later Malachi (3:7) link the desired return of the people to Yahweh to the return of Yahweh to his people. The latter concept implies that Yahweh has temporarily turned away, a condition represented by the destruction and exile.

These first occurrences of the root *šwb*, "to return," are only the first two of four in the oracular opening of Zechariah. The plural imperative followed by the first-person singular in verse 3 together underscore the reciprocity that is supposed to characterize the relationship between God and Israel (see COMMENT). The plural imperative is repeated in verse 4 (see NOTE), where it refers retrospectively to the call made by the earlier preexilic prophets to turn away from evil ways. The people in those days did not heed the words of the prophets, however. The fourth occurrence of *šwb* in the Call for Obedience is in verse 6b (see NOTE), where it is applied to the generation of Zechariah. In that verse it is made clear that the Yehudites are indeed giving heed to the prophet's words, which they had failed to do in times past.

Thus, *šwb* is clearly a key word in this and succeeding verses, where it has shifting yet interrelated emphases. Its fourfold repetition within only four verses enables the prophet to a) reveal God's promise of reciprocity; b) refer to the fact of the noncompliance with God's word of the preexilic generation; c) establish the important fact that a change of heart has occurred in the present generation concerning the restoration in a way that relates it to the failure of the previous generation to turn or return to Yahweh; and d) anticipate the return of Yahweh to the community since the people have now turned toward him.

The two appearances of *šwb* in verse 3 are important not only because they emphasize the theme of Judah's present turning to Yahweh (verse 6b), but also because, as familiar terms of preexilic prophecy, they are framed by traditional formulas: "Thus spoke Yahweh of Hosts" occurs twice and "Oracle of Yahweh of Hosts" once. The prophet's dependence on older oracular formulas is noteworthy here and elsewhere throughout the work. It supports the view that Zechariah considered himself a true prophet in the classic tradition.

4. *Don't be like your ancestors.* This statement is identical to the opening words of 2 Chron 30:7. There King Hezekiah calls upon the descendents of pre-721 Israel not to repeat the evil deeds of their fathers and brothers but instead to "return" to God so that God may "return" to them. Either the Chronicler has drawn upon Zech 1:3–4, or else both the Chronicler and Zechariah are drawing upon common materials that exhibit awareness of past events.

earlier prophets. A designation for the Yahwistic prophets of the preexilic period who were active in calling for repentance. Jeremiah in particular was no doubt one of those prophets included in the term, since the Deuteronomic flavor of Zechariah's quote from his prophetic predecessors can be seen in a number of Jeremiah's oracles, such as 7:3,5; 11:8; 15:4ff. That Zechariah uses such a quotation indicates that his audience is well aware of the prophetic tradition and that the legitimacy of that tradition is recognized; see our NOTES to "prophets" in 7:7,12, and to "words" in 7:12. Beuken (1967:97) takes this phrase as well as its repetition in 7:7 and 12 to be an insertion by the final redactor of Zechariah 1–8. First Zechariah (cc 1–8) has surely undergone final editing along with Haggai (see Introduction), and the correspondences between Zechariah 1 and 7–8 may be the result of that activity. However, we cannot accept Beuken's fourth-century dating of that editing or its direct association with the work of the Chronicler—i.e., the final editor or compiler of the Chronicler's work, including Ezra-Nehemiah (see Introduction for discussion of the compilation of Haggai-Zechariah 1–8).

proclaimed:. The use of the verb *qr*ʾ, "call out, proclaim," may be technical (cf. NOTES to "proclaim" in 1:14; 7:7,13). Here it is apparently employed to signal the precise content of earlier prophetic statements regarding Israel's turning. The same sequence of elements occurs here as in 1:14: *qrʾ lēʾmōr* (rendered by colon), plus "Thus spoke Yahweh of Hosts." The repetition of these elements in Zechariah suggests a formulaic context for "proclaimed" which is new to Zechariah and which identifies the internal quote that begins "Turn away" and ends "evil deeds." The layering of quoted materials, and the accompanying citation of source and authority, is characteristic of Zechariah's prophecy. He is conscious of his own prophetic experiences as well as those of earlier prophets; and he endeavors to combine them without seriously interrupting the flow of the narrative or dialogue.

Turn away. This is the third of four occurrences of *šwb* (cf. NOTES to "Return to me . . ." in 1:3 and "they returned" in 1:6b) in Part One. It appears within a quote from one of the earlier, preexilic prophets. This established beyond any doubt the time frame of events associated with this "turn away." Because it falls within an interior quote, it must refer to the preexilic shortcoming of noncompliance with God's word. Although *šwb* as a key word plays an important part in this oracle, this particular usage is not paired with a reference to divine turning. The pairing of the first two usages of *šwb* in 1:3 denotes the interrelationship of Yahweh and his people (see NOTE to 1:3); so too does the "returning" of 1:6, for which the pairing with God's return is not completed until 1:16 (see NOTE).

evil ways . . . evil deeds. The terminology again reflects Jeremiah, especially 25:4–5 and 35:15, and also Ezek 33:11. The specific nature of those sins which led to punishment includes, according to Jeremiah, injustice, oppression of the disenfranchised, theft, murder, adultery, and idolatry. Does Zechariah wish to accuse his audience of similar offenses? Apparently not, but the idea of social order—i.e., the absence of those sins—is as important for Zechariah as is the temple project. Zechariah 7–8 reflects his concern for establishing a legal basis for social harmony, and this initial oracle, with its correspondences to Part Three, evidently shows that concern (cf. first NOTE to 7:1). Zechariah here recalls a past sequence in order to invoke the principle of Yahweh's power to carry out what appears in his Law and what he transmits through the prophetic medium. While not indicting his contemporaries for the same catalogue of sins, he nonetheless urges recognition of the binding nature of traditional law.

If we may accept the preexilic past as the setting in time to which the two expressions refer, we may also anticipate their repetition in verse 6b without the adjective "evil." Once again the literary flair of the prophet may be observed. In verse 4 the preexilic example of misdeeds is drawn with a view toward comparing them eventually with the changed attitude of the restoration (v 6b), a generation which did return and which is prepared to be judged by Yahweh according to its "ways" and "deeds." The new awareness of the generation of the restoration is reflected in the fact that they acknowledge that God has dealt justly with them ("their fathers") in the past—i.e., has given them what they deserved; so too do they deserve what they get in *their* generation. There may be a veiled reference here to the difficulties that ensued between 538– 520 B.C.E., or prior to the Second Return. The repetition of *ʾbwtykm* at the beginning of verse 5 and at the end of verse 6a is an effective *inclusio* for the oracular quotation of verses 5–6a.

5. *Your ancestors . . . ? And the prophets . . . ?* These two ironical questions along with a third one in verse 6a are intended to convey in the most effective way possible the lessons of the past. Unlike one's ancestors or even the prophets, who all perish, God's word is eternal (v 6a). By rhetorically raising these issues the prophet is demanding the attention of the listener, who will doubtless realize the import of the contrast that has been drawn between God's enduring "words and statutes" on the one hand and the ephemeral nature of human life on the other. Curiously, the prophets who are usually linked with God or God's word are here on the opposite side; they are paired with the ancestors in their mortality.

6. *words and statutes.* Unlike the now-deceased ancestors and prophets mentioned in the sharp rhetorical questions of the previous verse, Yahweh's will as concretized in "words" and "statutes" has enduring authority and power. The Deuteronomic language in the citation behind this statement (Deut 28:15) has "commandments" and "statutes." The substitution here of "words" for the more common "commandments" has a special force in this initial Call for Obedience. The shift in terminology already

apparent in the Deuteronomic literature appears to continue the linking of Law and prophecy as done by the Deuteronomist, who sees Moses as lawgiver, judge, administrator of the governor, and as prophet *par excellence*. The oracular message emphasizes the ongoing reality of the "word of Yahweh" in the generation of the return (see NOTE to 1:1). God's word as mediated by the prophet has achieved an important and quasi-independent status, a situation which implies that prophetic revelation is still the authentic medium for the transmission of God's word. That the word has become attached to God's commandments, as it were, expresses one of the pressing realities of the restoration period: reestablishing community law in the land was not a simple matter without monarchic authority, and the prophetic missions of Haggai and Zechariah seem to authenticate both prophetic and pentateuchal tradition, which they understand to be valid now and in the future, as they were in the past.

overtake. Hebrew *hiśśîgû* is a hunting term and reflects the language of Deuteronomy (28:15). There the curses of the covenant overtook the fathers. Zechariah's statement is elliptical here and the intention is for the hearers to understand that the failure to heed laws and statutes brought the curses of the covenant into effect and these "overtook" the hearers.

they returned. Commonly rendered "they repented." Because Zechariah has not stated the nature of the problem which has provoked his citation of Yahweh's punishment of the ancestors, the "return" to Yahweh in this verse is likewise vague. However, several considerations can be taken into account: 1. The oracle dates to about the time of the inauguration of temple restoration activities and before Haggai's last oracle. These words of Zechariah can perhaps be related to the mild indictments of Haggai of this period—namely, against the failure of the people to place Yahweh at the head of their community by being reluctant to prepare his house for habitation. 2. This oracle, a discrete segment of Zechariah's mission, precedes the lengthy set of visions and oracles of 1:7–6:15, all of which are related in some fashion to the temple. Because of its literary position, Part One stands as an introduction to the temple visions. 3. Ezra (5:1 and 6:14), in reporting the prophetic activity of Haggai and Zechariah, announces the results of that activity, namely, the work on the temple. Zechariah as well as Haggai thus played a role in bringing about these efforts. These considerations taken together allow us to suppose that Zechariah's initial oracle deals with the same issue that concerns Haggai. The disobedience from which the people must, and do, return is shown by their reluctance to invest their time and resources in the material, symbolic representation of God's presence and sovereignty. The turn of heart reported in Hag 1:12 is paralleled in Zech 1:6b and underscores the overlapping character of the two prophets. For Zechariah the issue has been resolved; he reports that the people have responded, and this introductory section of Zechariah really links the fact of Yehud's compliance with the call to work (as in Hag 1:12) with the questions that such work raises. In addition, because of the correspondences between Part One and Part Three, where Zechariah ultimately extends his prophetic call to the realm of covenant obedience and social justice, this oracle anticipates that concern which emerges two years later.

The root *šwb* recurs for the fifth time in the oracular climax to the First Vision (see 1:16), where God's return to Jerusalem is linked explicitly with the rebuilding of the temple. The result of the people's returning here in verse 6b, therefore, can be seen

1. Darius I's monument at Behistun.
Courtesy of Biblical Archaeologist

2. Cylinder seal of Darius I.
After Donald John Wiseman, Cylinder Seals of Western Asia,
London: Batchworth Press

3. Drawing of head of Darius I from relief at Behistun.
Reproduced in The Art of Ancient Iran Pre-Islamic Cultures *by Edith Porada,*
© *Holle Verlag GMBH, Crown Publishers, Inc., New York*

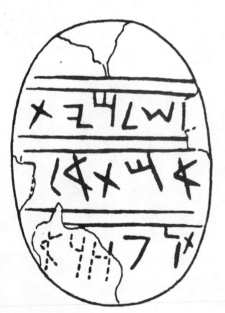

4. The Shelomith seal. Reading:
"Belonging to Shelomith, maidservant
of Elnathan the governor."
*Courtesy of Israel Exploration
Society*

5. Seal impression on store-jar handle. Reading: "Yehud/Yeho‘ezer/ the governor." Early fourth century B.C.E. from Ramat Raḥel. *Collection of Israel Department of Antiquities; exhibited and photographed by the Israel Museum*

6. Aramaic inscription on store-jar handle. Reading: "Yehud." Early fourth century B.C.E. from Ramat Raḥel. *Collection of Israel Department of Antiquities; exhibited and photographed by the Israel Museum.*

7. Bulla of Elnathan the governor.
Reading: "Belonging to Elnathan the governor."
Courtesy of the Israel Exploration Society

8. A hoard of bullae and seals from a postexilic Judean archive.
Courtesy of the Israel Exploration Society

there in v 16 as God returns with compassion to Jerusalem. The repetitive use of *šwb* has also served to tie the oracular Call to Obedience of Part One with a theme that appears in the first section of Part Two.

The logic of this interpretation, however, has not been noted before. Most commentators have seen great difficulty in understanding not only the subject of "they returned" but also the entire context and time sequence of verses 5 and 6. Instead, a rather popular emendation of *BH³* and *BHS*, that "overtake your ancestors" *(hiśśîgû ʾăbōtêkem)* of verse 6a be changed to "overtake you" *(hiśśîgû ʾetkem)*, changing "your fathers" to "you" as object of the verb, reflects these difficulties (Mason 1977b:33). Others have converted "they returned and said" to the imperative mode, "therefore return and say" (Rudolph 1976:66, 70–71), in order to bring the time sequence down into the period of the prophet. Some understand the phrase "they returned" to indicate the change of attitude already represented in the generations before the prophet (Mitchell 1912:113). A further solution suggests that the entire verse has been inserted by the redactor or compiler (Beuken 1967:105ff.; Petitjean 1969:50ff.) in a much later period. As a confession, it is argued, verse 6b has marked similarities with cultic confessions of the postexilic period (cf. Ezra 9; Neh 9; and Dan 9) and indicates both an awareness of the sins of former times and a recognition of sin in the present time (cf. van der Woude 1980).

The interpretation offered above accords with our conclusion (see Introduction) that the editorial framework of Zechariah 1–8 reflects the conditions just prior to the time of the rededication of the temple in 515 B.C.E.—namely, the end of the sixth century— a situation completely analogous to that in the Book of Haggai. This view is divergent from that which would place the organization or redaction of the book a century or so later (Beuken 1967), or from that which would understand the period of Zechariah as one of political turmoil and pervasive social unrest (Hanson 1975: *passim)*, or one in which idolatry and corruption have ruptured communal harmony (Barker 1977 and 1978).

according to our ways and our deeds. This expression resumes the language of verse 4 (see above NOTE to "evil ways . . . evil deeds") but omits the adjective "evil." The use of the repeated nouns minus their "evil" quality suggests a contrast between the preexilic and the restoration periods. By selecting stereotypical language and then altering it slightly, the prophet subtly conveys his insight into the present era: the sins of the present era are less outrageous than those of the preexilic age.

The repetition of the verb *šwb* at the beginning of verse 6b ("so they returned") reflects the language of verse 4b and denotes a change of attitude among his countrymen. Apparently verse 6b admits that Haggai's analysis of the situation was correct— i.e., that giving their own personal affairs precedence over those of Yahweh and his temple has brought about the contemporary state of affairs of crop failure and economic hardship. Yet the present generation has suffered less than previous generations; its sins are those of omission rather than commission. The covenant violations of the preexilic period were greater and more egregious. Yahweh in other words deals with people according to what they deserve. The point of Zechariah is that God is just and righteous in all his doings and will ultimately respond, reward, and bless those who respond *(šwb)* to him.

COMMENT

Both Haggai and Zechariah begin in the narrative mode. In this respect they resemble Daniel and Ezra-Nehemiah more than the preexilic and exilic prophets. The placement of 1:1–6 before Zechariah's visionary sequence, which also includes considerable oracular material, makes it an introduction, Part One, to the whole of Zechariah 1–8. It contains none of the specialized language and imagery of temple building that underlies much of Part Two of the Book of Zechariah (1:7–6:15), nor does it refer to any historical personage other than the prophet himself (v 1). The whole passage thus serves to present the prophet to the audience and to authenticate his credentials as a legitimate spokesman for Yahweh.

The first verse is especially revealing in the manner in which it dates "the word of Yahweh" revealed to Zechariah. As we have pointed out in our NOTE to 1:1, this is the only instance in either Haggai or Zechariah for which no day is provided to the otherwise complete chronological information, which normally includes three elements: day, month, year. At the same time, the Call for Obedience of Zechariah 1:1–6 comes chronologically before the conclusion of Haggai (2:10,20) and before the visionary sequence in 1:7. The omission of the date must somehow be related to the overlapping of the work of the two prophets, which is achieved canonically in the heading of 1:1. Their prophetic missions in time and in content are made interlocking and thus complementary. Although their oracles may have for a brief time circulated independently, a relatively short time elapsed before they were pulled together into the Haggai-Zechariah 1–8 composite.

We have already proposed that the Books of Haggai and Zechariah together have undergone some redactional work, primarily of an organizational character, prior to the promulgation of the received text, and that in all probability such activity was concluded prior to the celebration of the rededication of the temple in 515 B.C.E. The interlocking nature of the material in Haggai and Zechariah, however, strongly suggests the possibility that there was a common editor or compiler, possibly Zechariah himself or his secretary. That the compilation took place after Haggai's prophetic ministry had ended or after he simply had dropped out of the picture for some unknown reason is supported by the date and heading in Zechariah 1:1 and the headings in Zechariah 1:7 and 7:1. The earliest possible date for the preparation of one compendious work would be in the fourth regnal year of Darius—i.e., after December 7, 518 (Zech 7:1), while the latest date in our view would be March 10, 515 (Ezra 6:15), in the sixth regnal year of Darius, the year of the rededication of the Second Temple.

The oracular introduction begins by recalling God's anger (v 2) at those

preexilic Judeans who by their own evil deeds brought about their punishment
—namely, the destruction of the Jerusalem temple and the exile. The consola-
tory tone of the oracle is introduced in verse 3, which emphasizes Yahweh's
promise to "return" to his people if only they would "return" to him, a theme
repeated in Malachi 3:7. The reciprocal nature of such a turning in the relationship between God and his community establishes the potential for full
reconciliation. Although the seventy years of destruction are drawing to an
end, it is questionable whether the Yehudites at this point have turned back to
Yahweh. One biblical tradition (Deut 30:1–10) regarded the people's repentance in the exile as the basis for reestablishing a proper relationship with
Yahweh. Another view (Ezek 36:24–31) leaves all initiative to Yahweh, who
brings the people back to himself and to the land through his own divine
actions and spiritual cleansing. In the latter view, God's actions will cause the
people to repent of their evil ways and so return to Yahweh. The position
adopted by the prophet Zechariah offers another possibility for the reestablishment of Israel's relationship with God, for his generation had already begun,
under Haggai's prodding, to exhibit a new spirit of returning centered about
the temple project and God's symbolic presence in Jerusalem. The vocabulary
of returning thus plays a special role in the context of postexilic prophecy.

The fourfold repetition of the root *šwb* ("turn, return"), twice in verse 3,
once in verse 4, and once in verse 6b (see NOTES) serves as the literary vehicle
for contrasting the stubborn spirit of the preexilic age with the more compliant
spirit of the postexilic era. Whereas the earlier age brought about the punishment of destruction and exile because of their "evil ways" and "evil deeds" (v
4), the present age holds forth promise because the people have "returned" (v
6b). God has done to Yehud according to its deeds and ways, the people
having acknowledged the truth of what Haggai had been saying—namely, that
they suffered because Yahweh's temple, and therefore Yahweh, has not been
their central concern. The fourth occurrence of *šwb* in verse 6b links the more
recent postexilic situation with preexilic Judean history and enables the audience to apprehend the ground of hope provided by the prophet in his application of the oracular retrospection of verses 3–6a to his generation. Zechariah
echoes Haggai ("your ways," 1:5,7) here with the expectation that with repentance and returning, Yahweh will reward obedience according to its magnitude.

By offering a hopeful outlook for his own day, the prophet achieves the
desired aim of the oracle: to provide a transition between the utterance and
focus of Haggai and the tangential but differing concerns to which Zechariah
addresses himself. For Haggai the overriding issue was the resumption of work
on the temple; his considerable insight enabled him to link the resumption of
that work to the promise of God's blessing and his granting of "well-being"
(2:9). For Zechariah, however, the dominant issue of Haggai has evidently
been resolved. We encounter in the Call for Obedience oracular material that

is reflective and retrospective, but the prophet never, neither in 1:1–6 or elsewhere, repeats the theme of the resumption of temple work. Resumption of
work on the temple—the major thrust of Haggai's mission—in short is presupposed and regarded to be a success. For Zechariah, the prevailing issues in
Part Two (1:7–6:15) are the significance of the temple work already begun and
the organization of a community with a restored dwelling place for its god.
The prophet there employs the visionary mode, rich in imagery, to evaluate
the meaning of the temple project for the Yehudites.

Zechariah 1:1–6 occupies a critical position both in Zechariah 1–8 and in
the larger compendious work, Haggai plus Zechariah 1–8. Although linked to
Haggai by the common theme of temple work, which is implicit in verse 6b
(see NOTE), the Call for Obedience also constitutes a vehicle for thematic
transition. It anticipates the next stage in restoration history which underlies
the visions and which has a temple refoundation ceremony (see Introduction
and NOTES to 4:7–8 as well as to Hag 2:15,18) as the pivotal event linked with
Yehud's changing fortunes in the Persian Empire. The refounding of the temple was not the same as the completion and rededication of the temple itself,
which is nowhere mentioned in the Book of Zechariah. The absence of any
direct allusion to a refoundation ceremony in 1:1–6 suggests that the oracle of
Part One probably stems from the earliest stage of Zechariah's prophetic career; and the date of November–December 520 provided in the heading cannot be easily dismissed. The placement of 1:1–6 within the work of Zechariah,
however, must be part of a compilation of the entire work—i.e., after December 518 (7:1) and before the rededication of the temple in 515. The stimulus
for the final organization and publication of Haggai and Zechariah must
surely have been the imminent temple rededication itself. Our NOTE to 1:1
reviews in detail the factors involved in analyzing the chronological heading
and the sequence of materials from the two prophets.

Understanding the chronological problems and possibilities associated with
the redactional history of Haggai-Zechariah 1–8 enables us to comprehend
better the fact that oracular materials (vv 2–6a) have been integrated with
third-person material from the hands of the compiler (1:1) and also material
that may be a self-comment on the whole by the prophet himself (v 6b?). This
initial Call for Obedience with Retrospection represents one of the most complicated literary compositions of Zechariah in its usage of an intricate series of
quotations, beginning in verse 3. At least five internal quotations can be discerned. If verse 6b ("So they returned and said . . .") is treated as an additional comment of the prophet with an internal quote, six of these quotations
appear within four verses. Not only is this section replete with quoted speech,
but also the quotes are layered: there are quotes within quotes within quotes.
It is not easy to keep track of where the layers terminate. This section is a
nightmare for translators trying to signify the change in quoted material
through the limited devices of English punctuation. Because this layering of

quoted speech seems so difficult for the modern reader to penetrate, we must ask ourselves why the prophet and his secretary or compiler have gone to such lengths to produce this rather dense arrangement. We have already pointed out in the Introduction to the entire composite work that the mixing of narrative prose style with oracular materials is one of the most distinguishing features of these works. Though this general stylistic feature may help us understand to some extent the texture of Part One, this section goes far beyond a simple combination of oracular and narrative prose. Other factors must be considered if we are truly to comprehend the prophet's words.

An important clue in such an endeavor is provided by the text itself. The reference in verse 4 and again in 7:7 and 12 to "earlier prophets" reveals that Zechariah and/or his secretary-compiler were well aware of the legacy of classical prophecy. Both the prophet and his followers saw themselves as belonging to the long line of true prophets. For the prophet in this introductory block of oracular material, throughout the oracular attachments to the visions, and in the concluding chapters (cc 7–8), the pronouncements of his predecessors serve to legitimize the prophet's views about the present age and provide a means to invoke the memory of God's power in carrying out the stipulations of his covenant with Israel.

The three ironical and rhetorical questions that constitute internal quotations within verses 5 and 6 are sharply effective literary devices for bringing the lessons of the recent past into the hearts and minds of the prophet's present audience. The people's ancestors have perished, just as have the prophets who bore God's message. Yet God's message, in contrast, stands apart from such human mortality and endures in every generation. The failure of the preceding generations to hearken to God's commandments resulted in the disaster of the Babylonian conquest, for it was the curses embedded in the covenant (see Deut 28) which overtook the preexilic Judeans and brought about the end of their political autonomy, the destruction of many lives and much property, and the cruel exile of many of the survivors. *That* word of God still exists, the prophet insists: it may be discerned in the present materials in the persistent dependency upon quoted oracular materials. The eternal authority for Zechariah of previous revelation is further asserted in the contrast between the mortality of human beings and the ongoing vitality of God's message.

Another clue to the style of this opening section, with its excessive use of internal and layered quotations, is provided by the text in verse 6. There the substitution of "words" *(dĕbāray)* for the more familiar "commandments" *(miṣvôtay;* see NOTE to 1:6 "words and statutes") seems to indicate an awareness of both a corpus of earlier prophetic materials and a body of covenant materials which together would have constituted the nucleus of the first two divisions of Scripture, and Law and the Prophets. Such an awareness of and interest in fixed bodies of literature was one of the main legacies of

Achaemenid rule (Cook 1983:72). The well-documented Persian efforts at codification of existing laws in the provinces ultimately came to be reflected in a much later assessment, as by Diodorus, of Darius I in this connection as one of the great lawgivers. For Zechariah, the repeated citation of Yahweh's previous revelations constitutes an overt example of inner biblical exegesis. This feature of Zechariah's oracular statements is highly developed in Part Three, which comes two years later and may have been directly stimulated by Darius's support for the use of traditional laws and cultic materials by provincial officials (cf. NOTE to the date of 7:1).

Another situation contributing to the extraordinary use of quotations in Part One may be the increasing tendency in the postexilic period for the word of Yahweh to be mediated to humanity through a growing array of supernatural, or angelic, beings. The appearance of mediating figures dominates the visionary mode of Part Two of Zechariah. Perhaps it is anticipated in this introductory section, not by any direct reference to an angelic spokesman for Yahweh but rather by the atmosphere that the layering of quoted speech creates. Verse 2, for example, would make better sense were it the command given by an angel to Zechariah and not the direct words of Yahweh instructing the prophet to speak; the third-person reference to Yahweh in verse 2 as well as the double "speak" phrases of the beginning of verse 3 are awkward in the present arrangement. We might even speculate that an angelic speaker was once specified in the text but that he was left out by the compiler who intended Part One to remain fully distinct, stylistically, from the visions of Part Two in which an Interpreting Angel plays an integral role.

One final factor that may have influenced the layering of quotations in 1:1–6 as well as elsewhere in Zechariah is contemporary stylistic convention. The Persian Empire, with its far-flung provinces and administrative officials, produced documents which typically contain intricate series of conversations and reported conversations. Since as many as five people could have been involved in the composition of a letter, epistolary style regularly required the introduction of quoted materials (Hensley 1977:96–97, 143). While Zechariah himself is not a government official, he obviously was in close contact with Zerubbabel and Joshua in their administrative capacities. It is reasonable to assume that he had access to the missives of the imperial court, particularly in the likelihood that the temple, or the homes of its officials until it was restored, served as the archive for official materials such as were available for use in the compilation of Ezra (e.g., Ezra 1:2–4; 4:11–22; cf. 4:7–10, 23). Furthermore, Zechariah is acutely aware of the structure of the empire and its internal workings, as the imagery in the first and last visions in particular indicate (see, e.g., NOTES to 1:8). By layering quotations Zechariah would thus have utilized a practice, common in official circles, which underscored the authority, despite the intermediaries involved, of the ultimate source of a message. For government officials of history, Darius was that source; for Zechariah it was Yahweh.

In either case, quoted materials would help simultaneously to express the authority and to reveal the content of a pronouncement.

In this initial section the prophet does not yet turn directly to the changed circumstances of the postexilic administration in which there is no role for a Davidic monarch. This is especially revealing since in the compendious Haggai-Zechariah work, Part One of Zechariah falls directly after the final oracle in Haggai (2:20-23) in which the monarchic hope appears to be most fully developed (see NOTES and COMMENT). Haggai 2:20 is set approximately one month later than Zechariah 1:1; but it hardly seems possible that events changed so drastically within that short time span that would allow for such differences to emerge. Rather, Zechariah and his compiler or secretary were perhaps more attuned to the political realities of the day, more pragmatic in their approach than was Haggai. Such a contrast may be drawn narrowly between Haggai 2:20-23 and Zechariah 1:1-6. We may discern a similar persistent contrast between the two prophets despite their compositional integrity.

Zechariah and his followers are pragmatic in accepting Zerubbabel as governor and Davidide along with Joshua as high priest as the acceptable agents of local civil and religious administration within an imperial Persian framework of authority. Zechariah, as we shall see, accepts the radically altered circumstance of the restoration period in which no king and no fully independent state are possible. But he will seek to reconcile this situation to expectations and hopes shaped by past experience. Although the exilic prophets also preached in a time when there was neither king nor political independence, the return of the land and the achievement of limited political autonomy represented a new situation, a situation recognized and hailed by another biblical prophetic figure as having the power of salvation (Isa 44:28; 45:1).

Scholarly discussion about this initial oracle has tended to focus upon the meaning of "they returned" in verse 6b (see NOTES). Our analysis of that verse takes seriously both the impact and success of Haggai's utterances and the internal chronology of Haggai-Zechariah 1-8. That is to say, by November 520 the Yehudites had somehow been stirred to action and had already begun to collect materials for work on the temple rebuilding. Moreover, Haggai had no doubt impressed upon them the necessity of adhering to God's words in all aspects of community life (see NOTES to the priestly ruling of Hag 2:10ff., although that ruling actually would have followed Zechariah's first oracle). Since part of the result of Haggai's and Zechariah's prophetic activity is the return to work on the temple (Ezra 5:1 and 6:14), now given its symbolic interpretation by Zechariah as the representation of God's presence and sovereignty, it thus seems warranted to understand verse 6b in these terms. In our view it is not necessary to emend the text to accommodate alternate views of time sequence or meaning. Zechariah is referring to the immediate past, the time leading up to the renewal of temple building. The omission of the "evil" of verse 4b in the language of 6b surely reflects, as we have pointed out in NOTES, that the sins of the postexilic period were less reprehensible than those of the preexilic age. In either case, God metes out justice, according to what the disobedience deserves; Zechariah's countrymen truly have learned such a lesson and have responded to the prophetic call.

In sum, the Call to Obedience serves multiple purposes in its position as an introduction to Zechariah 1–8. First, it provides a critical linkage with the Book of Haggai. The ministries of the two prophets overlapped, and the dates provided in their works suggest that a composite work was promulgated sometime before the completion of the temple around 515 B.C.E. Second, as an introduction to Part Two of First Zechariah, which includes the sequence of seven visions plus prophetic vision with related and interspersed oracles and excurses (1:7–6:15) as well as an introduction to Part Three, the Address to the Delegation from Bethel and Supplementary Oracles (7–8), it establishes the tone and direction of the whole. In this regard the change in heart and commencement of building activities associated with the temple in Haggai can be presupposed. It is the meaning of that work for all factions of Yahwists that must be addressed. Third, the prophet's reference to earlier prophets and reliance on covenant language places Zechariah and/or his secretary-compiler within the mainstream of classical biblical writings, the Law and the Prophets, and exemplifies the vitality of traditional materials for the postexilic community.

That these initial introductory six verses do so much is no insignificant achievement. Indeed, by mixing prophetic and pentateuchal language the prophet has characterized his mission as one which integrates disparate yet overlapping areas of human existence. The communal and religious identity during the postexilic era was ultimately to survive without the office of prophet and without the institution of kingship, at least until the Hasmonaean era when the latter appeared. Zechariah's overt utilization of authoritative tradition and his effectiveness in doing so must be given due credit. He helped to shape an innovative community organization which could exist and flourish even without full political autonomy.

Part Two

Zech 1:7–6:15

THE VISIONS WITH ORACULAR SUPPLEMENTS

2. FIRST VISION: HORSES PATROLLING THE EARTH
(1:7–17)

Superscription to the visions

[7] On the twenty-fourth day of the eleventh month, the month of Shebat, in the second year of Darius, the word of Yahweh came to the prophet Zechariah ben-Berechiah ben-Iddo [and Zechariah said]:

First Vision

[8] I looked out in the night and behold: there was a man mounted on a red horse! He was stationed in the shadows among the myrtles; and behind him were red, sorrel, and white horses. [9] Then I said, "What are these, my lord?"

The angel-who-speaks-with-me said, "I will show you what they are."

[10] Then the man who was stationed among the myrtles answered and said, "These are the ones which Yahweh sent to roam about the earth. [11] They reported to the Angel of Yahweh who stood among the myrtles and said, 'We have roamed about the earth and all the earth indeed rests quietly.' [12] Then the Angel of Yahweh answered and said, 'O Yahweh of Hosts, for how long will you show no compassion for Jerusalem and the cities of Judah, with whom you have been angry these seventy years?' "

[13] Yahweh answered the angel-who-speaks-with-me with good, comforting words.

Yahweh responds: three oracles

[14] The angel-who-speaks-with-me then said to me, "Proclaim: 'Thus spoke Yahweh of Hosts,

I have shown great zeal for Jerusalem and Zion,

[15] and I feel great wrath against the nations which rest securely with whom I felt but little wrath although they fostered evil.

16 'Therefore, thus spoke Yahweh,
 I have returned to Jerusalem with compassion.
 My house will be rebuilt there—Oracle of Yahweh of
 Hosts—
 For a line* is stretched out over Jerusalem.'
17 Proclaim again: 'Thus said Yahweh of Hosts,
 My cities will again overflow with bounty;
 Yahweh will again comfort Zion, again choose Jerusalem.' "

NOTES

1:7. *twenty-fourth day of the eleventh month, the month of Shebat, in the second year of Darius.* February 15, 519. This is the fullest superscription in Haggai and Zechariah; it provides the day of the month, the month's number, also the name of the month, and the year according to the reign of the Persian monarch. This date puts the visions that follow into the chronological position of having occurred immediately preceding the beginning of the New Year. The significance of temple building in relation to New Year's rites has long been noted (e.g., May 1938 and Halpern 1978). Consequently, a date just prior to the New Year would be appropriate for the visions of Zechariah, since they are so closely associated with the restoration work on the Jerusalem temple, and apparently come as a response to the temple refoundation ceremony of December 18, 520.

The chronological heading, one of three in Zechariah, introduces the second and longest (1:7–6:15) section of First Zechariah's work. Two months have elapsed since the last prophecies (Hag 2:10,18,20) of the Haggai-Zechariah 1–8 composite, and about three months have passed since Zechariah's own initial prophecy. The temple refoundation ceremony, which apparently had produced the two theophanies to Haggai on December 18 as well as the repeated references to that date, was now an event of the past. Zechariah's prophetic imagination is free to deal with the meaning of the temple project in relationship to the traditional understanding of the temple's role in society.

The date begins with the day of the month, followed by the month itself, and concludes with the year. It shares this sequence only with the information provided by Hag 2:10 (and 18,20), which denotes the temple foundation ceremony (see NOTES to 2:10). Hag 1:15 apparently has the same order, but the position of the year there (see NOTE) at the end probably is related to the way it serves double duty for the date of Hag 2:1. Zech 1:1 lacks the day, though were the day included it would follow the day-month-year pattern of this verse and Hag 2:10. The citation of day and month before the year rather than after it is curious. The opening and closing date formulas (Hag 1:1 and Zech 7:1; see NOTES) of Haggai-Zechariah 1–8 emphatically start with the regnal year. We can speculate that the dates opening with reference to the day and month are more concerned with internal Yehudite affairs exclusive of Persian directives than are

---

* Reading with qere *(qāw)* and LXX.

the dates opening with specification of a regnal year. See also our COMMENT and NOTES to the dates in Hag:1 and in Zech 1:1 and 7:1.

the word of Yahweh came. Cf. second NOTE to 1:1.

[and Zechariah said]:. The sequence between verse 7 and the first-person account of the vision in verse 8 and following is problematic, probably because verse 7 is part of the editorial framework that introduces the prophet's visions, accepted by the editor as Yahweh's words. Our supplying this phrase is meant to be helpful to the reader and does not reflect either the Hebrew text or any of the versions. An alternative solution would be to drop the preceding clause of message transmission entirely ("the word of Yahweh came to the prophet Zechariah ben-Berechiah ben-Iddo"), connecting the first part of the verse with Zechariah's own introduction to the first vision in the next verse, as is found in Isaiah 6:1 (see Mitchell 1912:116). The clause that would be dropped bears the marks of the compiler's hand insofar as it refers to Zechariah in the third person. Such a suggestion, however, does not adequately recognize the fact that the dates in Haggai and Zechariah are supplied in order to convey important historical information. The dates as well as the message transmission clauses are integral parts of a literary structuring of Haggai-Zechariah 1–8 by an editor if not by Zechariah himself.

8. *I looked out.* Or, "I saw" (Heb. *rāʾîtî*) introduces this vision and is used, either directly or indirectly (with the angel telling Zechariah to see something or asking him what he sees), at the outset of all seven visions (2:1,5 [RSV 1:18, 2:1]; 4:2; 5:1,5; 6:1). The prophetic vision of chapter 3 also uses the verb "to see," although there it appears in the Hiphil ("he showed me," 3:1). The verb is followed by *hinnēh,* rendered "behold" by us, RSV, and other English versions and also indicated in our translation by the exclamation point (!). Although the ensuing vision involves a nighttime setting (see next NOTE), the use of the *rʾh* ("to see") terminology surely points to a wakeful prophetic experience rather than to any somnambulistic or dreamlike state on the part of the prophet.

The prophet as "seer" (cf. 1 Sam 9:9) is a dimension of Israelite prophecy that goes back to the general phenomenon of Near Eastern prophetic activity (Orlinsky 1965:153–74) and continues in the occasional oracles of the classical prophets which arise from their "seeing" in something a portentous message from Yahweh. While these prophetic visions tend to be evoked by mundane objects (Amos 8:1–2; Jer 1:11–12), there is no lack of visions with supramundane or celestial contents (Isa 6:1ff.; Amos 9:1; and Ezek 1:1).

in the night. The Hebrew word *hallayĕlâ* is perhaps the only direct indication in the visions of the time of day in which they occur. Chapter 4:1 appears to contain indirect information suggestive of a nighttime setting, but we reject such a possibility (see NOTE to "from sleep"). Because "in the night" is used here at the outset, it is often taken as a temporal introduction to the series of visions, all of which may have occurred in one night. Many treatments of Zechariah in fact entitle the ensuing material the "Night Visions." It is not clear that all the visions in fact occurred in one night, although the use of this word here seems intended to give that impression. However, the word for "night" appears with the definite article but without a pronoun or preposition. While it could therefore mean "this night"—i.e., signify the time of day, evening rather than morning, and not darkness or night as a setting in which the vision appears (cf. 1 Sam 15:16)—it more likely indicates "by night" as a condition of darkness that contrasts with daylight. Among the many adverbial uses of "night" in prepositional phrases, the appearance of "night" without the affixed preposition is relatively rare. In addition to the "this night" possibility to which we give little credence, there is a small set of usages in which *hallayĕlâ* denotes nighttime, specifically because of certain actions which are to take place secretly, under cover of darkness. The escape of the Judean warriors (and perhaps King Zedekiah as well) from Jerusalem under Babylonian siege was effected through a secret gateway "by night" (2 Kgs 25:4 = Jer 52:7); and the rebuilding of Jerusalem's wall under Nehemiah had aroused such opposition from certain quarters that the day laborers were not allowed to return to their homes after work but rather remained in Jerusalem, sleeping with their weapons handy and serving as a reserve guard "by night" (Neh 4:16; 4:22 in translation). In light of the vocabulary that follows depicting the darkness of a myrtle thicket which hides Yahweh's emissaries or informants, "in the night" introduces a similar element of secrecy appropriate to the account of the horseback messengers who are the chief figures in the ensuing vision.

man. The identity of this individual on horseback is a matter of some confusion. Subsequent figures in this vision, the Interpreting Angel (vv 9, 13, 14) and the Angel of Yahweh (vv 11 and 12), perhaps can be identified with each other, at least in the present stage of the text, which perhaps represents a conflation of visionary materials. The man on horseback, who is surely also an angelic being (cf. Gen 19:1; 32:25 [RSV 32:24]), would then be a distinct actor in this vision; yet in verse 11 he appears to be the same as the Angel of Yahweh. The problem is further complicated by the sudden appearance of the Interpreting Angel as the object of the prophet's query in verse 9. Zechariah does not introduce the angelic actors nor does he give them proper names, although the angels he depicts may emerge in later literature, such as the Book of Daniel and some intertestamental writings: the angel Michael, Gabriel, and others (see Dan 8:16; 9:21; 10:13; 12:1). The lack of specificity in Zechariah's use of angelic figures perhaps befits their character as divine beings, which must remain beyond full ken. The role of the Angel of Yahweh in Yahweh's Council emerges in chapter 3; see NOTE to "Angel of Yahweh" in 3:1.

mounted. The verb *rkb* is often translated by "ride." However, its primary meaning is "to mount, to be positioned upon something" in both Hebrew and Ugaritic as well as in Akkadian *(rakābu)*, Aramaic, and Arabic (Barrick 1982). For this passage, the image of a man seated on a horse rather than moving on his steed is far more appropriate than what would be conveyed by "to ride." Although it includes a description of movement that the horsemen have carried out, the vision itself is his delineation of the scene before him. *'md* ("to stand, be stationed"), is another word offering no hint of locomotion.

in the shadows. Hebrew *mĕṣūlâ* is obscure; it is a *hapax legomenon* probably derived from *ṣl* or *ṣll,* "to be or grow dark," and gives the impression of a low, shady place. The LXX, probably influenced by 6:1, translates the next phrase "between the mountains" rather than "among the myrtles"; nonetheless it understands the term to mean "dark" by rendering "shady mountains." Alternatively, NEB, RSV, NJPS, and *BDB* read *mĕṣillâ* from *ṣwl,* meaning "deep" or "hollow." Either reading fits the MT "among the myrtles," which do grow along watercourses in low places. A rather different reading is offered by Rudolph (1976:72). He proposes *miṣlâ,* "in the prayer places" *("an der Gebetsstätte"),* which is derived from Aramaic *ṣlh,* "to pray." However, the use of "shadows" has a direct implication of darkness, reinforced by the following phrase "among the myrtles," which is absent in the translations that provide "deep" or "hollow" as well as in Rudolph's reading. The implications of "shadows" are preferable here, especially because of the intensification provided by the succeeding words and also because of the context of the four horses (and probably horsemen) who are Yahweh's global informants.

The vision of the horsemen spreading out over the whole world apparently reflects knowledge of the elaborate intelligence and communications system worked out by the neo-Babylonians and especially by the Persians (cf. NOTE to "Accuser" in 3:1). Speed and secrecy were the key features of that system. The dimension of secrecy is conveyed graphically in this vision by the deep darkness of myrtle shadows. Similarly, "in the night" (cf. NOTE) provides a setting of nighttime with its obscuring darkness. A vocabulary stressing low visibility and therefore the requisite secrecy helps to develop the overall theme of Yahweh's omniscience that this vision conveys. Divine knowledge of all human activity is expressed in language derived from a human emperor's procedures for keeping informed of events in this realm (Oppenheim 1968). While there is nothing inherently secretive about Yahweh's acquiring knowledge of worldly events, human unawareness of God's constant surveillance allows for the aptness of this metaphoric language.

myrtles. The "myrtle" is an evergreen shrub *(Myrtus communis)* growing in low places or on hillsides. Its special significance in antiquity may derive from its regenerative qualities and its resistance to fire (Hareuveni 1980:84–85). Myrtle branches were among the greenery cut to make booths for the Feast of Tabernacles, according to Neh 8:15 (and in contrast with Lev 23:40), and the myrtle figures among the trees which flourish in the eschatological age (Isa 41:19; 55:13).

What can be its specific contribution to the scene painted in this verse? Its use here is no doubt related to the thickness of its low-lying foliage, for it is a shrub and not a tree. Indeed, in rabbinic tradition the enigmatic "thick tree" *('ēṣ 'ābōt)* of the four species (Neh 8:15) is identified with the myrtle, an identification acceptable to a modern talmudic botanist (Feliks 1981:277) and a tradition underscoring the reputation of the myrtle for having dense foliage. In addition, its year-round verdancy would have been a feature essential to the nuances of this vision, which took place in winter (February, 519 B.C.E.). That is, the usefulness of the thick myrtle leaves for hiding horses or horsemen would have been diminished in winter had the shrub been deciduous. Just as the element of darkness can be related to secrecy (see above), so too the appearance of a myrtle thicket provides the idea of cover and concealment. "Among the myrtles" and "in the shadows" together emphasize the hiddenness involved in the proper function of a system of intelligence for a human ruler and thus for the cosmic ruler, Yahweh. The two phrases serve as a kind of hendiadys expressing complete darkness.

red, sorrel, and white. Identifying the kind of horses indicated here and in chapter 6:2ff. and 6ff. presents considerable difficulties. How many horses or horse colors are meant to be featured in this vision? The Hebrew text of this verse would indicate that only three different kinds of horses appear, a fact that would be at odds with the related four chariots of chapter 6 and seemingly with the notion of patrolling all the earth, which is normally represented by its four corners or directions (see below, NOTES to chapter 6). The ancient translators present rather divergent pictures in their rendering of this verse and the ones in chapter 6. McHardy (1968:174–79) has made an ingenious though unlikely case for the possibility that the confusion has arisen from the misuse of abbreviations. In certain cases in the Hebrew Bible, abbreviations for common or stereotyped phenomena may have been used in early textual traditions but then were incorrectly interpreted by later scribes who sought to write out the full words. McHardy has argued vigorously that four color-words rather than a mixture of equine colors and patterns were original to this vision and to the last one.

For this verse he proposes that the second use of "red" be replaced by *'ămuṣṣîm*, which the LXX translates, and which is actually a mistaken expansion of the abbreviation *'m*, which would stand for *'ămānâ*, or "yellow." Since *'āmōs* is also a color word designating a shade of red (Brenner 1982:112), the same abbreviation could have signified "red," thereby creating even greater textual confusion. The "sorrel," *śĕruqqîm*, should be replaced by "black," on the grounds that a scribe read *š* as an abbreviation for "black," *šĕḥōrîm*. "White" presents no problem. In sum, McHardy asserts that the text would have read "a man riding on a red horse . . . and behind him were yellow, black and white horses." He notes in this matter of color nomenclature that Joel 2:4 compares horses with locusts, which can be categorized by color: yellow, red, white, and black. By analogy, he reasons, this vision should depict four major equine colors which would correspond to the four directions in which these horses roam. Significantly, the directions themselves were rendered by such abbreviations by ancient writers (preserved in postbiblical works such as Enoch [30:13]), which probably contributed to some of the confusion about the directions in the horse and chariot vision of chapter 6 (see NOTES to 6:2–3, 6–7).

As ingenious as McHardy's proposal is, the fact remains that only three colors are listed in the MT and that they are not all primary colors. In our translation we have adhered to the Hebrew text despite the harmonizations suggested by various modern commentators and ancient versions. The existence of three colors rather than four should not obscure the fact that there are still four horses—the red one on which the man is mounted and the three behind him. Furthermore, the use of "sorrel," a mixed-color word, rather than black may have been offensive to translators who sought a pattern of color usage, but not to Zechariah, who merely wished to portray three distinct horses.

The directional problem likewise may be one that exists only for those who seek to align this vision with the last one. In chapter 6, the listing of horses of four different colors makes sense in that compass directions are given and "four winds of heaven" are cited. In contrast, this vision, although proclaiming divine omniscience, does not do so in terms of compass points. The horses that "roam about the earth" (v 10) apparently are three and not four in number and can themselves represent totality. Three is indeed a number symbolic of completeness in Semitic tradition. An instructive analogy can be found in Ezek 5:1–3, where the MT records that Ezekiel divided his hair into thirds and the LXX regularly changes it to "fourths." Global scrutiny in the First Vision is distinct from the concept of the world represented by four directions or quadrants as in the Seventh Vision. Therefore, the use of three horse colors for the three horses that perform the mission of checking on the condition of the world is perfectly acceptable and perhaps even preferable to the use of four.

The significance of the three horse colors of the MT remains elusive. McHardy's theory that Zechariah 1:8 originally had the four basic equine colors is clever but does damage to the existing text. Hareuveni offers a more tenable solution (1980:115–17). The vision takes place in the eleventh month; and the name of the month—Shebat—is given, emphasizing that time of the year. In uncultivated areas, by the end of Shebat the landscape is ablaze with color. The color scheme of a field in Shebat is distinctive, and contrasts with the range of colors that appear earliest in spring, at the end of the preceding month of Tebet, when yellows, lavenders, whites, and some reds dominate. In Shebat, the red blossoms of tulips and anemones increase greatly in quantity while the pastels of early spring have disappeared. White almond blossoms and broom brushes and also white anemones appear in profusion. The natural vegetation of the tenth month created a palette of mixed red and white.

Let us look at the horses again. "Red" and "white" would correspond to the primary colors of the Shebat landscape in areas that were cultivated. What about "sorrel?" That color is a secondary term in the red range. As a horse color term, it apparently represents a combination of red and white; cf. Arabic *'ašpar*, which designates horses that have a ruddy tinge over white *(BDB* 977). The third horse color would represent precisely the mix of red and white that would meet the eye looking upon a field of red and white blossoms. Horses that were on a secret surveillance mission in Shebat would best blend into the natural background if they were red, white, and a mix of red and white—i.e., sorrel. An interesting Kabbalistic custom, which took place on the eve of Tu B'Shvat ("New Year of Trees," on the fifteenth day of Shebat), provides a striking analogy to the red-white-sorrel grouping. The Jewish mystics of Safed held a meal, akin to a Passover Seder, in which they drank four goblets of wine: 1. red wine, 2. white wine mixed with a bit of red, 3. half red and half white wine, and 4. mostly red with a tinge of white. The color gradations of red and white mirror the landscape that prevailed at the time of this nature festival. Perhaps the three horses of Zechariah's First Vision likewise are intimately related to the vegetation of the eleventh month.

horses. The four-footed animals of this vision were hardly everyday riding beasts in ancient Palestine, where the normal mode of transport, for humans and for burdens, was the donkey. Horses were used almost exclusively for military purposes in the ancient Near East, where they formed an integral part of the cavalry, as the Assyrian reliefs show (Yadin 1963:302), and were also essential to the royal chariot corps (see NOTE to "chariots," 6:8). Their use for transportation was generally restricted to the royalty and the very wealthy (Thompson 1962:646). Never used as a plow animal and rarely used for pulling anything but a chariot, the horse in the Hebrew Bible is nearly always mentioned in military and/or royal contexts. However, it is also a symbol of speed, and it is this association along with the military-royal one which is important to the First Vision.

In Job 39:13–18, for example, the horse's swiftness is compared unfavorably with that of the ostrich; but since the ostrich is one of the swiftest animals known to man and can attain speeds of fifty miles per hour, the horse does not suffer greatly from the comparison. Amos (2:15) cites the horse for its swiftness in normally enabling its rider to escape a difficult situation, and Jeremiah (12:5) similarly assumes the advantage of a horse in any race. Perhaps most significant for understanding this passage is the account in 1 Kgs 20 of the conflict between Ben-hadad, king of Syria, and the Israelite King Ahab. Ahab was able to capture most of the fleeing Syrian soldiers who sought to escape in their horse-drawn chariots, but Ben-hadad himself, on a horse without a chariot, succeeded along with other horsemen in escaping (1 Kgs 20:20). Horses, especially without chariots, represent swiftness.

The fact that this First Vision has many points of contact with the last vision, both having equine groups going out as divine emissaries, makes those two visions serve as a framing structure for the entire visionary sequence (cf. NOTE to "four chariots," 6:1). However, one of the major distinctions between the First and Seventh Visions is the presence of chariots, the normal biblical complement to horses, in the last vision and their absence in this one. The appearance of these four equidae without the expected vehicles thus alters the imagery from the royal-military symbolism of the horse-with-chariot to the swiftness quality of the horse alone. Indeed, if the hallmarks of a ruler's effective information system are secrecy and speed, the horses clearly denote the latter, with "night," "in the shadows," and "among the myrtles" (see second, fourth, and fifth NOTES to verse 8) denoting the former. Such language in the opening vision contributes to the concept of Yahweh's full awareness of the worldwide arena of human existence. The omniscience of God is represented by metaphors of swiftness and secrecy, which are the essential characteristics of the mechanisms on the plane of humanity for keeping a ruler informed, especially as they were developed during the period of the Persian Empire (cf. Oppenheim 1968).

9. *angel-who-speaks-with-me.* The notion of divine beings possessing some of the same characteristics that Yahweh exhibits and appearing in human form as messengers of Yahweh to humans runs throughout the Hebrew Bible. Many of the theophanic narratives of Genesis and Judges, for example, feature angelic beings who bring God's word directly to patriarchs or judges. However, this phrase, the angel-who-speaks-with-me *(mal'āk haddōbēr bî)*, or Interpreting Angel, represents a new stage in the function of angelic figures in the transmission of messages. This angel enters into dialogue with the prophet, who himself is a messenger of God (cf. Hag 1:13), in order to clarify a vision and so transmit Yahweh's will. The distinct content of the prophet's vision is not clear to him without the interpretation of the angel, who is also a figure in the prophet's visionary experience. Such an interpreting messenger, or *angelus interpres,* is a prominent feature in much of apocalyptic literature or apocalyptic eschatology (cf. Hanson 1975:250ff.). The delineation of heavenly beings with specific roles, however, is only one of many characteristics of later apocalyptic writings. Thus the appearance of the Interpreting Angel in Zechariah in and of itself is not to be taken as an indicator that this prophetic work is apocalyptic.

The role of angelic beings is one of the most distinctive aspects of the Book of Zechariah, but it has clear antecedents in prophetic tradition. Zechariah's use of angels is surely anticipated in Ezekiel and the preexilic traditions about the "Angel of Yahweh." However, the extent to which Zechariah develops the character of angels as divine messengers and informants may be a function of political conditions in the exilic and postexilic periods. Angels help Yahweh control his universal realm, just as human couriers and spies allow an emperor to direct events in his empire. Once Jerusalem fell, the inhabitants of Judah would have become all too familiar with the surveillance and messenger systems of the Babylonians and then the Persians. Zechariah theologizes an imperial communications network in the role he gives to angelic beings serving Yahweh, the universal sovereign.

10. *the man who was stationed.* While the verb is "stood," the reference here is to the same being as in verse 1 and so designates the man on horseback. He and his horse are standing amidst the undergrowth of myrtle. He reports on the activities of Yahweh's emissaries. While the text does not specify riders for the other horses, one must suppose that the horses were mounted and that their riders are delivering the report given in the plural ("we have roamed") in verse 11. The vagueness of the text is only apparent. Probably in the language of cavalry, which was a major element in the Persian imperial army, references to horses sent on a mission implied the human riders as well.

to roam. Literally, "to go back and forth." This line appears again (v 11) in this vision and several times (in 6:7) in the Seventh Vision. The use of the Hithpael of *hlk* suggests the totality of the territory covered by this equine scouting expedition. The horses and their riders have gone to and fro, and, by the force of such an implicit merism, have looked everywhere. Cf. Job 2:2, where Satan appears before Yahweh in the Divine Council after having "roamed to and fro" in all the earth. In Job, both the Divine Council setting and the specific meaning of the word "earth" contribute to a sense of the universal scope intended there. Note also its use in Gen 3:8 where God patrols the garden. A similar spirit of universalism is conveyed here. In none of these instances is the one walking—God or Satan or a horseman—simply out for a stroll; rather he is looking for something or keeping his eye on things.

11. *Angel of Yahweh.* Chief angelic figure, probably the "man" of 1:8 (cf. NOTE, and also see 3:1).

among the myrtles. This repetition of "among the myrtles" for the third time serves to place the angelic figures within the visionary scene as well as outside of it. The angel is exterior to the vision in that he converses with the prophet, who as witness to the vision is outside it, concerning the meaning of what the prophet sees. Yet he is also a figure who exchanges speech with the personae of the vision. The fluidity of his role, whereby he moves back and forth from the prophet to what the prophet sees, is conveyed by using the same phrase of location ("among the myrtles") for the angel as for the horsemen. His role outside the visionary field itself has already been established by his dialogue with the prophet in verse 9. Within the vision, "Angel of Yahweh" as the surrogate for Yahweh himself designates this figure, whereas in relationship to the prophet as interlocutor, "angel-who-speaks-with-me" tends to be used. Note the sequence in verses 12–13.

all the earth. "Earth" (*'ereṣ*) here and in the preceding verse has a global dimension, probably in antithesis to heaven as God's domain. The horse patrol surveys the whole terrestrial expanse. If the three horses (cf. NOTE to v 8) represent totality, they signify the universal scope of this phrase (Ottosson 1974:393–97).

rests quietly. Political/military conflict has subsided (cf. Judg 3:11). The international political situation suggested by the report of the patrol is one of stability. The initial unrest accompanying Darius's accession to the throne had been resolved, and Darius had quelled the rebellious activities of the Egyptians and others. The very fact that temple work resumes now in Yehud (see our COMMENT to Hag 1:1–11) indicates a Persian policy meant to mollify the indigenous leadership throughout the empire in order to prevent further uprising. Whereas Cyrus's military might had for the most part assured local subservience, Darius achieved stability in this realm through careful organization of provincial units and the granting of local autonomy.

12. *for how long.* Literally "until when," *ʿad-mātay* followed by a verb or a verb implied through aposiopesis (as Ps 6:4 [RSV 6:3]; 90:13) is an idiom used to question, and thereby to protest, the continued existence of an undesirable or virtually unbearable situation. The idiom is often attached to an apostrophic address to any individual or, frequently as in this case, to God. Its frequent usage in Psalms (6:4 [RSV 6:3]; 74:10; 80:5 [RSV 80:4]; 82:2; 90:13; 94:3) always involves a plea directed toward Yahweh. Prophetic request for divine response or aid rarely (Isa 6:11) utilizes this idiom. Note that despite the prophetic context of Zechariah, the angel and not the prophet utters the impassioned cry in this instance. The Angel of Yahweh stands before God, and in the manner typical of the psalmists' importunings, pleads on behalf of the cities of Judah and Jerusalem as their advocate or defense attorney.

show no compassion. The verb *rḥm* ("to love, show compassion") is strongly associated with Yahweh in the Hebrew Bible and offers a profound indication of God's passionate nature, particularly in his love for humanity (Freedman 1955; cf. Andersen and Freedman 1980:187ff. on Hosea's use of *rḥm).* The question here supposes that this anthropopathic attribute of God, namely compassion, has been suspended, a condition reported in the second part of the angel's question, verse 12, which records the sustained anger of Yahweh (see NOTE below to "have been angry"). The angel's question takes for granted that God has suspended his affection and kindness toward Israel and is asking how long God will continue to be angry at his own people. The dire circumstances and hence the human suffering suggested by these two verbs elicit the notion of anguish and anticipate the comfort that will be provided by God's response in verse 13. The termination of God's anger and of his withholding of love is signaled in the oracles at the end of this vision, where *rḥm* recurs as the noun *raḥămîm,* "compassion."

Note that it is the Angel of Yahweh and not the prophet who acts as intercessor; he poses the question and is subsequently comforted. The angel is the one who is sorely distressed at the long removal of divine favor from Israel. Yet the angel is an extension of God's being, he is Yahweh's alter ego. That he suffers suggests in a rather subtle way the possibility of divine suffering at the plight of Israel. When Yahweh is confronted by the query of his chief angel, he responds positively and immediately.

Jerusalem and the cities of Judah. This is a patently political designation for the realm of the Davidic ruler (Noth 1966:138) and occurs, albeit not always with "cities," very frequently in Isaiah and in Jeremiah and elsewhere. It seems that the angel's question is not here concerned directly with the welfare of the inhabitants but rather with their political identity. The latter condition, or rather question, is of great importance for those residing in the province of Yehud. Their autonomy had been severely curtailed by the events of the past generation. Now, with Darius's encouragement, work on the rebuilding of the temple had begun. The question of the monarchy, an associated expression of Judean autonomy, was thereby reopened.

have been angry. The verb *zʿm,* "to be angry, indignant," is used seven times in the Hebrew Bible with Yahweh as the subject. Like *rḥm* (see above NOTE in this verse on "show no compassion"), it is part of a biblical vocabulary revealing the attributes of God in relationship to mankind, for the objects of divine anger expressed by *zʿm* are, except in one case, personal. Wiklander (1980:108) suggests that an early meaning of "curse," derived from the image of Yahweh as righteous judge, has been extended by late biblical times to a more general concept of wrath, although certain usages in postexilic prophecy, such as this one and Mal 1:4, possibly retain a vestige of its earlier meaning. If that is so, it only serves to emphasize the intensity of Yahweh's rage, which in this passage appears as an antonym of Yahweh's equally intense love or compassion.

seventy years. This figure has often been taken (e.g., Mitchell 1912:124–25; Thomas 1956:1062) as a utilization by Zechariah of the reference in Jeremiah (25:11–12 and 29:10) to a seventy-year period. The difficulty with such a suggestion stems in part from the fact that the Jeremiah passages refer to a period of seventy years of Babylonian rule, beginning with the events of 597, and not of Judean exile. That span would thus have been completed at the time of Cyrus, nearly two decades before Zechariah's prophecies. Thus Zechariah's utilization of the seventy years' concept must be taken in a different way, as a stage in a series of applications of a symbolic seventy-year span to specific dates in Israelite history (see Ackroyd 1958:23–27).

The symbolic nature of "seventy" has long been noticed; e.g., recently by Fensham (1977). It represents a complete or whole span of time, such as the years of an individual's full life (Gen 5:12; 11:26). There is strong evidence to suggest that it was part of a general idiom in the ancient Near East that designated the waning of a nation's political power in terms of the full spending of a god's anger against a particular political entity (Malamat 1982:218). Lipiński (1970) has pointed out that the inscription of the Assyrian king Esar-haddon (681–669 B.C.E.) mentions that the god Marduk should have been angry with his land for seventy years. Being merciful, however, Marduk reduced the number to eleven. Similarly, Isaiah's reference to the fate of Tyre (23:15–17) involves a seventy-year period of political obliteration. Those seventy years are symbolic and not literal. They are like the "days of one king"—i.e., a full span, during which time the god's anger, his withdrawal from the wayward nation, abates and his presence is restored to the reconstituted polity, whether Tyre, Babylon, Judah, or any other conquered state.

Zechariah's usage of the seventy-year span, here and in chapter 7 (vv 3 and 5), is a step in the ongoing reinterpretation of Jeremiah's symbolic expression of Yahweh's anger, or at least of a commonly held notion that seventy years was a maximum period of divine anger. One cannot be sure that Zechariah is consciously drawing upon Jeremiah, although in light of Zechariah's explicit citation of "earlier prophets" (see NOTES to that phrase in 1:4 and 7:7) it is difficult to believe he is not. Both prophets are concerned with the duration of the destruction and exile, but their perspective is somewhat different. Jeremiah is looking at the length of Babylon's hegemony as well as the extent of exile, whereas Zechariah is talking about the unmitigated suffering. Jeremiah had quite naturally projected a count that would bring God's anger to an end when Babylonian might was overthrown. The Babylonian Empire had come to an end, but that event had not resulted in a restoration of Judean political independence. Jeremiah's seventy-year prophecy had not exactly been fulfilled.

Zechariah anticipated that the rebuilding and rededication of the temple would be the events to bring the end of God's wrath. His calculation would have used, appropriately, the destruction of the temple in 587/6 as the onset of divine anger, rather than the exile of Jehoiacin in 597, which was the starting point for Jeremiah's reckoning of seventy years. Jeremiah did not need to deal with the end point, but Zechariah did, and his use of 587/6 makes seventy years a particularly potent symbol in light of the fact that the seventy years would nearly have elapsed at the time of his prophecies. The imminent end of seventy years must surely have been a strong motivating factor in the rebuilding efforts in that the rededication of the temple might coincide with the end of that time period. The very appearance of so many date formulas in both Haggai and Zechariah indicates that these prophets and/or their editor were well attuned to what year it was, could well calculate the amount of time that had passed since Jerusalem fell, and were probably activated to considerable extent by the expectations aroused by their historical acumen. As it turned out, the dedication in 515 was remarkably close to the projected date. The fact that Ezra (6:15) reports a 515 date (the third of Adar in the sixth year of Darius I = March 12, 515; see Cross 1975:16) and not a 516 one certainly reflects on Ezra's veracity; he preserved the actual time of the event and not the ideal time, which would have been a year earlier (contra Ackroyd 1958, who argues that Ezra's date is a chronistic fabrication). Similarly, the absence of that date in Haggai and Zechariah 1–8, as we have asserted elsewhere (e.g., in our Introduction), shows that those prophetic books received their final form in advance of the completion and dedication of the temple.

Further reworking of the seventy-year concept occurs in 2 Chron 36:21 and in Dan 9:2. In these passages, the period of seventy years is viewed as a precise figure, referring to the desolation of Jerusalem (and the temple) and not to the ascendancy of Babylon as Jeremiah had specified. The dedication of the temple nearly seventy years after its destruction had made its impact so that Jeremiah's prophecy, altered somewhat in its citation, could be seen as fulfilled.

13. *Yahweh answered.* The identity of the speaker here is clearly God. However, the transition to the use of the phrase "angel-who-speaks-with-me" (Interpreting Angel instead of "Angel of Yahweh") for the figure addressed by Yahweh has caused some conjecture about levels of redaction in this vision. Rather than pointing to redactional interference, it more probably reflects the complex nature of the levels of mediation of God's word, within the visionary field itself and in relation to the prophet's apperception of the vision. Since the prophet himself is normally depicted as conversing with the Interpreting Angel rather than the "Angel of Yahweh," this verse and those that follow are taken to be a resumption of Zechariah's account, begun in verses 8 and 9.

words. The noun for word, *dābār,* when used with Yahweh, functions as a technical term that designates a prophetic word of revelation (see Schmidt 1978:111). *Dābār* in general characterizes the prophet in the same way that *tôrâ* is associated with the priest and *ʿeṣâ* ("counsel") with the sage. Consequently, the fact that Yahweh is the source of the "words" in this verse gives them a prophetic character. The Interpreting Angel becomes both the recipient and then the transmitter (in v 14) of God's word; but the important feature of prophecy, the presentation of God's word to a human audience, is not realized until the angel in turn gives the message to Zechariah who is charged with proclaiming it. The mediating role of an angelic being is in this way inserted into the chain of prophetic utterance. The "words" with which Yahweh answers the Interpreting Angel, if they are indeed prophetic, cannot stop with their immediate reception by the angel. Verses 14–17, which contain the proclamation of the "words" by the prophet, are therefore an essential complement to the information given in verse 13, that Yahweh has spoken to the angel—i.e., that he has provided "words" or prophecy which must yet find their intended destination.

14. *Proclaim:.* The imperative of *qrʾ,* "to call out," is here followed by *lēʾmōr,* "to

say" (rendered by a colon; cf. NOTE to "called out" in 1:4). This introduction to an oracular pronouncement of Yahweh is relatively rare in biblical prophecy. It constitutes an additional stage of the prophetic transmission of God's word. The typical pattern of message delivery in prophetic works is "Thus spoke Yahweh," followed directly by the *ipsissima verba* of God. The pattern is altered in this instance by the insertion of the common "proclaim" before "Thus spoke Yahweh." The prophetic sense of being a mediary between Yahweh and the people is thereby given more direct expression. Not only does God speak to the prophet and then the prophet exclaims his words, but also the prophet experiences Yahweh's explicit instructions that his message is to be broadcast. One can see a similar situation in Jonah 3:2 and in Jer 11:6, although in neither of those instances is the imperative "proclaim" followed by an actual oracular statement.

What can this exceptional announcement of an oracle mean? We are reluctant to attach too much importance to a prophet's creativity in varying the formulaic language of biblical prophecy. Yet two possibilities deserve mention. First, consider the use of "proclaim" insofar as it represents an added step in the prophetic process of a divine statement arising in a prophet's consciousness and then being verbalized to a human audience. This additional layer accords with the general tendency in the postexilic period for angelic beings to arise as intermediary figures in oracular contexts (see NOTE above to "angel-who-speaks-with-me," verse 9) and also with the specific delineation of prophets as divine messengers (cf. Hag 1:13 and NOTE to Zech 3:1). Since the Interpreting Angel in this instance is explicitly conveying the word of Yahweh to the prophet for his utterance, the use of "proclaim" is inseparable from this development in postexilic prophecy. Second, the particular selection of the word "proclaim" rather than "speak" (cf. Hag 2:2) or some other word calling for a statement to be made, has a possible relationship to the physical form in which the oracular words existed. Consider again the information in Jer 11:6; God's command to the prophet to proclaim a message is paralleled by his order to make the words of God's covenant known. Since the latter were surely part of a written document, the suspicion arises that this rare "proclaim" in a prophetic context may have some connotation of a written message that is to be read out. A similar possibility exists for the use of "proclaimed" below in 7:7 and 13 (see NOTES). *Qr²* frequently has precisely that meaning in nonoracular contexts, where it refers to the reading aloud from a book or scroll (e.g., Jer 36:8,10; Neh 8:3,8). In this connection, that is, a prophetic message possibly in written form, the words of Hab 2:2 are relevant: "Write the vision; make it plain upon tablets." These words to Habakkuk, like the proclamation of Zechariah, are consequent upon a question put to Yahweh concerning how long a given condition will obtain.

Another consideration remains. The imperative command "proclaim" is found only once again in Zechariah, below in verse 17, where it is part of the context established in verse 14: the Interpreting Angel provides an oracle from Yahweh and tells the prophet to recite it. Despite the prominent role that the angelic figure plays in all of Zechariah's visions, this is a rare if not unique instance in which he mediates an oracular pronouncement (cf. 2:8–9 [RSV 2:4–5], in which an angelic figure within the vision relates an oracle—but only to a single individual). The apparent communication by the angelic messenger of Yahweh's words in the Third Vision concerns a different cast of characters and not an ultimate delivery of the message to a general audience. Similarly, the investiture passage of chapter 3 includes an Angel of Yahweh conveying God's words to Joshua; but the prophet is not part of this chain of communication nor is Joshua exhorted to pass on the message.

All of this suggests, though it cannot do much more, that Zechariah's usage of "proclaim" verges on the technical. It may denote the presence of a well-defined intermediary—i.e., angelic figure—and perhaps also a written text.

I have shown great zeal. The intense nature of God's relationship with Israel is proclaimed in this expression of God's zealous (Heb. verb from the root *qn'* is used with a cognate accusative derived from that same root) involvement with Jerusalem and Zion. The covenant context of such language has been pointed out by Petitjean 1969:79–81 and Baldwin 1972:101–3. Yahweh's "zealous" or "jealous" regard for Israel is established already in the Decalogue (Exod 20:5; and Deut 5:9; cf. Exod 34:14) and leads to powerful statements of Yahweh's active response to Israel's covenant obedience or disobedience (e.g., Deut 29:19–28 [RSV 29:20–29]). "Zeal" describes Yahweh's affective nature. He feels strongly and reacts vigorously to the behavior of his people. So God's compassionate beneficence as well as his wrath is contained in the notion of Yahweh's devotion or "zeal" for Israel; the tone and measure of Yahweh's passionate reaction depends on whether his people uphold or break the covenant. In Zechariah 8:2 (see NOTE) the intensity of God's love is expressed even more emphatically, for an additional clause with *qn'* is added.

Jerusalem and Zion. While these terms may legitimately be taken together as a reflection of Israelite Zion theology (cf. Roberts 1973), whereby Jerusalem's cosmic significance in Yahweh's realm is proclaimed, the two words may more appropriately be taken as distinct and complementary entities rather than as synonymous expressions. That is, Jerusalem is a broader term, representing the monarchic holdings of the Judean kings; and Zion is the mountain of God's temple. Together, the two aspects of the city's identity create its role as political-religious center of the nation. Cf. below, 8:3, where very similar language occurs.

The order in which the two words occur is unusual. The normal sequence "Zion . . . Jerusalem," appears in Zech 8:3 and also, e.g., in Joel 4:17 (RSV 3:17), Amos 1:2, and Ps 125:1–2. In this set of three oracles, the Zion-Jerusalem combination appears again, at the end of verse 17. By beginning and ending the oracles with "Jerusalem," the prophet is emphasizing Jerusalem. Although the oracles don't actually begin with "Jerusalem," that city's name is the second word, which makes it very close to the beginning, and "Jerusalem" is the last word. The oracles are thus framed with the name Jerusalem. His attention to Jerusalem is further displayed by the two additional mentions of Jerusalem, in verse 16 in the second oracle. Consequently, "Jerusalem" comes at the beginning, middle, and end of the set of oracles. Zechariah could hardly be more forceful in his emphasis, and he has understandably reversed the usual order of Zion-Jerusalem in this verse in order to achieve his goal.

The attention to Jerusalem perhaps highlights another feature of the three oracles. The oracular unit, integrated as it is into the literary structure of the vision itself, is an unusual feature of the First Vision. The oracular material used in the other visions (but perhaps not 2:8–9 [RSV 2:4–5]) tends to be less directly connected with the vision itself, the case in point being the Addendum of 2:10–17 (RSV 2:6–13). We might speculate that the global purview of the initial vision is so sweeping that the prophet feels constrained to anchor it, by means of these oracles, to Jerusalem. As the visionary sequence unfolds, the universal scope of the visions will ultimately come to focus upon Jerusalem and the temple (see Introduction). The oracles that are part of the First Vision anticipate that eventuality; in their concern for Jerusalem, they assure the prophet's audience that the divine omniscience he perceives in the form of swift equine messengers has significance for the fate of Jerusalem.

15. *and I feel great wrath.* Together with verse 14b, this phrase produces a contrast between Yahweh's attitude to Jerusalem and Zion ("I have shown great devotion") on the one hand and to the "nations" on the other hand. Both units in the contrast employ a Hebrew verb followed by a cognate accusative formed from the same root. Here the root is *qṣp*, a biblical term for wrath, particularly that of Yahweh. As a Qal verb referring to God's anger, it occurs only in Third Isaiah (five times) and Deuteronomy (1:34), although the noun *qeṣep* is well distributed in the Hebrew Bible. The verb alone is perhaps somewhat less strong than *z'm* which, as in verse 12, indicates Yahweh's rage. The addition of a cognate accusative, however, strengthens the verbal idea and thereby intensifies God's ire. In the vision (v 12), God's anger with Jerusalem and the cities of Judah is equated with his lack of "compassion" for them. Now, in the oracles that complete the vision, God's wrath against the nations will allow him to restore his "compassion" for Jerusalem (v 16).

against the nations. This appears to be an unspecific and generalized reference to Persia in all of its imperial extent, with the plural "nations" reflecting the considerable conquests of Assyria or Babylonia and the incorporation of them into the empire (see NOTE to "horns of the nations" to 2:4 [RSV 1:21]). The "great wrath" which God feels would derive from the fact that Persia despite its apparently tolerant attitude—at least from the perspective of biblical authors—nonetheless has denied Yehud full independence and the possibility of reestablishing the Davidic monarchy. The present tense of the verb (in v 15a) makes it probable that it is the Persians against whom God's wrath is directed. But the change to the perfect tense (past) and the addition of the qualifier "little" in the second half of the oracle (v 15b) complicates the task of identifying the "nations." Two additional proposals can be considered: 1. An obvious solution would be to understand verse 15b as applying to an earlier period. In such an understanding "the nations" would refer to the Assyrians and Babylonians who had been instruments of God's wrath and judgment against Israel. 2. Another interpretation would allow "nations" to be equated with Persians and thus to be the antecedent of verse 15b. In such a case we would construe God's initial response to the Persians (538–520 B.C.E.) to be less wrathful—i.e., less negative hence more favorable. Verse 15b thus would be more retrospective and might reflect the cautious optimism that originally greeted Persian domination of the Levant soon after Cyrus's decree in 538 B.C.E.

rest securely. While using a different vocabulary, this phrase picks up and explicates the report of the horse patrol in verse 11 that the land is quiet. The word translated "securely," *ša'anān,* can simply mean safety, under God's protection, as in Isaiah's eschatological prophecies (32:18; 33:20). However, it more commonly has an ironic nuance, as here, in referring to the false or arrogant assumption that the condition of security will be sustained. In 2 Kgs 19:28–31, for example, a prophecy against the smug Assyrians is followed by an assertion that God will not allow that situation to persist; his "zeal" for Israel will bring about a reversal of the Assyrians' fortunes. Another example is Amos 6:1, "Woe to those who are at ease in Zion."

they fostered evil. Literally, "they helped to/for evil." The verb *ʿzr* means "to help" and is a common and straightforward biblical word. Yet its combination here with "evil" (*rāʿâ* preceded by *lĕ*) finds no parallel. The positive notion of helping has been twisted into a negative condition. Ackroyd (1968:176) employs a credible solution first suggested by Eitan (1924:8ff.), in which an alternate root for *ʿzr* is suggested on the basis of Arabic *ghazura:* "to be copious." Using this root requires a Hiphil for the verb but no consonantal changes *(hēmmāh ʿāzrû lĕrāʿâ),* and the resulting clause would read "they multiply calamity." Another suggestion, offered by Driver (1940:173), emends to *zārēʿû* (from *zrʿ,* "to plow") and translates "to sow, plot (evil)."

These suggestions are plausible; but the text can stand, as an unusual yet legitimate expression, without emendation. Since both the original Hebrew and the suggested emendations agree in their negative assessment of the deeds of the "nations" of verse 15a (see NOTE), the need for emendation becomes less critical. The strange pairing of "help" with "evil" may be an intentional ironic depiction of Persian policy toward Yehud in the period between Cyrus's conquest and Darius's accession. That which appeared to be so positive to many in Yehud, namely the termination of enforced exile and the decree allowing the temple to be rebuilt, in reality did not alter the evil being perpetrated against the people of Yahweh. If full restoration of political autonomy under Davidic rule is the criterion by which the policy of the Persians toward the Yehudites is to be measured, then the apparent benevolence of Persia in granting certain privileges fell short of this goal and so in reality only perpetuated the misfortune of the exile and destruction. Zechariah's language would then demonstrate his sensitivity to the predicament of the provincial status of Yehud, a sensitivity he demonstrates repeatedly in his visions and oracles. He is a realist, encouraging his countrymen to seize the opportunities afforded by the political currents of his day; yet he never relinquishes the ideal, the hope for the restoration of a Davidide as Yahweh's royal representative on earth.

16. *Therefore, thus spoke Yahweh.* The interpolation of this phrase between two poetic oracles is often taken (as by Elliger 1975 and Mason 1977b ad loc.) as a sign that the second one (v 16) is an addition, as is the one in verse 17. However, the complicated mediational layering of this vision can be equally responsible for this second oracular attribution. The content of the second oracle complements and completes in an essential way the meaning of the first; the third oracle likewise cannot be separated from the first and second. In addition, "therefore" *(lākēn)* is a connective commonly used in biblical prophecy to introduce a new section (Andersen and Freedman 1980:235–36, 266). The contents of that new section are asserted to be consequential to those of the previous one. Because *lākēn* precedes the oracular attribution, the existence of a discrete section in verse 16 is established and the attached *kōh ʾāmar yhwh* follows naturally, since Zechariah is replete with citations of divine authority for oracular pronouncements (see especially Zech 8). The fact of Yahweh's return to Jerusalem in this oracle is established as following from his universal sovereignty (verse 15). The absence of "Hosts," however, from this formula is unusual and has been imitated in Zech 8:3 (see first NOTE to that verse).

I have returned. Cf. 1:3. Yahweh's presence is to be manifest once temple building has been resumed, according to Haggai. This oracle, according to the date of 1:7, suggests that Yahweh has already returned to Jerusalem since the temple project is already well under way. The refoundation ceremony of December 520 (see NOTES to Hag 2:10 and Zech 4:7) has taken place, and the prophet has every reason to assume that Yahweh's presence and favor are being restored to his people.

The verb *šwb*, "return," completes the two sets of counterpoised returnings found in the beginning of Zechariah and serves to connect the opening section (Part One, Call for Obedience with Retrospection) to the visionary sequence of Part Two. In the oracular material of 1:3 (see NOTES to "return . . . return"), Yahweh charges the people of Zechariah's day to return to him whereupon he will return to them. We learn in verse 6b that this in fact comes to pass: "they returned . . ." in accord with God's word. And now we are informed that Yahweh too has carried out his promise to return. The balance between the actions of the people and the response of Yahweh has been achieved:

People return	*Yahweh* returns
1:3	1:3
1:6	1:16

compassion. God's absence from Jerusalem and the desolation of the exile is equated in verse 12 above with God's ongoing anger and lack of compassion for Jerusalem and Judah. The fortunes of Jerusalem (and his cities, verse 12) are reversed, with the root for "compassion" recurring. This time it is not negated; God's anger against Zion has ceased and concomitantly his intense love has been restored. The language of the oracles such as *rḥm* here (and in verse 12) and *nḥm*, "comfort," in verse 17 (cf. v 13) serves to link the oracles with the vision. The oracles are integral to the vision and constitute the seventh and climactic instance of direct speech in this second section of Zechariah (see COMMENT).

My house. I.e., the temple. See NOTE to Hag 1:4.

will be rebuilt. There is no need to render this in future perfect ("will have been rebuilt"), since God's presence returns to Jerusalem once the Yehudites acknowledge his full sovereignty by commencing temple restoration.

line. Although we have adopted the qere form *qāw* ("line"), it is difficult to know which reading is presupposed by LXX since the Kethib *qwh* can have the same meaning. The Masoretic pointing may have been influenced by the Niphal which follows, *ynṭh*. If the Kethib form *(qāwâ)* was considered, it was rejected because it was the wrong (fem.) gender. Hence the qere.

The line *(qāw)* here is the builder's string, symbolically stretched out to demarcate the line of the walls of the city. The stretching out of the builder's line is one of the initial steps, beyond procurement of materials, of the construction process. The use here of "line" is not to be confused with the act of measuring, since the word for measurement *(middâ),* sometimes coupled with *qāw* (as in Jer 31:39), does not appear here. Job 38:5 is instructive, since measurement and stretching a line are found sequentially as complementary steps in construction. Measurement of the temple in Jerusalem would not be necessary since the line of the building, if not most of the superstructure (see our NOTES to Hag 1:4; 2:18) was visible to the temple workers of Zechariah's day. Thus the rebuilding of all of Jerusalem may be intended by this image.

17. *again*. The fourfold repetition of *'ôd*, "again," in this verse is striking and seems to express the prophet's understanding of continuity between the preexilic and postexilic communities, a continuity to be symbolized by the restored temple. See NOTES to 4:7, especially "premier stone." The first *'ôd* precedes the verb; although *'ôd* normally follows the verb it modifies, its position here may be influenced by the *lākēn* ("therefore") introducing the previous, or second, oracle. This *'ôd* apparently is meant to function similarly as a connective. Moreover, it links the third oracle, which begins "proclaim," with the introduction to the first one in verse 14, which begins "Proclaim." Consequently, its position before the verb heralds its link with the first oracle as well as the second. See Hos 3:1 where it is also difficult to determine whether *'ôd* goes with what follows or precedes.

overflow. This form of Heb. *pwṣ* is used uniquely here, since elsewhere the verb means "to scatter in defeat" (as in Ezek 34:5 and Zech 13:7). However, one usage in Proverbs (5:16) depicts a spring overflowing with water. The image here is of the economic prosperity of the Yehudite settlements now that Yahweh's face is no longer turned away from his people in anger.

bounty. Hebrew *ṭôb*, "good." Dahood points out (1965:25) that the "good" *par excellence* in Palestine is the rain. Thus the image suggested in the Proverbs occurrence of the preceding verb ("overflow" with water) would be completed by the use here of the Hebrew word for "good," though we render it in its somewhat more extended meaning—that is, the economic prosperity which follows upon ample rainfall.

comfort. The language of the oracle picks up the Interpreting Angel's report of verse 13 and contributes to the continuity between vision proper and concluding oracles (cf. NOTE to "compassion" v 16). The association of comfort (verb *nḥm*) with Zion and Jerusalem is a theme of exilic and postexilic prophecy (Isa 40:1–2; 52:9; 66:13) which sought to deal with the suffering and anguish of the destruction.

choose Jerusalem. The language and wording of Zechariah here is unique to prophecy as it specifies the election or selection, *bḥr* ("to choose") of the holy city Jerusalem (Petitjean 1969:71ff.), though the root does occur with Judah and David in Ps 78:68,70. Precisely the same idiom is repeated in 2:16 (RSV 2:12) and 3:2, and one may detect its implicit theology elsewhere in Zechariah (e.g., 8:2,15) as well as in preexilic prophecy. The motif of choosing Jerusalem also occurs in historical texts where it is associated with the dedication of the temple (1 Kgs 8:44,48; 2 Chron 6:6,34,38). It is appropriate that the First Vision concludes with this phrase, for it provides an excellent recapitulation of the themes that unfold in verse 16: a) the return of God's presence to Jerusalem, b) the rebuilding of the temple, and c) the image of the measuring line in Jerusalem. The choosing of Jerusalem provides both an answer to the question posed in verse 12 and a fitting conclusion to the initial vision, reflecting both divine approval for the temple building in Jerusalem and sanctification of the city as a whole. Zechariah ultimately renames the holy city in 8:3, the "City of Truth" (see NOTE), and expresses in more detail the idea of Jerusalem's special role.

COMMENT

Superscription to the visions, 1:7

It is hardly coincidental that of all the headings in Haggai and Zechariah, 1:7 is the most complete (cf. Hag 1:1,15; 2:10,20; Zech 1:1; 7:1). It is the second of three in Zechariah and falls chronologically approximately two and a half months later than 1:1 but only one month after Haggai 2:10 and 20. Whereas the heading in 1:1 ostensibly serves the more comprehensive purpose of introducing both the oracular and visionary portions of the book, 1:7 by introducing the visionary sequence fills a more specific role. It provides vital information regarding the relationship of the visions to an external event, which we take to be the temple refoundation ceremony (described in our NOTES to Zech 4:7). The excitement generated by that recent event would constitute the underlying stimulus for the visions and oracles of 1:7–6:15.

The date provided in 1:7 is February 15, 519 B.C.E., or around one month prior to the spring New Year. The date of February 519 need not be taken to apply to the entire visionary sequence, though such a possibility cannot be precluded. Zechariah's inspiration for the visions doubtless comes in response to the activities which accompanied the ceremony of rededication on December 18, 520, approximately fourteen months earlier. No further date is provided until 7:1; the details of the ceremony of refoundation are not alluded to until chapter 4.

One other item is possibly affected by this heading if we are to take the chronological framing of Zechariah seriously. If 1:7 is the heading for the visionary cycle which concludes in 6:8 with the Seventh Vision, then the Crowning (6:9–15) occurs after the visions but just before the final heading of 7:1. Yet we regard that critical segment as the final element of Part Two (see NOTES and COMMENT below) and the conclusion to the whole (1:7–6:15). Because so many critics have argued that 6:9–15 is a part of Zechariah that has been heavily tampered with, our inclusion of it within Part Two therefore implies that it falls under the heading and hence chronology of 1:7, which precedes both visions and attached oracles, i.e., a little more than a year after the ceremony of refoundation. One of the clear implications of such a literary assessment is that the symbolic crowning of 6:9–15, if it represents an actual event, could theoretically have taken place on the very day of the temple refoundation ceremony, in 520, but the oracular account of it was integrated into the central portion of the visions only somewhat later. From the point of view of the editorial framework of the whole of Zechariah, therefore, the visionary sequence together with all of the oracular portions which have been attached to it begins with 1:7 and concludes with 6:15.

The editorial framing of Part Two may be observed in the abrupt change from the third person in verse 7 to the first person in verse 8 (see NOTE to "[and Zechariah said]").

First Vision, 1:8–13

The sequence of seven visions, all of which adhere to a common literary pattern, begins for this first one, as for most of the succeeding ones, with the prophet's first-person narration of his extraordinary experiences of the imagination. With deft narrative strokes, in the space of one biblical verse Zechariah presents the complex tableau which constitutes this First Vision. His audience thus immediately sees, along with the prophet, the salient features that have composed themselves to convey a message to him. The audience cannot but wonder, along with the prophet, what the significance of this composition is. The ensuing dialogue between prophet and angelic messenger responds to the curiosity naturally aroused by the initial portrayal of a strange scene. That dialogue simultaneously satisfies the interest of the audience, which has been likewise stirred up by the abrupt and concise depiction by the prophet of what has appeared to him.

What then are the features of this initial vision? A prominent aspect is clearly the setting of darkness. We learn of this through several distinct elements that appear at once in the description of what Zechariah sees. "In the night," as we have shown in the NOTES, refers to the darkness of this vision and not to a general nighttime setting for all the visions. "In the shadows" intensifies the sense of reduced visibility. Finally, "among the myrtles" adds further to the sense of utter blackness, for the myrtle was well known as a dense shade-creating shrubbery. In the economy of words with which Zechariah presents the components of all his visions, the occurrence of these three separate pieces of information, all pointing to the darkness of the setting, demands our attention. Indeed, the very connotation of invisibility that they provide would almost seem to contradict the essential fact that Zechariah *sees* something in the midst of such unlikely conditions.

The strongly suggested darkness of this vision thus simultaneously achieves two purposes. First, it obviously contributes a crucial element to the set of facts which make up the First Vision. Second, it subtly creates an awareness of Zechariah's unique role. The characters of the vision stand in utter darkness, a condition essential to the message which will unfold. Yet Zechariah sees them clearly. He sees the individual equine figures and can even identify their colors. The first feat may have been feasible even on the darkest night. The second would not have been possible; three different animal colors could not have been sorted out, given such low visibility.

As we shall soon see, Zechariah's ability to discern details even when the setting so strongly precluded the possibility of seeing anything makes his audience aware at the outset of the visionary mode. Although some of the subsequent visions as they are described by the prophet immediately convey the fact that they are removed from reality (e.g., the Fifth and Sixth Visions), others depict more ordinary objects or people and do not at once allow the visionary mode to become evident. This initial vision perhaps belongs to the latter category, although the particular combination of figures may push it somewhat toward the first category. Nonetheless, the clarity with which the prophet observes the fully obscured figures indicates that a narrative of the imagination ensues. We do not mean to suggest either reality or unreality in using the word "imagination." Rather, the reality of the prophet's experience arises within his own mental process and not from objects he sees in the world around him. Although his visions are thus distinct in this sense from reality, in another sense they are intimately linked with his world. For events and circumstances in the Persian Empire and the tiny subprovince of Yehud have provided the stimuli and searing questions to which the visions provide answers.

Perhaps the best analogy for Zechariah's visionary experience is the dream-world, which contains a mixture of the real and the unreal, the remembered and the imagined. When one enters this world, one suspends disbelief while never forgetting that it is a dream. Similarly for visions: they are supernatural yet contain real objects and people, so they may be quite natural in their settings yet feature supernatural characters and strange objects. Within the visionary world, in other words, any combination of natural and unnatural items can appear. The very juxtaposition of the expected and the unexpected often provides the shock to rational thought which expands one's thought processes and allows the meaning of the vision to emerge.

Other features of the vision are worthy of special comment. The major figures of this scene, moving about in darkness, are horses. Textual transmission (see NOTES) has blurred the language, but the intent of the text is to depict three horses of three different colors. As a set of three, they roam the entire world. Three, the smallest number with a beginning, middle, and end, represents totality: the horses with their riders go everywhere, see everything that needs to be seen. Compare Zechariah's use of four, another symbolic number: the four "winds of heaven" of 2:10 (RSV 2:6) and the four chariots of the last vision. The three horses of the First Vision make an essential contribution: individually they epitomize speed, collectively they denote a speed which takes them throughout the world. They also adumbrate other instances in which the prophet's symbolism is built upon the use of a symbolic number to suggest universality, as in the Seventh Vision.

The group of horses performs yet another function. It constitutes, with the four horses and chariots of the last vision, an *inclusio* or envelope construction. The First Vision in fact does have four horses, although only three seem to perform the scouting mission. These two sets of equines, each part of a vision dealing with Yahweh's universality (see below), frame a complex sequence of prophetic visions and oracles. All of them have been evoked by specific events within a tiny area of the Persian Empire. All of them deal with the implications of a restored temple for a people in whose extraordinarily strong traditions a monarchy looms large. The answers to and comments on this situation, which appears to be rather localized, come from a god whose purview is global. Rather than being a series of particularistic and fanciful episodes, the visions of Zechariah all operate with the understanding that Yahweh is the universal deity. His intentions for Yehud are part of his cognizance of worldwide developments. Zechariah's visions are thus placed within a universal framework. This postexilic prophet continues in his own way the broad conception of Yahweh's sovereignty already given eloquent voice by the prophets of the exile, notably Jeremiah, Deutero-Isaiah, and Ezekiel, who each in a different way stresses the universality and the supreme authority of the God of Israel.

The universal scope of the First Vision appears in both the implicit symbolism of the vision as the prophet relates it to us, and then in its explicit interpretation. Darkness and horses represent secrecy and speed. These two features are the hallmarks of a political intelligence system, such as was especially well developed in the ancient world by the Persians, whose extensive imperial territories demanded surveillance in order for the regime to maintain control. The ruling Persian officials, like their Assyrian and Babylonian predecessors, depended upon a far-flung network of anonymous informers. Sometimes known as "eyes of the king," they lent their efficiently obtained knowledge of all parts of the empire to the concept of God's awareness of all human activities (see NOTES to "seven eyes," 3:9, and "eyes of Yahweh," 4:10). In short, Yahweh's omniscience is proclaimed by the figures of horses covering directions in darkness. The terse interpretation in verse 10 confirms our understanding of the imagery: Yahweh sent them all over the world. The universal sovereign must be cognizant of all that transpires within his realm. The anthropomorphic language of the visionary image portrays Yahweh as supreme ruler, sending emissaries to gather information from the four corners of the globe. His omniscience is established; it will be complemented in the final vision by another dimension, his omnipotence. Together, these framing visions present an image of Yahweh's universality and constancy, which serves as a given for all the intervening visions and oracles.

The prophet's dialogue with an angelic figure is the next feature of Zechariah's visions that the audience meets. No description or anticipation of the Interpreting Angel's presence or role is provided. The prophet, having related in direct language the contents of his vision, immediately poses a query. We are not aware of the angel's presence; but since the prophet abruptly turns to him with his question, we realize that Zechariah is not alone in the visionary setting. In this vision as in all subsequent ones, there are others, especially angelic beings, who play a central role in what transpires.

The Interpreting Angel, literally the angel-who-speaks-with-me, is an integral part of the vision. He functions in two essential ways. First, inside the

visionary scenarios his presence moves the action forward. Although, technically speaking, only one vision (the Sixth, or Ephah, Vision) actually involves
progressive action, many of the visions proceed from an opening scene to an
exchange between the vision's actors and the angel, the last being in addition
to the basic dialogic structure that reveals the vision's apparent meaning. This
first vision includes all such exchanges: the angel speaks with the horsemen,
addresses Yahweh, and communicates to the prophet a series of oracular statements that must be proclaimed to the prophet's contemporaries. Second, the
angel is paired with the prophet to create a situation for dialogue concerning
the meaning of the vision. This function transmits the internal features to an
external audience. It provides the literary structure whereby the prophet's
progress toward insight into God's ways and plans vis-à-vis his people and all
the world can be made comprehensible to the prophet's audience. Zechariah
stands firmly within prophetic tradition in this sense. His comprehension of
God's will is not for his own edification but for the benefit of God's people.
The variation in the pattern of prophetic revelation for Zechariah comes in the
intervening figure of the Interpreting Angel. However, the concept of dialogue, insofar as it involves two parties, should not lull us into believing that
Zechariah alone is the recipient of a message from God. The message is to be
proclaimed, and the prophet does so in an innovative and effective way. He
utilizes the traditional biblical concept of angelic messengers but he expands
it, emphasizing the angel's role as interpreter and intermediary between God
and prophet.

The message of this initial vision is thus provided through a series of exchanges among the prophet, God, the angel, and the horsemen. In just a few
verses, all of these personae interact. The characteristic Hebraic use of dialogue to present a scene is in full operation. The following list summarizes the
speaker-listener pairings, with the arrows pointing from speaker to listener:

1. Prophet ⟶ Angel
2. Angel ⟶ Prophet
3. Horseman ⟶ Prophet (and Angel?)
4. Horseman ⟶ Angel
5. Angel ⟶ Yahweh
6. Yahweh ⟶ Angel
7. [Yahweh] ⟶ Angel ⟶ Prophet ⟶ [Yehudites]

Four separate lines of communication are established, in a series of six instances of direct speech: 1. Zechariah opens (v 9a) with his question to the
Interpreting Angel; 2. the angel responds to him (v 9b); 3. the lead horseman
then explains himself and his companions, presumably directing his words to
Zechariah since the angel knows full well who the horsemen are (v 10); 4. the
horseman then reports to the angel, here clearly representing Yahweh, on the
success of the equine mission (v 11); 5. the Interpreting Angel thereupon

queries Yahweh about his future plans, given the results of the mission as they have been presented (v 12); and 6. Yahweh himself provides an answer, first directly to the angel who has obviously shown some negative emotion upon considering the state of the world as reported by the emissaries (v 13).

Note that a seventh and climactic instance of quoted speech follows immediately in verses 14–17. This section involves a complex chain of auditors and not the two parties of each of the preceding quoted statements or questions. The Interpreting Angel in this oracular section addresses the prophet with the words of Yahweh, which are to be proclaimed to Zechariah's audience. Thus the final instance of quoted speech in this series (Yahweh responds: three oracles) is the culmination of the First Vision, from both a thematic and a literary viewpoint.

This series of quoted direct speech, in addition to allowing the message of the vision to unfold, provides an insight into the function of the Interpreting Angel. The angel is a party to all the dialogic pairings created by this vision, with the possible exception of the third one. That he represents Yahweh is made clear, indirectly but unambiguously, by the information in verses 10 and 11. It is Yahweh who charges the horsemen to survey his realm, and it is the angel to whom the horsemen give an accounting of their mission. This subtle shift creates the desired impression that the angel is indeed a facet of God's existence, empowered to speak with God's words. His credentials are thus presented to the prophet's audience.

What then is the message presented by this series of exchanges following the initial presentation of the vision's setting and personae? The concept of divine omniscience, implicit in the connotation of speed and secrecy of the hidden horses, is made explicit. The horsemen have been everywhere at the command of Yahweh. They have discovered stability in the world. This fact provides our first insight into the relationship of the prophet to the sociopolitical world of the restoration period. The global quietude that God's emissaries observe, together with the date of February 519 B.C.E. given by the compiler in 1:7, can be related to the stability achieved by Darius I by the end of his second regnal year. Those difficulties he had encountered in the period of his accession, which perhaps fanned hopes among some subject peoples including the Yehudites that their independence might be reestablished, had evidently been resolved as his third year in office approached. A situation of imperial Persian strength, a concomitant cessation of hostilities, and thus a sense of quiet and peace prevailed as Zechariah begins this second phase of his prophetic career.

This information, supplied in the vision by the metaphor of Yahweh's equine informants, is in Yahweh's possession. Yahweh's angelic representative now shifts his position to that of being a prophetic spokesman. The classic biblical interrogation of Yahweh, beginning with Abraham and moving through Moses and many of the classical prophets, finds its voice here in the angel's dissatisfaction with Persian imperial stability. Persian strength meant continued dominance of Yehud by foreign rulers. Yahweh had wrested autonomy from Yehud, had cut off the Davidic monarchy in a powerful move to punish her failure to adhere to his covenant. The ensuing exile, in the classical prophetic interpretation, would serve as adequate punishment for the previous sins and crimes of the people. God would then be in a position to bring them back from exile because of his great love and original commitment to the fathers and hence to Judah and Israel. The people had now returned to Yahweh, as the first part of Zechariah's ministry (1:6) makes clear. The temple restoration project is believed to be the signal to Yahweh that his people have indeed returned to him. And they wait expectantly for his turning to them—i.e., his restoring their preexilic state and status. The angel's sharp question to Yahweh in verse 12 comes from such an expectation and from the anguish created by its lack of fulfillment. For long years the people of Israel have been bereft of their homeland and their dynastic state. Now, since the days of Cyrus, a portion of Palestine has been reopened for Judahite habitation. But full self-rule to accompany the territorial occupation has not followed. We can feel the painful confusion of the Yehudites, who have turned to building God's temple at the urging of his prophets and who have expected the emergence of an independent kingdom ruled by a Davidide to accompany this symbolic reassertion of God's presence among his people, in the poignancy of the angel's question, "O Yahweh of Hosts, for how long . . . ?" (v 12).

The prophet's description of Yahweh's response confirms our impression, formed by the content of the angel's question, that the Yehudites as represented by the angel are sorely distressed by their uncertainty over the import of their temple work. The words with which Yahweh responds are said to be "good" and "comforting." In this highly unusual insertion of a subjective description by Zechariah of the content of oracular material, the prophet permits us to catch a glimpse of the emotional agony of the moment. Led partway toward autonomy by Darius's policies of encouraging the local Jerusalem shrine to function again, the Yehudites followed their cultic traditions in setting out to build the temple. But those traditions are embedded in a monarchic matrix, and they feel God's anger persisting with a monarchic restoration not likewise assured. Zechariah's mission phase two, the visionary sequence, thus begins in the midst of this turmoil of the spirit.

We have deemed it necessary to comment extensively on various facets of Zechariah's First Vision, for it introduces the complex materials, both visionary and oracular, that constitute the second block, Part Two, of First Zechariah. Many of the features will reappear. The vision of horses patrolling the world is only the first of seven visions, which are so identified by certain literary characteristics exhibited by them all. We hope that the reader will consequently be alert to the special stylistic features of the visionary mode (cf. Introduction) as Zechariah developed it. Visions are hardly new to prophecy, but Zechariah has presented his visions with unsurpassed skill in order to resolve the profound religio-political dilemmas that confronted him. The initial vision shows us the interwoven roles of prophet, Yahweh, and Interpreting Angel that we shall meet in the other six visions as well as in the prophetic vision of chapter 3. While the First Vision is a unit of material with its own discrete visionary composition, it is not meant to stand alone. Its meaning, which stresses God's universality and omniscience as the Yehudites struggle to understand what their situation in 519 B.C.E. means in relation to their traditional understanding of their national identity, is fully comprehensible only as the first piece of a richly textured whole.

Yahweh responds: three oracles, 1:14–17

The inclusion of oracular material within the framework of the entire visionary cycle is one of the distinguishing features of Zechariah 1–8. The next segment of oracular material in the visions occurs in 2:8b–9 (RSV 2:4b–5), and a large block of oracles constitutes an expansion to the first three visions (2:10–17 [RSV 2:6–13]). Other oracular sections integral to the visionary sequence include the Supplementary Oracle of chapter 3 (3:8–10), the Zerubbabel insertion of chapter 4 (4:6b–10a), the oracular quotation in 5:4, and the oracular portion of the Crowning (6:9–15). Verses 14–17 contain three oracular statements, each introduced by a formulaic clause signaling Yahweh's words as conveyed through a prophet. The placement of these verses in their present position and order either by Zechariah himself or by his secretary or compiler in the context of the First Vision demonstrates great literary skill. These materials integral to the whole chapter both amplify and require ideas enunciated in the visionary section. Whether or not this act of literary creativity occurred more or less simultaneously with the utterance of the vision itself or sometime prior to 515 B.C.E., when the final compendious work was being prepared for publication (see COMMENT to the Call for Obedience, 1:1–6) is a question that cannot be answered definitively (see also Introduction).

The first oracle (v 14) is introduced by the formulaic "Proclaim." It is also mediated by the Interpreting Angel, and is the only instance in which the angel is involved in this way outside the visions in Zechariah (although compare the communication of an oracle by an angel in 2:8–9 [RSV 2:4–5]). If the content of the First Vision may be understood as reflecting the theme of God's omniscience and worldwide dominion, then the shift in the opening of the first oracle to God's concern for Jerusalem and Zion effectively asserts that Yahweh retains his particular concern for Israel despite, or along with, his universal sovereignty. The language of God's devotion is expressed in positive covenant terms, underscoring the good that will derive from divine love.

In contrast with the positive tone and reassuring content of verse 14, the second half of the first oracle, verse 15, reports the anger which God feels. But the reassurance is sustained by the fact that divine wrath is directed not toward Israel but rather toward the nations that are resting "securely." Verse 15 therefore resumes a theme begun in verse 11 where the equestrian patrol reported that "all the earth rests quietly." Both verses 11 and 15a reflect the measure of stability which had been achieved by Darius at the end of his second regnal year. Verse 15b is retrospective and subtle. It appears to allude to the period before Darius when Cyrus and his successors, despite their apparently benign actions toward the dispersed Judeans and the remnant in Yehud, nonetheless continued suppression of the Davidic monarchy, which had been overthrown by the Babylonians. The absence of a Davidic ruler had called into question the validity of the Davidic covenant itself. The "seventy years" concept of the vision, denoting the time during which Yahweh has shown anger to Judah by denying her independence through the hands of the ancient empires, is echoed in the language of the first oracle. The prophet has again portrayed the role of divine anger in human events, but in the oracle it is the "nations" rather than "Jerusalem and the cities of Judah" against whom God's wrath is directed.

The second oracle in verse 16 is introduced by "therefore" before the oracular heading and hence is often taken to be a later interpolation. However, there is a powerful thematic connection between this oracle and the vision, just as we found to exist between the first oracle (v 15) and the vision. The language of God's "returning" picks up and completes a theme that was central to the oracular beginning of Part One at the beginning of this chapter. The addition of "with compassion," moreover, ties this second oracle to verse 12 where the absence of God's compassion during the seventy-year period of exile was a sign of God's displeasure. The returning of God "to Jerusalem with compassion" thus signals the beginning of a new era. The sign of God's favor is the restoration of the temple, now explicitly referred to for the first time in Zechariah. The mention of the temple together with the direct reference to a builder's "line" constitutes a marked and balancing departure from the universal scope of the First Vision. The effect is quite striking, and it serves to link the First Vision with the central Fourth Vision, with its specific temple setting. The interweaving of language that is common to both the vision and the oracle suggests common authorship, with the oracle perhaps being prompted or evoked by the content of the vision. It would be difficult to imagine an independent origin for this or the other two oracles in view of the close linguistic affinities between oracles and vision.

The third oracle in this grouping is found in verse 17. Like the first one, it is introduced by "Proclaim" followed by a formulaic clause. The fourfold repetition of the Hebrew word ʿôd ("still, again") emphasizes the continuity between earlier idealized times of prosperity in the land and the good fortunes about to befall the land once more with the return of Yahweh to his Jerusalem abode. Unlike the Call for Obedience of Part One (1:1–6), which deals with earlier times by recalling Israel's preexilic behavior and its disastrous consequences, the contact here with the past clearly has a positive tone, for it anticipates the happy effects of God's renewed favor toward a people returned to him. With the rebuilding of the temple, Yahweh will enable the cities of Yehud to be blessed with abundant crops (cf. Hag 2:19). The theme of economic prosperity linked with work on the temple is one that is central to the message of Haggai. Because the theme of temple building is only introduced in verse 16, in the second oracle, it would seem that verses 16 and 17 are related by virtue of thematic continuity but also by virtue of the language of "comfort" which resumes the similar language of the end of verse 13, thereby linking the end of the vision with the end of this third oracle.

In addition to noting the various points of contact among the three oracles and between the oracles and the preceding vision, we wish to call attention to the development in the three successive oracles. The first one, with its depiction of the waxing and waning of divine anger against the "nations," deals with the recent past. Our NOTES to verse 15 show how the relationship between Persia and Yehud during the years from Cyrus's rise to power in 538 until the beginning of Zechariah's prophetic ministry in the wake of the events of Darius I's accession provides the external conditions which best accord with the sense of that oracle. God's role in the immediate past—and not the more remote past of the preexilic or even the exilic period—is thus proclaimed. The contents of the next oracle, with "therefore" performing its natural function of suggesting consequence, follow from those of the first. Divine anger at the fortunes of Yehud under the first sixteen or eighteen years of Achaemenid domination has brought about the present situation of God's direct presence in Yehud by virtue of the restoration of his dwelling in Jerusalem. The third oracle can thus portray a future of well-being.

This temporal development from recent past to imminent future is held together by the recurrent mention of Jerusalem as well as by the various contacts of language that have been noted. It is Jerusalem to which God's devotion is assured; it is the rebuilt Jerusalem to which God returns; and it is the choosing of Jerusalem which signifies the recovery of the economic bounty that accompanies divine favor for much of the prophetic thinking. Unlike the preceding and succeeding visions, which specify the politics of Judah and Israel, only the oracles name Jerusalem. This inordinate emphasis on Jerusalem gives it a symbolic quality, and the oracles verge on the eschatological in their avoidance of the political boundaries of historical existence.

The role of a symbolic Jerusalem within the oracles of the First Vision finds additional and fuller development in the oracular expansion of the first three visions (2:10–17 [RSV 2:6–13]), especially in 2:15–16 (RSV 2:11–12) which echoes in oracular form the message of the First Vision. Again, the interweaving of the universal with the particular emerges as characteristic of Zechariah's overall approach and prophetic insight.

3. SECOND VISION:
THE FOUR HORNS AND THE FOUR SMITHS
(2:1–4; RSV 1:18–21)

2 ¹ I raised my eyes, and I looked, and behold: four horns! ² Then I
said to the angel-who-speaks-with-me, "What are these?"
He said to me, "These are the horns which have scattered Judah,
Israel, and Jerusalem."
³ Then Yahweh showed me four smiths, ⁴ and I said, "What are these
coming to do?"
He said: "These are the horns which scattered Judah so that no one
could lift his head, and these [smiths] came to make them tremble, to
cut down the horns of the nations who raised the horn against the land
of Judah to scatter it."

NOTES

2:1 (RSV 1:18). *I raised my eyes*. This phrase introduces three other visions (2:5
[RSV 2:1], 5:1, and 6:1). It also occurs in a slightly different form as a command of the
Interpreting Angel, below in 5:5. Five of the seven visions are introduced with the
notion of the prophet looking (up) at something, probably at eye level as in Gen 18:2
and not up in the sky. The First Vision likewise contains an element describing the
prophet's act of looking. Only the complex central or Fourth Vision begins in a completely different manner, "The angel-who-speaks-with-me again roused me." See
NOTES to 4:1.
Four horns. The symbolism of horns as representative of divine might, derived from
the power suggested by horned animals (cf. Sasson 1968:385–87), has a long history in
biblical literature and in Near Eastern mythology and iconography. Early Hebrew
poetry (e.g., Deut 33:17; cf. 2 Sam 22:3 = Ps 18:3 [RSV 18:2]) preserves the notion of
might in battle, as do epithets of El and Anat in Ugaritic poetry (Miller 1967:418–23
and 1971:177). The iconographic depictions of gods or kings wearing headpieces with
two or four horns, as on the Megiddo ivories (Loud 1939:10), is clearly part of the
symbolic expression of the supreme power of the wearer of such caps. Yet the use of
four horns in this vision does not seem to depend on such a manifestation of the horn
symbolism. The inappropriateness of a four-horned cap behind the prophet's vision is
apparent because of the way Zechariah uses sets of "four" items in the visions: four
horsemen, although not four horse colors, in the First Vision (see our NOTE to "red,

sorrel, and white," 1:8); four winds in 2:10 (RSV 2:6); four chariots and four winds in the Seventh Vision, 6:1,5. In all these cases the use of four, derived from the concept of the four directions and thus the four corners of the earth, conveys the notion of *all* the earth or the whole earth.

While a four-horned headpiece may not lie directly behind the prophet's vision, another sort of physical symbol is involved. The fate of the horns according to verse 4 (RSV 1:21; see below) informs us that some fabricated object did exist and was then rendered useless. Several biblical references to "horn" in the singular (e.g., Ps 75:5,6 [RSV 75:4,5]; 89:18 [RSV 89:17]; 148:14) refer to an object which could be raised on high as a symbol of might. Perhaps "horn" designates some sort of royal battle standard, as in the case of the implements commissioned by the king Zedekiah in 1 Kgs 22:11 (although Keel [1974:123–46] believes this refers to a horned crown). Alternatively, however, the references may be to the horned cap of might, with "horn" in the singular denoting the whole horned headpiece, with its two or four horns. In that case four horned headpieces would be the visionary objects. Niditch (1983:122–24) has recently concluded that the horns of this vision are to be understood only in the context of divine warrior imagery, with the power of the divine warrior as "the bull" lying behind the image. Just as in Zech 1:14–15 God declared his zeal on behalf of Israel, so too here does Yahweh vow to turn his power against the enemies who either scattered the Israelites or who would do so. Another recent monograph (Porter 1983:64–69) places the horn imagery as it represents Israel's enemies in the general context of animal imagery in the Bible, particularly in the Book of Daniel (Dan 7–8). Both Niditch and Porter discuss dimensions of the horn symbolism which reveal how powerful a symbol the horn was.

However its symbolism might be explained, "four" with "horns" suggests all the (military) might of the world, especially as monopolized by an imperial power— whether Assyria, Babylon, or Persia—which appears to rule the world. The military dimension of this symbol of power is paramount. It represents conquest and the accompanying subjugation of defeated peoples which, under the empires of the mid-first millennium, meant the mass deportation of substantial portions of the population. Since Judah, Israel, and Jerusalem are named separately, "horns" appears to designate all three imperial powers, Assyria, Babylon, and perhaps also Persia, which exiled or continued the exile of those three. Since verse 2 (RSV 1:19) informs us that these "horns" have brought about the exile of Israel as well as of Judah and Jerusalem, the policies of both the Assyrian and the Babylonian empires are represented. Furthermore, the tenses of the verbs in verse 4b (RSV 1:21b) indicate past action, again signifying that surely Babylon, with respect to Judah there, is the foreign power in question.

Can Persia also be included in the "horns" designation of an imperial power with which God's agents (see NOTE to "smiths," verse 2 [RSV 1:19]) must deal? Haggai and Zechariah 1–8 uniformly reflect a Persian administration of Yehud which was in most respects benign and beneficial. Indeed, the biblical record in general reflects, if anything, too positive an attitude toward Persia in its treatment of Cyrus's edict to end the Judean exile and to support the rebuilding of the temple. If this vision includes Persia in its depiction of the empire as a power which scatters people and which needs to be overcome, it offers a perspective that would differ from the other literary units of Haggai and Zechariah 1–8.

Although the simplest reading of this vision would have it be retrospective, it can, for several reasons, also suggest the prophet's own time. First, the language in verse 4 (RSV 1:21), as we shall explain below, is difficult. Second, despite Persia's benign patrimonial rule (see Introduction), the conquered nations would still have feared the power that controlled them. Third, Persian authorities from Cyrus onward did not hesitate to relocate segments of the population (see following NOTE) as it served their imperial goals (Kuhrt 1983). Nevertheless, any application to the present era of the term "horns" would appear to be as an object lesson, a reminder of God's power, rather than as a suggestion that Persia had relocated Yehudites and that Persia was about to be overthrown. The last possibility can only be an implied or indirect one.

The translation of "horns" by the Targum as "kingdoms" has no doubt inspired much of the later exegesis, including that of the Patristic commentators, who identified the "four horns" with the historic enemies of Israel—e.g., Assyrians, Babylonians, Medes, and Persians; or Egyptians, Assyrians, Babylonians, and Persians; or Medes, Persians, Greeks, and Romans, depending on the presupposed historical context.

2 (RSV 1:19). *scattered.* Derived from agricultural terminology ("to winnow," to separate the wheat from the chaff), "scattered" refers here as elsewhere in prophecy (e.g., Ezek 5:2,10,12; 6:8; cf. Jer 15:7) to the exile of Judah among the nations. This expression of exile is also found as a covenant term in Leviticus (26:33), where it depicts part of the devastation God will cause should Israel disobey God's words. The theme of "scattering" figures prominently in this Second Vision. The root *zrh*, "to scatter," appears three times, once in this verse and twice in verse 4 (RSV 1:21). In all three occurrences it is associated with "horns," which provide the instrumentality for the scattering. In this verse, the threefold object of the verb, Judah, Israel, and Jerusalem, signifies that it refers to the past dispersal of God's peoples. The prophet intends to be inclusive by listing the deportations inflicted upon the northern and southern kingdoms and upon Jerusalem. Presumably, the Assyrians and the Babylonians are the world powers represented by the "four horns" of this verse. However, the identification of the "horns" of verse 4 (RSV 1:21) probably involves Babylon alone; see NOTES below to verse 4 (RSV 1:21).

The policy of exiling portions of a conquered people, as practiced by the imperial powers of the ancient Near East, was a prominent feature of the aggressive phase of empire building, of establishing control over subject states. Following military victory, the imperial power regularly deported large groups of people from their homelands. The implementation of mass deportation served purely imperialistic purposes (Oded 1979). Whole communities were transferred, at least by the Assyrians, in order to punish rebellion and permanently weaken the defeated power so that its people or leadership would not be able to offer any further opposition to the empire. Deportation also created exiled communities that tended, in their new living situations, to be loyal to the imperial power upon which they depended for the rights and privileges, often considerable, which they enjoyed as they set about to reestablish their livelihood. Deportees were often, for this reason, settled in strategically sensitive areas. Exiled groups served a variety of other purposes, by providing skilled and unskilled labor both for urban needs and for the development of unsettled regions. In many instances the leadership along with the qualified people, those who could do something useful and well and who were thus of potential value for work and business in other parts of the empire, were the ones deported, while the poorest and least competent were left behind. Yet, a tendency to transport entire communities, thereby to promote greatest ease in adjustment and rapid accomplishment of productivity, can also be observed. The specific uses to which exiled groups were put varied, but the imperial goals behind the complex system of deportation were clear. Assyria, and her imperial successors, aimed to dominate "the four rims of the earth" (Oded 1979:74).

Judah, Israel, and Jerusalem. Some LXX manuscripts (Alexandrinus and Marchalianus) omit "Jerusalem"; another attests "Jerusalem" but not "Israel." Naḥal Ḥever Greek, however, has all three as does the Hebrew. Many understand Israel here to be a gloss, since it does not occur in the repetition of this statement of scattering (= exile) in verse 4 (RSV 1:21); others would omit both Israel and Jerusalem, since the latter also does not appear in verse 4 (RSV 1:21), although it perhaps has dropped out there. The manuscripts and versions have changed the text because the combination and the order of the three names is unusual. More to be expected would be "Israel and Judah" or "Judah and Jerusalem." The latter would be most appropriate for the time, as witness its frequent use in Jeremiah. Moreover, in Zechariah 1:12 the prophet uses what may be a standard phrase, "Jerusalem and the cities of Judah." If we have a conflate text "Israel" would be the secondary element, but since it comes between "Judah" and "Jerusalem" a conflate reading seems unlikely. In short, the originality of the three elements has much to commend it, as awkward as it may seem. The prophet may simply have wanted to be inclusive by inserting "Israel" between "Judah and Jerusalem," the stock expression of his day. Such an insertion would account for northerners who lived in Judah after the destruction of the kingdom of Israel in 722 and shared in the suffering of the Babylonian conquest. It would also accommodate northerners who returned to Palestine under Persian rule.

3 (RSV 1:20). *Yahweh showed me.* Abruptly a second set of characters appears in the prophet's visionary field. Many of the visions have two sections, in which two distinct elements of the vision are separately explained (Fourth Vision), or an action or oracle involving the vision's initial subject is presented (Third Vision), or a two-part drama unfolds (Sixth Vision). Yet the Second Vision stands alone in its portrayal of two distinct images, horns and craftsmen, which will ultimately interact. This unique feature is accompanied by the startling appearance of Yahweh as the one who exhibits the second set of personae for Zechariah's observation. The other visions are introduced by the prophet's seeing objects or characters, and the simple Qal of the verb "to see," *rʾh,* is employed. Here the causative Hiphil of *rʾh,* "showed," with Yahweh as subject, brings to the fore Yahweh's role in providing the prophet with his visionary experience. In so doing, it anticipates the Investiture Scene of chapter 3, which is properly within the series of the visions of Zechariah for contextual, thematic, as well as stylistic reasons, but which nonetheless is not numbered among the actual visions because of its divergent literary structure. Chapter 3 begins, as we show in our NOTE to 3:1, with Yahweh himself showing Zechariah the Heavenly Court.

The direct appearance of Yahweh rather than an angelic figure has two effects. First, with respect to the vision itself, it emphasizes divine action. This is precisely what is conveyed by the imagery of the "four smiths" (see following NOTE) whom Yahweh himself displays to the prophet; it is also what is suggested by the prophet's question in verse 4 which asks about the imminent deeds of the smiths rather than about their identity. Second, it indicates in a general way the fluidity between Yahweh and the angelic figures as mediators of divine will. Yahweh here performs the role played by the Interpreting Angel in the other visions: the prophet questions him about the vision's characters, and he provides an explanation. A similar blurring of the distinction between angel and Yahweh occurs in the language of the First Vision, 1:10–11, where Yahweh makes the assignment to the horsemen and the latter report back not to Yahweh but to his angel.

smiths. The word here signifies craftsmen *(ḥārāšîm)* and refers specifically in this case to smiths, or metalworkers (cf. Isa 44:12 and 2 Chron 24:12) since the horns are understood to be made of metal, probably iron as in 1 Kgs 22:11. Zechariah's use of this word for skilled workers becoming agents of destruction may have been suggested by the image in Ezek 21:36 (RSV 2:31) of "skilled destroyers" (cf. *BDB:* 360, which translates "hammer").

The meaning of these symbolic figures can be ascertained by noting three features of their presentation in this vision. First, the use of "four" to indicate the number of craftsmen implies totality (see NOTE to "four horns" in 2:1 [RSV 1:18]). Second, the introduction of the craftsmen is preceded by the unusual opening of verse 3 (RSV 1:20; see above NOTE) in which Yahweh himself and not the angelic emissary reveals these four personae to the prophet. Third, the immediate reaction of the prophet is a question, unique in that he asks not about the identity of the visionary figures but rather about their purpose (see NOTE to "what are they coming to do?").

These features together link Yahweh, his totality, and his activity, and suggest the symbolic meaning of "smiths": they are divine agents carrying out God's will. They can represent, in the past, Babylon or Persia, which each brought to an end an ancient imperial power. And they also can represent an unspecified future divine action against a world power. We have accordingly inserted "smiths" in brackets in verse 4, understanding them to be the referents of Hebrew *'ēlleh,* "these."

The craftsmen have reversed the policies of the conquering empires of the first millennium, a monumental task that only Yahweh's agents could have accomplished. Most commentators (e.g., Niditch 1983:124; Porter 1983:66) conclude that the "smiths" function symbolically as nothing less than agents of divine destruction. They sharpen the horns of the divine warrior, making them more deadly; or they directly render impotent the "four horns," Yahweh's enemies. The precise way in which destruction is brought about depends on the understanding of the verb we have translated "to cut down" (see NOTE) in verse 4.

The identity of the four horns, as we have already suggested in the second NOTE to 2:1 (RSV 1:18), can include Assyria, Babylon, and also Persia. Because this vision describes a past action of Yahweh's agents, Assyria and Babylonia and not Persia would be the obvious objects of Yahweh's power via the "smiths." Similarly, Babylonia and Persia in turn would be the historical forces of conquests which represent God's agents acting to destroy imperial might. Could the horns of verse 4 (RSV 1:21), as the objects of the craftsmen's activity, signify Persia as well? Probably not, but the lack of clarity surrounding the verbs "to make tremble" and "to cut" makes it difficult to rule out that possibility. However, the "smiths" in verse 4 (RSV 1:21) destroy the scatterers of Judah, a fact which indicates that only Babylonia, and not Persia nor even Assyria for that matter, could be meant as the "horns" which were objects of the smiths' activity. Persia in that case is the only world power that could represent the smiths, who had destroyed those who had deported the Judeans from their homeland.

4 (RSV 1:21). *what are these coming to do?* This question of the prophet addressed to Yahweh constitutes the only time in the visions in which there is a query about the purpose of the visionary figure(s). In the Hebrew this subtle stylistic shift is reflected in the addition of the complementary infinitive "to do" *(la'ăśôt)* after "coming." Usually it is the identity of a visionary figure—horses (Vision 1), lampstand and trees (Vision 4), scroll (Vision 5), ephah (Vision 6), horses and chariots (Vision 7)—or the place to which a figure is going, as with the man of the Third Vision, that is the object of the prophetic inquiry. The normal prophetic question is "what?" Here the questioning seeks to understand the purpose of the four smiths and the question assumes action on the part of those workers, whose very designation implies activity (see preceding NOTE). The significant departure from the regular pattern arouses curiosity and in addition places emphasis upon the deed to be performed. That action is described in verse 4b (RSV 1:21b; see NOTE below to "to arouse them"). Similarly the intrusion of Yahweh himself as the one who provides this second group of visionary subjects in the Second Vision draws attention to the special task of the craftsmen as direct agents of Yahweh.

The verb for "coming" *(bā'îm)* is a masculine plural participial form, which gives it a present meaning. In contrast, the action described in the answer provided by the Interpreting Angel involves past action. This shift is another source of difficulty in understanding the Second Vision, for it confuses the identification of the visionary characters with the real world of political powers. If the "smiths" are coming in the prophet's own time to do something, then how could they be the Persians? No easy answer is forthcoming. Zechariah's perception of time may not have demanded the same kind of progression between past and present that the Western mind expects. If the cutting down of imperial (Babylonian) horns by the (Persian) smiths is the event recalled by the end of this verse, the present coming of smiths in this query would communicate the prophet's understanding that divine agents are always at work in the world. Imperial domination, even by the Persians, will one day too be cut down by Yahweh's might.

scattered. This is the second of three occurrences of this word in the Second Vision; see above NOTE to "scattered" in 2:2 (RSV 1:19) and also below. At this point the prophet has narrowed his consideration of his exiled countrymen to consider only those deported from the southern kingdom, Judah. His ultimate concern is with the restored self-governance in Yehud, a place which is within the territory of the preexilic kingdom of Judah and not of Israel. The horns perpetrating this dispersal would then be the military might of the Babylonians, although the deportation policies of the Persians cannot be ignored (see NOTE to "horns," 2:1 [RSV 1:18]).

so that no one. The emphasis of this expression is on the individual. Although the Hebrew is somewhat unusual, *kĕpî* is nearly identical with *lĕpî* (cf. Exod 12:4). Zechariah has reversed the more normal order (see *BDB:*805), but this is not sufficient grounds for questioning the MT. The import of the phrase is the emphasis on the individuals who have been sent into exile as a result of the imperial policies put into effect by the seventh- and sixth-century conquerors of Israel.

lift his head. That is, "be independent." The Hebrew idiom denotes the personal autonomy of individuals; compare Jehoiachin's autonomy (Jer 52:31) when he is brought out of prison or the restored autonomy of Pharaoh's butler when he is reinstated in his position (Gen 40:20–21). Some would argue that the corporate autonomy or political independence of Judah is at issue here. Yet the emphasis of the preceding expression *kpy ʾyš* identifies the subject as an individual (i.e., each person of a group rather than the group as a whole), and the reference to the stirring up of exiles below (see NOTE to "arouse") supports our understanding of this idiom as referring to the individual autonomy of deported Judeans. The meaning of personal autonomy can also be found in the usage of this phrase in the census-taking narratives of Numbers (e.g., 1:2,49; 26:2; 31:49).

to make . . . tremble. The subject of "came to make them tremble" is "these [smiths]" (cf. NOTE to v 3 [RSV 1:20]). The Hiphil infinitive of *ḥrd*, rendered here "to make tremble," has occasioned much discussion by commentators. Part of the difficulty lies in identifying the object of the verb (see next NOTE) as either Judeans, or as the "horns," or enemies of the Judeans. In the latter case, the verb can either have connotations of destruction ("to rout") if the smiths cut down the horns representing imperial domination, or of trembling on the part of the enemies in the face of such destruction. Some commentators seek to ameliorate this ambivalence by changing *lh-ḥryd* to *lhkḥyd*, "to be totally destroyed" (see Kaufmann 1977:308–9; cf. the reconstruction perhaps overly ingenious of Niditch 1983:118). The meaning of this verb, and the reference of its object "them," require consideration.

The root *ḥrd* in the Qal means "to tremble, quake," or "to be terrified." The Hiphil usually means to "drive in terror, rout," but there are numerous attestations which suggest that a more extended meaning for the Hiphil is possible also. The Qal usage provides a series of instances in which animate and inanimate objects tremble: mountains shake (Exod 19:18), persons tremble under divine influence (1 Sam 14:15), etc. Humans, in particular, respond by quaking before God's word, so great is their terror of God's command (Isa 66:2,5). The Qal therefore describes an action or condition of moving (the forms in Isaiah are statives; cf. also Ruth 3:8) which presumes a prior condition of repose.

If the Qal describes a condition of agitation, the Hiphil denotes that such agitation or movement is being effected: "to cause to tremble, shake," or "to cause to be aroused, to arouse." In some passages a military connotation, "to drive in terror, rout" (e.g., Judg 8:12, Ezek 30:9, etc.), is possible; and that is the sense preferred here by many commentators. There is a series of usages, however, which support a Hiphil meaning that is consonant with the extended Qal meaning noted above and fits the contextual situation, with the "horns of the nations" trembling at the approach of smiths who have the power to overcome them. The absolute Hiphil participle frequently occurs with the negative *(ʾên maḥărîd)* as an idiom for "not disturbing the peace of" or leaving in an untroubled, unagitated state of being *(BDB:353)*, e.g., Lev 26:6; Deut 28:26; Nah 2:12 (RSV 2:11); Job 11:19; Jer 30:10 = 46:27; Mic 4:4; Zeph 3:13. Many of these passages describe the repose and security of individuals when God's covenant is obeyed, especially in an eschatological future, as in Mic 4:4, "Every one shall sit under his vine and under his fig tree, and none shall make them afraid" (RSV). The reading in the latter part of the verse in Micah is simply *'ên maḥărîd* in Hebrew and might better be translated, "no one to disturb him" (NJPS)—from his peace—or "no one to make him tremble." In short, the repose of an empire, seemingly in control of all the world, is profoundly disturbed by the approach of divine agents.

them. The word *'ōtām* is difficult because what it refers to is in some doubt. Despite the fact that *'ōtām has a masculine plural suffix, it is possible to understand "them" as anticipatory, agreeing with the following "horns of the nations" (qarnôt haggoyîm)* which is feminine plural. Such a shift of gender is attested in the late books of the Bible (Niditch 1983:118). Alternatively, one could construe the masculine plural as connecting specifically with the absolute masculine plural, *haggoyîm* (editor's suggestion). In either case, it agrees with "horns of the nations," which most probably refer to an earlier epoch in Judean history and represent Babylonia.

A less likely possibility would allow "them" to refer back to the exiled Judeans and be understood as a resumptive. "Them" would then represent the three scattered groups, "Judah, Israel, and Jerusalem," who would be roused from their state of repose in Babylon. Such a case need not necessarily preclude the preferred understanding of "them," described above, since *lhḥryd* ("to make tremble" or, alternately, "to arouse") itself is ambiguous. But the other problems which arise, in identifying the vision's symbols, become unwieldy at best if "them" has the exiles as its antecedent.

to cut down. Literally "to cast down," or "to cut," from the root *ydh*, one of two occurrences in the Piel (cf. Lam 3:53). The LXX has "to sharpen" *(lěhāḥēd)* for "to make tremble" *(lěhaḥărîd)* but adds "for their hands," apparently misunderstanding the second infinitive *lydwt* as pertaining to "hands." The intrusion of the plural accusative *'ōtām* between the two infinitive constructs is difficult, and the LXX at an earlier stage might have read *'ētîm* ("axes") instead of *'ōtām* ("them"). In any case the fact that "smiths" are the subject of the finite verb "came" means that the first infinitive ("to make tremble") must refer like the second infinitive (literally, "to cut") to the imperial power, "the horns of the nations," here representing Babylon directly. (See following NOTE.) Although the syntax is awkward, the intrusion of the pronominal suffix between the two infinitives facilitates the presentation of the second object ("horns of the nations") of "to cut," which is introduced by the accusative marker *'et* and obviates the need for a conjunctive *waw* ("and").

The meaning of the verb *ydh*, "to cut," is difficult to determine. Others translate it "to cast down" (RSV) or "to hew down" (NJPS), but throwing or casting down is inconsistent with the image of smiths. Niditch takes it to be a corruption of *lěhahădôt* and emends (1983:118). The lexical information about *ydh* provides no assistance. It appears only twice elsewhere, one other time in the Piel as noted above and once in the Qal in Jer 50:14, where it apparently means to "shoot" arrows. Unfortunately, the reading in Jeremiah is in some doubt. Some manuscripts read *yěrû*, which more accurately reflects the meaning "they will shoot." However, the vocalization may in fact be a qere for *yěrû* and the real reading, if the root is *ydh*, could be a Piel imperative. In Lamentations, another roughly contemporary book, the root is clearly used in the Piel (Lam 3:53) and is parallel to *ṣmt*, which is usually translated "put an end to." RSV translates it: "They flung me alive into the pit, and *cast (ydh)* stones at me." We render "cutting" chiefly to continue the imagery of metalworkers and their handiwork. By adding "down" to "cutting," perhaps we do not greatly distort the meaning of "throwing down," or "casting" since the severed horns of the conquerors would no longer be "raised" (see below) against a foe. Made useless by the smiths' activity, they would perforce be put down.

Our argument for delineating "to cut down" in this specific way rests upon our identification of "horns of the nations" in this verse with Persia (see following NOTE). The alternative view of the preceding "them," whereby the pronoun refers to Judah, is difficult to support in light of the meaning "to cut down." Persia had not been seriously threatened or her might curtailed. Therefore *lydwt*, "to cut," must refer to the Persian destruction of Babylonia in the days of Cyrus. Cyrus's conquest is viewed as the work of divine agents. The vision thus presents a standard postexilic view concerning the rise of Persia and the fall of Babylon. Zechariah, like Haggai, was well aware of the imminent end of the seventy-year prophecy and would have had on his mind events that marked the beginning of that period as well as those he expected to mark the end. The image of smiths as divine agents who bring about the end of Babylonian hegemony most easily fits the postexilic view of the Persians, whose power was considered even greater than that of the Babylonians. After all, the Persians conquered Babylon. While they had not restored Yehud to independence, they had not made her situation any worse. Persia appears as a positive force, a suitable candidate to serve Yahweh's purpose, in contrast to the Babylonians as a destructive force.

horns of the nations. The term "horns," as we have noted above (NOTE to "four horns," v 1 [RSV 1:18]), represents military power and might. When it occurs with "four" it signifies a totality of power—that is, an imperial force. Because the beginning of verse 4 (RSV 1:21) most likely depicts the Babylonian conquest and deportations, the phrase "to cut down the horns of the nations" refers to the overthrow of Babylonia and the ascendency of Achaemenid rule.

The use of the plural "nations" *(gôyîm)* to represent Babylonia seems strange but reflects the nature of the Babylonian imperial government, which exerted its control over preexisting units without dismantling them entirely or subjecting them to far-reaching restructuring. The Babylonian Empire, as it was constituted by the time of its conquest by Persia, could easily be perceived as a conglomerate of subject "nations." The expression "horns of the nations" therefore signifies the might of an empire consisting of many vassal nations, in this case Babylonia.

raised the horn. This is the fifth occurrence of the word "horn" *(qeren)* in this second vision, though the only one in the singular. The repetition of words designating the visionary object is an important characteristic of the symbolic vision form in Zechariah. There is no attempt to economize in the repeated use of the significant terms.

The participle form *hannōśĕ'îm* ("raised") governs the action and takes its understanding and tense from the main clause, from *zērû* ("scattered") and the imperfect *waw* conversive "came." The horns which symbolize a power that scattered Judah can only refer to Babylonia, the kingdom responsible for Judah's deportation.

to scatter. For the third time in this vision, *zrh*, "scatter," appears and provides emphasis to the fact of Judah's exile. Perhaps Zechariah, at the eve of the temple's completion and after nearly two decades of rebuilding in Yehud, no longer needs to focus upon the Babylonian destruction of nation, city, or temple. Rather he stresses the exile, which is also an important concern at the end of the visionary sequence the Crowning (6:9–15).

COMMENT

The brevity of the Second Vision obscures at first the complexity of the language and the elusiveness of the images which the modern reader must strive to analyze and interpret. The straightforward dialogic presentation enhances its communication of the prophet's visionary experience. "Horns" and "smiths" are apparently mundane objects and personages which should reveal their symbolism without undue difficulty. Yet both the language and the images pose problems for the exegete. The figures by virtue of their very ordinariness cannot be identified on their own; their significance in the vision can emerge only through understanding their integration into the literary and contextual framework. And the language, notably that of the vision's explanation in the second half of verse 4 (RSV 1:21), is replete with indefinite references and relatively obscure vocabulary. Short of resorting to wholesale emendation, these difficulties can be met only by strong contextual assistance.

Admittedly, working back and forth between etymology and context can result in some circularity of reasoning. Yet this attempt to reconcile the vision with the historico-political reality has several advantages that offset the problem of circularity. First, the absolute dating of the visions provides a fairly accurate picture of the world that Zechariah saw—namely, the Persian Empire at the apex of its period of organization and control under Darius I in the late sixth century. Second, the other oracles or visions attributed to Zechariah demonstrate his strong historical consciousness, so we can presuppose that the images of this vision are related to past events and politics he saw as important for the history of his people. Third, the visionary mode allows for the fact that certain things do not reflect a judgment of what the prophet expects will really happen but rather an expectation of things that ought to happen. Lack of clarity, in such a case, is a feature of Zechariah's thinking about certain things which is just as possible and as important as the specificity which he displays concerning other matters.

One further methodological possibility for dealing with this vision lies in the fact that it is one of a series of seven visions. The reconstruction of the prophet's times and thoughts depends to a great extent upon other biblical texts as well as on external information, but it also benefits from the nature of the visionary sequence as a carefully structured whole. Again, the problem of circularity is not to be overlooked. Looking at the Second Vision in the light of its position within a set of visions demands caution in using mutually tentative interpretations to support each other. Nonetheless, since an overall scheme to the set exists, even though the particular contributions of this vision to that scheme may be vague, the information provided by the structure of the whole contributes to the task of making sense of a seventh part of the whole.

The purview of the visions has been suggested by the charts in our Introduction. A universal scope is introduced by the initial vision and resumed in the concluding one. The intervening five visions move within an increasingly more confined range against that universal backdrop. All of the visions have as their ultimate concern the content of the central, focal one, the temple in Jerusalem, as well as the high priesthood which is the subject of the Prophetic Vision that stands at the center of the series along with the Fourth Vision. They all are addressed to the implications that a restored temple has for the widening circles that are the realms surrounding it: the immediate realm of Jerusalem and the province of Yehud, the larger realm of the Persian Empire, and the ultimate realm of Yahweh's sovereignty. Within this structure the Second Vision deals with the second largest of the superimposed circles surrounding the temple (Yahweh being the largest), namely Persia, the imperial regime of which Yehud and its temple were a part.

Like the Sixth Vision, which also helps to clarify the position of Yehud within the empire, the Second Vision consists of two parts introduced sequentially. The prophet first reports that he sees "four horns." No further information is given, and the prophet immediately begins his interrogation of the Interpreting Angel, whose presence is taken for granted. The Hebrew word for horns can admit of several meanings in the biblical world, as we have indicated in our NOTE to "four horns." While a number of nuances may lurk in the background, a militaristic one emerges because of the explicit explanation given by the prophet in verse 2 (RSV 1:19) and also in the reprise uttered by Yahweh at the very end of verse 4 (RSV 1:21).

The horns in this vision are symbolic, in a maximalist understanding of the objects of their domination, of the military expansion of supranational powers such as those that destroyed Israel and most of Judah, and a hundred years later Judah and Jerusalem itself. The end of the vision, however, focuses on the subjugation of Judah. This narrowed focus makes the Babylonians the imperial evil, and the demise of Babylon at the hands of the Persians emerges as the meaning of the smiths' destructive powers as God's agents.

The prophet is well aware of the destruction wrought by the Babylonians upon Judah, Jerusalem, and the temple. His retrospective of 1:1–6 and his oracles dealing with the rebuilding of Judah and of the temple (e.g., 1:16,17) are based upon his recollection of the devastation suffered in 587 B.C.E. Yet this vision ignores that aspect of Yehudite history and deals exclusively with the scattering of the conquered people. The prophet has shifted his attention exclusively to the policy of deportations practiced by the imperial government of the first millennium which were usually an immediate accompaniment of the military operations that established the supremacy of the conquering power. His attention is not focused upon the subsequent techniques of governance that the imperial government imposes upon its territorial holdings. As we have explained in our NOTES, the policy of exiling served the imperial purposes of political powers which sought to dominate the world. World powers in that way moved perilously close to Yahweh's dominion. The prophet's depiction of the empires or "horns" in this vision helps to clarify the relationship of God's control to even the most benign of imperial governments.

The mechanism of imperial subjugation must now be related to the dynamics of the Second Vision. Doing so depends to a certain extent upon establishing the identity of the political entities giving rise to the military symbolism of the horns. As we observe in the NOTES, the information in verse 2 (RSV 1:19; "These are the horns which scattered Judah, Israel, and Jerusalem") suggests that Assyria, Babylonia, and Persia might all be involved. Indeed, all those empires had well-documented policies of shifting some of the populations that they dominated. For the Assyrians and Babylonians, those deportations appear to have been carried out in the process of initial military advance. The narrative in the Book of Kings is explicit in its description of the deportation of Israelites and Judeans (2 Kgs 17 and 24–25). The vision, however, is clearly dated to the Persian period, as is all of Zechariah 1–8. More precisely, the visions belong to the end of the second year of Darius I. Can the horns then really represent all of the imperial powers who deported Zechariah's forebears? Can this vision be applied at all to the Persians, for whom the Bible reserves praise because of an opposite policy, repatriating people to Yehud?

In trying to answer these questions we wish to reiterate several facts. First, verse 4 (RSV 1:21) differs from verse 2 (RSV 1:19) in its specification of the objects of the scattering. In the latter there are three objects: Judah, Israel, and Jerusalem. In the former, which is Yahweh's concluding response by way of explaining the smiths, the fact of scattering appears twice more and Judah alone is the object. We take this to reflect Zechariah's overriding concern with the restoration community, namely the former southern kingdom, or Judah, which was allowed to rebuild the temple. The vision reflects the postexilic period and the community centered around Jerusalem. The obvious point of the last verse, then, is that Babylonia has been destroyed, with Persia as the instrument of that destruction. The verbal sequence of 2:4b (RSV 1:21b) is presented with past tenses, so that the historical and, from the Yehudite perspective, momentous overthrow of Babylon is recounted. That overthrow was prefatory to the return of exiles, the granting of semiautonomy to Yehud, and permission to rebuild the temple. Why does Zechariah, in light of this, persist in his emphasis on the scattered people?

Two explanations can be offered, neither of which precludes the other. The first lies in the fact that the policies of Cyrus and Darius I did not bring about a complete return of Judean exiles to Palestine. The Crowning Scene in chapter 6 deals in part with the relationship of the community of exiles to their homeland under the changed circumstances of a rebuilt temple with Yahweh's presence and sovereignty restored. Part Three of Zechariah similarly considers the renewed authority of traditional law that accompanied the temple's restoration and what it may have meant for groups outside Jerusalem. Our NOTES and COMMENT to 6:9–15 and 7:1–6 treat these issues to some extent.

A second consideration derives from an understanding of Persian policies. Let us not forget that the verb of the prophet's question in 2:4a (RSV 1:21a) suggests a present situation, the coming of God's agents, the smiths, in Zechariah's time, in Darius's reign. Is there something about Persian imperial policy that has caused Zechariah to dwell upon the problem of deportations, albeit with a review of past events?

Persia enjoys such a positive reputation in the biblical record that it is difficult to overcome the impression of the benevolence of Persian rule. Cyrus is lauded by Second Isaiah as Yahweh's anointed one, who has come to fulfill the divine plan (Isa 44:28; 45:1). Ezra has Cyrus proclaiming and fulfilling Yahweh's charge (1:1ff.). However, the nature of Persian rule was not consistently so benign or selfless as the ancient Hebrew writers would lead one to believe (Kuhrt 1983). The Persians indeed restored some peoples to their original territories, if these peoples were in key locations and if their repatriation served strategic purposes. They also deported peoples, particularly in the wake of localized rebellions which had to be quelled (Herodotus IV.204; V.13–16; VI.20). At the end of Darius's second year, a series of insurrections had only recently been quelled by the Persians (Cook 1983:50–57). In dealing with the rebellion, Darius continued the deportation practices that had been used so successfully in the past. Herodotus reports, for example, that the Barcans of Libya were moved to Bactria, and this was only one of several population transfers noted by Herodotus and other ancient sources (Kuhrt 1983:94). Darius's clever institution of favorable policies toward certain groups such as the Yehudites was matched by military action and selective deportations against other groups.

Not only was Darius active in implementing policies that were destructive for some peoples, he was also responsible, especially in the early years of his reign, for imposing administrative structure on his vast holdings. The organization of Persia was relatively loose under Cyrus and his successor Cambyses. Systematic control of the territories acquired through conquest can be attributed to the genius of Darius I (Cook 1983:41). Early in his reign, he took bold steps to partition the empire into provinces which were created through favorable groupings of peoples as much as with respect to purely geographical logic.

While we do not mean to imply that Persia threatened Yehud with further deportation or with a greatly altered system of governance, we do suggest that Zechariah's repeated reference to deportation is conditioned by contemporary as well as past historical events. That is, the events of Darius's first two years led Zechariah to perceive that even Persia was capable of instituting such measures. The "horns" of military battles and deported citizens, which intermittently characterized the sustained Achaemenid hegemony, were visible in the first two years of Darius's rule as they had been during the Assyrian and Babylonian eras. This vision need not be limited in its frame of reference to the traumatic experience of Judah with the Babylonians. It can also refer to the continuing awareness, at least on the part of Zechariah, that Yehud's security was not absolute as long as it was dependent upon a foreign power. The ambivalent and elliptical condition of the Hebrew text, especially in verse 4 (RSV 1:21), conveys the open-ended nature of Yahweh's past punitive actions against the aggressors. Zechariah is pleased with what Persia has allowed, even encouraged, Yehud to do. But in the final analysis even the Persians could turn against Yehud.

The Second Vision, while specifying the past conquest of the wicked Babylonians, is sensitive to the possibility of further interference with the "land of Judah." That phrase in verse 4 (RSV 1:21) is the only such instance in which it is found in Haggai or Zechariah, and it may allude not only to the past scattering of population but also to a potential reapportionment of Judean territory. Zechariah was conditioned by his knowledge of the history of the preceding two hundred years to admit that drastic measures could be implemented against his people. In his day, disaster does not recur; their fortunes appear to be miraculously reversed. But Zechariah is not fully confident that the fortunes of Yehud will hold. And even if they don't, he recognizes that the restoration of the temple and the establishment of semiautonomy is not yet the fulfillment of Yahweh's plan for his people. One day Jerusalem will be fully autonomous and Yahweh's supremacy rather than Darius's will prevail in the world. The present "coming" of the smiths allows for the possibility that Persia too must inevitably be subject to Yahweh's agents.

The image of the smiths appears abruptly after the angel's explication of the horns. They enter Zechariah's visionary field directly through Yahweh's instrumentality, the only visionary objects or personages in all the visions so introduced: "Yahweh showed me" (v 3 [RSV 1:20]). Yahweh's direct association with the smiths is clearly established. The smiths are God's personal emissaries, sent to destroy those who have exiled Judah. Because these agents of God's might are so closely connected with the source of their power, the question of their identity, with which we struggled in the NOTE to "smiths," almost becomes a moot point. The replacement of one foreign power by another is a consequence of Yahweh's plan, and the Persian armies are merely acting out that plan. Sooner or later Yahweh himself will garner the acknowledgment presently directed toward Darius, and the Persians too will have their horns cut down by God's agents.

Zechariah's Second Vision does not fully separate past events from expectations of what might happen in the future. The recognition that Yahweh has brought about Babylon's downfall means that Yahweh will inevitably end

Persian subjugation of Yehud, however mild that might be. The vision has an eschatological tinge which relates it to Part Three of Zechariah 1–8 as well as to many of the oracles. Like Haggai, Zechariah includes things that were not completely encased in the realities of the political situation but were not thereby less real to him. The prophetic vision ranges beyond historico-political realities without compromising or distorting them. Surely a prophet such as Zechariah, who responds so effectively in support of temple restoration and Yehudite reorganization, must have seen in those events the seeds of a larger change in the historical order. A prophet living in the century when two of antiquity's superpowers replaced two others could hardly deny the future possibility of still another world-shaking reversal.

4. THIRD VISION:
THE MAN WITH THE MEASURING-CORD
(2:5–9; RSV 2:1–5)

[5] I raised my eyes, and I looked, and behold: I saw a man with a measuring-cord in his hand!

[6] Then I said, "Where are you going?"

He said to me, "To measure Jerusalem, to determine its width and its length."

[7] Then behold: the angel-who-speaks-with-me was going out—and another angel was going out to meet him—[8] and he said to him, "Run and speak to this official:

Jerusalem will be inhabited, with its villages,
    an abundance of people and beasts in her midst;
[9] I will be for her—Oracle of Yahweh—an encircling
    wall of fire,
and as Glory will I be within her."

NOTES

2:5 (RSV 2:1). *raised my eyes.* See NOTE to 2:1 (RSV 1:18).

measuring-cord. Two words *(ḥebel middâ)* are used together to indicate a measuring device, but the first word alone actually provides the important nuance for understanding the phrase and consequently the imagery. In contrast with the use of builder's "line" in 1:16, this cord or string *(ḥebel)* is used for measurement; indeed, "cord" is often found in the Bible as a measuring device even without *middâ* ("of measurement").

The word is also found more than several times (Deut 32:9; 1 Chron 16:18; Ps 105:11; 78:55) in association with the term *naḥălâ* ("inheritance"). Although it is very difficult to judge the ascendancy of such an expression between the early days of the poetry of Deuteronomy to its later usage in Zechariah or the Chronicler, a case can be made for the "measuring-cord" in Zechariah to have a range of meaning which includes that provided by the expression "cord of inheritance," the territorial dimension of God's apportionment to Israel with Jerusalem at its center. A *double entendre* may be intended here. The man with the measuring-cord, while absorbed with the terrestrial demands of measurement, at the same time carries a device symbolizing Judah's inheritance of God's historic apportionment to Israel. In this case the Third Vision would anticipate not only the oracle of 2:10–11 (RSV 2:6–7), which appears to be directly associated with it, but also the statement in 2:16 (RSV 2:12), in which Yahweh allots to Judah his special portion ("inheritance") and selects Jerusalem as its sacred center (see NOTES and COMMENT to 2:10–17 [RSV 2:6–13]).

6 (RSV v 2). *Where are you going?* All the visions are dialogic: in four of them the prophet initiates the conversation, in the other three the Interpreting Angel speaks first. In two of the latter (Visions 4 and 5), it is the angel who actually poses the question concerning the identity of the visionary object or character. Considerable variation is evident in the manner in which the question that opens the dialogue is put forth. Yet the questions themselves are all introduced by "what" *(mâ)* with the single exception of this vision, which is introduced by *'ānâ,* "where, whither." The *he* of direction attached to the interrogative *'ān* indicates movement and so draws attention to the activity performed by the man carrying an instrument of measure. Neither the man himself nor the cord in his hand constitutes the symbolic images of this vision, although the presence of the man with his tool would seem to point to some significance in the act of measuring. The act of measuring in the abstract does not convey the full meaning of the man's activity. The *object* of his activity is essential for grasping his, and the vision's, message. The particle "where," unique in introducing Zechariah's visions (although it does appear in the second part of the ephah vision, 5:10) directs our attention to the object of the man's measuring and allows us to comprehend his specific task and its significance.

The force of "where" in bringing the man's specific action rather than his identity to the forefront as the chief visionary symbol is supplemented by the verb that follows. "Going" continues the sense of movement of the interrogatory pronoun and pulls us farther toward the place where the man is heading in order to perform his symbolic act. This movement toward a specific place likewise makes his measuring of Jerusalem, rather than just any measuring, the crucial element of the vision.

This question also represents another variant in the dialogic pattern found in all the visions. It is here alone that we see the prophet conversing directly with a visionary character. He does not offer the expected query to the Interpreting Angel. Instead, he directs his question to the man in the vision. It is difficult to ascertain exactly why this exceptional situation exists, especially since the very visionary mode itself would imply some separation between the prophet and that which he perceives. Our only clue is that the question itself is exceptional. Because the process of apperception is not complete without the prophet's awareness of the man's destination, his questioning of the man provides information he needs in order for him to have "seen" this vision. Only then would the expected question to the Interpreting Angel be appropriate, but such a question has been obviated by the prophet's address to the man. The Interpreting Angel nonetheless provides a response, itself atypical. He conveys an oracle via another angelic figure to the "official," whom we identify with the man of verses 5 and 6 (RSV vv 1,2).

The prophetic interaction with a visionary figure, unique as it may be to the set of Seven Visions, anticipates Zechariah's involvement with the actors in the Heavenly Court and Investiture Scene of chapter 3, which stands with the Fourth Vision at the center of the visionary sequences. While that chapter is not to be included in the visionary sequence proper (see NOTES to 3:1 and COMMENT to 3:1–7), it resembles three of the visions in certain of its features, the apparent participation of the prophet within the imagined scene being one of them. In it, we see further evidence of the lack of rigid demarcation among the various genres which are skillfully interwoven to form the Book of Zechariah.

To measure. The measuring of Jerusalem graphically anticipates that which will eventually fill out those measured dimensions—a rebuilt city with a restored temple. Such a concept is also found in Ezekiel's temple vision, although the measuring device there (cc 40–42) is a rod rather than a cord. Ezekiel's "son of man" is the one who performs the act of measuring in his vision; perhaps the man in Zechariah's vision corresponds to the one in Ezekiel.

its width and its length. These specific components of area measure are not to be construed as having a direct connection with the temple rebuilding project, for the process of restoring the temple was already under way. However, the relationship of the temple to the political or monarchic dimension of which the preexilic temple had been an element was not so clear. The boundaries of Jerusalem in this vision can be related to the royal estate of the house of David (cf. Ishida 1977:122–36) which will one day be restored; it is in the divine plan. This understanding of the measuring of Jerusalem is contingent upon the eschatological nature of the angelic explication in verse 8 (RSV v 4). It is not necessary to see in this measurement process a reference to any actual attempt in Zechariah's day to restore the walls of the city, as suggested by Thomas (1956:1064) and Baldwin (1972:106) among others. The width and length refer to its total area—that is, its size rather than its perimeter—insofar as verse 8 (RSV v 4) denotes the population that will inhabit that area. The measurer's survey creates an imagined and future Jerusalem, albeit one whose ultimate existence is initiated by the events of the restoration. The building of temple walls may have stimulated expectations of re-erecting city walls, and the measuring required for both is the link between the two.

The fact that the "width" precedes the "length" in this verse may provide a specific clue as to what is being measured. In Ezekiel, various measurements are given for an ideal, future territory and its components, which include a building precinct, a city with its open spaces and tribal allotments. The holy portion of the land (Ezek 45:1; 48:9,13) is consistently measured with length, the larger figure, preceding width. That seems to be the normal sequence: the larger figure comes first and is designated "length." However, Ezekiel provides the size of the city territory, which contains one sacred district. The rest of the territory, apart from Yahweh's precinct, is to be "5,000 cubits wide and 25,000 cubits long, (and) shall be for ordinary use for the city, for dwelling and for open country" (Ezek 48:15). The width precedes the length, apparently a departure from the normal order. Because this verse specifies width before length, and because there is a reference below to a Jerusalem greater than the city itself (cf. v 8, "with its villages"), this verse therefore would denote the future city along with its adjacent land.

The ordering of width before length also shows a relationship to the Fifth Vision which, in the overall structure of the visions (see Introduction), can be paired with this vision. The Fifth Vision also contains a set of measurements, and in that case the order is the opposite: length precedes width. The appearance of measurements and their chiastic arrangement helps to link the two visions.

7 (RSV v 3). *another angel.* A second angelic figure, in addition to the Interpreting Angel, makes his appearance and creates the impression that the angel who speaks with the prophet is only one, although probably the most important of a host of angelic beings who serve in the court of Yahweh. Zechariah preserves three designations for such figures: "another angel" of this verse, "angel-who-speaks-with-me" of all the visions, and "Angel of Yahweh" of the First Vision and the Investiture Scene of chapter 3. The second and third may be identical, however (see Notes to 1:8, "man," and 1:13, "Yahweh answered").

was going out . . . was going out. The verb *yṣ'* ("to go out, go forth") is used frequently in Zechariah's visions to designate movements of visionary figures, both animate and inanimate (cf. 5:5,6,9; 6:1,5,6,7,8). In this vision, the divine emissaries are in motion, suggesting God's active role in the world. As soon as the principal angel starts moving, the subordinate one does also, so that he can meet his superior and be available to receive orders and run errands if necessary. Except in 6:7, the verb appears in its participial form.

8 (RSV v 4). *he said to him.* The speaker is understood to be the Interpreting Angel, the chief angelic figure of the visions, since the closest antecedent to the subject of this verb is the object pronoun of the previous verb in verse 7 (RSV v 3) (*lqr'tw,* "to meet him"). He issues a command to "another angel," the second angelic figure of the preceding verse. The second angel responds to the command and proceeds to address the "official" in the vision.

Run. The verb *rwṣ* ("to run"), particularly when followed by a verb indicating speaking as in this case, often implies that the person running is performing the function of messenger. One of the classic passages exemplifying this specific dimension of "run" is 2 Sam 18:19–32, in which Ahimaaz, the son of Zadok, and an unnamed Cushite vie to bring messages to King David from his general Joab. The root *rwṣ* appears eleven times in that episode, all relating to the human couriers who transmit information from its source to an intended recipient. Such usage of "run" depends on the literal act of speedy locomotion. However, the messenger aspect of the verb can have a more extended meaning in some instances. It can designate the fact of a message being carried without actually intending that the person involved set off at a jog. The mission of the messenger *par excellence,* the prophet, is so designated in Jer 23:21, where prophetic parallelism links "ran" with "prophesied":

I did not send the prophets,
yet they ran;
I did not speak to them,
yet they prophesied.

In light of this passage in Jeremiah, the appearance of "run" in the present verse signifies the prophetic role of the angel. He is one of the intermediaries who carries God's message from its heavenly source to its earthly audience. This point is further corroborated by the nature of the message, delivered in 2:8b–9 (RSV 2:4b–5), which is called a prophetic oracle (n'm yhwh, "Oracle of Yahweh," v 9 [RSV v 5]). That it is an angel and not the prophet who is ordered to "run" and deliver the oracle reveals the functional equivalency between prophet and angelic beings, with the latter ultimately replacing the former as Yahweh's emissaries in Jewish literature of the late postexilic period. A similar fluidity between prophetic and angelic roles underlies the dramatic investiture passage of chapter 3.

this official. The identity of this figure is not readily apparent. Some would identify him with the prophet himself (e.g., Mitchell 1912:38); the relationship of Zechariah to Jeremiah is the chief reason for that interpretation. In Jeremiah's call (Jer 1:6) the prophet-to-be, who was already designated a prophet in his mother's womb, protests that he is only a na'ar, the word we render "official" but which (see below) can also mean "youth." Since there are many obvious and explicit connections between Jeremiah and Zechariah, na'ar here may refer to the latter and be an allusion to the former. The strong emphatic particle "this" likewise suggests that the following substantive refers to a character already identified in the vision. Only Zechariah would fit that description. He is the narrator who has also, already in verse 6 (RSV v 2), exchanged words with one of the visionary figures and in so doing has become a visionary figure himself. Yet the oracle that the "official" is to deliver has been transmitted by a second angel and only indirectly by the Interpreting Angel. Since the latter always and characteristically speaks directly to the prophet, it is unlikely that in this instance a mediator, who serves no other purpose in the vision, gives the message to the official. The Interpreting Angel and Zechariah have a relationship that is the epitome of dialogic exchange. The second angel must therefore be addressing someone other than the prophet.

Another possibility is that a new figure has been added to the sequence, if the presence of the relatively rare and thus forceful demonstrative (hallāz, "this") before "official" has the force of separating out the individual so designated. Yet the introduction of a previously unidentified person is also not tenable. The basic rule in sorting out the visionary personae is parsimony (editor's suggestion). How few different characters can one get away with? A new individual should be accepted as the "official" only if none of the previously introduced persons fits.

By this argument, one other figure is a candidate to be the "official": perhaps the man holding the measuring-cord (vv 5–6 [RSV vv 1–2]) is also the one to whom the second angel delivers an oracle. This proposal has been made by Rudolph (1976:85), among others, although he does not justify his choice. There is, however, much to commend it. It clarifies the addition of the second angel, whose role would be to speak to the other person in the vision (the man with the cord) and so preserve the special link between prophet and Interpreting Angel. Furthermore, most of the visions, brief as they are, consist of two parts, with some accompanying degree of interaction between the figures of the first and second parts. For that reason, the official would have to be the person who measures, otherwise the expected integration of the two parts of the vision would not be achieved. In addition, the content of the oracle amplifies and explains the measurements taken by that person, and in that way complements the measurer's role, even though the act of measuring is not part of the oracle itself. The one performing the measurements would provide the necessary link between the visionary act and its symbolic meaning. This way too the prophet would hear the oracle, which his angelic mentor would want him to, because he was still on the scene, listening as well as looking.

The word for "official," na'ar, is itself difficult. If it in fact refers to the man who measures, then it would not have its frequent meaning of "young man" or inexperienced youth, the latter being Mason's unconvincing explanation (1977b:41–42). Instead, the term na'ar can be a technical term for an official of the court or of the temple, or of both (cf. 1 Kgs 20:14ff.; a fourth-century inscription from Tel Dor; and the Kition inscriptions of the fourth–third century, Donner-Röllig: 1964 37:A.8,12; B.11). The general idea of na'ar is supported by the na'ar of Boaz who is in charge of the reapers (Ruth 2:5–6). Ziba, the na'ar or steward of King Saul, is the only such na'ar specified by name in the Hebrew Bible. Albright's interpretation of the na'ar seals at Tell Beit Mirsim and Beth Shemesh, now also found at Ramat Raḥel, as having a royal connotation has recently been challenged by Avigad (1976b). Seals having the meaning of steward or official have also been found in Ammonite and trans-Jordanian contexts. In Israel, of special interest and in nonroyal contexts, are the eighth-century seal of Benayahu, na'ar of Haggai, and the seventh-century seal of Malkiyahu (Avigad 1976b:296–97). The notion of an official, therefore, is appropriate to the figure of the man who measures, for the latter is involved in the reconstruction of Jerusalem, its walls, and perhaps the temple too. Since the message the na'ar receives tells him something about the size and the defense of Jerusalem and its urban context, it is reasonable to suppose that this individual is none other than the man who is determining the size of Jerusalem. The latter is surely acting in some authoritative capacity; he is an "official" rather than a "youth."

villages. Literally, unwalled villages or hamlets (cf. Deut 3:5; Ezek 38:11). Urban centers were surrounded by such agricultural settlements whose inhabitants contributed to the urban economy (Frick 1977:93). Normally, the word employed to designate the satellites of Jerusalem as an urban center is 'îr (Jer 19:15), which would imply that these subunits of Jerusalem's territory were themselves fortified—that is, they were politically subsidiary but economically independent units relating to Jerusalem as capitol city (Frick 1977: passim; cf. NOTE to "cities around it," Zech 7:7). The use here of pĕrāzôt, which specifically denotes an unwalled settlement, reflects the demographic pattern that emerged in the Judean hills beginning in the sixth century. While occasional small agricultural settlements existed around Jerusalem in the Early Bronze Age, and others were established in the Iron I period, the preponderance of the agricultural units surrounding Jerusalem apparently date from the Persian period (Edelstein 1982:212). This information helps to clarify the altered political-economic role of Jerusalem in the postexilic period. As capital of the Judean kingdom, it drew economic subsistence from its cities, the cities of the realm, since Jerusalem itself had an immediate hinterland that was considerably less arable—i.e., in which agricultural productivity required greater effort than in the farmlands around "her cities." With the termination of Judean independence and the restructuring of the territory into Yehud under Achaemenid rule, Jerusalem's lifeline of foodstuffs from politically dependent cities was cut off. The growth of agricultural terraces, fenced farm areas, and unwalled hamlets in the Judean hills around Jerusalem, beginning in the sixth century, testifies to the necessity for Jerusalem to secure her own food supplies by developing her formerly sparsely utilized hinterland.

In addition to reflecting settlement patterns in Yehud following the exile, the concept of unwalled settlements continues the poetic imagery of this section, in which Jerusalem likewise is unwalled. The language portrays an eschatological Zion, in which the normal existence of walls and the strife they imply is precluded. A city by definition (Frick 1977:30–42) in ancient Palestine was a fortified settlement, surrounded by walls or other defense works.

Preexilic Jerusalem, with its satellites, had the political and economic structure of a Canaanite city-state, a structure which resulted in perceptions of Zion that drew upon Canaanite mythology and produced the notion of Jerusalem as a divinely chosen center (cf. North 1967:138). The unique role of Jerusalem was achieved because it was the capital city of a monarchy (= kingdom) and was part of the royal (= federal) district. As such it differed from provincial capitals, from tribal enclaves, and even from religious establishments such as Bethel and Beersheba. Its fortunes rose and fell with those of the monarchy. Although the economic and political centrality of Jerusalem may have ended with the events of the sixth century, the ideological components of that centrality if anything were increased by the destruction of Jerusalem and Judah. The restoration of Jerusalem and ultimately of the monarchy was inextricably bound up with the conceptualization of Yahweh's ongoing relationship with his people.

The specification of unwalled villages consequently does not pertain to a situation in which defenses would be unnecessary. Jerusalem itself will be fortified, albeit with God's protection rather than stone walls. These villages, which in the present age have grown up to fill an economic need, will in the future age denote the opposite, the lack of need. The population of Jerusalem will be so great that it will spill out and fill the satellite villages too. The second clause, "abundance of people and beasts within her" (see below, NOTE to "beasts") explains why Jerusalem will have villages in the future.

The placement of the word "villages" in Hebrew, before the singular verb ("will be inhabited"; literally, "sits" or "dwells"), which itself precedes the subject "Jerusalem," is difficult. The plural *pĕrāzôt* is an amplification of Jerusalem. The lack of a connective or particle here reflects the poetic texture of the angelic utterance despite its incorporation into the narrative of the vision. The tendency to omit particles is characteristic of prophecy in general and we must supply them as the context requires. We have done this in our translation by adding "with." The overall structure of the tetracolon which is composed of verses 8b–9 (RSV vv 4b–5) is as follows:

pĕrāzôt tēšēb yĕrûšālēm	3 + 2 + 4 = 9
mērōb 'ādām ûbĕhēmâ bĕtôkāh	2 + 2 + 4 + 3 = 11
wa'ănî 'ehyeh-lāh . . . ḥômat 'ēš sābîb	
	3 + 2 + 1 + 2 + 1 + 2 = 11
ûlĕkābôd 'ehyeh bĕtôkāh	4 + 2 + 3 = 9

The language is both poetic and figurative, and it brings the vision to an eloquent conclusion.

will be inhabited. The future condition of Jerusalem is eschatological and involves both the restoration of a Davidide and the existence of the temple. It builds upon notions of the eternal habitation of Jerusalem such as expressed by Jeremiah (17:25–27). "Jerusalem" is the subject of this verb, which is actually a simple Qal imperfect. It means, literally, "Jerusalem dwells/sits (with) its villages."

abundance. The poor agricultural land immediately surrounding Jerusalem could not support a population much larger than its original Jebusite size (ca. 2,000, Broshi 1978) without the support of contributing city-states. Indeed, that land may not have been extensively developed at all until the political-economic exigencies of the Persian period (see above NOTE to "villages"). Broshi (1978:10–15) estimates the population after Nehemiah's rebuilding to be ca. 4,500; the inhabitants of Jerusalem several generations earlier would have been considerably fewer in number. A vision of a populous Jerusalem, in contrast to the postexilic reality, implies a Jerusalem with a restored economic basis to support an enlarged population (perhaps as many as 25,000 in the reign of Hezekiah, so Broshi 1978:11–13). That is, Jerusalem as a royal city-state at the head of a network of cities is the social unit underlying the image of a demographically flourishing locale (cf. "Jerusalem and her cities," Zech 7:7). Population increase, in addition, is a sign of wealth and prosperity. The future Jerusalem will be so prosperous it will be filled to overflowing with people and animals.

beasts. The mention of "beasts" together with "people" lends support to the connotation of the economic factors underlying the image of a well-populated Jerusalem. Many animals—a sign of wealth—as well as people can exist in Jerusalem only if they are supported by an agricultural hinterland larger than that to which Jerusalem had been reduced in Zechariah's time. The envisioned restoration of that hinterland implies that Jerusalem will again have city-state status. The impossibility of such an event under Persian imperial domination makes this poetic utterance clearly eschatological, as do the other elements it contains. "Abundance of people and beasts in her midst" suggests great prosperity and offers a reason for the addition of "villages" to "Jerusalem" in the first clause.

9 (RSV v5). *I will be for her.* Literally, "and I, I will be for her" *(waʾănî ʾehyeh-lāh).* The use of the verb "to be" *(hyh)* with God as speaker, followed by a preposition with a pronominal suffix, is suggestive of the use of the divine name EHYEH. In Exod 3:14, the sequence *ʾhyh šlḥny ʾlykm* ("EHYEH [I AM] sent me to you") is related to the revelation of God's name. Hos 1:9 has a similar structure, *wʾnky lʾ-ʾhyh lkm.* Andersen and Freedman (1980:143, 198–99) translate the Hosea passage "and I am not Ehyeh to you," and Freedman suggests (editorial communication) that *eʾhyeh* here be rendered "Ehyeh" rather than "I am": "As for me, I am EHYEH for her." "Ehyeh" as a divine appellation has the same form as the verb "to be" in the first person. Zechariah may well have used *ʾhyeh* to echo the Exodus and Hosea passages and the naming of God. Yet, this verse departs from the Exodus and Hosea ones in not dealing with the name of God. Hence our translation provides the verbal meaning ("I will be") of the Hebrew word, which occurs again in the next line. God's divine presence is emphasized; "within her" = "in her midst" also appears twice in this oracle.

wall of fire. Jerusalem too, in addition to her satellites, will be unwalled. Yahweh's presence replaces a stone fortification, the outward sign of a city or city-state's political independence and self-defensive capability. "Fire" is a vehicle of divine presence here, as in Exod 3:2–4 (burning bush) and 13:21f (pillar of fire). God's sovereignty is contained in this image; he will provide the services of royal ruler. The metaphorical depiction of Yahweh as a "wall of fire" transfers the security and autonomy implied by a wall to the presence of Yahweh. With God himself as guarantor of Jerusalem's integrity, the existence of actual fortifications becomes meaningless. The wall imagery contributes a political dimension, which is complemented by the religious aspect of God's presence ("Glory will I be within her"; see following NOTE), to the eschatological Jerusalem. The external security and independence represented by "wall" are paired with the internal presence of God.

Although numerous attempts have been made to understand the Third Vision in terms of an actual attempt to rebuild the city wall at this time (Lacocque 1981:71f.; Elliger 1975:110), with the man with a measuring-cord as the architect in charge of such efforts (see above NOTE to verse 6 [RSV v 2] and also the literature cited in Kaufmann 1977:277 and 319, n. 19), there is no evidence to support such theories. Similarly, recent attempts to understand this vision in a divine warrior context (Hanson 1975) involve too narrow an understanding of "wall." While the military dimension is present, "wall" has wider political implications and represents the city or city-state as a relatively autonomous unit. Note that the objection to the wall building of Nehemiah's time (Neh 6:6) is predicated upon the assumption that wall building is an assertion of rebellion and political independence.

Glory. Another designation of God's presence, this time in specific relation to the temple in which God's glory dwells. Although the temple is not specifically mentioned, God's glorious presence in Jerusalem as a whole is an extension of his dwelling in his earthly house; similarly, the whole city in a sense is the temple quarter (Fisher 1963:40). "Glory" *(kābôd* in the priestly writings) is always present in the tabernacle, and a similar condition must have existed for the temple. For Ezekiel, the Glory is a necessary presence in the temple; without it, the temple does not enjoy its proper sacred status. In earlier biblical texts, glory is a divine attribute reflecting God's majestic power; later biblical texts have it as an actual designation for God or his presence (see Mettinger 1982:80–115). Haggai uses "glory" several times in connection with the temple, though in a slightly different sense; see Hag 2:3,7,9, and NOTE to 2:7. In this verse, the Glory of God's presence is within Jerusalem; and Yahweh in the previous line surrounds Jerusalem as guarantor of her integrity vis-à-vis the external world (see preceding NOTE). Together, God's total involvement with Jerusalem is portrayed.

will I be. Hebrew *'ehyeh* is perhaps the divine name; cf. first NOTE to this verse. This is the third use of a first-person form: "I" as an independent pronoun is the first word in this verse, and the verb "I will be" occurs twice. "Glory" as a name for God also appears. An overwhelming expression of the divine presence is the message of this bicolon. The plenitude of the preceding colon is inextricably linked with God dwelling in this holy city.

within her. The Hebrew is the same as for "in her midst" in the preceding colon (2:8b [RSV 2:4b]). The repetition of the phrase connects the two bicola so that the conditions described in the first one become contingent upon the condition, divine presence, in the second one.

COMMENT

This is the briefest of all the visions. But brevity in this case hardly is synonymous with simplicity, and the five verses of the Third Vision are composed of a complex configuration with respect to both form and content. To begin with, they contain oracular as well as visionary materials. Further, a relatively large cast of characters is involved in evoking the vision's theme and putting forward its meaning. Finally, the characters of this passage interact in a pattern unique among the seven visions. We shall consider all these special features in turn.

The combination of oracular and visionary elements is actually present in the First Vision and also, it would seem, in the Fifth (5:4); and the first three visions as a group are expanded by the oracles of 2:10–17 (RSV 2:6–13). The integration of vision and oracle, with the latter being a component of the former, is in itself not at all atypical of Zechariah. Nonetheless, the organization of material in this vision is set apart from that of the others which include oracles in two ways. First, the oracle is directed toward a single individual; second, its spokesman is a figure other than the prophet himself. In these respects it is much closer to the Fifth Vision than to the First or to the Expansion of 2:10–17 (RSV 2:6–13). The statement identified as oracular in the Fifth Vision is clearly an integral part of the dialogic structure whereby the Interpreting Angel transmits the intended meaning of the vision's object. Because of its similarity in this aspect to the flying scroll vision and because of the two ways in which it differs from the oracles of the first half of the visionary sequence, we conclude that the contents of 2:8b–9 (RSV 2:4b–5) are essential to the vision and are intended to be the explication for the measurement of Jerusalem which is the symbolic action that constitutes the major theme of the visionary scene.

Next we consider the personae of the vision. The prophet of course is present, as the one who has had the visionary experience and who reports it to his audience. Yet he also, surprisingly, plays a role within the field of the vision itself. Upon seeing the man with the measuring-cord, who appears at first glance to be the thematic focus, he doesn't ask the Interpreting Angel "what" he is seeing. Rather, he speaks directly to the man. In this way, he both interacts with the vision's main character and provides a clue that the character himself is not the true focus of the vision. Zechariah has not actually "seen" the vision until he knows what the man with the measuring cord is meant to do with his mundane equipment. In this way, the exceptional participation of the prophet in the vision, through his conversation with the man who measures, draws our attention to the act of measurement and signals that the measurement of Jerusalem is the central image.

In addition to the prophet, the man who performs the task of marking Jerusalem's perimeter plays a key role. As we have asserted above, he himself is not the crucial figure but the activity he carries out is the key to the vision. Then angels appear: first the Interpreting Angel with whom we are already quite familiar from his appearance in the first two visions and whom we shall encounter in all the succeeding visions as well as, possibly, in the Investiture Scene; and second, "another angel" whose ready availability contributes to the sense that both of these angelic beings are representatives of what must be a whole company, or host, of angelic figures surrounding Yahweh and assisting in the mediation of his will to mankind or at least, as with Zechariah, to a prophet who himself is transmitting God's revelation to a human audience. Though only the two angels have delineated roles, they conjure up the existence of an extensive though undefined supporting cast attached to Yahweh's court and prepared to enter the human realm in an instant. Further, the ambiguity posed by verse 8a (RSV v 4a), in which the antecedents of the speaker and the one addressed in "he said to him" are not clear, implies a fluidity among the angelic beings, whereby their characters and roles are not firmly established. Such a fluidity and interchangeability are reflected in the story told by Micaiah in 1 Kings 22, where a large group of spirits is present at the Heavenly Court, and all seem to participate in the proceedings. Their identities are not clearly marked out, and they seem to share a variety of characteristics.

The final character is the "official" of verse 8 (RSV v 4). His identity is most problematic, and our NOTES have shown the likelihood that he is the same as the individual with the measuring tool of verse 5 (RSV v 1). Not only is his identity not made directly clear but also his appellation requires exegetical judgment. Is he simply a "young man" as the Hebrew text implies at first glance? Or is there reason to suppose that a more technical nuance is attached to his title? The latter possibility seems likely to us, hence our translation, "official," which allows for his association with the measurement of Jerusalem to operate at more than just the physical level of marking the city's territorial boundaries. The symbolic level of his role will be considered shortly.

This extensive set of participants in the Third Vision is arranged in two units of interaction, followed by an implied third unit. Zechariah and the man holding the measuring device speak with each other. Then the two angelic figures interact, with the result being an oracular statement which reverts back to the measuring man of the first unit and consequently to the prophet himself, whose visionary purview is linked with that man. That the prophet has constructed this complex structure within a few short verses testifies to the skill by which this episode and the visionary sequence as a whole reveal their significance to his audience.

The Third Vision is the third stage in a progressive narrowing of the scope of the prophet's visionary focus: from the worldwide span of Yahweh's universal sovereignty, through the role of Yehud within that world, and now to the political-religious center of the tiny province, Jerusalem itself. Only the climax is yet to come, in the central vision, which takes us inside God's holy habitation, the temple. Although the broad field of the prophet's imagination has closed in upon Jerusalem, that city is not meant to stand in isolation from the world around. The very structure of the visions, as suggested in the diagram in the Introduction, can be compared to a set of concentric circles, in which the innermost circles cannot be separated from the outer ones but rather are superimposed upon that which the larger ones signify.

The eschatological image of Jerusalem in this vision is grounded in the real world of the Persian Empire in the late sixth century. It was a city surrounded by unwalled settlements established in the infertile hills around the city in order to sustain a population normally dependent upon a network of satellite cities contributing to its subsistence. Jerusalem of the postexilic era may have been a provincial center, but its revenues from other provincial towns were now to be shared with the imperial government. It could not survive without the development of its immediate hinterland. But in the vision, the satellite settlements reflect great economic prosperity rather than need. Its villages are unwalled and so too is Jerusalem itself. The city battlements, the sign of political independence in the ancient world, were not restored along with the temple. This situation must have constituted a painful anomaly for the Yehudites. How could the temple, which throughout its history had served to legitimize the monarchy and so signify the independent status of the southern kingdom, exist in a polity lacking both monarch and autonomy?

The prophet answers such concerns in this vision. Yahweh himself, by virtue of his immanence in the Jerusalem temple which is about to be made inhabitable for him once again, will as a "wall of fire" represent the city walls of Jerusalem. The figurative language of the oracle that completes the vision provides an answer. The postexilic dilemma is resolved by emphasizing the unique participation of Yahweh in Jerusalem's history, a participation which carries into the future and provides the assurance that Jerusalem will ultimately exist according to full expectations. The prophet envisions a day when the city will be bursting with plenty. Jerusalem will support an abundance of inhabitants as only an independent state can be presumed to do, and it will be restored to full self-rule. The latter feature is implicit in the former. It may also be contained within the vague figure of the one to whom the oracle is ostensibly addressed. This "official" may be an allusion to a certain group of royal retainers periodically visible in the Deuteronomic history of the monarchy. His presence within the vision, executing the focal act of delineating Jerusalem's territory, may subtly provide monarchic connotations. Jerusalem's much-reduced role under Persian rule is hence not taken as permanent.

The prophet also asserts in this vision that Yahweh is as involved as ever in Jerusalem's ongoing history. The Yehudites should not be dismayed by their city's seeming powerlessness in the postexilic world. By its very existence, with Yahweh's dwelling restored, it contains the potential for an eventual resumption of its traditional place as capital of a Davidic kingdom. Masterfully, Zechariah has interwoven vision and oracle in the Third Vision to create a simultaneous mood of acceptance of the present circumstances and anticipation of an improved future, with the transition from present state to future ideal lying within the realm of divine activity. He does not call for disruption of Persian rule in order to bring about Jerusalem's sovereignty; rather he depicts the restoration of the temple, with God's glory inside, as the deed which will ultimately bring about Jerusalem's centuries-old centrality in a Davidic state. Yahweh's role as city wall spans the gap between present reality and eschatological ideal.

The vision of the man measuring Jerusalem has the effect of unifying the historic role of Jerusalem as the capital and symbol of a political state with its eschatological significance as the holy center, the site of God's earthly dwelling and locus of his universal rule. Late biblical Judaism (cf. Isa 60 and Jer 3:17) idealized the historical image and used it to portray Jerusalem as the "metropolis of the world," a designation suggested by Talmon (1971:312) in his provocative examination of Jerusalem's symbolism. In Jeremiah 31:38–40 the future Jerusalem is envisioned within the borders of the historic Jerusalem and a measuring line traces its biblical boundaries. In Zechariah's vision, the measuring cord defines the city's circumference. The whole city is to be holy and it will all be Yahweh's domain, more than simply the temple which is the focal point of God's presence. The image in the oracle, of the entire city rather than just its sacred precinct being inhabited by and surrounded by God's presence, creates an ideological or eschatological Jerusalem that is earthbound. Its historical significance is retained in the suprahistorical conceptualization.

5. EXPANSION ON THE THEMES
OF THE FIRST THREE VISIONS
(2:10–17; RSV 2:6–13)

[10] Hey! Hey! Flee from the land of the north—Oracle
   of Yahweh—
For I have spread you out like the four winds of
   heaven—Oracle of Yahweh.
[11] Hey! Escape to Zion, O dwellers of Babylon.

¹² For thus said Yahweh of Hosts, after [his] Glory had sent me, concerning the nations who despoil you, "Whoever strikes you also strikes at my[a] open eye. ¹³ For I will indeed wave my hand against them, and they will become spoil to their own servants." So shall you know that Yahweh of Hosts has sent me.

¹⁴ Shout and rejoice, O daughter of Zion;
For indeed I am coming to dwell in your midst—
Oracle of Yahweh.

¹⁵ Many nations will be joined to Yahweh on that day.—"They will be a people to me, and I will dwell in your midst."—Then you shall know that Yahweh of Hosts has sent me to you. ¹⁶ Yahweh will make Judah his inheritance on the Holy Land and will again choose Jerusalem. ¹⁷ Hush, all flesh, before Yahweh, for he stirs himself from his holy abode.

NOTES

2:10 (RSV 2:6). *Hey! Hey!* Hebrew *hôy hôy* is a characteristic prophetic interjection, found in all three of the Major Prophets (Isa, Jer, Ezek) and in six of the twelve Minor Prophets (Amos, Mic, Nah, Hab, Zeph, Zech). Only once (1 Kgs 13:30) does it appear elsewhere, and there it introduces a statement concerning a prophet. *Hôy,* a standard word for "woe!" or "alas!" can variously indicate a lamentation, an oracle of doom, or an exhortation (cf. Gerstenberger 1962:249–63; Clifford 1966:458–64; Janzen 1972; Zobel 1978). Normally *hôy* is followed by a preposition plus a noun, a standardized construction which identifies the group or classes of people to be alerted by the interjection. The statement then goes on to describe some characteristic or action of the group that has been cited. Usually some evil deed toward Yahweh is the activity given as the reason for the "woe" that will come upon the perpetrators of the deed.

In this verse, *hôy hôy* is used in a slightly different way. As in seven other of the fifty-one biblical occurrences, it is an independent interjection, not followed by the standard citation of miscreant groups and deeds. In fact, it is directed toward the exiles, who will be restored to Zion. *Hôy* hardly means woe for the exiles, although it implies woe for those who hold the Judeans captive (see vv 12–13 [RSV vv 8–9] below). Since it is not linked with a substantive, it can be something other than a prophetic lament here. The translation "hey" is accordingly preferable to the usual "woe." "Hey" has the quality of calling people to attention. Before the commands, here and in verse 11 (RSV v 7), to leave Babylon, an interjection of arousal is appropriate. "Hey" in English also can connote exultation, an emotion that might be experienced by deported people about to return to their homeland.

The prophet himself (see "sent me" in v 12 [RSV v 8]), and not the angelic figure

---

[a] "My" is a restoration of an original Hebrew *ʿêni,* which appears in the MT as *ʿênô.*

who delivers the previous oracle of the Third Vision, is probably the one who utters this sequence of oracles which begin with the double interjection. The succeeding oracular material in verses 10–17 (RSV vv 6–13) develops in reverse order themes set forth in the first three visions. Verses 10–11 (RSV vv 6–7) expand the Third Vision; verses 12–13 (RSV vv 8–9) develop the Second Vision; and verses 14–17 (RSV vv 10–13) deal with the First Vision. This threefold division relates to the content first and foremost, although stylistic considerations can also be taken into account. Many commentators have divided these verses in different ways (for the variety of such division, see Petitjean 1969:91–94); among them, Sellin (1930:469–72, 490–93) suggests a division akin to ours although for different reasons (see our COMMENT).

Flee. Hebrew *wĕnūsû,* with a copulative *waw* before the imperative verb, heightens the intensity of the clause which lacks a protasis (GKC § 154).

land of the north. An expression used frequently in Jeremiah (cf. Bright 1965:3–4, 50, 359) and also again in Zechariah (6:6,8), it refers to the place or direction from which invaders enter Palestine (Jer 6:22). It also frequently represents the place from which exiles shall return (e.g., Jer 3:18; 23:8). These two meanings are related in that some of the invaders of Judah/Israel took into exile many of the Judeans and Israelites they had conquered. These conquering powers traveled along the major routes from Mesopotamia that skirted the Syrian desert so that they entered Palestine from the north. Therefore, the eastern or northeastern imperial conquerors of Palestine were seen to be approaching from that direction. It is the place to which the Judeans, to whom this oracle is addressed, had been carried into exile.

The phrase "land of the north" is poetic in Hebrew, since "north" is a definite title but lacks the definite article. "North" could possibly be considered definite by itself, but it is also a common noun and poetic usage in this passage would be perfectly appropriate.

This designation, equated with Babylon in verse 11 (RSV v 7), probably refers to the place of dispersion in a geographical rather than a political sense. The urgency of the language ("flee" and "escape") may reflect a crisis, such as the impending fall of Babylon in 538. However, if the first oracle in this set is linked, as we believe it is, with the Third Vision, then it would be eschatological, urging all those still in exile to return to the restored Zion, to contribute to Jerusalem's "abundance of peoples" (2:8b [RSV 2:4b]). The language itself, however, can very well have been influenced by other oracles deriving from historical situations, such as those found in Jeremiah (e.g., 50:8,28; 51:6,45) and Deutero-Isaiah (e.g., 48:20). The eschatological character of this oracle is further indicated by the way in which the exile is reported in the next line. Yahweh himself is the cause of the spreading out of the people, and the dispersion is global ("four winds"). The cosmic overtones of that description of exile make it transcend historical realities.

I have spread you out. The Piel use of *prś* ("to spread out, scatter") is relatively rare though its meaning is not in doubt. The language is reminiscent of the Second Vision (2:2,4 [RSV 1:19,21]) where the image of Judeans "scattered" *(zrh)* in Babylon underlies the entire vision (see NOTE to "have scattered" in 2:2 [RSV 1:19]). This oracle employs a similar verb to express the reality of the diaspora, but the emphasis here is on the return to Zion (v 11 [RSV v 7]) and on Yahweh as the one responsible for the exile, rather than on the historical circumstances which brought the Judeans into exile.

LXX presupposes a different root, *kns,* and reads "I will gather you from . . . ," just the opposite of the MT.

four winds of heaven. The four compass points underlie the concept of the four winds, which conveys the idea of "everywhere, in all places." The exile is global, perhaps because the Babylonian and Persian empires appeared to dominate the whole earth. Or, more likely, the language is cosmic and eschatological, since God is the cause of the exile (see two preceding NOTES). This same phrase appears in 6:5; see also the Second Vision and compare Ezek 37:9 and Jer 49:36.

11 (RSV v 7). *to Zion.* The Hebrew has no preposition, a situation compatible with the fact that the verse is poetic in character. A preposition before "Zion" would be expected (and the LXX supplies one) in prose but not in poetry. As it stands, "Zion" is an accusative of direction and not the object of a preposition.

Insofar as this verse introduced by "Hey" parallels verse 10a (RSV v 6a), it completes the delineation of the movement of the exiles: in 10a (RSV v 6a) they leave the land of the north; in 11 (RSV v 7) the objective of that departure, Zion, is specified. Other translations (NJPS, NEB), however, render "Zion" as vocative. Zion alone, not coupled with Jerusalem (see 1:1–4), can have a broad, symbolic meaning, referring to the land as a whole to which the exiles will return; but it is always a land centered around Jerusalem (Zion). The meaning of Zion in this verse is informed by the depiction of Jerusalem and its villages in the Third Vision (2:8).

dwellers of Babylon. Hebrew has the singular *(yôšebet)* here and also for the preceding verb "escape." However, Babylon, which is equivalent to "land of the north" of 2:10 (RSV 2:6), is designated by the phrase *bat-bābel,* literally "daughter of Babel." "Daughter" plus a toponym is a common biblical figure in which the collective inhabitants of a place are represented by the personification (Haag 1975:334). Jer 46:19 presents an analogous situation for the inhabitants of Egypt, in which a singular participle has collective force (also cf. Jer 48:18). This analogy causes some difficulty in understanding who the "dwellers of Babylon" are, since the Jeremiah passage evidently refers to all indigenous Egyptians. The context of this verse would seem to make only the Judeans exiled to Babylonia the focus of the prophetic exhortation. Cf. "daughter of Zion," below, verse 14 (RSV 2:10).

12 (RSV v 8). *For.* This is the first of four occurrences of Hebrew *kî* in the second oracle of 2:10–17 (RSV 2:6–13). The second occurs at the start of the oracular quotation, in Hebrew before "whoever." The other two are in verse 13 (RSV v 9), "for" and "that."

after. Hebrew *'aḥar,* normally a preposition or adverb, introduces a subordinate clause. This somewhat awkward conjunctional usage establishes a time sequence and finds support in Jer 40:1 and 41:16 and in the versions. The suggestion of some (Ackroyd 1962:647 and Sellin 1930:491–92, among others), that *'aḥar* be changed to *'ăšer,* would ease the syntactical problem but remove the concept of successive prophetic activity. The position adopted here is similar to that of Petitjean (1969:117), who cites a number of parallel texts in support of the conjunctional use of *'aḥar* (Lev 14:43; Job 42:7; Jer 40:1; 41:16). Others have argued for a prepositional usage (Mitchell 1912:142; Scott 1949:178–79; Chary 1969:70). Baldwin also adopts the prepositional usage, and her understanding of *kābôd* as "heaviness" follows Chary in translating "with insistence he sent me" (1972:109). Rudolph (1976:88–89) understands *'aḥar* as an editorial addition. Compare the RSV, which is similar to our position, with the translation "He who sent me after glory" of the NJPS.

Glory had sent me. "Glory" *(kābôd)* represents divine presence, the Glory of Yahweh which manifests itself to the prophet and stimulates prophetic activity. Perhaps the most explicit presentation of such a process occurs in Isa 6, where the prophet is overwhelmed with a sense of God's all-pervasive presence and cannot help but become an apostle of God's word. As we have suggested in our NOTE to "Glory" in 2:9 (RSV 2:5), where "Glory" also appears as a divine title, without the definite article and probably elliptical for "Glory of Yahweh," this term is characteristic of priestly writing and also of Ezekiel. In this verse it is the subject of the verb "sent me" *(šlḥny).* Note that in the next verse "sent me" occurs again, with "Yahweh of Hosts" as subject. "Glory" and "Yahweh of Hosts" for that reason can be equated. There may also be a literary connection with Exod 3:13–15, where "sent" is repeated three times to describe Moses' role of going to the people as a messenger from God, who is called EHYEH (cf. first NOTE to 2:9 [RSV 2:5]). Moses, Isaiah, and Zechariah are all "sent" from Yahweh's presence to the people with a message. The situation underlying this imagery of prophetic mission is the Heavenly Court. Yahweh is the sovereign whose judgments are communicated to his people or to other groups by special emissaries (cf. NOTES to "sent," and "messenger," Hag 1:12,13 and to "word of Yahweh," Hag 1:1).

concerning. The problem of Hebrew *'el,* which normally means "to" and which might imply an otherwise untestified meeting of the prophet with Persian officials (if "to the nations" would be seen as completing the thought of the verb "to send"), can be resolved by translating it "concerning" on analogy with Isa 37:33 and Jer 22:18; see the discussion in Rudolph (1976:88) and Mitchell (1912:146). One Hebrew manuscript, St. Petersburg, transcribes *'al;* cf. Jer 1:7 where *'al* is used with "send" to describe the prophetic charge to Jeremiah.

On the other hand, *'el* as "to" frequently completes "send" in reference to a prophetic mission. Exod 3:13–15 has *'el* after all three occurrences of the verb "to send." And "to" need not imply that the prophet actually went on a journey to a foreign land, since prophets regularly delivered oracles to foreign nations without leaving their own land. Prophets "sent to" another nation may be a literary cliché, especially since the message in such cases is intended for the prophet's own people as much as for the distant power.

The latter possibility may be more natural, but in Late Biblical Hebrew the reading we have chosen makes just as good sense. Furthermore, the ultimate result is that an oracle is delivered to the Yehudites, not to the "nations." Zechariah's prophetic mission is to his countrymen throughout. Unlike Jeremiah or Amos, his oracles and visions concern his own people. It would be a departure from the nature of this prophetic role to have him sent "to" the nations, although there would be nothing at all unusual about his oracles containing statements "concerning" the nations.

nations. The identity of "nations" is somewhat vague. While the language that follows is akin to Jeremiah's oracles against Babylon, the nation that had originally conquered Judah (e.g., Jer 50:9–16), any foreign policy that exacted tribute continued to despoil the subservient peoples. The vagueness of the language allows for the possibility that "nations" can also include Persia at some unspecified time between 538–520 B.C.E. or in the future. The use of the present participle of "despoil" (see following

NOTE) tends to support such an interpretation. However much the Yehudites might have been pleased at Persian rule in comparison with Babylonian rule, they still remain a conquered nation within Achaemenid territory and so under foreign dominion. The Edict of Cyrus permitting the Judeans to return to Yehud was the major factor influencing the positive Yehudite assessment of Persian rule (but cf. NOTES and COMMENT to 2:4 [RSV 1:21] and Kuhrt 1983).

Still, this oracle need not be understood in so specific a way that "nations" can refer only to Persia or some other foreign power. The truth of the matter is that Judah was rather like booty passed from one conquering nation to the next. Despite the decree of Cyrus in 538 B.C.E., many Judeans (among whom was Zechariah himself) did not return until the second wave of emigration in the days of Darius. In addition, many never returned. The dispersion had not ended in Zechariah's time.

despoil. The participial form of *šll* can indicate ongoing action rather than a specific past act of taking booty. Elliger (1975:117) translates this in the present, although many others see it as a reference to Babylon and render it in the past tense. If "nations" also includes Persia or any future superpower, this oracle expresses the belief that all foreign domination of Israel must someday be abolished. Such an attitude is reflected in the visions in which Zechariah's support of the status quo is coupled with an eschatological affirmation that God will one day restore Judah's independence under a Davidide; see NOTES to the Zerubbabel insertion in 4:6b–9.

strikes . . . strikes. The verb *ngʿ* usually implies a violent action. Although Zechariah adopted a pragmatic position toward Persia's apparently benign policies, his strong awareness of the history of the preceding century at the same time gave him a wary attitude toward any foreign power. Yehud remained in Zechariah's view Yahweh's special trust, "the apple of his eye" (see following NOTE). So long as the community was not in mortal danger he was prepared to support the unique arrangements of Achaemenid control. But the Persians were still a foreign power and could not be absolutely trusted. The content of both verses 12 and 13 (RSV vv 8–9) accords closely with the visionary treatment of the subject in 2:1–4 (RSV 1:18–21), especially in 2:4 (see COMMENT to Second Vision).

my open eye. The value and vulnerability of the eye are conveyed by an idiom which is capable of more than one specific rendering. Hebrew *bābâ* may be related to the Aramaic word for "gate," hence our translation "open." However, many versions translate the word as "pupil" which modern commentators relate to the Arabic. Deut 32:10 contains a similar phrase *(ʾîšôn ʿeynô)* denoting the preciousness of Yahweh's charge, Jacob. Also relevant is Ps 17:8 *(ʾîšôn bat ʿayin),* which contains a phrase that could account for, by the dittography of *beth,* the present hapax legomenon. The first-person possessive makes this God's eye, and the original text no doubt read "my eye" and referred to God, thus creating an anthropomorphism intolerable to the medieval copyists. They believed that there should be no such explicit references to the body of the deity, who was conceived as essentially incorporeal. They changed the text in such cases in the least disruptive way, mainly by altering pronominal suffixes as they have here. Although the general meaning of the expression is not in doubt, it may be justifiable to understand *bt* or *bbt* as the "pupil" of the eye, an equivalent to *ʾyšwn.* The pupil is the most central element in the eye. It is possible that *bbt* is a partially reduplicated form, like *ypyp* from *ypy.*

13 (RSV v 9). *indeed.* Hebrew *hinĕnî,* which contains the first-person-singular pronoun, together with the participle of the following verb ("wave") form a *futurum instans* (GKC § 116p). This construction designates events that are imminent and certain to happen, as expressed in English by "indeed."

wave my hand. God will arouse (destructive) action against those who so much as touch his people. Waving the hand is a signal that sets such forces in motion, as in Isa 13:2 (cf. Isa 11:15 and 19:16). That Yahweh is the initiator of the military activity implied by this idiom is assurance that the activity will be carried out. The entire verse (13 [RSV v 9]) constitutes a divine pledge to Yehud that God is the instrument of her well-being. Should circumstances change and Persian policy be altered or another power replace Persia and oppress Yehud, God will effect action that will enable the conquered peoples to make the conquerors "spoil to their own servants."

spoil. Cf. verse 12 (RSV v 8), NOTE to "despoil."

to their own servants. That is, to those that serve them. Those who serve another nation are the conquered peoples, exploited through the exaction of taxes which become the ongoing booty taken by the dominant power. The image here of Yehud, as servant to superpowers, becoming herself the object of riches pouring in has an eschatological cast similar to that of Hag 2:7–9 (see COMMENT and NOTES to that passage). The idea of the servant's becoming master is the essence of retributive justice in the ancient Near East.

So . . . me. This formulaic statement is found also in 2:15 (RSV 2:11), 4:9, and 6:15. None of these instances is in the actual visions, and so the formula appears to be a characteristic of the nonvisionary sections of Zechariah (Amsler 1981:75–76). The statement itself is directed toward the issue of prophetic legitimacy, in which acknowledgment of the truth of the oracles will confirm the speaker as an authentic prophet (cf. Num 16:28–29; Jer 28:9). In this verse the theme of God's sending the prophet is repeated and completed. Confirmation of the prophet as God's spokesman goes back to the classic case of Moses in Exod 3–4.

14. *Shout and rejoice.* This pair of imperatives, along with the following phrase "daughter of Zion," creates the image of an atmosphere of joyous excitement among those who witness God's beneficent presence. It bears marked similarity to other prophetic expressions of the same idea, notably Zeph 3:14 and Zech 9:9. The verb "shout" *(rnn)* is found frequently in Psalms—e.g., Ps 84:3 (RSV 84:2); 98:4 and 8. The latter reference is significant in that it precedes the announcement of God's coming *(bʾ),* as does this usage in Zechariah. From a literary viewpoint, the coupling of imperatives followed by an exhortation to the "daughter of Zion" can also be found in Mic 4:10.

daughter of Zion. In some instances (e.g., Mic 4:8) this phrase may indicate a "Second Quarter" of Jerusalem, a spreading of the city northward to accommodate increased population and/or refugees from Samaria (as Zeph 1:10; cf. Cazelles 1964:57). However, in Hebrew poetry it usually is a personification of Jerusalem or Zion. See above, verse 11 (RSV v 7), the NOTES to "daughter of Babel" and "Zion."

indeed I am coming. For the coupling of ". . . indeed" *(hinĕnî)* with a participle, see NOTE to "indeed," verse 13 (RSV v 9). This common construction nearly always, as in verse 13 (RSV v 9), has an ominous force, indicating Yahweh's intended punitive actions. Its usage here is an exception, apparently meant to intensify the assurance that God's coming is an event about to be realized in the future. This expression, along with the following verb, "dwell," arouses speculation concerning the historical situation or point of reference for this section (vv 14–15 [RSV 10–11]). If God's coming or dwelling is linked to the restoration of his dwelling place, the temple in Jerusalem, the language would seem to indicate that this oracle, like the visions, is an early one—that is, it stems from a time (cf. NOTE to 1:7) prior to the temple rededication and possibly from the time when temple reconstruction commenced. It was the latter activity, if not a temple refoundation ceremony itself, which was the stimulus for the visions. In its placement here the eschatological portent of the message of God's royal sovereignty in Jerusalem is stressed.

to dwell in your midst. The primary locus of God's presence among the people is the national sanctuary of Israel, be it tabernacle or Jerusalem temple. The notion of the indwelling or tabernacling God comes from an early stage in Israelite history (Cross 1981). Although its earliest associations have a clear tabernacle context, this terminology need not be limited to the priestly corpus, as some have suggested (von Rad 1953:38–40; see in this connection Exod 29:44–46). The increased frequency of *škn* language in the First Temple period, however, indicates how the older premonarchic terminology was adopted to accommodate the theological concerns of the later period in which the movable shrine was replaced by a permanent temple. In its connection with the Jerusalem temple, *škn* reflects the tendency, under the influence of Canaanite religion, for Israel to localize God's presence; it nonetheless preserves the notion of God's transcendence. The association of God's earthly dwelling with Jerusalem and the temple is most fully elaborated by Ezekiel and is reflected in this oracle of Zechariah (vv 14–17 [RSV 10–13]) as well as in a comparable prophetic utterance in 8:3. Ezekiel's vision of the restoration of Israel in chapter 37 is climaxed in verses 24–28 with an eloquent statement on the renewal of the covenant, at which time God's presence will return and "dwell" among his people. The tabernacling terminology in Ezekiel is set in a future, Davidic context in which the nations will ultimately recognize God's sovereignty. This note of universality is picked up by Zechariah whose words come from a time when the new tabernacle, the Second Temple, was fast becoming a reality. Now God's presence is connected with the holy city in the "Holy Land" (v 16 [RSV v 12]), as it is in 8:3 together with "the holy mountain." In verse 14 (RSV v 10), ("to dwell") *škn* is linked to the verb *bw'* ("to come"), and in 8:3 *škn* is paired with *šwb* ("return"). Together these oracles present a complementary view of Yahweh's return to the "place of his abode" (2:17 [RSV 2:13]) where he is enthroned as sovereign.

15 (RSV v 11). *Many nations.* Perhaps equivalent to "all the nations" of Haggai (2:7–8), where a similar universalistic statement about the widespread recognition of God's sovereignty occurs. This concept recurs in Zechariah (4:14 and 6:5 "Lord of all the earth," see NOTE) where it likewise contributes to the idea of Yahweh's universal rule. In Zech 8:22 (see NOTES to that verse), "many" is used with "peoples" and a parallel word "manifold" is coupled with "nations"; further, in verse 20, "many" occurs with "cities." Again, the theme of Yahweh ruling the whole world from his earthly locus in Jerusalem (where he "dwells" in the temple) is expressed. A sixth-century Babylonian inscription published by C. J. Gadd (1953:123–34) records the dedication of an Ishtar temple at Uruk and contains a comparable notion of royal sovereignty's being recognized by the widespread bringing of tribute ("the abundance

of the four regions, the products of mountain and of sea") to the ruler of Babylon, who will then deposit them before the "Lord of Lords."

joined to Yahweh. A contemporary oracle in Third Isaiah (56:3–8) details the importance and nature of the eschatological acknowledgment by all nations of Yahweh's sovereignty in Jerusalem. The words "joined to Yahweh," for Third Isaiah as for Zechariah, mean that the foreign nations will be equivalent to Israel in their status before God. Both prophets employ covenant language following their use of "join," and both include temple language—Zechariah using *škn,* "dwell" (see above v 14 [RSV v 10]), and Third Isaiah using a sequence of explicit terms of prayer and sacrifice, including a designation of the temple precinct as God's "holy mountain." Similarly, in Jer 50:5 "join" involves the eternal covenant of Israel and Judah with Yahweh in Zion.

on that day. This standard phrase (cf. NOTE to Hag 2:23) establishes the eschatological nature of this passage.

They will be a people to me. This is covenant terminology and is the same as that used in Jer 31:33 and 32:38 for the eternal or new covenant between God and his people. However, for Zechariah as well as for Third Isaiah, the covenant with Yahweh has been universalized: "Many nations" are to be joined to Yahweh (see above NOTES to this verse) in the covenant, here and in Isa 56:6,7 ("foreigners," "all peoples").

I will dwell in your midst. See NOTE to verse 14 (RSV v 10). The repetition of the statement of God's dwelling in Zion replaces the normal complement "I will be their God," as in Jer 31:33 and 32:38, of the preceding covenant expression. That is, God's role as party to the covenant is equivalent to the sovereignty he exercises from his earthly abode in the Jerusalem temple.

Then . . . you. Although this statement contains the plural of "to know" and adds "to you," it is virtually identical with verse 13b (RSV v 9b); see NOTE to that verse.

16 (RSV v 12). *make Judah his inheritance.* Literally, "inherit Judah as his portion." The more abstract concept of "Zion" in verses 11 and 14 (RSV vv 7,10) is here replaced with the somewhat more concrete "Judah," as befits the language of inheritance supplied by the verb *nḥl,* "possesses." "Inheritance" is derived from the mythological notion of territory owned by a (Canaanite) God (see Clifford 1972:29–73) and as reflected in the Song of the Sea (Exod 15:17). As a noun, it frequently represents the land given by God to Israel (e.g., Judg 20:6). However, this Zechariah passage contains one of only three instances (cf. Exod 34:9 and Ps 82:8) in which *nḥl* as a verb is used with the subject Yahweh. The object of the verb here is "Judah," which denotes a community of people rather than a territory, inasmuch as the following phrase ("on holy soil") indicates the territory involved. A similar situation obtains in Exod 34:9, where Moses pleads with Yahweh to come into the midst of the people and to inherit *(nḥl)* them. A people rather than a place is thus the object of the action of inheriting, taken by the indwelling deity.

The phrase "make . . . his inheritance" in Hebrew consists of the verb *nḥl* ("inherit") with *ḥelqô,* "his portion." That is, Yahweh's particular inheritance in a world full of territorial or ethnic entities is Judah. The early Hebrew poem of Deut 32 (vv 8–9) introduces this idea: "When the Most High gave to the nations their inheritance . . . For the Lord's portion is his people." Note that this passage about the Exodus precedes the metaphor describing Jacob as the pupil of Yahweh's eye; cf. above 2:12 (RSV 2:8).

the Holy Land. A unique designation in the Hebrew Bible for Yahweh's earthly territory, this phrase (*'admat haqqōdeš*) is picked up in rabbinic literature as a central motif in both *halakah* and theology (E. Meyers and Strange 1981:155ff.; and Cohen 1961). Although it is usually assumed that the notion of a "holy land" becomes gradually spiritualized by New Testament and rabbinic times (Davies 1974: *passim*), an increasing amount of archaeological evidence from these periods shows that the place of "holy land" in both the Jewish and Christian traditions of Roman and Byzantine Palestine is realized in very specific ways. Chief among the customs that testify to an amplified view of the power of the "holy land" are reburial in Palestine, pilgrimage to holy places, and the practice of building pilgrim churches or sanctuaries which commemorate sacred events and theophanies of biblical times. Many of the atoning powers which become attached to the concept of "holy land" in rabbinic theology derive from the exegetical traditions surrounding the famous verse in Deut 32:43, "and the land will make atonement for his people" (see E. Meyers 1971).

Despite the sole biblical occurrence of the term "Holy Land" in this verse, a few other places in the Hebrew Bible contain analogous articulations of God's territory. The best parallel is to be found in Ps 78:54, where the phrase is "holy border" or "territory" (*gĕbûl*). There the context enables us to understand "holy land" as the area around Sinai, the earliest possession of the Israelites (cf. Rudolph 1976:91). The Psalms passage is based on Exod 15:13 and 17 (see Cross and Freedman 1950); those two verses in turn are based on Exod 3:5, where the original holy land is specified. The sacred territory around Sinai (Ps 78:54), *gbwl qdšw*, is also to be equated with the *nwh qdšk* of Exod 15:13 ("holy abode" in RSV). The transfer of this archaic terminology to Jerusalem occurred only after the capture and settlement of the Jebusite city and the subsequent erection of the temple there. Similar terminology has been preserved in Jer 31:23, where the restored temple and city are referred to as *nĕwēh-ṣedeq // har haqqōdeš*, "abode of righteousness" and "holy mountain." Zechariah himself, in 8:3 (see NOTES), designates Zion as the "mountain of Yahweh of Hosts" and "Mountain of Holiness."

Another similar expression, "Yahweh's land" (*'ereṣ yhwh*), occurs in Hos 9:3 and is also unique in the Hebrew Bible; it can be understood in the broadest of terms—namely, as a region embracing all of Israelite territory (see Andersen and Freedman 1980:524–25). All told, the vocabulary expressing the sanctity of a place originated in Israel's formative experience in the wilderness.

It is difficult to accept the suggestion of Petitjean (1969:148ff.) that the expression "the Holy Land" in 2:16 (RSV 2:12) is to be understood as an equivalent of the expression "the Mountain of Holiness" in Zech 8:3. To be sure, "holy mountain" can be construed as the place of Yahweh's abode (2:17 [RSV 2:13]), as the abundant parallels he has offered attest. However, such an interpretation is far too narrow for the present context in verse 16 (RSV 2:12), in which all of Judah's territory or portion is involved. Even though the postexilic territory was far more constricted than in the days of the monarchy, the eschatological context demands a broader interpretation (see NOTE to 8:3). Further, the role of Jerusalem as a distinct entity *within* the broader designation of "Holy Land" becomes explicit in the second half of this verse. Jerusalem is the sacred epicenter from which the holiness of the whole of God's possession emerges.

It is difficult to know why the prophet uses the word *'ădāmâ* ("ground, land") for "land" rather than *'ereṣ* ("land"). *'ereṣ*, with a genitive denoting a political or social entity that occupies a given geographical space, can represent sovereign territory. However, *'ădāmâ* is more exclusively linked to the spatial aspect, designating the actual ground or soil—more specifically the arable land—on which a country or nation exists. As land, or property, *'ădāmâ* can be connected with the owner of such land, such as peoples or tribes. However, since territories held by a political state can and usually do include nonarable land or wilderness, this word seems never to have a political meaning in the Bible (Plöger 1974:93).

While *'admat haqqōdeš* ("the Holy Land") in Zechariah is unique, it finds a nearly equivalent parallel in the burning bush episode of Exodus, where it lacks only the definite article before "holy" (Exod 3:5). The Exodus passage shows that the holiness is transmitted to the ground surrounding the spot of God's epiphany, the bush that is not consumed; and the area is called holy because of the presence of the deity there. Similarly for Zechariah, the holiness of the space extending out from Jerusalem is effected by Yahweh's habitation in the midst of his people in the Jerusalem temple (God's "Holy Mountain" according to 8:3, see NOTE).

choose Jerusalem. God will (again) make Jerusalem, the city of his earthly abode, the temple, the place which symbolizes divine sovereignty over Judah and all the world. Cf. NOTES to 1:17 and 3:2. The emphasis in Zechariah on the choosing of Jerusalem serves to offset the feeling that must have been strong during and after the exile that God had rejected Jerusalem.

17. *Hush.* Hebrew *has*, like English "hush," is onomatopoetic and suits the rhetorical nature of prophetic oracles, especially when it comes with "before Yahweh" as it does also in Hab 2:20 ("before him") and Zeph 1:7 ("before the Lord God"). These other two prophetic usages similarly denote reverent silence before God's presence in his holy habitation. Cf. NOTE below to "holy abode."

all flesh. That is, all mankind or all living beings. This common phrase indicates the universality of God's sovereignty. While God's reign may emanate from Jerusalem, everyone will strike the appropriate hushed pose of acknowledgment before his presence. The expression *kol bāśār* ("all flesh") occurs forty times in Hebrew Scripture. It is often used, as it is here, to contrast man with God in order to emphasize human distance from God (see Bratsiotis 1975:327).

stirs. The verb *'wr* is sometimes used in a military context to indicate arousal for conflict (e.g., Judg 5:12 and Isa 51:9). However, a wider range of potential activities, including love (e.g., Cant 2:7 and 3:5), are contained in the verb. The root idea is the existence of the vitality or energy that can be poured into any activity. Habakkuk (2:19) contrasts the inability of an idol to respond to a supplicant with the potency of Yahweh, before whom all are silent (v 20) in recognition of his utter vitality (see above NOTE to "hush" and also the following NOTE).

holy abode. God's heavenly habitation, as in Deut 26:15. The notion of the heavenly dwelling place of God, upon which his earthly temple is modeled, is borrowed from Canaanite mythology but has parallels in many other religions of the world. "Abode" *(mĕʿôn)* can sometimes refer specifically to the Jerusalem temple (Ps 26:8) rather than to its celestial model, and some (Elliger 1975) would take this Zechariah example in that way. However, because Zech 2:17 (RSV 2:13) is similar to the Zephaniah passage

(1:7) noted above with "hush," where the eschatological portrait of Yahweh himself preparing a sacrifice implies a heavenly rather than earthly shrine, a celestial locus is to be understood for Zechariah's usage.

Nonetheless, some imprecision in the term "heavenly abode" characterizes at least some of its biblical uses (Petitjean 1969:154–59), and it is not always clear whether heaven or earth is the place where God has his house. The fact is that the lines between the two are necessarily blurred, when a Jerusalem temple replicates in microcosmic form the supraterrestrial habitation of God (Wright 1961:169–84). The existence of an earthly shrine allows mankind to come near to God's presence in a tangible and emotionally necessary way, for the material temple structure both symbolizes and partakes of the reality of a heavenly structure and thereby makes real God's potent presence within it (cf. Deut 26:15 and Ps 68:6 [RSV 68:5]).

COMMENT

The placement of these eight verses immediately after the Third Vision and directly before the scene of Joshua and the Priestly Vestments of chapter 3 must be taken into account in evaluating the material in verses 10–17 (RSV vv 6–13). Most commentators would regard these oracles as complementing the first three visions and even ascribe authorship to Zechariah himself (Beuken 1967:317ff.; Petitjean 1969:8, 94ff.). Yet there is considerable disagreement as to the process by which they came to be included within the general framework of the visions of Part Two. Petitjean, who has written the definitive treatment of the oracles as distinct from the visions of Zechariah, only speculates that they could have been written before or after the visions (ibid., 8). Most approaches to Zechariah presuppose a separate context for the composition of the oracles, and many still posit separate authorship.

The mixing of oracular speech with the visions is, however, ipso facto one of the most distinctive features of Zechariah. These two forms of prophetic utterance, combined in a single work, are to be regarded at the very least as reflecting aspects of prophetic activity which could have occurred either very close in time to each other or even simultaneously. Such a working hypothesis may be entertained for Part Two as a discrete unit. The superscriptions to Part One (1:1) and to Part Three (7:1) imply separate times for their composition. Similarly, the superscription to the visions (1:7) would seem to apply to all the materials contained therein, including 6:9–15.

By choosing to treat the oracles in 2:10–17 (RSV 2:6–13) as a separate chapter within the overall unity of Part Two, we are perforce suggesting that they are integral to the whole of Part Two. The oracular Expansion represents the largest block of nonvisionary material in all of Part Two; but the material within this block is not simply a single long oracular pronouncement. In reality it is a series of oracles that recapitulate, in reverse order, the themes and content of the first three visions.

Verses 10–11 (RSV vv 6–7) begin this section with a bold, direct call to the exiles to leave their temporary homes in the land of the north, Babylon, and to return to Zion. The use of the double prophetic interjection *hôy hôy* ("Hey! Hey!") at the beginning of verse 10 (RSV v 6) and the single *hôy* at the beginning of verse 11 (RSV v 7) gives a sense of urgency to the oracular imperative. By vividly drawing attention to the fact that the exiles have been "spread out" or "scattered" like the "four winds of heaven," the oracle reflects the universal scope of the First Vision while at the same time echoing the theme of Israelite dispersal found in the Second Vision (2:2,4 [RSV 1:19,21]). In calling for a return to Zion, the oracle also expands on a theme contained in the Third Vision: the focus upon Jerusalem itself and the eventual repopulation of Jerusalem and its environs (2:8 [RSV 2:2]).

The urgent tone of verses 10 and 11 is achieved not only by the repetition of *hôy* but also by the twofold appearance of the formulaic announcement of God's word, "Oracle of Yahweh," in verse 10. Zechariah himself had presumably taken a lead in promulgating the idea of return by joining Haggai, Zerubbabel, and Joshua in a second major wave of emigration from Babylon to Yehud at the beginning of Darius's reign. No doubt he felt committed to the idea of resettling the land. Hence it should not be surprising to find these sentiments, based on a major life experience, expressed in both his visions and his oracles. Leaving Babylon would have been no easy task for the exiled Judeans, for it entailed leaving homes well established and livelihoods firmly secured. For many it meant leaving behind a life that had brought success. Accordingly, many exiles would have been reluctant to leave their familiar and even comfortable surroundings for the uncertainties and vicissitudes of settling a remote land only minimally tended during the many decades since the Babylonian destruction. Whether in the visions or in the oracles, in his references to the Babylonian diaspora the prophet is confronting a central issue of his day. The official Achaemenid policy of allowing repatriation to Yehud and encouraging temple restoration brought a choice to those resident in exile: to continue to reside under the known conditions of life in Mesopotamia or to move back to the ancestral homeland in Palestine.

Some scholars have postulated that Zechariah's prophetic activity had begun already in exile, while allowing that the second return itself would have been influential in inspiring his prophetic activity (Ackroyd 1968:148–49). We would be skeptical of the former possibility with respect to this oracle, for we hear in the imperatives of this oracle pulling its distant audience to Zion the voice of one who has already made the return and one who is involved in the temple restoration project. It is that project which has captured the attention of the prophet and given the urgency to his language, whether it be heard by fellow returned Yehudites needing assurance that they have chosen wisely or by exiles still pondering the choice. The relationship of all Yahwists to a renewed community in Palestine in Darius's time, after all, permeates Zechariah's oracular utterances, visionary experiences, and prophetic actions.

The second section of the oracular Expansion in verses 12 and 13 (RSV 8,9) relates to the content of the Second Vision in a direct way. In the vision God's agents are identified as "four smiths" who have destroyed Babylonia and secured Persia's limited, in comparison, exertion of power over Yehud. In symbolic language Zechariah introduces one of the basic premises of his total prophetic work: that Judah's acquisition of limited autonomy as the subprovince of Yehud has been won through divine assistance and exists with divine approval. Acceptance of the political reality also signified a potential end to the dispersion or "scattering" of his people outside the land of Israel. The ending of the dispersion means that Zion, which is the theme of the Third Vision, is the goal of those returning in the oracle of verses 10 and 11 (RSV vv 6,7) of the Expansion. Verses 12–13 (RSV vv 8–9) then discuss the potential limitations of the Persian rule which permitted a return to take place.

The two verses (2:12–13 [RSV 2:8–9]) that constitute the second oracle of the 2:10–17 (RSV 2:6–13) Expansion are neatly framed by an opening introduction which includes "[his] Glory had sent me." The clauses of this unit are further bound together by the fourfold repetition of the particle kî ("for, that"), with the heart of the oracle being contained in the words of God reported in verses 12b and 13a (RSV vv 8b–9a), "Whoever strikes . . . to their own servants." Zechariah's amplification of the Second Vision is couched in the authoritative language of a prophetic oracle and consists of three prose clauses.

In this brief oracle, Zechariah communicates God's assurance that Judah still occupies a special place in Yahweh's scheme of things, notwithstanding Persian rule. Although it may seem as if being a conquered nation is akin to being taken as booty, Yahweh's special relationship with the people of Israel means that no conquering power can now harm them. Israel is the "apple of his [God's] eye" (RSV v 8), never out of divine vision and so never removed from divine care. In the event that any nation threatens Israel or does damage to her, Yahweh will intervene to reverse the situation and make that nation subservient to Judah. Such a threat goes considerably beyond verse 4 (RSV 1:21) of the Second Vision (2:1–4 [RSV 1:18–21]), which alludes to Persian replacement of Babylon as the power dominating Yehud. In the oracle a balance is provided to the vision, a balance that enables the prophet to account to his audience for any future eventuality, even one which Zechariah might consider unlikely. In the vision it is the agents of Yahweh who limit the imperial exercise of power. Here in the oracles Yahweh directly provides protection and justice for his people.

Once again the oracles provide an opportunity for hermeneutical expansion upon themes contained within the visions. Because they are so complementary to the visions, the precise process of literary transmission by which they have come to be included in their canonical ordering cannot easily be assessed. It would seem, however, that the oracles have been inspired by the visions and, strictly speaking, are later. But because the two forms of prophetic composition are so interconnected, the time separating them may be so short as to be completely insignificant.

Verses 14–17 (RSV vv 10–13) provide a fitting conclusion to the whole of the oracular Expansion while developing several themes which are central to the First Vision with its attached oracles: God's universal dominion, and the return of his presence to Jerusalem. The latter appears in the oracular responses, especially the second and third (vv 16–17 [RSV vv 12–13]), and the former is presented by the vision itself. In all they serve as a transition to the two central units of Part Two, the Investiture Scene with Joshua (chapter 3), and the lampstand vision (chapter 4). Presumably the whole visionary sequence has been evoked by a ceremony of refoundation of the temple, which Zechariah views as the beginning of God's renewed dwelling in the midst of his people.

The opening oracle in verse 14 (RSV v 10) announced with joyous excitement the imminence of the long-awaited return of God to Zion: "I am coming to dwell in your midst." The language of God's return is rooted in the older premonarchic terminology of God's "tabernacling" (Heb. *škn*) and is symbolic of God's association with tabernacle and temple. The "return" of God announced in the oracular introduction of Part One (see COMMENT to 1:1–6) is now translated into the more concrete imagery of God's indwelling. Zechariah's enthusiasm is conceivably the result both of the temple work at last under way and also of the refoundation ceremony recently celebrated, as it had not yet been in November–December 520, to which Part One is dated.

The theme of universality, which appears most clearly in verse 15 (RSV v 11), is coupled with covenant terminology to express Yahweh's special relation with Israel: "They will be a people to me." First the "nations will be joined *to* (*'el*) Yahweh" one day. They will belong to Yahweh in a particular way (*vĕhāyû lî lĕ'ām*), as a "people" to him. The *gôyîm* ("nations") too will not only come closer to Yahweh but apparently will share in the special arrangement which had heretofore characterized Israel as a "people" (*'am*) in her relationship to God. This eschatological picture is inclusive, for it embeds the destiny of Judah with its specialized problems into an international matrix.

Although it is often presumed that only the oracles portray the theme of universality of Zechariah, the notion of God's universality is at the core of the First Vision and is implicit in the expression "Lord of *all* the earth" which appears elsewhere in the visions (4:14 and 6:5). It recurs most noticeably in oracular form in the conclusion of Part Three (8:22–23). A similar theme is also found in Haggai (2:7–8), where "all the nations" is equivalent to "many nations" of Zechariah 2:15 (RSV 2:11). Both the nations and Israel will one day share the benefits of God's return to Jerusalem, where he will "dwell" (*škn*) permanently in his earthly abode, the Jerusalem temple (v 15b [RSV v 11b]).

That the theme of universalism may be somewhat more explicit, or perhaps more fully developed, in the oracles than in the visions is a supposition that overlooks the fundamental compatibility of the two modes of prophetic utterance in Zechariah. The end result is a convincing interweaving of universalistic presentations rooted in a focus upon the particular manifestation of God in the place of his choosing, in the Holy Land and in Jerusalem. This combination of theological concerns is achieved in the final two verses (2:16–17 [RSV 2:12–13]) of the Expansion. Verse 16 (RSV v 12) commences with the statement that God has taken Judah as "his inheritance on the Holy Land." The verb is *nḥl* ("to possess"), and this is one of only two instances in the Bible in which God appears as its subject (cf. Exod 34:9). The idea of God's "possessing" his people and providing them with a specific "portion" (*ḥelqô*), which is derived from Canaanite myth, emerges in this verse in the only appearance in the Hebrew Bible of the term "the Holy Land" (*ʾadmat haqqōdeš*). The particular place through which God manifests his now universal covenant love is the land which has Jerusalem, the site of his holy temple, as its center. The expression "his holy abode" (*mĕʿôn qodšô*, v 17 [RSV v 13]) is sufficiently ambivalent that it may designate either God's heavenly or his earthly abode, or both. Hence the final verse succeeds in balancing the rather terrestrial statement of verse 16 (RSV v 12).

Verses 14–17 (RSV vv 10–13) contain elements of thought which perhaps seem contradictory to the modern reader but which posed no such difficulty for the ancients. Although there seems to be a tension between universalism and particularism and between God's immanence and his transcendence in the oracle, for biblical man such notions were complementary and not incompatible. The prophet has succeeded in welding all these concerns into a single acceptable vision of the future.

The Expansion (vv 10–17 [RSV vv 6–13]) when taken as a whole, albeit divided into three subunits, is both a commentary upon the first three visions and a climax to them. Moreover, it anticipates the scenes and visions yet to come. In this unobtrusive way the oracular Expansion has been included in Part Two so that some scholars still regard it as part of the Third Vision (e.g., Baldwin 1972:105; Mason 1977a:40). By so doing they follow a nineteenth-century scholarly consensus, which was challenged as early as Mitchell (1912:140). An alternative approach, which regards these verses as a collection of oracles many of which circulated independently and only later came to be included in the Book of Zechariah, predominates today. Such a view begs the question of a redactor or compiler without requiring the reader to reflect on the role of Zechariah in such a process.

The oracular Expansion, like the three oracles at the end of the First Vision (1:14–17), can be characterized as a prophetic commentary on the first three visions, or as a kind of inner biblical exegesis. Consequently the time of composition or utterance must be technically later than the material upon which it comments. The prophet could well have composed these oracles *in medias res* —that is, during the course of his visionary experience and/or the time when his prophecies were collected and edited. The time span in which all the elements of Part Two would have been composed, according to the chronological framework of the Book of Zechariah, is between February 15, 519 (1:7), and December 7, 518 (7:1). Within that span, two stages may be discernible. The oracular Expansion is the climax of a first stage consisting of the first three visions, two of which have substantial oracular components. The prophetic vision of Joshua's investiture (chapter 3) initiates another stage in the composition of Part Two.

The dominating event inspiring all the visions but in particular influencing the two central visionary episodes must have been the temple refoundation ceremony. Both the Vestment Scene (chapter 3) with its supplementary oracle (3:8–10) and the Fourth Vision, the Lampstand and the Two Olive Trees (chapter 4), focus on the temple itself. The central Fourth Vision has an identifiable oracular component, the so-called Zerubbabel cluster or insertion (4:6b–10a); but none of the last three visions contains a discrete oracular component. The Crowning Scene of 6:9–15 serves as an oracular conclusion to the last three visions, and also as a transition to Part Three.

The oracular Expansion in this reconstruction emanates from the period just after the ceremony of refoundation. By recapitulating and expanding upon themes in the first three visions, the prophet goads the unreturned exiles (vv 10–11 [RSV vv 6–7]), comforts the returned people by reaffirming God's protecting love in the arena of history (vv 12–13 [RSV vv 8–9]), and announces God's imminent return to the place of his traditional abode, the temple mount (v 17 [RSV v 13]). He proclaims that God's presence in Zion will bring together the nations along with Israel to Yahweh (v 15 [RSV v 11]). Finally, the prophet reconfirms God's unique scheme of redemption: the selection of a particular parcel of land, the land of Judah's inheritance, as the place and vehicle for the working out of God's will (v 16 [RSV v 12]).

Such pronouncements are not the result of an isolated literary or prophetic outburst. Rather they represent the considered notions of someone profoundly involved in shaping contemporary events. However, the placement of these three oracular statements seems to presuppose cognizance of a larger literary whole, namely Part Two. To be sure, contained within three verses of the Expansion are elements, especially the opening exhortations of verses 10, 14 and 17 [RSV vv 6,10,13], that may have their origin in historical events. Nonetheless the present oracular format has been utilized to serve a higher literary purpose, to wit, the articulation of a parenthetical goal which was treated only partially in the preceding visionary material. Discrete forms of biblical literature have been put to diverse uses in the presentation of the whole. Up to this point in Part Two we have identified three ways in which oracles have been employed: 1. internal quotes within the visions (e.g., Third Vision, 2:8–9 [RSV 2:4–5]); 2. material external to a vision but necessary to it (e.g., First Vision, 1:14–17); and 3. supplemental material designed to complement and expand upon ideas or themes in the visions (the Expansion, 2:10–17 [RSV 2:6–13]).

The oracles in general have been the cause of much restructuring at the hands of modern critics. Indeed, the second and final oracular summation in Part Two, the Crowning (6:9–15), has been one of the most tampered-with portions in the whole of Hebrew Scripture. The Expansion, a summation of the first half of Part Two, seems to have escaped such extensive efforts at textual reorganization only because its contents are less controversial. Yet the importance of 2:10–17 (RSV 2:6–13) cannot be ignored, for it comprises a retrospective review of the first half of the visions as the prophet's worldview gradually focuses in on his chief concern, the restoration of the temple.

6. JOSHUA AND THE PRIESTLY VESTMENTS: A PROPHETIC VISION
(3:1–10)

Heavenly Court and Investiture

3 ¹ Then he showed me Joshua, the high priest, standing before the Angel of Yahweh, and the Accuser was standing on his right to accuse him. ² Yahweh said to the Accuser, "May Yahweh rebuke you, O Accuser; Yahweh who chooses Jerusalem will rebuke you! Is this not a brand plucked from the fire?" ³ Now Joshua was clothed in filthy garments as he was standing before the angel, ⁴ who spoke out to those standing before him saying: "Take the filthy garments off him;" and to him he said, "Look, I have removed your iniquity from you and I have clothed you in pure vestments."

⁵ Then I said, "Let them put a clean turban on his head," and they placed the clean turban on his head. Thus they clothed him, while the Angel of Yahweh stood by. ⁶ Then the Angel of Yahweh charged Joshua: ⁷ "Thus said Yahweh of Hosts, 'If you walk in my ways and if you keep my service, then you will render judgment in my House and you will administer my courts; I will give you access to those who are standing here.' "

Supplementary Oracle

[8] " 'Take heed, O Joshua the high priest, you and your associates who are seated with you—for they are men of portent—for I am indeed bringing my servant the Shoot. [9] As for this stone which I set before Joshua, on this one stone with seven eyes, I will make an engraving'— Oracle of Yahweh of Hosts. 'Thus will I take away the iniquity of that land in one day. [10] In that day'—Oracle of Yahweh of Hosts—'you will call out, each man to his companion, to the one under the vine and to the one under the fig tree.' "

NOTES

3:1. *he showed me.* The opening to this passage is problematic for several reasons: 1) the subject of the verbal action is not specified; 2) the Hiphil of the verb *r'h* ("to cause to see, to show") opens the narrative, in contrast to the introductions to the first three and the last three visions, which use a Qal form with the prophet as subject; 3) the verbal idea is not supplemented by the adverbial emphasis of *hinnēh* ("behold," "I") as it is in the other visions (though not exactly the same way in each of the others). In addition, the form of the ensuing vision lacks the four-part literary scheme that characterizes the first three and last three visions (see Introduction). Further, the investiture that is portrayed, like the Fourth Vision, deals with real personnel and objects and not with elaborate imaginary characters, situations, or items as in visions 1–3 and 5–7. Finally the introduction to the vestment ceremony vividly portrays a Heavenly Court scene, which is seen only dimly if at all in other Zecharianic materials.

Despite these formal differences, which have led us to exclude chapter 3 from the sequential numbering of the visions, this prophetic vision is nonetheless very much a part of the visionary sequence. The opening of 3:1, "he showed me," continues a structure observed in Zech 2:1 and 3 (RSV 1:18,20), where "I raised my eyes, and I looked, and behold" (2:1 [RSV 1:18]) has its counterpart in "and he showed me" (2:3 [RSV 1:20]). Then in 2:5 (RSV 2:1) "I raised my eyes, and I looked and behold" appears again; and the next "and he showed me" does not occur until here in 3:1.

| 2:1 (RSV 1:18) | *w'ś' 't—'yny w'r' whnh* | 2:3 (RSV 1:20) | *wyr'ny* |
| 2:5 (RSV 2:1) | *w'ś'   'yny w'r' whnh* | 3:1 | *wyr'ny* |

The beginning of the prophetic vision is in this way connected with the preceding (Third) Vision, thus integrating Joshua's investiture into the entire visionary cycle. Yet, the differences noted above between chapter 3 and the other visions, and also those discussed below, especially the first-person shift in verse 5 (see NOTE to "I said"), contribute to the uniqueness of this prophetic vision and secure a special place for it apart from the sequence of seven visions.

Who is the speaker in this vision? Some (e.g., Peshitta) suppose that an angel addresses the prophet, insofar as this vision is understood to resume the vision sequence interrupted by the insertion of the oracles of 2:10–17 (RSV 2:6–13); at the end of 2:9 (RSV 2:5) an angel was speaking. However, our analysis of the placement of those oracles would not admit of such a suggestion. Another suggestion has the Interpreting Angel resuming his role (Baldwin 1972:113). Yet the Angel of Yahweh as distinct from the Interpreting Angel appears as an independent character farther on in the opening statement; and the Interpreting Angel has no legitimate role in this vision, since the question and explanation pattern in which he plays a crucial role in the Seven Visions is absent here. The only other serious possibility is that it is Yahweh who is speaking to the prophet, a view reflected in the LXX and Vulgate. Yahweh's direct appearance to the prophet, as also implied in 2:12 (RSV 2:8), is most appropriate in view of the prophet's direct participation in the scene described. In his involvement in the proceedings, Zechariah continues the tradition of preexilic prophecy in which prophets, without intermediaries, become intensely aware of God's plan and go on to join in its realization (Tidwell 1975). Note that in Amos 7–8, Yahweh is four times the subject of this same verb in the Hiphil. The Amos example supports the identification of the speaker in this verse as Yahweh. The Hiphil form helps provide the intensity with which the prophet experiences a divine commission (cf. Lindblom 1962:145), a situation which differs from that of the Seven Visions. Our designation "prophetic vision" serves to identify the special character, distinct from the "visions," of what follows. That is, the prophet is an actor in, and not simply a witness to, a visionary scene.

Joshua. Cf. NOTE to Hag 1:1.

high priest. The Hebrew hakkōhēn hagādôl is literally "great priest" but usually is rendered "high priest." It designates Joshua here and seven other times in Haggai and Zechariah (Hag 1:1,12,14; 2:2,4; Zech 3:8; 6:11). Although it becomes a common designation in rabbinic and later times, its biblical attestations are relatively rare. In the Pentateuch, Aaron and his successors, Eleazar and then Phineas, are never called by any name other than simply "the priest," except in Lev 21:10 (hkhn hgdwl). The Leviticus usage, however, is not a title but rather is only a designation (de Vaux 1961:397). Indeed, even in Ezra 7:5, where Ezra's priestly lineage is reviewed, his forebear Aaron is called "chief," or "first," priest (hakkōhēn hārōʾš), the title found in the description of deportation of priestly officials in 2 Kgs 25:18 (= Jer 52:24), in conjunction with the title "deputy" or "second" priest.

Although the Chronicler, and Ezra and Nehemiah, do employ this designation, their usage is reserved largely for officials or in contexts that postdate Haggai-Zechariah. Even when they mention preexilic priests they are even then not consistent in their utilization of "high priest," and they are more likely to use "chief priest" or "the chief" rather than "high priest." As a matter of fact, only for Hilkiah, in the time of Josiah, does the Chronicler use the latter title (2 Chron 34:9). As for the Deuteronomic history, only in two notable cases, Hilkiah (2 Kgs 22:4,8; 23:4) and Jehoiada (in the days of Jehoash; 2 Kgs 12:11 [RSV 12:10]), does the "high priest" designation appear. However, Amsler points out (1981:80) that in neither of those cases is the more usual title "the priest" absent; he therefore suspects an editorial addition of "high" priest by a postexilic hand. Whether or not that is the case, the title "high" for the priests Jehoiada and Hilkiah points to a special function that they have, namely the administration of collected revenues for temple repairs. Otherwise "high priest" does not denote the head priest, who instead was probably called "priest of" with a place name, on analogy with Amos 7, where Amaziah is "priest of Bethel."

The innovative utilization by Haggai and Zechariah 1–8 of this term for the chief priestly officer in Jerusalem can perhaps be related to one further and final set of passages in which it appears, Num 35:25,28 (and LXX, Syriac, and Samaritan Pentateuch, cf. v 32) and Josh 20:6. Both these passages deal with the very ancient custom of blood revenge and the six cities of refuge. The Numbers text does not list the names of the cities, but the Joshua passage does. It is thus possible to establish that all six cities (three in trans-Jordan and three west of the Jordan) are Levitical towns spaced out on either side of the Jordan. For the west of the Jordan group, an ancient sacred connection of the three cities is clear (Kedesh, Shechem, Hebron), and a similar sanctity may be presumed for the trans-Jordanian sites (de Vaux 1961:163). The establishment of the Levitical cities, with the Cities of Refuge having special functions in providing safety for involuntary killers, goes back at least to early monarchic times (so Albright 1945) and probably to premonarchic times, although the full list of forty-eight cities is later— eighth century, according to Petersen (1977). The six cities served as regional centers for the Levites, and their functions were wider than merely the sacerdotal.

Within the concept of refuge cities, the protected manslayer is given refuge for an indeterminate period of time, until the death of the "high priest," *hkhn hgdwl*. The title in this context hardly refers to a Jerusalem chief priest, particularly if a pre-Davidic context for these passages is supposed. Rather, the title designates the chief priestly figure among the Levites in those cities that are mentioned. The word "great," taking *gādôl* literally, rather than "high" perhaps would express better the leadership achieved by virtue of skill or reputation (cf. Jer 5:5; Exod 11:3; Esth 9:4) in the case of those regional priestly officials.

Haggai and Zechariah both revive the ancient term in direct association with Joshua, the dominant priestly figure at the time of the restoration of the temple and of the establishment of a new administrative apparatus for the province of Yehud. They do so in the awareness, for which the Chronicler's and Ezra-Nehemiah's patterns of usage supply evidence, that "high priest" and "chief priest" are not synonymous. Their utilization of the former term, therefore, reflects an administrative nuance which existed apart from the priestly hierarchy of the Jerusalem temple, where it appears only when the chief priests are involved in the extrasacerdotal duties of collecting funds and instituting building projects—precisely the sort of activities Joshua must undertake with Zerubbabel during the restoration. The collection of funds for temple work, above and beyond the normal income accrued through offerings, is the job of a priestly administrator with fiscal responsibilities in addition to ritual ones. It is also, under Persian rule, a task that the governor (Zerubbabel) would probably not have performed, since his involvement with taxation lay in his responsibility for supplying specified revenues to the imperial government, a task evidently introduced to the satrap system by Darius ca. 522 (see Introduction; cf. Cook 1983:82 and n. 11). Haggai and Zechariah may have revived "high priest" as a general title, not just a separate title used only when the "chief priest" had extra financial tasks, because in the Persian period the chief priest took on as his regular role the fiscal responsibilities only irregularly attached to the chief priesthood during the period of the monarchy.

Over the years, a rather extended and inconclusive debate has continued as to whether or not increased priestly control of fiscal affairs is reflected in the corpus of stamped jar handles and in the Yehud coins. Avigad (1957) first proposed to identify Uriaw (ʾwryw) on a Jericho jar stamp (possibly dated as early as ca. 500 or as late as 450 B.C.E.) with Uriah of the priestly family of Meremoth of Ezra 8:33 but later (1976a:22) modified his proposal by saying that Uriah could be a tax collector either for the temple or for secular authorities.

Similarly, Avigad proposed that the Yehud coins of the late Persian period also reflected increased ecclesiastical authority in fiscal administration (ibid., 149). His argument regarding the coins was based upon the identification of Yehezqiyah (yĕḥizqiyyâ) on a coin of Beth Zur with Hezekiah the priest and contemporary of Ptolemy I (Jos. Contra Apionem 1.187). Since Hezekiah's name has subsequently been found on coins from Tell Jemmeh bearing the title of "governor," Avigad has modified his views somewhat (1976a:29). Now he suggests that Yehezqiyah might have given up one of his titles to the new Greek authorities, presumably the title of "governor" (cf. the review of this material in Stern 1982:202ff. and 226ff.). In light of our analysis of Haggai and Zechariah, perhaps it is time to reassess the credibility of Avigad's earlier views.

To summarize, the postexilic prophets, in using an ancient priestly title, reflect the broadened administrative powers of the priesthood, which no longer functions in tandem with a monarch, in the restoration period (cf. NOTES below to v 7).

standing before. This technical language (ʿmd lpny; cf. v 4 below) reveals the setting of the prophetic vision, the Heavenly Court over which Yahweh presides as chief judge. This setting is deeply grounded in mythology, with Yahweh's Heavenly Court corresponding to the council of 'El (Robinson 1944:151–57; Cross 1953:274–77 and 1973:186ff.; Tidwell 1975:346ff.; Mullen 1980). The concept of an assembly or council of the gods was a common motif throughout the ancient Near East. The issue before the Court concerns Joshua and the office of the high priesthood. The adversary is haśśāṭān or the accuser; the advocate is the malʾāk, Yahweh's messenger or herald. The appropriateness of the Heavenly Court scene derives from the gravity of the issue being considered. A new role for priesthood and Joshua's fitness for it are at stake, and only God himself can sanction the shifts entailed. The prophet himself is involved; he participates in mediating the divine decision that will have the ultimate effect of admitting the priest, too, into the Heavenly Court. There is, however, no real case to be made against Joshua although the accuser no doubt thought there was (see COMMENT); this is not an instance of the divine lawsuit (Wright 1962). The accuser is "rebuked" in verse 2 before the proceedings even get under way; God's judgment, the main function of the Court, has already been made. Hence the main focus of this prophetic vision is the carrying out of God's decree through the act of dressing Joshua. His new clothes and headpiece symbolize his continued and expanded role as high priest. The language of Near Eastern myth has served to heighten the drama of the scene and to underscore the importance of the historical details which lie obfuscated somewhat by the remarkable visionary language.

This occurrence of ʿmd is the first of six usages of the verb in the Prophetic Vision. It is the most common word in Hebrew literature for reflecting the technical procedures of participating in the Court. Just as people appear before the king and enter his court (cf. 1 Sam 16:21–22, where "David came to Saul and stood before him," and Jer

52:12), so heavenly figures are admitted to the assembly over which Yahweh presides. The verb for "stand" recurs in this verse and is found again once each in verses 3, 4, 5, and 7. It is a key word, making the audience fully aware, from first to last, of the Divine Council setting and of Yahweh's exalted presence. Twice, here and in the next verse, the verb refers to Joshua and so emphasizes that what is to be done to him is the result of God's appraisal and decision.

the Angel of Yahweh. The figure designated here as *malʾāk-Yhwh* appears to be distinct from the *angelus interpres,* or Interpreting Angel, who plays no role at all in the prophetic vision of chapter 3. However, if the Interpreting Angel is really the same as the Angel of Yahweh (cf. NOTE to "man" in 1:8), then the Interpreting Angel is present in this vision but is not called by that designation because he does not play the role of interpreting visionary objects or characters. Whether or not the two designations refer to the same angelic being cannot be resolved. All that can be said is that the Angel of Yahweh in this council scene has a different function from the Interpreting Angel in the other visions. The substitution of one angelic designation and role, Angel of Yahweh, for the usual Interpreting Angel of the Seven Visions contributes to the uniqueness of the literary form of this vision. It is one of several features that have led some commentators to question the authenticity of this vision among the Seven Visions (Tidwell 1975:346, n. 20). While its literary discreteness is clear, any consequent separation of chapter 3 from authentic Zechariah materials is probably unwarranted (see Introduction).

The Angel of Yahweh is indeed a familiar biblical figure who stands at the head of the entourage of the Divine Council (Wright 1950:34–41; Cooke 1964; Kingsbury 1964). The phrase *malʾāk-Yhwh* is the most frequently used designation of an angelic figure in all of Hebrew literature and Zechariah employs it already in the First Vision (1:11,12). The frequent use of angels as mediators becomes characteristic of exilic and postexilic prophecy. Perhaps as Yahweh becomes more transcendent, the members of his council take on more active and specific roles. Ezekiel is the first to employ such a figure to mediate his visions (40:3ff.), and Haggai is called *malʾāk-Yhwh* in 1:13 (see NOTE to that verse). The prophet Malachi seems to retain the basic meaning of the word in his very name, "messenger," or someone sent with a divine commission. The further development of the idea of messengers with specific duties and commissions becomes an integral part of Jewish apocalyptic. Angelology is a central feature of much apocalyptic, with the Book of Daniel being the most developed example of this phenomenon in canonical scripture.

the Accuser. One of three cases in the Hebrew Bible in which this term occurs in reference to a figure in Yahweh's court, the other two cases being the prologue to Job (cc 1–2) and 1 Chron 21:1. Although many translators have felt justified in calling this figure "Satan," the less personified translation "Accuser" seems more suitable here for conveying the meaning of the Hebrew *haśśāṭān* (cf. for example, NEB with NJPS). Only in 1 Chron 21:1 does it appear without the definite article as a proper noun. Here and in Job it is still a common noun, with the definite article making it a title, "the Accuser," as "the Prosecuting Attorney." The occurrences of the noun as well as of its cognate verbs *(śṭn* and *śṭm)* reveal a set of meanings that are derived from the hostility of one who is an opponent. The earliest usage of the noun is in Num 22:22,32, in the context of the Balaam oracles. Other relevant passages include 1 Sam 29:4; 2 Sam 19:23 (RSV 19:22); 1 Kgs 11:14,25; and 1 Kgs 5:18 (RSV 5:4).

The best analogy to usage in a legal context is Ps 109:6, where *śāṭān* is parallel to wicked: "Appoint a wicked man against him; let an accuser bring him to trial" (RSV; cf. v 29, where the accusers are clothed in dishonor). Weiser (1962:690) has understood the accused to be the psalmist himself. In Ps 38:21 (RSV 38:20) and 71:13, the verb *śṭn* is used to designate personal adversaries. The same range of meanings is conveyed by the verb *śṭm,* as in Gen 27:41; 49:23; 50:15; Ps 55:4 (RSV 55:3); Job 16:9; 30:21.

In assessing the meaning of the noun *śāṭān* in Job, Zechariah, and 1 Chronicles, a measure of increasing independence leading finally to a personification in the later literature is usually assumed (but see Rudolph 1976:94–95 and Gaster 1962:224–28). The absence of the definite article in 1 Chron 21:1 has led Gaster (1962:224) to reject this occurrence as a proper noun. Yet the figure in this context is surely hostile to Yahweh's chosen one; and from a linguistic viewpoint, the lack of the definite article does not weaken the distinct image in Chronicles of a *śāṭān* figure (Hurvitz 1974:19). Because of the appearance of the figure in Job, the existence of *haśśāṭān* as a figure in popular folklore, as well as in the Divine Council literature can be assumed. Neither in Job nor in Zechariah is the Accuser an independent entity with real power, except that which Yahweh consents to give him. The figure thus originates with the Divine Council and *śāṭān* represents one of the "sons of God" who is given increasing power as in the Prologue of Job, where Yahweh has given him control over a variety of negative and hostile forces in the world. While a growing delineation of the forces of evil or hostility is to be discerned in Zech 3, the Prologue to Job constitutes the premier example in the Hebrew Bible of such power being vested in a negative personality. The emerging personification of the figures in the Divine Council, both positive and negative, is a major feature of exilic and postexilic biblical writing, and the Book of Zechariah bears unmistakable testimony to this process.

The development of a demonic figure in Hebrew literature of the sixth century and later can be related to the actual figure of an "accuser" in Mesopotamian bureaucracies (Oppenheim 1968:176–79). Such figures do not seem to have existed, at least in institutionalized form, before the neo-Babylonian period. At that time, they began to appear in documents as functionaries who observed the inhabitants of a realm. The observing seems to have taken place in secrecy, so that those being observed were unaware of it and thus the connotation of spying accompanies this institution. While theoretically the process was an ambivalent one—both good deeds and improper acts could be reported to the king—in practice it was normally the alleged misdeeds that were noted and thus the demonic implications were strengthened. Unseen informers told the king about individuals who were then subjected to some sort of punitive action. This negative dimension clearly applies to the process of satanic delineation and individualization in Hebraic literature. However, the general concept of official knowledge of events in a political realm, of which the accuser figure in Yahweh's court is a part, can also, in its portrayal of divine omniscience, include both the positive and negative implications of God's awareness of all that takes place in the arena of human activity. The notion of divine and cosmic omniscience, with the attendant feature of the speed and secrecy with which information was conveyed by the institutionalized informers or accusers of the Mesopotamian imperial system, appears in Zechariah's visions in the figures of the horses and chariots in the first and last visions (see NOTES *ad loc.)* and in the "eyes of the Lord" of the Fourth Vision (see NOTES to 4:10b; cf. 3:9).

For this verse, several commentators address the possibility that the Accuser can be identified with a specific hostile individual or individuals—that is, opponents of Joshua (Jepsen 1945:106; Kaupel 1930:104ff.; see also Hanson 1975:253–61). The biblical metaphor is very difficult to penetrate at this point, making it impossible to draw conclusions with any certitude as to the identity of any opposition to Joshua. Indeed, it is not clear whether it is Joshua himself or the office of high priest that is being scrutinized. If Joshua himself is being examined, then the Accuser may be implicating the Persians themselves, who appear to have had to sanction the appointees to important provincial offices (Cook 1983:41,71). However, it is more likely that it is not Joshua himself but rather his office that is being observed, as it is now prominent because of the exigencies of administering the temple restoration, which is under review. One could imagine concern over an enlarged priestly office from any number of quarters, from traditionalist or disaffected priests, from landowning citizenry, even from royalists who would see in such priestly powers the curtailment or preclusion of hope for a monarchic regime. However, the Accuser need not stand for any special interest group; rather, it would represent the powers of the court itself, Yahweh's sovereignty. The Accuser in the biblical passages in which he appears acts as the Public Prosecutor, an agent of the highest executive authority. From time immemorial, in the ancient world until the present, a figure equivalent to a Public Prosecutor has been the first officer of any court. It is hard to imagine any developed society in which such a person did not play a role. The Accuser is clearly the leading figure in this case, despite his dismissal. Yahweh himself and not the Angel of Yahweh rebukes him; for the Angel of Yahweh is the Public Defender or advocate—the second, not the first, officer in any court.

The role of the Accuser as prosecutor raises the question of what might have happened before the action begins. Why is Joshua there at all, and what kind of case might the Accuser, on behalf of Yahweh, have against him? The text never tells us what the Accuser's case is, so it can be reconstructed only on the basis of the rebuttal that it receives. The Angel of Yahweh apparently calls upon Yahweh to rebuke the Accuser for bringing charges on two issues, which are interrelated: first, the Accuser must have argued that Jerusalem has been rejected permanently by Yahweh and so cannot and should not be restored. Such a doctrine, which would be in keeping with preexilic prophecy and perhaps Lamentations too, would apply to the temple and to the priesthood as well. Just as Shiloh was destroyed, never to be rebuilt, so Jerusalem and its temple have been repudiated by God. Any efforts to restore either would be contrary to God's will; temple restoration would be nothing short of blasphemy. The rebuke includes the assurance of Yahweh's choosing Jerusalem, which would be an answer to the hypothetical charge that Jerusalem and the temple should remain in ruins. Second, and more easily discernible, would be an accusation about the restoration of the priesthood and/or Joshua's fitness for the office of high priest. Viewed in a narrow way, the Accuser might have argued that Joshua had been in exile and was permanently contaminated by the experience, so he could not ever be qualified to assume the office for which he was next in line. There was ample precedent in the rejection of Eli and his line (1 Sam 2:27–33) for the permanent dismissal of Joshua and his line. On broader grounds, the Accuser could have said that the destruction of Jerusalem and the temple was also a judgment against the priesthood that functioned there. The monarchy had also been repudiated, and so had the priesthood. God is not now restoring the monarchy, so how could the priesthood be restored? Either way, the emphasis on Joshua's purity suggests that the Accuser objected to the priesthood's role.

The Accuser's case on both issues would have been quite strong, for there is much in the Primary History and in the preexilic prophets upon which he could have developed his argument that Yahweh had permanently terminated Jerusalem, the temple, and the priesthood. The Accuser's case is thrown out, however, because Yahweh has changed his mind. He has decided that the period of disgrace and banishment and ruin has gone on long enough. So the charges can be dismissed, and the Accuser is now in the wrong while the Angel as advocate takes over. Yahweh has indeed chosen Jerusalem. He has not rejected it and never intended to do so (cf. 1:17 and 2:16 [RSV 2:12]), and the statement of God's choosing Jerusalem has become thematic in Zechariah. The Accuser appears in a bad light in this passage because he is unaware of the change in policy. The mood of rejection has finally passed, and the idea of Jerusalem's election has been revived. The older order is no longer dominant; that the new age has arrived is proclaimed in the vivid imagery of the investiture passage. The rebuke of the Accuser is so quick to come, before any case is actually put forth, that Yahweh's resounding approval of the priestly role, and of the temple, is established. Joshua's subsequent donning of priestly accoutrements is couched in the traditional language of the Divine Council, and this also lends legitimacy to his office. In addition, Zechariah's prophetic role within the Council in chapter 3 contributes toward authenticating the high priest. See NOTES to the succeeding verses.

standing. Once again the verb *'md* ("stand") appears as technical language associated with the Divine Council. Here the verb is accompanied by the preposition *'l*, as in 4:14.

on his right. "Right" signifies hand or side (e.g., Ps 21:9 [RSV 21:8]; 89:13–14 [RSV 89:12–13], etc.). Ps 109:6, which provides the best context for understanding *śṭn* in a legal sense, has *śāṭān* standing at the right also. Although the Western reader might expect a hostile power to be on the left side, such is not the case. The positioning of the Accuser on the right derives from the fact that he is the first officer of the court (cf. above, NOTE to "the Accuser"), whereas the defender (Angel of Yahweh) is the second officer.

2. *rebuke you.* The verb *g'r* is rendered in the jussive although it could also be indicative. The preposition *b* before the objective pronoun for "you" denotes the object of Yahweh's rebuke. The combination of verb, preposition, and object appears twice, emphasizing the finality with which the Accuser is put in his place. God's outburst in the court scene is tantamount to his rejection of the Accuser's charges (see NOTE to "the Accuser" in v 1). The prosecutor, in his accustomed role, was about to bring evidence against Joshua's position and against Jerusalem as a favored city. God's rebuke is not directed toward the function of the Accuser per se, but rather to the way in which he is carrying out his responsibilities. He is using irrelevant and dated evidence; he has not rebelled against Yahweh's authority.

In prophecy, *g'r* ("to scream, cry out") nearly always is an anthropopathic term which denotes divine invective against those who stand in the way of Yahweh's plan. God's very cry against someone constitutes a rebuke, a word strong enough to cause whatever has aroused God's cry to cease. Other instances of such sharp outcry include Jer 29:27, where a priest rebukes a prophet, and two instances in Malachi (2:3 and 3:11), where divine rebuke is directed against priestly abuses. While g⁽r itself does not imply cursing, it evidently contains the seeds of such usage. The divine pronouncement of 3:2 becomes an incantation in later Jewish literature and is found in the Aramaic magic bowls from Nippur (Caquot 1978:52; cf. T.B. Berakhot 51a and 1 QM 14:10).

who chooses Jerusalem. Yahweh's choosing of Jerusalem appears above in the oracles of 1:17 and 2:16 (RSV 2:12; see NOTES). The emphasis on Jerusalem as the favored city of God and the place for the holy temple seems obvious. Yet for the restoration community, the certainty that Jerusalem would resume its historic role was slow to come. After all, God had rejected Jerusalem nearly seventy years before, just as he had rejected Shiloh (cf. Ps 78:59–61,67–68; Jer 26:6). Yahweh never chose Shiloh again. How could the people be sure that Jerusalem would once more emerge as a special place? The Accuser must have argued that Jerusalem was to share that fate of Shiloh; and Yahweh must set him straight (cf. NOTE to "the Accuser," 3:1).

a brand plucked from the fire. This statement would seem to be a variant form of the proverbial saying in Amos 4:11, "and you were as a brand plucked out of the burning." Only the word for fire is different: here ʾeš, in Amos, śĕrēpâ. The saying has particular relevance to Joshua because his grandfather, Seraiah, was among those who were slaughtered by Nebuchadnezzar (2 Kgs 25:18–21; Lam 2:6,20; and 1 Chron 5:40–41 [RSV 6:14–15]). The fact that Joshua survived in exile to return to Jerusalem in the capacity of high priest is hardly accidental, according to the prophet.

The related verse in Amos describes the rescue of some Judeans in a situation comparable to the overthrow of Sodom and Gomorrah, which was a destruction characterized by the spectacular use of fire and brimstone falling from the heavens on the doomed city. The image of "brand plucked from the fire" is a vivid one and suggests that Joshua's availability to serve as high priest did not come about easily. The sources provide no direct information and one cannot do much more than speculate. Because his grandfather had been executed, his family may have been regarded with suspicion by the authorities. The imagery suggests a narrow escape from a dangerous situation. Perhaps it reflects the transition from Babylonian to Persian rule, a transition in which Zechariah has more than passing interest (cf. 2:4,10–11 [RSV 1:21; 2:6–7]). If Joshua and his family had been in a precarious position under Babylonian rule, Persian ascendancy may have served him. Miraculously, it would then seem to at least some of his contemporaries, including Zechariah, that a direct descendant of the last chief priest in Jerusalem was ready to serve again in the restored temple. Whatever misgivings accompanied Joshua's role, the point is that the high priesthood becomes a sign of divine favor in Jerusalem, the place Yahweh has chosen.

3. *filthy.* The Hebrew ṣôʾîm here and in verse 4 designates an extreme condition of dirtiness. That word can be used to designate excrement, as in the law of Deut 23:14 (RSV 23:13); cf. 2 Kgs 18:27, qere. His utter filthiness, to be contrasted with the state of purity reflected in the new vestments in which he is garbed later, need not signify moral or ethical transgressions on the part of Joshua. Rather, the change from foul to pure clothing symbolizes the shift in the priest's status from the mundane world to the sanctified or holy realm of the house of Yahweh. See NOTE below to "pure vestments," verse 4. This shift is comparable to the notion of prophetic uncleanness in the Heavenly

Court scene of Isa 6:5–7, where Isaiah's sense of being unfit *(ṭāmēʾ)* is removed by the purification of his person: the burning coal touches his lips, which represent his speech and thus his thoughts. Likewise, in Isa 4:4 the daughters of Zion (and not their clothing) are filthy and are cleansed, to be made fit (holy) to live in Jerusalem by God's judgment. Compare too the cleansing of the heart and spirit of those to be brought back from exile by the sprinkling of water, in Ezek 36:24–27; Kaufmann (1977:282) suggests that the application of water to the persons themselves and not to their garments denotes the removal of their personal guilt.

Joshua's uncleanness is perhaps better related to his having lived the first part of his life in Babylon, as the preceding verse emphasizes with its proverbial saying. The implications for a priest of life in exile can be ascertained from a passage in Amos (7:17). The judgment against Amaziah, the priest of Bethel specifies, as the final blow in a series of disasters, that he will die "in an unclean land." He will lose his wife to harlotry, his children to the sword, his land to opportunists, and himself to the impurity of exile. It must have been a particular disgrace for priests to live in a foreign land.

By selecting Jerusalem, God makes Jerusalem and its territory "holy," a concept clearly expressed in the "chooses Jerusalem" passage of 2:16 (RSV 2:12). Therefore, Joshua's return to Jerusalem in and of itself represents a move to a place of great sanctity from a place, outside the "Holy Land," of great impurity. Even further, his role as high priest will bring him in greatest proximity to God's holiness and thus necessitate his symbolic purification.

standing. See NOTE to "standing" in verse 1.

angel. Probably to be understood as "the Angel of Yahweh," since in verse 1 Joshua is described as "standing before the Angel of Yahweh."

4. *who spoke out.* The Hebrew does not supply a subject here though the Peshitta supplies "angel." It can be assumed that the antecedent is the last mentioned angel at the end of verse 3. The verbal pair (literally, "he answered and he said"), translated together "spoke out," is reminiscent of the language of the dialogue between Zechariah and the Interpreting Angel. However, since this prophetic vision, although containing dialogue, does not conform to the form of the Seven Visions, the presence of those two verbs is not sufficient to provide evidence that it is the Interpreting Angel who now speaks.

those standing. That is, the other members of the Divine Council or the other divine or angelic beings present in Yahweh's court. Cf. NOTE to "the Angel of Yahweh" in verse 1.

filthy. See NOTE to verse 3.

to him he said. Now the angel addresses Joshua directly. In the words that follow, the angel's claim to have removed Joshua's iniquity by having his dirty garments taken away indicates that the angel speaks in the name of Yahweh. Indeed, throughout this vision there is a flow of divine identity from Yahweh himself to the angels of his court. The interchangeability of Yahweh and his angelic representatives is an old theme, and it is curious to see it contained in this scene along with an increased delineation of the roles played by angelic figures. Zech 3 may be a transitional piece. As in earlier biblical texts, the Angel of Yahweh performs earthly tasks for God, speaks for him, and serves as an alter ego while still remaining distinct from God. The argument between God and Moses over the way the Israelites are to enter the promised land is a good example of the nature of the angel-Yahweh relationship in earlier books of the Bible. The angel will lead the people and do all the miraculous things along the way that only God can accomplish; yet he is not the same as God himself, for God explicitly does not lead the Israelites (see Exod 32:23–33:3). In Zechariah some of this partial blurring of lives between angel and God is retained. Yet the Accuser as Prosecutor and the Angel of Yahweh as Public Defender have defined roles. Their distinctiveness anticipates the sharply differentiated positions and the hierarchical structure of the angelic hordes in later periods. By the second century, as in Daniel and the Apocrypha, the angels get names and identities and specific tasks assigned to them.

iniquity. Just as the "filthy garments" in which Joshua was clothed are symbolic of the impure state, to be contrasted with his subsequent ritual fitness to do God's service, his "iniquity" is introduced here, not as a description of his personal sinfulness but rather as the abstract counterpart to the unclean apparel. Such an understanding of "iniquity" *('āwōn)* appears justified from the importance of the priestly headgear, which is introduced in the next verse as the only specified individual item of the clean wardrobe that will replace the contaminated clothing. In the description of the Aaronic vestments in Exod 28:36–38, the turban is to be fitted with an inscribed gold plate. That plate, probably part of the crown which was placed over the turban (Exod 29:6; cf. 39:30), serves to remove the guilt *('āwōn)* that was attached to the holy sacrifies. Aaron's inscribed headpiece is the material, visible object that symbolized the ultimate purification of holy offerings. Presumably Aaron's holiness, represented by the crowning object of his raiment, was such that he could absorb and render as naught the "guilt." The whole series of actions and appurtenances associated with the inmost part of the tabernacle (= temple) were permeated with carefully organized symbolic value (Haran 1961 and 1980:175–87; 205–20), and the dressing of the chief priest in traditionally specified garb was an integral part of establishing the holiness of the sanctuary and all who were connected with it. In this particular case, the additional responsibilities that Joshua was to have as "high priest" and as legitimate functionary in the eyes of the Persian Government which was permitting him to serve in that office would intensify the symbolic value of the investiture. Other aspects of this process are discussed below in our NOTES to verses 5 and 6. The association of the engraved stone, perhaps equivalent to the inscribed plate/crown of the turban in Exod 29 and to the stone set "before Joshua" below in verse 9, with "iniquity" (also *'āwōn)* is likewise part of the symbolic realm of priestly garb.

Joshua's guilt is a complicated and comprehensive matter. It includes the personal contamination he has suffered, especially as a priest, by living far from the earthly locus of holiness and purity, Jerusalem and the temple (cf. NOTE above to "filthy," v 3). Because he is the leading priestly official, he is representative of all priests as well as of the people. Their collective impurity is also involved. In normal times, the offenses of the people, as individuals and as a group, threaten to diminish the purity of the temple. Impurity is an external force which must be removed (Levine 1974:76–77) lest the sanctuary be threatened with impurity. The priests had to deal with this collective guilt. In Num 18:1,23 the Aaronides are instructed to bear the "transgression/guilt of the sanctuary" *('āwōn hamiqdāš)*—that is, the responsibility for any violation of purity. The impurity at issue would include what we would label moral impurity as well as ritual uncleanness. The two were not separate in biblical religion (see COMMENT to

Hag 2:10–19). After the exile, the impurity of the people would have been that much more threatening. The exile itself was a punishment for sins and guilt, and living in a foreign land further contributed to the atmosphere of uncleanness. All this iniquity needed to be purged and removed in connection with the actual restoration, as well as with the symbolic restoration of the temple as a holy place. Joshua's role in expiating past sins and present contamination of himself and of the people would have been enormous—too enormous, some might have thought. Nothing less than the removal of iniquity in God's Heavenly Court can establish Joshua's success in achieving the purity required for him to be instated in his office.

and I have clothed. The MT is difficult but it can be supported (cf. suggestion in *BHS*). The verb *whlbš* is the Hiphil infinitive absolute and carries the force of the verb *hᶜbrty* ("I have removed") in the preceding clause. It is good biblical Hebrew.

This statement of how Joshua is clothed is followed in verse 5 by, first, a command to put on his clean headpiece. Next, the carrying out of that command is recorded. Finally, the report that "they clothed him" appears. These four statements constitute a pattern: clothed; places headpiece; headpiece placed; clothed. The act of clothing begins and ends the series. In literary terms this forms an envelope which accomplishes two things: 1) it emphasizes the central act, the positioning of a clean turban, with all its symbolic value, on Joshua's head; and 2) it makes the instruction to clothe Joshua a general statement about his entire new wardrobe, of which the turban is only one part, although the most important part. When Joshua is stripped of his filthy clothes in verse 4, a filthy hat would have been included in the items he removed. Acknowledging the literary structure clarifies what otherwise appears to be a confused or illogical sequence of events, with Joshua being clothed, then receiving a headpiece, then being clothed.

pure vestments. Hebrew *mahalāṣôt* is derived from a root *hlṣ* and occurs only here and in Isa 3:22, where it is included in a list of finery that the ladies of Jerusalem possess. Since the root can mean "withdraw, draw off," *BDB* (323) has concluded that the noun *mahalāṣôt* represents a "robe of state"—that is, something that is taken off in ordinary life. However, that explanation does not fit the opposing notions of clean and unclean which permeate this scenario. Thomas (1931–32:279–80) points out that the Arabic cognate to *hlṣ* with the meaning "withdraw" has a primary sense of "to become clear, pure, genuine, white" and is actually used of garments (Lane 1863:I *ii* 785–86) in its adjectival form. Furthermore, the ancient usage of the root to designate some pure or purified item may find support in Assyrian *halāṣu*, "to purify" *(CAD* VI:40,50–51), especially of oil *(šamnâ halṣa)*, the primary meaning being "to press out," the derived meaning, "to purify." The term *mahalāṣôt* designates the purified garments, the "pure vestments" with which Joshua is clothed once his filthy or impure ones have been removed. Since the term does not appear in any of the detailed descriptions of priestly vestments in Exodus or Leviticus, the term clearly cannot refer to a specific type of garment but rather to the state of the apparel so denoted.

5. *Then I said.* The use of the first person at this point in the vision is unexpected and for most commentators represents the impulsive intervention of the prophet into the text. The versions have had great difficulty here, either omitting (LXX) or converting to the third person (Vulgate and Peshitta). The key to understanding this form is the setting of this prophetic vision in the Heavenly Court. Tidwell (1975) has suggested that Zech 3:1–7 constitutes a fully developed *Gattung* known as the "council-

genre" (354). In his analysis, verse 5 is absolutely integral to the text, thereby obviating any necessity to separate out verses 6 and 7 as suggested by Ackroyd (1962:566b) and Beuken (1967:290–91). The closest parallels in prophetic texts are found in Isa 6:1–11 and 40:1–11, which also share the striking use of the first person by the prophet. Other analogous texts include 1 Kgs 22:19–22; Job 1:6–12, 2:1–7; and Zech 1:8–13 and 6:1–8. In Tidwell's argument, the prophetic outburst in the first person is the climax of the entire vision and is much more than a simple literary device to point out the significance of the turban, except that the clean turban itself *is* the central symbol of the vision. Even in other instances in Zechariah (cc 1 and 6), despite the interlocution of the Interpreting Angel, he asserts that the same genre and phenomenon can be observed.

Despite many higher critical misgivings about its placement, Zech 3:1–7 plays an integral role in the overall scheme of the visions. Along with the following Fourth Vision, it stands in the middle of the visionary sequence. Together, chapters 3 and 4 are a kind of centerpiece. In chapter 3 the prophet himself emerges abruptly in the unfolding drama of Joshua's investiture. In so doing, he represents the active and direct involvement of the prophet in transmitting the will of God as it emanates from the Divine Council. Zechariah thereby stands in the line of preexilic and exilic prophecy. Thus this prophetic vision differs from the Seven Visions in providing a closer link with the modes of earlier classical prophecy.

Let them put. Literally, the beginning of verse 5 reads: "And I said, 'They will place . . .'" The MT *yśymw,* as pointed out, is indicative and not jussive, which would be *yāśēmû,* without medial *yod,* as we read.

clean turban. That is, "pure turban." The use of *ṭāhôr* ("clear, pure, shining") to describe the turban is typical of priestly contexts where ritual purity and not hygienic cleanliness is involved (C. Meyers 1976:27–28): the adjective functions in much the same way that *ellu* does in Akkadian *(CAD* IV:106). Another possible rendering, "shining headpiece," can also be considered. In certain contexts *ṭāhôr* ("shining") designates bright metals such as sapphire, as in Exod 24:10. It also depicts the brightness of lapis lazuli, as in Ugaritic *ṭhr* or the variant *zhr,* which appears in reference to the sacred *iqnim* stones (Gordon 1965: texts 51:V:81 and 77:21–22). Turban here is *ṣānîp* rather than *miṣnepet,* the normal word for turban, to which a metal plate *(ṣîṣ)* and/or crown *(nēzer)* is added according to Exod 29:6 and Lev 8:9. Perhaps *ṣānîp* for turban designates a composite headpiece, including that part of it, whether stone or metal, which shines and which is the specific, symbolic component that relates to the priest's function, described in verse 9 below, in ridding the land of iniquity. Zechariah's departure from the terminology of the priestly texts, however, may be intentional and significant.

The ceremonial aspect of the priestly vestments and headgear was of great importance for the role of Joshua and also for the legitimacy of the temple project for which his administrative powers were to be used. Throughout the ancient Near Eastern world, the rank or status of officials, and of their gods (Oppenheim 1949:172–93) was communicated through carefully chosen and prepared items of apparel. The garments of gods were akin to those of the royal and priestly figures, sometimes one and the same, who served them. The establishment in Israel of elaborate and ornate costumes for the chief priestly officials had ancient roots and, like other features described in the tabernacle texts of Exodus, goes back at least as far as the days of the Solomonic temple (Haran 1980:3–42, 189–94). The garments worn by the priests probably changed very little over the centuries, although some slight elaboration or modifications might have been made. Once introduced, the costumes stayed much the same, ritual garb being highly conservative by nature, until they were wiped out by the destruction. The priestly information about their appearance may depict the latest form in which they existed, but since that form did not change appreciably, the elaborate nature of the priestly garb is a condition that would have existed from earliest times. Hence there is no reason to suppose (as do de Vaux 1961:400, and others) that the ornamental garments associated with the high priest represent a transfer of royal garb to the priesthood in the postexilic period because of the loss of the monarchy.

Limited lexical information is available to us for identifying ṣānîp as "turban." It is attested in three other instances, two of them in a general way as a designation for a fine article of clothing (Isa 3:23; Job 29:14). The third use is in the qere of Isa 62:3, "You shall be a crown of beauty in the hand of the Lord,/and a royal diadem in the hand of your God" (RSV). The Isaiah passage has ṣānîp (qere; kethib has ṣĕnîp) as a "diadem" modified by "royal"; it also has ṣānîp the parallel to crown (ʿăṭeret; cf. NOTE to "crowns," 6:11). The resulting image is that of an official headpiece with monarchic associations. Because of this, and also because Joshua is given a crown in the Crowning of chapter 6, the ṣānîp of this vision appears to be a conscious departure from priestly terminology. Joshua's turban is linked with the Aaronic one in that the Hebrew root is the same, yet the word Zechariah has chosen is somewhat different. The shift ideally suits the situation. Joshua as "high priest" both continues the traditional role of "chief priest" (cf. NOTE to "high priest" in 3:1) and also incorporates into the scope of his office some responsibilities previously assumed by the Judean kings. The turban designated ṣānîp would therefore symbolize, as official garb is meant to, such an alteration in the priestly role.

they clothed him. Literally, "they dressed him in garments." The sequence of outfitting Joshua would seem to be headpiece first, followed by the rest of his garb. That order would appear to contradict the instructions of Exod 29:5–7 and descriptions of Lev 8:7–9, in which the turban with crown is the last item to be placed upon Aaron. This apparent reversal of the pentateuchal order evidently was of some concern to the Greek translators who insert, before the instructions for putting the turban on Joshua's head, an order to clothe him with a long robe. However, the term "garments" *(bĕgādîm)* is a general word for clothing and does not refer to any specific item of priestly apparel according to the priestly source. Exod 29:5 initiates the instruction for garbing Aaron with the words "Take the garments" *(bĕgādîm)* and then proceeds to enumerate the individual items (coat, robe, ephod, etc.), ending with the headpiece. From this we can conclude that the Zechariah passage is not meant to be a sequential listing of the clothing of Joshua. Furthermore, the structure of verses 4b–5, which begin and end with the verb "to clothe," suggests that the sequence of acts serves literary purposes and does not reflect a literal ordering of what took place in the vision (see NOTE above to "and I have clothed" in v 4). In short, the repetition of "clothed" in this verse indicates that Joshua was properly attired in clean or purified garments (see NOTE to v 4 "pure vestments") and draws attention to one significant item in the assortment of layers and trappings worn by the priest, namely the headpiece, because of its particular symbolic value in relationship to "iniquity" (see NOTE to "iniquity," v 4).

Another apparent divergence from the ceremonial sequence of Exod 29 and Lev 8 is the absence in this passage of any mention of anointing, a ritual which accompanied the investiture of Aaron. De Vaux suggests (1961:399) that the silence of Zech 3 in this regard means that Joshua was never anointed into his priestly office. Joshua is already called "high priest" at the outset of this chapter and also in Haggai, which comes from a slightly earlier date. He was already considered the chief priestly official, whether or not an official ceremony of investiture complete with anointing had ever taken place. If Joshua was born in 570 as Cross suggests (1975:17), with his father having been born near the beginning of the sixth century, it is likely that Joshua would have succeeded to his priestly position well before his return from Babylon. While he was probably recognized as high priest, or at least in line to be high priest once all the limitations of the impurity caused by his living in exile had been dealt with (see NOTE to "iniquity" in previous verse), there would be a question whether he would have been invested with authority and insignia while on foreign soil. The Persians may have officially granted him the right to occupy his inherited position, but the formal recognition of his own people may have been contingent upon his return to Jerusalem and his taking up of administrative tasks. Beyond that, a ceremonial induction may not have been possible until the temple's renewal was made factual by the refoundation ceremony (see Hag 2:10,15–19, NOTES and COMMENT) which took place shortly before Zechariah's visions and to which his visions are a response. On the other hand, anointing may not have been a standard practice for priests except for Aaron, the first priest. The brief description in Num 20:26–28 of Eleazar's succession to his father's position does not mention anointing. Furthermore Ezekiel makes no mention of anointing, although he is careful to point out the special vestments that distinguish the priests (Ezek 44:17–19). Finally, the Talmudic sages reluctantly admitted that several important constituents of the preexilic temple—the ark, the cherubim, the Urim and Thummim, and the anointing oil—were absent in the postexilic temple. They assumed that the anointing oil was hidden away with the other sacred objects: the ark, the manna, and Aaron's rod (T. B. Horayoth, 12a; Yoma, 52b).

The dressing of Joshua depicted in this vision may not be an installation ceremony at all. Rather it could depict an enrobing for a special temple ritual such as had not taken place since the temple structure itself was rendered unusable in 587. On the basis of Ezek 44:17–19, it can be asserted that the symbolic ceremonial garb of the priests was used only for their ministry in the sanctuary itself and not for the activities of the courtyard (at the altar). Although the altar was being used and Joshua had already been functioning in his priestly office for some time, the temple itself was in disrepair and there would have been no occasion for him to have donned the full assortment of ritual apparel for entering the inner sanctum. Nor would there have been opportunity or need, until the reality of a rebuilt temple was certain, to recognize Joshua's fitness in a ceremony of installation. The reason now for the investiture passage must be related to the restoration of the temple itself and the recognition of Joshua's role in the temple and in the administration of Yehud based in the temple. That refoundation ceremony linking the old temple with the present one and stressing the continuity between the two would have been the appropriate occasion for his investment (see below our discussion of verse 9 and of 4:7). Whether or not any previous or provisional installation took place cannot be ascertained.

stood by. Another instance of the vocabulary of the Heavenly Court (see NOTES to v 1). The Angel of Yahweh has been observing the procedures and is now ready to insert his—that is, God's—charge to Joshua.

6. *charged.* The Hiphil of *ʿwd*, a denominative from *ʿēdâ*, "testimony," has an official ring to it; often witnesses are involved. The verb anticipates the solemnity and authority of the ensuing message, an official job description, delivered to Joshua.

7. *If . . . then.* This conditional sentence is not altogether clear in the Hebrew since the division between protasis and apodosis is somewhat uncertain. The versions have noted this difficulty in their translations. The two clauses following "if" (*ʾim,* which is repeated in Hebrew before the two verbs, "walk" and "keep") could conceivably be followed by the next two clauses introduced by "then" *(gam* before both verbs, "render judgment" and "administer"), with the apodosis being constituted by the last clause in verse 7. However, the shift from *ʾim* to *gam* seems sufficient cause to understand that the second set of clauses denotes the scope of Joshua's authority, so long as he obeys God's word. His ability to carry out his specified role will be uniquely aided by the access to the Heavenly Court indicated by the final clause (cf. following NOTES). Ackroyd (1968:187) makes a further point in favor of this arrangement. He suggests that the firm statement in the second set of clauses about the priesthood would be suitable to Joshua's postexilic status as a strong figure and that it would be unlikely to have that role itself be part of the protasis of a conditional statement.

The internal content of the four clauses introduced two each by *ʾim* and *gam* consists of an *ab ab* arrangement. The first clause of the first set corresponds to the first clause of the second set, and the second members of the two sets likewise correspond. This correspondence concerns the meaning of the two members of each set with respect to the range of priestly duties. The first members deal with an expanded aspect of the priests' role in administering (civil) justice; the second part of each pair treats the cultic dimension of the priests' function.

walk in my ways. While this can be a general term for following God's commandments, it can have specific reference to the wide range of legal matters with which the priesthood at this point would have had to deal. A pivotal text is Exod 18:20, which describes a premonarchic system of civil justice. Moses instructs men to represent him, or to take on some of his responsibilities in arbitrating disputes, by teaching them the laws and how to use them—that is, "the way in which they must walk." Likewise, during the period of the judges those "saviors" of Israel performed some unspecified (judicial) tasks to which the people gave no heed in that they turned aside "from the way in which their father had walked." The language of walking in God's ways involves the administration of justice.

The role of the Levitical priests in *instructing* the people in God's law has been discussed above (see COMMENT to Hag 2:10ff.). During the monarchy the king appears to have taken on the ultimate responsibility for *executing* God's law and providing justice (2 Sam 8:15; cf. Whitelam 1979). With the termination of the monarchy, the royal responsibility for internal justice and order also came to an end. Insofar as Persian policy encouraged continuity of local law systems in the provinces (cf. first NOTE to 7:1 and Cook 1983:72), and since the civil administrator or *peḥâ* was mainly concerned with economic matters (taxes) and the relationship of the province to the imperial authorities, the priestly officials who were the tradents of Israelite law were likely to have taken on (or resumed?) judicial-legal powers within the community that were broader than the cultic dimension of their activities (cf. NOTE to "flying scroll," 5:1).

keep my service. This phrase refers to the duties involved in carrying out the cultic functions associated with the temple itself. The pentateuchal texts assign the Levitical priests the tasks of maintenance associated with the tabernacle (e.g., Num 1:53 and 3:8, etc.) and the tent of meeting (Num 3:7,8). Although the relationship between priests and Levites in carrying out the "service" in the postexilic period is not clear (see Ezek 44:14–18) the nature of that service as it includes physical maintenance and perhaps ritual acts seems to be beyond question (see Haran 1980:60).

render judgment in my House. This is a difficult phrase (tādîn 'et-bêtî). The verb dyn is elsewhere used in legal matters to denote the exercise of judgment or justice. Its predominant meaning is to specify, in the context of a lawsuit, the rendering of an authoritative and binding decision (Liedke 1971:446ff.). Thus the object of such verbal action would be the case itself, when the cognate accusative (dîn) appears, or else the party being judged. God himself often appears as the ultimate executor of justice (e.g., Deut 32:36; Isa 3:13), and the king too is depicted in the role of giving judgment (Jer 21:12; 22:16). Zech 3:7 is unique in having a priest as the subject and in having an institution or building as the object, although the long-standing association or Levitical priesthood with judgment can be found in Deut 17:9–10 (cf. Halpern 1981:231–32). The use of the independent personal pronoun, which is always emphatic, before the verb suggests that something unusual is being predicated on the priesthood. Our translation, which supplies "in," should not obscure the problem of understanding what aspect of the priestly responsibility is being set forth. To make the verb a general word for "govern" (see BDB 192) is to neglect its important juridical content. Thus the "govern, rule, administer my house" suggested by many translations and commentators is unacceptable in that it does not adequately portray the charge to the priest to execute judgment (so understood by Mason 1982:147). With the removal of the king as chief judicial officer, the likelihood (see NOTE above to "walk in my ways" in this verse; also see our Introduction) is that the priesthood filled this gap in social organization and that the temple precinct rather than the palace became the seat of justice. The chief officer of the temple ("my House" = God's House) thus bore the final responsibility for the execution of justice and so regained a function held by the monarchy during the era of the Davidic kingdom (cf. NOTE to "twenty cubits long . . . ," 5:2). Although on local levels, at least until Josiah's reform, appellate judgment continued the premonarchic practice of being in the hands of the local priesthood.

administer my courts. This directive clearly pertains to the priestly administration of temple affairs, which included not only maintenance of the sacrificial system but responsibility for collection of revenues as well. The term ḥāṣēr, although it can refer to a specific inner precinct of the priests only (e.g., Ezek 10:3,5), is used here in a more generalized sense. The expression "to administer (tišmōr = you will keep) my courts" is unique in Scripture but nicely parallels "to keep (tišmōr = you will administer) my service" in verse 7a where the idiom is both warranted and well attested (e.g., Lev 8:35, 18:30; Num 18:5; Deut 11:1; Ezek 40:45; Mal 3:14; etc.). The sense of tišmōr, "you will administer," is as unusual as the entire expression itself. The plain sense of the phrase could hardly be "to keep my courts" in the way that custodians maintain a facility. The totality of the specialized ecclesiastical functions is implied by the term "my service"— i.e., preparation of the sacrifice, lighting the lamps, purification, etc. Designating the public place (in "my courts") where such activities occur may be a way of representing the range of public activities of the priests: their role in explanation or teaching of Scripture (see COMMENT to Hag 2:10–19) and their collection of revenue and offerings. Unlike the temple itself, which was off limits to the general public, the temple court-yards were the places where the people interacted with the priesthood and came closest to God's presence. The charge to Joshua concerning the courts apparently represents his responsibility for all the business and activities in connection with the public.

Many of these duties listed for Joshua impinge upon what would have been the responsibility of the king in the preexilic period. The job description of 3:7 represents an absorption of certain royal prerogatives or responsibilities by the priestly establish-ment. This verse is not so much concerned with the legitimacy of either Joshua or of the priesthood; the preceding verses deal dramatically with that issue. Rather, the four clauses of 3:7 reflect the problem of the relationship between ecclesiastical office and civil office and the division of responsibility and authority in light of the status of Yehud as a subprovince of the Persian Empire. The words of Yahweh to Joshua repre-sent an accommodation which the traditional biblical views of the relationship between monarchy and priesthood made to the political realities of the late sixth century. The civil role of the governor was hardly as broad as that of the king had been, and the priesthood took up the slack. Those (e.g., Rudolph 1976:97; Mason 1982:147) who contend that royal privileges had to be given to the priesthood to strengthen it have not properly assessed the dynamics of the shifting configuration of civil and priestly func-tions under Darius's rule. The resulting theocratic form of provincial government in Yehud was as much a result of Persian interests and limitations as it was of indepen-dent local attempts to elevate priestly authority. Yet the outcome was an increase in the scope and status of the legitimate priesthood despite the retention of a combined civil and ecclesiastical governance.

access. The versions (LXX, Syriac, Vulgate) apparently read an intransitive Piel participle, *mĕhallĕkîm*, on analogy with Eccles 4:15, literally, "those who wander." Rudolph (1976:93) among others has argued for the Piel participle, but the transitive meaning "to lead" makes no sense here. The d-stem Pail is twice attested in the Aramaic of Daniel (3:25 and 4:34), rendered *mahlĕkîn* and pointed identically with the present instance. All these interpretations, however, require an implied or assumed comparison: "I will make you like those who." It is possible that there was an original *k* after *lk* of the word "access," but the simplest solution is suggested by *BDB* (237): that the word is a plural noun meaning "goings," and hence "access." The singular form would be *mahălak*.

Beuken (1967:294) is bothered by such an interpretation because of the powers it gives to Joshua. He maintains that the underlying dynamic of all the visions is the fact that they are grounded in a real-life situation that does not suit the present scene when interpreted as we have done. Beuken concludes that the scene reflects a later theologi-cal viewpoint, and he suggests a "chronistic redactional setting" (296–97). However, so many other features of both Haggai and Zechariah point to a prominent place for the high priest that his reluctance to accept the originality of this scene seems unwarranted.

to those who are standing. That is, the members of the Heavenly Court; see our NOTE to "standing before," verse 1. This priestly access to the Divine Council is innovative. Previously only prophetic figures, including Zechariah as in verses 1 and 5, are portrayed as present in the council scene. Not even kings had access to the Divine Council. The expanded role of the priest with respect to judgment necessitates his becoming privy to God's judgment, which is often represented in biblical parlance by the Heavenly Court, an important aspect of the function of the Divine Council. Just as the prophet is God's messenger, communicating God's judgment concerning Israel to the people and especially to the king as the official ultimately responsible for the carrying out of justice, so now the priest must execute justice and thus needs to have access to divine will. In the absence of a monarch in Yehud, therefore, it is quite understandable how priests and especially the high priest came to assume more and more judicial power (see above NOTE on "clean turban").

The text raises a question about the manner of priestly access to God's court and his supreme judgment on earthly matters. On the face of it, it appears as if Joshua himself were to have the same privileges as prophets, who in the classic tradition were the only human observers of the Divine Council proceedings. No administrators of Judah, whether royal or priestly, are depicted as entering Yahweh's council. Even David and Solomon, who in some sense enjoyed a special relationship to Yahweh, are nevertheless visited by prophets with messages from Yahweh. Other kings explicitly consult prophets who perform the service of securing a decision about something. The standard procedure, even though he is the highest authority in the land, is for the king to call upon divine authority. He consults a prophet, who has direct access to God and who then reports the word of Yahweh to the king.

In light of this, it would be highly unusual for the priest to be granted identical access. Yet that may be the case for Joshua, who appears at a significant transition point in the reworking of governance patterns in Yehud. Still, if Joshua's increased responsibilities entail an absorption of certain functions previously performed by the king, then one would expect that Joshua would have the same relationship to prophetic pronouncements that the king previously had. With the transfer of some royal authority to the ecclesiastical administrators would have come the transfer of access to Yahweh via the prophets. Perhaps the text is elliptical here and intends that very situation, with prophets now addressing Joshua as they formerly spoke to kings and in that way constituting his access to the Divine Council. This explanation would ameliorate the apparently untenable awarding of direct access to a priest, but would it really reflect a change? After all, the prophet Haggai was already addressing his oracles to the high priest and also to the governor as well as to the people. Did the priest need special access? So we are left with the sense that the end of 3:7 in fact does accord Joshua an unprecedented position. If it isn't entirely consistent with classical models, it is because the exigencies of the postexilic period demanded forms, and sanctions for them, that departed from tradition. Such a departure was not complete, however; there is always the model of a premonarchic figure such as Samuel, who was priest and prophet, to consider.

8. *Take heed.* This directive, addressed to Joshua, is strengthened in Hebrew by the

addition of the emphatic *nāʾ* to the imperative form of the verb *(šmʿ,* "hear"). Attention is thus focused upon the recipient of this oracle, namely Joshua (and his colleagues). Whereas Haggai's words to the Yehudite leadership included both Joshua and Zerubbabel as well as others, Zechariah here focuses upon the priestly segment of the community. In 4:6 Zechariah delivers an oracle to Zerubbabel, but that statement lacks the specific call for attention found in the imperative introduction to this oracle to Joshua. Just as the preceding investiture passage revolves around Joshua's assumption of a priestly position with increased authority and status, the oracle that follows likewise sets Joshua in a premier place. His priestly companions are also charged with a significant role. The need to reconcile the priesthood's expanded responsibilities in the postexilic period with the traditions of monarchic powers provoked this oracle to the priests as a supplement to the preceding vision.

the high priest. It is precisely Joshua as "high priest," whose responsibilities are at variance with those of the chief priest during the monarchy, to whom the promise of the ultimate renewal of the Davidic monarchy must be addressed. See the discussion of "high priest" in the NOTES to 3:1; cf. 3:7.

your associates who are seated. The literal translation of the verb *yšb* ("sit") here denotes the official capacity of the priestly hierarchy and does not necessarily indicate that the entire company of priests is present when Joshua receives this prophetic announcement. The concept of officials "seated" may reflect a courtroom or judicial function, such as expressed in the language of "sit in judgment" (cf. Exod 18:13–14; Isa 28:6). We find comparable usage in Ezekiel (8:1; 14:1; 20:1). The same verb is used of a gathering of the elders, who sit before the prophet in order to receive an oracle from God. The function of the priesthood in the restoration community, as laid out in verse 7 above (see NOTES to that verse), surely involved juridical responsibility, a responsibility that was larger than in the preexilic community when ultimate legal authority resided with the monarch himself. The existence of a "college of priests" (Amsler 1981:83) in the Second Temple, with whom Joshua and his successors sat in deliberation, is supported by the evidence of a century later from Elephantine. The Aramaic documents from that Egyptian community includes letters addressed to the high priest in Jerusalem and his colleagues *(knwth;* see Cowley 1923:30–31). Yet the ideal of justice for the monarchic period rested upon the king's exercise of authority, as expressed in the words of the psalmist, who states that the thrones of judgment are the "thrones of the house of David" (Ps 122:5). It is precisely the contained validity of that monarchic ideal with which Zechariah must deal, in the absence of an actual monarchy, just as he underscores the need for the adjustment of that ideal to the reality of the wider priestly authority in Yehud under Persian rule.

Although we have retained the basic physical meaning "to sit" in our translation of *yšb*, and have also suggested that it may be elliptical for "to sit in judgment," we suggest that it could easily bear the rendering "rule, exercise authority." In the NOTE to "leaders of many cities" in 8:20 below, the important subset of usages of *yšb* in participial form to designate the formal or informal authorities in a community is described. The officials so designated are often kings and princes. But the term is wider than that, even though the primary derivation of the verb comes from the idiom "to sit on the throne" (= "to rule"). Not only kings and princes per se sat in office; all sorts of officials could be so characterized. As Gottwald demonstrates (1979:531), the scope of leadership designated by *yšb* includes military officers, judicial figures, or even people of unspecified position whose ability to exert authority is based on nonformal qualities. The verb *yšb* in this setting may well be a technical designation for a group of leaders, in which case the translation would read, "you and your associates who rule with you."

with you. Literally, "before you." This phrase, just as in Ezekiel's description of the elders seated in council "before" the prophet, contributes to the sense of an official body of priests under the direction of a senior officer, in this case Joshua as "the high priest."

they are men of portent. This difficult phrase presents both a grammatical problem and an exegetical one. If the oracle is presented as addressed to Joshua *and* his colleagues, then a third-person pronoun ("they," *hēmmâ*) would be awkward (cf. the discussion and suggestions in Petitjean 1969:163–65), as in the Syriac, which reads "you" (pl.). Rudolph (1976:98) would allow for a third-person pronoun to be used in conjunction with the second-person vocative of "you and your associates." However, one can also understand that Joshua stands alone before the prophet, whose words are intended to be conveyed to the official body of priests by their leader, who recognizes the authority of the priestly assembly he convenes (cf. Mitchell 1912:155–56, 160). The whole phrase, then, would be in apposition with "priests."

The meaning of the word *môpēt* ("portent") in this context is very difficult. The word has two sets of Old Testament usages. The first, usually paired with *'ōtōt* ("signs"), refers to God's miraculous intervention in history on behalf of the Israelites, notably in delivering them from Egyptian bondage (e.g., Exod 7:3), sometimes through the human assistance of Moses and Aaron (as in Exod 4:21). The Deuteronomic writer repeatedly uses *môpēt* (= "wonder") along with "signs" in his recital of the Israelite escape from Egypt (Deut 4:34; 7:19; 26:8; 34:11; etc.), as do the psalms with Exodus themes (78:43; 105:27; 135:9). A related, though somewhat independent, set of passages focuses upon human beings, chiefly prophets, as those in human history who indicate God's intended actions which will be carried out in the future. Isaiah's naked and barefoot behavior (Isa 20:2–6; see also 8:1–20) and Ezekiel's departure from Jerusalem with an emigrant's set of belongings (Ezek 12:3–15; see also 24:15–24) are primary examples of prophetic personages constituting signs of God's expected actions. Also relevant is the description in 1 Kgs 13:1–5 of an unnamed prophet giving a "sign" that the altar at Bethel would be torn down; in this case the anticipated event does in fact take place, demonstrating the validity of the sign provided by the prophet, or "man of God." In all these cases, the event prefigured by the prophetic "sign" was an unhappy one, destruction or exile.

This latter group of usages, along with the first group, which in a sense are related to destruction (Egyptian) albeit to the advantage of the Israelites, has led to the common supposition that *môpēt* as "portent" is an indicator of ominous events. However "portent," along with the Hebrew word it translates, can more generally indicate prophetic character, for good as well as for evil. In 2 Kgs 20:8, the gravely ill Hezekiah requests from the prophet Isaiah a sign (*'ōt*) that he may be healed; the parallel account in Chronicles (2 Chron 32:24) uses *môpēt* to refer to the prophetic communication to the king of a sign that God will not only heal him but also deliver Jerusalem from the Assyrians.

In either case, the premonitory function of prophets is taken by most commentators (e.g., Baldwin 1972:116) to relate to the succeeding phrase which presents the idea of God's bringing his servant the Shoot (see below). However, as Petitjean has pointed out (1969:169–70), the use of *môpēt* here seems to have a unique context, for which none of the other biblical passages employing that word can provide direct assistance. While we would agree that the Zechariah context stands apart from other biblical usages, we nonetheless would point to a feature of those occurrences that does bear upon this postexilic passage. All of the preceding appearances of *môpēt* deal with a means of communicating God's will or judgment to mankind, and the prophets figure prominently as the instruments, in their actions or demeanors as well as in the dominant mode of their words or oracles, of the divine message to the people.

The period of the restoration of the temple and the reconstitution of community life followed the organization of the pentateuchal literature and the former prophets during the exile—i.e., what Freedman calls the Primary History (1983). Recognition of the authority of the legal materials therein as the mode of judgment and justice, apart from a monarchic system, was a major challenge of the postexilic age and culminated in the promulgation of the Torah by Ezra in the fifth century. An authoritative body of Torah, of legal materials, was in the process of becoming the official repository of divine will, or judgment of the affairs of mankind. Whereas in the preexilic period the prophets loomed as the ultimate recourse in the seeking of God's purposes, the emerging status of the Torah literature as the community rule in the postexilic period gave to the guardians and promulgators of that literature, namely the priests, the function of communicators of divine will that had previously resided with the prophets. The Isaianic passage (8:1–20) in which Isaiah and his children are considered "signs and portents" (v 18) also exhorts the people (vv 19–20) not to turn to mediums or wizards but rather to consult Yahweh, to take note of Isaiah as a message (and messenger) from Yahweh, of the "teaching" *(tôrâ)* and "testimony" *(tĕʿûdâ)*. In the time of Zechariah such functions are becoming associated with the priesthood (cf. Hag 2:11 and NOTES).

Zechariah's utilization of the phrase "men of portent" thus reflects the process of priestly absorption of a function previously associated chiefly with the prophets. Such an understanding of *môpēt* is related to the delineation of Joshua's increased authority as revealed in the use of the term "high priest" (see NOTE to 3:1) and the charge given to him in 3:7 (see NOTES). Joshua's access there to the Divine Council gives him an entrée, formerly associated with prophets, that he needs in the prophetic dimension of his position as mediator of divine judgment. Joshua is not alone in this task, and the other priestly officials at whose head he stands share in this judicial role and constitute a judicial-administrative group. "Men of portent" therefore reflects the prophetic dimension of the priests' responsibilities in the postexilic period, rather than denoting any specifically predictive element. Since this situation represented a departure from the preexilic role of the priesthood, there must have been difficulty, as much of Zechariah seems to reflect, in adjusting to rearranged administrative structures. The succeeding statement about the Shoot is also a response to such difficulties.

Our interpretation is not meant to imply that priests replaced prophets in the postexilic era or that the role of either changed abruptly or dramatically in the opening decades of the restoration. Haggai and Zechariah are holding forth, and the people are responding. The same can be said for the slightly earlier ministries of Deutero-Isaiah and Ezekiel as well as for the somewhat later appearance of Malachi. All of these prophets belong to a tradition and share a basic set of beliefs and values. Yet development over time also exists, with the later prophets showing an increasingly greater awareness of and dependence on sacred literature, although earlier prophets too incorporated traditional elements. The growing prophetic dependency upon authoritative sources in the postexilic period coincides with the gradual shifting of emphasis and authority from prophecy to priesthood. The end stage of that shifting took place about a century later under the aegis of Ezra.

The tendency observed already in Haggai and Zechariah toward priestly ascendency over prophet and king prevails at the time of Ezra and can be related to the virtual disappearance of identifiable prophets or monarchic hopes in the fifth century. The line of David seems to have evaporated; there may be royal descendants still around, but any hope for an immediate monarchic restoration has been abandoned. The disappearance of prophecy is far more difficult to describe, but the availability of written, sacred tradition as revelation from God must have been one crucial factor. The policies of Darius I (see NOTE to 7:1) in encouraging the local legal system to be put into effect, and the positive Yehudite response under Haggai and especially Zechariah to a Persian policy leading toward the establishment of semiautonomy, worked together to create an acknowledgment of the authority of Torah (which would have included prophetic as well as pentateuchal writings).

Zechariah's portrayal of an increasingly authoritative priesthood, particularly in chapter 3, represents a transitional period in the relationship of the community to Torah legislation and to the associated authority to uphold the validity of that material. In its early preexilic stages, going back perhaps to Moses himself, sacred literature was probably seen as more of an inspiration, and as an interpretation of national history, than as legally binding prescriptions and models. At least beginning with the monarchy, legal and executive authority lay with the king and his appointed officials who may well have relied on sacred tradition to carry out their tasks. By the time of Ezra, when the monarchy was effectively eliminated from the picture along with prophecy, the literature itself became the fixed and ultimate authority, the binding law of the Jewish community from that time forward. That Ezra focused on the Pentateuch had the effect of making Yehud a direct heir of the wilderness community led by Moses—a priestly state within the Persian Empire. The sixth century saw developments that anticipated the fifth-century events. Prophets and Davidides were still visible and vocal, but they were already moving toward the sidelines—especially the latter, since there was no longer a kingdom. Sacred literature was on the way to becoming the legal constitution of the community, and the priests as guardians of that literature were beginning to dominate all the leadership responsibilities connected with administering the Torah.

I am indeed bringing. This statement by Yahweh occurs twenty-nine times in the Hebrew Bible and usually has negative implications (Preuss 1975:38). However, in three instances dating from the exilic period (Jer 31:8; 32:42; and Ezek 37:5) the statement is strongly positive in its announcement of some highly desirable aspect of Israel's future condition that will be a reversal of her present state. The usage in Zechariah similarly rings a positive note in its looking ahead to a time when the present unfortunate condition of a nonmonarchic community will be altered by the presence of a Davidic scion.

The participial form of the verb can be compared with the introductory unit ("I am about to shake") in the series of verbs in Hag 2:21–23 that culminate in the announcement of the choosing by Yahweh of Zerubbabel as his servant. Haggai is explicit in naming Zerubbabel, whereas Zechariah leaves the matter open, using two terms of Davidic import ("servant" and "Shoot") in contrast with Haggai's usage of one term ("servant") along with the name Zerubbabel.

my servant. A royalist term, linked with David and appropriate to the problem of dynastic continuity which has provoked this oracle and which has elicited the use of the term "Shoot" *(ṣemaḥ).* See our discussion in the NOTE to Hag 2:23, where "servant" appears in specific reference to Zerubbabel but without the second word ("Shoot") used here by Zechariah.

the Shoot. This designation, *ṣemaḥ,* is based upon an agricultural term meaning the first growth of the vine, grain, or tree, or simply the new growth of the vine or tree, hence "sproutage," as in Hos 8:7 (Andersen-Freedman 1980:481–99) or "foliage." The Syriac and Targum preserve a secondary meaning, "shining." It is often translated "Branch" or "Rod" and has been taken as a play on the name Zerubbabel, "seed [or offspring] of Babylon" (Mowinckel 1959:120, 160; see also NOTE to Hag 1:1), if not as an oblique reference to Zerubbabel himself and his dynastic claims to the throne of David (Bright 1965:143–44; 1981:371). The basic sense of the noun is clearly agricultural, but its associations in the prophetic literature concern the monarchic hope, the future or coming king. The combination of the two meanings, agricultural and dynastic, is both compelling and apt (C. Meyers 1976:151–53).

The metaphoric use of the term *ṣemaḥ* to represent dynastic legitimacy is documented in an early third-century B.C.E. Phoenician inscription form Lapethos in Cyprus where it occurs with the term *ṣdq,* the two words together meaning "legitimate heir" (Donner-Röllig 1968: No. 43,1. 11). Originally discussed in 1893, the text is sixteen lines long and is incised into a partially carved door molding. The relevant line follows mention of a King Ptolemy, without year designation, and the act of bringing dedicatory sacrifices to the altar of Melkart, ". . . for my life and the life of my offspring forever, and the legitimate heir or seed *(ṣmḥ ṣdq)* and his wife and his blood . . ." This inscription is widely cited in support of the interpretation of Jer 23:5 and 33:15, where the "Shoot" is understood to be the Davidic scion. Similarly, a fifth-century B.C.E. Phoenician inscription from Sidon (Donner-Röllig 1968: No. 16) conveys the legitimacy of the dynastic heir, *Bōd 'aštart, Ytnmlk,* by the expression *bn ṣdq.* The term *ṣdq* alone meaning "legitimate heir" also occurs at Ugarit but is more relevant to the Jeremianic passages cited than to this one. For a review of the literature on the subject see Petitjean (1969:199–202).

The repetition of the term *ṣemaḥ* in Zech 6:12 with the imperfect form of the verb, *yîṣmaḥ,* and the fact that in the present instance it follows the royalist designation "my servant" (cf. Hag 2:23), have led to the widespread impression that the prophet is offering his support not only for a monarchic political component in the enterprise of restoration (Kaufmann 1961; Uffenheimer 1964), but perhaps for an explicit messianic component as well (Bright 1981:371). Both of these hopes, it would seem, should they have been explicitly expressed by the prophet, would have been sure to engender the hostility of the Persian authorities. Numerous biblical parallels provide evidence that Zechariah's choice of this word represents his genuine sense of continuity within the

Israelite prophetic tradition. The root ṣmḥ occurs in the context of the future expectation of a Davidic scion in Isa 4:2 and Jer 23:5 and 33:15; botanical or agricultural
imagery frequently expresses the idea that the future king would be "a shoot from the
stump of Jesse" (e.g., Isa 11:1,10), a Davidide of the Bethlehemite line. The real issue,
however, would seem to be the extent to which the prophet is reflecting feelings about
the Davidic dynasty present not only here and in Zech 6:12 but also in Hag 2:23. The
appointment of Zerubbabel as governor by the Persian authorities was surely not intended to arouse secessionist feelings in a population that occupied a strategic territory
on the route to Egypt and Africa. On the contrary, the motivation of the Persians
stemmed from their desire to pacify the subprovince and command its loyalty. The
Persians sought to conciliate Yehud to a certain degree by exploiting the feelings of
exiled Judeans concerning return to their land and the hope of at least some Yehudites
that the House of Yahweh might be restored. From the perspective of Persia, therefore,
Zerubbabel was an important instrument in realizing imperial policy. Zerubbabel could
well have been groomed for his position as governor in the royal Persian court as was a
later governor, Nehemiah (Cook 1983:71). Zerubbabel's Davidic ancestry as grandson
of Jehoiachin was known to all: to the Persian authorities, to the prophets Haggai and
Zechariah, and to the Yehudites who were now witnessing the completion of their
temple and were experiencing the first fruits of apparently tolerant Persian rule (cf.
NOTE to "raise the horn," 2:4 [RSV 1:21]).

Zechariah, therefore, is not necessarily identifying Zerubbabel as the Shoot who will
bring about the return of kingship, for that possibility would have been unlikely under
Darius's policies. Rather, the prophet is employing lively prophetic imagery to point to
a future time when kingship might well be reestablished. Meanwhile, Yehud was to be
administered internally by the priest Joshua and, to a lesser degree, by Zerubbabel.
Joshua's role (see NOTES to 3:7) included a wide range of judicial and administrative
responsibilities. Zerubbabel's obligations, though primarily external—e.g., raising
money for the Persians—still involved him in raising taxes and other payments from
members of the local community. The governor and priest would have had to coordinate their activities. Zerubbabel, as civil leader, was the titular head of state so far as
the Persians were concerned. The second "crown" of monarchy is set aside in the
temple for another time, yet to come (Zech 6:14; see NOTE below). Whether or not
Zerubbabel might himself live to see such a day, and whether some of his contemporaries thought he might, we cannot say. Zechariah employs prophetic future-king imagery
by postponing the day of restored kingship and by not identifying Zerubbabel by name
as the royal figure.

By retaining the ideal of kingship to be reestablished at a future time, and by simultaneously accepting the reality of its absence in the present, Zechariah resolves the
anomaly of a temple's being restored without a monarch's direction. The prophet has
been very careful in stating his case. A monarchic participant is needed for temple
building, and the Davidide Zerubbabel can fill that position. It is only a symbolic
participation, but one that leaves open the possibility that a descendant of Zerubbabel
will occupy the royal throne. Zerubbabel's role in the temple refoundation ceremony
gives it the necessary royal sponsorship. The future hope is proleptically realized in
that event. Zechariah is hardly provoking insurrection. Rather, he is affirming two
things: first, that the ceremonial events surrounding the temple restoration have been

efficacious because of Zerubbabel's involvement as well as because of Joshua's investiture; second, that Zerubbabel's present position and limited authority, though not ideal, have the potential for becoming the legitimate kingship of an independent state.

The position adopted here is similar to a degree to that of Bentzen (1930:493–503), who long ago eschewed any notion of Zerubbabel as a royalist figure supported in rebellion against Persian rule by the prophet and people. By recognizing Zerubbabel's status as governor, the Yehudites avoided confrontation with the Persians. De Vaux advances a similar view of Zechariah's acceptance of the status quo (1972) in his meticulous documentation of the "liberal" policies of Darius I with respect to conquered nations and defended the historicity and plausibility of the decrees of Cyrus the Great and Darius I (cf. our NOTES to "horns of the nations" and "raise the horn" in 2:4 [RSV 1:21] and COMMENT to the Second Vision). Albright, although bothered by an apparent disparity between the person of Zerubbabel, whom he calls "a cautious man of middle age," and the perception of him by Haggai and Zechariah, whom he refers to as "fiery prophets" (1963:88), concludes that the Persian authorities' ultimate aim was to consolidate power in the hands of the priesthood (ibid).

However one might treat the position of Zechariah vis-à-vis Yehud's status in the empire, it is important not to push too far a reconstruction of the prophet's political stance. Zechariah has expectations of God as well as of the people. Not that the people were to be inactive—he encouraged this return to Zion and their work on God's house. Perhaps the prophetic line can be seen as a middle one: opposed to those who would do nothing but sit and wait, and equally opposed to those who would rise up in arms. After all, it would have been a good prophetic tradition for Zechariah to espouse the view that God would have a hand in this dilemma. Some things are best left to the divine spirit, as Zechariah asserts in 4:6, "Not by might and not by power but by my spirit." Whatever would happen would be brought about by Yahweh's decision as much as by human activity.

9. *this stone.* The attempt to identify this stone and understand its meaning in this verse has elicited an enormous scholarly discussion, which is summarized extensively by Petitjean in the context of his analysis of verses 8–10 (1969:161–206). The problems in dealing with the stone are related to the difficulties surrounding the placement of verses 8–10 and the complexities of its connection with verses 6b–10a of chapter 4, which interrupt the flow of the Fourth Vision. In Zech 4:6b–10a, Zerubbabel is mentioned explicitly with respect to temple restoration and in the process "stone" appears twice (see NOTES to 4:7b,10). Furthermore, the stone of 3:9 is said to have "seven eyes" (see NOTE below), a phrase very similar to the one describing the seven eyes of Yahweh that appear in the Interpreting Angel's explication, immediately following the Zerubbabel insertion of 4:6b–10a, of the seven lamps of the menorah.

While the present placement of verses 8–10 follows the investiture passage and develops at several points the theme of that scene, the language of the oracle, particularly since verse 9 has a stone with seven eyes, signals a close connection of that verse with the Zerubbabel insertion into the temple lampstand vision that follows. The ambiguous position of this oracle with respect to the preceding scene on the one hand and to the Zerubbabel passage of 4:6b–10a on the other hand has led to a rather sharp division of scholarly opinion about the stone, the pivotal term upon which the various theories for textual rearrangement and the concomitant diverse interpretations are based. Two major views concerning the meaning of "stone," which is not in this verse identified by any qualifying words as it is in 4:7 and 10, emerge. Though the individual scholars who propose one or the other viewpoint do not necessarily provide identical reasons for so doing, nor do they express their conclusions in exactly the same way, nonetheless we can summarize these two stances and refer the reader to Petitjean's detailed review of nearly all possible arguments (ibid) or to Amsler's more recent and more compact review of the research (1981:83–86).

To those for whom the present attachment of this oracle to the preceding Joshua vision is of paramount importance, the "stone" set before Joshua is a reference to a component of the high priest's garb. Since the robing of Joshua is the central activity of the preceding passage, this supplementary oracle must supply an important detail of that investiture ceremony. The stone, then, would be part of the high priest's apparel; it is a gemstone associated with the crown or turban (cf. v 5 above) of the high priest. Exod 28:36–38 describes an ornament *(ṣîṣ)* engraved with the words "Holy to the Lord" and placed upon Aaron's turban, which was upon his forehead and which served to remove guilt *('āwōn;* "iniquity" below and in v 4 above). The Exodus text provides many points of connection with the "stone" of this verse and supports the contention that Zech 3:9 is a continuation of the description of Joshua's presentation as high priest. Similarly, the two engraved onyx stones of the ephod fasteners (Exod 28:9–12) and the twelve engraved gemstones of the breastplate (Exod 28:17–21), both sets of which list the names of the twelve tribes, may be part of the conceptual reference to the chief priest's garb. The distinct plurality of stones in the Exodus passages would be intentionally contrasted with the one "stone" here; and the omission of that one stone's identity would be necessary, in that it would refer to a variety of gems that are likened to seal stones in the Exodus passage: in addition to onyx, eleven other kinds of gemstones are listed. In this way, the significance of the twelve tribes in the engraving of the stone and consequently in Aaron's function within the careful organization and structuring of the cult would be replaced with whatever is intended by the "seven eyes." Since the latter phrase (see below) would appear to refer to Yahweh, the enigmatic single stone of 3:9 would symbolize the specific reality of God's approbation of Joshua's role. Just as the meaning of the high priest's ephod and breastplate stones is thus shifted as the attention here is focused on one stone, so too the "iniquity" that the headpiece stone of Aaron's raiment removes is perhaps extended here to symbolize a more pervasive sinfulness (see below "iniquity of this land").

However close the points of connection between the stone of verse 9 and the evidence for high priestly apparel in Exodus and in the preceding section may be, the case for another interpretation that would preclude such a connection can likewise be made. Because verse 8 refers to an unnamed Davidide ("my servant the Shoot"), and because the Zerubbabel passage of the next chapter is widely held to be out of position there and hence more properly to be associated with verses 8–10 of chapter 3, the stones of chapter 4 are consequently understood as the referent of the stone of verse 9. Some would even omit Joshua's name from this verse, allowing for a more direct and exclusive association between Zerubbabel and the symbolic "first stone" or "dividing stone" of 4:7 and 10. Those stones themselves are somewhat enigmatic (see NOTES); suffice it to say at this point that, however their specific meaning may be educed, their association with the construction of a major public building is undisputed. The stones of chapter 4 and therefore that of 3:9 are all objects involved in the restoration of the temple. If not an actual building stone, such an item might alternatively be the cosmic rock or point on which a sanctuary is built (cf. 4:7ff.). In another variation on this interpretation, the engraved or incised stones are compared to the tablets or stones of destiny of Mesopotamian tradition, particularly as they affirm that it is the god's will for temple construction to be initiated.

As convincing as many of the arguments are which identify the stone in verse 9 as a priestly gemstone, so too are the arguments which suggest that the stone was part of the temple construction. We have been unable to find any further points or nuances of exegesis or of arrangement of the text that would help to settle the matter in favor of one view or the other. However, we can suggest a way of considering the issue which is in line with our analysis of Zechariah's prophetic mission and which does not necessitate opting for one interpretation over the other.

The very ambiguity of the word "stone" in its present placement may well be intentional. The prophetic missions of both Haggai and Zechariah were centered upon the process of the restoration of the temple in Jerusalem, and those two postexilic prophets were concerned with not only the immediate or pragmatic steps involved in a construction project but also with the ideological setting and meaning of such a project. The restoration community was fully aware of the need for continuity between the new building and the preexilic temple institution. Acknowledgment of that continuity was evidently essential not only to establish the efficacy of the new structure but also, and just as important, to supply the motivation for undertaking its rebuilding despite its ruin and after many decades in which sacrifice and ritual had been abandoned (except, it seems, for altar sacrifice; cf. NOTE to Hag 1:9).

The postexilic restoration of the temple had to be effected under far different conditions from those under which the first temple had been erected and indeed, different from conditions which conformed to temple building ideology throughout the ancient Near East (see Lundquist 1983; NOTES to "House of Yahweh," and "to be built," Hag 1:2; and COMMENT to Hag 1:1–11). The erection of such a major edifice was always a task carried out by kings and constituting a legitimating role in their dynastic claims. That dimension of the sacred enterprise tied the existence of a temple to a monarchic polity in a way that was as inextricable from the typology of temple features (enumerated by Lundquist 1983) as were the other items of that typology, such as divine blessings (cf. NOTE to Hag 2:19, "I will bless you."). Zechariah in particular is the prophet who deals with the problem of the expected monarchic sponsorship by espousing the participation of a governor *(peḥâ)* who was a Davidic scion but who was not allowed to ascend the throne (cf. NOTE above to "Shoot," 3:8).

The question of how a community could erect a "national" temple without a monarch, as we have already asserted, is the dominant issue in the prophecies and visions of Zechariah. That the resolution is neither clear nor simple is perhaps more a function of our failure to appreciate the thought patterns of a sixth-century prophet than a result of any confusion on the part of Zechariah or his redactors. The ambiguity in Zechariah, such as surrounds the identity of the "stone," is more apparent than real. Zechariah supported the proposition that the temple of Yahweh was to be restored, and thus subscribed to the idea that a Davidide must commission that temple's construction and function. Since the restoration of a Judean monarchy in the early years of Darius was not possible, the ideological bond between king and temple had to be retained in an innovative way. His resolution appears ambiguous because it accommodated both the ideology and the actuality. But his time perspective, spanning both future and present to form a whole piece which contains both king and temple, allows him to include all the elements needed for temple building. Those elements seem mutually exclusive for 519 B.C.E., but not if an open-ended future is involved. The work on the building begins and progresses without a king. Broadening of priestly authority in a theocratic format compensates for the immediate administrative needs. The belief in the future restoration of the Davidic monarchy satisfied for the present the ideological need for a royal temple builder.

Zechariah succeeded in supplying a solution to the problem of the postexilic temple's failing to adhere to the temple-king typology through his carefully worded and dramatically presented visions and oracles. In addition, he had the advantage of precedent. The building of the temple of Solomon was thoroughly embedded in ancient Near Eastern temple-building ideology. Yet Israel had had a prior experience in her tradition of building a shrine without benefit of a king. The tabernacle was commissioned by Moses, who may have performed all the functions of a king but was never called by such a title. Moses supervised the construction of a perfectly legitimate sanctuary, upon which to some unknown extent the Solomonic temple must have been modeled. In addition, there was a tent shrine (Jos 18:1) or temple (1 Sam 1:9) at Shiloh before the days of the monarchy. Israel's early political experience differed from that of the Near Eastern states that were characterized by adherence to temple typology, and so she could depart from strict compliance to all its features. The postexilic community therefore knew that a sanctuary could be built without a king and be dedicated by priests alone. The promulgation of the Primary History shortly before the restoration would have contributed to that knowledge, especially since the pentateuchal part of the Primary History focused on Moses' success while the rest of that document revealed the dismal failure of the monarchy. Should one even want a king after the dubious record that kingship had compiled? The decision to give weight to Mosaic traditions over Davidic ones, while not discarding the latter, had already been made by Zechariah's day. The tantalizing possibility of independence that emerged as Persia replaced Babylon inspired Davidic traditions and made Zechariah deal once more with the ever uneasy priestly-royal symbiosis.

The stone of 3:9, therefore, can be understood as participating in both the priestly and the monarchic realm. It is the priestly stone marking the reality of Joshua's dominant role in terms of the internal organization of the Yehudite community. And it is simultaneously the building stone which the reigning monarch would be expected to set in place in the temple that legitimated his reign. The absence of a specific qualifying word attached to "stone" allows for the inclusion of both meanings, a situation which may seem illogical in isolation from the visionary context but which within that context served to reconcile reality with ideology for the people of Zechariah's day.

I set before Joshua. Yahweh is the initiator of this action, which concerns the high priest and the restoration of the temple. Joshua is named, and the object of the verb is the ambiguous stone discussed above. The placing of the stone by Yahweh himself provides divine sanction for the building activities represented by the stone as well as for Joshua's role in carrying out the restoration process. The inscribed stone of this

verse relates to the ceremonial legitimation of the temple work which, as we have
explained, is part of a typology of temple building which included the legitimization of
the dynast as temple builder. Evidence from ancient Near Eastern sources shows that
the name of the king, in his capacity as high priest responsible for temple construction,
was emblazoned upon inscribed stones in the temple precinct (Falkenstein and von
Soden 1953:115). In light of such analogies, the appearance of Joshua alone in this
verse is further testimony to the way in which the priestly role in temple building after
the exile is distinguished from the monarchic emphasis on Solomon (or David, in the
eyes of the Chronicler, 1 Chron 22:1–6) in the case of the first Jerusalem temple.
Joshua's administrative role is being upheld; cf. the end of our NOTE to "engraved"
below.

   one stone. This additional information about the stone is probably intended to set its
singularity against the plurality of stones found in the Exodus description of Aaron's
garb (first NOTE to 3:9). Lipiński (1970) uses the idiom of Judg 9:5 to offer another
interpretation of this phrase. His assertion that it is a time indicator is ingenious but
not convincing, if only because it disrupts the associated imagery. The single inscribed
stone here contrasts with the sets of inscribed stones in the high priest's ephod shoulder
pieces (two stones, each of which signifies by means of an engraved inscription six
tribes) or on his breastplate (twelve stones, each engraved with a name of a tribe). At
the same time, it may refer to the dedicatory stelae or stones introduced to some temple
precincts and inscribed with the names of the dynast responsible for the sacred edifice
(see above). In either case, the singularity of the stone set before Joshua is being
emphasized, maybe to symbolize the unity of the community of which Joshua is the
high priest. Since, however, this stone can likewise be related to the building stone in
the Zerubbabel passage of chapter 4, the focus on *one* stone would be analogous to the
role of a single fragment of the ruined preexilic temple which would have been ceremonially brought forward and laid into the renewed structure (see NOTE to "first stone"),
symbolically conveying the continuity between the two. The representation of a whole
building by *one* component would be similar to the case of Ezek 4:1, where one brick
set before *(ntn lipnê)* the prophet represents an entire city, Jerusalem. Yet, again,
Joshua and not a king is the recipient of the stone in this passage; in that sense, the
institutional continuity of monarchy with respect to temple building is absent.

   seven eyes. Literally the words read "seven [pairs of] eyes" since ʿ*ênāyim* is conven-
tionally taken as a dual. In keeping with an interpretation of the stone so described as a
gemstone, some would read "seven facets" (e.g., Ackroyd 1968:189). Lipiński
(1970:25–29) suggests that ʿ*ayin* is "spring," and represents the cosmic imagery of the
temple encircled by the cosmic waters flowing from seven springs. The former suggestion may not be possible in terms of Hebrew usage, and the latter involves a difficult
rendering of the preceding and succeeding phrases in order to provide a suitable context for such an interpretation. Further, both possibilities limit the range of meanings
that "stone" otherwise, and perhaps intentionally, provides. In fact, ʿ*ayin* ("eye") is a
versatile word in any language, providing a variety of metaphorical usages (collected
briefly by Baldwin 1972:117), and it would not do justice to the style of these verses to
limit its openness by a specific rendering of "facet" or "spring."

   A grammatical problem is posed in this phrase by the improper gender agreement
between the cardinal number "seven" and the feminine dual plural form of "eye"

(ʿênāyim). Normally *šebāʿ* is masculine and construed with feminine nouns, and *šibʿâ* is feminine and construed with masculine nouns. Hence the present situation is anomalous, because the latter form of "seven" is construed with a dual form *ayin*, which is a feminine noun. The expected form would be *šebāʿ* in this situation. Its recurrence in Zech 4:2 with *mûṣāqôt*, a feminine plural noun, is also contrary to standard usage. This inconsistency with classical biblical Hebrew suggests that the early postexilic age was one of confusion with respect to agreement/disagreement between numerals and the nouns they qualify. The inconsistency may only be apparent, and it may actually represent a shift from an earlier standard so that in late Hebrew feminine numbers go with feminine and not masculine nouns.

This unusual pairing may be intentional, in order to relate it to the seven lights of the lampstand in the Fourth Vision. In the following chapter the seven lights of the lampstand are explicitly identified as the seven eyes of god *(šibʿâ-ʾelleh ʿênê yhwh)* and "seven" is the feminine form, referring to *nērōtêhā*, the plural of the masculine noun "lamps," but having a feminine plural form. Perhaps the 3:9 usage has been affected by the chapter 4 language. Indeed, in terms of the meaning of "seven eyes" in 3:9, the relationship of that term to the explicit mention of the "eyes of Yahweh" in the Fourth Vision cannot be ignored. The notion of God's eyes, seven of them, reflecting his full or complete divine vision, is a metaphoric expression for God's omniscience as well as his omnipresence. A stone either with seven facets or with a design of seven eyes or pairs of eyes (given the dual form of "eye") would signify God's involvement with and approval of the construction of his earthly dwelling. A temple-building typology includes the notion that divine favor and assent must be associated with such an enterprise, and in his dedicatory prayer at his completion of the first temple of Yahweh in Jerusalem, Solomon offers his pleas to God that "Thy eyes may be open night and day toward his house" (1 Kgs 8:29; note there the use of the root *pth*, "open," which is suggestive of the language of the following phrase in which *pth*, possibly as a root distinct from that signifying "open," is used). Several other biblical passages likewise attest to the metaphoric usage of God's eyes to indicate divine presence, specifically in the temple: Ps 11:4; 5:6–8 (RSV 5:5–7). Of course there are many additional instances, notably in Psalms, in which the presence of Yahweh everywhere is represented by his "eyes" (e.g., 34:16 [RSV 34:15]; 66:7). One passage outside the psalter is particularly interesting in relation to this verse; in Deut 11:12 God's eyes are said to be upon the land and so assuring its fertility, a situation akin to that of the restoration of peacefulness and fruitfulness that accompanies, in temple-building typologies, the building or restoration of a divine dwelling (cf. our NOTE below in this verse to "remove the iniquity of the land"—i.e., to allow the land to prosper).

make an engraving. The ambiguity surrounding the meaning and symbolism of "this stone" in the first half of the verse is paralleled by the doubt surrounding the precise nature of the engraving that is referred to here. The uses of the noun *pittûaḥ* together with the Piel verb *pth* as a cognate accusative are fairly limited and have a technical meaning. Literally the text reads: "I will engrave its engraving." The traditional reading of the MT is supported by several Greek manuscripts (Symmachus and Theodotian) and the Vulgate. The Peshitta, which is very difficult ("I am opening its gates"), is comparable to Aquila and to a lesser extent the Targum. The LXX is equally difficult, reading "I am digging a trench"; it lacks a personal suffix, though the notion of "cutting" or "digging" probably derives from a strict meaning of the Hebrew root *ptḥ*.

Although many kinds of engravings are referred to in the Bible, including those executed in wood (1 Kgs 6:29; Ps 74:6; the wood was undoubtedly overlaid with gold), the vast majority of references are to the medium of stone (Exod 28:9,11,21,36; 39:6,14,30). The Chronicler includes metals as well in his list of materials on which engravings were done (2 Chron 2:6 [RSV 2:7], 13), thereby providing further lexical support for the variety of materials that could be used in this process—probably some sort of inscribing or incising—in biblical times. We have already indicated (see above, NOTE to "this stone") that among the items to be engraved or inscribed which could have been intended by the designation "stone" were the plate of the high priest's turban, the shoulder-piece stones of his ephod, and the gemstones on his breastplate. Similarly, the information that the stone was to be engraved or incised could apply to either a limestone building stone or a commemorative stela. Either possibility would reflect practices known in the Persian period and well published; see Stern 1982:196–228 and Donner-Röllig 1968, Parts I and II.

The question evoked by this phrase, which is derived from the practice of inscribing solid objects (whether of stone, wood, or metal), concerns the nature or content of such an inscription. One cannot go beyond the realm of conjecture in dealing with such a question. However, the likelihood that the engraving was epigraphic and not pictographic in nature, and more specifically that it was a name, is perhaps somewhat more than mere conjecture. In the texts in Exodus which set forth the details of priestly garb, the writer is at pains to stress that the engraved stones are marked with tribal names. The communication of this information is accomplished through parallel phraseology: the stones were engraved, and they were thus like signets. Since signets (cf. NOTE to Hag 2:23) legally represented their owner, the design and words on them identified that individual. Hence an engraving on stone, at least with respect to the high priest's apparel, would be some mark of an individual. Alternatively, a building inscription would contain the name of the builder (king) responsible for the building, as the many foundation deposits from Mesopotamia indicate (Ellis 1968). A mark or name indicating an individual, human, or god is thus likely, and it is only the identity of that individual which remains conjectural. Even if such a stone commemorated a high priest, it is not assured that the name "Joshua" was so inscribed, since the inscription on his turban piece contained God's name. That latter inscription, the name of God, is equally a possibility, especially since the guilt removal associated with this stone can be connected with that inscription on the turban (see above, vv 4–5). Finally, the association of this passage with the Zerubbabel section below may imply that Zerubbabel's name appeared.

The ambiguity of the stone thus persists in the issue of the identity of the one memorialized on the stone, though the probability that it was to be an individual's name rather than some long statement or dedicatory phrase can be sustained. In any event, since the nature of the oracle is visionary, we need not read into the text a historical event. Prophetic language, therefore, provides the appropriate medium for expressing an ambiguity such as the one which existed as the Yehudites hoped for a revived monarchy and realized that it was not possible under Persian rule.

We would add one further observation to this discussion of "engraved." If we are correct in our deduction that an individual's name was inscribed on this stone associated with Joshua, especially if it was a signet or seal, we can discern in that fact another dimension of Zechariah's use of stone imagery. In the preexilic period the appearance of personal names on seals or signets, as recovered in archaeological excavations, was fairly widespread, whereas in the Persian period such artifacts tend to be without inscription (Stern 1982:200). Those few containing names from the late sixth and early fifth century may have belonged to high officials. Cross (1966:204, n. 12), in analyzing two seals bearing a legend among over 125 seals or impressions found at Wadi Daliyeh, suggests that Persian policy dictated that only high officials could hold inscribed seals. If this was the case, Zechariah's employment of language that can be associated with stones that bear personal names may be another example of the way in which he provides sanctions for Joshua's position in the restoration community. Since inscribed stones were restricted, it seems, to official usage, Joshua as recipient of the engraved stone apparently is receiving authoritative powers.

take away the iniquity of that land. The ideas in this passage must be understood in light of the removal of Joshua's "iniquity" *('āwōn)* in 3:4 above (see NOTE). There Joshua's "filthy garments" are symbolic of his impure state prior to being cleansed, or made fit, for assuming the high priestly office. "Iniquity" in that context is a very complex issue, dealing less with personal sin or wrongdoing, and more with the accumulated uncleanness of both Joshua and the people he represents as high priest as the result of exile. The uncleanness derives both from the sinfulness which, at least on the part of the ancestors of the exile, brought about deportation, and from the impurity caused by living outside the homeland, i.e., the Holy Land (cf. 2:16 [RSV 1:20]).

In the present context the focus has shifted away from Joshua alone and includes the eschatological "Shoot" of verse 8, the enigmatic "stone" of verse 9, and the "iniquity of the land" in the latter part of verse 9. We have pointed out above that although "the stone" set before Joshua can have a high priestly association, it can also signify the preeminent stone of the foundation of the temple (see NOTE to "this stone" in 3:9). Petitjean (1966:53–58; 1969:179–85) and Halpern (1978:170) have proposed that in such a setting, the remission of guilt is related to the Mesopotamian phenomenon of the resolution of social disorder upon the founding or refounding of a temple. Most recently, Lundquist has dealt with this idea as part of a common Near Eastern temple typology: if the calamitous destruction of a temple is viewed as the "result of social and moral decadence and disobedience to God's word" (1983:4), then the restoration of that destroyed institution is seen as reversing the destructive disorder. The persistent appearance of such a theme in Mesopotamia provides a conceptual backdrop for what is being uttered in the second half of verse 9. The Hebrew root *mwš* ("take away"), which is presupposed by the Vulgate, closely parallels Akkadian *māšu,* "exorcise."

Another important feature of this statement, in contrast to the removal of Joshua's iniquity in verse 4, is the use of the phrase "of that land" to denote that from which the iniquity is to be removed. The removal of iniquity from a territory at the time of temple building also appears in the cuneiform literature. Not only is social order restored at such an occasion, but also the arable land is revitalized so that its yield increases abundantly. In Gudea Cylinder A we read "when the foundations of my temple will be laid, abundance will come. The great field shall bring forth for thee (fruit)" (as translated by Bewer 1919:129). The "land" will yield abundantly as a result of the new temple activities (cf. NOTE to Hag 2:19 and see below NOTE on v 10). The addition of the phrase "of that land" provides an appropriate transition to the idyllic vision of the land which follows in the next verse of the Supplementary Oracle, verse 10. In this connection, note that Deut 11:12 associates the eyes of Yahweh with the fertility of the land (ʾrṣ), the word used here and also in Zech 8:12, where the theme of abundance appears again. The eyes of Yahweh, symbolic of God's presence, are associated both with temple building and fertility of the land. The removal of iniquity from the land involved both these aspects of the temple's role as a central organizing institution in the ancient Near Eastern world. The construction of a temple was closely associated with the promise of economic prosperity and productivity and also with the establishment of social order. Zechariah in this oracle at the end of verse 9 is also asserting the fitness of his people to restore their temple after the years of sin and exile which have rendered them, or their ancestors, unfit even to live in their land.

10. *In that day*. The correct interpretation of this expression in the present instance hinges upon one's overall understanding and exegesis of the Supplementary Oracle, Zech 3:8–10. Those who would identify "the Shoot" as the Messiah would tend to translate "on that day" and identify it with the messianic day of the end of time (Rudolph 1976:102–3; Ackroyd 1968:191; Kaufmann 1977:287), the dawning of a new age. In such an understanding the expression has a technical connotation of the "last day," that metahistoric moment which witnesses the end of historic time and ushers in posthistorical time.

Lipiński (1975:29) and Baldwin (1972:118), however, have pointed out that "in that day" really means "on the *same* day." Petitjean (1969:189) more specifically relates the expression *bayyôm hahûʾ* here and in Zech 6:10 to the day of the refoundation of the temple, a view with which we are sympathetic, although we construe the activities of "that day" in a slightly different way (see above NOTE to "the stone" in 3:9). The expression might refer to a specific moment in time which initiates conditions leading to the beatific image that follows. In the common Near Eastern temple typology, stability and abundance attend temple foundation and/or dedication. If the purpose of the Supplementary Oracle is to relate the activities of the refounding of the temple to a present that is only in transition to an anticipated future, then "in that day" can also refer to the eschatological future that we may associate with the Shoot. Joshua's present is indeed full of promise and hope but the language of verse 10 suggests that it will give way ultimately to another future.

each man to his companion. In the new and improved circumstances that are to be ushered in, people will speak to one another in harmony. This common expression (cf. "against the other," 8:10,17) conveys the idea of social stability, as evidenced in close, harmonious interpersonal relations and reciprocity (cf. Zech 2:15 [RSV 2:11]; 6:15; 8:22–23; and Mal 3:16). The phrase provides an important link to the stereotypical expression that follows. The plural verb ("you will call out") which introduces the phrase indicates that this part of the oracle is addressed to a general audience of Yehudites. Verse 10 thus stands somewhat apart from verses 8–9, which concern the high priest and his entourage.

to the one under the vine and to the one under the fig tree. The vision of contentment closely parallels the text of Mic 4:4 and 1 Kgs 5:5 (RSV 4:25). Similar words (in 2 Kgs 18:31) are attributed to the Assyrian king who tries to lure the Israelites away from

King Hezekiah: "Make your peace with me and come out with me; then every one of you will eat of his own vine, and every one of his own fig tree . . ." (RSV). The picture of peace and stability along with fertility and abundance of food accords well with the imagery of this verse (cf. "take away the iniquity" above). Hag 2:19 likewise identifies the day on which abundance will begin with the day on which the temple work begins, the twenty-fourth day of the ninth month of the second year of Darius—i.e., December 18, 520 (2:18; see NOTES to Hag 2:18–19). Then and only then will a situation of plenty replace a circumstance of want (1:6). The vine and the fig, the pomegranate and the olive (2:19) symbolize the bounty that springs forth when God's dwelling on earth is rebuilt or rededicated.

In addition to abundance, the temple is associated with a state of harmony and stability (Lundquist 1983). The patent similarity of this verse to Mic 4:4, which represents one of the most majestic visions of the messianic age in Hebrew Scripture, cannot go unnoticed. However, the passages in 1 and 2 Kings, in which much the same phraseology of "vines and fig trees" occurs, clearly refer to historical albeit idealized situations. Although Zechariah is clearly cognizant of the Israelite belief in an idealized, eschatological future, in the oracle of 3:6–10 he projects its realization to a much later date. The striking prophetic language of an ideal future would be used by Zechariah as added emphasis to his commitment to temple restoration and in support of his urging the people to carry through on that task. The imagery of abundance is resumed in the oracle in Zech 8:12, and details of the future time in its universalized and eschatological form are provided in 8:22–23 (when all nations will go to Jerusalem to entreat the favor of Yahweh). It is to that time and to that day that the temple rebuilding will someday lead. Clearly *that* day is rendered nearer and more attainable by the situation which has been effected by Persian political wisdom and decisions and by the Yehudite response to Persian policy.

COMMENT

Heavenly Court and Investiture, 3:1–7

Zechariah 3 is unique among the visions and oracles that constitute this prophet's work. While it dramatically and unmistakably proclaims the content of a visionary experience, it nonetheless stands well apart from the structure that characterizes the sequence of the other (seven) visions. Several features can be observed to remove this passage from the typical visionary mode of Zechariah. We shall consider those features before turning to the vision's content and meaning, for its literary discreteness in and of itself has significance for the overall structure and focus of Part Two (1:7–6:15).

First, unlike the presentation of the Seven Visions, this passage does not introduce a person or object to the prophet's consciousness as a vehicle for conveying a message concerning the issues of his day. While the contemporary world of Zechariah permeates the narrative of this chapter, it does so in a much more overt way than do the visions proper. A key official is mentioned by name (Joshua) and his role as high priest is explicitly established. The

specific meaning of some of the props in the scenes may escape our comprehension, but that is a result of our great distance from Jerusalem of the sixth
century B.C.E. Presumably the prophet's audience was more familiar with the
various items of priestly garb and their significance than we are.

Second, while objects and persons are critical to the passage's intent, their
importance is revealed not through identifying and explanatory statements or
oracles but rather by means of the parts they play in the dramatic action that
unfolds in the heavenly arena. In turn, the message is conveyed to an earthly
audience through the prophet's witness. Although the Sixth Vision possesses a
measure of movement in the two scenes through which its message unfolds
before Zechariah's eyes, and several other visions imply that some activity is
taking place, the Seven Visions nonetheless are largely static. Such movement
as there is in the other visions is symbolic, and the message is not embedded
specifically in a visionary course of events as it is for chapter 3.

Third, the prophet is cast in a double role: he is witness to the scenes of this
vision and simultaneously is an actor in them, or at least in the second part of
the investiture passage. Perhaps there is a hint of such a combined function in
the Third Vision, in which the prophet directly addresses a character in the
visionary field: he opens the dialogue by asking where the man with the measuring-cord is going (2:6 [RSV 2:2]). However, that apparent exception to the
prophet's single role as witness to the Seven Visions and not participant in
them is in reality not an exception, since the prophet's part there is only to
assist in revealing that a symbolic act rather than person or object is the focus
of the vision. The prophet does not himself participate in the action. Zechariah
here is present as the first scene opens, and he initiates the climactic action of
the second scene on the basis of what he observes there.

Fourth, Yahweh himself is a direct actor in the drama. In most of the Seven
Visions, his presence is strongly felt, particularly through oracular pronouncements integrated into the visionary narrative, as in Visions 1, 3, and 5. Yahweh
also actually appears in several of the Visions, specifically Visions 2 and 7. Yet
even in those appearances his role is subsidiary to the symbolic objects that
dominate all of the Seven Visions and does not constitute an intrinsic contribution to the meaning of the visions. Instead it is the Interpreting Angel, as
God's representative, whose presence dominates the Seven Visions so that
Yahweh himself becomes an offstage actor whose presence is felt but who
remains unseen. The role of Yahweh in chapter 3 stands in sharp contrast to
that situation. Yahweh, not an angel, appears at the outset, to introduce the
prophet to the scenes that follow. And Yahweh is on center stage in the first
scene, where he confronts the Accuser and issues a resounding pronouncement that affects the subsequent action. In that pronouncement, however,
Yahweh peculiarly refers to himself by name in the third person, even though
it is clear that he is the speaker. Perhaps this is an accommodation to the
mode of the Seven Visions, where the Interpreting Angel does the speaking.

Fifth, the action is moved forward through the interaction of rather a large cast of characters for a drama that plays from start to finish within seven biblical verses. While interaction among visionary figures finds a place in several of the Seven Visions, their action—or rather their symbolic meaning—is elicited through the framework of a dialogue between the prophet and a particular angelic figure, the "angel-who-speaks-with-me." This Interpreting Angel is essential to the structure of the other Seven Visions, hence his absence in this one further sets it apart from the rest of the visionary experiences of Zechariah. In drawing attention to the missing presence of the Interpreting Angel, we do not wish to neglect the fact that other heavenly beings are present. The "Angel of Yahweh," who has a leading role, may be related to a persona of several other visions, such as Vision 1 and perhaps Vision 3. However, we take this point of contact with other visions to be only one of several which would be expected since they are all expressions of visionary experiences. We reiterate that the absence of the Interpreting Angel is a significant divergence from the Seven Visions. Even if the Interpreting Angel is to be identified with the Angel of Yahweh, he is never called "Interpreting Angel" in this vision. The absence of the Interpreting Angel is the other side of a coin: the prophet's direct involvement is the first side. Since the prophet is a participant in the scene after he comprehends on his own the proceedings that he witnesses at the start, the mediating role of a personal interpreter, of an angel to explain things to him, is superfluous.

The combined force of these features has made us hesitant simply to designate 3:1–7 as a vision. Its importance apart from the seven other visions must be noted, yet its correspondence to them in general theme and tone cannot be ignored. Hence we call the visionary scene of this chapter a "prophetic vision," thereby indicating both its experiential nature and also the role of the prophet within it. The other visions are of course also prophetic, but they are more aptly labeled "symbolic visions." Zechariah 3 is not given a number within the visionary sequence, yet it has for good reason been placed within that sequence. For some critics the divergences from the visionary sequence have either not been fully noted or have been deemed not of sufficient consequence; thus many commentaries count eight visions, with this as the fourth or even the fifth by virtue of rearranging the MT and inserting chapter 3 after chapter 4 (e.g., Mitchell 1912; Beuken 1967; Baldwin 1972; Rudolph 1976; Mason 1977a). There are in fact eight visions, but this one is so different as to merit a separate label. The result is that Zechariah Part Two (the visions) is composed of seven visions plus one vision. The numbering itself, however, is not so important as the recognition that one vision is extremely distinct. The text itself makes no mention of how many visions the prophet has experienced, and any system imposed on them cannot be other than a scholarly construct.

Because the designation of chapter 3 as a fourth vision has considerable support, it may be helpful to discuss its place in the overall structuring of Part

Two as well as to analyze its internal features in order to justify further our reluctance to include it among the numbered visions. In our Introduction, the structure of the Seven Visions is graphically arranged in two charts. In both of them the special properties of the number seven, long recognized in the Semitic world, can be perceived in the way they have been effectively and subtly utilized by the prophet to represent his view of the world and of the integral part of Yehud, Jerusalem, and the temple within that world. Yet there are critical dimensions of that central focus, the Jerusalem temple, which affect more than that building itself, and the prophet has used several means to interweave them into the visionary sequence. Those dimensions include the facets of community life and expectations which must be *altered* as a result of a temple's being restored under Persian imperial domination and not as an institution of an independent kingdom. In other words, the roles of both priest and king must be reconceived. Zechariah artfully achieves this both in the visionary sequence—in the climactic Fourth Vision, which is the only one set directly in the temple—and in several other prophetic inclusions such as this Prophetic Vision, the Zerubbabel insertion of chapter 4, and the Crowning scene of 6:9–15.

The issue Zechariah faced with respect to priest and king was the shifting configuration of ecclesiastical and civil leadership, with the accompanying restructuring of offices and responsibilities. Such shifts in institutional patterns characteristically involve uncertainty and tension on the part of the population affected. Zechariah's function in part was to support the changes and allay the fears. In carrying out this mission he departed from the customary patterning of the visions. Instead he used the somewhat more dramatic and certainly more direct expression of God's plan that the Heavenly Court and Investiture followed by the Supplementary Oracle provides. It is still within the structure of a vision, although a vision differently conceived, a vision of the Heavenly Court. In this way, the prophet musters the strongest possible heavenly sanctions for the earthly decisions that his audience must make. His shift in the use of the visionary mode parallels his encouragement of the shift in leadership roles. Although the lampstand vision stands alone in the center of his wide visionary field, the scenarios of chapter 3 precede it and inform its startling imagery of two equivalent and equally authoritative leaders in a theocratic state. Yet the lampstand vision remains an ideal for the restored temple. It mentions no names; only this prophetic vision along with the Supplementary Oracle (3:8–10), the Zerubbabel insertion (4:6b–10a), and the Crowning scene (6:9–15) can reconcile the realities of Yehud with the ideals, revised though they may be, of traditional prophetic expectations inextricably bound up with the concept of Yahweh's dwelling restored in Zion.

Viewing this chapter as somewhat distinct from the Seven Visions, yet containing information integral to them, allows the sequence of seven to retain its special character and permits the central one to stand alone with its image of dyarchy. Furthermore, our arrangement recognizes the Prophetic Vision as a unit which accords with the other elements of Part Two that are interspersed into the visionary materials but are distinct literary pieces. Finally, as a special and unique unit, as a prophetic vision, it involves the prophet directly in giving divine authority to the resolution of a sensitive political issue. *Rebuilding the temple* required divine sanction through prophetic messengers. Yet a temple had strong and immediate precedent. *Restructuring the community* in a manner without immediate precedent demanded the most unassailable divine authority. The prophetic vision of chapter 3, merging Zechariah's particular visionary genius with the mainstream of Hebraic prophecy, provided an authenticity suitable to the issue it addressed.

Let us review the cast of characters, some of whom we have already mentioned in this discussion. The prophet, of course, is now both witness to and participant in the drama, and Yahweh himself has the crucial role. In addition, at least one angelic figure is specified, in verses 1 and 4; and the probability is that many more (a host of) divine beings constitute the supporting cast. In verse 4 a plural participle designating those "standing" represents an unspecified number of angelic figures. Likewise, the plural subjects of the verbs "put," "placed," and "dressed" in verse 5 do not refer to the "Angel of Yahweh" who is standing nearby, but rather to an ancillary and vague company of other angels. We simply are not told and cannot know how many there are; and indeed, Yahweh's angelic courtiers should not be so limited.

One further member of the cast, "the Accuser," is specified. Our NOTES to "the Accuser" in verse 1 review the evidence for the gradual personification of the concept of opposition to Yahweh's will. It is enough to reiterate here that, in the context of Yahweh's court, the function of "the Accuser" is not so much to represent demonic forces per se as it is to provide a vehicle for demonstrating Yahweh's awareness of *all* facets of the case before him and to represent as Prosecutor that unstated case, known only from Yahweh's response to it. Finally, and perhaps most important, the central figure of the prophetic vision is Joshua the high priest. Apart from the editorial superscriptions in 1:1 and 1:7, this is the first appearance by name of a historical figure in Zechariah. His centrality to this vision bespeaks the importance of his historical role as well as contributing to the distinctiveness of the literary context. The issue of the high priest's position in contemporary Yehudite society was evidently one fraught with tension, so that it has worked upon the prophetic imagination of Zechariah and evoked this extraordinary portrayal of his understanding of God's will with respect to the priesthood.

The setting for the drama that will communicate God's will to the prophet's audience is nothing other than the Heavenly Court of Yahweh. Zechariah stands in good prophetic company in his utilization of this image, which is ultimately grounded in the mythological language describing the structure of the Canaanite assembly of the gods, though the actual figure of an accuser is not found in Canaanite mythology. Various elements of the technical terminology depicting God's court appear in this vision, and we refer the reader to our NOTES on such words as "standing before," "Angel of Yahweh," and also "the Accuser," all in verse 1, for an indication of the vocabulary of the Divine Council setting.

The concept of Yahweh effecting his will in the arena of human affairs is given the reassuring dimension of divine justice through the imagery of the Heavenly Court. Yahweh's decisions vis-à-vis humanity reflect consideration of all ramifications. That Yahweh does not act without full knowledge of a given situation is emphasized by the courtroom scene and the angelic minions who compose it. God has gathered data from every conceivable corner—from the "four corners" of the world, as the opening and closing visions assert—and on the basis of such complete information, only a judicious and fully authoritative ruling can issue forth.

The prophetic vision of chapter 3 brings us into the exalted chambers of the Heavenly Court. The prophet establishes the setting at once: all the major characters are introduced in the opening verse: Joshua, the Angel of Yahweh, and the Accuser, with Yahweh himself showing these actors to the prophet Zechariah. Joshua is the first mentioned of those pointed out by Yahweh, and his centrality to the ensuing drama is established forthwith. Two contiguous but distinct scenes take place, to be followed by an oracular statement that reveals the significance of what has happened.

In the first scene (vv 2–4) Yahweh immediately proclaims by his sharp dismissal of the Accuser that whatever charges may have been brought concerning Joshua cannot even be entered into the record. The Accuser is not allowed to speak. He is rebuked, so God obviously knows what he was planning to say, and his unspoken arguments are further forestalled by the great irony of the rhetorical question about the "brand plucked from the fire." If an individual is rescued from grave danger there is a purpose, and nothing can be allowed to thwart that purpose. Joshua's return to Jerusalem is the key to the divine sanction for his being installed as priestly leader.

At this point props are introduced in the form of Joshua's tainted clothing, bearing the filth caused by the "fire," probably a metaphor for exile from which he has escaped and hardly suitable for a representative of the people who will soon stand ceremonially before Yahweh in his earthly habitation, the temple. The mention of Joshua's iniquity and the emphasis on clean garments reveal Joshua's plight. A child of the fire, Babylon, he is unclean from living in an unclean land, the descendant of sinful and impure people. But he has not suffered the fate of his priestly forebears. He has lived to return. But can he shed the corporate uncleanness of his people? Will God allow this? Has divine anger abated? The rhetorical question has shown what God's response is to these questions raised necessarily by Joshua's unclean condition, and his angelic assistant then assumes the authority for divesting Joshua of his unfit apparel. As the scene closes, Joshua is addressed directly for the first time. The angel who had ordered his divestment speaks to Joshua and in so doing lets the audience know that not only will the symbolic offensive garments be shed, but also a new set of priestly raiment representing purity and fitness will be donned.

The next scene (vv 5–7), which begins with the prophet himself assuming a speaking part, is linked to the first scene. The first scene ends with statements about clothing Joshua, and that is how the second one begins. The prophet has witnessed God's judgment and now takes up the arduous prophetic task of interpreting that decision to the community of God's people. Zechariah issues the orders for a special headpiece to be placed upon Joshua's head. In so doing, he acts upon what he has learned by being onstage for the first scene. Because he knows of God's approval, he can initiate the delineation, via the symbolic apparel of high office, of Joshua's role. The prophet's command is obeyed and then the Angel of Yahweh delivers the charge, another divine pronouncement setting forth in words what the vestment of Joshua has represented visually.

The prophetic vision reveals in dramatic form the mediational activity involved in prophecy, with the first scene corresponding to his taking steps to have God's judgment carried out in the human realm. The prophet is assisted in both these facets by the heavenly beings surrounding Yahweh and attending him in the domain of his Divine Council. These features of the prophetic process somehow do not come as a surprise. Perhaps they had not been so extensively and finely drawn before, but earlier Hebrew prophets have more than hinted at their existence. What astonishes us, then, is the final statement of the second or vestment scene, announcing that Joshua too shall have access to the Divine Council and the presence of Yahweh. The high priestly prerogative of entering the earthly sacral sphere of the interior of the Jerusalem temple will now be enhanced by Joshua's admission to the Divine Council. This establishes a dimension to the high priesthood unprecedented in the biblical sources.

Having said so much about the unique form of this dramatic prophetic vision and its extraordinary depiction of the interaction of divine and human characters, we can consider its historical meaning. First let us examine the circumstances in Zechariah's world that evoked this special vision. Our premise is that this vision's exceptional quality, its partaking of the visionary mode and yet transcending that mode by virtue of its particularly rich mixture of the human experience with the divine, signifies that it is rooted in an intensely critical period in the restoration era. If the irruption of the divine into the earthly realm is a concomitant of crucial transition periods in human history, then the prophetic vision of chapter 3 must signal such a transition or shift in the life of the Israelite community.

In fact it is not so difficult to determine what that shift might be. Our review of the history of this period in the Introduction highlighted the well-known facts of the Judean exile to Babylon following the destruction of Jerusalem and termination of the monarchy, and of the subsequent restoration in Palestine of a semiautonomous unit of the Persian Empire called Yehud. This province, or more likely subprovince, was superimposed in part upon the territory and populace that had constituted the Davidic monarchy. Hence its internal organization achieved stability insofar as it could capitalize upon existing remnants of community structure. The need to formalize a system of self-governance was particularly acute during the early years of Darius. This emperor attended to the arrangement and administration of the vast territories and multitudinous national groups that composed the imperium, whereas his predecessors, caught up in the momentum and power of conquest, had treated lightly, if at all, the organization of the territories.

Darius's political and economic policies with respect to Yehud brought about organizational emphases or changes: 1. Restoration of the temple, a politically strategic ploy from the viewpoint of the Persians, brought the role of chief priest to the fore; Joshua was an important administrator, along with Zerubbabel, of that project and also was soon to resume the full responsibilities of a functioning high priesthood, once the temple was restored. 2. The Yehudites, like other imperial subjects, found themselves required to deliver tribute, or regular tax revenues, to the empire for the first time after 522 B.C.E. Zerubbabel as governor and titular head of the government would have been charged with that responsibility as well as other responsibilities in a civilian administration. This left Joshua with supervision of the normal temple revenues and also of the extra financing for temple work. Since the temple was not now part of a royal administrative complex, Joshua probably had access to and control of a significant part of the annual budget of the province. With Zerubbabel's financial role being defined by his obligations to Persia, Joshua's as chief priest were redefined by the internal workings of the Yehudite economy. 3. The desire of Darius to establish peace in his empire and loyalty among his subjects involved not only his selective encourgement of local institutions but also his attention to the internal stability of the conquered peoples. Wherever possible, local systems of justice were encouraged. For the Yehudites, the ancient Torah laws were already authoritative in some form, but the Judean king as locus of judicial authority no longer existed. The priests thus resumed and extended the adjudicatory powers inherent in their traditional roles. That they ruled on cultic matters is obvious, but they also had in the premonarchic period resolved difficult cases (e.g., Num 5:11–31; Exod 22:6–12 [RSV 22:7–13]; cf. the roles of Eli and Samuel as priests and judges). As teachers and/or custodians of pentateuchal materials, they were able to fill the gap left by the cessation of royal legislative and judicial powers (cf. NOTES to "flying scroll" and "twenty cubits" in the Fifth Vision, 5:1–2).

These converging factors at the outset of Darius's reign led to a redefinition of the chief priest's range of authority and responsibility in the postexilic period. The changes no doubt had gradually begun to take shape during the decades after the destruction of Judea and perhaps even more visibly once the Persians controlled Palestine after 550. Yet the broad redistribution of powers that can be glimpsed in various passages of postexilic prophecy becomes official during the temple restoration process. Without a king to effect the temple building, the priest must step in as Yahweh's earthly representative. The chief priest of the monarchic period has truly become the "high priest" of the restoration. The Persian recognition and encouragement of the temple work constituted an overt external authorization of Joshua's expanded power; Zechariah's visions, and this prophetic vision in particular, functioned within the community as ideological justification for the transition.

The drama of the Heavenly Court and Investiture scene leaves us with a further question, which cannot easily be resolved. Do the heavenly scenes Zechariah has envisioned and expressed in the vivid narrative of his prophetic vision reflect any actual earthly ceremony? Since there is no independent witness for Joshua's induction into office, we cannot do more than speculate. Joshua in fact was already recognized as high priest and by that time (after February 15, 519 B.C.E.) was functioning in that capacity, for Haggai's prophetic utterances of August 29, September 21, and October 17, 520 B.C.E., address Joshua by that title. The donning of robes of office, an act vividly described in Zechariah's vision, suggests that an investiture took place.

In the absence of other information, we suggest that the recent temple refoundation ceremony (see NOTE to 4:7, "premier stone"), in which Joshua shared the symbolic role normally associated with a monarch, was a time of great concern for a people. For them the concept of temple building and refurbishing was inextricably bound up with a Davidide. Zechariah's sensitivity to such anxiety gave rise to this visionary experience of Joshua's heavenly vestment. The vision was a message to the people from Yahweh. God himself had presided at an investment ceremony in which Joshua with his broad powers and responsibilities was clothed in pure garments and a special headpiece. His fitness for the postexilic office of high priest, based in the temple about to be restored for Yahweh, was symbolically established as the clean robes replaced his impure clothing; and the extension of the priestly role was sanctioned as a headdress with a new designation was placed upon his head. Should these symbolic actions have left any doubts in the minds of those who witnessed them via the prophet's words, the reporting of Yahweh's charge to Joshua and of Joshua's ongoing access to Yahweh's council should have finally removed them. Joshua had at some point in his life been delivered from great danger. Perhaps the exile is all that is meant by the "fire" from which he was saved, or perhaps he had actually been thrown into the Persian prison. Either way, his rescue was part of God's plan, and the removal of all uncleanness and guilt so that he could serve at the temple was also God's will.

In sum, we see no reason to rule out an actual installation ceremony. The people's fears about whether or not they could restore the temple and whether or not their sins had been removed could only be handled through the visible means of a priestly inauguration. Work on the temple itself was initiated with a ceremonial refoundation. Shouldn't the restoration of a high priest to the ancient office likewise be marked with a public ceremony, particularly if the scope of his office had altered so it now needed recognition and acceptance? Although it is hard to imagine any effective substitute for a formal public event, an alternative view would have Zechariah's reporting of a heavenly investiture serve the same function of assurance and sanction.

Zechariah was an accepted prophetic figure in a period in which the authenticity of Israelite prophetism was firmly established (see Harrelson 1982). Zechariah himself appears not to have been questioned in his prophetic role. On the contrary, he is later cited by Ezra for his success in rallying his countrymen. His visionary experience of Joshua's formal accession to the Heavenly Court could have been tantamount, in its strong symbolic value, to any earthly ceremony that might have been arranged. Because of the place of prophecy in the community and because of the acknowledgment of Zechariah as a true prophet, his visions would have been taken as the sacred and valid expression of the will of Yahweh. Maybe the best conclusion is that the two things, earthly investment plus prophetic vision of heavenly investment, worked in tandem to achieve the desired effect.

Supplementary Oracle, 3:8–10

This oracle constitutes the first of three additional major oracular units within Part Two. The second, the so-called Zerubbabel cluster, is included within the framework of the Fourth Vision (4:6b–10a); the third is the oracular summation contained in the Crowning scene (6:9–15). Unlike the oracular portions of the First and Third Visions and the oracular Expansion of the first three visions (2:10–17 [RSV 1:18–2:13]), which are rather more abstract and which in any case do not allude to historical personages by name, these other three oracles, two of which are part of the central, Fourth Vision, directly concern the two most important leaders of the day, Joshua the high priest and Zerubbabel the governor. Furthermore, they all—especially this one and the Zerubbabel passage of chapter 4—make reference to the act of the temple restoration as well as to an actual ceremony of temple refoundation.

The placement of these three verses at the end of the prophetic vision of Joshua and the Priestly Vestments has not unexpectedly occasioned much critical discussion since the days of Wellhausen. Although many recent treatments of the Supplementary Oracle have proposed to treat it as if it had once been contiguous with the Zerubbabel insertion of chapter 4 (vv 6b–10a), we have chosen to deal with it in the context of the prophetic vision of chapter 3 because of our understanding of the brief redactional history of Zechariah 1–8.

The canonical arrangement of the Book of Zechariah has included the material at the end of the prophetic vision and not in the Fourth Vision where it is often placed. We feel this is a fact that cannot be readily dismissed.

In the Introduction we have argued that First Zechariah (cc 1–8) together with Haggai was promulgated or presented in its final form some time immediately prior to the rededication of the Second Temple in 515 B.C.E. but after the ceremony of refoundation in 520. Rearrangements of the text presuppose an intermediate stage in the history of transmission of the text that was either the result of scribal error (Halpern 1978:169–70, n. 13) or represented an earlier form of redaction (Kaufmann 1977:254–84 and others). Similarly, it has also been suggested that verses 8–10 existed independently at an earlier stage (Rothstein 1910:87–89). Since an earlier version of all or parts of Zechariah still remains nothing more than a hypothetical possibility, we propose to understand the text in its present order. Prophecies in this period could well have achieved written form and arrangement very soon after their utterance (cf. NOTES to "proclaim," 1:14 and 7:7,13).

Before explicating the Supplementary Oracle in its canonical context, we will briefly indicate the dominant alternative form of organization. Verse 3:8 is usually considered the introductory directive for a larger oracular cluster which consisted of both 4:6b–10 (the Zerubbabel insertion) and 3:9–10, the concluding verses of the Supplementary Oracle. If the scribal error theory is to be entertained, the assumption would be that a scribe unwittingly skipped from "seven eyes" of 3:9 to "seven eyes" of 4:10b. Given the fact of the repeated treatment of "stones" in both segments (twice in 3:9, once in 4:7, and once in 4:10a) the opportunity for scribal error in transmission would have been great. But even more than this, it is argued, the two oracular clusters constitute a core of material that is basically concerned with Zerubbabel's role in the temple rebuilding process, whereas chapter 3 in particular is concerned with Joshua's role. There is in short an intolerable tension reflected here between Davidic monarchism and priestly rule that intrudes into the flow of the visionary presentation.

Our approach to a problem which undeniably exists in both Haggai and Zechariah 1–8, however, has been to understand such tension to be present because of the unique circumstances of Persian administration in the provinces. Zechariah and his scribe or compiler, possibly one (or more) of his disciples, fully understood the implications of the Achaemenid restructuring and supported it, not with a view toward complete and permanent acceptance but with the hope that one day the present conditions would give way to a situation in which a Davidic leader could resume the royal privileges not then available to him. Zechariah's support of the status quo therefore was no conventional pro-establishment position. Rather, by presenting an acceptable picture of the present he has eased the transition to a more acceptable future. This he does with daring and creative genius. The Supplementary Oracle is the first of three oracular attempts to temper support for an expanded priestly role and acceptance of a civilian governor with future hope for Davidic leadership.

The oracular conclusion to chapter 3 begins in verse 8 by calling upon Joshua and his priestly cohorts to harken to God's words. The call is directed only to the priestly leadership. There is no mention of Zerubbabel, to whom the Insertion in chapter 4 (4:6b–10a) is clearly addressed. The promise of the future restoration of a Davidic "Shoot" is thus made to the person in whom new authority and power resides, Joshua, and to his associates who will assist him in the manifold duties of the high priesthood, which have just been emphasized in the prophetic vision (vv 1–7) that precedes the oracle. Joshua's weighty responsibilities are accompanied by the astonishing fact, reported in verse 7, of his being granted access to the Divine Council. That a priest thereupon shares this prophetic prerogative signals the increased authority of the priesthood within the restructured restoration community. We refer the reader to the NOTE to "access" (3:7) for a discussion of the configuration of priestly, prophetic, and monarchic interaction. Within the oracle itself, in verse 8, the newly acquired juridical functions of Joshua and his colleagues are reflected in the way in which "portent," a term heretofore associated with the prophets as communicators of divine will, is employed. The present context demands a new understanding which relates it to the priesthood and so to the altered circumstances of the restoration period. Zechariah's terminology reflects the beginning stages of a development which was to be of paramount significance for the late biblical period: the priestly absorption of some prophetic functions.

Zechariah's oracle does more than confirm the implications of Joshua's new authority, however. The acceptance of priestly rule is grafted onto a statement which implies an ultimate reversal of the present order: "I am indeed bringing my servant the Shoot." The participial form of the Hiphil verb *bw'* plus *hinnēh* points to a future time when a Davidic scion will come to assume the dynastic throne. Here and in Zechariah 6:12, the term "Shoot" *(ṣemaḥ)*, which has obvious royalist associations (cf. Hag 2:23 where the term is "my servant"), addresses the distress of many about the present circumstances which prevented Zerubbabel from ascending the Davidic throne. Familiar prophetic terminology (cf. the use of *ṣemaḥ* in Isa 4:2; Jer 23:5; 33:15) provides assurance that the present political system should be perceived only as an interim measure.

The tension in such an arrangement is reflected in the ambivalence in the meaning of the single stone set before Joshua in verse 9. Enormous scholarly debate has arisen over the identification of this stone and its relation to the stone(s) (4:7 and 10) of the Zerubbabel insertion. The absence of any qualifying words before "stone" in the Supplementary Oracle compared with "premier stone" in 4:7 and "tin-stone" in 4:10 has made the task all the more difficult. In general, those scholars who have maintained a connection between the Heavenly Court and Investiture of 3:1–7 and the Supplementary Oracle in

3:8–10 have related the single stone of verse 9 to the priestly apparel of Exod 28:9–12, 17–21 and 36–38. Such a stone would signify divine approval of Joshua's new role. On the other hand, scholars who would relate the oracle to the Zerubbabel insertion of chapter 4 have sought to explain the enigmatic single stone of chapter 3 in the context of customs associated with ancient temple building and the role of the monarchy in such ceremonies. The stones of chapters 3 and 4 might be identified with a building stone, a foundation deposit, even the cosmic rock on which a temple is erected. Most of these interpretations have been collected for the reader in the NOTES to each mention of "stone" in the text.

The strength of the arguments on both sides has suggested to us that the meaning of "stone" in this oracle may be intentionally ambivalent. Inasmuch as temple building or rebuilding was usually considered to be a task for kings in the ancient Near East, it is quite probable that the appearance of a single stone in the context of the vision of Joshua's vestments is intended to shift that task into the priestly purview. By partaking of the imagery of the priestly apparel, the "stone" as a reflection of Aaronic garb achieves a sense of continuity with the premonarchic priestly past. At the same time, it discreetly and judiciously depicts the role of a new principal in such activity, the priest and not the king. The "stone" can also anticipate the explicit mention of Zerubbabel in temple building activities in the insertion to the Fourth Vision. Zerubbabel's participation, however, must be seen in light of the demurrer of 4:6b: "Not by might and not by power, but with my spirit"—that is, God in a time of his choosing will bring about the return of full sovereignty to Judah with a Davidide. Meanwhile, Zerubbabel the Davidide will participate only in the limited way available to him under Persian administration: as governor of Yehud.

The second mention of the word "stone" includes the very difficult "seven eyes," which occurs again in the Fourth Vision in verse 10b. Once again, many different interpretations, which depend on the understanding of stone as gemstone or stone as building stone, appear in the scholarly literature. Some translations render "seven eyes" as "seven facets," thereby giving credence to a gemstone identity for the stone. Yet it is equally possible that "seven" is intended to carry several levels of meaning. Recognizing the special significance of the number seven in the ancient world and its usage within the visionary sequence, we may also take "seven eyes" or "seven pairs of eyes" (which would mean seven heads!) to represent divine presence or divine favor —that is, God's pleasure or presence at a ceremonial refoundation of the temple. A similar case has been made for a multivalent quality of the word "engraving."

To summarize our consideration of these three terms of verse 9—"stone," "seven eyes," and "engraving"—we reiterate that any one meaning that would exclude other connotations cannot be definitely established for any of them.

The prophet, it seems, has used language that admits of a range of associations. His subtle presentation of words that can refer to either a priest's or a monarch's role in the crucial and symbolic task of refounding a temple is evidence of his own achievement. He has enormous sensitivity to the Yehudites' difficulties in accepting the shifting configurations of such leadership and in putting off their expectancies for a Davidic monarch, and he has summoned his own powers of discourse in order to sustain both traditional hopes and contemporary demands.

The creative genius of the prophet is perhaps most evident in the conclusion to verse 9: "Thus will I take away the iniquity of that land in one day." As we have already noted, the oracle has been directed to Joshua, who is also the focus of the prophetic vision in verses 1–7. But in the oracle Joshua's role is presented in an even broader context, a context which constitutes an ultimate limitation to his priestly powers: the Shoot has been attached to the prophet's view of the future. Just as Joshua's "iniquity" had been removed in verse 4 above, now the iniquity of the entire land will be removed when the eschatological Shoot is included. Through the repetition of the key word "iniquity" all elements have become integrated into a single oracular utterance: a) Joshua's ritual cleansing in preparation for the high priestly office has been related to the cleansing of the land; b) the removal of Joshua's "iniquity" has been set in a new context which includes the figure of the Shoot; and c) both Joshua and the Shoot have been associated with the themes of social order and abundance which are presented in verse 10. All of these features, Joshua, the Shoot, and the picture of world harmony, reappear together in the final oracular presentation of Part Two, the Crowning (6:9–15).

The removal of the iniquity of the land and the consequent stability and productivity are features closely associated with temple building in cuneiform literature. At such public occasions as temple foundations or refoundations, the social order was understood to be restored and abundance in the land was anticipated. The biblical reporting of the *Pax Solomonis,* in association with the Solomonic construction of the first Jerusalem temple, shows the extent to which the Israelites shared such views. For the restoration period, this text along with Haggai 2:19 and Zechariah 8:12 reflect that ideological evaluation of the temple's restoration. Zechariah's utilization in verse 10 of language evocative of the benefits of temple work is addressed to Joshua and so endorses his pivotal role in the administration of Yehud and restoration of the temple. Yet it is also the language of prophetic eschatology and allows the Davidic Shoot a place in the ultimate restoration. The somewhat confusing use of the terms "in one day" and "in that day" again appear to reflect an ambivalence which is part of the prophetic design.

The themes of the Supplementary Oracle are integral to the prophetic vision of chapter 3. They complete the prophet's assessment of the reorganized high priesthood by showing its ultimate reassociation with a monarch. Moreover, the view presented in chapter 3 as a whole accords completely with the dyarchic picture painted in chapter 4, where Zerubbabel has been cautiously included again in the Oracular Insertion, and with the dramatic Crowning scene of chapter 6, in which a second crown has been set aside for a future Davidide. Consistency and constancy are the distinguishing features of these blocks of oracular material. They have been included in their present arrangement in Part Two with care and finesse. Whether this ordering occurred at the same time as or shortly after the conception and written expression of the visions cannot be ascertained with absolute certainty. Nonetheless, it is apparent that they constitute an essential complement to the visionary materials. They answer questions left unresolved by the visions.

The visions assert the divine acceptability of the temple project within a restored Yehud, and the oracular blocks of chapters 3, 4, and 6 relate that acceptability to the different patterns of the past, which also have been attained through Yahweh's guidance. The tension between the divergent arrangements is restored through the superimposing of future language upon present conditions. The Supplementary Oracle of 3:8–10 is permeated with ambivalent words and terms which constitute exegetical stumbling blocks for the modern reader but which allowed the prophet's listeners to reconcile the seeming contradictions in the circumstances of their age.

7. FOURTH VISION:
THE LAMPSTAND AND THE TWO OLIVE TREES
(4:1–6a,6b–10a insert,10b–14)

Vision

4 ¹ The angel-who-speaks-with-me again roused me, as one who is aroused from his sleep. ² Then he said to me, "What do you see?"

I said,ᵃ "I see a lampstand all of gold with its bowl on top of it! There are seven lamps on it, each of the seven with seven spouts, for the lamps which are on top of it. ³ And there are two olive trees by it, one to the right of the bowl and one to its left." ⁴ Then I replied to the angel-who-speaks-with-me: "What are these, my lord?"

⁵ The angel-who-speaks-with-me replied to me, "Don't you know what they are?"

ᵃ Reading with qere and other versions as over against MT which has third person imperfect.

I said, "No, my lord."
⁶ Then he replied to me:

Oracular Insertion: Zerubbabel and the Temple

This is the word of Yahweh to Zerubbabel: "Not by might and not by power, but with my spirit," said Yahweh of Hosts. ⁷ "Who are you, O great mountain? Before Zerubbabel [you are] surely a platform. Thus he will bring forth the premier stone to shouts of 'Right! Right!' "

⁸ Then the word of Yahweh came to me: ⁹ "The hands of Zerubbabel have founded this House; his hands will complete it. Thus you shall know^b that Yahweh of Hosts has sent me to you. ¹⁰ For whoever has scorned such a day of small things will rejoice upon seeing the tin-stone in the hand of Zerubbabel."

Resumption of the Vision: Explanation of Lamps and Trees

[Then he replied to me] "These seven are the eyes of Yahweh which range through all the earth."
¹¹ Then I responded to him, "What are these two olive trees, on the right of the lampstand and on its left?" ¹² And I asked him a second time, "What are the two branches of the olive trees which empty the gold by means of two golden conduits?"
¹³ He said to me: "Don't you know what they are?"
I said, "No, my lord."
¹⁴ Then he said, "These are the two sons of oil who stand by the Lord of all the earth."

NOTES

4:1. *again roused.* There is some disagreement concerning the translation of *šwb* ("return") along with the second verb *ʿwr* ("rouse"). Rudolph (1976:103–4) and others translate *šwb* as we do. NJPS and Rignell (1950) translate otherwise, giving the ordinary meaning of the root, "return." The present instance contrasts with the somewhat similar usage in 5:1 and 6:1 where *šwb* appears contiguous with the following verb (cf. Gen 26:18; Eccles 4:1,7). In this instance the placement of the subject, "the angel-who-speaks-with-me," between the two verbs provides a stylistic variation that draws attention to the meaning and content of this vision.

^b Read with two MT mss. which have plural and all the versions except LXX. The confusion may have arisen due to similar oracular formula in 2:13,14 (RSV 2:9,11).

There is perhaps a more obvious point to be made. Since the prophetic vision of chapter 3 interrupts the sequence of seven visions, this stylistically novel opening of the Fourth Vision provides the necessary literary linkage with the first three visions. The use of *šwb*, whether translated "again" or "returned," reintroduces the angelic figure and forms a verbal sequence that continues the visions but also shows awareness that the scene of Joshua's investiture had been interrupted.

as one who is aroused from his sleep. This phrase, along with reference to "in the night" at the beginning of the First Vision (1:8), has led to the common view that all of Zechariah's visions are nocturnal (i.e., "Night Visions"). However, we have shown above (NOTE to 1:8) that the reference to "night" is restricted to the initial vision, for which it provides the setting of darkness necessary to the imagery of that vision. In this verse, the reference to sleep is in the form of a simile and should not be taken as the indication that the prophet was actually asleep. Nor does it provide a contrast between wakeful and somnolent states, between alertness and dullness. Rather, it expresses the prophet's awareness that his visionary experience is as different from normal experience as wakefulness is from slumber. His grasp of the true state of affairs is greatly enhanced by what he learns from the visions. The implication is that the ensuing vision enables the prophet to understand and accept the innovative message it contains, a conception that hitherto had been beyond his comprehension. Chapter 4 complements the prophetic vision of chapter 3. Together, these two visions provide a view of dual leadership of Yehud, with the roles of priest and governor well defined. The role and status of Joshua are described in chapter 3, with the matter of civil leadership being dealt with only in a vague or indirect way. This chapter balances the previous one by offering additional and more precise details about the role and status of Zerubbabel (see especially NOTE to "Shoot," *ṣemaḥ*, in v 8).

2. *lampstand.* Insofar as Zechariah's visions are related to the Jerusalem temple, the appearance of a golden lampstand or menorah surely involves a major temple appurtenance. The difficulties posed by this passage for most exegetes are twofold. First, the textual irregularities associated with the menorah's description are indicated. Second, the real lampstands of Israel's cultic history are related to this visionary object: the lampstand of the tabernacle, the lampstands of the preexilic temple, and the lampstand of the Hasmonaean/Herodian temple of the later postexilic period. These two problems are related and stem from attempts on the part of both ancient and modern translators and tradents to objectify—that is, to describe in specific terms—the appurtenance that figures in Zechariah's vision.

The textual problems—the suffixes for several of the words, the number of times "seven" occurs, the form of the word for "spouts," and the arrangement of items in relation to one another—will be dealt with in their respective places. Suffice it to point out that such difficulties typically emerge in the transmission of, and in particular the translation of, technical material. Perhaps the best and most extensive analogy is the Septuagint's peculiar treatment of the technological aspects of the tabernacle texts in Exodus (cf. Gooding 1959:8). In such cases, the later generations responsible for translating or reproducing the Hebrew text were not familiar with the specific object described in the text or with the techniques used to produce it. Therefore they interpreted the terms and reconstructed the object to a certain extent on the basis of the material culture familiar to them. Thus the temple appurtenances of the Hasmonaean and

Herodian eras, during which the Septuagint was shaped, have influenced the way in which temple/tabernacle passages are handled. Similarly, the Chronicler in some ways tried to reconcile his information about the preexilic temple with his knowledge of the postexilic structure. A case in point for the Chronicler concerns the menorah itself: In 2 Chron 4:7 and 20, the construction of ten Solomonic menorahs is reported; but in 2 Chron 13:11, Abijah in referring to an aspect of the priestly service speaks of a single golden lampstand. The pentateuchal description of a single menorah in the tabernacle derives from authentic premonarchic tradition regarding tent or tabernacle usage (C. Meyers 1976:181–85). This factor explains the persistence of the single lampstand in the whole series of postexilic temples, in contrast to the multiplicity of lampstands in the preexilic temple.

The efforts to identify the concrete reality behind Zechariah's description are surely rendered even more complicated because of the visionary setting of the information. Other biblical texts presenting the menorah constitute intentional descriptions of real objects, whether existing or anticipated. Here we are dealing with a vision which, while based on reality and reflecting real objects and circumstances, nonetheless also has an imaginative element which inevitably transforms the underlying image so that it is difficult to distinguish the imaginative and often imaginary elements from the ones drawn from reality. Consequently, Zechariah's description would have to be considered less reliable than those embedded in the tabernacle texts of Exodus (Exod 25:31–40 and 37:17–24, cf. Exod 26:35; 30:27; 39:27; 40:4,24,25; Lev 24:1–4; Num 3:31; 4:9; 8:2–3 and Levine 1965) and the Solomonic narrative (1 Kgs 7:49, part of a nine-chapter unit, cc 3–11 of 1 Kgs, presumably based on the no longer extant Book of the Acts of Solomon, so Porten 1967 and Liver 1967). However, sorting out the points of resemblance and distinction between Zechariah's lampstand and those described in other biblical sources can help to ascertain the prophet's position in the sequence of cultic traditions.

The lampstand of Zechariah's vision does not correspond exactly either with that of Exodus or those of Kings. It probably can best be understood as involving elements from both along with certain characteristics of its own. It shares with the other cultic lampstands of the Bible the concept of *mĕnôrâ* as a generic "stand," a cylindrical tube or shaft, flaring at the lower end to provide a stable base and at the upper end to afford the support of light-bearing vessels (C. Meyers 1976:57–93). The Hebrew word for lampstand does not include the vessel it supports; in its ceramic prototypes as well as stone or metal equivalents it is related morphologically to stands that held a variety of functional objects such as incense burners, tables or trays, and bowls. Thus the word menorah itself does not include branches, lamps, bowls, or any other things which may have rested upon it or been attached to it. The Zechariah lampstand shares this feature with all biblical lampstands, including that of the tabernacle, for which the branches are presented as attachments to a stand and not as integral parts of the thing designated *mĕnôrâ*, as well as with the single noncultic example mentioned in the Hebrew Bible, the lampstand of Elisha's chamber in 2 Kgs 4:10.

The cultic object of Zechariah 4 is clearly a single appurtenance with seven lamps surmounting it, albeit in some complicated fashion (see following NOTES). In this feature it is comparable to the single lampstand of the Book of Exodus rather than to the ten stands of the account in 1 Kings. It seems to lack branches, however, and in that respect is like the stands of the Solomonic temple, which do not have them so far as the descriptions go (C. Meyers 1979). Just as in the tabernacle menorah, the lamps are part of a complex vessel *(gullâ* in Zechariah, *gābîaʿ* in Exodus) which rests upon the menorah or stand; yet the Exodus passages do not indicate uniformly that the actual lamps were of gold (compare Exod 25:37–38 with 37:22–23), whereas the 1 Kings 7 account does specify golden lamps. Further, the number of lamps, whether it be seven or forty-nine, does not clearly correspond with either of the other biblical descriptions. The priestly texts of the Pentateuch allude to a stage in tradition with a single light (Exod 27:20 and Lev 24:2, which may refer to the *ʾOhel Moʿed* or Tent of Meeting as distinct from the Tabernacle; cf. 1 Sam 3:3, which mentions a single lamp in the Shiloh sanctuary, and Haran 1960) and are ambiguous about the placement of seven lamps. The Solomonic narrative does not specify the number of lamps per stand and in fact the archaeological evidence of Iron Age cultic lamps would suggest a seven-spouted saucer lamp for each stand rather than one or more lamps set somehow on each of the ten stands. Strictly speaking, the Solomonic temple would then have had ten lamps, each a multispouted one.

In light of these considerations, the place of Zechariah's particular stand in the cultic tradition of ancient Israel can be ascertained with some certainty. The ten lampstands of the preexilic temple could not have been known to the prophet through direct experience. Surely they no longer existed. They may have disappeared from the Jerusalem temple long before the Babylonian destruction (Haran 1963). Even if they were among the vessels captured by Nebuchadnezzar's army, it is unlikely that they were preserved and returned to Jerusalem under the Persians, as recounted in Ezra 1:7 (cf. 5:13–16). The account in 2 Kings 25 of the looting of the temple indicates that the bronze objects were dismantled but carried to Mesopotamia in recognizable form (v 16), whereas the gold and silver objects probably were melted down and then transported (v 15). Since at least some of the major cultic appurtenances (the incense altar and the table for the bread of the Presence, according to the Exodus descriptions of the temple vessels, and also perhaps the menorah itself; cf. C. Meyers 1976:31–34) were probably wooden forms overlaid with gold, the valuable metal alone would have merited transport to Babylon. For those objects, the Babylonians would have discarded the wood while saving the precious metal, "gold . . . as gold, silver as silver" (2 Kgs 25:15). The many vessels listed in Ezra would thus denote subsidiary ones, perhaps those relating to the courtyard ritual and not more which were the central objects of the ritual acts that took place within the *hêkāl* or main room of Yahweh's house. In short Zechariah himself, living in the latter stage of the exile and during the early restoration period, had never actually seen any of the lampstands of the preexilic temple. In addition, the lampstand of the not yet restored postexilic temple obviously may not have been known to him. It is the very issue of that temple's restoration which had initiated his prophetic ministry. The cultic instruments were hardly ready if the temple work itself had barely begun, although the initial stages of design and fabrication may well have been underway.

What then were the sources upon which Zechariah based his visionary depiction? Although he had not himself seen the lampstands of the sixth-century Jerusalem temple, he surely had access to sources, written or oral, which gave witness to their appearance. The Deuteronomic history, or one or another of its sources, with its description of the temple in 1 Kings was available; it probably had just recently been promulgated as part of the Primary History, from Genesis through Kings. Furthermore, as Hag 2:3 and Ezra 3:12 remind us, there were still people alive in Zechariah's day who had seen "the first house" and perhaps had also seen its furnishings. Oral reminiscences passed along by eyewitnesses would also have been accessible to Zechariah.

Despite the more recent existence of the Solomonic temple and the more current sources describing it, Zechariah's vision of the lampstand was influenced much more by the single lampstand tradition of the Pentateuch. In his reliance on the archaic record of premonarchic sanctuaries, the prophet apparently was making a deliberate choice. He didn't invent the idea of a single lampstand but rather utilized the sources that presented such an object. Zechariah's choice can be attributed to a number of factors. First, the tent and tabernacle traditions were associated with Moses and Aaron rather than with a king, and that leadership pattern was more akin to that of his era than the monarchy would have been. Second, the menorah depicted in pentateuchal sources had not suffered the ignominy of destruction at the hand of foreigners. It was better to identify the menorah of the restoration with a premonarchic tradition for which there was the weight of authority and success than to persist in a tradition associated with the monarchy, which became corrupt and led eventually to the disastrous failure marked by the collapse of the kingdom and the devastation of the temple and its appurtenances. Third, the menorah of the tabernacle texts was of greater antiquity and that may have lent it greater authenticity. Although the descriptions of tabernacle and temple menorahs were both to be found in the Primary History, which combined Pentateuch with Former Prophets, the authority in Zechariah's day of the pentateuchal materials as a distinct unit within that corpus must have been more compelling. Fourth, the use of the older menorah tradition left the future open. The tabernacle/tent had eventually been replaced by the temple, which had probably incorporated what remained of the tabernacle in Solomon's time. If Zechariah saw the postexilic temple as the correlate of the archaic premonarchic shrine, he could envision a temple-to-come which would be built by a Davidide who had not yet come but who would ascend the throne in due course (cf. 3:8 and especially 6:12–13). Finally, the single lampstand would have been somewhat less ostentatious and surely less costly than ten such golden objects, a consideration not irrelevant to the economic and political situation of the restoration. Riches pouring into Jerusalem were part of Solomon's achievement and Haggai's eschatology (Hag 2:6–9); but the reality of the late sixth century was one of economic hardship (Hag 1:6,9–11; 2:15–17).

For all these reasons, Zechariah had envisioned a lampstand which, while it does not conform completely to the descriptions in the pentateuchal sources, is closer to those sources than it is to the monarchic temple sources. This period of postexilic history saw the emergence of a written authoritative legal tradition. The same political activity which had stirred the Persians to encourage the restoration of a Yehudite temple in the early years of Darius I had also led the Yehudites to pay closer attention to their legal heritage (see our Introduction, our Notes to 5:1, and also Cook 1983:61, 72). The prophet Haggai, in his metaphoric use of priestly and legal procedure, is clearly aware of that tradition. Zechariah too shares the postexilic attention to community law, as witness the Fifth Vision (The Flying Scroll, 5:1–4). Thus the tabernacle texts in substantially their present form, with their presentation of a wilderness shrine and its appurtenances, would have been the dominant influence on Zechariah's generation of temple builders.

For all its reliance on the single lampstand portrayed in the Pentateuch, the visionary lampstand of Zechariah 4 also probably reflects, with its multispouted lamps, features of the stands that existed in the monarchic temple. To a certain extent, Zechariah's lampstand is a conflation of the two traditions, the premonarchic and the preexilic. Or at least it represents a combination of an archaic written source with the late Iron Age technology of cultic lamps. The various reconstructions of the Zechariah lampstand by North ([1970], who reports on earlier attempts at reconstruction, as by Galling and Möhlenbrink, and then offers his own) bear little resemblance to the first-century witnesses of the Second Temple menorah (e.g., the graphic testimony of the Arch of Titus or the coins of Antigonus and the literary testimony of Philo and Josephus or the Mishna). These first-century C.E. witnesses deal only with the last in a series of golden lampstands of the postexilic temple, since that building, once restored, was subjected to repeated plunderings by the Greeks (cf. 1 Macc 1:21–22,54 and 4:38) and consequently to successive refurbishings and refurnishings, culminating in the elaborate and monumental Herodian edifice. Zechariah's vision, as a Persian-period interpretation of the sources available to him, could well have anticipated the sixth-century building that was in the process of being constructed with sixth-century technology. He might have had access to or even influence on the plans for the cultic objects. However, centuries later the refurnishing of the temple was more heavily influenced by Hellenistic and Roman technology, with the result that the menorah finally took on its familiar seven-branched, seven-lamp form, with a tripodal or stepped base (see Sperber 1965).

In terms of its imagined material form, the lampstand of the Fourth Vision, even if somewhat exaggerated or distorted because of its visionary characteristics, is best understood as being transitional between the corresponding preexilic and late Second Temple forms. Similarly, its symbolic value appears to bridge the tabernacle and the late postexilic meanings. The thematic identity of the lampstand in the former lies clearly within the botanical realm, as the vocabulary of its description and the morphology of its branched arrangement attest (C. Meyers 1976). The tabernacle lampstand represented a tree form, and as such it conveyed the notions of cosmic orientation and of divine presence. In this way it contributed a requisite feature, the sacred tree or tree of life, to the typology of sacred buildings in the ancient world. For the postexilic lampstand, known chiefly from the Hasmonaean and Herodian eras, the thematic identity shifted to that which in preexilic times was mainly its instrumentality —i.e., to its light-bearing qualities. Both texts and graphic remains from the postbiblical period attest that the symbolic value of the menorah was derived from the light that its lamps provided (Goodenough 1954:71–98 and 1965:79–83; M. Smith 1957–58), thus signifying through an alternative channel, light rather than tree, the similar message of God's presence in the sanctuary.

The Zechariah lampstand, it should be noted, preserved the tree symbolism somewhat indirectly, in that its own properties are not arboreal. The description includes none of the terms such as "branch" or "fruit" that provide the botanical character and thus the tree symbolism of the tabernacle lampstand. Yet the lampstand of this vision is closely and perhaps literally (see v 12) associated with two olive trees. Their presence in the vision links the menorah graphically with the rich symbolic world of sanctuary trees. Tree symbolism apparently had disappeared from the lampstands of the preexilic temple. Those stands were probably not branched, and their lamps were important as light-providing vessels. Furthermore, the Jerusalem temple, unlike the movable shrines which preceded it, had its own courtyards with living trees (Ps 52:10 [RSV 52:8]; 92:13–14 [RSV 92:12–13]) as well as wooden walls and doors carved with palm trees and open flowers (1 Kgs 6:29,32,35). In Zechariah's vision the tree symbolism is reintroduced by transference. The menorah itself is dominated by its elaborate lamps (either seven or forty-nine), which are a direct indication of the light symbolism that reflects, as does the tree symbolism, divine presence and also emphasizes divine omniscience (cf. "seven eyes" in 3:9 and 4:10b). The olive trees provide the arboreal motif. The whole group, lampstand flanked by two trees, contains the tree-of-life symbolism combined with the light-giving symbolism. This arrangement is a new expression of earlier traditions, in which the lampstand alone contained both symbolic components.

all of gold. This quality of the lampstand differs from the other biblical lampstand descriptions in that it doesn't specify "pure gold" as do the priestly texts *(zāhāb ṭāhôr)* and the Solomonic narrative *(zāhāb sāgûr).* Those specifications of purity are probably technical designations of the source of the gold. The absence in Zechariah of such information befits the visionary aspect in that the prophet is not describing or prescribing an actual artifact. Surely he would assume that the menorah was made of the finest gold, no matter how it was obtained.

That the lampstand is made entirely of gold puts the object of the prophet's vision firmly within a special cultic setting. Ordinary lampstands were rarely made of metal, and even most of the cultic stands recovered archaeologically are ceramic. A golden lampstand would have been an unusual object even for a temple. It could only have been intended for an extraordinary temple, which for Zechariah is the House of Yahweh.

its bowl on top of it. The Hebrew text of this phrase is very difficult. The reading we have chosen is found in the Vulgate and some Targum mss. over against the LXX, the Syriac, and other Targum mss. that omit the pronominal suffix of "bowl." The MT has a *mappiq* in the *he* which supports not only our reading but also a reconstruction of a bowl on top of a stand yet integral to it. The proper form of the noun is *gullâ,* which is the same as *gullāh* in verse 2 except for the MT pointing with *mappiq.* It is possible to understand the presence of the suffix, however, even if it is not written. If we can accept the MT pointing, our emendation in the singular to *gullātô* would be in order. However, the simplest solution is to read *gullâ* without *mappiq,* leaving the MT consonantal text intact.

Despite these textual problems it is clear that this feature is closely associated with the stand but distinct from "it." From the root *gll,* the word translated "bowl" designates a curved or rounded object. It is also used for a component of Jachin and Boaz, the enigmatic temple pillars (1 Kgs 7:41). It is related to Akkadian *gullatu,* which means "ewer" or, probably in a derivative sense, a curved architectural feature associated with a column—perhaps an astragal or a bowl-shaped capital (CAD V:128–29). Other biblical references (Josh 15:19 = Judg 1:15; Eccles 12:6) reflect similar curved or bowl-shaped objects. The artifactual material perhaps related to this feature would be the bowls or lamps, often with basal projections that rested upon or were inserted into the open tops of cylindrical stands (R. H. Smith 1964:9 and Stern 1982:128, fig. 203). However, another possibility is equally attractive: a meaning known in Akkadian for the bulbous ring of an astragal is used here in Hebrew to designate a kind of kernos; cf. our discussion below in the NOTE to "seven."

It is curious that the word *gullâ* is used here instead of the term *gābîa'*, which denotes the corresponding feature of the menorah of the tabernacle texts. That term likewise has an Akkadian cognate, *gabūtu (AH* II: 890), the *locus classicus* for which is the black obelisk of Shalmaneser III, which depicts Jehu's homage and contains a listing of vessels carried off as tribute from Jerusalem, including "golden bowls" *(gabu-āti hûrasi;* see *ANET*:281). The reasons for Zechariah's choice of *gullâ* rather than *gābîa'* are not clear. However, the use of the former word in the description of the pillars Jachin and Boaz in 1 Kings allows for some speculation. Those two extraordinary pillars were very important elements in the Solomonic temple-palace complex in Jerusalem. They represented gateposts in their placement at the entrance to the inner court of *'ûlām* of the temple. They thereby signified Yahweh's entry into his earthly abode at the time of the temple's dedication. In that way, they conveyed the essential notion that Yahweh legitimized the monarchic regime which had constructed his house as part of the capital city (C. Meyers 1983).

As symbols of dynastic legitimacy, the pillars Jachin and Boaz, which had been broken up and carried off to Babylon in 586 (2 Kgs 25:16) could hardly have been restored in the postexilic temple. That temple did not serve a Yehudite monarchy except in the hopes that a future Davidide would ascend a Jerusalem throne. Without a dynastic king on the throne, there would have been no purpose or function for such pillars. The Persians would have seen these as provocative. Although Zechariah may have expected that the new temple, to be built by the Shoot (see 6:12–13), would have the pillars, there is no indication that they were restored in any actual temples of the postexilic period, from Zerubbabel to Herod. Since the literary sources, especially for the Herodian temple, are extensive and detailed, the lack of positive evidence can be construed as a strong argument that Jachin and Boaz did not ever exist after 586.

Zechariah's lampstand vision nonetheless utilizes a technical architectonic term from the descriptions of the temple pillars which could not in reality be erected as the temple was being rebuilt. Perhaps the prophet in this way incorporated the idea of future monarchic restoration into the menorah as symbol of divine presence. One cannot be sure that this was Zechariah's intention, however; the word association may be accidental or coincidental. The use of *gullâ* and not the expected *gābîa'* may be more important in suggesting that the priestly writers were not dependent upon Zechariah for their menorah descriptions, and that pentateuchal tradition is not derived from postexilic temple practice. Instead, Zechariah appears to have been influenced (see previous NOTE)—though not slavishly as this word choice indicates—by pentateuchal materials.

seven lamps . . . seven . . . seven spouts. The threefold repetition of "seven" in the MT, unlike the Septuagint which preserves only two, causes some difficulty. The first "seven" clearly indicates the number of lamps, a reading supported by the Vulgate and the Targum as over against the Septuagint and Peshitta, which omit the pronominal suffix. The retention of the suffix is necessitated by the reading *gullātô* for *gullâ,* but the context would allow us to presume the suffix in the latter even though it is not written.

The third "seven" poses no problems, for it denotes the number of spouts. The second "seven" is the difficult one. It is unattached to a substantive in the Hebrew, is omitted by the Greek, and consequently is deleted by the editor (Elliger) of *BHS* and by many commentators. There is no easy solution to this dilemma, and the LXX may in fact be secondary precisely because it is better and simpler. Our translation retains the middle "seven" of the MT, which perhaps is recapitulating the preceding "seven lamps" in a distributive fashion (see North 1970:184–85 and cf. 2 Sam 21:20 // 1 Chron 20:6). In this case, the second "seven" would be associated with the seven lamps in order to indicate that each of these lamps had seven spouts. If so, the confusion—or the insertion of what appears to be an extra numeral—may stem from the technical nature of the lamp arrangement being described, an arrangement based on later Iron Age or Persian-period lamps which differed from the Hellenistic lamps most familiar to later scribes and translators. The oil lamps of the Persian period in Palestine represent the culmination of the millennia-long tradition of open saucer lamps, with the wick held in place at the rim by a pinched fold in the clay. The introduction of imported closed lamps with wick nozzles from Greece led, in the succeeding Hellenistic period, to the displacement of the ancient saucer lamps by the closed form (Stern 1982:127–29).

We shall return to Persian lamp technology for our discussion of the spouts, but shall first consider another possible explanation for the problematic three "sevens" of this passage. In addition to the number seven, the number two also figures prominently in this vision. Five occurrences of "two" can be noted, in verses 3, 11, 12, (2 times), and 14. All of these create pairs of symbolic objects or figures representing the dual leadership of Yehud (see our COMMENT on this vision) which this vision legitimates. According to the prophet, the two leaders of the restoration community exercise their authority because Yahweh has acknowledged the validity of their roles. The vision portrays this through the image of Yahweh's presence, represented by a golden lampstand, between the "two"—two trees, branches, conduits, sons of oil. But Yahweh's presence is evoked even more specifically by his "seven eyes," the seven lamps of the menorah prefigured by the seven eyes of the enigmatic stone of 3:9 (see NOTE). Also, there are five mentions of "two," and the mentions of "seven" (= God) which the "two" flank and represent appear five times in the text. Taken together with 3:9, this vision would have only four occurrences of "seven" were not the middle instance in this verse included. Awkward or unnecessary as it may seem, it may serve to augment the number of sevens to five and so provide the necessary balance between the symbolic representations of Yahweh on the one hand and his two viceroys on the other hand. The prophet would thus have attained the desired symmetry between the major elements of his visionary experience: God, and the Yehudite leadership authenticated by God.

To return to the matter of spouts, we reiterate that the Persian-period lamp technology in Palestine still adhered to the open lamp tradition. Hence the seven "spouts" are to be understood as the notches made in the rim of the lamp bowl for holding the wick and not as closed nozzles. Persian lamps are noted for their very sharply pinched wick holes, which anticipate the ensuing predominance of nozzled lamps. The Hebrew *mûṣeqet* ("spout") is formed from the root *yṣq* ("flow, pour"), which frequently appears in connection with oil, particularly the oil of anointing or sacrifice (e.g., Gen 28:18; Exod 29:7; Lev 2:6; 1 Sam 10:1). The lamp spout guides the flow of oil from the saucer along the wick to the wick end where the flame burns. That conduit or channel holds both wick and oil, the latter being supplied from the saucer or bowl, and the former terminating at the wick hole or spout, where the flame provides light. The wick hole is designated "spout" in archaeological language, but this need not indicate a tubelike nozzle (cf. "tube" in v 12). A similar though less convincing result is obtained by Möhlenbrink, who derives *mûṣeqet* from *ṣwq*, "to be in straits," with the noun conveying the idea of narrowness (1929:285). His suggestion deprives the word of its connections with oil and anointing, both of which are important elements in the explanation of the Fourth Vision offered by the Interpreting Angel in verses 10b–14.

Seven-spouted lamps, which this verse specifies, were not common artifacts in the biblical world. Yet they do occur from the Middle Bronze period onward, notably in cultic contexts. The predominance of seven-spouted examples among multispouted lamps suggests the symbolic significance of that number; and indeed the biblical record is replete with instances in which seven appears symbolically, representing totality or completeness (see NOTE to "seven eyes" below in v 10b). The specification in Zechariah of an arrangement of seven seven-spouted lamps has no archaeological analogue and must be comprehended as part of the creative dimension afforded by the visionary presentation. In this significant feature of the central vision, the prophetic imagination intensifies the symbolism of seven lights with this multiplicity of flame; each of seven lamps with seven wick holes. Zechariah has taken the seven-spouted cultic lamp, which he may well have known from experience, and multiplied it by a factor of seven. His vivid imagination has enhanced the symbolic value of seven by envisioning a menorah with forty-nine spouts, from which forty-nine flames would burn. The Jubilee year is analogue to this kind of symbolism. Because the seventh or sabbatical year was special as a year of remission of debts and release of slaves (Deut 15:1–2,12–14), the completion of forty-nine years, a cycle of seven sabbaticals, brought the exponential sabbath, nothing less than a Jubilee. This year had extra sanctity and was ushered in by the blast of a "ram's horn" *(ybl)*, which was reserved for extraordinary occasions, rather than by an ordinary trumpet *(špr)*. It was marked by the restoration of property, the cessation of agrarian activity, and the proclamation of "liberty throughout the land to all its inhabitants" (Lev 25:8–12; cf. Lev 27:7–24). The forty-nine-year period may have originated in a primitive pentecontad calendar, but that does not diminish the importance of the fact that it is clearly derived from a seven times seven reckoning. As such it is the climactic unit in a number symbolism based on the significance of seven. Similarly, the forty-nine wicks or lights of Jeremiah, on a lampstand representing God's presence and omniscience, provide the maximum sense of divine presence.

The material reality stimulating this exaggerated vision is a conflation of a seven-spouted lamp with a kernos-like arrangement. A kernos is a hollow, circular, tubelike vessel perforated on its upper side with holes or receptacles for the receiving or pouring out of liquids. Normally kernoi are not associated with lamps, at least not in the Iron Age examples which predominate in the existing corpus. However, an unpublished kernos fragment from En-Gedi (reported in Stern 1982:124) consists of a ring surmounted by lamps and obviously intended for illumination. Since the form of those lamps is of the ordinary Persian open type, it has been possible to redate to the Persian period two similar vessels, one each from Tell-es-Safe and Tell Sandahanna, which had previously and erroneously been attributed to the Hellenistic period or the Iron II period by their excavators early in the twentieth century. The existence of kernos rings with a series of attached lamps in the Persian period may provide evidence for the nature of the object in Zechariah's vision that holds the seven-spouted lamps, which represented continuity with the lamps on each of the stands of the Solomonic temple. The *gūllâ* of Zech 4:2 perhaps is not a bowl at all, strictly speaking. Rather the term may designate a kernos, otherwise unknown in the biblical lexicon. The exact meaning of *gūllâ* in this setting has not been fixed (see above); insofar as its Akkadian cognate sometimes denotes an astragal, it represents exactly the shape of a kernos if one omits the column shaft associated with an astragal. Zechariah would thus have adapted the *gābîaʿ* ("bowl") of the pentateuchal lampstand source to the Persian-period technology for multiplying wicks on a single light-bearing vessel, a technique which improved the relatively poor light-giving capabilities of a single wick. This combination of features— multispout lamp with multilamp kernos—has created an object unique to the prophetic imagination, the scriptural description of which puzzled the post-Persian tradents and translators unfamiliar with the technology underlying the visionary artifact.

3. *two olive trees.* The two olive trees which appear in this verse figure prominently as thematic items in the whole of chapter 4. They figure directly in the question and answer dialogue of verses 11 and 12 where, in addition to inquiring as to the nature of the two trees, the prophet asks about "the two branches of the olive trees *(šibbălê hazzêtîm)."* The Interpreting Angel finally answers the query in verse 14 with the very difficult expression (see NOTE below), "These are the two sons of oil." Although the full expression *ʿṣ zyt* ("olive tree") is not used here, since the word for "tree" is omitted, there is no question that "olive tree" is meant, as in many other places in the Bible (cf. Jotham's parable, Judg 9:8–9, where *zayit* is rendered "olive tree," and Hos 14:7 [RSV v 6], where "olive" without "tree," conveys an image of beauty). Hence, the use of "olive" alone to represent the olive tree here is quite regular, though it contrasts with Haggai 2:19, which prefers the fuller Hebrew *ʿēṣ hazzayit.*

The olive tree theme provides a broad range of meaning and a rich symbolism by virtue of that species' enduring properties and economic value in the Mediterranean world. Its fruit and the derived oil still constitute basic dietary staples in the Middle East and are also primary market commodities. Its leafy beauty and its other physical and economic attributes have inspired much biblical imagery. Because some trees apparently survive for as long as a thousand years, the olive tree represents continuity. The durability of olive trees is enhanced by the fact that in severe drought they can withhold their fruit in order to preserve their own vitality. Yet, as the trees mature, the gnarled trunks become hollow and susceptible to destruction by strong winds or by fire; and it is this feature of older trees which lies behind Jeremiah's famous metaphor of Judah's vulnerability (11:16): "'A green olive tree, fair, with good fruit,' Yahweh has named you. With the sound of a great tempest he will set fire to it and its branches will be consumed." The very fragility of the aged olive tree, however, is linked with qualities of propagation that serve to underscore its longevity rather than moribundity. An olive tree can theoretically survive for an unlimited length of time, because as its trunk becomes increasingly broad and hollow, its roots near the base of the trunk produce young shoots which surround the trunk and ultimately replace it when it collapses or burns. The renowned longevity of the olive tree allows it also to represent the righteous life (cf. Feliks 1981:216) in that the upright man is blessed by God and so will endure.

In short, the olive tree had powerful connotations of permanence and righteousness in the biblical world. The placement of two olive trees alongside the lampstand in this vision provides a sense of stability, continuity, and longevity. Furthermore, this association of olive trees with the temple is hardly novel (see Psalms 52 and 92). Because the symbolism of the menorah (see first NOTE to v 2) has shifted by this time from tree imagery to light imagery, the typological connection of temple with sacred tree is preserved in Zechariah's vision by the olive trees flanking the menorah. However, this vision specifies two trees, an unexpected situation from the viewpoint of temple typology, in which a single sacred tree or plant is normally found. The numerical qualification forces the prophet's audience to seek further symbolic meaning or significance for the "two" trees; and indeed verse 14 below provides that enigmatic identification, "two sons of oil." Whom do the two trees represent? Had there been only one tree placed alongside the menorah, which symbolized God's presence, the "Shoot" (see NOTE to 3:8) as legitimate Davidic scion might have provided a reasonable candidate. However, the vision contains two trees which, according to the identity suggested by verse 14, must represent the figures of two community leaders, notably high priest and governor.

Although anointing was a ritual associated with both priest and king (see NOTE to "two sons of oil," v 14), the treatment of a governor in this way would have been unlikely. In this connection, it is to be noted that the Fourth Vision is interrupted after 4:6a by the insertion concerning Zerubbabel and the temple and is resumed in 4:10b with the theme of the two olive trees/two sons of oil linking the two segments of the vision. The preceding chapter (3:1–10) has presented Joshua and the priestly vestments as a way of legitimizing an expanded priestly role in the organization of postexilic Judah. The logical inference to be drawn from the canonical arrangement of the text of chapter 4 is that Joshua's role was not the sole focus of Zechariah's interest in community leadership. The centerpiece vision addresses the monarchic question not treated in chapter 3 by supporting the structure of Yehud with high priest and governor as joint leaders. Zechariah himself is certainly not encouraging royalist rebellion by the oracular Zerubbabel insertion (4:6b–10a) or by this visionary reference to dyarchic rule. The quiescent tone of 4:6b ("Not by might and not by power, but by my spirit") reveals the prophet's pacifist stance. However, through the ambivalence of the visionary style and by the selection of evocative and compelling images, the prophet achieves the difficult task of supporting simultaneously the nonmonarchic status quo and also the dynastic ideal. The dyarchy represents a necessary stage in the scheme of Israel's contemporary history. The new Jerusalem temple, and the theocratic provincial state under Joshua's priestly leadership and Zerubbabel's governorship, is but an intermediate stage in the ongoing drama which will lead finally to the fulfillment of God's plan. Jerusalem's independence will be achieved, and full Davidic rule will be restored.

by it. The preposition used here, *ʿal,* has caused some difficulties for exegetes who would understand it to mean "above." However, the sense of "alongside," or on either side, is obvious from the context in this verse and in verses 11 and 14. The symbolic meaning of the "two olive trees" renders somewhat irrelevant the attempts of others to measure the height of olive trees in relation to the supposed stature of the lampstand (see North 1970:186). "Right" and "left" appear again in verse 11 indicating the importance of conceptualizing the two trees as flanking the lampstand.

bowl. The use of *gullâ* here instead of menorah is unexpected and cannot be readily explained. If the word *měnôrâ* represents only the cylindrical stand which supported the lamps, then "bowl" here is a *pars pro toto* designation in which the most important or prominent part of an object represents its entirety. Whether the object designated "bowl" is an open receptacle or even a closed kernos ring (see NOTES above to "bowl" and "seven" in v 2) is less important than the fact that the Hebrew word for "bowl" provides a link with the preexilic temple. It does so by using a term that was prominent in the description of the temple pillars, which legitimized the monarchy by marking God's entry into, and presence in, the temple. Both menorah and pillars symbolize, in different ways and among other things, God's legitimizing presence. Zechariah perhaps uses a word common to both to denote the menorah in order to identify that portion of the menorah's symbolic range which is most important in this setting.

4. *"What are these . . . ?"* As in 1:9, 2:2 (RSV 1:21), and 6:4, the prophet's description of visionary objects is followed by this query to the Interpreting Angel. In addition, this vision employs the same question, although also directly designating the objects in question, in 4:11 ("What are these two olive trees?"). The dialogue between prophet and angel, which is one of the major literary features of Zechariah's visions, characteristically employs the question-and-answer format to achieve its purpose, namely, the presentation of the vision's subject matter and then of its meaning. In this central vision, the questioning takes on a particularly intensive quality because of the presence of a more complicated set of questions (see the following two NOTES and first NOTE to 4:14).

my lord. This direct form of address between Zechariah and the Interpreting Angel has a decided ring of familiarity, for Zechariah uses it frequently (cf vv 5 and 13 below, as well as above in 1:9). In the following verse and in verse 13 the angel's rhetorical answer ("Don't you know what they are?") to the prophet's question is followed by the prophet's response, "No, my lord." Twice in chapter 4, the twofold repetition of the question is followed by "No, my lord." Such repetition helps to confer on the Fourth Vision an importance and literary centrality that none of the other visions has. In this case, however, "my lord" is attached to a question which elsewhere is not followed by this term of address (cf. verse 11). Perhaps this first usage of "my lord" in chapter four is meant to balance a fourth appearance of the root, in reference to God, in verse 14.

The use of "lord" in direct address occurs frequently in Scripture and is applied to kings more than fifty times (cf. Gen 24:12 for contrasting usage in a single verse). It is an especially appropriate term for God in its sense of "master" or "owner," and it is certainly no coincidence that "two sons of oil" of verse 14 are standing before the "Lord of all the earth" (see NOTE below). In this case, the singular form *ʾădōnî* ("my lord") appears. According to the convention of the Masoretes, the singular is used when a human is addressed, whereas the plural *ʾădōnay* appears as an indication of honor or majesty when God is meant. "My lord" as part of Zechariah's speech to the angel appears once in the First Vision, three times in this central vision, and once again in the last (Seventh) vision. Such a pattern appears to be part of the literary framing apparent in the arrangement of the Seven Visions.

5. *"Don't you know what they are?"* This is the one of only two instances in Zechariah's visions (see v 13 below) in which the Interpreting Angel answers a question with a question. Clearly this is a rhetorical technique designed to underscore the centrality of this vision and its imagery of the two olive trees flanking the lampstand. The addition

of this stylistic element at a midpoint in the visionary sequence is one of several literary devices (cf. vv 1 and 13, and COMMENT) pointing to the pivotal role played by this fourth or central vision in the overall sequence of Seven Visions. It is no coincidence that the Fourth Vision falls squarely in the middle of the sequence. This question is also the angel's second question to the prophet in this passage, and it is balanced by Zechariah's twofold questioning of the angel in verses 11–12. These sets of questions intentionally frame the Zerubbabel insertion.

The angel's answering question differs from Zechariah's question in an important way. The prophet simply says *mh 'llh* ("What are these?"), but the angel adds *hmmh* when he asks his question in response: *mh hmmh 'llh,* literally "(Don't you know) what they are, these?" The prophet's question is sufficient for our normal purposes, but the angel goes beyond conventional questions and is chiding Zechariah: It is as if he were saying, Here you are, a prophet who has access to the Divine Council; how can it be that you don't know the meaning of this simple little vision that you have just described? The *hmmh* serves as a copula connecting *mh* ("what") with *'llh* ("these"). It also acts as an emphatic, adding stress to the angel's questions and providing a note of mock incredulity. The angel exposes the prophet's unexpected ignorance. At the same time, the author creates and maintains suspense. The prophet is frustrated in having his question answered with a question, which itself is a mild taunt. The audience shares the prophet's frustration by having the explanation delayed, for if the prophet can't figure out the meaning of the vision, how could anyone else? Both prophet and audience must wait until the playful angel gets around to providing the explanation, which will not come until the final verse of this chapter. Other devices, including a parallel set of questions plus question-in-response (v 13), further put off the true revelation of the vision's significance.

The pairing of questions has implications for understanding the canonical ordering of this vision, which is interrupted by oracular material in the Zerubbabel insertion. This interruption at 4:6b presents the literary critic with serious problems. To begin with, the separation of this unit from the preceding and following verses means that the usual MT divisions of verses must be ignored. The scholarly literature invariably refers to the Oracular Insertion as Zech 4:6b–10a. Customary procedure would be to divide the verse at the *athnach* which precedes "Not by might . . ." but we have divided the verse after "Then he replied to me." For simplicity, however, we are retaining the customary nomenclature. Similarly, the verse labeled 10b ("These seven . . .") is technically not the second part of verse 10. That verse divides according to the MT after "These seven . . ." and not before it. However one divides it, the passage about Zerubbabel and the temple interrupts the flow of the lampstand vision and has led many scholars to rearrange the text (cf. first NOTE to verse 4:6).

That the repetition of the prophet's question by the Interpreting Angel is not answered until the resumption of the vision in 4:10b may in fact be related to the canonical order with its intervening text on Zerubbabel and the temple. The excursus on Zerubbabel may represent an attempt at harmonization in the canonical or editorial process (see below NOTE to "Zerubbabel" in v 6b) whereby Zerubbabel is not extraneous to the understanding of the whole. Or it could equally be the prophet's own insertion, for the same reason.

my lord. See NOTES to verses 4, 13 and 14, where *'ădōn* ("lord") also appears. This second usage of "my lord" parallels exactly its third usage in verse 13. Together they frame the Oracular Insertion.

6. *word of Yahweh.* This expression, *dĕbar*-Yahweh, which occurs again in verse 8, is characteristic of Zechariah's oracular style in contrast with his visionary style. It occurs only in blocks of nonvisionary material (1:1; 6:9; 7:1,4,8; 8:1,18) and contrasts significantly with other introductory formulas (see Petitjean 1969:238–41). It also corresponds to the usage in Haggai (e.g., 1:1,3; 2:1,10,20), where the expression serves to frame the entire literary structure of the two chapters. Here in chapter 4 its usage signals that the following verses do not fall within the visionary mode. It is no wonder then that considerable scholarly opinion would judge the Insertion (4:6b–10a) to be misplaced and intrusive (see COMMENT to the Supplementary Oracle, 3:8–10 and preceding NOTES to 4:5). The interweaving of the visionary and oracular styles is, however, one of the most characteristic features of the Book of First Zechariah, and the appearance of one style after the other in the same unit does not mean that either had a separate context and that we now have a crude mixture of elements which did not belong together originally (cf. the transition between the Third Vision 2:5–9 [RSV 2:1–5] and the oracular expansion 2:10–17 [RSV 2:6–13]).

The placement of a major oracular insertion within the context of the central Fourth Vision nonetheless poses difficult literary questions. Did Zechariah's composition of the lampstand vision include this insertion from the beginning? Or did Zechariah himself as editor of his own work (cc 1–8) place this insertion in its present context on the eve of the temple's rededication in 515 B.C.E.? Or has another hand, presumably that of a redactor, placed these verses in their present arrangement to accommodate the shift away from Zerubbabel reflected especially in the Fourth Vision? Or, finally, do these verses (vv 6b–10a) represent part of a larger oracular unit which at one time was attached to the Supplementary Oracle (3:8–10)?

The approach adopted here finds no reason to reject Zechariah himself, or less probably a disciple, as the one who placed the materials in their canonical arrangement. Since this activity would have been concluded prior to 515 B.C.E. and hence soon after their composition (see COMMENT to Zech 1:1–6), we take the arrangement of the parts of this chapter as the author's intention (cf. COMMENT to the Oracular Insertion). The possibility that the insertion was originally placed within the vision rather than being put there at the time of redaction must also be entertained. The insertion in that case would be the centerpiece of a visionary envelope (editor's suggestion). The opening of the construction would be the vision of 4:1–6a, and the explanation of 4:10b–14 would constitute the closing section. The two sections would have been deliberately separated in order to frame the important and essential information contained in the Oracular Insertion, 4:6b–10a. Although long-held conceptions of biblical literature viewed the Israelites as writers who only moved directly from one statement to the next, and in the same literary style, more recent appraisals recognize the deliberate juxtaposition of styles. Units which appear distinct cannot automatically be treated as if they were independent of the preceding and following passages.

Zerubbabel. While the human identity of the figures of the two olive trees remains nonspecific, as befits their symbolic character as well as the visionary mode, the Oracular Insertion is forthright in its introductory words. Zerubbabel is identified as the one to whom the oracle is addressed, and his actions are of central concern, for he is mentioned by name three additional times in this inserted passage. All of these occurrences of Zerubbabel's name in 4:6b–10a are without the patronymic and without the use of the designation "governor." The contrast with Haggai's usage is striking. Haggai mentions Zerubbabel seven times in all, sometimes with patronymic and title (1:1,14; 2:2), sometimes only with patronymic (1:12; 2:23); once as governor (2:21) and only once as Zerubbabel alone (2:4). Zechariah's avoidance of such familiar terms and titles cannot be mere happenstance. For Zechariah the expectation that Zerubbabel or any Davidide would ascend the throne and reestablish kingship is one that is remote if not impossible. The monarchic hope can only be realized in some future time. Zerubbabel's title and patronymic have been omitted because Zechariah does not want to evoke hopes regarding Zerubbabel's role which he would consider unrealistic (see NOTE to "Zerubbabel ben-Shealtiel" in Hag 1:1).

The direct attention to Zerubbabel presents an intrusion into the series of visions that derives from Zechariah's precarious role in encouraging temple restoration under a non-Yehudite political authority. None of the visions includes specifically named persons, yet the pragmatic questions of the day required a similarly pragmatic response from the prophet. Such response took the form of prophetic oracles which interrupt the visions at appropriate points, and translate supermundane visions into practical reality. Joshua's primary role as high priest received a lengthy oracular validation in the preceding chapter. The role of a governor who was a Davidide and who was involved in the restoration process also had to be reconciled with the belief that temple building and dynastic legitimacy were inextricably intertwined. The oblique reference to Shoot in 3:8 was evidently not enough; the fuller statement of the Zerubbabel insertion was needed.

The unique Fourth Vision, with the static symbolism of lampstand and trees, is less vague than the other six visions for which the explanations are not always readily apparent from the ostensible content of the figures they contain. Furthermore, the objects of the other visions do not involve identification with humans, and they are more abstract and less concrete than the central vision. The intense questioning (see vv 4, 5, 11, 12 and 13) of the Fourth Vision also forces the prophet as well as his audience to consider the characters in the restoration events.

The way in which the Fourth Vision differs from the others makes it possible that the Zerubbabel insertion belongs to a very early if not original stage (cf. preceding NOTE) of the organization of Zecharianic materials. The imaginary world of the visions and the real world of a Yehudite province with a temple project intersect in chapter 4. The preceding Joshua chapter is also part of that intersection, and the crux—the issue of the expected role of a king in a temple project—is a direct insertion into the Fourth Vision with its portrayal of two leaders. One leader had been dealt with in chapter 3, where Joshua's role is sanctioned as a matter of political expediency. Since a Davidide's role as king would only have a theoretical or futuristic resolution, Zerubbabel's function as *peḥâ* allowed Yehud to carry on its temple project under Persian sponsorship and with Persian approval. At the same time it signified to the prophet's audience the expectation of a future restoration of autonomy.

Not by might and not by power, but with my spirit. This is surely one of the most quoted statements from Scripture and one of the gems of the Book of Zechariah. Jewish tradition in particular has a fondness for this verse, which has become identified with the theme of the holiday of Hanukkah, the Jewish Festival of Lights celebrated in December in commemoration of the rededication of the Second Temple by the Maccabees after its desecration by the Seleucid Greeks in 168 B.C.E. The chapter as a whole has been inserted by the rabbis into the tradition as the prophetic reading for the sabbath of Hanukkah. Although the festival of Hanukkah also celebrates a great military victory of the Jews over the Seleucids, it is significant that the rabbis apparently chose this chapter with its vision of quietism to tone down the militaristic dimension of the festival and to stress the fact of God's spirit. From the rabbinic perspective, victory was achieved as much by the pouring out of God's spirit as by military might.

The present oracle, which is addressed to Zerubbabel, contains a message that may be understood in terms of the then current political realities. As Zerubbabel was a political appointee of the Persian government, his mission to assist in the restoration of the Temple of Yahweh could be understood only in terms acceptable to the Persians. The words "might" and "power" probably constitute a hendiadys. Hebrew *ḥyl* ("might") often means army or military force. The combination of "power" and "might" is to be understood as "military might" or "powerful armies," either of which would signify political autonomy since the presence of an army is the distinguishing mark of an independent state. The point is that this was not the time or occasion for the exercise of force. Yehud at that time was not fully autonomous and had no army. Although many commentators have taken this sentence and these terms to suggest that Zerubbabel was about to launch or had already launched a rebellion against Persian authority and rule, we find no support here or elsewhere for such a conspiracy theory. Rather, the thrust of the first half of the verse conveys merely the reminder that in *this* period—i.e., the restoration period—the normal attributes of an independent political entity were lacking for Yehud.

The concluding phrase "with my spirit" conveys God's reassuring words to Zerubbabel and the Yehudites. Zerubbabel the *peḥâ* (governor), as a Davidic descendant, must have been aware of his impact upon his fellow Yehudites. God's approval of the status quo is provided, along with recognition of the legitimacy of the dynastic claim for some future time (cf. use of *rûaḥ* in Hag 2:5 and Zech 6:8). Such an oracular pronouncement is not to be construed as a denunciation of Zerubbabel but as a sign that God's active presence and favor still are to be discerned in the temple restoration project. God's "spirit" is his involvement in and control over human events. Yet is the idea of a Davidic dynasty thereby to be forsaken? This accompanying question is the focus of the next oracular portion of Zechariah (6:9–15, The Crowning), which follows the uninterrupted sequence of the Fifth, Sixth, and Seventh Visions. There the unnamed Shoot will assuredly hold royal office at some future time (see below).

7. *great mountain.* The apostrophic address to this feature of Jerusalem's topography arises from the concern over the manner in which the temple restoration process was to be effected. The term "great mountain" belongs to the category of symbolic designations for the temple or its situation on Mount Zion. It is especially informed by the frequency with which the theme of a temple as embodiment of the cosmic mountain occurs in texts from the ancient Near East, such as those referring to a temple as "the great house . . . a mountain great" or "House of the Great Mountain of the Lands" (cited in Lundquist 1983: n 10). Ancient Israel clearly shared this conceptualization, with the temple at Mount Zion in Jerusalem incorporating the holy Sinai

mountain and its heavenly temple (Freedman 1981:21–30; Clifford 1972). The psalms are replete with phraseology joining temple with mountain (e.g., 48:2–3 [RSV vv 1–2]; 24:3; cf. Isa 2:2–3 and Zech 8:3; cf. also Jer 31:23).

The specific circumstances in which the address is made to the great mountain arise out of a temple-building context and can be understood by examining the procedure involved in temple building in the ancient Near East. The initial procedure of constructing a new temple, on a site where a temple had never before been erected, appears to have consisted of an enormously laborious and often elaborate process of creating a suitable foundation for the temple. The lengths to which the ancient engineers went to prepare the building site appear to have been far in excess of the load-bearing requirements of monumental architecture. The extraordinary efforts of the preliminary stages of temple building are not illumined directly by any textual material. However, the indirect evidence suggests that the preparatory labors are related to the typology of temple buildings. Closely related to the cosmic mountain symbolism is the concept of temple as the locale of the original foundation and ordering of the world, where dry land first emerged from watery chaos. A temple's earthly location is hallowed, representing as it does that original cosmic stability (see Lundquist 1983, especially nn 11–14). Temple construction participated in this typology by satisfying mythological requirements, by erecting enormous platforms with clean fill to signify the primeval emergence of the inhabitable world. In the flat plains of Egypt and Mesopotamia, great earthen platforms or sand beds provided the primeval mountain on which the temple had to be built (see Ellis 1968:147–50).

For Israelites, mountains were the equivalent of the artificial platforms of Mesopotamia in terms of the homologization of man-made edifices to cosmological notions. The construction of the Jerusalem temple on a hilltop in Jerusalem, like most mountaintop shrines in the Canaanite sphere, fulfilled the typological requirements of temple building by virtue of the topography rather than as the result of mammoth earth-moving operations. This does not preclude leveling operations and the introduction of substantial fills for hill-country shrines, but it does relegate such actions to the functional rather than the ideological sphere. The Jerusalem locale for the temple, this verse reiterates, constitutes the necessary great or cosmic mountain requirement for the building project. The complement of this idea is "platform."

Zerubbabel. Cf. NOTE to verses 6 and 9.

surely. The adverbial quality of the *lamed* attached to the following word ("platform") provides emphasis for that word. It functions like the Assyrian *lu* and the Arabic *la* (*GKC* § 143e; see also the discussion of the emphatic *lamed* in Dahood 1970:400). Such usage is attested elsewhere in the Hebrew Bible and appears to be more prevalent in later texts—e.g., Eccles 9:4; 1 Chron 7:1; 2 Chron 7:21; and Ezra 1:11. The emphasis that "surely" offers in this case may be a response to the uncertainty of the temple's status in building situations such as this one, in which a temple is being constructed on an ancient site where a previous temple had stood. The rubble of the ruined building must be carted away, and a certain amount of further demolition also takes place. Because such actions could be interpreted negatively as the further destruction of the temple, their legitimacy had to be assured.

platform. Hebrew *mîšōr* is derived from *yšr*, "to be smooth, straight" and denotes a flat or level place. The noun normally refers to flat land or tableland, such as the segment of the trans-Jordanian plateau between the site of Heshbon and the Arnon River (as in Deut 3:10; 4:43; Josh 13:9,16, etc.). Some commentators interpret the statement in a figurative way, and understand it to say that mountains become plains in the presence of Zerubbabel's masterful skill and efficiency. We likewise accept that *mîšōr* connotes flatness, but would place such a connotation within the technical language of temple-building procedures. The term is used in an extended sense; it is the flattened place upon which a building is constructed—i.e., its "platform." In Mesopotamia and Egypt the foundation stage of temple building (cf. above under "great mountain") consisted of the erection of an enormous platform *(temen* in Sumerian and in subsequent Mesopotamia building texts), representing the primal emergence of dry land and assuring the temple its microcosmic status.

Zechariah states emphatically that the temple mount is indeed the legitimate "level spot" or "platform" upon which the House of God is to be reestablished. Such flatness may include reference to an actual leveling procedure that was part of the site preparation. At the same time it equates the temple mount with the ideological credentials of temple construction. The notion of "premier stone" (see NOTE) is likewise related to the reutilization of a temple locale. Much of the terminology of this Zerubbabel insertion as well as the Joshua material of chapter 3 is illumined by reference to Mesopotamian texts and excavations. Particularly since Zerubbabel was born in exile (and perhaps raised in the royal court there) and since the temple is to be rebuilt in conformity with Persian policy, such direct influences of Mesopotamian language and concepts should not be surprising.

bring forth the premier stone. The identification of the action and the object of the action, the stone called *hāᵓeben hārōᵓšâ,* has puzzled commentators for generations and has inspired a myriad of interpretations. These have been conveniently summarized by Le Bas (1950). Many of these interpretations are based upon ancient versions that have great difficulty not only with the translation of this phrase but also with the understanding of the verse as a whole (see Petitjean 1969: *ad loc.).* Several Greek mss. insert "stone of inheritance," possibly reading *yĕrēšâ* or *mârāšâ,* "inheritance," for *hrᵓšh,* "premier." The Syriac reads "stone of equality and harmony." The Targums have made this expression purely messianic. Symmachus has "highest stone" or "capstone" and the Vulgate translates "first stone." The "premier stone" has been variously interpreted as foundation quoin, topstone, the jewel of the breastplate, the gem for the crown, the legendary foundation stone of Jewish lore, building material for the temple, symbol of the temple, the plummet, the rock of the altar of Holy of Holies, a symbolic stone, the messiah, the Kingdom of God, Israel, the "pyramidion" of Isa 28:16.

The publication of Ellis's *Foundation Deposits in Ancient Mesopotamia* (1968) has stimulated a fresh approach, which recognizes Mesopotamian influences or analogies to the action and object reflected in Zech 4:7 (see Petitjean 1969, Lipiński 1970 and 1975, Petersen 1974, and Halpern 1978). The specific situation reflected in this verse is the dilemma of temple restorers faced with the ruins of a previously existing temple. Near Eastern archaeology provides countless examples of the extraordinary continuity of temple sites. Once a sanctuary was constructed at a given site, that precise location was tenaciously preserved and reused when another sanctuary was erected to replace the building that had been destroyed or had fallen into disuse. The decline or destruction would occur when the polity—economically, politically, theologically—collapsed or perished. Emergent states or conquering kingdoms went to great lengths (Ellis 1968:12–17) to preserve the temple sites. They erected new temples in exactly the same places, so as to ensure the sanctity of the holy places and buildings and thus secure the sanction and blessing of the deities so honored.

The pragmatic dimension of such an undertaking took various forms in the ancient world, depending at least to some extent on the condition of the sacred site on which a new temple was to be built. There may also have been ideological reasons, for which only conjecture can be made, for the great efforts—apparent in archaeological remains as well as in Mesopotamian building inscriptions—involved in the reutilization of a temple location. If the temple had been largely demolished and silted over, to the extent that its exact location could not be easily determined, the original functions were often sought through extensive excavations and leveling. The neo-Babylonians who had to deal with the ruins of the preceding millennia of Mesopotamian civilization were especially vigorous in restoring temples on the exact outlines of the preceding buildings. Nabonidus's mammoth efforts exemplify this; not only did he excavate deeply, he also aligned the new temple precisely with the old one: "I searched for its old foundation, I dug down eighteen cubits into the ground, and Samas . . . revealed to me the foundation of Naram-Sin, son of Sargon, which no king before me had seen for 3,200 years. . . . I laid its brickwork on the foundation of Naram-Sin, son of Sargon, not protruding or receding an inch" (Ellis 1968: Appendix A, No. 38).

Less extreme measures could also be taken. If the walls were at least partially extant and structurally sound, then they could be reused to some extent. However, reuse certainly involved some further clearing of the debris that naturally accumulates at such a site and also the dismantling of unstable parts of the existing walls. Such activities often meant, in essence, at least the partial taking apart of the remains of the former sanctuary. Since any destruction of a god's shrine was a great insult to his power and likely to bring his vengeance and wrath, demolition even for the purposes of rebuilding was risky. It might provoke the deity whose shrine it was. Therefore the whole process, the use of stable existing walls and the accompanying removal of debris and structurally unsound elements from the old temple's ruins, had to be handled with great care and delicacy to secure the blessing of the deity upon the new political power.

The building of temples involved rituals at many stages, beginning with the decision to build. The sole surviving Mesopotamian text describing temple-building rituals deals with the case in which ruins are reused. This text, much cited by scholars dealing with Zechariah's temple visions, is from Warka. Dating from the Seleucid period, it is one of two copies of a somewhat earlier document from Babylon. Although it postdates Zechariah by several centuries, it is presumed to be a conservative text describing a ritual which represents age-old practices. In this text the professional singer—*kalû*—chants "soothing songs" while a ritual is performed that will link a new temple building with an old one (Ellis 1968:34, 184). The ritual involved the removal of a brick, the major building material in Mesopotamia and the equivalent of stone in Palestine, from the ruined building and setting it aside for reutilization in the new temple. Two interrelated purposes were accomplished by this rite: material continuity between the previously existing temple and the new one could be assured, and the proper preparation of a vast foundation was symbolically effected since the previous building could be considered identical with the succeeding one.

The rebuilding of a temple on an old site was thus accompanied by a ritual which would not have been required for a brand-new sanctuary and which was carried out in place of the elaborate physical and ritual preparation of new building sites. It is just such a ritual which appeared in the Warka text and which the Zechariah materials as a whole reflect. Not yet a ceremony of rededication, which would occur only after the building was completed, a refoundation ceremony achieved through ritual the reestablishment of the sanctity of an old site. Equivalent to a cornerstone laying, it marked the initiation of construction by making the existing ruins constitute the foundation of the building project. In Mesopotamia, the temple builder is to "remove *[ha-si-in]* the first brick *[libittu maḥritu]."* The latter term also appears in the Gudea Cylinder, where a new temple is being erected and Gudea carries in the "first" brick. This single important object is the prototypical element in the temple's construction and the embodiment of the temple's existence. Presumably, in the Warka text, which involves the restoration of a temple, the adjective *maḥru* signifies "former" or "previous"—i.e., a brick from the earlier temple but not necessarily the original "first" brick involved in the original foundation ceremony (Ellis 1968:24–29). Whether for pristine temple or rebuilt temple, a "first brick" is the conceptual prototypical construction object.

Similarly, Zerubbabel's bringing out a "premier" stone is the focal point of a Yehudite temple refoundation ceremony. While it may not be a cornerstone (ʾeben pinnâ as in Ps 118:22 and Job 38:6; cf. Jer 51:26) from the preexilic temple, it symbolizes all the stonework of that edifice which will subsequently be incorporated into the restored building. Conceptually the new temple will be identical with the old, and the continuity of the two structures will be assured. The refoundation ceremony, with its premier stone, is part of the same concern for establishing a link with the old order that is exhibited by the careful attention to the reusing of old vessels for the new temple. The tradition of God's presence in Israel and the temple, bruised by the trauma of exile, was authenticated in a refoundation ceremony. Perhaps even more than the later dedication event, the ritual refoundation was an event of vital significance for the life of the postexilic community and surely for the prophetic mission of Zechariah.

shouts. The use of the Hebrew *těšūʾâ* (in the plural) is most unusual and appears to be clearly intentional. It occurs elsewhere only in Isa 22:2, where it has the meaning of city sounds, and three times in Job where it conveys a variety of nonhuman sounds (30:22; 36:29; 39:7). In no other instance do we find the word used to connote a kind of public exclamation. The considerable confusion in the versions about this word apparently can be attributed to the fact that none of the ancient translators knew what its precise meaning was, especially because it follows the equally enigmatic "premier stone." The root would appear to be *šwʾ,* meaning either "to devastate" or "to ruin," as *BDB* 996. The root *šʾh,* meaning "to make noise" or "to cause a din" is also appropriate and has a derivative sense of devastation (*BDB* 980–81). Many of the versions (e.g., Syriac and LXX) in fact render "shouts" as a genitive associated with "premier stone." It is not impossible, therefore, that at one point in the history of the text "shouts" had a meaning of "ruin" or "desolation" as in *měšôʾâ.* Indeed, Ps 74:3 presents us with a vivid picture of the ruins of a temple that may well depict the destroyed First Temple. In such a hypothetical reconstruction, which, however, the present text would not allow grammatically, verse 7b might be paraphrased in the following way: "He will bring forth the premier stone of the ruin to shouts of right, right!"

It is revealing to examine the text of Ezra 3:10–12 in connection with the ceremony of rebuilding. Both the Mesopotamian (Ellis 1968:13, 16–17; Petitjean 1969:247–48) and the biblical evidence indicate that great emphasis was laid upon the ceremonial rites which accompanied the symbolic act of removing and relaying a premier stone— i.e., a stone of the former temple (see above). The text of Ezra provides these details: the priests went out in their priestly apparel with trumpets and the Levites went forth with cymbals to praise Yahweh. All the people sang together and shouted out a great shout *(tĕrûʿâ)* because the foundation of Yahweh's temple was laid. If the prophet coined a new word for "shouts" using a root whose associations are so clearly with ruins, then the new poignancy of the word would have been apparent to all who heard it. Unfortunately, there is no direct textual support for "premier stone of the ruin."

'Right! Right!' The twofold repetition of the word *ḥēn* followed by the particle *lamed* plus the feminine suffix has caused innumerable difficulties for commentators and translators. The LXX, for example, reads "the grace of it the equal of my grace." Both the ancient versions and the modern critics have been especially impressed with the expression *ʾeben ḥēn* of Prov 17:8 (so Petitjean 1969:247; cf. NJPS) and accordingly translate "beautiful." Others have simply taken the repetition to be interjectory and render it "bravo." Rudolph captures the correct sense of the word as divine favor, from the root *ḥnn*, but has missed entirely the ceremonial context of the verse (1976:111).

The meaning of *ḥēn* is quite certain, and the single word often occurs as part of the idiom "to find *favor* in the eyes of." However, the twofold repetition is unique to the present context, where it is an example of the practice in Biblical Hebrew of repeating single words to express entirety (*GKC* § 123c) or to intensify the expression to the highest degree (ibid: § 123e and passages cited there). This passage utilizes both aspects of repetition. The exclamation points in our translation are meant to suggest the intensity of the utterance as well as the totality of the divine favor so signified. In much the same way that "surely" provides intensification earlier in the verse (see above), the repetition here is part of the heightened emotionality surrounding the temple refoundation ritual which this passage reflects. The uncertainty surrounding the issue of cultic renewal and attending the reestablishment of a divine dwelling on an old site is met with the strong assurance that God accepts and favors the construction plans; God gives his full approval. Accordingly, the *lamed* plus feminine singular suffix (literally, "for it") which follows the repetition of "Right!" in the Hebrew text refers to the stone (a feminine noun) that is of paramount symbolic importance. That "premier stone" is thus decreed acceptable in this stone removal ceremony. The reader should note that "for it" does not appear directly in our translation.

The repetition of *ḥēn* may be further evidence of the ritual context of this verse. The apostrophic address to the building site ("O great mountain") at the beginning of verse 7 and this twofold appearance of a monosyllabic, emphatic cry at its end together evoke a sense of some sort of ritual utterance. Indeed, the description in Ezra 3:10–12 of the resumption of temple work provides evidence of a verbal (musical) dimension for the refoundation, a situation analogous to the Mesopotamian involvement of the *kalû* singer.

8. *Then the word of Yahweh came to me.* Verse 8 introduces the second half of the oracular material in verses 6b–10a. It contrasts with verse 6b, which is directed to Zerubbabel, the present oracle being directed to the prophet himself. Many therefore

suggest that verses 6b–7 are an oracular unit distinct from verses 8–10a and so favor a drastic rearrangement of the insertion itself. Petitjean (1969:263–68), for example, has reversed the order of the oracular material in the insertion and suggests the following: 4:8–10a,6b–7. Mitchell originally made this suggestion (1912:191–94) and proposed to place the insertion after 6:14. Most recently Petersen (1974) has suggested that although the present order might be maintained, the two oracles are to be understood as having originated independently and as containing two different messages: verses 6b–7 constitute a challenge to Zerubbabel and verses 8–10a an oracle of weal pertaining to Zerubbabel's foundation deposit.

These and many other attempts to rearrange the text or to separate out the oracular material in the insertion fail to perceive the essential unity of purpose and thematic continuity within the cluster. Yahweh is an extension of the "word of Yahweh" in verse 6b (see NOTE above) and all the oracular material within the insertion pertains to the ceremony of refoundation and to Zerubbabel's unique role in it. The present arrangement of the oracular material within the framework of the vision is entirely in order, and there is no need to alter it or to place it elsewhere.

The Hebrew text of this formula is repeated word for word in 6:9 (see NOTE), another oracular section of Zechariah and one which, like this one, is addressed to the problem of readjusting the major monarchic component of the preexilic state to the realities of the postexilic community. While this passage may resolve the issue with respect to the present moment and in terms of the symbolic participation of Zerubbabel in the temple refoundation, the ultimate conception of Yahweh's people having a Davidic ruler in the full political sense is deferred to the somewhat parallel oracle of The Crowning (6:9–15). The nature of this formula in introducing a prophetic oracle is also appropriate to the two other instances (8:1 and 8:18) where it is found in Zechariah albeit with "of Hosts" added to "Yahweh."

9. *hands of Zerubbabel.* Just as important conceptually for the Yehudites as was the material continuity between the old and new temples, a matter underlying the preceding oracle to Zerubbabel, was the matter of institutional continuity. Consequently the role of Zerubbabel as Davidic scion involved in temple building, although without monarchic status in the eyes of the imperial Persian authorities, elicited prophetic statement. The simultaneous sanction and limitation of Zerubbabel's participation emerges in verse 6 above and in these two verses, 9 and 10a.

The typological pattern in the ancient Near East whereby temples were constructed by gods and/or kings or equivalent leaders (Kapelrud 1963:56ff. and Hurowitz 1983:123–57) is reflected for the Israelites in the essential roles of Moses and Solomon in tabernacle or temple building and also in the Chronicler's desire to add legitimacy to the Davidic reign by recording temple-building activities attributed to him. It is noteworthy that the connection between temple building and the role of the king is made explicit in Ezra 5:11 in the context of the postexilic rebuilding of the temple, although it is Solomon who is portrayed as the "great king." As we have already noted (see NOTE to "high priest," 3:1), in the postexilic community the high priest became responsible for internal administration in and for the temple building project. Yet could the latter take place without a monarch? The ambivalent language of the prophet 3:8–11, to which the Zerubbabel insertion is directly related, deals with this delicate issue.

Similarly here, the expected royal dimension of temple building is signified by the direct participation of Zerubbabel, even though he is not king (see below, NOTE to "small things"). The graphic use of "hands," along with its repetition in this verse and again (in the singular) in verse 10a, belongs to the language of temple building rites. The building of any public structure in the ancient world must be ascribed to a specific ruler responsible for the carrying out of the project. As Ellis points out (1968:20ff.), the royal figure is the founder or builder of a building in more than an official or extended sense. Not only did those ancient kings order the work and provide for its completion, they also were frequently participants, at least ceremonially, in the manual labor involved. In Mesopotamia the kings themselves, according to the evidence of the building inscriptions, carried materials and formed the bricks. The involvement of Zerubbabel is of this order. The use of "hands" is literal, not synecdochic, and expresses the requisite monarchic participation in temple building. One can imagine considerable uncertainty over the legitimacy of Zerubbabel as *peḥâ* for this role. The prophetic sanction in this passage is extended from the suitability of the site to that of the supervisor.

have founded. This is not necessarily a literal description of laying a foundation. Rather, by the ceremonial reutilization of a stone taken from the preexilic temple, the new building could legitimately use surviving portions of the old and yet symbolically be founded anew (cf. Hag 2:18). Since temple restorers in the ancient world seem to have taken great pains to recover and reuse the foundations of the previous sacred structure, the founding of subsequent new temples was always, conceptually, a refounding of a prior structure.

will complete it. The participation of Zerubbabel in the initial building stage and in the final one represents his full involvement. It is typical of texts dealing with temple construction to summarize the full range of activities by denoting its foundation (or refoundation) and its completion. The pairs of verbs in 1 Kings (*bnh–*klh in 6:9,14 and 7:1, which appear to equal the Aramaic of Ezra 5:11; cf. the similar *yussad . . . kālâ* in 1 Kgs 6:37–38 and 2 Chron 8:16) are different from this pair (*ysd . . . *bṣʿ). Neither the 1 Kings usages nor the analogous Akkadian terminology are consistent in their choice of words or their pairing of terms. However, the formulaic quality of a couplet designating the start and finish of a project seems assured even though it does not extend to the specific components of that formula. There was evidently latitude in the choice of the words composing the pair.

Thus . . . me. This statement has occurred three times in the oracular portions of Zechariah. Thus far (cf. NOTES to 2:13,15 [RSV 2:9,11]) it never appears in the visionary sections. As a prophetic formula it serves to legitimate oracular material; in the present instance this consists of the latter half of the Zerubbabel insertion, which is introduced by another formula, "Then the word of Yahweh came to me." All of the oracular portions of Zechariah consist of prophetic activity distinct from the visions. Their insertion into the visions may be a separate stage, formally speaking, in the organization of the full prophetic work. However, the oracles can be considered integral to the prophet's message. They complement the visions and need not be considered later editions of originally separate materials.

10. *whoever has scorned.* The individuals designated by this phrase are those who have trouble accepting either or both of the two ideological assumptions which the preceding verse of the Zerubbabel insertion presuppose—viz, the suitability of the

temple site and the legitimacy of the overseer of the building operations (see above). The verb "scorn," from the root *bwz,* indicates rejection. Compare Esau's treatment of his birthright (Gen 25:34; the root is *bzh)* or the numerous accounts of God's word or human oaths being broken (Ezek 16:59 and 17:16–19; these are also from the root *bzh).* Examples of *bwz* can be found in 2 Kgs 19:21; Prov 6:30, 11:12, and elsewhere. There seems to be a link between the two roots, which have the same meaning.

It is very difficult to determine what part of the populace might be counted among such scorners. Since the Yehudites in general knew their preexilic monarchic state had been legitimized by a temple, the prophet may simply be promulgating a revision of that conception. The efficacy of the temple renewal could well have been questioned, since nearly all who claimed descent from the Judahites were aware of the temple-dynastic connection, which is a major feature of the Primary History. Most people were probably acquainted with the contents of that corpus.

such a day of small things. The expression "day of small things" *(lĕyôm qĕṭānnôt)* is unique to this passage. It signifies the misgivings of some regarding the momentous quality of the present day. The use of *lamed* before *yôm* ("day") as an emphatic particle recalls a similar use in verse 7a above (see NOTES to "surely" and "platform"). It is preferable to understand it as such rather than as indicator of the direct object of the verb *(GKC* § 117n; the use of the emphatic *lamed* is discussed in § 143e and also by Dahood [1970:406]), which is generally regarded as an Aramaism. The phrase "day of small things" may be a deliberate ironic or sarcastic adaptation of what may have been a common saying, namely that the Day of Yahweh would be a time of "great things," since the substantive "great things" appears a number of times in the Bible in reference to God's redemptive acts or cosmic powers (e.g., Deut 10:21; Job 5:9; Ps 71:19; 106:21).

The refoundation ceremony undoubtedly aroused concern over the role of Zerubbabel. As a Persian appointee, he was not quite the same as the royal rulers who figured in temple founding or refounding rituals in the ancient Near East. Some people would have regarded the refoundation ceremony as of little consequence, because the necessary royal figure was lacking, or if present, then in an inconsequential and peripheral way (in the person and potentiality of Zerubbabel). What should be a momentous day ("day of small things" in this situation conjures up its opposite day of "great things") is thus perceived as an unimportant occasion. But Zechariah see things differently. He is confident that Zerubbabel is an appropriate figure in this ceremony and that the monarchic interest in the proceedings has been adequately safeguarded. The effectiveness of the prophet in convincing his audience of this is difficult to ascertain, except for the optimistic "rejoice" that follows and indicates success. What is clear from this passage, and from the entire Zerubbabel insertion, is that Zechariah was dealing with a serious skepticism on the part of Yehudite society. If the oracles contained in this Zerubbabel cluster were originally uttered independently of the Fourth Vision, the present form of chapter four would have taken shape at a time when these concerns were still current. Such a context would have been early—i.e., before the composition of Part Three in December 518 and certainly before the dedication of the rebuilt temple several years later. However, the context of the temple refoundation ceremony itself seems most likely. This passage has stimulated considerable effort among scholars to identify a particular group or faction within the Yehudite community that opposed either the temple building project or the nonmonarchic status of Zerubbabel. Although there may be evidence from other quarters to suggest some internal divisiveness, this verse seems to indicate skeptical evaluation rather than active opposition.

the tin-stone. The phrase *hāʾeben habbĕdîl,* "the tin-stone," refers to a stone of some kind, but just what it was is not at all clear. Just as for "premier stone" above in verse 4 and the enigmatic stones of 3:9, the ancient translators found difficulty in rendering the Hebrew and achieved rather different results. Similarly, modern analysis has coped in divergent ways with the obscurity of the term; see Petitjean 1969:230–37 for a summary of the possibilities. The most cogent explanations, among those cited by Petitjean as well as subsequent studies, are those in which full recognition is given to the context of ceremonial refoundation. One such explanation follows the Syriac, and at least one Greek tradition involves a slight emendation so that the word rendered "tin" instead became a form of the root *bdl,* "to separate, divide." In other words, the term would be another designation for the "premier stone," that which is separated out from the old building in order to be reused in the new. Another interpretation is less dependent on the ceremonial context: the tin-stone is a weight or plummet such as builders use (cf. Vulgate, Targum, LXX; see also Rudolph 1976:111 for discussion and alternative readings).

A further possibility presumes a technical usage no longer familiar to the translators and only available to modern exegetes through the archaeological discoveries in the ancient Semitic world. "Tin-stone" is not composed of a substantive with an adjective or two substantives in construct. Rather, the phrase consists of two nouns, each preceded by the definite article. The second noun ("tin") denotes the material from which the object represented by the first noun is made. In other words, the object is a piece of metal rather than an actual rock. As such it can be related to the variety of objects which, either singly or in any number of combinations, constituted the sacred building deposits made in conjunction with the founding or refounding of temples. The purpose or meaning of such archaeologically recovered deposits, a corpus of which forms the body of Ellis's work (1968), defies specific explanation, particularly in light of the wide assortment of items which appear in these deposits: precious metals, precious stones, inscribed metal or stone tablets, clay prisms, cylinders and cones, comestibles, valueless bits of shells, beads, and stones, and pegs or nail-like figures. Perhaps the most one can say for them is that while their specific symbolism is lost to us, they must have contributed by virtue of their deposition in the walls or foundations of a temple to the significance of the building.

Objects of precious metal or stone could also signify the wealth or success of the enterprise. But it is difficult to conceive of any analogous meaning for the nonprecious metals or odd scraps of glass or other materials that were often included. Tin itself appears in various corpora of deposited material, but it never appears alone. The only instances in which a metal object is found by itself are in the peg deposits, where copper or bronze nails sometimes constitute solitary deposits. The objects in such cases perhaps represent the notion of fastening or securing the temple permanently (Ellis 1968:77–93). However, this type of building deposit is not attested after the old Assyrian period, long before Zechariah's day. Although later monarchs in Mesopotamia, including the Persians, were aware of the ancient practice of placing pegs in temple walls or foundations and may have reinstituted it, the vagueness of the object in Zerubbabel's hand precludes any firm identification of it with an item, peg or otherwise, known from ancient building deposits. Yet, since this section of Zechariah is full of the language of temple foundation ceremonies, this last stone in the succession of items that figure in chapters 3 and 4 is likely related to that important aspect of temple refoundation which is otherwise absent—namely, the deposition of a symbolic object in the walls of the new structure. If we knew more about the use of tin or dross metal objects in the sixth century B.C.E. construction business, perhaps then we would understand better the significance of Zerubbabel's tin-stone. Obviously its meaning was well known to Zechariah's audience, since the prophet assumes immediate recognition of its import and anticipates that its appearance in Zerubbabel's hand will have a dramatic impact.

These seven. The "seven" refers to the seven multispouted lamps of verse 2 (see NOTE to "seven lamps . . . seven . . . seven spouts") and begins the reply of the Interpreting Angel to the query posed by the prophet in verse 5 and introduced by the clause "Then he replied to me" that constitutes verse 6a. Although the two olive trees were the last visionary objects described by the prophet (v 3), the explanation of what the prophet has seen follows the same order as the presentation of the vision. The meaning of the seven lamps on the menorah is first conveyed to Zechariah, and then the significance of the olive trees is revealed following further interrogation by the prophet.

Although this vision is frequently called the lampstand, or menorah, vision, the actual focus of the imagery is not the golden menorah itself but rather the lamps that surmount it. The angel's explication does not mention the word menorah, which is the actual stand, or the *gullâ* ("bowl") which is the immediate receptacle for the lamps. Whatever symbolism is inherent in the menorah itself is not a direct part of its visionary role for Zechariah. This fact may be comprehended in two complementary ways: 1) The menorah, originally the branched symbol of a sacred tree of life, had by late biblical times become important chiefly because of its light-bearing function (C. Meyers 1976:176–79, 185–88). That is, the menorah's instrumentality came to dominate its morphology, so that the prophet sees its lamps, rather than the stand itself, as the meaningful element. 2) The lampstand is flanked by two trees, which have absorbed or preempted the arboreal imagery of the menorah.

eyes of Yahweh. This expression is analogous to the "seven eyes [of God]" as reflected in 3:9 (see NOTE to "seven eyes"), where it is a metaphoric expression in an oracular context for God's omniscience and omnipresence. Its appearance in the Fourth Vision indicates the continuity between the visionary and oracular styles. In both contexts the expression is associated with the presence of God and the favor he shows toward the temple-building enterprise. Although most commentators take this expression to refer to the seven lamps of verse 3 (see NOTES and Baldwin 1972:117, 123), which it certainly does in the Fourth Vision, its broader metaphoric connotations are indicated by the response of the Interpreting Angel which follows.

range through all the earth. The notion of God's omnipresence is underscored by the use of the Hebrew verb *mĕšôṭĕṭîm,* "range," which might also be translated "scour." The entire phrase (v 10b) minus the number "seven" appears in 2 Chron 16:9 with the verb form in the feminine plural. It also occurs in the masculine plural in a late third- or early fourth-century C.E. synagogue inscription from En-Gedi (Chiat 1982:223). The text in the Chronicler is especially apposite because it goes on to add that Yahweh's eyes move about all the earth in order "to show his might in behalf of those whose heart is blameless toward him." The expression thus would seem to have a certain currency in the Persian period. When all of verse 10b is taken together it provides an expression of divine presence and favor, not only as it applies to the temple rebuilding project, which is symbolized by a major appurtenance of God's House, the menorah, but also as it applies to the two principals in that activity, Zerubbabel and Joshua (cf. v 14 and NOTE to "two sons of oil"). Zechariah's support of the status quo in Yehud reaches its culmination at the very end of this chapter—i.e., in verse 14.

11. *"What are these two olive trees?"* This is the first of two questions put by Zechariah to the Interpreting Angel in verses 11–12, in Resumption of the Vision. Together, these two questions balance the twofold questioning of Zechariah by the Interpreting Angel in the Vision section (4:1–6a; cf. first NOTE to 4:5).

olive trees. Again, as in verse 3 above and verse 12 following, the trees are indicated by the term "olive" alone, without the Hebrew word for "tree" (cf. NOTE to "olive trees," v 3). Although it is common parlance for the tree to be identified by its fruit, it is also possible that in this instance the fruit is meant to be highlighted along with the noteworthy qualities of the tree itself. In light of the vocabulary of the next verse and of verse 14, in which the oil produced from the fruit of the olive tree is either implied or specifically designated, the role of the olive itself is as important to this vision as are the qualities of the tree.

the lampstand. The position of the two trees with respect to the lampstand is explicit; it can be compared with verse 3 above, where the word "bowl" *(gullâ)* designates the entire object flanked by the trees. Yet the word *měnôrâ* itself may also represent not the entire object but rather only the stand or support for the lamp-bearing component. In this case, verse 3 together with this verse—*měnôrâ* on the one hand and *gullâ* on the other—make it clear that the trees are situated on either side of the composite object.

12. *I asked him a second time.* The double questioning by the Interpreting Angel in the first part of the vision is balanced by the twofold query of the prophet when the vision resumes in verse 11 and here (cf. first NOTES to vv 5 and 11). This intensification of the interrogation is related to the unique style and the central position of the Fourth Vision in the sequence of Zechariah's visions. The prophet uses this device in order to emphasize the importance of what is contained in the answers to the questions and also to bracket the oracular materials of 6b–10a.

two branches. The second repetition of the prophet's question regarding the olive trees (cf. v 11) provides important additional information about the trees that is not contained in the initial description of the trees in verse 3 or in Zechariah's first question in verse 11 (see NOTES). Here two "branches" of the trees *(šibbălê hazzêtîm)* are specified. The usage of the term *šibbōlet* to connote a feature of an olive tree is unique to Zechariah. The word usually refers to spikes of grain, as it does in Isa 17:5, Ruth 2:2, and Job 24:24. It also occurs ten times in the story of Pharaoh's dream, which is interpreted by Joseph in Gen 41. The story of the seven spikes of grain parallels the story of the seven kine, resulting in Joseph's well-known prediction of seven years of famine following seven years of plenty. The imagery thereby suggested is that of sustenance, which olive trees indeed provide with their fruit. We have already noted how olives and olive oil were essential to the Palestinian diet and economy as a staple foodstuff and as a leading market commodity. The lampstand represented God's presence among his people. Divine favor has returned as a result of the newly resumed building activities and ushers in a period of agricultural plenty such as anticipated by the prophet Haggai (2:19, see NOTE). But it is not simply a favorable economic situation to which this word alludes. That the image includes *two* of these branches serves to connect them with the two trees of verse 3, with the two conduits of the next clause, and with the two "sons of oil" of verse 14. The next clause elaborates on the relationship of the trees to the menorah, as does the explanation of the pair of trees (and of branches) in verse 14.

empty. The root *ryq* ("empty out, pour out") is used exclusively in the Hiphil. It is sometimes found with a liquid, as in Mal 3:10 where it is used when describing rain; consequently the suggestion that "oil" should be substituted for "gold" has seemed plausible. However, the word is used for the removal of other contents from a container, as in Gen 42:35, where Joseph's brothers empty their sacks, divulging the contents to be money as well as grain. If "gold" here symbolizes money or wealth, then the trees provide wealth (by means of conduits) in the same way that money came forth from the grain bags of the Genesis story.

The analogy with the story in Genesis is also helpful in understanding the very difficult Hebrew syntax of the entire sentence. In the Genesis story "sacks" are the direct object of the verb *(hēm měrîqîm)* whereas in Zech 4:12 we have *'ăšer . . . měʿălêhem,* literally "from upon which they are emptying . . ." The antecedent of the participle form *hmryqym* is *šbly hzytym* ("branches of the olive trees") and the verb also relates to *šny ṣntrwt,* "golden conduits," which are used to "empty" the trees of their harvest ("liquid gold"? See NOTE on "gold" below) into the golden fixture which is at the center of the vision. The conduits literally transport the "gold" to the bowl *(gullâ)* of the lampstand, thereby creating a physical link between lampstand and trees.

the gold. The difficult imagery of gold pouring through a channel has led some translators, including the RSV, to emend "gold" to "oil" in keeping with the olive tree context. However, such an attractive alteration has no support from the ancient translators; and the original intention of the text to specify "gold" as the item transferred must be taken seriously. The placement of *hzhb* ("the gold") in the final position of verse 12 without a sign of the direct object makes it even more difficult to understand the specific intent of the word. However, the connection between trees and menorah has been established in several ways. They are both made of gold, and the trees are positioned on either side of the menorah. Since olive trees produce a commodity and lampstands, or at least the lamps they support, consume a commodity, the emptying must involve the transfer of that commodity, if it be one required by the latter and produced by the former—i.e., from trees to lampstand. Olive trees in fact produce olives and oil, and sanctuary lamps function only if they are supplied with pure olive oil (cf. Exod 27:20 and Lev 24:1–4). The frequent suggestion that "gold" should be read "oil" is not acceptable, but the idea shows proper insight into the situation: a substance which could only be oil must flow through the branches of the olive trees, through the conduits, and into the proper receptacles on the lampstand.

Why then does the text read "gold" rather than "oil"? The symbolism of the golden paraphernalia of this vision is extended by having all the objects directly connected with the lampstand made of gold. The lampstand itself is all of gold, and the conduits which probably touch it as they empty the "gold" are also golden. It is only fitting, then, for the commodity which actually enters the lampstand's vessels to be "gold." In addition, pure olive oil is golden in color, although there is a tinge of green as well, depending on the degree of refining. While one might not automatically call the color golden, it is a fair approximation, particularly in this temple setting dominated by golden appurtenances. In sum, "gold" in verse 12 is the object of the emptying *(hmryqym)* and refers to the color and not the substance of that which is being transferred from trees to lampstand. The substance is oil, which is alluded to by the presence of the olive trees and their branches in this verse, and which is specified in the identification of the trees as "sons of oil" in verse 14.

by means of. It seems most sensible to understand *běyad,* "by means of," as indicating instrumentality as does NJPS, although LXX and others translate "at the side of." The more common rendering "by the side of" is suggested by *BDB* 391, which cites Ps 141:6 and Job 15:23 in support of such a translation. Neither of those examples, however, would justify altering the meaning here.

golden conduits. The word *şantěrôt* is a hapax legomenon. Virtually all versions translate it by terms for pipes or tubes. The LXX and other versions add "golden oil funnels," probably under the influence of "spouts" in 4:2 *(mûşāqôt)* and in the desire to clarify the nature of the physical contact between lampstand and olive trees. Although the MT is less explicit and detailed than the versions, a physical connection still seems implicit. The word rendered "conduits" is formed by the insertion of *t* into *şinnor* *(BDB:*857), itself a rather obscure word that is known chiefly from its appearance in 2 Sam 5:8, where it refers to a feature of the Jebusite water system in Jerusalem. The obscurity of the word itself prevents us from visualizing its graphic form, and the rendering "conduit" is intended to be broad enough to allow for any number of tube-like or pipelike possibilities. The place to which these "conduits" bear their contents is not overtly specified. We must assume, therefore, either that the lexical tools available to us simply are deficient for this, as for many other technical words, or that the vagueness is intentional as befits the visionary context. Nonetheless the two branches/ trees, by their association with a pair of conduits, are performing a function that obviously is related to the golden menorah they flank. The connection can be made, if for no other reason, on the basis of the material of which the conduit is made and the commodity which it carries (see below); both are "gold" as is the menorah itself.

13. *Don't you know what they are?* Just as in verse 5 (cf. first NOTE to 4:5) in the first half of the vision, the Interpreting Angel answers Zechariah's query with this question and not yet with the explanation that the prophet obviously seeks. The double questioning in each segment of the vision and the unusual query of the angel as response to the prophet's question are both literary framing devices, highlighting this central vision and, by inclusion, making the Zerubbabel insertion integral to the whole.

my lord. The polite usage of *'ădōnî,* "my lord," after "No" in response to the angel's query "Don't you know what they are?" echoes its usage in verse 5 above, while a nearly identical sequence occurs. Together they form an envelope around the oracular insertion. "My lord" appears also in verse 4 above (see NOTE), but in a slightly different way, for there it is attached to a question ("What are these, my lord?").

14. *two sons of oil.* Verse 14 is the climax of the Fourth Vision. It constitutes the final answer of the Interpreting Angel regarding the "two olive tree/branches" and is

couched in the same kind of symbolic language as the entire vision. The two trees are now identified with a particular designation for oil and are called "sons of oil" *(běnê-hayyiṣhār)*. Our reading is found in Symmachus and the Latin. LXX and Syriac have "sons of fathers." Other versions are overtly messianic and the Targum for example translates "sons of princes." There is no indication that either figure has been anointed in reality, although many translations and ancient versions so interpret. Such an act would surely have constituted an open challenge to the Persian authorities. The view of Kutsch (1963) that, even though there was no actual anointing ceremony, the text indicates that two figures (Joshua and Zerubbabel) were acknowledged as anointed is also to be rejected in light of the visionary context and also because of the particular nuances of the word for "oil."

The term *yiṣhār* ("oil") has a specific connotation; it designates the fresh new oil of olives and is so used in Hag 1:11 (see also Hos 2:10,24 [RSV 2:8,22]); Jer 31:12, etc.). In one instance (2 Kgs 18:32), it is preceded by the actual word "olive" and clearly designates olive oil. "New oil" is associated with the blessing that comes with God's favor as crops produce their full yield (see Andersen-Freedman 1980:243, 287 on this point and also de Vaux 1961:399). It is precisely such blessing that both Haggai and Zechariah believe will be forthcoming upon the restoration of God's earthly dwelling place, the Jerusalem temple. In this connection, the parable of the vineyard in Isa 5 is relevant. In verse 1, "oil" *(šemen)* is preceded by *ben* (literally "son"); but the resulting phrase means "very fruitful" or "very productive" and not literally "son of oil." The Zecharianic use of "sons" with "new oil," however, involves both meanings. It generalizes the fertility implied by the new oil, and it also designates, more specifically, two individuals who accompany God's restored presence among his people.

Another aspect of the "new oil" terminology is its relationship to the priestly share of temple offerings. As a first fruit due the Levitical priests (Deut 18:4; Neh 10:38 [RSV v 37]; cf. Deut 12:17 and 14:23), it was part of the tithe system, which was developed after the reform of Josiah or Hezekiah in order to maintain the Jerusalem priesthood. One of the crucial organizational issues of the postexilic community was the support of the priesthood; the Nehemiah citation and a mention in the Chronicler's extensive excursus on Hezekiah's reorganization of the temple personnel (2 Chron 31:2–20; see v 5) both list the new oil among the commodities that constitute temple revenue. Without a king's portion (that is, the contributions made by the king; cf. 2 Chron 31:3), the financial stability of the temple in the postexilic period had to be secured largely through priestly revenues. Yet the function of the two "sons of oil" in this vision is to provide sustenance for the central object, which symbolizes divine presence. That function in practice would have meant that they provided for all the temple services and sacrifices. In short, the imagery of "sons of [new] oil" assures that official responsibility for the maintenance of the temple will continue the preexilic practice except that now it will be shared by two leaders.

Had the prophet wished to indicate unequivocally that the two figures were anointed, officially inducted into two offices—presumably those of high priest and king, for which anointing with oil was practiced—he could well have chosen *šemen* ("oil"), which designates the liquid of anointment (Exod 29:7; 1 Sam 10:1; 2 Kgs 9:1,3; Ps 89:21 [RSV v 20]; etc.), or *māšîaḥ*, "anointed one" (*BDB* 603). Instead, the language used evokes the imagery of divine favor to be bestowed upon those who rebuild God's house and reestablish stability in the land. The double leadership that will effect this project is thus given divine sanction—both trees stand next to God (see below, "Lord of all the earth")—and the financial support for the ongoing function of the restored institution perhaps is also assured. The priestly leader is placed on a par with the political administrator, an arrangement authorized by the Persian authorities. This arrangement diverges from the preexilic pattern, in which the authority of the kings usually was greater than that of the chief priests and where royal anointment could signify designation for office and not merely inauguration (Halpern 1981:14, 49). Yet, there is precedent for such a bilateral operation in the premonarchic period and also at times in the monarchy, both north and south, when strong priests exercised considerable authority and autonomy within both the ecclesiastical and secular spheres. The "two sons of oil" are not yet two messianic figures, a development which later figures prominently at Qumran and in apocryphal literature, where a Davidic messiah is accompanied by a Levitical messiah. It is perhaps a tribute to the high regard for the words of Zechariah that in the Testament of Levi (8:8–9) an olive branch serves as one of the symbols of the royal priesthood of Levi.

stand by. As in chapter 3, the verb ʿmd ("to stand") signifies a Divine Council scene. Although in the former instance "before" establishes the position of Joshua as an individual in Yahweh's presence the use here of ʿal ("by") is appropriate to the two figures situated near Yahweh. A royal court, with ruler and courtiers, is designated in this fashion in Judg 3:19 where Eglon, King of Moab, appears with his attendants, "all who stood by him." The Heavenly Court is likewise indicated in 1 Kgs 22:19, where the prophet Micaiah reports having seen Yahweh enthroned with the heavenly host "standing by him." Further, those attendants are situated "on his right" and "on his left." This additional information about the positioning of those with access to Yahweh recalls the description in verses 3 and 11 of the two olive trees on the left and on the right of the lampstand, which symbolizes the divine presence. The two trees then must represent two figures who stand in close relationship with Yahweh.

Lord of all the earth. ʾădôn meaning "lord" has already appeared three times in this Fourth Vision, twice in the first segment of the vision (vv 4 and 5) and once (v 13) in the resumption of the vision. All those references concern the prophet's polite address to the Interpreting Angel. Now, in the climax to the series, the fourth usage designates Yahweh. "Lord" as a title for Yahweh is found several times in conjunction with "all the earth." God's universal power and sovereignty are emphasized by this designation in Ps 97:5 and Mic 4:13. A similar universal and political thrust characterizes the other place where the epithet is used, in the story of the Israelites crossing the Jordan; there the "ark of Yahweh, Lord of all the earth" (Josh 3:13; cf. 3:11) is brought across the river, demonstrating to all observers that Yahweh empowers his people to expel the inhabitants of the land. Zechariah himself repeats the term in the last vision, where God's emissaries are stationed by "the Lord of all the earth" (6:5). The universal implication of the term as it appears in the Fourth Vision with the two designated officials emphasizes that Yahweh's sanction, since he is supreme ruler, of a twofold community leadership supersedes the political reality under Persian domination. God's spirit in verse 6b and God's dominion here provide the ultimate authority for Yehud in the days of Darius.

COMMENT

Vision 4:1–6a

Zechariah presents his audience with the centerpiece of the visionary sequence in chapter 4. Not only its central place as fourth in a series of seven visions but also a number of internal features of its presentation proclaim that in this vision the prophet has finally reached the culmination if not the conclusion of his extraordinary visionary experiences. The special features of this vision, which set it apart from those visions which precede and follow, have all been examined or alluded to at various points in the NOTES. It will be useful to collect those data here, as part of our consideration of the centrality of the Fourth Vision.

First, this vision is unique in not being introduced by the first-person assertion of the prophet that he has witnessed some visionary objects or personae that are invested with significance beyond their mundane identity. Instead, the prophet requires special or additional assistance in the very act of taking in the tableau before him. The Interpreting Angel, whose role has previously been to explicate the contents of the visions, here appears before Zechariah has even set eyes upon that material. A similar situation appears to obtain in the Sixth Vision, where the angel directs the prophet to look up; but that instance does not include the arousing of the prophet that is found in 4:1 and that forms the distinctive introduction to the Fourth Vision. The angel must create in the prophet the proper state of mind, the intensely sensitive perceptiveness and receptivity essential for comprehending the complex and symbolic array that greets his eyes. Only the prophetic vision of chapter 3 has a similar introduction. Although the parallel is not exact, the opening of that chapter (3:1) presents a divine force acting upon the prophet. The manner in which the angel secures Zechariah's attention in the Fourth Vision thus makes this vision closer than any of the others to the special form of the Divine Council scene and underscores that the message that will unfold is provided by Yahweh.

Second, the dialogic structure which characterizes all the Seven Visions diverges for the Fourth Vision as it allows the meaning of the prophet's experience to be divulged. The normal pattern has the prophet, after seeing the visionary material, pose a question to the Interpreting Angel, who is the means for revealing to Zechariah the significance of what he sees. Only the Fifth Vision would also appear to vary the pattern, for there the angelic figure first asks the prophet what he sees and effectively removes from Zechariah the initiative of interrogation. Yet that variant can be related to stylistic purposes internal to the Fifth Vision, and in any case it in no way resembles the elaborate double questioning which makes the dialogic arrangement of the Fourth Vision stand apart from that of the others. To be more specific, the simple question-and-answer format is rendered more complex by the fact that the angel twice—once in the initial vision (vv 1–6a) and once in its resumption (10b–14)—responds to Zechariah's questions with a question of his own, "Don't you know what they are?" In addition, the angel's questions in response to Zechariah's contain an emphasis that adds to the suspense that both prophet and audience must feel as they await the explanation. Further, the prophet himself asks three different questions, more than in any other vision. Altogether, this extensive interchange between prophet and Interpreting Angel draws the audience as completely as possible into the prophetic task of comprehending this vision. Its message is the one upon which all of Zechariah's prophecies hinge, and so such devices of discourse as the extended dialogue and the duplication of queries function to draw extra attention to the resplendent objects and their meaning.

Third, if the structure of the vision is elaborate, so too is the scene which composes it. Although the Fourth Vision is not alone in having a multiplicity of images juxtaposed to form the content of the prophet's imaginative experience, it is alone in presenting its objects together and then explicating them individually. Furthermore, the images are described in considerable detail, especially the initial lampstand component of the vision. They share this feature with the first and last visions, where the specific colorings and positions of four horses or pairs of horses are carefully delineated. In this way, Visions 1 and 7 frame the entire sequence and also point to the central vision, which likewise contains images with characteristics that must themselves be described for the prophet's audience. This literary congruity of the First, Fourth, and Seventh Visions accompanies a measure of thematic correspondence, as we shall consider more fully below, with respect to the matter of divine presence and omniscience.

Fourth, the literary correspondence of the First, Fourth, and Seventh Visions in the descriptive material accompanying the visionary object is paralleled by the prophet's use of the phrase "my lord" to address his angelic tutor. Only in these three visions does Zechariah so designate the Interpreting Angel, upon whom he must depend for his comprehension of the significance of what he perceives. Both the initial and final visions include a single instance of the angel being called "my lord." The central vision contains three such examples, thereby intensifying the angel's role and thus stressing the authenticity of the message as mediated by an authoritative source, an angel of the Lord. This dimension of the angel's credentials is further suggested by the fact that Yahweh himself is called "Lord" in this vision. The same word for "lord" (ʾădôn) appears in the final verse of this vision underscoring God's omnipresence; and again in the last vision Yahweh is so designated (Zech 6:5) in connection with the universal scope of his power. The appearance of the word "lord" constitutes a selected and balanced arrangement, connecting first and last visions and highlighting the central one. This structure is not only literary but also thematic, in that the sovereignty implicit in the title is a crucial element of the three visions in which the term appears.

Fifth, the nature of the visionary objects per se is remarkable in the Fourth Vision. The other visions portray objects or persons which are not necessarily noteworthy in and of themselves; rather, they take on their significance perhaps through some tentative symbolic connection but only emphatically through the explanation provided by the Interpreting Angel. This may also be the case for the olive trees, which together are a major although secondary feature of the vision. Yet the central image itself is hardly a mundane object. A lampstand of precious metal with an intricate ordering of multispouted light-giving vessels can only be a unique artifact. Even if it does not replicate an actual menorah that stood in one of Israel's series of national sanctuaries, there can be no doubt that it is meant to be just such an appurtenance. Consequently the identity of this vision's central object as a specific and unique piece of cultic furniture is readily apparent. Its symbolic value within the visionary scene is predicated upon its existence as a live symbol. It may derive further significance from the meaning provided in the vision's explications, but the starting point for understanding or comprehending its powerful presence in the vision clearly stands apart from the others. So important is its message that the evocative visionary object must bear the special quality of having inherent symbolic content, which is then augmented by the particular details of its appearance and context as uniquely provided by the Fourth Vision.

Finally, not only does the lampstand differ from the other objects or individuals viewed by the prophet in his vision as it possesses inherent symbolic value, but also it is exceptional for its static quality. The golden lampstand in the center of this central vision does not itself move. All the other visions involve or imply motion of some sort—the patrolling of horses in the first and last visions, or the various other actions viewed or at the least anticipated in the other visions. The menorah diverges from this pattern; it stands fixed and immobile in the center of the prophet's visionary field. It represents the presence of Yahweh himself, as we shall discuss in some detail below, and as such its immobility suggests the permanence and eternity of God's existence, especially as manifest within his earthly dwelling. In sharp contrast with the dynamic qualities of the other visions, the Fourth Vision's lack of movement conveys the absolute stability of the divine presence. The world may move and change, but the initiator and cause of its movement remains the same. The lampstand's static quality implies divine stability. God's presence is not, however, static; there is some movement within the vision. The difficult ending of verse 12 describes gold (= oil; cf. NOTE to "gold," v 12) pouring forth from branches of the olive trees. Yet even this movement of "gold," a feature which we shall discuss below, does not suggest a process with a beginning or end. The flow is ongoing and continuous, and as such it complements rather than contradicts the sense of permanence evoked by the unmoving lampstand. If the flow of golden oil is related to God's presence, through his "trees" which flank him, then that flow too would be a continuous and uninterrupted condition as long as those trees are in their proper place.

All told, those aspects of the central vision within the sequence of Seven Visions make evident its position as a literary and thematic centerpiece. We can also, in both these respects, relate it to the overall structure of the visions we have noted in our Introduction. The outermost pair of visions, numbers 1 and 7, have a universal purview that forms the backdrop for the intervening visions. The next pair, numbers 2 and 6, concern relationships between Yehud and the imperium of which it is a part. The third set, numbers 3 and 5, deal with Yehud itself if not more specifically its capital, Jerusalem. In such a set of visions, conceived as concentric circles with ever-narrowing areas, the central vision can present us only with the pinpoint of the cosmos, the temple in Jerusalem, the earthly locale of the divine presence. Symbolized by the lampstand, which is localized in the holy of holies, God's presence extends its influence and effect in ever-widening circles until his universal involvement is achieved or attained.

Having established the special place of the Fourth Vision among Zechariah's visionary experiences, we can now turn our attention to the actual scene which composes it. With what imagery does the central vision respond to the many forces that draw our attention and expectations to this one among the seven? As we have already noted, the prophet does not simply announce what has appeared to him. He is first brought into the proper state of alertness so that his receptivity will be assured. Then, again, he does not at once describe what has emerged in his consciousness. Rather, God's emissary first interrupts with the request that he recount what he has seen.

The first word of his description, the object of his "I see," immediately dispels the suspense created by the prolonged introduction of verses 1–2a in which the angel arouses the prophet and then asks for his report. The designation "lampstand," or menorah, stands at the forefront of its detailed description which appears in the rest of verse 2 and that of its context which is then related in verse 3, and we must attempt to ascertain what it signified to a prophet in the late sixth century B.C.E. While the seven-branched menorah had undoubtedly become a premier Jewish symbol by late biblical times, a role that endures even to the present day, the lampstand of this vision does not coincide exactly with that object in form, and one must question whether its rank as a paramount cultic appurtenance can therefore be assumed.

The fact that Zechariah's lampstand is "all of gold" provides the first clue that this object is part of the array of interior furnishings of the temple. Rare would be the private lampstand made of anything but clay; indeed, the descriptions in both the tabernacle texts of Exodus and the Solomonic temple passages of 1 Kings specify that the lampstand(s) for Yahweh's dwelling were golden. Furthermore, the multiplicity of associated lamps—seven to be exact for this single stand—likewise points to a special cultic context. In addition, the literary positioning of the vision at the center of three pairs of visions with narrowing foci places the temple as the scene of the Fourth Vision. Consequently, the foremost object of the Fourth Vision can be none other than a golden lampstand of the interior of the Jerusalem temple.

The difficulty in comprehending this object with respect to its meaning for Zechariah comes not so much in identifying it with a temple appurtenance but rather in relating it to the appurtenances of the temple which is to be replaced by the restoration work to which Zechariah is so strongly committed. Solomon's temple contained ten golden lampstands. While the Solomonic temple was altered and renovated several times during the several centuries of its existence, there is no reason to suppose that any of the ten lampstands was removed. Zechariah's utilization of this single golden stand is thus rather astonishing. In the midst of a community which is seeking to restore the preexilic temple and to establish continuity with the edifice destroyed by the Babylonians, the prophet's imagination brings us within the sacred precincts of such a building and shows us a solitary gleaming object.

Why did Zechariah depart from the tradition of the First Temple? It is hard to imagine that he would invent a new feature. Rather, he would hark back to a tradition even older than the Solomonic one. That is, Zechariah's vision of one menorah may be drawn from descriptions known to him and may indicate the availability to him of the priestly traditions in the Torah literature. To be sure, the Fourth Vision depicts an object which does not agree in all its features with the lampstand of the tabernacle texts. The differences can be understood, first, on the grounds that distortion or exaggeration might be expected in a vision and, second, on the grounds that the prophet inevitably adapted an archaic object to the technology of lamps and stands familiar to him in the Persian period (see our NOTES to "lampstand," 4:2). Although it is possible that the priestly writer used the prophet's vision or the furnishings of the postexilic temple for his description, it is more likely to have been the opposite. A priestly writer of the late sixth or early fifth century would have had no reason to distort or alter what he saw in the temple or read in a prophetic text. Zechariah for the above reasons could hardly have avoided making such changes. If the existence of Torah literature has influenced the prophet, the temple menorah's becoming part of his visionary experience would be one of several hints in Zechariah that he has drawn upon an authoritative tradition.

Zechariah's imagination has alighted upon the golden lampstand to bring him into the center of his world, the Jerusalem temple. Its appearance immediately has that effect. But its role in this vision does not end with that circumstance. The details of the lampstand provided by verse 2 clarify its cultic identity; the description of its situation, presumably within the temple, points to a symbolic significance that goes beyond what is implicit in the menorah itself. The lampstand, we learn further, is flanked by two olive trees. More specifically, its "bowl" appears between the two trees, one to its left and the other to its right. This information accomplishes two purposes: 1) the importance of the lampstand, indicated already by the centrality of the vision itself, is underscored in this conception of two attendant items, designated only in relationship to the central one; and 2) the "bowl" or *gullâ* component of the lampstand becomes the feature of the lampstand to which the trees are directly related.

A golden lampstand, replete with bowl and an array of blazing lights, appears between two trees which themselves have rich symbolic possibilities. What more can be said about this visionary array, aside from the temple setting in which it so clearly belongs for reasons contained both within and external to the Fourth Vision? As a visionary tableau imbued with symbolic significance apart from the particular role it plays for Zechariah, it nonetheless is inextricably part of the Seven Visions. Therefore its significance cannot be fully revealed until the visionary structure has been completed. The dialogue between prophet and angelic figure must proceed, and the Interpreting Angel must give his explication and so provide the authoritative message underlying the brilliant contents of Zechariah's Fourth Vision.

At this point the vision is abruptly interrupted. The real world penetrates the prophet's visionary consciousness. Data essential to the ultimate comprehension of the angel's explanation are lacking; the Insertion, as we understand it, provides the essential information. The uniqueness of such an interruption can be added to the list of the Fourth Vision's exceptional qualities and need not be taken as a secondary or editorial addition. If anything, the extraordinary contents of the vision demand the presence of the inserted material. The general symbolism of lampstand and trees must find its particular and authoritative meaning through oracular as well as visionary data, through direct contact with reality as well as from the supramundane atmosphere of the prophetic imagination.

Oracular Insertion: Zerubbabel and the Temple, 4:6b–10a

This is the second of three major interrelated units of oracular material in Part Two of The Book of Zechariah (cf. COMMENT to 3:8–10 and 6:9–15). As we have already noted, there are also significant blocks of oracular materials, notably Parts One (1:1–6) and Three (cc 7–8), which appear to have been composed or originally uttered independently of the temple reconstruction and refoundation context of the Seven Visions. In addition, other oracular materials appear to have been inspired by the visions themselves (e.g., 2:10–17 [RSV 2:6–13]). The present oracular unit consisting of two interdependent oracles (vv 6b–7 and 8–10a) is to be understood both within the context of the chapter 4 vision and as one of three oracular units that are concerned with presenting and justifying the new Yehudite political restructuring to the restoration community. By suggesting that the insertion is related to the Supplementary Oracle of 3:8–10 or the Crowning scene of 6:9–15, we do not mean to imply that all these units either once existed as a larger single unit or were necessarily composed at the same time. Rather, we propose to read each of these units in the canonical position in which it appears and to treat each as an individual and essential attempt to deal with specific aspects of the political restructuring process that affected Yehudite perception of the present and future. They ground the visions in the reality of the late sixth-century organization of the Persian province of Yehud.

The Supplementary Oracle in 3:8–10 dealt with the role of a future David-ide, the Shoot, vis-à-vis the greatly strengthened high priestly office. Joshua's being granted access to the Divine Council (3:7) dramatically signals his ex-panded role. Yet the prophet has presented the transition from monarchic to priestly rule in a cautious and tradition-bound way: he has tempered accep-tance of high priestly rule within Yehud with a reminder of the future role of the house of David in bringing about full restoration. He has done so in the rich language of the ceremony of temple refoundation. In the absence of a king, the one normally involved in the ceremonial initiation of temple building or restoration, the future Davidide (rather than Zerubbabel the present Da-vidic governor) has been associated with the mysterious stone of 3:9, which was set before Joshua and which can have both priestly and monarchic as-sociations (see NOTES to "this stone" and "one stone" in 3:9). Zerubbabel is not mentioned by name in the context of the oracle which completes the prophetic vision of chapter 3.

In contrast, Zerubbabel is mentioned four times in the Oracular Insertion of the Fourth Vision. Chapter 3 concerns the preparation and legitimization of Joshua for an altered high priestly office (see NOTE to "high priest" in 3:1). Chapter 4 deals with both Joshua and Zerubbabel—i.e., high priest and gover-nor—but here Joshua is not once mentioned by name. Chapter 4 presupposes the material of chapter 3; the two chapters apparently did not have a separate existence apart from each other. The vision itself implies a temple and there-fore priestly context, yet two individuals (see NOTE to "two olive trees" in verse 3 and "two sons of oil" in verse 14), presumably Joshua and Zerubbabel, are featured. The exegesis of the Insertion, however, reveals that the Zerub-babel material is rooted in the ceremony of temple refoundation. Together, chapters 3 and 4 portray the participation of both Joshua and Zerubbabel in a ceremony which, in a country with a monarchy, would have been dominated by a king. A high priest would have been involved in such ceremonies reestab-lishing the temple as the place of sacral operations, and even in the monarchic period high priests played important roles beyond the sacerdotal ones. Yet it is difficult to conceive of a temple foundation or refoundation event not domi-nated by the royal figure who would normally have received the charge to build a sanctuary and who would have commissioned the priesthood and others to carry out the charge. The attention paid to Joshua in chapter 3 implies that his role in this case of temple rededication went beyond what would have been expected of him as high priest. The royal participation in the ceremony, we suggest, has been divided between Joshua and Zerubbabel, the latter being unable at present to participate as a true king. Zechariah justifies both roles in chapters 3 and 4—Joshua's as greater than might be supposed, and Zerubbabel's as more limited and yet valid in light of future expectations.

It is no wonder that scholars want to rearrange the text by placing the Zerubbabel materials in one unit and the Joshua materials in another. But the reality of the postexilic situation was such that a priestly officer and a Davidic governor were together entrusted with the administration of Yehud by the Persian Government. Because there were no exact precedents for such a situation in Israelite history, some reluctance to implement this dyarchic pattern of administration no doubt existed. The Supplementary Oracle of chapter 3 addresses the related problem of expectations about the revival of monarchy, as does The Crowning of chapter 6 (especially vv 12–15)—expectations that were stimulated by the presence of a Davidic scion with only partial authority in the midst of the restoration community. Zechariah's resolution of this problem is to eschatologize it, to place it on the agenda of issues that can be resolved only in the future. The Oracular Insertion of chapter 4 helps clarify Zerubbabel's administrative role in the present temple refoundation context. His direct involvement in the ceremony of refoundation perhaps assuages fears that no Davidide would be present at that momentous event. In many respects the oracular sections of chapters 3 and 4 place the new administrative setup within the traditional categories and so help to make it acceptable.

The complementary nature of the prophetic vision of chapter 3 and the Fourth Vision of chapter 4, however, with respect to their content and purpose, cannot obscure the fact that stylistically verses 6b–10a constitute an intrusion into the vision of The Lampstand and the Two Olive Trees. These verses cannot be understood as a response to the inquiry addressed to the prophet by the Interpreting Angel in verse 5. The response and interpretation commence only in verse 10b. Higher criticism has sought to deal with this glaring interruption. Investigating how the text came to be the way it is has produced no consensus, and most suggestions propose to rearrange the text (see NOTES and COMMENT to 3:8–10 and NOTE to "Then the word of Yahweh came to me" in 4:8). However, from a literary viewpoint, the intrusive nature of the Zerubbabel oracles in chapter 4 does not by virtue of that fact demand their excision or rearrangement. On the contrary, chapter 4 in its present form is a classic envelope construction. The opening and closing units correspond with each other, as for example in the repetition in verse 13 of the questioning by the Interpreting Angel in response to the prior questioning of the prophet that had already appeared in verse 5; together they frame another unit which is in the middle. Because such constructions are common in the Bible and in the literature of the ancient Near East, the idea that they must have arisen through deliberate or accidental textual confusion becomes less defensible. The material in Zechariah 4 appears in this way because of purposeful arrangement and not through later careless or thoughtless handling of prophetic materials. Chapter 4 as a whole should be seen as a single literary construct.

We have proposed that Zechariah himself, perhaps with the assistance of one or more of his disciples, was involved with the editing and compiling of his own works and probably also those of his sometime colleague Haggai. We have also suggested that this task would have been concluded, at the latest, prior to the temple rededication in 515 B.C.E., perhaps a few months before the dedication if the editing was completed in anticipation of that event. A date of 516 for the "publication" of Haggai–Zechariah 1–8 would not be far off. It could also have been completed as early as shortly after the latest chronological heading (7:1) in First Zechariah—i.e., after December 7, 518 B.C.E. If the Zerubbabel insertion ever existed apart from the Fourth Vision—and we have argued against that possibility—it could have done so for only a very short time; they would have been combined no later than 516 B.C.E. Coming back to the matter of the insertion as an independent unit, like the Supplementary Oracle of 3:8–10, we would have to ask what the social setting of those oracles would have been if they indeed circulated or originated separately from the visions. Since the Oracular Insertion of chapter 4 so directly relates to Zerubbabel's role in the ceremony of refoundation and since the Supplementary Oracle of chapter 3 alludes to it, it is simplest to assume that it was that event in the spring of 519 B.C.E. which evoked the prophet's oracular response. Since the visions as a whole have the temple reconstruction as their inspiration, we again reach the conclusion that the visions and the oracles of chapters 3 and 4 arise from the same historical context. The two parts of chapter 4, therefore, must have been composed at approximately the same time. Furthermore, since both oracular units in chapters 3 and 4 as well as the visions themselves presuppose the same dyarchic pattern of administration which had been created by the Achaemenids, there is no convincing reason to suppose one *Sitz im Leben* for the oracles and another for the visions. The joining of the two parts would have taken place almost at the same time as their nearly simultaneous composition in 519. That is, the Insertion was included in the Fourth Vision at the very earliest stage in the brief redactional history of the Book of First Zechariah. If chapter 4 existed in its approximate if not exact canonical form at this early date, the task of final redaction involved putting all three parts of the Book of First Zechariah together and combining that form of the book with the Book of Haggai, thereby creating a single compendious and continuous prophetic piece, Haggai and Zechariah 1–8, nearly all of it concerned with temple affairs, in anticipation of the rededication ceremony.

The Oracular Insertion is introduced in a formulaic style that is especially characteristic of both Haggai and Zechariah. The "word of Yahweh" normally directed to the prophet is twice directed to Zerubbabel, whose name occurs in this section without accompanying specification of his role as governor or of his ancestry as a Davidide (vv 6b and 8). The unusual manner of direct address underscores not only the unique circumstance of Zerubbabel's role as Davidic governor but also emphasizes the following quotation of Yahweh of Hosts: "Not by might and not by power, but with my spirit." It is this oracular saying perhaps more than anything else in the insertion which reveals the political posture of the prophet.

The words "might" and "power" are part of a hendiadys and signify the military power that is the mark of a sovereign state. Cast in the negative, the saying is designated to remind Zerubbabel and his contemporaries that the trappings of statehood are being denied to Yehud only temporarily. Only through God's spirit can the status quo be changed. Meanwhile the realities of the postexilic period, in which only limited power is available and such power only through the apparent largesse of the Persian king, must be accepted. We need not understand the use of this statement as an attempt by a later editor to bring prophecy into line with a failed attempt at rebellion or conspiracy. Rather, it is part of an oracular unit designed to define and rationalize Zerubbabel's limited but important authority in the restoration.

For Zechariah and for the community, concern for the delineation of Zerubbabel's role is brought to the forefront by the temple restoration process, in which a community's monarch played the paramount role in the ancient Near East. This concern would no doubt have come to a head at the first official or ceremonial recognition of the temple project—viz., a ceremony of refoundation in which construction work officially began. We have described the ideology and ritual of that ceremony in considerable detail in our NOTES (see especially NOTES to "this stone," 3:9, "great mountain," "platform," and "premier stone," all in 4:7) and we refer the reader to our discussion there. We would only reiterate here that temple building in the ancient Near East was part of the royal administration of a god's territory. Consequently, a monarchic involvement in temple building was requisite. The Yehudites recognized the return of the divine presence along with his favor to their midst, and they sought to understand at the same time how their monarchic hopes could still be suspended.

In this passage we encounter Zechariah's resolution of the crisis implicit in a temple rebuilt without a king on the throne as Yahweh's viceroy. Although denied monarchic privilege, Zerubbabel is nonetheless given a role, created especially for him in the ceremony. Circumstances normally required that a king participate in such a ceremony, but that was not possible. Joshua is apparently present also as 3:9 would indicate. But the mere fact that Zerubbabel has become a principal figure in the ceremonial equivalent of a modern ground-breaking or cornerstone-laying ceremony cannot be separated from the fact that he is a Davidide. Even though he has not ascended the Davidic throne, it is he who brings forth the premier stone in verse 7 and who carries the tin-stone to its place of deposit in verse 10a. The Oracular Insertion thus both proclaims the Davidic role in the refounding of the temple and reminds the audience that such participation may lack external political legitimacy, but possesses the internal legitimacy of Yahweh's spirit. Zerubbabel's participation in a refoundation ceremony may well have aroused many monarchic expectations that were not to be fulfilled. The Supplementary Oracle in 3:8–10 and the oracular summation in The Crowning (6:9–15) address such expectations with eschatological language. The present Oracular Insertion is intended more to accommodate and reassure those who may have doubted the appropriateness if not also the efficacy of the present arrangement.

The language of the oracle is couched in technical terms the exact meanings of which may elude even the most serious modern reader of Scripture. The "great mountain" of verse 7 evokes the imagery of temple building and also conveys a sense of continuity in the placement of the temple at a key geographic point in Jerusalem. The rebuilding is to take place precisely where the former temple stood, and considerable human effort was expended in order to prepare the construction site for new work. Zerubbabel himself makes that hallowed site the proper "platform" upon which the restored temple must be situated. The Davidic scion thus is afforded a central role in the ceremony of refoundation.

It is Zerubbabel too who brings forth the "premier stone" to sounds of public acclamation. The identification of the stone, *hā'eben hārō'šâ,* has engendered innumerable interpretations for generations. Only recently, however, has attention been drawn to possible analogies with Mesopotamian practices relating to temple rebuilding (Ellis 1968; Petitjean 1969; Lipiński 1970; Petersen 1974; Halpern 1978; and Hurowitz 1983), so that the appropriate conceptual backdrop for much of Zechariah, and for 4:7 in particular, can now be discerned. The "premier stone," usually the first brick in Mesopotamia *(libittu maḥritu),* is a unit of building material that has been removed from the former temple ruins and then incorporated into the new building. Such an act provides a sense of physical continuity between old and new temples. It also marks the completion of the preparatory labors mandated by the refoundation of a ruined building.

The Zerubbabel insertion must be understood in the context of just such a ceremonial occasion, and the echoes of that occasion can best be discerned in the accompanying expression, "to shouts of 'Right! Right!' " The public acknowledged this particular moment in the ceremony of refoundation with loud exclamations of approval. Additional evidence for this occasion comes from Ezra's account of a celebration (3:10–12), which undoubtedly reflects the ceremony of refoundation rather than the one of rededication. The refounding is accompanied by much ceremonial rejoicing: the priests went forth in their ritual apparel with trumpets, the Levites went out with cymbals in hand, and all the people shouted out together in joy because the Temple of Yahweh was refounded. Although the term for "shouts" in Ezra is *tĕrûʿâ* and not *tĕšûʾâ*, as in Zechariah 4:7, the context and intent are undoubtedly the same. In Mesopotamia the professional singer is the *kalû;* in Yehud it is the Levitical singer (Ezra 3:10). The approval of the public and of all the principals is reflected in Zechariah's choice of the Hebrew *ḥēn,* which elicits also the sense of divine approval. Its twofold occurrence no doubt echoes its ceremonial utterance. Zechariah thus has preserved in verses 6b-7 possible excerpts from the pivotal celebration of refoundation that occurred in the spring of 519 B.C.E. These excerpts testify to the formal measures that were undertaken to ensure a sense of continuity between the old and new temples.

Verses 8-10a constitute the second half of the Oracular Insertion. Whereas verse 6b represents both the sanction and limitation of Zerubbabel's participation in the ceremony of refoundation, verse 9 represents symbolically a "royal" participation. The repetition of "the hands" of Zerubbabel asserts his direct involvement, just as in Mesopotamian practice the king himself carried the bricks and even formed some of them. Zerubbabel's direct participation, therefore, albeit as governor and not as monarch, is rooted in specific aspects of Semitic temple-building practice. The use of the two verbs "have founded" and "will complete" is also reminiscent of the monarch's role in temple building (cf. 1 Kgs 6:9,14; 7:1; 6:37-38; 2 Chron 8:16; Ezra 5:11) and helps to evoke supportive feelings for Zerubbabel's surrogate royal role. The prophet apparently assumes that Zerubbabel will still be in office when the work on the temple is completed. But it is only in the final Crowning scene (6:12-13) that full—i.e., monarchic—Davidic participation is assured, and there, as we have indicated, Zerubbabel is not mentioned, for such a monarchic role is reserved for another, future time.

Verse 10a addresses directly those within Yehud who may have doubted the legitimacy of this temple apart from a monarchy or who may have questioned the significance of Zerubbabel's circumscribed position. The Hebrew verb "to scorn" captures the sense of those who could not accept Zerubbabel's limited authority as governor or who rejected the efficacy of the temple renewal under Persian auspices. Many Yehudites were probably deeply committed to the temple-dynastic connection that was their only authoritative model for temple renewal. It is impossible to say whether or not their concerns were ever fully relieved by the Jerusalem authorities or the prophet's assurances. It does appear, however, that at least for another generation, a Davidide was kept close to the locus of civil authority. Zerubbabel's successor Elnathan was linked (by marriage?) to Shelomith, Zerubbabel's daughter, called *ʾamah,* meaning co-official, of Elnathan (E. M. Meyers 1985; see also NOTES to "Zerubbabel ben-Shealtiel," and "governor of Judah" in Hag 1:1). Perhaps a Davidic descendant (Shelomith) in such a position did serve to defuse the concerns of many traditionalists.

For those who regarded the day of refoundation as "a day of small things,"

Zerubbabel's transfer of the "premier stone" was perhaps not convincing. Yet the prophet has an optimistic assessment of the future, for the ceremony is not yet complete. They "will rejoice upon seeing the tin-stone in the hand of Zerubbabel" (v 10a). Not only was Zerubbabel involved in the removal of the "premier stone," which was to be included in the new foundations, but he was also to lay what appears to have been a foundation deposit, a "tin-stone," an object well known in Mesopotamian contexts (Ellis 1968:77–93) and probably included in the ceremony of refoundation. Such objects were very often metal nails or tablets and are referred to in the literature as "peg deposits." Apparently, Zechariah expected that even the skeptics would rejoice when they saw this object in the hand of Zerubbabel. The authenticity of Zerubbabel's participation will finally have become apparent. The premier stone represents the temple's connection with the past, and the tin-stone intended for the future secured the temple's—and Zerubbabel's—connection with the future existence of Yahweh's shrine.

It is difficult to ascertain the impact of the prophet's words on his audience. Inasmuch as verse 10a constitutes the final mention of Zerubbabel in the text of the Book of Zechariah, the prophet perhaps has succeeded in dispelling hopes for immediate monarchic restoration and in establishing general acceptance of the new pattern of leadership that was to obtain in Yehud for some time. In many ways the Oracular Insertion is a rhetorical tour de force. Its placement within the framework of the Fourth Vision, which espouses so explicitly the dyarchic pattern of leadership, is to be seen as intentional and probably original. In our opinion it reflects the prophet's awareness of and sensitivity to feelings of loyalty to the house of David. His support of the new leadership is grounded in a pragmatic view of the world situation in a time when Darius I had concentrated his power and organized the territories in such a way that his reign was to survive for nearly forty years and the Persian Empire was to endure for almost another two hundred years, collapsing only in response to the repeated attacks of Alexander the Great in the 330s B.C.E. Acceptance of that reality and adjustment to the implications of it place these words of Zechariah within the mainstream tradition of classical prophecy.

Resumption of the Vision: Explanation of Lamps and Trees, 4:10b–14

As abruptly as the presentation of the vision in verses 1–6a had been interrupted by the Oracular Insertion concerning Zerubbabel and the temple, so too does the explication of the vision abruptly resume once the information critical to our comprehension of that explication has been conveyed by the intruding oracle. Our COMMENT on that insertion considers at length its placement within the Fourth Vision, and we need only emphasize here that it appears to be integral to that vision despite its clear distinction from the visionary mode. The tendency of biblical scholarship to remove it from its present position is to be resisted.

In the vision, the lampstand is the first and apparently the major item described. Situated between the two trees, it looms as the central object not only in this vision but also in the entire visionary sequence in which the Fourth Vision is the focal point. Yet an explanation of the lampstand per se is not forthcoming; rather the "seven" are the items for which the Interpreting Angel provides an explanatory statement. In fact, the description of the full visionary tableau has already offered a hint that it would not be the golden menorah that would necessitate a comment by Zechariah's angelic companion. The trees in verse 3 are said to be on either side of the "bowl" which was placed on top of the lampstand rather than on either side of the lampstand itself. This hardly means that the trees were somehow floating in air at the level of the "bowl" where it surmounted the stand. The "bowl" surely is representative of the entire appurtenance, as the repetition of the trees' positions in verse 11 indicates. Yet this *pars pro toto* designation highlights the particular component of the object that bears the symbolic meaning essential to the working out of the explanatory section of the vision.

The focus on the "seven," which we understand to mean the seven lamps distributed around the lamp bowl or ring on its stand, draws our attention to the instrumentality of the menorah—that is, its light-providing properties. The single tabernacle lampstand that has, in our view, stimulated Zechariah's imagination was a potent symbol, through its treelike morphology, of the cosmic tree and the attendant and beneficial presence of Yahweh. These botanical qualities have been transferred to the accompanying olive trees in the Fourth Vision, and the concept of divine presence in connection with the menorah remains in its lamps.

The "seven" lamps of verse 2 have consequently been intensified in the prophet's imagination. He shows us not a simple arrangement of seven saucer lamps attached to a supporting ring around the perimeter of the stand's upper circumference. The lamps themselves have multiple wick supports, seven each. With seven being the Semitic number designating totality, the resulting seven times seven lights for these seven lamps reiterates in the biblical symbolism of numbers the utter completeness of that which the "seven" represents. And what are these seven? That is the precise question of the prophet to his angelic companion, and it is also the mildly taunting question (v 5a) with which the angel responds to Zechariah, "Don't you know what they are?" That second question reveals that the prophet *should* know their identity but that he in fact doesn't and presumably lacks the skills and background to allow him to grasp the angel's forthcoming explanation, and for that reason the Oracular Insertion must intervene.

The suspense is at last relieved when, as the vision resumes, the seven lamps are identified with Yahweh's "eyes." The lampstand as a whole may represent Yahweh's presence, but this focus on the full array of lights upon it stresses the divine omniscience that is the concomitant of God's presence. The language of verse 10—"These seven are the eyes of Yahweh which range through all the earth"—integrates the universality of God with his particular relationship to Jerusalem and its temple. The seven "eyes" echoes the terminology of 3:9, where the enigmatic stone before Joshua the high priest signifies, among several possible things, divine knowledge and approbation of Joshua's comprehensive role. Now in chapter 4 God's presence within the sanctuary is revealed in the symbolism of the vision. The temple's full acceptability to Yahweh as his earthly abode is graphically presented in the form of the blazing lights of the menorah. But the language takes us further. Yahweh's eyes "range through all the earth," and he is "Lord of all the earth" (v 14). Such terminology links the God of Jerusalem with the universality associated with Yahweh in the first and last visions. The very phrase "all the earth" appears once in the First Vision (1:11) and once in the Seventh Vision (6:5), so that its twofold occurrence in this central vision underscores the relationship between Yahweh's cosmic scope and the particular earthly spot from which his concern with human affairs emanates.

The "seven eyes" symbolism, drawn as we have indicated in our NOTES from the way in which imperial intelligence systems were conceptualized in the ancient world, appears at the beginning of the Interpreting Angel's explanation. The prophet acknowledges God's omniscience before the angel begins the task of explaining and interpreting visionary material for the prophet. The prophet again poses his question, this time asking what the two olive trees may be. This second question is rendered complex beyond the normal dialogic pattern in two ways: 1) As with the first query to the angel in verse 4, an unexpected question in return constitutes the angel's response (v 13a) in lieu of a direct answer; and 2) The prophet refines his inquiry by posing yet another question, the difficult description of the olive trees' branches in verse 12.

The information in verse 12 about the two branches of the olive trees with their golden conduits comes as a surprise. We of the prophet's audience have become accustomed to grasping a visionary component in its entirety before explication is requested. Here, the prophet adds to his description of the trees in the very process of asking the angel what are the marvelous branches that are part of these trees. The imagery of gold—i.e., oil—coming forth from the two trees signifies that the connotations of fertility or productivity associated with the menorah in its pentateuchal description have been transferred to the trees flanking it in the vision. This transition accords with the fact that it is the lampstand's instrumentality, as light-bearer, which provides its essential symbolic value for Zechariah.

The prophet's second question in verse 12 concerning the trees is in essence a rephrasing and amplification of the first question about them in verse 11. It is not simply a matter of identifying two ubiquitous Palestinian trees; rather, a special quality of those trees demands clarification. The answer ultimately provided for the prophet in the final verse (v 14) of the vision, in its reference to "oil," demonstrates that this qualification of the olive trees' properties is essential to their significance in the vision. "Oil" is the key, and the "gold" of verse 12 emphasizes the oil's color, which blends accurately with all the golden equipment at the center of the vision.

As with all of Zechariah's visions, the visionary objects or personae can and must be related to the contemporary world of the restoration community. Those correlations are not always easy to establish for the modern reader, as our analysis of the Second Vision in particular has revealed. However, we must assume that in the last quarter of the sixth century B.C.E. Yehudites in a Jerusalem subservient to Persian dominance would well have comprehended the visionary allusions. In this Fourth Vision, however, the Zerubbabel insertion and the immediately preceding Joshua passage of chapter 3 assure that the prophet's audience, his contemporaries and we modern readers as well can apprehend the points of contact between the visionary figures and the world that has spawned them and given them their vivid shapes in the prophet's consciousness.

The two olive trees, with their branches pouring forth golden oil, are explained at last in the final verse of this chapter. That verse (v 14) in a sense is the climax to the entire central portion of the visionary section, or Part Two, of the Book of First Zechariah. The central portion consists of both chapters 3 and 4 and concerns the roles of the priestly official Joshua and the gubernatorial figure, Zerubbabel, the latter serving Persian interests and to a certain extent Yehudite interest too. Just how much Zerubbabel represents the interest of his countrymen is the underlying issue of the Fourth Vision and its Oracular Insertion. The prophetic vision asserted Joshua's legitimacy, acknowledging his entry into the Heavenly Court. Now, at the end of the Fourth Vision, we find two figures flanking Yahweh. The language of verse 14, especially the term *hāʿōmĕdîm,* "who stand," reflects the same heavenly setting as the Heavenly Court and Investiture of chapter 3; and the "Lord" and "all the earth" terminology link this verse with Yahweh's global scrutiny of the first and last visions.

The message of verse 14 and therefore of the vision as a whole is complex and, at the same time, radical. The representatives for Yehud of Yahweh's sovereignty are now two in number, in contrast to the model of the monarchic period when the king stood as Yahweh's chosen one, his servant and his son, though there was a chief priest answerable to the king at that time also. The two figures flanking God, however, are not named, for Zechariah sees their positions as Yahweh's viceroys as generic offices, not tied to specific individuals. The high priest and governor henceforth, whoever they may be, are legitimate administrators of Yehud, the special earthly territory chosen by and belonging to God, from whence his universal dominion emanates.

The legitimacy of this dual or dyarchic leadership is proclaimed in two images. The trees flank Yahweh and so equally share the divine authority transmitted to those who have places in the Divine Council. That the two trees are on either side of Yahweh, who is represented by the golden lampstand, sets the message about the administrative legitimacy of priest and governor in a temple context. The restoration of God's house is a restoration of his sovereignty over the territory administered from Jerusalem, and the governance of that territory cannot be separated from divine approbation. This vision adjusts the Near Eastern temple-building ideology, or typology, which was clearly in evidence in ancient Israel, to the reality of the provincial status of Yehud, making the two community leaders the authentic equivalents of a Davidide, whose power was usually greater than that of the chief priest before the exile. The circumstances of the restoration brought about a change in the balance of power and authority. The general dominance of the king (House of David) over priest (House of Zadok) has shifted. Here royal and priestly figures are on a par. Certain royal prerogatives and responsibilities have moved to the domain of the priesthood, for the Davidic figure is now governor and not king. In subsequent years, with no Davidide at all in a high administrative position, the power of the high priesthood will increase even further. The basic structural relationship of a high priest and a king together leading Israel and serving Yahweh persists; it is only the balance between the roles of each that is continually adjusted to the personalities who fill those roles as well as to the political developments that define them.

The two trees not only flank Yahweh and share his authority; they are also "sons of oil." The latter image functions in two ways. First, both governor and high priest provide a constant flow of oil to the lampstand. They support both the temple and Yahweh's sovereignty. Their support will keep the lamps on the menorah permanently lighted. Second, the oil also represents fecundity and prosperity. As such, the trees are connected with divine favor and its attendant blessings. They prosper and that happy condition serves both Yahweh and the people. The prosperity connected with temple building, a theme running through much of Haggai's prophecy, is here directly associated with the two leaders of Yehud, signifying the acceptability to Yahweh of the temple itself and of its restructured administrative context. The eternity of Yahweh, conveyed in the static nature of the vision, is extended to the ongoing prosperity—the flow of gold or wealth—brought about through the two human representatives of divine sovereignty who together will serve Yahweh.

As we have noted, the vision itself does not specify individuals by name, although the directly adjacent materials—the prophetic vision of 3:1–10 and the Oracular Insertion of 4:6b–10a—clearly mention both Joshua and Zerubbabel. The vision thus retains the special character of all Zechariah's visionary experiences, which are oriented more toward heaven than earth, more toward the ideal than the actual, but which nonetheless are evoked by and addressed to earthly circumstances. The portions of his utterances that specify historical characters or occasions are intimately integrated into the visions, which artfully convey their various roles in the divine plan. Yet individuals pass from the arena of human events and so do not appear in the visions themselves, which are meant to transcend the immediacy of the events they reflect. Zechariah, despite the uniqueness of the extended visionary mode which dominates his mission, nonetheless stands firmly within Israelite prophetic tradition.

8. FIFTH VISION: THE FLYING SCROLL
(5:1–4)

5 ¹ Then again I raised my eyes and I looked, and behold: a flying scroll!

² Then he said to me, "What do you see?"

I said, "I see a flying scroll, twenty cubits long and ten cubits wide."

³ He said to me, "This is the curse which goes out over all the land, for every thief according to it has been acquitted, and every perjurer according to it has been acquitted: ⁴ 'I have brought it forth'—Oracle of Yahweh of Hosts—'so that it shall enter the house of the thief and the house of the one who swears falsely by my name. It shall lodge within each house and destroy it, both its wood and its stone.' "

NOTES

5:1. *again I raised my eyes and I looked.* Whereas the use of *šwb* with another verb may literally mean "return" in the peculiar introduction to the lampstand vision of chapter 4, its appearance here as well as in the last vision serves to indicate a repeated action, something occurring "again." As in 6:1, this verbal coordinate focuses upon a renewed looking up (literally, "I lifted my eyes"). Both this vision and the last vision use "I looked," resuming the pattern of the Second and Third Visions. All four of these continue with "behold . . . !" and a variant of that occurs in both the First and Sixth Visions, leaving only the central, Fourth Vision with a noticeably distinct introductory formula. Cf. first NOTE to 2:1.

flying scroll. The image of a scroll unfurled and flying through the air at first seems hardly appropriate to the sequence of visions that has gone before. There is nothing at all unusual about the word for scroll used here; *měgillâ* is the normal term for rolled papyrus (or parchment) as in Jeremiah 36, where it is used thirteen times (cf. usage in Ezek 2:9 and 3:1-3, where a scroll is eaten, and Ps 40:8 [RSV v 7]). The Septuagint translator is apparently bothered by the term in Zechariah, perhaps because it tests the imagination so severely when coupled with the word "to fly," ʿwp. As a result, or by confusion with the Hebrew word *maggāl* of Joel 4:13, the LXX has "sickle." The LXX is well aware of the Hebrew term for scroll, however, as witnessed by its translation of "scroll," meaning sheet of parchment or papyrus, for Jeremiah (MT 36:2,4,6,14 = LXX 43:2,4,6,14 and MT 36:23 = LXX 43:23).

The image of a "flying scroll" is unparalleled in biblical and nonbiblical sources. For several reasons, this strange object which is the focus of the Fifth Vision must be interpreted symbolically. First, the scroll's dimensions, if taken at face value, would present the image of a large billboard rather than a scroll; yet those dimensions, introduced by the stylistic device of the Interpreting Angel's query, are central to the concept of Zechariah's scroll and provide a connection with the temple (see NOTE to verse 2). Second, the notion of a self-propelled airborne scroll likewise defies logic; but the complete mobility implied is essential to the notion of comprehensiveness which is, in turn, vital to the message that is revealed by the angel's explanation.

The ultimate answer to the problem of the scroll's meaning is provided by the Interpreting Angel in his statement in verses 3 and 4. The "flying scroll" is none other than the "curse." The details of those verses make it clear that this "curse" is embedded in a covenant or legal document, for which two instances of covenant violation are specified (see below, discussions of "curse," "thief," and "perjurer"). The specific use of "scroll" in this vision is related to documentation procedures in ancient Israel. The word "scroll" is readily associated with ancient libraries or archives. Sheets of parchment or papyrus, stitched together, were rolled *(gll,* from which the term *mĕgillâ* itself is derived) so that they could easily be stored—perhaps in jars as in Jer 32:14, or on shelves. In high antiquity, archives or written materials frequently were kept in temple storerooms, as reflected in the account of the book of Scripture being discovered in the temple in Josiah's day (2 Kgs 22:8ff.). The scroll of Zechariah's vision is indeed comparable to the covenant document *(sēper)* of Josiah. The very word "scroll" thus conjures up an image of writing, or covenant, and of temple libraries.

It is precisely to this time in the history of Israel that so much of Israel's literary creativity and editorial activity has been attributed. The pentateuchal books had probably assumed their final form a generation earlier and the prophetic corpus was attaining its penultimate shape (Freedman 1963 and 1983). While some of that activity took place in Babylon outside the land of Israel (see NOTE to "all the land" in verse 3 below), with the return of the exiles and with the rebuilding of the temple, the time for recognizing the authority of the Law within community life was at hand. Both priest and prophet were drawn closer and closer in their service to the Law, with Haggai and Zechariah each reflecting this tendency of postexilic prophecy (see NOTES to Hag 2:10ff. and to Zech 3:1, especially "high priest") to communicate divine will as recorded in pentateuchal law. In addition, there is increasing evidence to suggest that the impulse to codify laws and to make laws or patents available in writing came from Darius I himself (Cook 1983:72). Preoccupied with imposing responsible government upon the administrative centers of his empire, Darius is remembered by Diodorus as one of the great lawmakers of ancient Egypt and by Plato in his seventh letter as the great lawgiver of ancient Persia (Cook, ibid; see also NOTES to Zech 7:1). Darius sought to bring stability to his realm by encouraging the internal stability of its components. He capitalized upon the indigenous legal systems of those political entities where he could, and thus for the Yehudites gave external sanction and immediate social application to the codification process already under way, if not recently completed. The result was the emergence of a fixed body of law, representing God's renewed covenant with Israel, which provided the force for social stability in Yehud by the end of the sixth century B.C.E.

The temple context provided by the peculiar dimensions of the scroll (see below) reflects the reorganization of the administration of social justice in the absence of monarchic authority. The priesthood was inexorably involved in carrying out the stipulations recorded in the Law. The identification of the scroll with divine law, in the context of the reestablishment of sacral authority, is contained in this vision in the detail of the scroll's propulsion. The motion of flying conveys the idea of omnipresence, specifically the idea that God is everywhere, in much the same way that the "seven eyes" of the Fourth Vision imply God's presence with respect to the temple. Compare Ps 18:11 (RSV v 10) = 2 Sam 22:11, where the superior mobility of the flying cherub is linked with Yahweh's presence. A "flying scroll" thus represents a law in effect everywhere (cf. "over all the land") in the reconstituted Yehudite community, organized internally through the temple and its functionaries.

2. *"What do you see?"* The question is posed by the Interpreting Angel, who begins the interrogation of the prophet Zechariah as he does also in the Fourth Vision. In all the other visions, it is the prophet who questions the angel immediately upon relating the scene which constitutes his vision. The departure in this case from the pattern of all but the centerpiece vision seems inexplicable, except by acknowledging the influence of the immediately preceding Fourth Vision, and precludes the otherwise expected prophetic query into the meaning of the vision's content. However, the fact that the angel opens up the questioning provides a mechanism for the emphasis on a specific detail of the "flying scroll." The prophet must repeat the statement of what he has seen. In so doing, attention focuses not on the scroll itself, the existence of which has already been noted by the prophet, but rather on the specific dimensions of the scroll. Those dimensions are presented as a critical element of the scroll's identity and meaning.

twenty cubits long and ten cubits wide. The strange detail of the size of the scroll appears as one of its important aspects because the questioning pattern, observed for all but the exceptional central vision, is reversed. The scroll's size is an integral part of the concept of a full scroll as embodied in this vision. While the length of the scroll (20 cubits = *ca.* 10 m.) may not be outrageous in terms of the length of actual scrolls (cf. the Isaiah scroll from Qumran, which is 7.34 m. long), the height (10 cubits = *ca.* 5 m.) is surely a preposterous figure. The delineation of an actual scroll, life size, is hardly possible. Yet the dimensions in and of themselves, as well as the item with which they are associated, are important for understanding the significance of the scroll in this vision. There are two ways in which the twenty-by-ten size can be examined: first, by assessing the symbolic value of those figures apart from the scroll; and second, by considering those dimensions directly in relationship to scrolls and their usage in sacral contexts. We shall follow both courses, and we point out that the explanations provided by one do not preclude the veracity of the explanations provided by the other. The very effectiveness of visionary objects rests upon their ability to convey what is beyond their manifest content.

The twenty-by-ten image, in and of itself, is one which can be related to the temple refoundation context of Zechariah's visions. In its connections with the temple, the twenty-by-ten size is one of several allusions to an aspect of the temple's function contained within this Fifth Vision. The description of Solomon's temple in 1 Kings gives a series of measurements for the various structural components of that temple as well as for the appurtenances to be used in association with it. Two of the sets of measurements may be relevant here: the size of the *'ûlām,* and the span of the cherubim.

Of the three main parts of the Jerusalem temple, which had a tripartite ground plan, one has exactly the same dimensions as this airborne scroll: "the *'ûlām* ("vestibule" according to RSV; also translated as "portico," "porch," etc.) in front of the hall of the house was twenty cubits long, equal to the width of the house, and ten cubits deep in front of the house" (1 Kgs 6:3). This *'ûlām* is of a character markedly distinct from the rest of the temple in its construction and decoration (C. Meyers 1983). Architecturally and conceptually it is a "forecourt" to the house of Yahweh, with the towering bronze pillars Jachin and Boaz at the entrance to the *'ûlām* serving as the gateposts or gateway to God's earthly dwelling. The temple thus consisted of its own forecourt (distinct from the more public temple courtyard *heḥāṣēr happĕnîmît,* 1 Kgs 6:36) plus the *hêkāl* ("hall"; "nave" in RSV) and *dĕbîr* ("holy of holies").

What might be the significance of the equivalency of the scroll's size with the length and width of the temple forecourt? The function of that space during at least part of the monarchic period may provide a clue. Because the enclosed parts of the sanctuary were off limits to the laity and even, perhaps, to most of the priesthood, the meeting place between priest and populace appears to have been the twenty-by-ten-cubit forecourt, or at least the area between that space and the great altar of the temple court. In premonarchic times, before the monarchical authority had virtually usurped all mechanisms of justice in Israel (Whitelam 1979:39–46), the tribal locus of jurisdiction at the town and clan level was situated with the elders at the town gate. However, the priesthood too was involved in the judicial process, especially for difficult or disputed cases or where resolution by divine oath was demanded (as in the cases of Jonathan [1 Sam 14], Achan [Josh 7], and the suspected adulteress [Num 5]; cf. the priestly "breastplate of judgment," Exod 28:30, and the swearing by Yahweh, Exod 22:10 [RSV v 11]). The space at the town gate where judgment was rendered is analogous to the space at the gate to God's dwelling—i.e., the *'ûlām* or forecourt area, where the priests secured Yahweh's judgment. Ezekiel's use of *'ûlām* as a part of the gateway system of the temple precinct supports the notion that *'ûlām* and gateway are complementary architectural features.

The association in this vision of the *'ûlām* or temple forecourt area with the flying scroll would represent the revival of the priestly role in the administration of justice. The progressive encroachment of monarchic juridical authority upon the priestly sphere of jurisdiction was virtually complete by the time of Jehoshaphat, whose reform made the priestly role in justice fully subordinate to that of the monarch (Whitelam 1979:45). The postexilic Yehudites, lacking a dynastic authority, renewed the ancient meshing of the sacral and judicial spheres. The priests were now called upon "to render judgment in my House" (Zech 3:7), a process which presumably took place between the altar and ʾûlām (cf. Joel 2:17, the precise location of the priestly presence needed to secure God's favorable judgment of his people). Further, the basis for the divine justice to be effected by the priestly office is God's law or covenant, as represented by the "flying scroll." The expanded priestly responsibilities, already attested by the designation "high priest" (see NOTE to Zech 1:1) and by the attention to Joshua in Zechariah 3, are here linked specifically to the legal sphere of Yehudite life.

A second dimensional connection between the Fifth Vision and temple, also based on the absolute value of the numbers, appears in the size of the two cherubim, those fanciful composite creatures whose wings were spread out over the ark within the děbîr, or Holy of Holies. The text of 1 Kgs 6:23–26 explains carefully that each cherub stood ten cubits high and that one wing of each was five cubits long. That is, each cherub was ten cubits wide, wing tip to wing tip, and ten cubits tall. Since the cherubim were identical in size and shape, and since they were positioned next to each other with their outer wings touching the walls of the děbîr and with their wings on the side next to each other just touching in the middle of the děbîr, the cherubs together occupied a space twenty cubits wide and ten cubits high. Just as for the dimensions of the ʾûlām, the size of the cherubim can also be related to Israelite legal traditions. The outstretched wings of the cherubim sheltered "the ark of the covenant of Yahweh" (1 Kgs 8:6–7) which contained the "two stone tablets which Moses placed there at Horeb, where Yahweh made a covenant with the people of Israel" (1 Kgs 8:9). If the cherubim represent divine presence and transport (Freedman and O'Connor 1984) in association with God's word on tablets, a twenty-by-ten flying scroll (a covenant document of some kind; cf. NOTE above to "scroll" in v 1) would be a postexilic equivalent. The scroll itself has replaced the ark and its tablets, which have disappeared from Israel, as the source of God's word; and its twenty-by-ten airborne size conjures up the winged guardians of the Mosaic tablets.

A second set of possibilities for understanding the scroll's dimensions emerges from considering the size in relationship to actual scrolls and to what Zechariah would have seen in his vision. The scroll was flying—that is, it was up in the sky—and it must have looked like a scroll because the prophet identified it as such. How is a scroll to be recognized? Its distinctive feature and the source of the Hebrew term denoting it (cf. NOTE to "scroll," 5:1) is that it is rolled. In other words, Zechariah did not see a twenty-by-ten billboard, a scroll completely unrolled, which then would not have looked like a scroll and would have had the wrong proportion for a scroll. Nor did he see an entirely closed or rolled-up scroll, since he apparently is able to read from it. In other words, Zechariah sees in his vision a partly unrolled scroll. The dimensions, therefore, are not that of a completely unrolled scroll. Although the height of ten cubits would be the same whether the scroll was unrolled or not, the other figure of twenty cubits would depend on how much of the scroll was unrolled. Does the twenty-cubit length give us any clues as to what the prophet saw? There are two possibilities, both based upon the ratio of length to height as two to one rather than on the absolute value of the figures, and we thank the editor for drawing our attention to them. Both these possibilities concern how much of the writing of the partially unrolled scroll was visible to the prophet.

The smallest amount of unrolling to be done if someone is to be able to read something from the scroll would be that which would expose one column. One situation thus would be that Zechariah saw a scroll with one column exposed. Later evidence shows that scrolls were written in columns, and it can be assumed that scrolls in Zechariah's day were written that way since such traditions tended to be conservative. Scrolls were read by rolling one end and unrolling the other, leaving one or more columns visible in between the two rolls that were formed at either end as the scroll was read. The minimum that the prophet could have seen, therefore, would have been a column. The biblical scrolls, unlike the other scrolls found at Qumran—and the Isaiah scroll is a good example—always have a ratio of length to width, or height to width, of two to one. The Isaiah scroll is just over ten inches high (that is, the scroll itself and not the column), and the columns are about five inches wide. This two-to-one ratio, which is verifiable from archaeological sources and perfectly applicable to biblical scrolls, could underlie the two-to-one ratio of length and width in Zechariah's vision. Rules for writing biblical scrolls must have been standardized for Qumran scribes and could easily have been the practice several centuries before the earlier Qumran fragments (some Samuel fragments, e.g., are probably from the third century B.C.E.).

This solution is very tempting but it ignores the fact that Zechariah says he sees a scroll and not a column of a scroll. A partially unrolled scroll would have to include the rolled-up parts on either side of the exposed writing. Those rolls would change in size relative to each other but their combined thickness would remain constant and would have to be added to the width of the exposed text if the width of the scroll is to be calculated. A second solution would preserve the two-to-one ratio by having the larger dimension be the width of the exposed text plus the two rolled-up parts, with the smaller dimension representing the height of the scroll rather than the width of a single column. If this were the case, how many columns would be exposed? The width of three columns of the Isaiah scroll, including margins, would be about sixteen inches, since the whole scroll is twenty-four feet long and contains fifty-four columns. The width of the rolled-up portion would then be four inches, which seems like a reasonable size for a thickness that cannot otherwise be calculated because it would depend upon variables such as how tightly the scroll is rolled and how long it is. If four inches is too small a number, then two columns of writing could have been exposed, allowing for about eleven inches of text and rolls totaling about nine inches. In either case, the visions would show a total scroll, partially unrolled, and not just a single column of writing.

Arguments in favor of a three-column exposure or a two-column exposure are speculative but worth considering. A case for the latter might propose that the two exposed columns constitute an imitation of the decalogue, which was written on two tablets. Such an explanation would coincide well with the suggestion offered above, that the twenty-by-ten image recalls the cherubim surmounting the ark and its stone tablets. Alternatively, the two columns could represent the two cases, that of the thief and perjurer, cited in verses 3 and 4 of the vision. An argument for the three-column width, in addition to the fact that the size of the rolled-up portions would be smaller and hence more likely than the rather large nine-inch measurement of the two-column possibility, is based upon the rabbinic traditions about how many columns should be visible when a Torah scroll is read. Three columns should be visible, at least when a scroll is read in a synagogue.

The arguments for the twenty and ten figures representing a ratio found in biblical scrolls does not mean that the symbolism inherent in the absolute dimensions is not also involved. The text of the vision specifies "cubits" and probably would not mention the unit of measure if it intended to portray ratio alone. In short, the ratio may represent the reality of how scrolls were made and read, whereas the actual numbers provide the temple connections and also the extraordinary size of a visionary scroll. The combination of reality and fantasy is exactly what one would expect in a vision. Like dreams, visions are rooted in experience but can have a fantastic aspect as well.

One further aspect of this visionary object also relates to its enormous size. What Zechariah sees is gigantic. While his figures may be based on real scribal techniques as well as on certain biblical measurements associated with the temple, he is looking at something that is a heavenly scroll and not an earthly one. Has he conjured up this image out of nothing? Since there is good biblical precedent for the idea of heavenly documents, in which God records certain things (cf. Exod 32:32–33, where the document, however, is a "book," *spr,* rather than a scroll), Zechariah may very well be drawing upon a long-standing tradition, familiar to us from biblical as well as extrabiblical sources, of books or scrolls in heaven. Zechariah is reading a scroll, a perfectly legitimate earthly occurrence. But the scene is a heavenly one and the scroll is a divine scroll, which Yahweh has "brought forth" (cf. verse 4), presumably out of an ark or box or wherever scrolls, even in heaven, would be kept. Its dimensions are suitable for heaven; and its contents, some form of the decalogue with the sanctions or penalties attached, are meant for earth. The vision puts the two qualities together, giving us heavenly sanction for earthly legal codes.

3. *curse.* The use of *'ālâ* in the angel's speech provides the mechanism for the identification of "scroll" with "covenant" *(bĕrît). 'ālâ* is a "curse" only in terms of its covenant grounding. That is, it is a "sanction/curse," the sworn statement of the covenant participants to abide by the document's stipulations lest certain sanctions be brought against them. The linkage of curse with covenant is perhaps most clear in the language of Deuteronomy 29, where Moses addresses the Israelites in the land of Moab. The Israelites are reminded that they are entering into a "sworn covenant," and that while one who hears the words of this "sworn covenant" may feel automatically blessed, a transgressor will be punished according to all the covenant curses/oaths (Deut 29:9–20 [RSV vv 10–21]; cf. the analysis of Brichto 1968:29–31). "Curse" thus represents the covenant in its breach, when those who violate its stipulations are brought to justice. Equating a written agreement with its sanctions can likewise be seen in extrabiblical materials (e.g., Cross and Saley 1970:42–49), and the Phoenician equivalent *'lt* means "promise" as well as "curse" (Scharbert 1974:261). "Covenant" *(bĕrît)* and *'ālâ* as sanction can clearly be used synonymously or, similarly, as complementary parts of a hendiadys as in Deut 29 (Scharbert 1974:264). Note also that in Nehemiah's day (Neh 10:30 [RSV v 29]) the community self-consciousness was achieved through entering an *'ālâ* to keep God's Torah with all its laws and judgments.

The suitability of this designation for covenant is determined by the two instances of covenant violation, theft and perjury, which follow. Both property offenses and swearing false oaths are disruptions of the social order with which sanction oaths were intimately associated in ancient Israel. Brichto (1968) emphasizes the extent to which the *'ālâ* is used as an "accusatory conditional imprecation" or "exculpatory conditional self-curse" in the negotiation of disputes, and such emphasis is indeed germane to this passage.

over all the land. The meaning of this expression is best derived from its overall context in the visionary sequence. The choice of the word *'ereṣ* for "land" seems to be influenced by the usage in 3:9, "Thus will I take away the iniquity of this land" (see NOTES), where it occurs in the Supplementary Oracle. In that context it is the removal of the iniquity of Yehud, and perhaps Samaria as well, in preparation for temple rebuilding that is the concern of the oracle. Also associated with the temple restoration is the idea that the "land" will yield abundantly in the day when the temple is refounded or completed (see NOTES to Hag 2:19 and Zech 3:10 and 8:12). Concomitant with the idea of abundance is the notion that temple rebuilding promotes social order.

It is the dimension of social order rather than economic prosperity which comes into clear focus in the Fifth Vision. The blessings of the covenant can only be realized when the Law takes hold in all of Yehudite society. In view of the covenant offenses mentioned in this verse—theft and perjury—the application of covenant law is presented in terms of its negative sanction—i.e., the "curse" or the prosecution of the offender. The Sixth Vision carries forward the application of covenant law in banishing "wickedness" from the land. The Law knows no exceptions and hence goes out "over all the land." No Yehudite was exempted from its jurisdiction, and bringing it to bear on everyday life provided a rigorous challenge for the authorities of the restoration community. Here, then, the prophet partakes of and revitalizes older prophetic concepts of social justice and, in his particular choice of theft and perjury as examples, reactivates the priestly responsibility for administering justice.

thief . . . perjurer. The first of this pair is simply denoted by the participial form of the verb *gnb,* "to steal," whereas the second citing of this lawbreaker in verse 4 utilizes the noun form *gannōb.* The second miscreant is referred to elliptically in this verse, but the citation of the liar in verse 5 makes it clear what covenant violation is under review: verse 5 completes the Niphal participle *hannišbāʿ,* "the one who swears," with *bišmî laššāqer,* "falsely by my name." Clearly the issue is that of lying under oath—i.e., perjury or false testimony. The use of the two terms together here probably means that they are interrelated matters, that the perjury in this passage is the so-called "oath of acquittal," in which the person under oath is the defendant. In certain cases an individual charged with a crime for which there are no witnesses is permitted to swear his way out of jeopardy. The writer of the decalogue clearly has such a situation in mind as the *Sitz im Leben* for the third commandment, with the separate issue about a witness giving false testimony being covered by the ninth commandment. The point of the third commandment is that Yahweh will not acquit a perjurer even if the miscreant swears himself innocent and is allowed to go free since there is no one to testify otherwise. The decalogue warns against those who use this technique to avoid punishment when they are guilty. It must have been a great temptation for those guilty of theft, or any other crime, to abuse this process and to go free when evidence sufficient for a conviction was lacking.

Zechariah, like Jeremiah (chap 7) and Hosea (chap 4) before him, is citing the decalogue in his plea for legal stability and social justice. He is making a compound charge, which is typical and representative. Someone commits a crime, theft, and goes free on his (false) oath of exculpation. It is doubtful that the prophet has singled out theft as the only such case in which the acquittal oath might be abused. Rather, the theft plus perjury combination is symbolic of a legal process basic to Israel's system of justice and its covenant with Yahweh. It is symbolic of a system which is concerned with the protection of the innocent and which can be effective only through the power of divine sanction against those who might abuse it. Zechariah raises this issue, perhaps echoing his prophetic forebears, because of his concerns for the establishment of social stability under a legal system for which Yahweh's authority is the ultimate source and recourse.

The combination of a crime lacking in evidence to convict plus an oath resulting in acquittal constitutes the kind of hard case with which Israelite juridical procedures dealt by invoking Yahweh. Very little can be said about how the oaths were administered, but since the Covenant Code has a man accused of theft coming "near to God" to proclaim his innocence (Exod 22:6–10 = RSV 22:7–11), we can suppose that such oaths were administered in solemn proceedings at a sanctuary under priestly supervision. Solomon, in his temple dedication speech (1 Kgs 8:31), refers to the adjudication of a dispute between two parties (*ʾîš lĕrēʿēhû;* cf. the positive use of this term for social harmony in Zech 3:10) under priestly supervision through the swearing of an oath (*ʾālâ*) at the altar of the temple. Note also that, although neither theft nor perjury is involved, the resolution of the issue of the woman accused of adultery is effected through the priestly administration of an oath (Num 5:11–31; see Frymer-Kensky 1984:24–25), providing another instance of priestly adjudication.

The Covenant Code and the dedication speech both give indirect testimony to the existence of an ultimate judicial function associated with the priesthood as well as with civilian leaders. When the elders or those responsible for the meting out of justice on regional or local levels could not render a decision, the parties were to appear before Yahweh, with the priests providing the means to a resolution. Immediately prior to the establishment of the monarchy, a council of elders at the gate of a town would have referred their case to the local sanctuary; with the establishment of the monarchy and the temple, the *ʾûlām*—gateway to God's chief earthly house—becomes the locus of such final adjudication. The sanctuary setting lent majesty and awe to the appellate procedures, which were conducted by the priests, with the resolution given by Yahweh himself. However, the monarchy evidently did not tolerate this priestly role in judicial affairs for long, and the resolution of difficult cases eventually became the responsibility of the king (Whitelam 1979), although the priests must have retained authority to settle routine cases. The judicial role played by the king during the monarchy is shifting back to its sacral position in the postexilic era. With the Persians encouraging law codification and internal implementation of legal systems and judicial proceedings (cf. NOTE to "scroll" above, verse 2), the priests were in the unique position of having access to the written body of precedents and ruling—i.e., pentateuchal law or covenant documents—and also of having the traditional function of playing an important role in community adjudication.

The selection of these two cases, or rather their combination of charges, among many possible covenant violations, seems to be directed specifically at the potential involvement of a supreme adjudicating body in addition to representing an issue which was at the heart of the Israelite concept of justice. In a literary sense, "theft" and "perjury" form a synecdochic pair intended to present just such a situation. Appearing as they do in a temple context, in Zechariah's temple vision and in conjunction with an " *ʾûlām*—scroll," they have the force of offering divine sanction to the restored sacral dimension of the judicial process.

according to it . . . according to it. The Hebrew *mizzeh kāmôhā* is very difficult and is best understood in context—i.e., according to the wording of the oath or "curse." The suggestion that the two phrases are meant to convey two different sides of the inscription on the "flying scroll" (NJPS, NEB) has no justification whatever. Also the suggestion of others (Mitchell 1912:169, 171; Rudolph 1976:115–16) that the present text is a corruption of Zech 7:3 meaning "already how long" *(zeh kammeh)* or simply originally *mizzeh kammeh* is unconvincing. The present translation literally may be understood as referring back to the oath—*mizzeh,* "on the one hand," *kāmôhā,* "according to it" (so Ackroyd 1968:203; RSV). It is *mizzeh,* therefore, that picks up the force of the doublet—i.e., on the one hand the "thief" and on the other hand the "perjurer" as a symbolic pair (see previous NOTE) rather than as two random or separate cases.

acquitted. Both ancient and modern translators have been bothered with this word, which may mean either "to be purged out" or "cleaned out" in the Niphal and "to leave unpunished" or "to hold innocent" or "to be acquitted" in the Piel. The verbal root *nqh* is doubly irregular and hence difficult to parse. Its occurrence twice in the present verse has caused much difficulty. The MT pointing allows for construing it either as a Piel or a Niphal perfect 3 masc. sing. The context of the entire verse favors the Piel, and the meaning must belong to the legal sphere. It, therefore, must mean "has been acquitted," which would result in the accused party going unpunished; cf. NOTE above to "thief . . . perjurer." The law would allow defendants to exculpate themselves by oath, a procedure intended to protect the innocent but which unfortunately could be exploited by the guilty. However, when criminals have so subverted the system, divine justice will catch up with those who have made a parody of what was intended by falsely invoking Yahweh's name (see verse 4).

4. *brought it forth.* The idea of bringing out "it," the "curse" or covenant mentioned in verse 3 (see NOTE), implies that ordinarily it was kept somewhere. This may be an oblique reference to a heavenly ark, in which God's copy of the document, the heavenly scroll, would have been kept (see NOTE to "flying scroll," verse 2).

enter the house. The entrance of the (covenant) "curse" into the house of the "thief" and "perjurer," or perjurious thief, is meant to convey the impression that one who violates the covenant is not immune, even in his own home, to the all-embracing applicability of covenant law.

falsely by my name. The addition of two Hebrew words *laššāqer* ("falsely") and *bišmî* ("by my name") adds to the participle of "swear" *(šbʿ).* The full juridical connotations are lacking in the mention of the perjurer in verse 3, where the participle alone appears. The noun *šeqer* is common in legal contexts, and the phrase "by my name" introduces the sacral dimension of oath-taking. Contested cases, or those lacking in evidence or witnesses, involved sworn testimony by God's altar; see above NOTE to "thief . . . perjurer," verse 3.

destroy. The verbal root *klh* provides the emphasis on totality, and the major components of a dwelling are meant to be the metaphoric objects of the covenant's full justice. Nothing that a thief/perjurer has produced shall survive the reestablishment of God's covenant law and its enforcement. The effect of this statement is not so much to indicate specific punitive action as it is to emphasize the full return to a just society by the restoration of a system that protects the innocent.

its wood and its stone. The two major building materials for Palestinian dwellings are given here as the constituent elements of a covenant-violator's house. The concept of divine justice restored uses the image of an individual's house in its assertion that sinners will be annihilated. This image possesses a sharp irony in the present context of the temple visions of Zechariah. The process of restoration itself, with the stones and wood of God's dwelling providing a complete and functioning national monument to God's active presence in Yehud, is accompanied by the reassertion of covenant authority for the community and consequently for the removal of the existence—the wood and stone material that houses them—of those who disrupt social stability.

COMMENT

The Fifth Vision brings a welcome change from the intense focus which the preceding two chapters had placed upon the absolute center of Zechariah's world. The roles of Jerusalem, the temple, and the leaders were undergoing reexamining and restructuring in the restoration community. That process demanded the ideological refinement and support provided by the prophetic oracle of chapter 3 and the lampstand and trees vision, with its Zerubbabel insertion, of chapter 4. Those densely symbolic passages established the status of the central organization and personnel of the postexilic polity of Yehud; the prophet now turns to the meaning those central features have for the wider circles of human existence—Jerusalem standing, in the prophet's worldview, at the center.

The reader is again referred to our discussion in the Introduction of the literary arrangement of the Seven Visions (see pp. li–lviii). The Fifth Vision is a companion piece, according to that analysis, to the Third Vision. Both these visions concern the realm immediately surrounding the center in Zion—that is, the community which constituted the province or subprovince of Yehud and which was governed by an administration newly constituted under the imperial policies of Darius I. However, since the vision's theme, which we shall consider more directly below, concerns the rule of law in the community, it would be fair to ask whether the vision doesn't have as its scope all Yahwists, whether in Yehud, or in other Palestinian territories, or across the Jordan, or still dispersed in Babylon, Egypt or elsewhere. All of that larger body of Yahwists would presumably recognize the authority of the literature which the scroll in this vision represents and so would be affected by the range of the scroll's movement in the visionary scenario. Yet the special relationship of this vision to the Third Vision in the symmetry of the visionary sequence, and also the language of the vision itself, provide information that may suggest a need for a more limited application of the Fifth Vision. The features of The Flying Scroll vision that connect it with The Man with the Measuring-Cord vision (2:5–9 [RSV vv 1–5]) must be examined before we can comment on the purview of the former.

First, inclusion of oracular material in the unfolding of the vision and its meaning is apparent in verse 4. The entire verse is presented as an oracular statement. Both the repetition within it of the terminology of verse 3, which initiates the Interpreting Angel's explanation of the vision's meaning, and also the syntactical organization whereby the pronouns and understood subjects of verse 4 refer to the "curse" of verse 3, make it clear that the two verses are integrally related. Consequently the oracular formulation of verse 4 is entirely within the visionary presentation. Although the First Vision ends with an oracle, only the Third Vision shares with this one such a direct and essential inclusion of oracular material: the speech to the "official" of 2:8b–9 (RSV vv 4b–5) is actually the explanatory component of that vision.

A second similarity between the Third and Fifth Vision involves the audience for the oracular material that is part of the visionary structure. Since the oracle of 5:4 constitutes the content of the "curse" of 5:3, it is necessarily part of the explanatory portion of the vision and hence is addressed to the prophet, Zechariah being the immediate recipient of the angel's interpretation of the visionary object. The prophet himself, in his presentation of the entire vision, addresses a much wider audience; yet that fact should not obscure the role of a single individual, the prophet, as the one who first hears this oracle. Similarly, in the Third Vision, an individual is the sole recipient of the oracle of Yahweh. In that case, the oracular material is addressed to a certain "official." Zechariah, naturally, thereby hears the original utterance of the proclamation, for he participates uniquely in that vision and may even *be* that official, although we have virtually rejected such a possibility in our discussion of that person (see NOTE to "official," 2:8 [RSV v 4]). Whether or not Zechariah is the one to whom the oracle is addressed, it is clear that the Third Vision portrays it as being directed toward an individual. As in the Fifth Vision, it is only by implication that the prophet charges his larger audience with the contents of the oracular statement.

A third point of contact arises from the movement or action implicit in the description of the visionary object (Vision 5) or person (Vision 3). The scroll is not simply a length of parchment or papyrus; its distinction is that it is moving, or "flying," to be exact. Its symbolic purposes for the vision cannot be ascertained unless one includes property of flight as one of the characteristics of the scroll, which is a heavenly scroll and no ordinary earthly object. Similarly, the man of Zechariah 2:5 (RSV v 1) with a measuring cord in hand is a meaningless character in and of himself. The extraordinary intrusion of the

9. Attic silver tetradrachm of late sixth century B.C.E. struck at Athens and found in Jerusalem. 9a: obverse, archaic head of Athena; 9b: reverse, owl facing right with olive spray at left.
Courtesy of the Israel Museum, Jerusalem

10. Fourth-century hemiobol struck in Jerusalem ca. 340 B.C.E. as a Jewish coin. 10a: obverse, facing head of Hezekiah the governor; 10b: reverse, Hebrew inscription: "Hezekiah the governor" (YḤZQYH HPḤH).
Courtesy of the Israel Museum, Jerusalem

11. Fourth-century silver hemiobol struck in Jerusalem between 350 and 333 B.C.E. 11a: obverse, falcon with spread wings, with inscription "YHD" to right; 11b: reverse, identification uncertain.
Courtesy of the Institute of Archaeology, Hebrew University, Jerusalem

12. Seven-spouted lamp from Tell Dothan, Late Bronze–Iron I.
Courtesy of Dothan II Publications

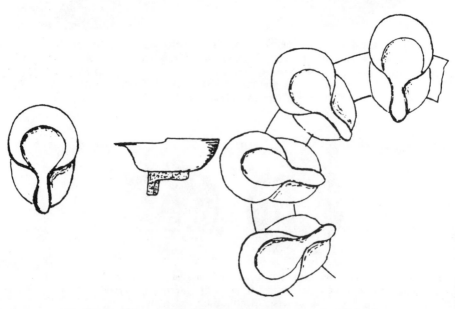

13. Persian (?) period multi-spouted lamp from ancient Palestine.
After Bliss and Maclister

14. Illustration of Zech 4 from Cervera Bible, Cerva, Spain, 1300 C.E.

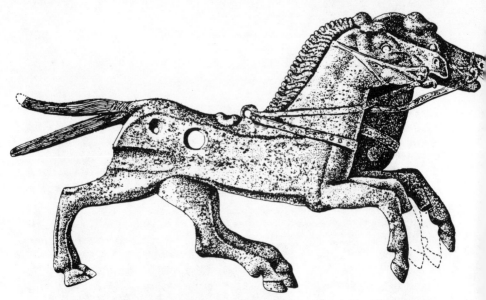

15. Horses in the Persian Empire, drawing from two bronzes at Persepolis.
Courtesy of the Oriental Institute, University of Chicago

16. Discovery of foundation deposit from Persepolis.
Courtesy of the Oriental Institute, University of Chicago

17. Foundation deposit of the mail hall at Persepolis laid by Darius I.
Courtesy of the Oriental Institute, University of Chicago

prophet into that vision functions to make the act of measuring a characteristic of the visionary person and, as a trait, essential to full comprehension of the vision's significance.

A fourth connection between the Third and Fifth Visions arises from the language used in the prophet's narration of his dialogues with the Interpreting Angel in the case of this Fifth Vision and with the man who measures in the Third Vision. In 2:6 (RSV v 2), the visionary persona reports that he has measured a given territory, first its width and then its length. The scroll vision, at exactly the same point in its dialogue, reports that Zechariah sees an object of specified dimensions, first its length and then its width. In short, both visions offer a set of measurements, and the ordering of length and width is chiastic. The set in chapter two apparently reverses the usual order, which means that length (the longer number) precedes width (e.g., Exod 26:2,8; 1 Kgs 6:2; Ezek 40:6–7; 48:9, but compare Ezek 45:1, where the size of the "holy district" of the land is specified in terms of length and then width with Ezek 48, where width precedes length in the discussion of the dimensions of the tribes in the restored community). While this may seem a fine point, and while the things being measured do not correspond, the existence of this hint of symmetry in these two particular instances is worth noting in conjunction with the other correspondences.

A final item is rather less specific but nonetheless noteworthy. The sense of community evoked in the Third Vision is one composed of individuals, people as well as their livestock, for the corporate population of Jerusalem and its satellites is indicated by the designation of its components, "people [literally, "man"] and beasts." That language, as in Haggai 1:11 and Zechariah 8:10, brings us close to the persons who, one by one, compose a population. The Fifth Vision has a corresponding interest in the individual, albeit in a negative sense. Just as chapter 2 (v 8 [RSV v 4]) describes a territory inhabited by man and animal—i.e., substantives in the singular—so chapter 5 (vv 3 and 4) refines the concept of "all the land" by reference to the individuals who will be sought out by the scroll's pervasive presence. The substantives and participles in 5:3 and 4 are predominantly singular, the thief and the perjurer as well as the house inhabited by such a wrongdoer. The collective group of those who disobey the law of God and the government is denoted by an emphasis on the individual violators.

These characteristics shared by the Third and Fifth Visions might not, individually, be convincing arguments for the link between those two visions. However, the combined weight of the correspondences cannot be dismissed as coincidence. The similarities of language and theme create a conscious and purposeful connection between the visions which flank the central section (cc 3 and 4) of Part Two of Zechariah. Nor can we ignore the strong correspondence that exists between the First and Seventh Visions (see COMMENT to those visions). In other words, the balancing of visions on either side of the central one in chapter 4 and its companion piece in chapter 3 is a feature that is clearly discernible in the outermost set of visions. Note also that the set, the Second and Sixth Visions, that comes between the outermost pair and the innermost pair under consideration here likewise exhibits points of contact, perhaps more muted than in the other sets but nonetheless present and significant (see COMMENT to Visions 2 and 6). In sum, the internal connections between the Third and Fifth Visions as well as their integration into a larger scheme which entails the pairing of members in inverse order together lead to the conclusion that those two units of Zechariah's visionary sequence should be considered as complementary segments of a whole.

Because of this relationship between Visions 3 and 5, the question raised above concerning the scope of the scroll's authority can now be resolved. The phrase "all the land" of verse 3, even though the word for "land" is the same 'ereṣ used to designate God's global sovereignty as in "Lord of all the earth" of 4:14 and 6:5, denotes in this context a circumscribed portion of all earthly territory. The Third Vision literally concerns the demarcation of Jerusalem and its territory (satellite settlements), which must be understood as Yehud— that is, the province or subprovince administered from Jerusalem under the organization made by Darius of his imperial holdings. Consequently, in the companion Fifth Vision the population held accountable to the "scroll" is that occupying "all the land"—that is, the inhabitants of Yehud.

If this be the case, then the nature of the authority of the "flying scroll" is being expressed in rather an extraordinary way which can perhaps be better appreciated by means of a direct consideration of that visionary object. Our NOTES to 5:2b have carefully investigated the language in which Zechariah describes this fifth experience of his prophetic imagination. The scroll in and of itself represents the prevalent method of documentation in ancient Palestine. In light of both the subsequent explication of the scroll connecting it with law, and the information available to us about Darius's reputation for imposing stability in his territories by encouraging the utilization and enforcement of local legal systems (see NOTE to chronological heading in 7:1), the specific kind of documentation represented by this airborne roll of parchment or papyrus is clearly a codification or at least a collection of legal materials, all of which have the authority of the divine covenant. In this case, Yahweh's own copy, the heavenly scroll, is shown to the prophet.

Can we identify the scroll's contents any more specifically than that? Such a task is not unlike the problems facing those who seek to relate the "book of the law" found in Josiah's day (2 Kgs 22:8, cf. 2 Chron 34:15) to portions of the canonical Bible. In this case, direct evidence is lacking and we can only infer from the general scholarly opinion concerning the process of canon formation. While the range of theories concerning the date of an authoritative Pentateuch is considerable, the exilic and/or postexilic periods predominate in the spectrum of possibilities. Perhaps already in the middle of the exile the

Pentateuch had assumed its enduring position as the beginning of an account of Israel from its prehistory through its termination with the collapse of Judah (as recorded in 2 Kgs 25). In any event, given Darius's concern that indigenous legal systems be made authoritative for the people who had traditionally adhered to them, it is reasonable to suppose that the Torah literature, or at least the legal portions thereof, is the specific body of law represented by the scroll of the prophet's vision. This would appear to mean that biblical authority is being promulgated in this vision only for Yahwists resident in Yehud, according to our understanding of this vision's scope in general and the meaning of the phrase "all the land" in particular.

Is it possible that such a limited application of Torah authority can be intended? While the answer to that question is that it would be highly unlikely, according to analysis of the entire scroll imagery and explanation of this vision, the question nonetheless points to a fundamental issue of this period. The dispersed Yahwists had persisted in their loyalty to Yahweh through the years of the exile even though God's personal earthly territory in Judah had been wrested from the hands of a Yahwist nation. Now a semiautonomous Yahwist state has been reestablished in Palestine and once again integrates God's covenant rule with a political administration. The Yahwists outside Yehud would have had to deal with the implications of that development for their own acknowledgment of Torah authority.

Explicit information concerning that dilemma is hard to find for the late sixth century, at which time the existence of possibly three diaspora communities (Egypt, Babylonia, and Asia Minor?) can be documented although little of their internal structure can be deduced. The situation improves considerably when examining the Egyptian community at Elephantine in the fifth century (Ackroyd 1970:279–90), yet even then the picture that emerges does not allow us to suppose anything more than that the Torah and its laws were only partially enforced. The mere existence of a temple there and the evidence of syncretistic names implies that the authority of the Torah at Elephantine was at sharp variance with what obtained elsewhere.

Furthermore, in the Babylonian diaspora where no temple was built, new categories of religious expression emerged in response to the trauma of exile and of existence without a central religio-political office to govern the life of the people. These new categories were manifested in the emergence of synagogues in their earliest form of existence, probably as places of assembly in which prayer and worship were conducted apart from a "temple" for sacrificial rites (Gutmann 1975). The separation of a part of a religio-political community from its geographic territory and organization thus signified the onset of processes leading to the compartmentalization of "religion" as a system of beliefs and values separate from the mechanism of sociopolitical control.

We are on firmer ground in examining the insights into this problem afforded by the vision itself. The "flying" quality of the scroll is particularly relevant at this point. It represents the *all*-pervasiveness within Yehud of its authority. The scroll is heavenly and possesses the omniscience of its divine source. Might the converse of this, then, be that outside Yehud its stipulations do not have such total application? Consider also that the explication of the scroll's meaning in the vision is based on the breach of its contents. The ultimate test of the authority in a community situation—whether or not the sanction for obedience to the legal systems can be carried out—can be made only in this "land," Yehud, where the theocratic dimension of a broad priestly role in the restoration community provides the requisite sociopolitical channels for the enforcement of the tenets of Torah literature.

The remaining feature of the scroll as depicted in this vision, which has not yet been brought into the discussion, is now directly apposite. The particular dimensions given for the scroll, twenty by ten cubits, cast it into the sphere of priestly function by relating it to that locale of identical size within the temple's ground plan in which the ultimate priestly authority in the judicial system of preexilic Israel had once resided, before the monarchs of Judah had gradually usurped the last judicial word (see the second NOTE to 5:2). The dimensions also reflect the span of the cherubim, protecting the ark containing the covenant, in the holy of holies of the temple. The twenty-by-ten measurement does not point to a 200-cubit-square scroll but rather creates an analogy between the scroll and a space of similar length and breadth in the sacred space of the temple precincts. This passage contributes to the corpus of allusions, in both the oracular and visionary materials to Zechariah, to the expanded role of the priesthood in the postexilic restructuring of leadership in Yehud. When combined with the prophetic vision of chapter 3, and especially verse 7 of that chapter ("If you walk in my ways and if you keep my service, then *you will render judgment in my House* and you will administer my courts" [italics ours]), and also with the image of two olive trees as Yahweh's agents in the Fourth Vision, this vision shows the increase of priestly authority beyond what it had been toward the end of the monarchy if not already from the time of the Solomonic structuring of the Israelite kingdom. The monarch had become the primary locus of national authority and governance, but now the Persian-appointed replacement for a king attended to matters such as revenues, which directly related to Persian control, thereby leaving the bulk of internal administration to those who retained and transmitted traditional covenant law during exile—namely, the priests. The two-to-one ratio of the scroll's dimensions, in addition, is apparently appropriate to real techniques for copying documents onto scrolls and for the reading of such documents once they are prepared. The exaggerated size, however, takes the scroll of this vision out of the realm of reality and places it in the fantastic world of heavenly scrolls.

The particular cases cited in the explanation of the scroll in verse 3 have been carefully chosen to represent those instances of legal prosecution likely to require ultimate resolution by priestly ruling. In this way they further contribute to the graphic connotation of a temple locale for the scroll implicit in its measurements. In the last analysis, as the oracle of verse 4 makes clear by the very oracular form in which it is presented, it is Yahweh himself who oversees the judicial process. The house for Yahweh that is being restored brings legitimacy to its priestly functionaries in their widened roles. Furthermore, according to the literary imagery of the prophet in this vision, that restored House will bring about social stability. The insistence of Haggai that people whose own houses are in good order cannot neglect the need to make God's dwelling inhabitable is echoed here. God's dwelling is now to be completed. God's presence will at the same time go forth into all the houses of the people, to seek out those who violate his law and abuse its unique protective techniques. Such sources of instability will be removed from the land. The temple restoration, as inaugurated by a refoundation ceremony, will affect all facets of life. With God's authority restored through his law and its priestly administrators, only the houses of the righteous will stand to enjoy the imminent abundance and peace of a community that has responded to God's demands as spoken through the words of his prophets. The scroll, representing a theocratic covenant, is as all-embracing for Yehud in the Fifth Vision as it was for the premonarchic Israelites in the Mosaic appropriation for Israel of the covenant idea.

9. SIXTH VISION: THE EPHAH
(5:5–11)

⁵ The angel-who-speaks-with-me came forth and said to me, "Raise your eyes and look. What is this that goes forth?"

⁶ I said, "What is that?"

He said, "This is the Ephah which goes forth." He also said, "This is its appearance in all the land."

⁷ Behold, a lead weight was lifted, and this is one woman seated in the Ephah. ⁸ He said, "This is Wickedness," and he thrust her down into the Ephah and cast the lead-stone in its mouth.

⁹ I raised my eyes and looked and behold: two females were going forth with wind in their wings! And their wings were like the wings of a stork; they lifted the Ephah between earth and heaven. ¹⁰ Then I said to the angel-who-speaks-with-me, "Whither are they taking the Ephah?"

¹¹ He said to me, "To build for it a temple in the land of Shinar. It will be constructed and it will be set there upon its base."

NOTES

5. *came forth*. This vision, like the central fourth one, is not initiated by the prophet's own accounting of what has appeared to him. The Interpreting Angel is involved in presenting to the prophet the visionary material. Yet the mode of that presentation differs from the Fourth Vision in both the description of the angel's activity and the report of his directive to the prophet. The angelic figure appears in Zechariah's visionary field, announced by the verb "came forth," from the root *yṣʾ*, "to go out, to go forth." Because of the Hebrew sentence structure, with verb preceding subject, the action of the angel is the initial word in the visionary account. As an active verb, "came forth" creates a pattern of activity or movement which is sustained throughout the vision. That verb is repeated three further times: again in this verse, where the visionary object is moving; in verse 7 where that object is further recorded as moving; and in verse 9 where the two winged creatures transport that object eastward. In addition, a fifth instance of verbal motion uses another verb, *hlk*, in verse 10. While only the Fourth Vision is fundamentally static (see above, pp. 262–63), this Sixth Vision involves movement that is seen rather than reported or anticipated as in Visions 1, 2, 3, and 5. Even the last vision, in which *yṣʾ* is also found, presents an action that is reported rather than witnessed directly by the prophet. The opening Hebrew word of this vision, English "came forth," thus sets the tone for its dynamic content. That this vision is divided into two scenes, verses 5–8 and verses 9–11, likewise contributes to the sense of ongoing activity or unfolding drama.

Raise your eyes and look. This is the only vision in which the prophet is ordered to direct his attention toward something, i.e., the object of his vision. This command is more forceful than the "he showed me" of the Fourth Vision, the only other place in which the angelic figure is involved in the initial prophetic perception. This unique imperative opening formula must be related to the complex structure as well as to the peculiar dynamic quality of this vision, which shows the perceived object to be in motion. It is not so much that the prophet must be sharp-eyed in order not to miss the moving object. Rather, the movement in and of itself is a significant component of the vision. The prophet must take in at once both the object *and* the fact of its motion, even though the means by which it moves is not apparent until the second stage of the vision, beginning in verse 9. The prophet first must "look" and absorb the scene of an Ephah going forth; in verse 9 the means of locomotion is introduced to the prophet and then the destination is perceived.

The formula "raise . . . look . . . behold" appears in all the other visions except the central one. Only here, however, is "behold" *(hinnēh)* separated from the two verbs of the formula. Not until the beginning of verse 7 does "behold" appear. The separation of the three parts of the formula has the effect of splitting up the disclosure to the audience of what it is that the prophet is asked to identify. After the initial verbs and then one question, we learn as does the prophet that an ephah is involved. However, that in itself does not constitute the significant visionary object. The contents of the

Ephah must be known or else the vision is meaningless. But the contents are not visible. At this point in the description, "behold" appears and introduces a unit, verses 7-8, which reveals what the Ephah contains (cf. NOTE to "behold," verse 7).

What is this. The Interpreting Angel's introductory command is followed by a question about what the prophet sees even before the object has been described. In two other visions a question by the angel comes after the opening formula. In the preceding vision (The Flying Scroll) the angel asks what the prophet sees, but the object has already been revealed. The Fourth Vision lacks the introductory formula ("raise . . . look . . . behold") and uses the angel's question to introduce the visionary object. In the present case, the angel's question apparently compensates for the fact that the third part of the introductory formula does not yet appear. The question, therefore, initiates a dialogue which will allow the angel to describe the visible object, the Ephah. Only in verses 7-8, when "behold" completes the introductory formula, does a description of the contents of what the prophet sees appear. Thereafter, in verses 9-11, the typical dialogic structure emerges, with the prophet's statement of what he sees, his question to the angel, and then the angel's explanation. Verses 5-8 form a complicated introduction, necessitated because a prior action must be revealed in order for the visionary object to be comprehended.

goes forth. The identity of the object of this vision is immediately and uniquely associated with movement (cf. first NOTE to 5:5). Other visions have some motion, but only in this one are the questions that constitute the dialogue, here and in verse 10, concerned with what the object is doing rather than with the nature of the object itself.

6. *"What is that?"* The prophet immediately interrogates the angel so that the visible object can be identified. Although this question looks as if it is the same as the prophetic queries that follow the opening formula and description of the visions' objects in all but the Fourth and Fifth Visions (see NOTES to 4:2 and 5:2), the question in verse 10 about *where* the object is going is the real question of the angel-prophet dialogue. This question is preliminary; as part of the introductory scene of verses 5-8, it is used to elicit a description of the object and its contents. The focus of the vision, however, is the movement of the object and not its symbolic significance apart from that movement. Hence the present question put by the prophet anticipates his real question about the meaning of the vision in verse 10.

The prophet's question here at the beginning of verse 6 is the second question of the opening of the Sixth Vision, following as it does the angel's question in verse 5. These two questions balance the twofold answer provided by the Interpreting Angel in verse 6. The angel has two things to tell the prophet each preceded by "he said" (cf. NOTE below to "he also said").

Ephah. The choice of 'êpâ in this vision has perplexed generations of exegetes and has provoked an assortment of rather forced interpretations. The word itself is not difficult; it represents a barrel- or bushel-shaped container for grain or else the quantity of grain contained within such a vessel. Found twenty-seven times in the Hebrew Bible, "ephah" is in every case but this one clearly a technical designation for a volume or dry measure. Such a uniform usage in ancient Hebrew cannot be ignored in this passage. However, a literal interpretation of the ephah's size would appear to be impossible because a person is reportedly sitting within the container (v 7). Estimates of the ephah's capacity vary. Based on Albright's reconstruction of some rather fragmentary jars marked *bt* from Tell Beit Mirsim, R.B.Y. Scott has suggested (1959:29) that an ephah, if it is the same as a *bath* (cf. Ezek 45:11), would be 22 liters or 19.98 American quarts (dry measure), which is approximately ⅗ of a bushel. An older calculation by W. Nowack (in *Lehrbuch der Hebräischen Archäologie* 1894) arrived at 36.44 liters or 33.09 American quarts, which is somewhat more than a bushel. Neither method of arriving at the ephah's capacity is conclusive, and in either case the calculations allow for a space that would obviously be too confined even for a seated human figure. The possibility that the figure was not an actual person but rather a smaller than life-size figure (see below, NOTE to "woman")—that is, a statue or idol of a deity—does not fully resolve the issue of this mundane ephah image.

While the evident familiarity of the ordinary ephah measure does not allow that concept to be rejected, there is nevertheless another aspect of the word *'êpâ* which may also figure in this vision. The vision itself, like Zechariah's other visions, has a general temple setting (cf. Halpern 1978:179–80). The language of the last verse in particular supports the idea of a sacral context, and certain other elements (see NOTES below) such as the presence of a figure in the Ephah, the identity of that figure as Wickedness, the pair of winged beings, and the lead object, all have temple connotations. Those connotations would appear to be non-Yehudite, a situation appropriate to the Mesopotamian destination (see NOTE to "land to Shinar" below, v 11) of the Ephah. Because of these associations with pagan cultic elements, a suggestion made decades ago by Marenof (1931–32) seems worthy of reconsideration, especially now that the technical elements of temple restoration in the ancient Near East, as made known to us through Mesopotamian deposits and inscriptions, can be related to many details of Zechariah's visions and oracles, particularly in chapters three and four.

Marenof points out that the Sumerian word for one of the ziggurats in Mesopotamia, the shrine of the goddess Nin-Girsu at Lagash, is *E-pa,* "summit house." He suggests that this name became incorporated into the Assyrian language and from there into other Semitic languages in a manner related into Hebrew as *hêkāl* (= House of Yahweh or main room of the temple; see NOTE to Hag 2:18). Further, he calls attention to the Assyrian nouns *a-pu* ("cave") and *a-ptu* ("room") as well as the Arabic *afta* ("room"), and also to the denominative verb *apu* meaning "to build," which can be found in association with building a shrine. Specifically, Marenof proposes that Ephah designates the little room, an enclosed shrine or cella, which surmounted a ziggurat, a conclusion not far removed from the suggestion of Mitchell (1912:175) that verse 11 implies such a shrine. It is unlikely that an ephah measure would represent that cella: the possibility is precluded if *'êpâ* can linguistically be connected with the larger container—i.e., a cult room for the statue of a god atop a Mesopotamian temple edifice.

Even though the temple visions of Zechariah show marked familiarity with the general Near Eastern temple ideology in which Israel participated, and the postexilic setting admits of an even more direct awareness of Mesopotamian religious architecture, at least among the returned exiles, the connection of Ephah with a pagan shrine still cannot fully rule out the mundane meaning of *'êpâ* as measure. At best the word may be a *double entendre,* partly meaning an idolatrous cult room but also inescapably evoking the image of a grain container. The significance of the former emerges as the vision unfolds. But what can the latter indicate? One can do little better than speculate. Perhaps the very familiarity of the term in this strange visionary configuration was meant to startle the prophet and his audience, alerting them to the specific and far less common meaning of the word—i.e., its association with a Mesopotamian cult place. There is also an irony to be perceived in the notion of a measure of the temple cereal offering being turned around, containing instead the idol for whom the grain may have been intended, and being taken away.

In addition to the above possibilities suggested for the startling image of the ephah, the fact that it appears in a prophetic vision should be considered. Like the scroll of the previous vision, which is explicitly larger than life, the object of this vision is airborne. Anything the size of a real ephah would certainly be too small for the prophet to see, and in any case things in heaven tend to be conceptualized as being oversized. Even if ephahs had standard sizes and capacities, a heavenly ephah, one containing a woman at that, would surely be proportionately much larger than an earthly one. The prophet saw in his vision an ephah in the sky, which automatically meant that it was very much greater in size than an ordinary one. Consequently, a human figure could easily be conceived of as fitting within what he saw. This aspect of the ephah does not rule out the preceding discussion. If the appearance of an ephah rather than some other vessel as the container for the figure is not arbitrary, then the association of 'êpâ with temple architecture would still be a possible explanation for why Zechariah specifies "ephah."

The reader should note that our translation capitalizes "Ephah" to indicate the shrine frame of reference. Our discussion continues that practice, while using "ephah" with a lower-case initial letter when it connotes a measurement.

goes forth. The association of the object with movement is again presented by a verbal form used to qualify the noun (cf. first and last NOTES to 5:5 and also the verbs in verses 9–10).

He also said. The repetition of this clause to introduce further information about the Ephah is not necessary. It has the effect of dividing the angel's statement into two parts: the Ephah itself and its "appearance." In other words, the object has two components. Since the meaning "appearance" makes it difficult to understand the second statement as another component, perhaps it does actually signify what the Ephah contains: the content is the second component. However, "appearance" is not suitable as an indication of its contents, and the LXX rendering "iniquity," which would be related to the "Wickedness" of verse 8 and so designate the contents, appears to be a legitimate reading (see next NOTE).

its appearance. Although there is enormous disagreement among the versions as to the proper meaning of 'ynm, the MT need not be altered. Our reading is supported by the Vulgate (cf. Symmachus), though LXX and Syriac transmit "their iniquity" or "their guilt," undoubtedly reading 'ăwōnām. The Greek and Syriac have perhaps been influenced by the occurrence of 'āwōn in Zech 3:4 and 3:9. The Latin has read the Hebrew text, correctly it would seem, as 'ayin, "eye," but has overlooked its less literal meaning of "appearance" or "shining."

Most modern translators and commentators have preferred to emend the MT, as suggested by the editor of Zechariah in *BHS*, by changing y to w thereby forming 'wnm, meaning "their iniquity." A recent critic (Barker 1978:23) has defended this emendation by citing the support in the Targum Onkelos where the idea of a "false measure" is associated with the word "ephah." She also suggests that the LXX translation "adikia" ("unrighteousness") for 'wnm represents the supposed lawlessness that overtook the Yehudite community in the period of return, and has chosen to read into this vision a situation of social disturbance and struggle within the community which she believes is also reflected in the so-called Third Isaiah (Barker 1977; 1978:17). Other critics, who regard this vision as supplemental to the Fifth Vision, take the mention of "iniquity" and "Wickedness" as a reflection on the general nature of Yehudite society but tend to identify the verse as a gloss inserted by a mistaken copyist (Mitchell 1912:172–73). Although we have retained the difficult MT reading in this case, we note the fact that it is introduced by a second "he said," which gives it the character of a second fact about the visionary object (see previous NOTE). That second fact would have to be related to its contents, which are equated with "Wickedness," another form of "iniquity," in verse 8.

The masculine plural suffix is very unusual, especially since one would expect a feminine singular. In the visionary context, where symbolic language plays so vital a role, the use of the plural to convey a collective singular might be appropriate. There is ample precedent for this in the Bible (GKC § 135p). The Hebrew word for "eye," 'ayin, is extremely versatile, and it has a well-attested usage meaning either appearance or gleam of metal in particular (Lev 13:5,37,55; Num 11:7; 1 Sam 16:7; Ezek 1:4,7, 16,22,27; 8:2; 10:9; Dan 10:6). Another possibility is that the *mem* is not the suffix but rather an adverbial ending, or even an enclitic *mem*. Neither suggestion, however, helps with the meaning of the text. The plural suffix is all the more puzzling in view of the fact that the only plural words in this passage come in verses 9–10, where the "two females" are mentioned. While the feminine forms are used regularly in those verses, *hmmh* ("they") in verse 10 is anomalous, being masculine instead of feminine, in contrast with *lhnnh* ("their") in verse 9. It is therefore possible that we have a survival of the dual forms, which don't distinguish masculine from feminine, both in verse 10 and here in verse 6 (editor's suggestion). Yet a prospective use of the suffix would be unusual and it is problematic to have this noun referring to anything but the Ephah of the previous statement.

The form of the suffix remains problematic, and the meaning of the noun is still difficult. However, a much older suggestion offers a viable explication of the extremely difficult MT and has particular merit in light of our understanding of the term "Ephah." In some Mesopotamian sources the ziggurat is designated "conspicuous house" in ideograms. The expression *igi-e-nir* which literally means "house to be seen" may well have been expressed in Hebrew as *'yn* (Marenof 1931–32). If "Ephah" can be associated with a Mesopotamian shrine, the MT would correctly be referring to its visibility.

in all the land. As in the Fifth Vision above (5:3), the "land" (*'ereṣ*) at issue is restricted to that which is inhabited by the people who will be affected by the temple restoration and for whom the wickedness (of idolatry? See below, NOTE to "Wickedness," v 8) will end. Yehud and possibly Samaria as well are thus designated. Although it is not readily apparent that "land" here designates Yehud, our COMMENT to the Fifth Vision provides an analysis which concludes that Yehud, represented as Jerusalem and its satellites or hinterland, is the primary frame of reference for the phrase "all the land."

7. *Behold.* Our second and third NOTES to verse 5 indicated that *hinnēh* ("behold"), which is the concluding element in the introductory formula of most of Zechariah's

visions, is separated in this vision from the first two parts ("raise . . . look"). The splitting of the formula is the result of the complex introduction to the Ephah vision. The vision concerns the movement of an object, but that object itself must first be revealed. To complicate matters further, the contents of that object are not visible because they are explicitly sealed within by a cover that cannot easily be moved. Hence the contents must be shown to the prophet in a scene that is actually a flashback. Verses 7 and 8 constitute a compact chiastic unit, introduced and concluded by the "lead" weight or stone and presenting the woman = Wickedness forcibly contained within the Ephah by that heavy lid. Those verses describe something that would have had to have taken place before the prophet raised his eyes and saw the Ephah. The logical chronology would have the action of verses 7 and 8 preceding the prophet's seeing the closed Ephah being carried off to Shinar. Since such an arrangement is precluded by the fundamental structure of all the visions, a complicated introduction, with the opening formulaic verbs as commands and with "behold" delayed until this point, serves to convey the necessary information so that the action of the vision can be properly understood by the prophet. The splitting of the formula also has the effect of dividing the whole introduction (vv 5–8) into two parts: a. the Ephah itself (vv 5–6) and b. the contents of the Ephah (vv 7–8).

lead weight. The removal of this lid from the Ephah does not appear to fit naturally with either the *'êpâ* = measure or the *'êpâ* = shrine meaning of the Ephah. Perhaps the inappropriateness of lead for a cover is meant to emphasize the fact that an extraordinary device is being used to enclose forcefully and unalterably the Ephah's strange contents. The word for "weight," *kikkār,* is related to a verb *(krr)* denoting circular motion and is used to indicate a round object. A geographic district, usually that surrounding some focal point, can be indicated by the noun (e.g., the Jordan district, Gen 13:10,11). Such a usage may be an extension of the idea of the basic round shape of a bread load (as 1 Sam 2:36) or of a metal weight, and the latter is clearly the sense that this usage implies.

As a term for weight, *kikkār* normally represents a talent. There was great variation in the ancient world, both in the method by which the value of the talent was calculated and in the variance in weights of the specimens representing a talent or some fraction thereof. The Babylonians used both ordinary and royal talents as well as "heavy" and "light" standards (Sellers 1962:830–33; Scott 1959:34). The "heavy" (double) talent in Mesopotamia can be roughly estimated as averaging 60 kg. (132 lbs.), with the "light" (single) talent at half that (30 kg. = 66 lbs.) for the common weight. The royal standard would be slightly heavier, with the "light" talent weighing somewhat less than 1.0 kg. more than the "light" talent according to the common weight. Calculations of Israelite equivalents indicate that the "light" talent was used in Palestine, with computation based on the decimal rather than the sexagesimal system used by the Babylonians. Using a Hebrew shekel of slightly over 11 grams, a figure derived from weights recovered at Tell Beit Mirsim, the Hebrew talent of 3,000 shekels can be estimated at 34.272 kg. (75.6 lbs.). In at least some instances the Israelite reckoning appears to use Babylonian units, so the resulting weights would be the same, a condition no doubt desirable for economic and political purposes. The present context would presumably favor a correspondence between Hebrew and Babylonian measurement, since the object in question is moving between Palestine and Mesopotamia. Because the variation between Hebrew and Babylonian talents was small, its use in this passage would not be greatly affected if one were to assume incorrectly that the Babylonian standard is the one employed. The variation between the double and single talents, however, is greater; hence the meaning of the passage might well be altered if the correct interpretation of talent is not ascertained. Since a woman could, albeit with some difficulty, push aside a single talent of 66 pounds, the likelihood is that a double talent of 132 pounds better fits the implication that the woman could not remove the weight placed on her.

The *kikkār* as a talent or unit of weight was characteristically employed in reference to silver or gold (e.g., 1 Kgs 9:14), although it could also indicate a quantity of bronze (Exod 38:29) or iron (1 Chron 29:7). Most of the biblical usages for *kikkār* as a weight occur in the context of temple or tabernacle construction. This is the sole instance of "lead" in association with the talent measure and thus the certainty of its meaning as a weight has been questioned. A round object, or lid, rather than a weight has been suggested by some translations (e.g., NJPS; RSV equivocates, using "cover" in this verse but referring to it as a weight in v 9). However, both the temple context of the vision and the inappropriateness of lead as a cover for an ephah together provide sufficient reason to retain the "weight" connotation. Further, as a unit of measure it is in keeping with the normal meaning of ephah as a measure, although one deals with volume and the other with weight.

The introduction of "lead" *('ōperet)* in connection with "weight" may be an example of prophetic irony. Instead of the valuable metals usually meted out by the talent for temple building, the shrine for Wickedness (= idolatry; see below, NOTE to "Wickedness") is here associated with a metal which was relatively useless in the ancient world and which was considered to be a kind of worthless silver (Forbes 1950:176). Its heaviness simultaneously connotes its effective use in keeping the Ephah's inhabitant weighted down, captive in this container. Lead's peculiar properties also lent it a special magical role in the ancient world, a role that emerges in the second appearance of the word "lead" in this vision, in verse 8 (see NOTE).

"Lead" at the beginning of verse 7 is balanced by the recurrence of that word near the end of verse 8. Together, the words enclose a unit in which the contents of the Ephah are revealed to the prophet. The action of these two verses explains why the Ephah is significant: not because of properties which inhere in the Ephah as shrine or as measure, but instead because of its peculiar contents. The sequence of movements that takes place implies a past event. The lid is removed and then replaced so that Zechariah can see "Wickedness." Yet Wickedness is already contained in the Ephah; she is in fact imprisoned there. The placing of the woman in the Ephah had already taken place before this vision began.

lifted. The normal visionary introduction, used in the Second, Third, Fifth, Sixth and Seventh Visions, includes a statement (or command, as here in the Sixth Vision, v 1; cf. v 9) portraying the prophet looking at the object of the vision. The idiom for his looking is, literally, "I lifted my eyes," with the verb *nś'* used for "lift." That same root is also employed in the language of this Sixth Vision to further the narrative sequence. This dynamic vision is not presented in its entirety simply by having the prophet lift his eyes—that is, by his looking at an object which the Interpreting Angel then explains to him. Instead, the visionary object, or at least a feature of it, must itself be "lifted" up so that the contents of the Ephah can be revealed. But the lifting of the lead cover that is situated over the opening of the Ephah does more than allow for the visibility of the Ephah's contents. The "Wickedness" enclosed in this container, which needs to be transported, is hereby afforded mobility. She is not static. That she moves unless forcibly restrained is implied by the two active verbal ideas of verse 8, which describe how she is restored (permanently) to her place within the Ephah.

this is one woman. It is very difficult to render the Hebrew syntax into comparable English syntax because the demonstrative *z't* ("this") is in the predicate position. Our literal rendering would be paraphrased "there was this one woman . . ."

The text gives no clue as to the nature of the female figure situated within the Ephah. Because the Interpreting Angel identifies her with Wickedness (in v 8; see NOTE), which probably is an oblique reference to idolatry, this figure in an Ephah, seen as a shrine, would be a representation of a deity. If it is in fact a statue of a (seated) goddess (so Marenof 1931–32) such as would have been the sole occupant of the cella of a pagan shrine, the accompanying figures of winged beings transporting the deity represented in this way would be appropriate to the idolatrous imagery. In such a case, the female gender of the symbol of non-Yahwistic worship would have been determined by the female gender of the word ("Wickedness") that personifies this abhorrent practice. The transfer of a woman, or goddess, to Babylon and the establishment there of a shrine for her (cf. below, 5:11), balances the restoration of the temple in Jerusalem and the countermovement of Yahweh back to his land and his earthly dwelling. The identity of such a goddess is not revealed, but the equation of "woman" with "Wickedness" provides a clue (see below, first NOTE to 5:8).

While the association with a deity is strong, "one woman" could also refer to a human female in a way which would not be at variance with the implied idolatry that emerges from the language of this vision as a whole. The woman is about to be removed to Babylon, and the stork simile suggests that she never fully belonged in Palestine (see NOTE below). In this case, the female could represent "foreign women," presumably Babylonian wives brought back from exile by the returning Judeans. The use of the female, specifically a foreign woman, to represent the danger of the foreign culture is a feature of the postexilic period. The "strange" or "foreign" woman of Proverbs can be identified with non-Yahwist women present in Yehud and the threat they posed to community stability (Camp 1985). These women later figure prominently in the reforms of Ezra and Nehemiah as part of the company of "foreign women" who have threatened the integrity of Yahwism. In Ezra 10, in Nehemiah (13:23–27), and also in 1 Kings with reference to Solomon's non-Israelite wives (11:1–8), the presence of alien women is related to idolatry. For Solomon, the relationship is explicit—his foreign wives turn his "heart after other gods" (1 Kgs 11:4). For Ezra and Nehemiah the assertion that foreign wives interfere with sole loyalty to Yahweh is less direct, yet Nehemiah justified the increased emphasis on endogamous marriages in part by reference to Solomon's sin (Neh 13:26). The problem of such foreign influence did not originate in Ezra's day; note that Ezra lists four sons of Joshua (Jeshua) among the priestly offspring who had married outside their community (Ezra 10:18). The offending wives in Ezra and Nehemiah's day were evidently from other local groups (Nehemiah specifies Ashdodites, Ammonites, and Moabites, and Ezra employs the difficult phrase "foreign women from the peoples of the land"), but surely the problematic marriages in the early days of the return would have been with Babylonian wives.

The word "woman" in the Sixth Vision, with its focus on the removal of idolatry, can thus refer to two things: the causes of such "Wickedness," namely the integration of members of groups serving other gods into Yehudite families; and the result, idolatry. In either case the root of this disruptive situation, the woman and/or goddess, is about to be restored back to her proper position in the "land of Shinar." The use of the word "woman" rather than a more specific word for goddess or name of a deity is ambiguous enough, as befits the visionary mode, to allow for both meanings.

The peculiar qualification of "woman" by the cardinal number "one" does not seem appropriate to the Ephah context. It is questionable whether a single figure could have been inserted into an ephah as a measure, and more than one figure would be out of the question. Its possible simultaneous significance as a pagan shrine (see NOTE to "Ephah," v 6) likewise does not seem to warrant the specification of the number one in reference to the contents of the Ephah. However, the winged creatures that will ultimately carry it and its *one* "woman" *(ʾiššâ)* are presented as "two females" *(nāšîm)*. Since the gender of the composite creatures providing the transportation is linked to the gender of the persona to be carried, the singular number of that persona may have been provided in anticipation of the designation below of the flying women as *two*.

seated. This piece of information about the female figure's posture could describe a human woman's squatting position as might be required if the ephah were the measure in which she is contained. However, this is hardly an ordinary ephah. The sitting position is more likely related to the image of the Ephah as a cult room. A seated woman in that case would be a statue of an enthroned goddess, not unlike those known in glyptic representations of cult scenes from Mesopotamia.

8. *Wickedness.* The choice of the term *hāriš̄ʿâ* to personify the "woman" of verse 7 who sits in the "Ephah" provides the key to understanding the overall meaning of the vision. This noun occurs thirteen times in the Bible, but this is the only instance in which it is preceded by the definite article. We have rendered it here with a capital "W" to indicate the force of the definite article in personifying the noun. Although there is a broad range to the attested usage of *hāriš̄ʿâ* as "wickedness" in civil, ethical, and religious affairs, where it denotes the opposite of righteousness, it also can refer quite specifically to idolatry. Some scholars (e.g., Ackroyd 1968:204) therefore propose to translate *hāriš̄ʿâ* as "idolatry" in the present context.

The several biblical passages in which "wickedness" is associated with idolatry are instructive. At the end of chapter 8 of Deuteronomy (vv 18–20), the covenant of Yahweh is said to be valid so long as Israel does not walk after other gods; then, in chapter 9 (v 4) the "wickedness of the nations" is cited as the justification for Israel's inheritance of the land. In other words, *hāriš̄ʿâ* is understood to embrace the idea of idolatry, at least as far as the indigenous Canaanite population is concerned. Mal 1:4, although probably dating to the first half of the fifth century B.C.E. and thus postdating Zechariah, describes the area of Edom as the "region of wickedness," with an association of idolatry also (cf. use of *riš̄ʿâ* in Mal 3:15,19). Since "Wickedness" in the present passage is thrust into a container, sealed within it, and ultimately sent to Babylon (see NOTE on "land of Shinar" in v 11), it is reasonable in light of the above usages to understand the word as a technical term for idolatry. The motif of stuffing a figure of wickedness or idolatry into a vessel anticipates the motif of much later times in which an evil spirit is contained within a jar, waiting to be released as soon as the container is opened (so Ackroyd 1968:205). Mason (1977a:58) suggests that the image is symbolically like the land being cleansed from wickedness, meaning female impurity (Ezek 36:17), but there seems to be no reason for this aspect of "woman" to be accepted. Nor should the presentation of "wickedness" as a female be overstressed, as by Rudolph (1976:120) when he relates the image of this verse to the figure of the woman in the garden of Eden story (Gen 3:6). The female figure here thus can represent idolatry not because of inherent female wickedness or impurity, but rather because of the historical contamination of Yahwism caused by intermarriage with foreign women.

The text does not specify which, if any, goddess might be represented by the designation "Wickedness." However, the vision indicates that the deported figure will have a shrine in Babylon (v 11) and hints (cf. NOTE to "stork," v 9) that she is not native to Palestine. Therefore the chances are that insofar as the woman in the Ephah represents a deity, she would be one of the great Semitic goddesses, Ishtar (= Astarte), the reigning goddess of Babylon, or Asherah. The name of either one of those divinities, but especially Asherah, constitutes an anagram of *hāriš^câ*, "wickedness." That title may well be a play on the real name of one or both of those goddesses. The cult of Asherah, like that of Baal, had penetrated even the temple of Yahweh in the days leading up to the Babylonian conquest (2 Kgs 23:4,6,7; cf. 1 Kgs 15:13). Archaeological traces of the cult may be observed in the inscriptions and scenes from the ninth to the eighth century B.C.E. Kuntillet ʿAjrud and the postexilic Khirbet el-Qom inscriptions (Dever 1984). Jeremiah's concern about worship of the Queen of Heaven (Jer 7:18; 44:17,19,25) apparently refers to the cult of Ishtar (Bright 1965:56), which was very popular in Judah in the late monarchic period.

A specific link between "wickedness" and idolatrous cults is suggested by the story of the wicked Queen Athaliah (2 Chron 24:7; 2 Kgs 8:26), granddaughter of King Omri of Israel, mother of King Ahaziah. The negative description of Athaliah by the Chronicler as *hammiršaʿat* ("that wicked woman") utilizes a variation of the word *riš^câ* and establishes a close connection between wickedness and idolatry. Clearer still is the reference to her in 2 Chron 22:2–3 where, as counselor to her son Ahaziah, she advised him "to do wickedly" (v 3; *lĕharšîaʿ*) and to walk in the ways of the idolatrous King Ahab (her father). The connection between "wickedness" and idolatry is clear in those texts.

thrust . . . cast. The Hebrew word used in both instances is the Hiphil form of the root *šlk*, "to throw" or "to cast," which conveys action. The text of verse 7, in conjunction with verse 8, describes an action that relates how the woman/goddess happens to be shut up within a container for transport away from Yehud. In other words, the thrusting and casting are presented retrospectively. They are part of an introductory flashback scene (cf. first NOTE to v 7) that the prophet must see in order to comprehend the real visionary action, which he describes in the next verse. The end result of the preliminary action, in which a woman/idol is already enclosed in an Ephah, is given at the outset in verse 6. The series of actions is presented out of chronological order—a poetic device also found, for example, in the Song of the Sea, where the result of the main action is summarized (Exod 15:4–8) and then the poet describes the previous phase in which the Pharaoh's army pursued the Israelites (Exod 15:10).

lead-stone. This phrase almost at the end of verse 8 forms an envelope with "lead weight," which appears near the beginning of verse 7. The information of verses 7–8 composes a unit providing a retrospective view of why the Ephah is an important object in this vision; it allows the prophet to see inside it (cf. NOTE to "behold," v 7).

In this instance "lead" appears with "stone" (*'eben*) and not "weight." The combination "lead-stone," like the "tin-stone" of 4:10 (see NOTE), refers to a piece of metal and not to a lead-bearing rock or piece of ore. It is to be noted that the pairing of "lead" and "stone" in this verse is achieved by a construct chain, the use of which may be intended to put "lead" in a position of emphasis. "Tin-stone" of 4:10, in contrast, appears as two nouns in apposition. "Lead," whether emphasized or not, is found with "stone" to describe an object of great weight. As we have already noted, lead's high specific gravity and resulting heaviness make it an appropriate material for a metal object which is being used to ensure that the figure within the Ephah is contained securely. The image of a "lead-stone" in reference to a similar decisive action against God's enemies is deliberately broken up in Exod 15, where in verse 5 the Egyptians and their chariots go down like a "stone" and in verse 10 the enemy sinks like "lead." Since the reference is to the same people, the Egyptian army, the connection of lead and stone is substantiated: they went down (sank) like a lead-stone into the depths (great waters).

In addition to its heaviness, "lead" may appear in association with "stone" here because of certain other properties and associations. Lead was a highly suitable material for engraving. From Assyrian times on, it was considered an appropriate metal from which to make magical tablets, on which curses or prayers were inscribed (Forbes 1950:178). Job 19:24 provides an instructive example of the engraving of words on lead with an iron tool. Job wishes that his words could be inscribed with lead and thus achieve permanence (see Pope 1965:124 on the difficult addition of "rock," *ṣûr*, which seems to refer to the lead on which the iron "pen" records Job's words). Similarly, lead tablets were used for inscriptions in Mesopotamian temple deposits, thus rendering immovable and permanent the words inscribed on them in association with the construction of temples, or as lead blocks in the corners of temple buildings (Ellis 1968:176, 191). Such magical properties of lead, associated with permanence, may correspond to its usage in this vision. The fate of "Wickedness" (= idolatry) is unquestionably sealed by the lead lid covering the Ephah (cf. following NOTE).

in its mouth. The Hebrew is ambiguous as to where the lead-stone is placed, because the feminine pronominal suffix of "mouth" can allow it to refer to either "her" (= woman/goddess) or "Ephah." Since the general rule is to refer the pronoun back to its nearest antecedent, "Ephah" is probably the correct referent in this case. The lid which in verse 7 was lifted to reveal the seated woman is here put back in place. Since the woman/goddess herself does nothing at all in this vision but sit passively while she is confined and transported, the alternative possibility that the lead-stone might be placed in her mouth seems unwarranted.

9. *I raised my eyes and looked.* This is the only instance in the visions in which this formula is used twice. In verse 5 (cf. second NOTE to that verse) it appears as a command and prefaces the introductory scene, which includes the presentation of the visionary object (v 6) and the retrospective information about the contents of that object (vv 7–8). The formula is used again, this time in the narrative imperfect, at the beginning of verse 9, to complete the first usage. It reports compliance with the com-

mand and resumes the narration of the vision with the prophet's account of what it is that he sees. The Interpreting Angel had instructed him to look up; he had asked what it was that he saw; the contents were revealed; and now the prophet responds, offering his description, which is actually a description of an action and not an object, of what he sees. The twofold use of the formula "raise . . . eyes . . . look" provides narrative continuity between the two parts of the vision: the identification of the object, and the action to which the object is subjected. The odd separation between the command of verse 5 and the compliance of verse 9 is created by the necessity of inserting information that will make the whole vision understandable. The sequence itself, of command and fulfillment of command, may be the norm for all the visions, preserved in its entirety here because of the inserted retrospective details but omitted in the other visions where the time sequence is chronological. The second appearance of the formula in this vision not only completes the first, it also suggests the ongoing, though not sequential, activity in the prophet's visionary field and so contributes to the dynamic character of the vision.

two females. The removal of the Ephah and its undesirable contents is effected by two female winged creatures *(nāšîm)* who together carry their strange load to Shinar. The pairing of such composite creatures—humans with wings—finds a biblical analogy in the cherubim flanking the ark in both the tabernacle (Exod 25:18–22) and temple (1 Kgs 6:23–28) passages. The outstretched wings of those cherubim provide a throne on which Yahweh's glory or presence rests within his earthly abode (cf. 1 Sam 4:4, 2 Sam 6:2). Near Eastern art also provides ample evidence for the frequent pairing of such winged creatures in the ancient world (e.g., *ANEP* 38, 645–48, 650, 652, 654, 656), where they often flank the deity of the deity's shrine. Since the Ephah as a shrine or cella and the woman as idolatrous Wickedness both strongly suggest the cultic presence of a pagan deity, a pair of winged beings fits well with the imagery already established. Furthermore, composite winged beasts are often associated with mobility (Freedman and O'Connor 1984), specifically with the transportation of divine beings as in the instance of Yahweh riding on a cherub (Ps 18:11 [RSV v 10] = 2 Sam 22:11) or as in the strange image of composite beasts and wheels in Ezek 1–3. It seems quite appropriate that a figure representing foreign religion and idolatry should be transported by flying creatures of the type suggested by Zechariah.

Yet these creatures are not cherubim, which are masculine beasts in the biblical texts in which they appear; or at least the substantive denoting them is a masculine word. The reason for the female identity of Zechariah's composite figures is not readily apparent. Several suggestions can be made, and they may all have validity. First, the object being carried contains a female figure, "one woman" in verse 7. That rather awkward qualification of woman by *one* may be explained as an anticipatory contrast with the *two* female creatures, the "two females" *(nāšîm)* of this verse, who are to carry that *one* woman *(ʾiššâ).* Since "one" and "two" are counterparts in their enumeration of the personae, gender agreement of the designated personae provides logical completion of this counterpart relationship. Second, it is unlikely that the cherubim associated with the Yahwistic cult would be seen as appropriate bearers of the wicked, non-Yahwistic burden of this vision. Language distinct from any connection with the cherubim of Yahweh's dwelling would then be employed, and using the female gender allowed for such a distinction to be made. The use of female attendants here apparently separates them from Yahweh's attendants, who are almost always, if not always, male when their gender can be determined. However, this supposition creates a problem. If these are attendants of a goddess, the Wickedness within the Ephah, and if that goddess is powerless and impotent as she would have to be to a Yahwist's way of thinking, then how could her attendants have the power to carry her off? So perhaps these are Yahwistic figures after all, but not the male ones normally encountered in other biblical passages. Third, the stork image that follows (see NOTE below) depends to a certain extent on the behavior of the female of that species. The simile therefore works best with female winged creatures.

going forth. This is the fourth and final occurrence of the verb *yṣ'* ("go out, go forth") in this vision. First the angelic figure comes forth (v 5); next he urges Zechariah to look at something that is moving across his field of vision (v 5); then the Interpreting Angel identifies, for the prophet, that moving object (v 6). Now the winged creatures are "going forth" as they transport the Ephah. This is the climactic movement to which the original appearance of the Ephah, and the intervening lifting and replacing of its cover over the Wickedness it contains, are leading.

wind. "Wind" *(rûaḥ)* in association with wings produces the notion of flight. The particular kind of locomotion that the winged creatures are using as they remove the Ephah from the land is poetically conveyed. Alternatively, it is possible that "wind" together with "wings" might simply mean that the wings were outstretched, as suggested by Dahood (1965:107; cf. Pope 1973:339–40 and Dahood 1970 and Ps 104:3) in his discussion of Ps 18:11 (RSV, Ps 18:10), where he changes *rûaḥ* to *rewaḥ.* Note that the passage in Ps 18 refers to the swift movement of Yahweh who rides "upon a cherub." The winged creatures here function like the cherub, providing transport for a deity. While the imagery of the Zechariah passage is markedly similar to that of Ps 18:11, here the noun "wind" precedes "wings" and "wings" itself is preceded by the preposition *b,* "in." Thus Dahood's reading for Psalms would seem impossible here syntactically. Further, our rendering "wind in their wings" suits the dynamism characteristic of this vision better than would "wings outstretched."

in their wings. Composite beasts, part of the mythological imagery of the ancient world (Freedman and O'Connor 1984), are very frequently identified as such by the combination of human and avian characteristics. The latter is usually represented by wings, since the wings are the feature of a bird's anatomy which afford mobility. The threefold repetition of "wings" in this verse intensifies the sense of movement. The importance of movement throughout this vision is evident in several of its literary features, such as the repeated use of the verbs "go forth" *(yṣ')* and lift *(nś')* as well as the sequence of two scenes in the total vision (see above, NOTES to vv 5, 7, 9).

stork. The noun *(ḥasîdâ)* denoting this bird is feminine, and the connotations associated with the stork in the Bible (as well as in Western tradition) are of maternal behavior (Ps 104:17). The very name of the bird may be derived from the root *ḥsd,* "to be good, kind," because of the reputation of the stork for being affectionate and caring toward its young *(BDB:334).* The stork, it is to be noted, does not hatch its eggs in Palestine but rather is a migratory bird that produces its young elsewhere (Feliks 1971). It follows a north-south migratory pattern, flying north away from Palestine in the spring and back southward into the land of Israel in the fall. The reference in Jeremiah to the stork (8:7) demonstrates an awareness of the bird's habits. The simile of Zechariah's vision would appear to utilize these aspects of the stork's behavior. The stork's biological continuity involves hatching its young elsewhere, and the ongoing life of the Wickedness (= idolatry) is carried elsewhere as well by these stork-like creatures. Similarly, the bird's exit from Palestine is to the north, and the winged minions of this vision are bound for Babylon, following a northerly route as they leave Palestine, for travelers must head north before finally turning eastward in order to skirt the Syrian desert (cf. NOTE to "land of the north," 2:10).

It is difficult to know whether the prophet had all this imagery consciously in mind. The stork is mentioned in a simile, and so the chief point of comparison may simply be the "wings" of those birds. Storks are large birds with large wingspans, and their associations with the maternal role make us think of them as female. These facts alone make a "stork" meet the requirements of both the vision and the simile.

lifted. The word for "lift" *(nś')* appears here for the third time in this vision (cf. vv 5, 7) and concludes the sequence of actions which unfold before the prophet's eyes. The second scene ends, from the Palestinian perspective, with the airborne Ephah en route to its ultimate destination in Babylon (see "Shinar," v 11). Whatever is to take place there is related to the prophet by the Interpreting Angel but does not appear onstage in this dynamic vision.

10. *Whither.* This second query of the prophet to the Interpreting Angel (cf. v 6) parallels the literary pattern of the Fourth Vision where two questions posed by the prophet serve as framing devices which link the first half of the vision concerning the lampstand with the second half concerning Zerubbabel (see NOTES above to 4:5,13). Here in the Sixth Vision, the two questions relate to each of the two scenes of the vision. The "what" of verse 6 regarding the nature of the Ephah may be contrasted with this "whither" of the second scene, which concerns the final destination of the Ephah. The second question, by utilizing the interrogative "whither," accentuates the movement of the Ephah away from Palestine and also resumes the prophet's questioning begun in verse 6.

11. *for it.* The suffix on the preposition is feminine, and since neither "woman" nor "Wickedness" is mentioned nearby, the antecedent must be "Ephah," which is the last word in the preceding verse and which is the thing being transported to Shinar. Does this mean that a temple is being constructed for our Ephah? That would hardly be the case. Rather, since "Ephah" may refer to a cult room that in this case contains the image of a pagan goddess, it is clear that the shrine in Mesopotamia is being built for that deity. Without the woman = idolatry, the Ephah alone has no significance. Since "it" refers to "Ephah," the imagery suggests that the goddess together with Ephah within her cult room will be deposited in a newly erected Babylonian temple.

temple. The Hebrew word for a "house" *(bayît)* is used here as a designation for a divine residence or temple (cf. NOTE to Hag 1:9). Although no details are provided as to the nature of the structure to be built for the Ephah and its contents, it is clear that the purpose of building this "temple" is to provide an appropriate residence for a non-Yahwistic deity outside the land of Judah. Whether this reference implies a ziggurat or a shrine on top of a ziggurat (see above NOTE to "Ephah," v 6) is not so important as is the overall force of the Interpreting Angel's explanation, which establishes the idea that the goddess who is implicitly the woman in the Ephah has her legitimate place in Babylon.

land of Shinar. I.e., the land of Babylonia. Some of the versions (LXX, Syriac, Targum) in fact substitute "Babylonia" for "Shinar" (cf. Gen 10:10; 11:2; 14:1,9; Josh 7:21; Isa 11:11). The selection of Babylonia as the place to which the figure of "Wickedness" (= idolatry) will be expelled is hardly accidental. It was the land to which the Judeans themselves had been sent and the place from which they returned when Cyrus the Great permitted them to return to Palestine. If the "woman" in the Ephah of verse 7 represents not only Wickedness or idolatry but also (cf. NOTE to "this is one woman") the foreign wives, brought back by some returnees from Babylon, who are responsible in part for the attention to foreign goddesses in Yehud, then the return of idolatry and the "woman" to Babylon is a fitting solution. The source of the problem of idolatry is returned to the place from which it originated. At the same time, the building of a shrine for a non-Israelite deity in Babylon can be related to the construction of the temple in Jerusalem for Yahweh. Yahweh's people have returned from Babylon and so therefore has Yahweh. A countermovement of a deity from Jerusalem to Shinar balances the restoration of Yahweh to Zion.

it will be constructed. This Hophal from the root *kwn* resumes the technical language of temple founding that we have encountered throughout the visions but especially in chapters 3 and 4. It is recapitulated in the Hebrew in the prepositional phrase "in its place," *ʿal-mĕkūnātāh*, a noun derived from the same root which is a technical term for its proper cultic setting (see NOTE below). The active voice of the LXX suggests a possible Hebrew active, either *wĕhēkînû* or *ûlĕhākîn*, neither of which can be justified. The MT, however, is difficult mainly because the antecedent is unclear. Our translation presupposes "temple," the masculine *bayit*, as subject and antecedent. Just as Zechariah has used the language of Near Eastern temple ideology to describe a series of all-important events in the history of the restoration in Yehud, so too does he recount the construction of a temple in Shinar in the terminology associated with temple building.

Although several commentators have identified the temple as a ziggurat (Marenof 1931–32:264–65, especially n. 7), there is no need to understand the visionary language so specifically. A temple structure, whether ziggurat or not, would provide the appropriate imagery. It is this larger architectural element that is being "constructed," and it is the smaller shrine or Ephah with the goddess inside that is being transported to it via the two winged figures of verse 9 (see NOTES above to "Ephah," v 6, and "two females," v 9).

it will be set there. The present third-person feminine singular Hophal pausal form in the MT may be maintained if we understand "Ephah" to be the subject of the verb. The LXX presupposes the active voice and may have read *wĕhênnîhûha*—i.e., "they shall set it," a Hiphil. The disagreement in gender between the two verbs may also represent a *forma mixta* (*GKC* § 78 c.2) and so reflect an early attempt to harmonize a very difficult grammatical problem. The MT, by preserving a masculine verb alongside a feminine one, has thus maintained a semantic and gender distinction which was important to the early tradents and which separates out the pagan temple as a whole from an important component of it as represented by the "Ephah." This distinction is helpful in understanding the rather specific, technical meaning of "Ephah" as cult room, contrasted with its usual meaning of "measure," since there is also a feminine singular ending affixed to "foundation," doubtless because it too refers back to feminine "Ephah" as well as the female contents of the Ephah and not to masculine "temple." The MT in preserving these subtle gender distinctions created many problems for future exegetes and grammarians.

upon its base. Most commentators take ʿal-mĕkūnātāh to refer to a kind of "base" or "pedestal," as indeed the word is commonly used in the Bible (e.g., 1 Kgs 7:27–43, where it is used thirteen times in reference to the ten bronze stands of the Temple of Solomon). Although all the occurrences of the term are in cultic settings, a broader meaning which embraces the sense of "proper foundation" occurs in Ezra 3:3, where the verb and prepositional phrase utilize the same root—i.e., Hiphil of *kwn* plus *mĕkônâ*. The meaning there and in the present context is "to set in [rightful] place" (so RSV and NEB). In both these instances the word *mĕkônâ* provides the definition of the space on which something is to be erected or placed and hence is conceptually analogous to the word "platform" of Zech 4:7. Given the repeated use of temple language, the specialized terminology employed here is not unexpected. The main point of this concluding phrase, therefore, is that the "Ephah" with its seated woman/goddess has been restored to its correct place, not only far away in the land of Shinar but also in its very proper place within the temple precincts. Idolatry has been removed from Yehud, where it does not belong, to its rightful place in a foreign land which is not at this moment Yahweh's land. Just as Yahweh is returning (cf. Zech 1:3,16; 2:14 [RSV 2:10]) to Zion and to the restored temple along with his people who have come back from exile, so idolatry is placed in Babylon where it belongs.

COMMENT

The arrangement and language of the Sixth Vision exhibit certain departures from the general structuring of the Seven Visions as discourse between prophet and Interpreting Angel. While the Ephah vision does adhere to the overall dialogic structure, it nonetheless diverges in several subtle as well as overt ways. Since we have asserted above that the Fourth Vision, in its organization and theme, is intentionally unique, it is incumbent upon us to consider whether the divergencies of the Sixth Vision are meant to separate it out for some reason from the sequence of seven or whether they serve some other function. This issue cannot be resolved without looking at the specific features that set this vision somewhat apart from the pattern to which the other five (excluding the exceptional central vision) adhere.

The vision begins with an introductory scene that provides information about something that has happened and prepares the prophet for the proper understanding of what the actual focus of the vision is, namely the action that takes place in the second part of the narration of the vision. The introduction includes an initial and unusual imperative in which the angel instructs Zechariah to direct his attention toward something. This opening command may in fact be implied in all the visions, but it is present only here. The narration thus begins with what the *angel* does and says rather than with the expected announcement by the prophet that he looked up and saw X. The audience must shift its attention from the angel to the prophet and then back to the angel again (verses 7–8) before the focus of the vision is revealed.

Another apparent departure from the formulaic introduction to the vision is the placement of "behold." That interjection, which normally follows the information that the prophet has "lifted [his] eyes" and precedes the description of what he sees, seems to be missing. But no, it has been moved to the beginning of verse 7 so that it comes after the appearance of the major visionary object, yet before a subsequent and related object is introduced. The audience's full awareness of what the prophet has witnessed is still further delayed by the repetition, at the beginning of verse 9, of the "looked up" formula, heralding the appearance of additional personae within the visionary field. The splitting of "behold" from its normal position and the second occurrence of the introductory formula are both features found only in this vision. They serve to create a complex structure with a more complete introduction than is present in any other of the visions. The Sixth Vision is composed of a scenario that proceeds through two parts or acts, with the first act itself divided into two scenes. The following table indicates this arrangement:

Act I	vv 5–8	Ephah and its contents
scene 1	vv 5–6	Ephah
scene 2	vv 7–8	woman
Act II	vv 9–11	transport of Ephah

The vision clearly has a more complex structure than any of the others. The breakup and duplication of stereotypical language arises from the inclusion of an introductory scene which may be implied in the other visions but has been omitted from them. Why does the structure of the Ephah vision retain the full preparatory sequence? Two interrelated reasons have necessitated the use of an elaborate opening act. First, the focus of the vision, the thing which the angel must eventually explain to the prophet, is not the physical object itself but rather the movement of that object. However, the prophet must first be introduced to that object. The initial act of the vision is necessary and preparatory; in its first scene the prophet is shown the item that will be acted upon in the second act. Second, simply seeing the item does not yet provide the prophet with enough information to comprehend what happens to it. The significance of the action of Act II depends upon his knowledge of its contents, and so a second scene in Act I reveals what sits within the object presented in the first scene.

The vision actually begins in verse 9, where the prophet announces, as he does in the other vision, that he raised his eyes. Act I, or at least its second scene, functions as a flashback or retrospective and accomplishes the task of informing the prophet just what it is that the Ephah contains. If the prophet doesn't know that, he will have no idea why the Ephah is embarked on the journey described in Act II. The formal structure of the vision does not, therefore, represent a sequential chronological arrangement. The organization of the vision into acts and scenes gives it a dynamic quality, quite apart from the movement presented in the second act and the prior activity reported in the second scene of the first act. The formal structure itself, along with the vision's contents, contributes to the dynamism of the Sixth Vision. Certain other aspects of the language it uses have a similar effect. For example the verb yṣ' ("go out, go forth") recurs several times, including once in reference to the Interpreting Angel, a situation found only in this vision. This verb of action is only one of several interspersed throughout the narrative: note especially the use of "thrust" and "cast" in verse 8 and also the appearance of "lifted" and "taking" in verses 9 and 10 as well as that of "build," "constructed," and "set" in verse 11.

This information allows us to respond now to the question: Are the ways in which the Sixth Vision differs from the structure of most of the Seven Visions enough to set it apart from the others because it is intrinsically distinct, as in the case of the Fourth Vision? This appears not to be the case for the present vision. The series of literary characteristics that cause its distinctive quality does so with the intent of creating a strong sense of movement, which is crucial to the meaning of the vision, and also in order to deal with the problems of identification of objects which themselves are not the true foci of the vision. Since many of the other visions also involve action, the emphasis on motion in this vision is only one of degree and not of total differentiation from the others. Through structure, vocabulary, and variance of formulaic language, the Sixth Vision succeeds in drawing attention to the visionary activity the prophet sees.

Resolving this issue only leads to another: Why has the prophet utilized this complicated arrangement to stress movement? Or, what is the function of the dynamic quality of the Ephah vision? We can begin to approach the problem of meaning by recalling that the Seven Visions are organized in a pattern which exhibits correspondences between three pairs of visions, leaving the extra or central one and its companion prophetic vision as the climactic ones (see Introduction and COMMENT to the other visions, *passim*). Within this organization of the material, the present vision appears in closest relationship with the Second Vision (The Four Horns and the Four Smiths). The first and last visions deal with Yahweh's global presence, and the central three visions plus the Joshua vision of chapter 3 focus on Yehud itself with the temple at its center. In between those two groups, the Second and Sixth Visions concern Yehud's status vis-à-vis the world. For Zechariah that world coincides with the Persian Empire, which exercises imperial dominion over most of the known peoples and places of the sixth century.

A cursory comparison of Visions 2 and 6 reveals their shared international interest. Zechariah envisions four horns that have been the cause of the exile

of Judah, including the capital and royal estate of Jerusalem, as well as of the
northern kingdom of Israel. That imperial policy of shifting populations in
order to assure the cooperation of subject peoples will now be terminated; this
becomes clear to Zechariah as the four smiths, the agents of Yahweh, appear
along with the four horns in the visionary field. The chronological frame of
reference in that vision is not easy to reconstruct, but our analysis has led to
the conclusion that events in the earliest years of Darius I's ascendancy provide the political backdrop against which the prophet's visions interpret the
meaning of world events for his people. Persia at that time was establishing
administrative structures that would stabilize the empire through internal control rather than through the military power that Cyrus had exerted in order to
establish his dominion over much of the ancient world. Persian organization
of its territories meant some further imperial population shifts, particularly for
rebellious factions. But for the provincial territory of Yehud, Darius's policies
meant a reversal of the dislocations of the previous centuries caused by the
Assyrians and Babylonians. The Second Vision therefore reflects the possibilities that existed under Darius or in the future, as under Cyrus, for exiled
Judeans to return to Palestine and to reclaim their holdings in the province of
Yehud.

The Sixth Vision likewise has an international scope, in that it begins in "all
the land" which presumably means Yehud, and terminates in the "land of
Shinar," a designation for Babylonia which at this point is a geographical term
for some part of Mesopotamia, or a political term only in a historic rather
than a contemporary sense. The dynamic quality of this vision is designed to
underscore a definitive and inexorable transfer of the chief visionary object
from Yehud to its appropriate place to the east in the land between rivers. The
full meaning of that transfer can emerge only upon consideration of another
correspondence between this vision and its counterpart, Vision 2.

The Second Vision consists of two parts that appear sequentially, the four
horns and then the four smiths. They do not interact within the vision itself,
although their imminent confrontation is implicit, but they do constitute a
two-part arrangement that may be analogous to the two-act structure of the
Sixth Vision. Yet, since a pair of visionary objects is perhaps not the best
counterpart to a set of visionary events, and since the events are really more
than two in number because the first act of the Sixth Vision has two scenes, it
may be more appropriate to consider the two kinds of personae of the present
vision as the meaningful counterpart to the two sets of objects of the second
one. In other words, the "woman" in the Ephah plus the two winged females
would be the visual pair best compared with the two sets in the Second Vision.

With such a correspondence in mind, we recall the symbolism of "horns"
representing the foreign nations and "smiths" as agents of Yahweh. The
woman in the Ephah, as our NOTES have established, is a complicated figure
representing both idolatry as an abstract concept—i.e., Wickedness = idola-

try—and also perhaps the human agents, the foreign women, responsible in part for the introduction of idolatrous beliefs, practices, or loyalties into the community of Yahwists. If the correspondence between the visions is to be sustained, then the fanciful winged creatures who transport the idolatrous symbol from Yehud to Babylon must also be agents of Yahweh rather than attendants of the woman/goddess. This pairing is represented by the following chart:

Vision 2	Vision 6
a. horns = foreign nations	a. woman (= goddess) = foreign nations
b. smiths = Yahweh's agents	b. winged females = Yahweh's agents

As straightforward as this arrangement may seem, it is not without its problems with respect to the symbolism of the winged women. In the NOTE to the "two females" we have considered these fanciful creatures as belonging to the category of composite beings widely known in ancient Near Eastern iconography where they often flank a deity or the entrance to a deity's shrine. Such imagery is similar to that of the biblical cherubim, who uphold the throne/ark upon which Yahweh's presence or glory is enthroned. Yet in this vision the female gender of the composite figures apparently distinguishes them from their counterparts who support Yahweh on outstretched wings. And indeed, these "females with wind in their wings" are patently transporting a figure of "Wickedness," hardly an appropriate surrogate for Yahweh.

In light of all this, can the winged figures really represent Yahweh as the correspondence of imagery between the Second and Sixth Visions would suggest? The two figures of 5:9 are engaged in an activity during which the movement characterizing the vision as a whole reaches its climax, although not its conclusion. The woman (Wickedness) is forever removed from Yehud by the definitive action of the two females. As they appear at the opening of the second act, we are treated to a descriptive passage (v 9) that is more elaborate than the rather sparse prose of the vision to this point: 1. the females have "wind in their wings"; 2. their wings are akin to a stork's wings; 3. they are moving with their strange burden "between earth and heaven." The fullness of the narrative here signals the climax and points to the most important segment of the vision's movement, the journey from Yehud to Babel. Since a female symbol of non-Yahwistic worship and loyalty is the object being transported by female genii, the implication would be that idolatry is moving of its own accord, by its own attendants, to its Babylonian locale. However, by acknowledging the symmetry of the Second and Sixth Visions, the two winged females become, like the four smiths, none other than Yahweh's agents. This conclusion is borne out by the fact that the goddess or woman herself is seated, still and impotent, in the Ephah, as deities other than Yahweh must be.

Winged creatures associated with that deity would also be powerless; only Yahweh's attendants could carry her away.

The idea that the goddess is impotent points to a further problem. If this idolatrous being truly lacked power, why bother with her at all? This question suggests a dilemma of the monotheistic Yahwists of Yehud: how to deal with foreign gods and cults. If the "other gods" are really empty and powerless, if the images are nothing more than pieces of stone or wood, why should a prophet care about getting rid of idolatry? Why should Zechariah envision Wickedness carried away to Babylon and restored there? One explanation would be that while gods or goddesses are nothing more than inanimate idols, their rites and cults can nonetheless attract many and entrap them at the expense of Yahwism. Therefore idolatry must be contested and rooted out, not because the idols or deities themselves have power but rather because their devotees may and do have power. The woman/goddess in this vision symbolizes wickedness not because of anything she can do but rather because of what worship of her can do to the people who follow her within a community of Yahwists. Another explanation for the carrying away of idolatry from Yehud in this vision derives from the temple building context of all the visions. Many exiled Judeans had returned to Palestine and resettled in Yehud. Their God too had returned to Zion, and a temple was being readied for Yahweh. The movement toward the "Holy Land" (Zech 2:16 [RSV v 12]) had to be balanced by a movement in the opposite direction, the direction from which Yahweh and his people had come: "the land of Shinar." The carrying of Wickedness away to Babylon serves as the counterpart to the return of Yahweh to the land he had chosen and to his rightful temple in Jerusalem.

The balancing of Yahweh's return with idolatry's departure may have some bearing upon the understanding of Wickedness = goddess. We don't mean that the goddess herself can be identified but rather that the chronological or historical scope of the idolatry she represents can be ascertained. The companion vision, Vision 2, recapitulates the deportations of Yahweh's people going back to the eighth century. This vision can cover similar ground, since idolatry had always been identified as a cause of exile. While idolatry may still have been a problem in Zechariah's day, there is no doubt that it was a major issue in the earlier history of Judah and Israel. The earlier prophets cry out against apostasy and idolatry, and Jeremiah in particular protests the attraction of the Queen of Heaven. For Zechariah, the fact that the temple is being restored and that Yahweh is returning means that such idolatry is finally banished from the land. The prophet may have in mind residual or new idolatrous practices of his day; but he also is referring to the long history of cultic contamination in his community.

The image of God's minions removing idolatry contains magnificent irony. The two creatures hovering in the territory of the gods between land and sky, flying with the reliability and carefulness of the stork, are removing a foreign presence from Yehud not at the direction of any Persian or Babylonian deity, but rather at the behest of Yahweh himself. The affairs of the empire, which have allowed Yehud quasi-autonomy and a restored national shrine, are ultimately under the direction of Yahweh. Idols, the overt signs of non-Yahwist sovereignty, are removed from the land. The several literary measures used to convey movement in the Sixth Vision are appropriate to the vision's meaning. Bringing exiles back to Zion as in the Second Vision is not as strenuous as eliminating centuries of foreign influence from Zion, and so the intensified dynamic character of the Sixth Vision provides the atmosphere commensurate with the task.

The universality implied by the fact that Yahweh is ultimately responsible, via the quasi-mythological winged creatures, for ridding the land of "Wickedness" does not also imply exclusiveness. The woman in the Ephah appears on stage only in the first act; and it is in that act alone, set in Yehud, that she represents Wickedness. Her removal is a separate section of the vision. She is not destroyed; on the contrary her container, the ephah/Ephah, has a rightful resting place, a temple. Just as Yahweh has been accorded his traditional earthly abode in Jerusalem, so the gods who had invaded his territory can be worshipped, quite legitimately it seems, by their own peoples in their own territories. If Zechariah's oracular flights of eschatology (e.g., 2:15 [RSV v 11]) envisage all nations acknowledging Yahweh, his visionary expression of reality admits that Yahweh's universal existence is acknowledged only by his own people. Yet in that acknowledgment, as we shall see in the last vision, lies the potential for the eschatological sovereignty of Yahweh.

All told, the objects and characters of the Sixth Vision cannot easily be comprehended at first glance. Our NOTES have attempted to explain the connotations provided by these visionary characters, and the results of our investigation have been assumed in the foregoing discussion and need not be repeated here. Nonetheless, several observations on their common characteristics are in order. They all belong to the cultural continuum which spanned the Fertile Crescent, at least from its center in Palestine to its eastern terminus in Mesopotamia. The use of "ephah" as a *double entendre* for container and shrine surely is effective only for an audience cognizant of Babylonian temples. Similarly, the magical qualities of the "lead weight" or "lead-stone," in addition to its physical properties, would be most meaningful to those familiar with certain Assyro-Babylonian practices, particularly in association with temple foundings or refoundings. The winged genii are also figures, especially when not linked to cherubim, derived from a general Near Eastern iconography.

Because the images utilized in this vision are drawn from the larger Semitic world of which Yehud was a tiny part, the international perspective of the vision is enhanced. At the same time the matter of audience identity is at issue if Zechariah is assuming that the multiple connotations of the visionary figures will be familiar to those to whom he is reporting. Clearly those Yehudites most recently returned from exile would be those most aware of the connotations of both the inanimate objects and the living figures. They are the ones for whom the vision's theme would be most relevant, and they would be the ones who might have brought foreign elements into their ancient homeland, elements that must be thoroughly excised as the place of Yahweh in his restored temple among his reorganized people is reasserted. However, the application of this vision can be wider than that if the political as well as the religious import of a foreign cult in Jerusalem is admitted. Foreign powers regularly introduced their own gods into the territories they vanquished, as a sign of their extended dominion. Consequently the removal of non-Yahwist images from Yehud would have constituted a statement of autonomy, an expression of the semi-independence of Yehud with the Yehudite God alone residing in the land. This implication of the vision would surely have appealed to all Yehudites and encouraged them in their restoration efforts.

10. SEVENTH VISION: THE FOUR CHARIOTS
(6:1–8)

6 ¹ Then again I raised my eyes and I looked, and behold: four chariots were going out from between the two mountains! The mountains were mountains of bronze. ² With the first chariot, there were red horses; with the second chariot, there were black horses; ³ with the third chariot, there were white horses; and with the fourth chariot, there were dappled horses; [all] mighty ones. ⁴ Then I answered and said to the angel-who-speaks-with-me, "What are these, my lord?"

⁵ The angel answered me, "These are the four winds of heaven which go out from being stationed by the Lord of all the earth: ⁶ The one with the black horses was going out to the northland; and the white ones went out after them; the dappled ones went out to the southland. ⁷ The mighty ones went out, for they were eager to go to roam about the earth. Thus he said, 'Go! Roam about the earth.' So they roamed about the earth. ⁸ He called me forth and spoke to me: 'See them going out to the northland; they have placed my spirit in the northland.' "

NOTES

6:1. *Then again I raised my eyes and I looked, and behold.* The full introductory formula is exactly the same as that which begins the Fifth Vision, that of The Flying Scroll, in 5:1. Without the preliminary "again," which is actually a verbal idea in the Hebrew (literally "I returned," *'āšûb;* cf. 4:1), the opening clause also repeats exactly the words of the Second and Third Visions (2:1,5 [RSV 1:18; 2:1]). In addition, the formula appears twice in the Sixth Vision (5:5 and 5:9), although it is arranged somewhat differently there. Finally, two of the basic elements (the verb "to see," *r'h,* plus *hinnēh)* appears in the First and Fourth Visions (1:8; 4:2). The introductory formula of the last vision utilizes all of the components found in the several different arrangements that occur in the preceding six visions.

four chariots. The "four" of this vision is to be related to the four horses of the First Vision. Although only three different horse colors are specified in 1:8, four distinct equines (see NOTE to 1:8), or rather one horseman plus three horses, are part of the prophet's initial vision. The use of the "four winds" in verse 5 below further contributes to this imagery of "four," which represents the four compass directions and thus the entire world. The Second Vision also involves "four" entities, horns and smiths, which likewise symbolize totality (see NOTE to 2:1 [RSV 1:18]).

The new element in this vision is the appearance of "chariots" in association with four horses, but much of the language of the final vision is comparable to that of the first one, with four horses sent out on a global mission. As a whole, the thematic similarity of the initial and final visions provides a literary framework, or inclusion, for the visionary sequence, which begins and ends with visions proclaiming the universality of divine presence. However, the horses in the Seventh Vision are accompanied by "chariots" *(markābôt)* and not simply riders (cf. 1:8). Introduced collectively in this verse, the chariots are then enumerated according to the color of the horses drawing them in verses 2 and 3. While the actual chariots are not specified again, the directions in which the horses move in verses 5, 6, 7 imply that the vehicles to which they are harnessed are moving.

The presence of the chariots in this vision brings about a shift in the symbolic function of the four mounted emissaries of chapter 1. Riding "in the night" and "among the myrtles," those horsemen of 1:8–11 represent a divine intelligence service and as such convey the idea of Yahweh's omniscience (see NOTES to v 8). The chariots of chapter 6 contribute a new dimension to the global imagery, that of divine omnipotence. The chariot was a vehicle associated with political sovereignty. As the quintessential war vehicle, it was part of a ruler's military equipment; its prominence in the tribute lists of the Egyptian and Assyrian kings attests to its critical role in warfare. Indeed, the emergence of the extensive imperial states of the ancient world, such as the New Kingdom in Egypt and the Hittite and the later Assyrian empires, was possible in part because of the extensive use of horse-drawn chariots (Wevers 1962:553; Yadin 1963:74, 86–90, 297–99). Even in the Persian period, at least in the sixth century, chariotry persisted as a significant factor. The king went to war in a great chariot pulled by special horses (cf. Cook 1983: Pl. 33), and Darius I expressed gratitude to

Ahura Mazda for having granted him good chariots as well as good horses (on a plaque from Susa; see Cook 1983:102). Although cavalry, nonexistent in Cyrus's original army, eventually became the key to Persian military success, chariotry was retained on a small scale and for specific tactical purposes (Cook 1983:101–3).

The Bible repeatedly refers to the military aspect of the vehicle, for foreign rulers (e.g., Exod 14:25; 15:4; Josh 11:6; Judg 4:15; Nah 3:2) as well as for Israelites. The protest made by Samuel against dynastic rule links chariotry with the establishment of a monarchy (1 Sam 8:11). Jeremiah's fervent desire for the preservation of the Davidic monarchy, despite his denunciation of specific kings, is expressed in his hope that there will always be kings and princes on the Davidic throne, "riding on horses and in chariots" (Jer 17:25; 22:4). In Haggai's final oracle, the destruction of foreign powers is equated with the overturning of their horses and chariots (2:22). Chariotry clearly represents the ultimate or absolute sovereignty of a political entity that can forcibly carry out its policies and exercise dominion. Even the nonmilitary appearances of the chariot in ancient Near Eastern literature and art bear out this meaning. The chariot appears ceremonially in processions or in the hunt. Since only rulers and high officials are included in the iconographic record of the chariot in sport or ceremony, these nonmilitary examples must be seen as extensions of the basic royal-military function. The image of chariots as a metaphor for Yahweh's supreme might underlies such passages as Isa 66:15 and Hab 3:8, where divine power is exerted to effect God's will and demonstrate his ultimate sovereignty.

The four chariots thus add the concept of divine omnipotence to the idea of divine omniscience established in the opening vision. God's presence in all the world is composed of his knowledge of all that transpires on the one hand and his control over all that happens on the other. This combined conceptualization of the two components of divine omnipresence dominates the opening and closing units of Zechariah's temple visions. In the final vision, the might of earthly empires is transcended by divine power. This portrayal plays a key ideological role in the overall context of the visions. The Jerusalem temple refoundation (see our NOTES and COMMENT to chapter 4) contravened the normal association of major temple buildings with nation states, as understood from the ideology of temple building in the ancient Near East and just as clearly in evidence for the preexilic temple in Jerusalem (Lundquist 1982; Ahlström 1982). The refoundation of the temple after the exile would have called the ideology into question in two overlapping ways: If an independent polity is not legitimized by the reestablished temple, what sort of deity allows such a limited or quasi-independent community to exist? And, secondly, is the temple truly legitimate without a palace and the concomitant organs of statehood? A vision proclaiming the cosmic power of Yahweh provides an answer to these fundamental issues and allows the innovative idea of a temple institution apart from power-wielding government structures. The real power legitimized by the temple is God's sovereignty, which in turn constitutes sanction for the efforts to rebuild his earthly abode and also for the God-given Torah literature to be the standard for communal order. Yahweh's omnipotence is not at odds with the Persian policy that allows the Jerusalem temple to function once again, although in a different manner than had the preexilic house of Yahweh; rather, the postexilic temple is approved as being *within* the framework of the divine will.

were going out. The use of this verb *(yṣ', "go out, go forth")* in the previous vision was part of the expression of the dynamic quality of that vision. Here, the verb describes the activity of the chariots in a more static sense. It is the *fact* of their going forth which is reiterated repeatedly in the last vision. The word is used seven times—once in this verse, once in verse 5, three times in verse 6, once in verse 7, and a last time in the last verse of this vision, verse 8. This arrangement, given the symbolic quality of seven to indicate completion or totality, contributes to the sense of God's total control over the world scene. His emissaries are always "going out"; there is no decrease in their involvement with the nations that occupy the four corners of the world. This temporal totality of divine omnipotence balances the spatial totality provided by the "four" directions of the "winds" and "chariots" (see preceding NOTE).

Another dimension of the chariots "going out" in this verse may be noted. The verb *yṣ'* is probably part of the sunrise motif which is present in the imagery of the succeeding words: "two mountains," "bronze" (see NOTES). Since the participial form *môṣā'* can mean "sunrise" (Ps 19:7 [RSV v 6]) or the place from which the sun first appears in the morning—that is, the East (Ps 75:7 [RSV v 6])—the chariots representing God's presence surely initiate the dawn imagery in the process of their "going out."

from between. The compound preposition *(mibbên)* rather than the simple "between" is necessary to emphasize the direction or place *from* which the movement occurs and not just the fact that the chariots are passing "between" a pair of mountains. The "from" indicates that they are moving out, away from the mountains where they originated, toward some distinct goal. "From," following "going out," anticipates the vision's conclusion in verse 8, where "going out" makes the last of its seven appearances in this final vision and is followed by "to" *('el)*. "Going out from" (v 1) with "going out to" (v 8) constitutes an *inclusio* which frames the vision and also draws attention to the essence of the movement it depicts—from Yahweh's presence ("two mountains"; cf. following NOTE) to the distant "northland" (see last NOTE to v 8).

two mountains. The element of divine power introduced by the chariot motif appears to be sustained in the concept of these rather enigmatic mountains that flank the chariots emerging from the Heavenly Court of Yahweh (see v 5). A mythological meaning seems to lie behind these mountains, perhaps because the cosmic abode of deities is linked to great mountains (see NOTE to "great mountain," 4:7). A pair of mountains, more specifically, is found in Near Eastern sun-god mythology, in which the daily appearance of the sun (Shamash) is portrayed iconographically as the emergence of the solar deity (often in his chariot!) between a pair of cosmic mountains (e.g., *ANET* 683, 684, 685). Although mountains are not mentioned, Psalm 19 depicts Yahweh's global presence in terms that reflect the language of sun-god myth (Sarna 1967). Horses and fiery chariots are also linked with a mountain in the Elijah-Elisha cycle, with its supernatural elements (2 Kgs 2:11,12; 6:17). Similarly, chariots associated with the sun appear in the negative context of Josiah's reform, when Josiah orders that the "chariots of the sun" be removed from their position on the temple mount, where they appear to have flanked the entryway to the temple, the place from which Yahweh departed his earthly abode (2 Kgs 23:11). The interwoven motifs of divine omnipresence—four chariots and the sun-god—are supplemented by the mountain imagery. The shiny metallic quality of these mountains (see following NOTE to "bronze") makes their relationship to sun-god mythology likely.

The sun-god imagery helps explain what might otherwise appear to be a curious fact:

the vision suggests that God is associated with two mountains. Is the cosmic dwelling of Yahweh somewhere between two mountains so that the chariots he dispatched from his court must pass between them? The mythological traditions of Canaan generally connect the great gods with particular mountains: Casius for Baal, Amanus for El, ʾInbb for Anat. Yahweh too is usually associated with specific mountains, Sinai and then Zion (Clifford 1972:107–60). In contrast, Mesopotamian mythology draws from a human experience for which mountains were not central, and so lacks the same connections between gods and single mountains that characterize Canaanite and biblical texts. Mountain imagery in Mesopotamia may not even be an integral part of the symbolism of the cosmic center (Clifford 1972:1–25). Mesopotamian tradition does, however, have a place for the range of mountains on the east, the place of the sun's rising. The glyptic depictions of the sun-god Shamash coming from between the two mountains may be artistic shorthand, used to conceptualize the arrival of the sun from behind the peaks that rise at the eastern edge of the Mesopotamian plain. The universality of Shamash in Assyrian texts (e.g., *ANET:* 286–89) as well as the iconography inform this vision better than does the mountain imagery of Canaanite religion. "Two mountains" is a word picture equivalent to the stylized twin peaks of Mesopotamian mythological scenes depicted in art and representing the eastern mountains. As elsewhere in Zechariah (cf. NOTE to "Ephah," 5:6; NOTE to "stone," 3:9; NOTE to "premier stone," 4:7), the demography of Yehud with its returnees from Babylon has led to a frame of reference showing familiarity with Mesopotamian culture.

bronze. The Hebrew *nĕḥōšet* can mean "copper," the basic metallic ore from which its alloys, notably bronze, are made. However, most of the artifacts associated with this word in the Bible are understood to be "bronze," the alloy of copper and probably tin, since copper alone would not have provided the strength necessary for the objects said to be made of *nĕḥōšet.* The shiny quality of bronze was well known, as in 2 Chron 4:16, where the temple utensils made by Hiram for Solomon are said to be of "burnished bronze," and Ezek 1:7, where the four strange creatures are said to "sparkle like burnished bronze" (cf. Ezek 40:3). Note also that the awful failure of the rains to provide fertility in Deut 28:23 is conveyed by the phrase "the heavens over your head shall be brass *(nĕḥōšet),* " meaning that the heavens are bright with the ever-shining sun and are never darkened by rain clouds. The mountains of bronze in Zechariah's vision would thus be notable for their shining appearance, as if they were illumined by the sun's rays. These mountains, suggesting sunlight and divine omnipresence, contrast with the darkness and secrecy of the opening vision. The exertion of power implicit in the chariots does not require the cover of night; God's omnipotence is explicit and visible.

2, 3. *red . . . black . . . white . . . dappled.* Four colors of horses are indicated here, corresponding to the four points of the compass and perhaps also to the four horses (though not four horse colors) of the First Vision (see NOTE to "red, sorrel, and white" in 1:8 and to "four chariots" above, v 1). However, the MT here and in verses 6–7 below, as well as in 1:8, has suffered in the transmission of the information about the horses and their colors. In the Seventh Vision, the four types of horses are closely linked to the four directional quadrants of the world. Therefore one can assume that, despite the confused state of the MT, at one stage in the history of transmission there probably was a direct correspondence between four horses and the four directions represented by the "four winds of heaven" in verse 5. All of these correspondences serve to underscore the theme of this vision, God's omnipotence.

In this listing of the four kinds of horses (cf. below, vv 6–7), the first three colors present no difficulties. The fourth one, the "dappled" group of horses, has caused much conflict among the ancient versions and a variety of interpretations among modern translators. The difficulty arises because the word for the fourth kind of horse, bĕruddîm ("dappled" or "piebald"), is not actually a color word but rather a pattern word. As such, it seems out of place with "red," "black," and "white." Furthermore, bĕruddîm is followed by the word ʾămuṣṣîm (cf. next NOTE), which either can stand apart from the four preceding horse types or can be understood in association with bĕruddîm. Commentators have suggested a variety of explanations, with one or the other term being considered a gloss. One of the more ingenious solutions (McHardy 1968) would restore "yellow" for the two terms combined (cf. Rev 6:2–8, where the fourth horse is "pale" or "pale yellow").

The term bĕruddîm is not exactly a common word, but it was used to designate animals in the Bible (Gen 31:10,12). The coloration of animals involves a vocabulary for describing multicolored phenomena (Brenner 1982:169–71), and that vocabulary is found in the Bible only in reference to Jacob's and Laban's herds and to Zechariah's horses. The fact that "dappled" represents a horse description other than primarily a color term may be considered an argument in favor of its originality. If the fourth term were a gloss or later addition, a scribe would have applied the same logic modern critics bring to the verse: he would have inserted a fourth color term rather than a pattern designation. While white, black, and reddish-color horses easily come to mind, a fourth color is not so apparent. Yet spotted or dappled horses, of mixed color, would be equally common and therefore would constitute a fourth category, for which the logic would call for four commonly seen horses rather than four different color terms for horses, although a fourth color would be expected to be in the yellow range. The MT of Zechariah 6 does not contain such a word nor does the Hebrew lexicon provide an appropriate term for yellow at this stage (Brenner 1982:15, 102, 105, 169). Hence it remains simple and clearer to see bĕruddîm as original and to understand that it is a multicolor designation, "dappled."

A few observations about the development of color terminology may help to explain why the Zechariah text has suffered in transmission and has received such varied treatment in the versions. The Bible uses red, black, and white as major color nomenclature, as established by Berlin-Kay (cited in Brenner 1982:14–17). In an analysis of color terms in a sample of ninety-eight languages, "black" and "white" are the only two terms appearing in all languages. The inventory of color terms then expands in stages up to a total universal inventory of eleven basic color terms. The order in which the inventory grows always has "red" emerging next, after "black" and "white." However, there is no consistency in the following stage in the growth of color vocabulary: there is no universal fourth color, and the appearance of "yellow" or "green" as a fourth category in Hebrew apparently takes place sometime during the sixth century. Since many versions read "yellow" or "ashen" in Zech 6:3, they may be doing so from their post-sixth-century vantage point. That is, in Zechariah's day a fourth or "yellow" color would not yet have been established; but very shortly thereafter "yellow" was added to the Hebrew color lexicon (Brenner 1982:105) and is assumed by the postexilic tradents and translators who supply it in Zechariah 1 and 6, which seemed deficient to them given *their* color vocabulary.

No matter how one understands the appearance of the fourth horse, the presence of four horse groups is certain. This situation complements the opening vision, which may have four horses or horsemen but has only three horse colors. Together the first and last visions have seven horse groups (though not seven different ones). Similarly, the word "earth" (*ʾereṣ*) appears seven times in the absolute state (cf. NOTE to "Lord of all the earth," v 5) in these two visions: three times in chapter 1 and four times in chapter 6. The pattern of three + four = seven recurs, symbolizing perhaps the totality or completeness of the first and last visions, and of all that comes between them.

[all] mighty ones. The use of *ʾămuṣṣîm* at the end of this verse is difficult, but its usage in verse 7 clarifies its appearance here. It is used in reference to all four horse groups; it tells us that they are all "strong" or "mighty," which is what one would expect of heavenly couriers. Verse 6 has suffered in transmission (see NOTE, below, to "northland . . . southland," and to "after them," v 6), and four horses going out in the four compass directions are implicit only in the extant text. Nonetheless, the *ʾămuṣ-ṣîm* ("mighty ones") of verse 1 go through the whole earth, and not just to one direction. They cannot be one of the groups but rather they summarize or represent all four groups. Verses 6 and 7 help us understand verses 2–3. The summation "mighty ones" of verse 7 has its parallel in the final word of verse 3, which summarizes the four horse categories of verses 2–3. The word *ʾmṣ*, meaning "strong" or "mighty," should be retained as such and not read as another color word (contra Brenner [1982:112–13], who suggests *ʾamōṣ* as another word for red, etymologically unrelated to *ʾmṣ*, "strong" or "mighty").

4. *I answered and said.* The angel has not asked any question of the prophet. As in the central lampstand vision (cf. 4:4), Zechariah responds directly to the visionary material itself and not to any query posed by the Interpreting Angel. A similar situation occurs in the First Vision, although the question asked by the prophet there (1:9) is introduced simply by "I said" without the preceding *wāʾaʿan*, "then I answered." The absence of a question or statement put forth by the angel does not necessarily mean that the angel did not speak out before Zechariah asks this question. Rather, the form of the vision that we have may be abbreviated. Compare the Sixth Vision, which apparently retains the fullest form of the angel-prophet dialogue (cf. NOTE to "what is this," v 5). There the angel clearly initiates the exchange as he must have in this case, except that his initial comments are not preserved. The Sixth Vision alone keeps the full introduction for reasons intrinsic to the special focus of that vision.

"What are these, my lord?" This question repeats exactly the words of the prophet found in the First (1:9) and Fourth (4:4) Visions. The other visions all involve interrogation of one sort or another; but this specific form of questioning, which includes addressing the angelic figure as "lord," is to be found only in the enclosing visions (First and Seventh) and in the central one, where "my lord" appears three times (cf. NOTE to "my lord," 4:4). This literary arrangement draws attention to the interrelatedness of all the visions, with the central one being climactic.

5. *four winds of heaven.* As in 2:10 (RSV 2:6, see NOTE), these four cosmic winds represent the four compass directions. The movement of atmospheric currents, between heaven and earth as it were, suggests the freedom of movement and the speed as

well as the strength through which God or his messengers connect Palestine with all surrounding areas. The "four winds" connote a worldwide totality and, as a consequence, in this vision they suggest the universal scope of Yahweh's realm. The language of the last vision, in a series of vivid images—four chariots, four horses (or teams of horses), and four winds—conveys the omnipresence and omnipotence of Yahweh's sovereignty and complements the concept of omniscience introduced in the opening vision. The use of "winds" *(rûḥôt)* also anticipates the final verse of this vision where God's "spirit" *(rûaḥ)* or presence is equated with the movement of his subordinates (cf. NOTE to "placed my spirit," v 8).

from being stationed. A Hithpael infinitive of the verb *yṣb* plus *ʿl,* "to station oneself" or "to take one's stand at the side of" (see Hurvitz 1974:25 and cf. Job 1:6; 2:1; 2 Chron 11:13; Josh 24:1) describes the positioning of the horses and presumably chariots as well in God's presence. The setting suggested by this verb, along with the phrase following it, "by the Lord of all the earth," is that of the Heavenly Court, which appears implicitly in the opening vision and explicitly in the investiture of Joshua in chapter 3 (see NOTES to 3:1). Since the emissaries that span the globe have their place of origin in Yahweh's court, they function as the symbolic representatives of Yahweh, who is present throughout the world. In giving specific form to that abstract concept, they signify that whatever is achieved through the activity of the messengers must be construed as God's will, since the messengers come from their rightful place at Yahweh's side. One use of this verb is noteworthy: it describes the quiet or passive stance of those witnessing Yahweh's might, especially on their behalf (e.g., Exod 14:13; 1 Sam 12:7,16). Whatever notion of power the horses and chariots may evoke on their own, their effectiveness comes only from the fact that Yahweh is the ultimate source of power.

Lord of all the earth. Emphasis on Yahweh's universal sovereignty lies behind this designation for Yahweh. Yahweh's sovereignty evidently has a political dimension inasmuch as this title is similar to certain titles that are applied to a god as lord of the land in other ancient Near Eastern countries (so Lipiński 1965:425ff.). The context here and in other passages in the Hebrew Bible where it is found indicates that the biblical writers intend it to express God's worldwide sovereignty (Ottosson 1974:395; cf. the analogous title "King of all the earth" in Ps 47:3,8 [RSV vv 2, 7]). The political overtones of such sovereignty are particularly appropriate to this vision, which implies divine sanction for Persian rule, as well as in the central vision, the other place where this designation of Yahweh appears in Zechariah's visions (see NOTE to this phrase in 4:14). The use of this title is another example where the language of the central vision and that of the final vision converge, as they do for the formulaic query of the preceding verse, "What are these, my lord?"

In addition to setting the universal stage for the final vision, the use of *ʾereṣ* ("earth") in itself performs two other functions: it provides linkage with the initial vision, and it contributes to the impact of the last vision. "Earth" in the absolute state appears three times in the First Vision and four times in the Seventh, this instance being the first of those four occurrences. In addition, the specific forms in which "earth" is used constitute a chiastic arrangement between the two visions. In the First Vision, the first two occurrences have the form *bāʾāreṣ* ("about the earth," 1:10,11) with the same verb ("roam"); the third occurrence has *kl-hʾrṣ* ("all the earth," 1:11). In the Sixth Vision *kl-h'rṣ* ("all the earth," 6:5) appears first, followed by three repetitions of *b'rṣ* ("about the earth," 6:7) all with the verb "roam." The structure is *b'rṣ* . . . *b'rṣ* . . . *kl-h'rṣ* (chap 1:11) *kl-h'rṣ* . . . *b'rṣ* . . . *b'rṣ* . . . *b'rṣ* (chapter 6). The redundant language in verse 6, where "roam about the earth" appears to be repeated unnecessarily, may be the result of adding one *b'rṣ* in order to make up the full number seven. The resulting group of seven usages, composed of correspondences and repetitions which can hardly be accidental, helps to connect the outermost pair of visions which frame the visionary sequence. The connection is a thematic one, in terms of the universality denoted by the word "earth," and one of language, in which a key word is repeated seven times, representing totality in Semitic parlance. Note the similar sevenfold repetition, in this vision, of the verb *yṣ'* ("go out, go forth"; see NOTE to "going out," v 1).

"Earth" appears several other times in the last vision, but it is difficult to determine whether the position or repetition of the term in those other instances is significant. In verse 6 and 8, there are four additional occurrences of *'rṣ,* all in the construct with either "north" or "south." However, since at least two other such usages apparently have fallen out (cf. second and third NOTES to v 6), the reckoning of the total occurrences of "land," or of the number of examples in the construct cannot be certain. Any further importance inherent in the repetition of this word cannot be established.

6. *The one . . . going out to.* Literally: "The one with which the black horses were going out to." The Hebrew *'šr-bh* ("with [which]") at the beginning of the verse refers to "chariot," which is specified before each horse group in verses 2–3 and which is feminine singular. The preposition *(b)* is the same as in verses 2–3, where *b* ("with") appears before each usage of "chariot." The verb "going out" *(yṣ'ym)* is masculine plural and thus refers to the horses and not the chariot; the horses are the subject and the chariot is in an oblique case. The term *'šr-bh* should thus be understood distributively: "with it (the chariot) the black horses were going out; and the white ones, etc."

northland . . . southland. As in the oracle in 2:10 (RSV 2:6; see NOTE to "land of the north"), *ṣāpôn* ("north") here and in verse 8 below, where it appears twice, denotes the region of Babylonia or Persia. Although it may indicate the direction from which the enemies of Israel came, as it does frequently in Jeremiah (e.g., 6:1,22), it also signifies the place from which the exiles will return (e.g., Jer 3:18; 23:8). The route taken by either group would have been to Israel's north along the major ancient highways between Palestine and Mesopotamia. "Northland" in its simplest sense, including either of the two ways in which Jeremiah uses it, designates that nation state or empire at the eastern end of the Fertile Crescent whose political strength will affect or has already affected Judean integrity. Persia, for Zechariah, now occupies the northland, but it is not as an enemy in relationship to Judah. The prophecies of Deutero-Isaiah have identified the first Persian emperor in the most positive light (e.g., Isa 44:28; 45:1), and the inferential evidence of Ezra and of Haggai and Zechariah does not present Persia as a disaster-bearing foe. The particular significance of chariots with respect to the "northland" should not be dissociated from the fact that all four directions are traversed by chariots, though only two or three (see NOTE to "after them," below) are specified in the text as it stands. Yahweh's chariots are not, therefore, going out to do battle with a specified enemy. Rather, the "quiet" (cf. 1:11) state of affairs in the known world, reflecting the stability of the Persian Empire at this point in the reign of Darius I (see Cook 1983:67–77), is an expression and consequence of Yahweh's supreme dominion. The four chariots, as we have suggested (see NOTE to 6:1), represent general divine sovereignty based on Yahweh's supreme might and authority and not any specific military preparation against an enemy figure. The "divine warrior" imagery of Yahweh, suggested elsewhere by chariots (Hanson 1975:292ff.), is not particularly relevant to the chariot imagery of this vision, which serves as a complement to the horse imagery of the First Vision.

The use of "northland" and "southland," with no explicit reference to east or west, would seem to contradict or dilute the meaning of the "four winds of heaven" as the four compass points. The text has obviously suffered some depredations in this verse. The omission of east and west may be the result of simple haplography (cf. "after them," below). Another possibility is that the omission represents an adjustment of the global scope of the four winds, which correspond to four chariots, to the facts of topography and the location of Judah in Palestine. The roads upon which chariots might pass would have been the north-south ones, because the political powers that sought to dominate the Levant and that had the resources to field horse-and-chariot armies were either Egypt to the south or the imperial powers of Syria/Mesopotamia approaching from the north. Thus the north-south polarity of this verse, if it is a possibility for one stage in the transmission of the MT, would represent Yahwistic control over whichever powers might exist at the two ends of the Fertile Crescent, whether or not they were a threat to Palestine. In contrast, the last set of directional references (in 6:8) specifies only "northland" and apparently refers to the "northern" imperial power of Zechariah's day, viz. the Persian Empire under Darius I.

The terms "northland" and "southland" are both made up of the Hebrew word 'ereṣ (otherwise translated "earth" in this vision, vv 5, 7, 8 and elsewhere) in construct with a directional word. These two instances in verse 6, of 'ereṣ in construct with a directional word, along with two further ones in verse 8, appear along with four other usages of 'ereṣ in the Seventh Vision (cf. NOTE to "Lord of all the earth," verse 5). The repetition is striking, although it is difficult to ascertain whether the total number of occurrences is significant since at least two additional usages of "land" have probably dropped out.

after them. The commonly favored emendation supplies a direction—i.e., "to the west" *'l 'ḥry hym* (or *'l 'áḥôr*), to correlate with "north" (v 6) and "south" (v 7). The simplest emendation here, however, would be to suppose that the words *'rṣ* plus some directional signal had fallen out between *'l* and *'ḥryhm* through a haplography induced by homoearcton; note the sequence of words beginning with *aleph*. Four directions are clearly needed, for the entire passage is stylized: the use of four winds and four chariots demands the corresponding presence of four directions. Indeed, from Wellhausen onward commentators have regularly supplied *'rṣ* ("land") plus a direction. McHardy (1968:178) has pointed out that in a number of passages where the four directions are indicated, the Hebrew text is very difficult and questionable (so Josh 18:15; 1 Sam 20:41; Ezek 40:2,20,44; 42:10). Hebrew tradition apparently had no fixed order for indicating the four directions (compare Gen 13:14 with Ezek 47:15ff. and 1 Kgs 7:25; NT Rev 21:13 is apparently influenced by 1 Chron 26:14–16 and Ezek 42:16–19).

The problem for the Seventh Vision is that only two directions are explicitly indicated: the black horses go to the north and the dappled ones go to the south (see above NOTE to "northland . . . southland"). As we have already indicated in NOTES to 6:2–

3 and 1:8 there has been a good deal of confusion in the transmission of the colors and names in these texts. The group consisting of white horses was probably intended to be dispatched to the west. We have not put "west" in the translation because either the confusion occurred very early in the history of the transmission of the MT or, as is always possible, the original text in fact never had four individually listed directions. Nonetheless, it is likely that an original had the white horses going west and also included the fourth group (red horses), which would have gone to the east (cf. following NOTE).

dappled ones. The use of a pattern word (cf. NOTE to "red . . . black . . . white . . . dappled," 6:2–3) to describe one group of horses instead of a color word is irregular and unexpected, but could just as well testify to its originality. If 6:2–3 is original, as we have asserted, then the problem in this verse is not the presence of "dappled" as a horse category but rather the absence of a fourth horse. "Red horses" are missing from the grouping of four. The omission of the red group, which should precede the black horses in this verse because the horses otherwise are in the same order as in verses 2–3, can well be explained as haplography due to homoearcton. The scribe's eye would have jumped from the *he* at the beginning of *h'dmym* ("the red horses") to the *he* at the beginning of *hšḥrym* ("the black horses") with the corresponding loss of the whole clause. Thus one horse color has accidentally been dropped just as have one or two directions (cf. the suggestion of the editor of this passage in *BHS*).

7. *The mighty ones went out.* This statement, as we have indicated in our NOTE above to "[all] mighty ones" *('āmuṣṣîm)* of verse 3, summarizes the activity of all the chariot groups. Although verse 6 clearly has suffered some losses, the intention for four groups to be represented in that verse can be assumed. The root *'mṣ* has nothing to do with color, and its etymological meaning of "strong" or "mighty," rather than "numerous" or "many," makes good sense in this vision. Since the "mighty ones" go out through all the earth in this verse, *'āmuṣṣîm* can hardly refer to only one horse group but must represent all of them. The designation "mighty ones" provides a characteristic, not a color, that applied equally to the four groups of horses.

The verb "went out" is masculine plural, as is the next verb ("were eager"); similarly, the following two imperatives ("Go," "Roam") are masculine plural. These must all refer to the horses. But at the end of verse 7 the verb "roamed" is feminine plural and goes back now to include the chariots and can be related to the feminine plural verb in verse 1, which refers to the chariots there. In other words, verses 1 and 7 correspond and form an intricate envelope. They are both summary statements: verse 1 begins with chariots and a feminine verb, and then the horse groups follow in verses 2–3; verse 7 ends with chariots, or rather a feminine verb referring to them, with the horse groups preceding them.

were eager to go. Literally: "they sought *(wybqšw)* to go." "To go," infinitive of *hlk,* appears redundant and is omitted in some manuscripts (LXX[L] and Syr[H]). However, its presence immediately before another infinitive, "to roam," may be meant to balance the two imperatives ("Go," "Roam") in the next part of the verse. The subject of the finite verb ("were eager") must be the masculine "horses," since the verb is masculine and "chariots" is feminine (cf. preceding NOTE). The chariots are finally included at the end of verse 7, with the last verb of the verse, *wtbhlknh,* being feminine.

roam . . . Roam . . . roamed. The Hithpael of the verb *hlk* is used here three times. The first occurrence is an infinitive, paired with "to go" (see preceding NOTE) and referring to the horses as indicated by the finite verb *wybqšw* ("they were eager"), which is masculine plural in agreement with "horses." The second occurrence is a masculine plural imperative ("Roam"), paired with "Go" and likewise referring to the horses. The third occurrence, however, is third feminine plural and so cannot be a response to the masculine imperative that comes immediately before it. Rather, it links up with the feminine "chariots" and "were going out" of verse 1 (cf. two preceding NOTES). The shift in gender in this series of verbs in verse 7 is hardly a mistake but rather a fine structural touch meant to form an envelope with verse 1. Verse 1 begins and verse 7 ends with a statement about the movement of chariots.

The use of the Hithpael of *hlk* can be compared to a similar usage in Zech 1:10 (see NOTE), where it describes the thorough but covert surveillance of God's domain, the whole earth. In contrast to the movement of the horses in the First Vision, the roaming of the quartet of horse-drawn chariots in the Seventh Vision is overt, as indicated by the language (see NOTE to "mountains of bronze," v 1) and also by the fact that the very nature of the chariot makes its progress difficult to conceal. Therefore, while the "roaming" of the First Vision implies that the horsemen might go anywhere unseen, in order to accomplish their goal of observing events in the whole world, the visible movement in the Seventh Vision suggests a more regular patrolling, a traversing of fixed rounds. Indeed, many translations do employ "patrol." While we are in sympathy with such a rendering, we use "roam" in both the First and Seventh Visions in order to retain the enveloping language of the Hebrew text. Furthermore, in this context, the notion of going off in different directions (cf. Judg 21:24) would supersede any concept of fixed paths by which such going might take place.

This verse features an abundance of verbs: *hlk* three times in the Hithpael and twice in the Qal; *bqš; yṣ'*. The activity of the horses and chariots could hardly be more directly and insistently presented. Yet it is questionable whether the intensification of the movement of the chariots should require a triple use of "roam about." Might not a single repetition suffice as for "went/go?" The unusual and apparently unnecessary tripling of "roam about the earth" might be explained in two ways. First, the third occurrence of this phrase involves a gender shift, as we have pointed out above, and so brings the chariot, first introduced in verse 1, back into the picture. Second, this vision on its own and in conjunction with Vision 1 contains a sequence of appearances of the word "earth," which is the object of the verb "roam about." That sequence appears to require a total of seven usages of "earth" (in the absolute state) in Visions 1 and 7 together, a requirement which is fulfilled only by including this seemingly redundant instance. Therefore, the third repetition of "roam about the earth" has a triple function: intensifying the movement, linking verse 7 with verse 1, and supplying another appearance of a key word.

The possible monotony of three usages of the Hithpael of *hlk* is somewhat averted in that each assumes a different grammatical form in the Hebrew. The first is an infinitive, following directly the Qal infinitive "to go." The second is an imperative, used in asyndeton with the preceding imperative "go." The third is an imperfect and refers back to the feminine *mrkbwt* "chariots." Since the verb therefore cannot be understood as a response to the masculine imperatives immediately preceding, the response to the imperative must be the verbs which appear before them, that is, "went out," and "were eager." These are both masculine plural and refer to horses. In verse 7 the order of clauses is inverted, with the command coming after compliance. In English a similar effect is achieved through the use of particles and sophisticated tenses such as the pluperfect and future perfect. Hebrew does not have such a variety of forms or particles, but a similar effect can be achieved through a highly structured arrangement such as that of verse 7.

he said. This introduces the first of two internal quotations in the last two verses of the vision. The antecedent is "Lord of all the earth" of verse 5. The Interpreting Angel, beginning in verse 5, has described the four chariots as the emissaries of Yahweh. He now reconstructs the charge given by God to his minions, and it is Yahweh's commands which are about to be quoted. Just as Yahweh is the one denoted by "he said," so too is Yahweh the subject of "called me forth" and "spoke" in verse 8 (see NOTES).

the earth. The word for "earth" (*²ereṣ*) is found eight times in verses 5–8. It first appears as part of the title given to Yahweh in verse 5 (see NOTE). There, as in the Fourth Vision, the universal sovereignty of God over terrestrial, and thus human, affairs is proclaimed (see NOTES to 4:14 and 6:5). Two directional uses follow in verse 6, where "northland" (*²ereṣ ṣāpôn*) and "southland" (*²ereṣ hattêmān*) represent two, if not all, of the directions in which the chariots are moving. In this verse, preceded by the preposition *b* meaning "in" or "about," "land" signifies the entire world; and Yahweh's dominion over it is symbolized by his chariots traversing it. Finally, in the last verse (v 8) of this vision, "northland" (*²ereṣ*) appears twice (see NOTE), resuming the directional specificity of verse 6. Clearly, *²ereṣ* ("earth, land") fulfills a variety of interrelated functions in this vision as well as in relationship to the Fourth and also the First Vision. The repetition of the same Hebrew word in all these cases, all of which are concerned with God's sovereign presence and the symbolic expression of that presence, would seem to underscore the universality of divine dominion for human existence.

8. *He called me forth.* The Hiphil of the verb *z⁽q*, "to call, cry out," introduces the conclusion of this last vision. While the Qal of the verb would indicate a simple crying or calling out, the Hiphil with the following accusative "me" (*²ōtî*) involves the object of the verb in the verbal action. The speaker is Yahweh (cf. preceding NOTE). He is not calling out *to* the prophet, for that dimension of his speaking to Zechariah is expressed in the following words, "spoke to me." Nor does the Hiphil here indicate a general or intense cry, as it does in Jonah 3:7, where there is no object of the verb, pronominal or otherwise, in contrast with the present instance. The closest biblical analogy for the Hiphil of *z⁽q* followed by an accusative comes in the vocabulary of mustering, in which a military leader calls forth or summons members of certain tribes or units for military duty (e.g., Judg 4:10,13). The implication of such usage for Zechariah is that the prophet is to be fully alert and ready to hear the statement that follows, which appears not only as a climax to this vision but also, since this is the last, as a conclusion to the visionary sequence in its entirety.

The normal vocabulary of the visions, in which the prophet is addressed by the angelic figure, consists of the words "speak" (*²mr*) or "answer" (*⁽nh*). The closest thing to an exception to this pattern comes in the Fourth Vision, where the Interpreting Angel acts upon the prophet by rousing him (4:1) before he speaks. The arrangement of the present passage apparently is similar, with the prophet's full attention evoked before the words are uttered. The Fourth Vision differs in that the prophet's awareness is secured for the purpose of seeing the visionary objects rather than for hearing the interpreting message. The use of "roused" in 4:1 is appropriate because visual perception is required there, whereas the "called forth" of 6:8 is relevant to the auditory receptivity required in this context. In any case, the calling forth of the prophet in the last verse of the final vision is an exception to the way in which he is addressed in the previous visions and so draws the attention of the audience as well as of the prophet to the words that follow. In addition, it suits the unusual fact that Yahweh is speaking directly to the prophet *within* a vision. Although the interchange between Yahweh and the Interpreting Angel is sufficiently frequent to allow for the possibility that the latter is the speaker, the use of the first-person suffix with *rwḥ* ("my spirit") indicates that God is the one addressing the prophet this last time. Furthermore, the use of the verb *dbr* ("speak"), unusual in the visions, points to Yahweh rather than the angel as the subject of both verbs at the beginning of verse 8 (see following NOTE).

spoke to me:. This rather common phrase, the verb *dbr* ("speak") with the preposition and its object, followed by *lēʾmōr* ("saying," which we have rendered with a colon; cf. Hag 1:1; 1:3, etc.), is found only at this place in Zechariah's visions. However, with the noun "word" *(dābār)*, normally in construct with "Yahweh," instead of the verb, this combination is typical of oracular material in prophecy, occurring many times in Haggai as well as in the nonvisionary sections of Zechariah (e.g., 6:9; 8:1,18). The use of this clause here gives oracular weight to the final pronouncement. The angelic figure in this role as a divine messenger has advised the prophet throughout the visions. His mediating function has been prominent as he moves about, interacting with both Zechariah and some of the visionary objects or characters. Here, however, Yahweh himself provides the message, as indicated by the appearance of language used to introduce the *ipsissima verba* of Yahweh. In this final vision the mediating role of the angel has receded and the message of Yahweh has become direct and forceful. In addition, the appearance of the phrase "he called me forth and spoke to me," with Yahweh as subject, helps to explain the otherwise unexpected and difficult "my spirit," referring to God's and not the angel's spirit, in the statement that follows. Further, in giving the last statement the character of an oracle it provides a parallel with the oracular supplement of the First Vision, thus completing the envelope construction of the opening and concluding visions.

going out to. This is the seventh and final usage of the *yṣʾ* ("go out") in this vision. It completes the series of occurrences (cf. NOTE to "going out," v 1) that express the totality in time of God's knowledge and the control over his global domain. In addition, it balances the first usage in verse 1. There the "going out" was "from"—that is, "from between the two mountains" or from the court of Yahweh. Here the "going out" is "to" *(ʾel-)*, specifically to the "northland" which represents the earthly political power controlling Yehud (cf. last NOTE to v 8) and over which God's power extends.

placed my spirit. The Hiphil of *nwḥ* ("to rest") can be compared with the Hophal, which appears in the conclusion of the Sixth Vision (5:11) designating the ultimate deposition of the Ephah in Babylon. The cultic overtones that accompany this verb in the Ephah passage, where it refers to a pagan deity's image or shrine (see NOTE to "Ephah" 5:6, for a discussion of its identity), are extended here to the unseen presence of Yahweh, also in a foreign context. The verb does not in itself have a negative connotation. Therefore the commentators who see the verb and its object together as denoting the exercise of Yahweh's anger base their interpretation on their understanding of the noun *rûḥî* ("my spirit") and also "northland" (cf. following NOTE).

For some scholars (e.g., Elliger 1975:102; Rudolph 1976:122–23), the interpretation of *rûḥî* begins with an emendation suggested by *BH³* and *BHS* of "my spirit" to "spirit of Yahweh." However, there is no textual support for such a change, though there is a tradition of using abbreviations for *nomina sacra* in the Greek scribal tradition. The possessive pronominal suffix, referring to Yahweh, actually fits quite well the oracular character of this last statement as introduced by the unusual "he called me forth" and by the stereotyped prophetic language of "he spoke to me" (see the two preceding NOTES).

More controversial is the actual translation of the noun *rûaḥ* as "anger," "wrath," or "spirit." The former rendering, prominent in the older commentaries (e.g., Nowack 1903:265), is continued to some extent in more recent exegeses of the passage (e.g., Rudolph 1976:125) which base their arguments upon the supposed connection between *rûḥî* and *ḥamātî* in Ezek 5:13, where it is used with *nwḥ* in the Hiphil. Rudolph also points to the occurrence of *rûaḥ* meaning wrath in Judg 8:3, Prov 16:32 and 29:11. It was such an understanding of *rûaḥ* in Zech 6 that led some to interpret this statement as a judgment against the enemy, a possibility noted by Ackroyd (1968:183), who paraphrases "God's anger is appeased by bringing disaster there." Other commentators (e.g., Marti 1904:419), who translate the verb as an imperfect, lend an eschatological cast to this verse: God will ultimately rest when Israel's enemies have been subjected to his anger—i.e., judgment. The place associated with this event is the "land of the north" or "northland," and those words are understood to refer to the foes or conquerors of Israel, an interpretation with which we disagree (cf. NOTE to "northland . . . southland" above, 6:6, and also the following NOTE to "northland" in this verse).

Together with the following phrase "in the northland," God's "spirit" in this vision represents God's active presence in world events, a usage not unlike that associated with the appearance of *rûaḥ* both in Haggai (2:5) and also in the Zerubbabel insertion of Zechariah's Fourth Vision (4:6b). It is not necessarily eschatological—indeed, in this passage (see following NOTE) it refers to the present world—nor does it imply that either wrath or blessing is a dominant feature of Yahweh's active will or *rûaḥ*. Furthermore, the use of *rûaḥ* as God's "spirit" in this verse cannot be dissociated from the *rûḥôt*, the Hebrew substantive for "winds," of verse 5. When we encounter *rûaḥ* in this verse, we hear an echo of the "winds of heaven" mentioned above.

in the northland. These final words of the last vision echo the first few words of this oracular statement ("See them going out to the northland") and also the description of the horse-and-chariot emissaries of verse 6. Because "northland" can represent the political powers of Syria or Mesopotamia that sometimes have conquered Palestine, in the time of Zechariah that term would designate Persia (cf. NOTE to v 6). However, it is questionable here whether "northland" has a connotation of enemy. Persia does not appear in such negative terms in postexilic biblical literature, nor would the Persian imperial policy, which allowed Yehud to restore its national shrine and achieve a measure of community identity and self-rule, seem to warrant the arousal of divine wrath against Persia.

"Northland" as enemy, if it does not refer to the international scene of the prophet's day, might then be an eschatological designation of Israel's enemies in a symbolic and not a literal sense. However, Childs (1959) has shown that the use of the "enemy from the north" language in eschatological contexts in the postexilic period draws upon the language, not present in this passage, of the chaos myth or motif, the ancient Near Eastern tradition reflected in certain texts referring to a struggle between Yahweh's creative activity and the opposing primordial chaos. In particular, the verb *rʿš* ("to shake") is a technical term that has been assimilated into the chaos motif. It is never found in preexilic texts describing the enemy from the north, for the enemy in those passages is on the plane of human history. But in postexilic biblical writings, the enemy from the north "invariably" (Childs 1959:197) appears with a great shaking *(rʿš),* thus demonstrating that the "northland" has become suprahistorical because it has been fused with *rʿš.* Certainly in Haggai (2:6,21), that verb appears in an eschatological passage, though without "northland." "Northland," it seems, must appear with *rʿš* in postexilic eschatological contexts but not vice versa. In short, the absence of *rʿš* here would preclude an eschatological cast to this verse and thus make the identification of "northland" as enemy unlikely.

If "northland" is not a past or future enemy, its association with the Persian Empire of the present world seems to be a plausible interpretation. In the context of the visions in which the prophet is dealing with the need to understand the Persian policy allowing the Yehudites to refound their temple within traditional Yahwism, a reference to Persia would be quite in order. In addition, specifying the "north" as a direction would be intentional, given the four directional possibilities represented by the "four winds" and "four chariots" (see NOTES to 6:1,5) as well as the four sets of horses (see NOTES to vv 2–3 and 6, 7). If the four directions are narrowed to two (north and south, see NOTE to "northland . . . southland," v 6) in order to adjust the metaphor of Yahweh's omnipotence to the north-south highways of Palestine, which Israel's conquerors have used in the past with their chariots, then the focusing upon "northland" in this last verse would be a similar and further localization in accordance with present political realities. The power that dominates Palestine and the world in Zechariah's time is the one that is superseded by Yahweh's omnipotence.

The perspective in this conclusion to the visions is thus fully in accord with that of the others. The Yehudites' activities in refounding the temple and reconstituting their community internally, which appear to be the result of Persian initiative and authorization, are actually to be seen as reflecting the will of Yahweh. Rather than representing conflict, the "northland" actually reflects the sense in which the former conflicts have been resolved and the power of Yahweh holds sway (Mason 1977b:60–61). God's spirit in the northland gives legitimacy to the Yehudite efforts. No matter how powerful the Persian imperial domination may seem, the cosmic power of Yahweh, symbolized by the chariot patrols, lies behind Persian political decisions. While the subsequent Zechariah oracles (e.g., 8:22–23) may be eschatologically oriented in their hope that all nations will one day acknowledge the scope of Yahweh's sovereignty, the visionary material, including this verse which is oracular in texture, is rooted in and addressed to the world of the early postexilic community.

COMMENT

The prophet has allowed us to witness with him an extraordinary succession of visionary scenes. He has comprehended God's purposes for the crucial events of his day through the workings of his fertile imagination, and he has skillfully narrated these experiences with their decisive prophetic content to his compatriots. Having followed his account, vision by vision, his audience now is shown four chariots drawn by horses. The language and context are so strikingly similar to that of the opening vision that his hearers must surely conclude that they have come full circle and that this vision completes the visionary cycle. Just as Visions 5 and 6 could be paired thematically and structurally with Visions 3 and 2 respectively, so too can the Seventh Vision be linked with the First, thus establishing the *inclusio* framework for the corpus of Seven Visions. While this pairing of visions can be recognized because of certain similarities that exist between the members of the pairs, it must also be noted that there are important differences between the members of each pair. Those differences make the pairs complementary as well as parallel.

The appearance of a set of horse groups, albeit with the addition of chariots, is just the most obvious of several features shared by the opening and closing visions. Other correspondences include: the manner of the prophet's questioning, in which he addresses the Interpreting Angel with the title "my lord" (1:9; 6:4); the repeated use of the term "roam about," twice in chapter 1 and three times in chapter 6; the delineation of an opening setting, the shadowy darkness of a myrtle thicket in the First Vision (1:8) and the brilliance of bronze mountains (6:1) in the Seventh; the intimation that Yahweh's court is the ultimate setting for both the visions, with Yahweh himself having dispatched the equine figures (see 1:10 and 6:5); and the strong suggestion of a global scope, created in part by the sevenfold repetition of the word "earth" (*ʾereṣ*), here meaning all the world (1:10–11, three times; 6:5,7, four times), in addition to the appearance of "earth" in construct with several directional words in the last vision ("northland," "southland") whereby it forms another set of usages. Furthermore, the Seventh Vision ends with a pronouncement by Yahweh introduced by a unique occurrence of an oracular formula within the vision rather than with an angelic explication. In this way, the final vision is given an ending that parallels the oracular conclusion of the opening vision while at the same time providing an impressive finale to the Seven Visions, ending with the words of Yahweh himself and not those of the mediating figure, the Interpreting Angel, who has otherwise been so prominent in this corpus.

If the last vision is so distinctly paired with the first, its relationship with the central one likewise can be noted. Indeed, in a seven-part series, with the first and last enclosing the whole, we would *a priori* expect to find linkages between the outermost units and the middle one with its companion piece (chap 3, the prophetic vision) insofar as the structure of the whole serves to heighten the importance of the central part. Not surprisingly, such connections are in evidence. First, perhaps the most obvious point of comparison is the phrasing of Zechariah's question to this angelic interlocutor. In 1:9, 4:4, and 6:4, and nowhere else in the visions, the prophet asks "What are these, my lord?" Second, the suggestion of a Heavenly Court scene appears in all three places, created by the equines or chariots sent out from Yahweh's presence in Visions 1 and 7 and by the description of two symbolic figures who "stand by" Yahweh in Vision 4. This feature is one which the Fourth Vision's companion piece, the prophetic vision, develops rather fully. Third, God's universal presence and knowledge are major thematic components of all three of these visions. They are, in fact, the primary message of the First Vision; they are present in the "seven eyes" terminology of the Fourth Vision, where they are the counterpart of the "two sons of oil" in a vision which has a two-part visionary presentation; and they are implicit in the terminology of horses and of patrolling which the Seventh Vision shares with the First. Finally, the phrase "all the earth" meaning all the world (as opposed to "all the land," or Yehud, as in 5:3 and 6) is found only in these three visions and contributes to the global purview.

The interconnecting of Visions 1, 4, and 7 is more than an exercise in literary ingenuity. The prophet is able, by coordinating the visions, to unify the elements of his prophetic experiences, which are replete with significance for the people. The first and last visions also, as we have already proposed in our COMMENT to the First Vision, establish the fact of divine universality as a backdrop for all the visions. The particular problems of Jerusalem and Yehud that are the concern in one way or another in all the visions are set against the incontrovertible worldwide scope of Yahweh's knowledge and power. The concomitant divine sanction for the messages Zechariah apperceives and then relates to his audience is an intrinsic part of all the innovative developments that Zechariah proclaims in the process. This is especially important for the Fourth Vision, which would appear to have the narrowest focus of them all in its presentation of the temple scene, and which also offers the most direct and radical rearrangement of traditional patterns and expectations. The temple, one small spot on the earth's surface, is in this way seen as an integral component of God's entire, universal domain. The renewed understanding of the administration of God's particular territory, Yehud, within that global domain receives the affirmation that it is part of Yahweh's cosmic ordering of events (see our COMMENT to the Fourth Vision). The First Vision suggests omniscience, and the Seventh one with its chariots indicates omnipotence. These attributes in combination are directed inward in the overall visionary structure, across the interposed visions (2, 3, 5, 6), and they meet at the center to add their combined significance to the focal message of the central vision.

The role of the chariot vision in the full set is obviously of the utmost significance. At the same time, it has its own distinct purpose among Zechariah's visions. The message of the Seventh Vision depends upon two of its characteristics: the imagery of the chariots above and beyond that of the horses alone, and the oracular conclusion to the vision supplied by Yahweh in the last verse ("They have placed my spirit in the northland," v 8).

The chariot, as we have explained in the NOTES, is first and foremost an instrument of war that enabled political states in the ancient world to expand their territories and extend their dominion. The strength and skill of the charioteers were often the decisive factors in a military confrontation. Although the chariot upon occasion was used for ceremony or sport, those functions were derivative from the military one, so that only the governing elite used chariots for such purposes. The symbolic value of the chariot in the last vision emerges from the concept of military might and the attendant political control.

The basic imagery of the chariot is then refined by a series of associated details that the prophet sees and relates to us: (1) The chariots are four in number and, along with the four sets of horses designated by the four basic equine colors, represent a complete set of military equipment and hence complete power and dominion. Although the depiction of the colors of the horses may not have been transmitted accurately, the emphasis on the presence of four distinct horse groups is nonetheless clear, since the colors are listed twice in this vision, initially in verse 2 and again in verses 6–7. The symbolism of "four" as a global set is validated by the elucidating remarks of the Interpreting Angel in verse 5, where the four horse-and-chariot groups are equated with the "four winds of heaven." (2) Equating the four chariots with the "four winds of heaven" provides not only the assertion of totality but also the suggestion of spatial completeness. These four winds represent the four directions and hence the whole world. (3) The chariots, or the equivalent winds, are reported to be "going out" not fewer than seven times in the course of the vision. Again a totality is suggested, this time a temporal one: the chariots are *always* in motion, their might unceasingly exerted. (4) The chariots move out from between "two mountains," imagery suggesting divine presence and universality. The Interpreting Angel's statement in verse 5 confirms that impression: the chariots (= winds) are beside the "Lord of all the earth."

Recognizing these features of the chariots allows us to grasp the powerful imagery of the Seventh Vision. The chariots with their attendant details are a visual statement proclaiming that Yahweh's power reaches throughout time and space. But this proclamation alone is not the entire purpose of the Seventh Vision, which ends not with the angel's explanatory response to the prophet but rather with an oracular pronouncement by Yahweh. The generalization about God's universal dominion is therein given specific application to the prophet's own time. The "northland" is the direction singled out in this statement as the particular place in which God's presence, with its inherent might, can be discerned. For the period of the restoration, the northland represents the imperial dominion of Persia, whose rule over the Levant is expressed by this traditional term for the place from which Israel's conquerors come. The events of Zechariah's day have come to pass under the aegis of Yahweh's sovereignty. Persia's granting of semiautonomy to Yehud is not an act of independent imperial authority but rather an extension of Yahweh's will. Yahweh is the ultimate authority lying behind the manifold patterns and interactions of human history.

What has Persia granted to Yehud, with divine approbation? The answer to this question is important in what it excludes as well as what it includes. The prophet's visionary experiences, with their several oracular portions, have allowed us to sense the importance of the temple restoration process as the focal manifestation of Persian policy vis-à-vis Yehud. The rehabilitation of the Yehudite temple and its administration was, for the Persian, a political measure enabling them to promote stability and to achieve control over one part of their vast territorial holdings in the eastern Mediterranean (see Introduction). For the Yehudites, the Persian decrees assured that God's house in Jerusalem would be made functional once again. This meant the return of civil government and economic development to the priestly sphere, for the permitted restoration of the temple and its organization was not accompanied by permission to reinstitute the monarchic government that had been the integral accompaniment of the central Israelite shrine since the days of David and Solomon. Could temple without palace truly be what Yahweh intended for his people? If temple and palace together had been the essence of Judean existence, could the Yehudites accept one without the other as legitimate and proper? The visions as a whole, and now specifically this final pronouncement of the last vision, offer a resounding yes to such questions. The reorganization of national life under Persian dominion is surely a divinely ordained event.

Fortunately, a model for nonmonarchic governance was part of the Israelite past. Instead of inventing something, the postexilic prophets and leaders could reach back to an older tradition and adjust it to the new circumstances. The wilderness tradition of Moses and Aaron of the joint civil-ecclesiastical rule associated with the Sinai event provided the nonmonarchic pattern for the sanctuary and for a leading role for the priesthood. The Jerusalem pattern with the hope for a Davidic scion did not disappear, but its lack of viability for the postexilic community meant that the premonarchic pattern emerged strongly. The new governing structure on the one hand, and the emphasis on Torah literature on the other, were both ways in which the ascendancy of the older model became expressed after the exile.

Zechariah's visions all, in greater or lesser measure, confirm the fact that establishing the priesthood as the civil and religious authority of the state is acceptable. The visions may succeed in accomplishing this legitimization, ironically shifting the pattern of legitimization in the ancient world in which the temple was the symbol of the approval of the gods for a dynastic power. Here the prophetic vision provides sanction for the temple's role. Yet the question of monarchy would not so simply be dissolved. The visions are accompanied by oracles that address that question head-on, and this last vision is perhaps the most vivid case in point. The visionary sequence does not terminate Part Two (the visions) of First Zechariah, and a sequel or conclusion follows directly in the form of The Crowning passage of 6:9–15. The visions deal with Yehud and the temple, but the larger audience of all Yahwists cannot be ignored, and the persistent question of Davidic rule must again be addressed.

11. THE CROWNING
(6:9–15)

⁹ Then the word of Yahweh came to me: ¹⁰ "Take from the exiles, from Heldai, and from Tobiah, and from Jedaiah—you will go on that day and go into the house of Josiah ben-Zephaniah—[all of] whom have come from Babylon; ¹¹ And take silver and gold and make crowns. You will place [one] on the head of Joshua ben-Jehozadak, the high priest ¹² and say to him: 'Thus spoke Yahweh of Hosts:

> 'Behold, there is a man—Shoot is his name—and from his place he will shoot up and build the Temple of Yahweh. ¹³ He will build the Temple of Yahweh; and he will bear royal majesty and sit upon his throne and rule. A priest will be on his throne, and there will be peaceful counsel between the two of them.'

¹⁴ "The [other] crownª will be in the Temple of Yahweh as a reminder to Helem, Tobiah, Jedaiah, and Hen ben-Zephaniah."

¹⁵ Those who are distant will come to work on the Temple of Yahweh. Thus you will know that Yahweh of Hosts has sent me to you. This will be so when you truly listen to the voice of Yahweh your God.

ª The change from the MT plural requires no consonantal changes. The reading hā'ăṭeret is supported by the LXX and Peshitta; an old Phoenician singular may underlie the text.

NOTES

9. *Then the word of Yahweh came to me:*. This introductory formula is exactly the same as the one appearing in 4:8 in the Zerubbabel insertion. In addition, the two sets of oracles which constitute chapter 8 are each introduced by this formula, although its arrangement there differs slightly because of the addition of the words "of Hosts" after "Yahweh."

The Zerubbabel passage (4:6b–10a) within the Fourth Vision bears several similarities to the present passage, and the use of identical oracular formulas serves to underscore their thematic relationship. Both are concerned with the role the monarchic figure should play in the Yehudite reorganization demanded by the new circumstances of semiautonomy established within the overall dominion of the Persian imperial state. The oracle concerning Zerubbabel, enclosed by the central (lampstand) vision, addresses the immediate crisis of the role of a Davidic scion within the context of reestablishing the temple. The resolution of that crisis in the Zerubbabel insertion did not deal with the larger question concerning the monarchic model, ingrained in the culture and integral to the independent preexilic state, and its relationship to the present realities of Yehudite subordination to Persian rule. Furthermore the establishment of semiautonomy in Yehud raised questions about the status of those who remained in exile vis-à-vis the restoration community and its functioning temple. This oracle is as much a part of the visionary sequence as is the Zerubbabel insertion; while not visions in themselves, they are directed toward ideological issues precipitated by the temple refounding, which is the particular situation giving rise to Zechariah's visions.

10. *Take from.* The use of the infinitive absolute *lāqôaḥ* of the verb *lqḥ* ("to take") plus *mēʾēt* ("from"), without an intervening direct object, has caused much difficulty for the versions and the commentators. The infinitive absolute is to be read in the sense of an imperative, see *GKC* § 113.46; indeed, nine Kennicott manuscripts read the imperative. The verbal form itself, with the infinitive absolute functioning as an imperative, has been so translated in all the ancient versions. Analogies elsewhere in the Hebrew Bible (Exod 20:8; Deut 5:12; 31:26; Jer 32:14; Ezek 24:5) support such a rendering, and the suggestion of Ackroyd (1968:164) and Rudolph (1976:127) that *lāqôaḥ* is to be taken as a verbal noun and translated "something is to be taken" is therefore unwarranted. The origin of the imperative meaning of the infinitive absolute may lie in the shortening of the full expression, like *zākôr tizkōr*, which is a kind of intensified imperative [editor's suggestion]. That is, it would not be a substitute for the imperative but rather a shortened form of a different usage. This use of the infinitive absolute as an imperative is rare in Late Biblical Hebrew. The Chronicler, for example, never uses it in this way (Polzin 1976:43–44) and in fact rarely uses the infinitive absolute at all. This example in Zechariah, and the several examples of the infinitive absolute (not as imperative) in Haggai (cf. Hag 1:6), show greater affinity with earlier Hebrew than with the Hebrew of postexilic books.

More problematic is the absence of a direct object. The LXX sought to rectify this situation by supplying "things" after the verb. *BHS* and NJPS propose an emendation, changing "from" (*mēʾēt*) to "gifts" (*mattĕnōt* or *maśʾōt*). However, the verb can stand as it is, without a specified accusative, so long as this opening phrase of verse 10 is treated within the larger context of the series of instructions given by God to the prophet in verses 10–12. The verb "take" appears again at the start of verse 11, and it is followed there by the two items "silver" and "gold" (see NOTE to v 11). That fact must be considered along with the technical priestly expression, found several times in the Pentateuch (Exod 25:2; Num 18:26–28; Lev 7:34), for taking certain kinds of offering: the verb "take" *(lqḥ)* plus the compound preposition *mē'ēt,* composed of "from" and "with." In one instance, Lev 7:34, the direct object is also omitted but the context, in which the terms taken are specified earlier in the same verse, supplies the necessary information. We would therefore argue that the elliptical phrase "take from . . ." is similarly provided with the missing detail, the item to be so taken, by the repetition of the verb "take" at the beginning of verse 11, where it is clearly followed by a pair of direct objects. The omission of the objects after this first "take," although somewhat awkward from a purely prosaic point of view, would thus be intentional. As a literary device, a form of anticipation, it focuses attention on the silver and gold to be mentioned later.

At the same time, the delay in providing the objects of "take" allows the individuals involved in this passage to be introduced early in the narrative. Since this passage is addressed to the exiles and to the problem of *their* relationship to a homeland with a restored national shrine, the interaction of the prophet with the exiles, as a group or as several key individuals (see NOTES below to "exiles" and to "Heldai, Tobiah, and Jedaiah," v 10), takes precedence over the objects involved in this symbolic interaction. The prophet has altered the expected pattern of verb-object-prepositional phrase(s) by supplying the second item in the group in the second group of instructions (v 11). In this way the prepositional phrase "from" plus "exiles" and then the three individuals become the focus of the verbal idea instead of the direct object which would otherwise be the natural focus. In this special kind of prophetic oracle the persons addressed play a peculiar role, appearing as they do at the opening of this scene and again at its close (v 14; for the relationship of v 15 to this section, see NOTES below, v 15). This is another example of envelope construction, in which the closing materials balance and complete the opening statements. The meaning of the actions that the prophet is to perform is integrally related to the audience before which he is to carry out God's commands. That audience, therefore, is abruptly inserted into the opening imperative of the Crowning scene and appears again at its end.

This oracle consists of the direct words of Yahweh to the prophet without the intervening comments and queries of the angelic figure who played an important mediating role in the Seven Visions. That the opening words are in the form of a command to perform an action, which stands as the initial activity in a series, signifies the appearance of a particular genre of prophetic material, the symbolic action (cf. Hag 2:10–14; Jer 18:1–11; 19; Isa 8:1–4; 20). Usually the prophetic literature depicting such actions comprises three segments: the command to do a certain activity, a description of the order being executed, and an explication of the action's significance. Although the second element is not found here, as is sometimes the case for this genre (Amsler 1981:106), the other two elements are explicit. The divine imperatives begun in this verse continue in the next, and an oracle beginning in verse 12 within this scene conveys the message that completes the action. Because, by its very nature, a prophetic symbolic action demands witnesses, the introduction of the ones from whom Zechariah is to take some items and who will then observe what he does with them is an important part of this scene.

the exiles. The reference here seems to be to the community of returned exiles; and both the Targum and Syriac read "exiles," i.e., *mbny hgwlh.* However, the word *haggôlâ,* "the exiles," is a somewhat ambivalent term. As a singular noun it can refer either to the collective community of all exiled individuals (as in Est 2:6; Jer 29:1; Ezek 1:1; 3:11,15) or to the more abstract notion signified without the definite article of the condition of captivity or sojourn away from one's native lands (as in Jer 48:11; 49:3; 2 Kgs 24:15,16; Ezek 12:4, etc.). Because it can have these two distinct meanings, its usage in this particular passage is difficult to comprehend, particularly since it is not clear whether *haggôlâ* is meant to include all of the four individuals who are mentioned by name in this verse. The word *haggôlâ* immediately follows "take from" (see preceding NOTE) and precedes the names Heldai, Tobiah, and Jedaiah. Farther on in the verse, Josiah ben-Zephaniah is mentioned, and only at the very end does the presumably resumptive phrase, "who have come from Babylon," appear. The Hebrew of verse 10 thus allows for three possible interpretations of "exiles": 1. unreturned exiles who have sent offerings to the Yehudite community (cf. NOTE below to "silver and gold"); 2. a collective designation for the three individuals whose names would then be in apposition with "exiles," with these three being returnees according to the last phrase of the Hebrew text of verse 11 ("who have come from Babel," see NOTE); and 3. both unreturned exiles and a group of newly returned exiles, represented by one or two or three of the named individuals.

The matter cannot easily be resolved. The ambivalence of the Hebrew may be intentional, so that the crowns which are to be made with offerings represent the combined contributions of both exiled and returned groups, as the reprise of verse 14 perhaps indicates. However, the arrangement of the thrice-used preposition "from" in Hebrew would tend to support the possibility that not all of the named individuals are meant to be included in the "exiles" designation. The compound preposition *mē'ēt ("min,"* "from," plus *'et* "with") does not appear before the name of the first individual, Heldai, whose name is simply prefixed by the preposition without the accusative particle. But it is repeated before the names of the next two individuals. Heldai thus stands in closer relationship to "exiles" than to "Tobiah" and "Jedaiah," who perhaps were not intended to be included under the designation "exiles," even though they might have originally been in Babylon according to the final phrase (in Hebrew) of this verse. The absence of the *waw* ("and") which occurs in conjunction with both Tobiah and Jedaiah before Heldai also tends to confirm this. Heldai would then be a delegate from nonreturned Babylonian exiles, whose gifts are taken by Zechariah along with those of resident Yehudites, a group which would reasonably have included people who had returned on previous occasions, such as in the first wave of release from captivity under Cyrus. The inclusiveness of this verse thus involves exiles still in Babylon and those now living in Judah.

The ambivalence of the term "exiles" helps to demonstrate the unity of a community acknowledging Yahweh as God, apart from the form or identity of the political state in which those who acknowledge Yahweh may live. Those living in exile had maintained their memory of and association with Jerusalem as it had existed without a temple since 587. Now, with a temple refounded, the relationship of that exiled community to a Jerusalem with a temple had to be clarified.

Heldai. This individual is the first in a series of three men cited in Yahweh's charge to the prophet. All three names are taken as appellatives by the LXX. However, the first individual is distinct from the other two in several ways: his name follows immediately after "the exiles," with no intervening conjunction "and" nor with the compound preposition *(mēʾēt)* which precedes the names of the other two immediately following his name, although the preposition "from" has been affixed to his name. And he appears to have two forms to his name, for in the repetition in verse 14 of the names of those who witness Zechariah's deeds, the first individual is called Helem rather than Heldai. Although those two names are nowhere explicitly equated, indirect evidence appears sufficient to demonstrate that alternative forms of that man's name did exist (cf. Petitjean 1969:275–77). The mighty men of David, enumerated in 2 Sam 23:8–39 (= 1 Chron 11:10–41), included a man from Netophah called Heleb in the Samuel source (v 29) and Heled by the Chronicler (v 30). Together, those references reveal a personal name in which the first two consonants are stable but in which the third consonant varies probably through scribal error because of the similarity between *b* and *d* in the old Hebrew script. A further variant is recorded in 1 Chron 27:15, where "Heldai the Netophathite of Othniel" is listed as commander of the twelfth division of the Davidic kingdom. That passage, with a name exactly like that of the individual in Zechariah, further indicates that the name Heldai appeared in different forms, with only the initial two consonants remaining the same. While none of the other biblical references supplies a version of the name with *mem* (m) as the third consonant, the fact that several variants of the name Heldai did exist allows us to conclude that the Heldai of verse 10 is the same as the Helem of verse 14. Again, it is likely that scribal error is involved in the case of the third (and fourth) consonants. The Vulgate and Targum render "Helem" here, in the interest of providing consistency with verse 14, as does the LXX in treating the name as an appellative. Similarly, the Syriac changes the verse 14 rendering to Heldai, also to provide consistency.

Another possibility is that Heldai, the first individual designated after the term "exiles," has a name with two forms. One might speculate that he was known by one of them (Heldai) in Babylon and reverted to the other upon his return to Judah. Whatever the reason, his name in the text clearly stands in apposition with "exiles" and somewhat apart from the names of the other two people. On syntactical grounds alone, therefore, we would suggest that he is a delegate of exiles either still in Babylon or else very recently returned. This supposition may find support in a recent study of the onomasticon of Babylonian Jews, for forms similar if not identical to "Heldai" are either attested or suggested in Babylonian documents (see Zadok 1979:31, 116, 140). The *-ai* ending is probably a form developed in the exile, since it is a suffix common in Aramaic and late Akkadian. Heldai would then be an Aramized name, on analogy with *šabbātay,* which consists of the Hebrew word *šabbāt* and the suffix *-ai* (ibid.: 23; cf. NOTE to Hag 1:1 on the similar case of "Haggai").

and from Tobiah, and from Jedaiah. The other two men, who along with Heldai/ Helem (cf. previous NOTE) are to go with the prophet to Josiah's house (cf. following NOTE), both have theophoric names. If Heldai is meant to be a delegate of those still in Babylon or recently returned, then these two men would be local residents. But they too appear not to have been born in Judah, since the concluding clause of this verse, "who had come from Babel," is understood to apply to Tobiah and Jedaiah as well as to Josiah (cf. last NOTE to this verse). These first two individuals are apparently named nowhere else in the Hebrew Bible. The LXX, perhaps grasping their symbolic role here, renders their names with appellatives: "useful men" and "men who have understood it."

The name Tobiah itself is not uncommon, particularly in the exilic and postexilic periods. The "sons of Tobiah," for example, are among a group of exiles, returning with Zerubbabel, whose lineage is in doubt (Ezra 2:60; Neh 7:62). That Tobiah, however, was either deceased or remarried in Babylon and cannot be identified with the person of this oracle. Another Tobiah, in Nehemiah's generation, becomes the adversary of the Yehudite governor (Neh 2:10,19, etc.), and the apocryphal Book of Tobit deals with yet another gentleman by that name. Josephus and Maccabees both discuss the Tobiads of the Hasmonaean period. Outside the Bible, the name is found in the Lachish letters (letter 3, line 19) and the Zenon papyri. The Babylonian clan of Ṭu-ubria-a-ma may or may not be related to the biblical family (see Zadok 1979:62, 122, and Mazar 1957:231).

Similarly, Jedaiah is a name found in postexilic biblical literature, where it is associated with a priestly family, and also in Babylonian documents (Zadok 1979:14, 101). In 1 Chron 9:10, a Jedaiah appears to have been part of the earliest wave of returning exiles, and the name appears also in the priestly lists given by Ezra (2:36) and Nehemiah (7:39; 11:10; 12:6–7,19,21). Note that Jedaiah's name, unlike many of those associated with him in Ezra and Nehemiah, does not appear in the listing of returned priests who had taken foreign wives (Ezra 10:18–22). Though it is not possible to equate the Jedaiah of this passage with the figure of the Ezra-Nehemiah lists, the principle of papponymy which appears to operate for Tobiah (see below) may mean that he is indeed a member of that leading and faithful Jerusalem family.

Although neither Tobiah nor Jedaiah can be identified with other biblical characters bearing those names, it is certainly within the realm of possibility that these two individuals are from the same families for which those names are found in the postexilic literature. The very fact that no patronymics are given by Zechariah for Tobiah and Jedaiah may indicate that they were well-known personages whose names would be recognized without lineages (Mazar 1957:229). At least for Tobiah, biblical and extrabiblical sources provide information showing him to be from one of the most prominent families in Judea, from the end of the Davidic monarchy until the waning days of the Second Temple period. Mazar (1957), who has traced the sources for the Tobiads, argues that the Tobiah of Zech 6 is the grandfather of the Tobiah of Nehemiah's day and the grandson of an early sixth-century Tobiah who was the "arm" of King Zedekiah around 590. On the principle of papponymy, with the name Tobiah being passed from grandfather to grandson, the Tobiah of Zech 6 would fit in quite well, chronologically speaking. The following chart suggests the sequence of Tobiads:

Chart 13
Reconstruction of the Tobiad line
(based on Mazar 1957)

Head of Family	Source	Ruler	Approximate Date
Tobiah ("arm of the king") X	Lachish letters	Zedekiah	590
Tobiah X	Zech 6	Zerubbabel/Joshua	520
Tobiah (Ammonite "servant")	Nehemiah	Nehemiah	440
Jehohanan XX	Nehemiah (6:18)	Nehemiah	420
Tobiah (prince of land of Tobiah)	Zenon Papyri	Ptolemy II	259
Joseph	Josephus	Ptolemy III	230
Tobiah; Hyrcanus	Josephus; 1, 2 Macc	Antiochus III	200

X = missing one generation   XX = missing several generations

Mazar's arguments would make the Tobiah of Zech 6 part of an important family. Zechariah's witnesses have apparently been chosen carefully because of the great significance, both political and religious, of what he is going to do. The men whom he singles out would have been important people in the postexilic community. Tobiah is probably a powerful landowner from a trans-Jordanian district centered around ṣôr. He thus would represent a faction of Yahwists who held lands in Gilead and who had connections to the Judean crown going back into preexilic times.

The center of the Tobiad claims in trans-Jordan can be identified with the site of ʿAraq el-Emir, although the archaeological evidence does not substantiate a date for the remains that would make a settlement there contemporary with the early postexilic period. Its connection with the Tobiads rests on several points. First, its megalithic fortress or palace is known as Qasr el-ʿAbd, "Fortress of the Servant," in reference to "Tobiah the Ammonite servant" mentioned in Neh 2:10. Second, the word "TOBIAH" is cut into the rocky façades of two large halls or burial caves cut into the cliffs several hundred meters from the site (McCown 1957: fig. 7). Mazar would like to date the Tobiah inscriptions to the late sixth or early fifth century, but that dating has been disputed. Cross's proposal for a 300 B.C.E. date is also not secure, and a majority of scholars of paleography adhere to a fifth-century date (so Lapp 1976:528). Therefore, while the establishment of ʿAraq el-Emir as a settlement does not date to the early restoration period, it eventually did become the site of Tobiad dominion in Gilead.

The wealth of information about the Tobiads, and the strength of the evidence connecting them with trans-Jordan, allow us to see in the Tobiah of 6:10 and 14 the representative of a Yahwist faction not resident in Yehud. Although some Tobiads evidently remained in Babylon, as the Murashu documents (Coogan 1976:26, 52–53, 74–75 and Zadok 1979:62) indicate, many returned westward to their family estates in Gilead during the reign of Darius I. If Heldai represented Yahwists still in exile, Tobiah could conceivably be a delegate representing Yahwists returned from exile but not living within the small confines of the subprovince of Yehud. Jedaiah, the third member of this grouping, was evidently from among the earliest returnees and thus represented Judeans who had gone into exile and then come back with the Zerubbabel group or possibly earlier with Sheshbazzar in 538. If Heldai, Tobiah, and Jedaiah represent three different groups of exiles, might the fourth individual, Josiah, the only one whose house and lineage are noted, represent families that had remained in Jerusalem? Whether or not that be the case (cf. NOTE below to "Josiah ben-Zephaniah"), the three men of the first part of this verse seem to be a carefully chosen set, with each one representing a group of Yahwists who have varying relationships with the newly reorganized territory of Yehud and its temple that is being restored.

The three witnesses summoned by Zechariah, whatever their individual status, are all in the category of returnees. As such, they are part of the emphasis in the existing biblical literature on the role played by former exiles in the restoration of the temple and of Jerusalem. The prophets Jeremiah (Jer 39:10; 52:15–16) and Ezekiel (Ezek 11:15–25) consider the exiles the true Israel, with those left behind being only the nobodies. Surely all the identifiable leaders and participants in the major events of the late sixth and the fifth centuries were returnees.

you will go . . . and go into. The MT transcribes *ûbā'tā* twice. This repetition is often taken to be a dittography since LXX, Latin, Syriac, and Targum translate the term only once (so Mitchell 1912:189 and others). The Hebrew text, although obviously difficult in the eyes of the ancient translators, is fully intelligible as it stands, with two attestations of the verb. A number of analogous texts where a similar repetition of the verb "to come" occurs have been pointed out by Petitjean (1969:278), and these greatly facilitate our reading and acceptance of the MT (Gen 37:10; 1 Sam 4:12–13; 1 Kgs 2:41–42; 2 Kgs 4:32–33; 9:2; 10:21; Jer 46:20; Ezek 7:6–7; 33:33; Hab 2:3; Dan 11:10; Ps 126:6).

Our translation and organization of verse 10 are attempts to understand this twofold repetition of the verb *bw'* ("to come") as central to this oracle and as an essential part of the prophet's commission. The verb *bw'* lends itself easily to a rather broad range of meanings. The versions may actually be translating only the second MT *ûbā'tā* when, for example, they render "come and enter into" (so LXX, Targum, Syriac, and Latin), with the second verb expressed as a different word in Greek or Latin, etc., but actually meant to convey the nuance of the original Hebrew. God's instructions to the prophet at this point consist of two elements that explain "come"—when to come and where to go—so that the two appearances of "you shall come" correspond to these two aspects of the prophet's movement. It is equally possible and perhaps simple to understand the repetition of the verb as a form of emphasis. From a grammatical point of view, the object of both verbs *(wb't)* is "the house of Josiah." In ordinary prose, the sentence would have been written: On that day you shall enter into the house of Josiah. But in the stylized language of the oracle, the repetition of the verb and the addition of the independent pronoun "you" draw attention to the focus of this verse—namely, the prophet's going to Josiah's house. The same effect could have been achieved through the use of the infinitive absolute, but the simplest expression of emphasis in most languages is through repetition. Furthermore, the existence in verses 12–13 of a similar repetition of verbs, also with an independent pronoun, and in reverse order with respect to this verse, strengthens our argument that the text is original as it stands (cf. below, first NOTE to v 13).

The verb each time is in the singular and clearly refers to the prophet. However, this fact should not be taken as an indication that Zechariah alone is to go to Josiah's house. The resumptive "take" at the beginning of the next verse connects with "take" at the beginning of this verse and implies that the prophet's collection of gold and silver is linked with his going to Josiah's house. Therefore, the three principles of verse 10a (Heldai, Tobiah, and Jedaiah) along with Josiah ben-Zephaniah, as in verse 14, are to be witnesses to what Zechariah will do with the materials provided by the three representatives of the exiles.

on that day. This expression *(bayyôm hahû᾽)* elsewhere often has an eschatological meaning (see NOTE to Hag 2:23). Here it is a simple time indicator and as such should not be excised from the text as suggested by Mitchell (1912:189), nor disregarded as a gloss to verse 11b as does Rudolph (1976:127). The twofold use of "you will go," which has evoked much exegetical comment, has occasioned some unjustified readiness to dismiss the importance of this phrase. In fact, the phrase helps establish the relatedness of the actions performed by the prophet. On the day on which the contributions for the temple and the crowns are collected, "on that day" will the prophet proceed to the house of Josiah ben-Zephaniah. The sequence of the Hebrew verbs, with "you will come" as a perfect with the *waw* consecutive following an infinitive absolute ("take") used as an imperative, indicates the present action ("go") of the prophet, which is the logical and temporal complement of his taking *(GKC:* 331–33). The next four verbs in verses 11 and 12 ("take," "make," "place," "say") continue this sequence of contiguous actions which are all to take place on that one day, as reckoned in conventional noneschatological terms.

Josiah ben-Zephaniah. While the name Josiah is well known in the Hebrew Bible as the designation for the Judean king associated with the Deuteronomic reform of the late seventh century, no biblical figure other than King Josiah and this one is so named. The lineage of Zechariah's Josiah, unlike that of the three previously listed individuals of this verse, is established through the use of his patronymic, ben- (son of) Zephaniah. Unfortunately that additional information does not allow us to ascertain Josiah's identity with any more certitude than we have for the other three. However, we can perhaps identify Zephaniah with a priestly family and in that way learn who this Josiah is.

A priest named Zephaniah figures prominently in the biblical materials, from both Jeremiah and the Deuteronomic history, concerning the last days of the Judean monarchy. He was evidently the second priest in the Jerusalem hierarchy and was involved in the communication of various messages and complaints among several parties, which included the king Zedekiah, the prophet Jeremiah, and a group of exiles (Jer 21:1; 29:25,29; 37:3). In 2 Kgs 25:18ff. (= Jer 52:24ff.) it is recorded that he was one of the Jerusalem officials taken to the King of Babylon at Riblah in Hamath and put to death there. The last-mentioned citation does not reveal whether or not his family was taken with him. Its silence on that point could mean that only Zephaniah himself, as a key official, was among those seventy-two leaders carried away and executed as political prisoners by Nebuzaradan, captain of the guard of the Babylonian king in 586. Yet in most cases about which we know, the families too were taken into captivity along with the Judean leaders. Such certainly was the case for Jehoiachin, whose relatives went with him (2 Kgs 24:14–15). The same would have been true for the chief priest Seraiah (2 Kgs 25:18; 1 Chron 6:14–15; Ezra 7:1–6; cf. comments of Myers 1965:60). Since Zephaniah is mentioned in 2 Kgs 25 (v 18) along with Seraiah, we must suppose that his descendants too were in Babylon.

If the Josiah of this verse is indeed from the priestly family of Seraiah, he would probably have been the great-grandson, rather than the son, of the second priest of King Zedekiah's day. Assuming that papponymy was prevalent among priestly families in this period (cf. Cross 1966:203–5), the sequence can be reconstructed by having Zephaniah the second priest in his fifties at the time of his execution. His son, possibly named Josiah, would easily have been in his thirties at the time and could well have had a young son named Zephaniah. This son could then have had a son named Josiah, born in the seventies or sixties of the sixth century and hence a mature individual in his forties with children and grandchildren of his own by the time of Zechariah. It would be difficult to have the son of the second priest as the person of Zechariah's oracle, but a direct descendant several generations later, since the average generation in those days was probably twenty to twenty-five years or less, is quite conceivable for Josiah ben-Zephaniah. This chronology is obviously hypothetical but entirely plausible.

Although there is no explicit evidence for the identification of Josiah with the priestly family of Zephaniah, the hypothetical evidence pointing in that direction can be supported by other information contained in Zech 6. The prophetic action which is the key feature of this oracular passage is to take place in *his* house. Why is it that Josiah's house has been chosen for an event that will be laden with symbolic meaning? Perhaps his house is selected because Josiah is an individual holding an important leadership position in the postexilic community. The houses of the two main officials, Joshua the high priest and Zerubbabel, would be eliminated because they are figures involved in the oracle associated with the symbolic act. The next in the chain of authority in Yehud, since Joshua is the chief officer of internal administration (cf. chapter 3, NOTES and COMMENT), would be the second priest. If Zechariah's interest is to have the symbolic action take place in front of a group of carefully chosen witnesses, then having them gather at the home of an authoritative person in the community who would presumably also be a witness would add to the effectiveness of the action.

[all of] whom have come from Babylon. This phrase (ʾăšer bāʾû mibbābel) appears to specify the place from which all the individuals mentioned in this verse have come. It is difficult to ascertain whether or not Josiah is meant to be part of this grouping. The ambivalence of the Hebrew word gôlâ at the beginning of the verse (see above NOTE to "exiles") with respect to who is included in the term gôlâ is perhaps similar to the ambivalences of this phrase concerning those who have returned from Babylon. The antecedent of the plural Hebrew verb, "who have/had come," is rendered vague by the unusual Hebrew syntax which, influenced by the infinitive absolute at the outset of verse 10 and by the intrusion of the twofold "you will go" (see above NOTE to "take

from," and also the following NOTE), has placed this phrase at the very end of verse 10 with the name Josiah ben-Zephaniah immediately preceding. The versions have clearly had difficulty on this point. The LXX explicitly understands, with a singular verb for "come," that only Josiah had come from Babylon. The Syriac likewise deals with the awkward Hebrew word order by taking Josiah as the immediate antecedent; unlike the Hebrew, it has a singular verb for "come" as does the LXX. The Targum slavishly translates the MT and replicates its ambivalence, and the Vulgate too apparently follows the MT by using a plural verb (MT *'ăšer bā'û* = *qui venerunt*). Both the presence of the plural verb and the location of the clause at the very end of the verse probably indicate that all of the individuals mentioned in verse 10 are intended to be the antecedents of "have come." The first three words of the verse ("take from the exiles") and the last three ("[all of] whom have come from Babylon") form an envelope construction around the rest of the verse. Although the syntax in English is awkward, the Hebrew order evidently has been established to be inclusive of all the participants involved in the prophet's symbolic action.

11. *And take.* The word "take" *(lqḥ)* resumes the verbal idea introduced at the beginning of this oracle in verse 10. There, an infinitive absolute functioning as an imperative (cf. NOTE to "take from," v 10) constituted the opening command to the prophet and initiated a sequence of verbs in the perfect which together compose the set of symbolic actions the prophet is instructed by Yahweh to perform. The intervening words of verse 10, between *lqḥ* there and *lqḥ* as the first word of this verse, introduce the characters who are to witness Zechariah's deeds and who provide the materials which will enable him to carry out his actions, and the location where the actions will take place. The information provided in verse 10 was evidently central to the prophet's purposes and thus interrupted a normal flow which would have had *lqḥ* followed directly, as in this verse, by the direct object. The perfect form of the verb here continues the action of "go . . . go into" which together are consequent upon the first "take." The two uses of *lqḥ* together form a complete idea: the taking involves a) those who provide the material (v 10) and b) the material so provided (v 11).

silver and gold. The cultic context of the term "take" *(lqḥ)* followed by the compound preposition consisting of *mem,* "from," plus *'ēt,* "with," (= *mē'ēt)* has been pointed out above (NOTE to "take from"). Offerings of several kinds to the temple are said to be taken to the priests or Levites from "the people of Israel." The tithe is taken in Num 28:26ff. by the Levites, and the breast as wave offering (cf. Milgrom 1972) and thigh as peace offering are specified in Lev 7:31–34 as the priestly due. In addition to these specified offerings of goods, four other passages refer to single instances of offerings "taken from" various groups of individuals. These passages collectively form a pattern; they exhibit several common characteristics, although every passage does not necessarily contain all characteristics. These features are: 1. Silver and/or gold are the items offered. 2. The leaders of the Israelites and not the general populace make the contributions. 3. The offerings are not demanded but appear to be voluntary (freewill: *kōl nědîb libbô,* as in Exod 25:2; cf. Exod 35:22). 4. The offerings are occasioned by a special event: relating to the building, restoring, or dedicating of the sanctuary. 5. A nonpriestly leader is involved in the collecting of the items.

The first passage exhibiting these characteristics is Exod 25:2ff. (= Exod 35:4ff.), in which a freewill offering *(těrûmâ)* of gold, silver, and other precious metals and materials is taken by Moses from everyone whose heart is willing in order to provide the raw materials for the construction of the tabernacle. The participation of any Israelite other than one who is a leader is the exception to the pattern. Then, on the day when the tabernacle was anointed and consecrated, Moses took from the leaders ("princes," *něśî'îm)* of Israel offerings which consisted of wagons and oxen for the Levites to use in their service and also silver and gold utensils along with foodstuffs for the dedication of the altar (Num 7). All elements of the pattern appear to be present, if the metal vessels and foodstuffs are also considered to have been "taken" by Moses along with the oxen and wagons.

Next, following the Israelite rout of the Midianites, Moses and Eleazar take spoils of gold from the "captains" *(śārîm)* of the military units that had fought against Midian and then had taken booty (Num 31:51–54). The freewill nature of this offering is not specified, though it appears to be a voluntary act on the part of all the men of war who had survived with their lives (vv 49, 53) and to follow upon the mandatory portion of the general bounty that was set aside for the Levites and for Yahweh's tribute *(mekes,* Num 31:37–42) or offering *(těrûmâ).* Clearly this contribution of gold was not associated with any phase of sanctuary building. On the other hand, its one-time-only nature is preserved in an extraordinary piece of information, in light of what is contained in Zech 6:14 below, about the gold taken from the leader in verse 54: "And Moses and Eleazar the priest received *[lqh]* the gold from *[mē'ēt]* the commander of thousands and of hundreds and brought it into the tent of meeting, as a memorial *[zikkārôn]* before Yahweh" (cf. NOTE before, v 14, to "reminder").

The last passage to be considered is the only one not in the priestly portion of the Pentateuch. 2 Kgs 12 (3–17 [RSV 12:4–16]) recounts the refurbishing of the temple under Jehoash, who orders the priests, probably in consultation with the "high priest" Jehoida in his technical fiscal role (cf. NOTE above to "high priest," 3:1) to set aside special funds which include both assessed fees and also "money ("silver," *kesep)* which a man's heart prompts him to bring" (v 5 [RSV v 4]). That money is to be taken from people the priests know, presumably an elite Jerusalem group. All the features enumerated above apply to the verses in 2 Kings.

Before considering the relevance of these passages to the Zechariah material, one further dimension of this postexilic offering of silver and gold must be examined. In Ezra 1:4–6 it is implied that in Cyrus's day and to some extent at Cyrus's urging, freewill offerings were channeled to Jerusalem for the rebuilding of the temple. This process was effected through local leadership: some of the "heads of the fathers' houses of Benjamin and Judah, and the priests, and the Levites." Furthermore, with the return of Zerubbabel, "heads of families . . . made freewill offerings for the house of God" which consisted of gold, silver, and priestly garments (Ezra 2:68–69). Although it is not clear whether the Ezra 2 passages refer to the 538 B.C.E. returnees or a later group (cf. Introduction, pp. xxix–xv), it seems fair to assume that the idea of making a freewill offering of precious metals for a renewal of the Jerusalem temple was present in the postexilic community.

In light of this information in Ezra along with the four passages discussed above, the taking of silver and gold in the Zech 6 Crowning passage appears to belong to a specific but infrequent practice, one with religious and political overtones. All the characteristics of the practice are mentioned in the Zechariah passage. Silver and gold appear.

Certain leaders—Heldai, Tobiah, Jedaiah, and Josiah—provide the requisite materials. Presumably the precious metals are offered freely, as the specialized use of "take" *(lqḥ)* with silver and gold would indicate. The momentous event that occasions the offering in this case is the postexilic temple restoration or probably, to be more specific, the temple refoundation ceremony associated with temple-building projects in the ancient Near East (cf. NOTES to 3:9 and 4:7,10). Finally, Zechariah, though of priestly lineage, does not function as a priestly leader; perhaps his role is analogous in this respect to the prophetic role of Moses in the pentateuchal passages mentioned above, where Moses is charged with collecting the specified items.

What Zechariah must do with the silver and gold is clearly presented in a context in which the cultic function of a central sanctuary intersects with economic and political matters—that is, monetary contributions and community representatives. The description of the economic and political dimensions is crucial to the meaning of the prophet's deeds, which constitute an ideological statement about the relationship of all segments of the greater Yahwist constituency to the Yehudite community. That they were *not* one and the same became apparent with the temple refoundation, and the relationship between the two had to be clarified. Normal temple support was evidently provided for by internal Yehudite offerings. But external support, from the wider community of the *gôlâ* or from Yahwists not resident in Yehud, was also important. The latter group, not under the official legal organization of Mosaic or Torah law as it was established in Yehud, was nonetheless part of the full eschatological community in which monarchic (Davidic) rule would again exist along with the present rule of the priestly officials under Persian supervision (see NOTES to the following verse).

One final comment about "silver and gold" concerns their order. As in the majority of places in the Bible where both these metals are listed, silver comes before gold (cf. Dan 5:4 for reverse order). That order suggests that as a medium of exchange silver was more valuable than gold until the late period. Only in the Persian period (ca. 500 B.C.E.; see Gerber 1962:355), when access to new sources of silver increased the availability of that metal, did gold become valued, at least with respect to its role as an exchange commodity, more highly than silver. Late Biblical texts (Chronicles, Esther, Daniel) nearly always list gold before silver, whereas the opposite sequence prevails in earlier texts (cf. 2 Sam 8:10 with its parallel, 1 Chron 18:10). The relative rarity of silver objects found in archaeological excavations before the Persian period likewise attests to the scarcity of silver in Palestine. Zechariah would then have belonged to the old economy, in which silver had not yet become more plentiful than gold (cf. Isa 13:12).

This information is complicated by the fact that, despite its greater economic value, silver was never more desirable than gold as a precious metal. Because of its greater intrinsic attractiveness and maybe even because of its greater availability, gold was the preferred object for jewelry and for special royal and cultic trappings and furnishings in the ancient world, from Sumer to Egypt. As a result, the market value of gold apparently could at times exceed that of silver despite the relative rarity of the former (Kedar-Kopfstein 1980:36). Cultic texts in the Bible, of whatever date, tend to list gold before silver (e.g., Exod 25:3) because the former was more widely used for the cultic furniture and temple-tabernacle decoration.

Both the priestly crowns and royal crowns in ancient Israel were made of gold (Exod

28:36–37; Ps 21:4 [RSV v 3]). This fact may have some importance in dealing with the difficulties in determining whether the Hebrew for "crowns" in this verse (see NOTE below) is singular or plural. Silver may be mentioned before gold here because of its traditional place before gold in the pre-fifth-century economy. However, if this text may be considered a cultic text it tells us about at least one crown, which is to be used for the high priest (v 11b); and the sequence might be expected to be reversed on that account. An explanation of the silver-gold order might better take into account the traditional use of gold rather than silver for priestly and royal headgear. Why is silver mentioned at all? We suggest in our NOTE below to "crowns" that silver and gold were *not* combined in making crowns but rather that each metal was used to make a separate crown, a silver one for Joshua, who is mentioned first and therefore making it appropriate for silver to be listed first, and a golden crown for the future king (vv 13–14).

make. Although it might appear that the gentlemen specified by the prophet are the ones who are to perform the actual task of fabricating crowns of precious metals, it is unlikely that these men were in fact the actual silversmiths. They have been cited as the sources for the requisite silver and gold. According to our understanding, these individuals were representatives of segments of the Yahwistic community (see NOTES to v 10), and their importance in this oracle rests upon their position in the community with respect to place of residence and not upon their skill as metalworkers. Indeed, the command to "make" the crowns is in the singular and presumably is directed to the prophet himself. Note that in Judg 17:1–4, Micah's mother takes *(lqḥ)* 200 pieces of silver and has images made by giving the silver to a silversmith. In the present text that procedure would be implicit. Thus Zechariah is responsible for having the crowns made, and he would presumably find an appropriate artisan. The suggestion that Josiah is that artisan is to be treated skeptically, again because his role in this oracle stems probably from his priestly lineage and his leadership position. Yet the making of the crowns was an important part of the symbolic action of this scene, and the witnesses gathered at Joshua's house no doubt were brought there to see the manufacture of the crowns as well as to observe the crowning of Joshua and the sequestering of the second crown in the temple.

crowns. The MT plural *ʿăṭārōt,* despite concerted scholarly efforts to change it to the singular *(ʿăṭārâ* or possibly *ʿăṭeret),* is to be preferred (see NOTE to "the [other] crown" in v 14). The MT plural is supported by the LXX, though the reliability of the LXX as a witness to the original old Greek for the Minor Prophets is not great. LXX[LC], Syriac, and Targum have the singular, but confusion may have arisen if the singular *ʿăṭeret* is original to verse 14. The emendation to a singular, as suggested by many, would require the elimination of the plene *waw* of the existing plural. In contrast, our proposal to change the defective plural form in verse 14 to a singular (see below NOTE to v 14) does not require an alteration of the consonantal text of the MT. Indeed, the following singular verb *tihyeh,* in verse 14, requires a singular subject.

The lexicons and concordances list *ʿăṭārâ* as the singular absolute form of *ʿăṭārōt,* "crowns," with *ʿăṭeret* listed only for the singular construct. The editor of *BHS* proposes that MT plural *ʿăṭārōt* be emended to the absolute singular *ʿăṭeret,* here in verse 11, and that the defective plural *ʿăṭārōt* in verse 14 also be emended in the same way. Although *ʿăṭārōt* or *ʿăṭārōt* may sometimes represent an absolute singular deriving from the old Phoenician ending -*ot* (Ceresko 1980:184–85; Donner-Röllig No. 60) as is the apparent case in Job 31:36 (so RSV), attempts to emend the text here have been unduly influenced by verse 14 and by a felt need to harmonize the two verses.

A plural reading of the Hebrew text is also supported by the fact that the text goes on to indicate what was to be done with each of two crowns (vv 11b and 14). The prophet would be expected to report that "two crowns" rather than just the plural "crowns" should be made. Elsewhere Zechariah is quite explicit when enumerating objects (2:1,3 [RSV 1:18,20]; 3:9; 4:2–3; 5:7,9; 6:1,5). Why does he omit a numerical designation here? The answer may lie in the words specifying the materials to be used: silver and gold. The use of these two categories of metals provides the information that more than one crown was to be made. Why does it tell us this? The two metals could either be used together, to form a crown or crowns made partly of each metal, or separately, to make two crowns, one all of silver and one all of gold. Despite the greater abundance of gold (cf. NOTE above to "silver and gold"), most treasured objects in the ancient Near East before 500, including the crowns of both priest and king in Israel, were made of gold. Therefore it is likely that the collection of silver and gold for the purpose of making crown(s) meant that two separate crowns were made, one of silver and one of gold.

Zechariah's audience would have understood this; they would not have expected a crown of mixed silver and gold for either royal or priestly purposes. Yet they would hardly have expected a silver crown. What would that have signified? If the crowning of Joshua is meant to give him near-royal authority, perhaps the shape of the crown rather than its material (*ʿăṭārâ* rather than *nēzer*, if the former is used exclusively for royal power except for this verse) provides the insignia of royalty. Yet if it were made of silver, which is entirely possible, given the fact that silver was used but probably would have not been used with gold in the same headpiece and also that silver is mentioned first and that the use of a crown for Joshua comes first, those who saw Joshua in all his regalia would have known at once that he didn't have a fully proper monarchic crown, a gold crown. The latter would be reserved for a Davidide, as in verse 14.

An overwhelming number of critics have regarded the canonical MT form of this oracle with great suspicion. "Crown" in the singular has been the reading preferred by most scholars because the second half of this verse (v 11b), they argue, presupposes a single crown. To accommodate such a suggestion yet another emendation is required, the substitution of "Zerubbabel" for "Joshua" in this verse. Wellhausen (1892:185) was among the first to propose that the single crown was intended for Zerubbabel. Others followed his lead, offering a series of additional changes contingent upon a singular reading for *ʿṭrwt* (Mitchell 1912:185–86; Marti 1904:420; et al.). Verse 11b was not the only portion of the oracle that needed to be readjusted if one were to assume that Zerubbabel was the one who was to be crowned; verses 13–14 could not survive intact either (see NOTES below). The supposition underlying all emendations of the MT of verses 11–14 is that the Hebrew text has been heavily redacted to accommodate either the excision of "Zerubbabel" from the original text or the putative fact of his mysterious disappearance from the scene. Zerubbabel is presumed to be the principal persona in the crowning scenario, and Joshua's role has consequently been misinterpreted and underestimated. In reality, the dyarchic implications of the oracle, in which both

Zerubbabel, as governor and also as potential future Davidic monarch, and Joshua, as internal administrative leader of the Yehudite community appear, remain consistent with the previous Zecharianic material and also require virtually no changes in the received text.

Examination of relevant biblical texts, moreover, offers no contraindication for the manufacture of crowns for both a priestly and a secular, potentially monarchic, figure. Both priests and kings wore crowns. The terms used for those artifacts of the royal and priestly offices are most revealing. The usual terms for crown, as related to the royal office, are *nēzer* or *ʿăṭārâ;* neither presents a problem in the context in which it is found. The former, *nēzer,* is used to refer to both Saul's (2 Sam 1:10) and David's (2 Kgs 11:12 = 2 Chron 23:11) crowns and hence represents the insignia of royal power (see also Ps 89:40 [RSV v 39] and 132:18); it is also used to signify the crown on top of the priestly turban, *nēzer ʿal hamiṣnepet* (Exod 29:6; Lev 8:9). The latter, *ʿṭrh,* is frequently used as a term for royal power (e.g., 2 Sam 12:30 = 1 Chron 20:2; Jer 13:18; Cant 3:11; Ezek 21:31 [RSV v 26] where crown, *ʿăṭārâ,* is used together with turban, *miṣnepet;* etc.) but, except for this verse in Zechariah (6:11), it is never used for priestly power or authority. For this reason many critics have insisted that the subsequent crowning of Joshua as high priest could not have been original to this oracle. The term *is* innovative for priests; but precisely this kind of innovation is appropriate to the political situation of the restoration, which is not the same as the preexilic period.

If the peculiar confluence of terms used for both king and priest in this oracle appears to be rooted in an innovative political organization, it may in part be influenced by the fact that, in addition to wearing crowns, kings (Judg 9:8–15; 1 Sam 9:16; 10:1; 15:17; 16:1; etc.) and priests (Lev 4:3,5,16; 6:15 [RSV v 22]; etc.) were also both anointed. The chief priest, although not initiated into office by special crowning, was apparently consecrated in an anointing ceremony (Exod 40:13,15; Lev 21:10,12). If any term might have been expected to designate the "priestly crown," it would be the *nēzer* (Exod 29:6; Lev 8:9) of the priestly texts in the Pentateuch, where it occurs together with the expected term for priestly turban, *miṣnepet.* In Zechariah, however, already in the section on Joshua and the Priestly Vestments (3:1–10), a new term *(ṣānîp)* has been substituted for the priestly term *miṣnepet* (see NOTE to 3:5, "clean turban"). Note that in Isa 62:3, where *ṣānîp* occurs in parallelism with "crown of glory" or "glorious crown" *(ʿăṭeret tipʾeret,* cf. Jer 13:18), it is clearly used to signify royal power. This may be a case where the two words are in apposition ("crown, glorious one" = "glorious crown"), rather than constituting a construct chain, and hence provide additional support for construing *ʿăṭeret* as the absolute form in verse 14 (see below NOTE to "the [other] crown"). In both instances, Zech 3:5 and here, a nonpriestly or royal term has been applied to the high priest, a usage that must be intentional and fully within the prophet's overall purpose.

If chapter 3 represents the ritual or cultic preparation for Joshua's expanded role in a newly defined office of high priesthood (on this point see NOTES to "high priest" in 3:1, "clean turban" in 3:5, "render judgment in my House" in 3:7, and NOTES to Hag 2:10–19), then chapter 6:9–15 represents the symbolic acceptance and assumption of that role. Selecting the word *ʿăṭārâ* for Joshua's crowning in effect emphasizes Joshua's extensive powers in the reorganized nonmonarchic restoration community. The purely royal imagery and terminology is resumed only in verses 12b–13 where the "shoot" epithet is again applied to the Davidide (cf. NOTES to 3:8), who is not excluded from this scene but rather is included in terms of the expected future time in which he will build the temple and sit upon the throne. The ambiguity of the reference in verse 12, where it is not certain whether or not the oracle intends to relate the "Shoot" to Zerubbabel the governor, does not detract from the force of the utterance. The oracle certainly anticipates the eventuality that a royal heir will someday rule again. In the meantime, the other "crown" (see NOTE to v 14) has the equally important function of serving as a reminder of the anticipated restoration of the monarchy.

Rignell (1950:235ff.), who along with Kaufmann (1977:294–97), Eichrodt (1967:343), and Baldwin (1972:134) has defended the MT, concludes that the actual crowning of Joshua is only a symbolic action similar to that signified by the entry of the "men of portent" of 3:8, a text which also includes an eschatological figure, the "Shoot" (see NOTES above). The question of whether or not an actual crowning took place is one that defies certain resolution. Insofar as this is a symbolic prophetic action, the suspicion remains that an official coronation of Joshua as a reigning priest was not observed. However, the restoration period did see the emergence of a strong priestly ruler, so that by the time of the Hasmonaean dynasty the Maccabean rulers beginning with Simon (142 B.C.E.) or more likely with his son John Hyrcanus, called themselves both king and high priest. Though they were neither Davidides nor Zadokites, the priestly lineage of the Maccabees was not in doubt. They used their Aaronide descent to seize the power of the high priesthood, since certain biblical passages call for the high priest to be a descendant of Aaron. They exercised executive authority in the civil realm in addition to priestly authority, and from that power base eventually claimed all civil authority and ultimately granted themselves kingship. Serious opposition arose, from the Pharisees among others, only when the office of kingship came into the picture, since no traditional terms could be found to support that position; the Maccabees had no connection with the House of David. Yet their ability to combine priestly and civil authority, short of the actual claim to kingship, apparently had succeeded in part because it rested upon tradition established under the Persians and continued under Greek domination.

When the Persians granted semiautonomy to Yehud, the high priest assumed certain responsibilities formerly attached to the throne. Since Zechariah's visions and oracles repeatedly sanction a newly defined role for the priesthood, the possibility of an actual ceremonial recognition of Joshua's status cannot be precluded. Indeed, precisely because the priesthood was undergoing a transition in its range of responsibilities, a ceremonial inauguration or crowning would have given support to this alteration in the traditional role of the priesthood. Joshua's pivotal role as chief administrator of internal affairs would have been given visible and public acknowledgment by such a ceremony.

The symbolic nature of the action in this oracle provides the message that the regnal priestly crown of Joshua cannot be separated from the concept of monarchy even though the Davidic dynasty is still in a state of suspension. The crown of office worn by the priestly ruler is one of a pair. It is the placement of the other crown which carries the true symbolic intent of the vision. Joshua's crown embraces the symbolic and the actual, but the Davidic crown would exist only in the symbolic realm.

Those who would see that the crowning was originally that of Zerubbabel are influenced to a certain extent by the fact that he is no longer mentioned in biblical texts after Zechariah 4. They therefore postulate a disappearance which would have been the result of Persian authorities taking action to quell an insurrection, marked by the crowning of a monarchic ruler. The Persians, in this view, not only remove Zerubbabel from the scene but also suspend a Yehudite governorship until a later time, when a Davidide would no longer be the one to assume such an office (cf. the judicious remarks of Cross, 1975:15–16, who avoids such a conclusion yet views the Persians in a less than favorable light). However, for textual reasons and for historical and political ones, both of which we have educed above, we see no justification for altering the MT in order to reject a crowning for Joshua and insert instead a Zerubbabel coronation. Furthermore, the suggestion that *both* Joshua and Zerubbabel were crowned (as in Ackroyd 1968:196ff.) presents more problems than it resolves. This oracle, as in the oracles within the visionary sequence, appears to propose a limited role for the Davidic governor (cf. NOTE to "governor," *peḥâ*, in Hag 1:1) until an eschatological restoration of the monarchy. Whatever monarchic hopes may have naturally accompanied temple restoration are not sustained in Zechariah's portrayal of the terminology and trappings of the Yehudite office. That the crowning of a priest has no biblical precedent in terms of the vocabulary of headpieces of office is not a legitimate argument against a coronation of Joshua here. It is precisely because his office has wider powers that this text departs from previous usage and relates his official headgear to that of royal authorities.

You will place [one]. The inclusion of the pronominal object "one" in brackets is intended to clarify the text for the English reader. It stems from our exegesis of the MT in this verse (see NOTE to "crowns" above) and our understanding of the second occurrence of the word "crown" in verse 14 (see NOTE below). The singular pronominal object is frequently omitted in Biblical Hebrew (*GKC* § 117f.) when it can easily be supplied or inferred from the context, especially after *verba sentiendi (šmʿ)* and *dicendi* (*ngd,* Hiphil) and the roots *ntn* ("to give"), *lqḥ* ("to take"), *bwʾ* in the Hiphil ("to bring"), and *śym* ("to place or lay"). In the present instance, *śym* ("place") is the verb and there is no pronominal object following it. Although there is good precedent for the omission of the pronominal object, the shift in number from the antecedent noun ("crowns," plural) to the singular object "[one]" is not normal procedure. We would have expected either "you shall place one of them" or "you shall place a crown" (or "one crown"). However, the antecedent appears without the number "two" in the text (cf. above NOTE to "crowns") and so the specification "one" in this clause may not have seemed natural. The biblical writers did use ellipsis now and then, despite its potential for obscuring the meaning and leading to some confusion, as it has in this case.

How then can the object be supplied? The context here, when viewed together with that of verse 14, requires that the supplied object be understood as one of two crowns, either the (silver?) crown intended for Joshua or the (golden) crown of monarchy to be placed in the temple. Since Joshua alone is the focus of the action in verse 11b, it follows that a single crown, a crown designed in such a way as to lend authority to his role in the postexilic administration, is intended for him. The use of *śym* here without the object specified does not detract from the conclusion that the first of two crowns is intended for Joshua.

on the head. The Hebrew text is quite explicit in stating that the "crown" was placed on Joshua's head. The use of the root *śym* + *b,* "to place on," is well attested in the Bible (*BDB:* 962–63) in a variety of settings. Therefore the choice of the expression here is not surprising. In 3:5, however, Joshua's "turban" (*ṣānîp*) is placed on his head (*śym* + *ʿl*) in the account of the priestly vestments. The different language used in the present instance seems to be influenced by the fact that the pronominal object is not specified as it is in 3:5. "To place on the head" would seem to have a more elliptical sense in 6:12 than in 3:5 where it is the "turban" which is placed upon Joshua's head. It is possible that Joshua could have worn both turban and crown on some occasions and only the crown on others. The ambiguity here thus pertains to whether or not the crown was placed on top of the turban or directly on Joshua's head.

As chief administrator of the community and as high priest, Joshua would be expected to wear headgear that reflected both areas of power, the ecclesiastical as well as the civil. Having already assumed the *ṣānîp* or turban symbolic of his expanded role as high priest, Joshua now receives the *ʿăṭārâ,* the crown of civil authority. The issue of whether or not the latter was placed on top of the former in the present instance is secondary to the concern of the oracle, which is to sanction the civil authority, formerly held by the house of David, now to be exercised by a priestly leader.

The question of how Joshua can receive a royal crown and yet not be king arises from this situation. The high priest is not to exercise civil authority, which had formerly been reserved for the king. Yet he isn't thought of as king and, from what is known about resistance to the Hasmonaean introduction of the combining of priestly and royal authority, it is difficult to imagine that this crowning of Joshua was seen as a royal coronation. How are we to view, then, the fact that Joshua gets two headpieces, a priestly turban and a royal crown, while the governor apparently receives none? This is a delicate matter, and there must have been a way in which the Yehudites avoided implying that the high priest was king, in spite of the crown. Perhaps the suggestion made above (see end of NOTE to "crowns") that the two crowns were alike in form but different in material—one being of silver, the other of gold—provides the answer. The silver crown, mentioned first and used first (for Joshua), was like a royal crown in its shape, and was called *ʿăṭārâ* as were royal crowns. Yet, if it was made of silver as we have proposed, then it was clearly and visibly different from traditional royal (and priestly) crowns, which were made of gold according to the biblical sources and according to the evidence of archaeological and iconographic sources. The apparent choice of silver for the priestly crown would have signified the distinction between Joshua's exercise of some powers normally reserved for the king (and not to be exercised by the governor) and the future exercise of royal power by whoever would wear the golden crown reserved for the true Davidic monarch.

12. *and say to him:.* These words, prefixed to the introduction to the oracle of verses 12b–13, designate the recipient of the words of Yahweh as transmitted through the prophet. The antecedent of the pronoun is Joshua, who appears at the end of the previous verse as the recipient of a crown. "And say" continues the action of the verb "place." The crowning of Joshua is not complete without the prophetic words which follow and which place an ultimate limitation in the future, on the power that accrues to the high priest by virtue of his wearing the crown which, to a certain extent, is a royal insignia of office (cf. previous NOTE).

Thus spoke Yahweh of Hosts:. This standard formulaic introduction to the words of Yahweh appears in the first oracle (1:3,4), although without the supplementary *lē'mōr* (here rendered by a colon; cf. Hag 1:2), and in several other oracular insertions within the visions (1:14,17; 2:12 [RSV 2:8]; 3:7), also without *lē'mōr*. The use of *lē'mōr* is, in Zechariah, found after the stereotyped phrase "the word of the Lord came to me" (as in 4:8) or after the formulaic words introducing the Interpreting Angel's words (as in 4:13). Precisely the same form as in this instance appears in 7:9. The prophet thus varies the formulaic language found in biblical prophecy for indicating the content of a divine oracle. He does, however, use the somewhat more direct and anthropomorphic reporting that God "spoke," whereas the narrative introductions in 1:1,7, and 7:1 (and perhaps 8:1) use the slightly more abstract notion of God's "word" coming to the prophet.

Behold, there is a man. These words introducing the oracle lend a sense of drama and immediacy to the utterance that follows, concerning the dynastic hopes of the Yehudite community. Although similar to the oracle in 3:8 regarding "the Shoot" (see NOTE above), the absence of a verbal element and of the definite article here—*hinnēh 'īš*—lend a vague and unspecified quality to the statement. Zech 3:8 refers to the Davidic scion as "my servant the Shoot"; here it is *"a man—Shoot is his name."* The majority scholarly view, nonetheless, would identify "a man" with Zerubbabel. However, although it is possible that Zerubbabel did attend the crowning ceremony of Joshua, it does not necessarily follow that those assembled would have been further encouraged in their monarchist tendencies by an oracle drawing explicit attention to Zerubbabel's claims to dynastic leadership.

The monarchist terminology that follows is introduced in the present manner precisely with the intention of not arousing excessive royalist feelings in the present situation, one in which Joshua endorses a great hope for the future but eschews it for the present. The sense of imminency of time conveyed in 3:8 by the words "I am indeed bringing" or "I am about to bring" are replaced with "in his place"—that is, at some future time still unknown, a Davidide will assume his full position as leader of the community (cf. Jer 23:5; 33:15–17; and Zech 9:9).

Shoot is his name. Here the text may be avoiding the specificity of the well-known Jeremianic texts cited above—*ṣemaḥ ṣaddîq* and *ṣemaḥ ṣedāqâ*—and the explicit terminology of 3:8 (cf. NOTE to "my servant the Shoot")—*'abdî ṣemaḥ*—in its use of the rather unemotional *ṣemaḥ šemô*. Yet the text could well be elliptical, for it is clear from 3:8 that Zechariah associates the royal servant with the righteous shoot, God's servant. The intent in either case would be to deal with the delicate situation of a priest with some royal prerogatives, to deflate the emotional potential of the scene, and to impress again upon everyone the limited potential of the role of Zerubbabel in the restoration. If in fact Zerubbabel was present at the crowning, the oracular language recognizes in him only that which was possible at some future time.

from his place he will shoot up. The Hebrew text reads literally "from under him someone will sprout up." The compound Hebrew word "from under him" or "from his place" serves to indicate the future setting of the dynastic hope. That is to say, from his loins ("under him") or "after him," later on, another Davidide will arise or "shoot up," *yiṣmāḥ*. The latter is a wordplay on the noun "Shoot" *(ṣemaḥ)* and possibly on the name "Zerubbabel" ("seed of Babylon"), and its use emphasizes the anticipated role of such a person (cf. Dan 11:7). Indeed, the expression represents a kind of commentary on Jer 33:17, "David will never lack a successor to sit on the throne of the house of Israel" (Anchor Bible translation). The "throne" of the Jeremiah text is alluded to in the continuation of the Zechariah oracle in verse 13a (see NOTES below), just as the notion of perpetual Levitical succession (Jer 33:18) is picked up in verse 13b, where a priest will also sit upon a throne (see below, NOTE to "on his throne").

Since The Crowning of chapter 6 constitutes a conclusion to the entire visionary sequence, the historical context or setting of the oracle may be the period after the refoundation ceremony but prior to the date given in Zech 7:1—i.e., late in 519 or early in 518 B.C.E. By such time, nearly all problems pertaining to the rebuilding of the temple and the reorganization of the community would have been resolved. Zerubbabel's place in the newly reconstituted community is understandably understated and muted, since no role for him other than governor has been established.

and build the Temple of Yahweh. The theme of temple construction, underlying the visionary sequence of Zechariah, also permeates the oracles. The preoccupation of the Yehudite community during the restoration period as well as those Yahwists still in the lands of exile with the meaning of temple building has evidently provided the stimulus for much if not all of First Zechariah. This oracle from Yahweh is addressed to Joshua, presumably in the hearing of the witnesses gathered by the prophet. The apparent awkwardness of the divine speaker referring to his own temple in the third person is to be noted; but such shifts within oracular material are not unknown (cf. Andersen and Freedman 1980:170) and should not be used to infer that this concluding phrase of verse 12 is intrusive. Since "Temple of Yahweh" *(hêkāl yhwh)* occurs as a set phrase, referring to God's earthly shrine in Jerusalem, it would disrupt the language were "temple" to be used with a first-person possessive suffix. If the alternative phrase for God's house *(bêt,* "house") had been used as in Hag 1:9 with the definite article, a first-person possessive pronoun would have been expected. The choice here of the less common *hêkāl* for the temple as a whole building (and not the middle segment of the entire building as described in the Solomonic texts) is appropriate to the succeeding verses which describe the royal rule of a Davidide. Since *hêkāl* derives from a word meaning "palace" as well as "temple" (cf. NOTE to Hag 2:15), it denotes a god's palatial dwelling and provides the association of royal residence.

The building of this temple is a future and probably eschatological event. The identity of the "Shoot" who is to carry out the building work is not provided. Zerubbabel was apparently involved in the postexilic temple restoration, as the Zerubbabel insertion into the Fourth Vision proclaims (see NOTES to 4:6b–10). Yet his activity in this project was by virtue of his being governor under Persian dominance. He was not a royal ruler despite his Davidic lineage. As we have pointed out in our discussion of the Zerubbabel insertion, the inextricable connection of temple building with political sovereignty in the ancient Near East and in their own monarchic past evidently was a cause of considerable concern for the Yehudites, who were being asked to support a temple project which had no royal orientation. The prophet suggests that Zerubbabel's participation in that project represented the royal component demanded by ideological and traditional patterns. Yet Zerubbabel was clearly subservient to Persian rule. Therefore a Jerusalem temple along with the autonomous rule of a Davidide continued to be the conscious hope of the inheritors of the Deuteronomic tradition, with its promise of eternal Davidic rule. Since the present temple restoration did not conform to the arrangement established during the monarchy, a future construction with a full royal component was envisioned.

The future verbal idea of "to build," literally "he will build," continues from the preceding "he will shoot up" and carries over in the repetition of the verb to build *(bnh)* in the next verse (cf. first NOTE to 6:13). The relationship which the construction of Yahweh's house by a future Davidic king would have to the building presently being restored is not specified. While it may seem odd to the modern reader to find a prophecy that Yahweh's temple will be built by a Davidide when such an edifice is about to be completed, the biblical mentality did not preclude the erection of a new structure in addition to the existence of an actual temple in the restoration community. An entirely new structure would not have been literally required. Successive Judean rulers had periodically refurbished or altered the original Solomonic building, each time becoming temple builders and thus legitimate occupants of the royal throne. The reestablishment of Davidic rule in the future could not be conceived of without the legitimizing concomitant of temple building. The extent of such work, whether creating an entirely new structure or only modestly refurbishing an old one, would be far less relevant than the fact that actual work would take place. A renewed monarchy must have a temple building component; and this oracle represents Zechariah's assurance that the present temple work shall not detract from that which will ultimately accompany political autonomy. Although the monarchic and temple-building components form essential elements of the future vision that are in essential continuity with the monarchic tradition of Israel, the vision also contains an adjustment to that tradition. The following verse includes both priestly and royal figures in the imagined restoration and in so doing accommodates the alterations made in Yehudite organization under Persian rule. The prophet envisions a future that is influenced by contemporary realities as well as by past experience.

13. *He will build.* The repetition of this phrase is troublesome to many commentators, some of whom would follow the LXX in excising it (see the discussion and listing of those accepting the Greek, or the alternative of the Syriac omission of 12b, in Petitjean 1969:286–91). An apparently similar duplication exists in this verse for "on his throne." Neither doubling constitutes a grammatical problem, and an explanation of the utilization of these repeated phrases should be sought contextually. The delicate balance of rule in the future kingdom involves two figures, priestly and royal. Unlike the preexilic monarchy, when the king's authority superseded that of all other officials of the realm, the projected monarchy will have to incorporate the shifts in community governance established under the exigencies of Persian dominance in the late sixth century. The priestly powers have been enlarged and that increase of authority is to be sustained in the future, when the monarchy will be reestablished independent of any other political power.

In this prophetic vision, the dyarchic pattern is carefully delineated. Joshua's important role in temple restoration during the reign of Darius, as is clear from the prophecies of both Haggai and First Zechariah, must not be seen as a precedent-setting priestly domination of temple construction. The Solomonic, monarchic example has not been abrogated; in the future, the Davidic scion alone will be responsible for building the temple. If the statement to this effect appears twice in succession, it does so to emphasize a set of circumstances which revert to the preexilic pattern and are at variance with the experience of the prophet's audience. The duplication of words or phrases in order to emphasize or to express a special quality is normal in Hebrew syntax, especially in Late Biblical Hebrew (*GKC* § 123d, e). The exclusive role of the Levites in divine service is proclaimed in a somewhat similar manner by the repetition of the verb *nĕtûnîm*, "wholly given," in Num 3:9 and 8:16. See also the heightened intensity of the promise to Ezekiel, which is provided by the repetition of "blood" three times (Ezek 16:6). The duplication here shows that the future temple construction, unlike the present one, will be exclusively the manifestation and corollary of monarchic authority. A similar need for emphasis, in light of the tension between tradition and contemporary experience, can be adduced for the double use of "on his throne" (see NOTE below).

The repetition of "build" in verses 12 and 13, and the presence of the independent pronoun "he" together form a sequence remarkably similar to and in chiastic arrangement with the repetition of the verb "come" and the use of the independent pronoun "you" in verse 10. One is in the second person and the other is in the third, and one uses the conversive perfect for both verbs while the other uses the conversive perfect for one and the imperfect for the other. Yet both use verbal repetition plus a separate pronoun to emphasize the importance of the subject and of what the subject is going to do. In verse 10, the verb is followed by the pronoun at the beginning of the sequence, with the same verb without independent pronoun coming at the end of the sequence: *ûbā'tā 'attâ . . . ûbā'tā* ("*you* will go . . . and you will go"). Verses 12–13 have the verb alone without pronoun at the beginning of the sequence and the pronoun preceding the verb (in the imperfect) at the end of the sequence: *ûbānâ . . . wĕhû' yibneh* ("he will build . . . and *he* will build"). Despite the variations, the correlations are sufficiently precise and yet unusual enough to indicate that the same editor or writer has composed all the parts of this Crowning scene and also that the text in both places is likely to be original, even though the order and repetition may seem awkward and redundant.

bear royal majesty. Although the two components of this expression, "bear" *(ns²)* and "royal majesty" *(hôd),* are each well attested in Biblical Hebrew, the combination of the two is unique and suggests great care in providing a new idiom to characterize the future legitimacy of the Davidic scion. The expression is the second in a series which delineates the role of the monarchic rule. The first, we have noted, denotes dynastic legitimacy through the vehicle of temple building. The present idiom, which is continued in the two succeeding verbs ("sit" and "rule"), provides the future Davidide with the proper authority and partakes both of the royal connotation of the term *hôd* in the Bible and of the Mesopotamian idiom *(pulḫu/melammu),* which conveys monarchic authority in the royal Akkadian inscriptions and which finds echoes in seven biblical expressions of *hôd wĕhādār* (Job 40:10; 1 Chron 16:27; Ps 21:6 [RSV v 5]; 45:4 [RSV v 3]; 96:6; 104:1; 145:5). The aptness of the Mesopotamian material has been pointed out by Lipiński (1965:433–34) and Petitjean (1969:295–96).

The Hebrew term *hôd* occurs apart from *hādār* seventeen additional times in the Bible and conveys a sense of royalty as it is used in both divine and earthly settings. In two late instances, *hôd* is followed by *malkût* and expresses royal rather than divine majesty in a very direct manner (1 Chron 29:25; Dan 11:21). Although it sometimes has a divine warrior connotation (Warmuth 1978:352–56), it is the persistent royal character of the term that most informs its present usage. The passage in Num 27:20 that records God's instruction that Moses invest Joshua with "authority" *(hôd)* is especially helpful in understanding the meaning of the phrase "to bear royal majesty." By investing the Davidic scion with proper authority and legitimacy, he will be able to rule properly. That the term *hôd* so often designates Yahweh's universal cosmic power adds to the idea that the Davidide's earthly power is integrally related to and sanctioned by Yahweh's rule over all the world.

This phrase, like the preceding one concerning the building of the temple, has the independent pronoun *hû'* ("he") as the subject. Strictly speaking, the independent pronoun with the verb is unnecessary and the chief value of its presence is in emphasizing the subject. In this case, the force of the independent pronoun before the preceding verb ("he will build") could carry over to this verb, if needed. But it doesn't carry over. The use of the pronoun here again points to a deliberate arrangement of the verbs in this verse. "He will build . . ." is matched exactly by "he will bear . . . ," each with emphasis on the subject. These two verbs with pronoun subject are followed by two that are not so qualified: "sit" and "rule" *(wyšb-wmšl),* which are also parallel and matching. Furthermore, the two forms with the pronoun are imperfect whereas the forms without are conversive perfects. They have the same time and force but the form has been deliberately varied. The latter pair explicate and augment the preceding statement about the bearing of royal majesty: the king fulfills that statement by sitting on the throne and exercising his rule.

sit upon his throne. This is a standard phrase, found repeatedly in the Deuteronomic history and also frequently in Jeremiah, for designating succession to the royal, and especially the Davidic, throne. In this case the expression, composed of the verb "to sit" and the prepositional phrase "upon the throne," is broken up by the intrusion of the verb *mšl* ("to rule"). The writer could just as easily have put the words in a more convenient order, either by reversing the two verbs or by putting "rule" at the end, after "throne." The unusual order probably is original and shows the author's desire to vary stereotypical language, which otherwise can become monotonous and so lack impact. This device of breaking up stereotyped phrases is not uncommon in the Hebrew Bible, and the text should not be emended to make it conform to standard phraseology.

To "sit upon his throne" expresses the authority of monarchic rule. The literal image underlying this stereotyped language is the chair in which the king was seated as he meted out justice and otherwise exercised royal powers. The association of judgment with the throne of office appears in the description of Solomon's accession to his father's throne (1 Kgs 10:9); and in their eschatological expectations, both Isaiah (9:6 [RSV v 7]; 16:5) and Jeremiah (33:14–17) anticipate a ruler who will sit upon the Davidic throne and execute justice. Although the postexilic community has been somewhat restructured, with the responsibility for adjudicating internal matters resting with the priesthood (see NOTES to 3:7 and 5:2–3), the precedent for the monarchic exercise of supreme judicial powers (Whitelam 1979) is revived in this description of the future restoration of a Davidic king. With the return of dynastic rule will come the reestablishment of the king's responsibility for earthly justice. Since this phrase appears to be complemented by the following, or rather by the phrase "and rule," which is intrusive

in the Hebrew and has universalistic overtones (see following NOTE), the enthronement of the Shoot will involve authority external to the Yehudite constituency. Priestly
judicial rule as Zechariah knows it would have applied only to internal matters.

and rule. The root *mšl,* "to rule, have dominion" occurs over eighty times in the
Hebrew Bible. Consequently it is not easy to sort out the specific nuances of the verb
which distinguish it from the closely related *mlk,* "to rule, reign." We note, however,
that in reference to the reign of the Davidic kings, the verb *mšl* is used only of David,
Solomon, and Hezekiah, monarchs whose realms extended beyond the borders of Judah. Solomon ruled in his wisdom over the neighboring kingdoms that David had
subdued by military conquest, and Hezekiah appears to have held sway briefly over
Philistine territory. Otherwise, monarchic rule in Israel or in Judah is not expressed by
this verb, despite the fact that kings other than Solomon, David, and Hezekiah acquired territory outside Judah and Israel. Perhaps only those three succeeded in imposing an international political and economic structure over the newly conquered areas,
thereby justifying the use of *mšl.* Although the verb has limited use with respect to
Judean or Israelite kings, God's rule over *all* kingdoms is often denoted by *mšl* (e.g.,
Isa 40:10; Ps 22:29 [RSV v 28]; 59:14 [RSV v 13]; 1 Chron 29:12, etc.). In addition, this
verb signifies the imperial domination of other nations over Israel or Judah (e.g., the
Philistines: Ju 14:4 and 15:11; the Egyptians: Ps 105:2; Babylon: Isa 14:5 and Jer 51:46;
the nations: Ps 106:41).

Using the word in this way expresses the idea of rule or dominion of one party over
another distinct party or parties—that is, over a group of which the ruler is not naturally a part. It is especially well suited to the concept of imperial dominion, whereby an
emperor rules *(mlk)* over his own territory or people and exercises dominion *(mšl)* over
an extended territory made up of other groups. Yahweh's universal dominion is an apt
extension of such a concept as it is found in political, as distinguished from sapiential,
contexts in the Bible since it has a more figurative dimension in wisdom literature. Not
surprisingly, in his vision of the future Zechariah foresees a Davidide representing on
earth the universal sovereignty of Yahweh and utilizes the word *mšl* for "rule." That
root with its supranational overtones allows the prophet to echo, in his own way, the
eschatological sentiments of Hag 2:6–9 and 22–23, although Zechariah is obviously less
sanguine than Haggai as to the identity of the Davidide who will function as Yahweh's
earthly representative. The universal implications of *mšl* with respect to the Shoot's
broad responsibilities set him apart from his priestly colleague. The broadened responsibilities of the priesthood in the postexilic community may be sustained in terms of the
future vision, since Joshua's crown apparently will remain with him and he will occupy
a throne representing authority (see following NOTE), yet those responsibilities would
appear to remain internal to the Yehudite community and not extend to the community of nations as will the authority of the Shoot, who will have broad dominion.

A priest. The LXX supplies the definite article, perhaps assuming a specific reference
to Joshua ben-Jehozadak. Indeed, the LXX has an entirely different reading from MT:
"And the priest will be upon his right hand." The LXX seems to derive from a
different Hebrew text, or else it has been influenced by some other passage (cf. Ps
110:4–5, which has "priest" and "right hand"). The MT, however, has no article
before priest. The identity of the priestly official is thus rather indefinite. Such a situation is appropriate to the unspecified future time indicated in this oracle.

on his throne. This phrase, with reference to a priestly official, is the same as that just used concerning the royal figure in this verse. Much discussion and emendation exist in the scholarly literature dealing with it. Since it appears to place a priest on a par with a dynastic scion, its originality in the MT has been held as unacceptable by many modern commentators, some of whom (e.g., Beuken 1967:281) argue that the second occurrence of the phrase in reference to a priest is a deliberate alteration of the Hebrew text. The LXX reading (cf. previous NOTE), which omits "throne," offers support to exegetical views that doubt the authenticity of the MT. Other scholars (see summary in Mastin 1976) argue rather unconvincingly that the LXX has changed the received text. But Mastin himself has demonstrated the legitimacy of such a proposal by showing how the LXX would have come to render "on his throne" by "on his right hand." Therefore the LXX cannot be cited as evidence for a different Hebrew text. The editors of the LXX, anticipating the modern critics, were apparently bothered by the prospect of equating the priest with the king.

We admit the difficulty in ascertaining the relationship of priest to king but submit that rendering the Hebrew text as it is, "on the throne," does not interfere with the way in which this oracle depicts the two figures and their future roles. While "throne" has a decidedly royal cast in English (as also do *"Thron"* in German and *"trône"* in French), the Hebrew *kisse'* is the basic word for "chair" and takes on the meaning of throne only in royal contexts. It can just as easily be understood to designate the seat of any high official. To put it another way, the translation "throne" need not be specifically royal but can otherwise denote the official chair in which an administrator conducts his business and which thus comes to symbolize his incumbency and jurisdiction (cf. Neh 3:7). The use of the word *kisse'* to denote the chair of a nonroyal, priestly official does occur in the Bible, notably referring to the premonarchic period in the days when Eli was ministering to Yahweh at the Shiloh sanctuary (1 Sam 1:9; 4:13,18). The first reference, in 1 Sam 1:9, indicates that Eli's chair was positioned at the doorpost of the temple—a significant location in terms of Eli's priestly and judicial responsibilities (cf. NOTE to 5:2, "twenty . . . ten"). These references to Eli's chair clearly demonstrate that the chair was his judicial and sacramental seat and that its location in the temple precinct was quite intentional. Eli's "chair" could well have served as the model for the one on which Joshua is enthroned, for Eli is the best example we have for the postexilic high-priestly office with its civil as well as ecclesiastical prerogatives. That no priest during the monarchy is said to have occupied such a seat is possibly a chance omission, but more likely the result of the fact that the monarchy had taken over the judicial functions that a priest seated in a chair of office located near the entrance to the temple would have exercised.

The appearance here of a priest occupying a chair of office, or "throne," does not make him a royal figure equivalent to a king. Rather, it acknowledges the increase in his responsibilities in the postexilic community, for which the premonarchic situation provided a precedent. Yet the priest is described here solely in terms of his sitting on his throne, whereas for the royal figure the mention of enthronement is only one of several items marking his official royal role and legitimate position as a Yahwist monarch. Reading the Hebrew text as it is does not assign greater powers to the priest than to a king; it endows him, in recognition of the postexilic situation, with a larger role than during the monarchy. Consequently the future restoration of monarchy will entail a cooperative leadership between the two (see following NOTES). This second "on his throne" is contextually essential for depicting the priest along with a Davidic dynast. The repetition of the phrase is thus distributive, providing the concept of important and official roles for both priest and monarch.

In depicting a dual structure, Zechariah may be working from the arrangements created under Persian rule. But at the same time, his view of the future as well as his support for the contemporary structure of leadership in Yehud are based on what he believes to have been the pattern in premonarchic times. That was the wilderness period when Moses was civil leader and his brother Aaron was high priest, and the period of the Judges for which the prophet must have assumed that there always was a ranking priest alongside the intertribal judge or civil leader. Whether or not Zechariah was correct in his view of the distant past as a time of dual leadership, there must have been some historical substance to his view or it would not have survived in the traditions as it has. Nor is it likely that the pattern of joint civil and ecclesiastical rulers would have emerged as it did in the postexilic period without some basis in long-standing tradition.

peaceful counsel. Once again the prophet provides a unique combination of words to express the special nature of the harmonious relationship that will exist between king and priest in the ideal future state. Although the present era does not allow for the Davidide Zerubbabel to assume monarchic and political responsibility, the future, like the present, involves two major administrative leaders who will work amicably together. Such a relationship perhaps foreshadows the later dyarchic structure of the Qumran community, although in that community the priestly leader appears to have dominated (1 Q Sa 2:11–14; Testament of Judah 21:2).

The phrase *ʿăṣat šālôm* ("peaceful counsel"), however, implies more than a relationship between two leaders. It also suggests that those leaders are divinely inspired individuals whose very purpose is to bring about God's will and to effect his purpose in society. The word *ʿēṣâ* ("counsel") occurs frequently with God's name (*ʿăṣat*-Yahweh, "counsel of Yahweh"; cf. Isa 19:17; Jer 49:20; 50:45; Ps 33:11; Prov 19:21; and Ezra 10:3), and such references provide the model of divine sanction for collaboration between priest and king. Here, as in 4:12 (see NOTE above to "two branches"), two individuals are ultimately required to achieve the goal of harmonious rule (see Ackroyd 1968:198–99 and Rignell 1950:231–32).

between the two of them. The text is explicit in stating that peaceful harmony will exist between *two* individuals. Baldwin's suggestion that this verse refers to the unification of the role of king and priest in the person of the Messiah therefore is to be rejected (1972:136–37). Despite the fact that it is Joshua who is crowned, verses 12–13a recapitulate Israel's historic attachment to kingship, while verse 13b reiterates the continuing role of the priesthood. The elaboration of the role of the monarch when compared to the narration of the priestly coronation signifies that monarchist traditions of Israel were strongly entrenched and weighed heavily upon both the prophet and his audience. Yet the attitude reflected here shows that both institutions had their place in the use and thought of Israel.

14. *The [other] crown.* Reading singular "crown," *hāʿăṭeret* or the old Phoenician singular *hāʿăṭārōt*, in agreement with the following singular verb *tihyeh* ("will be"); see footnote to "crown" in verse 14 and NOTES to "crowns" and "You will place [one]" in

verse 11. The defective spelling of the MT here makes the choice of the *ʿăṭeret* somewhat difficult since the lexicons and concordances list *ʿăṭeret* as a construct form, though as a singular absolute form, however, it may be attested in Isa 62:3. In any case this "crown" represents the (golden?) crown of royalty as distinguished from the (silver?) crown of priesthood which has been placed upon the head of Joshua (cf. NOTE to "silver and gold," v 11).

The MT may reflect an old Phoenician singular absolute, *ʿăṭārōt* (so Petitjean 1969:281; Ceresko 1980:184; see also Donner and Röllig 1973: No. 60). A late Hellenistic (?) Phoenician text leaves no doubt that *ʿaṭrt* is to be read as a singular absolute with *-ot* ending:

Text: *tm bd ṣdnym bnʾ spt lʿṭr ʾyt šm ʿbʿl bn mgn/*
ʾs nšʾ hgw ʿl bt ʾlm . . . ʿṭrt ḥrṣ bdrknm 20 lmḥt

Translation: It was resolved by the Sidonians, the members of the assembly, to crown with a wreath *(šmʿbʿl)* son of Magon/whom the community appointed over the temple . . . a golden wreath *(ʿṭrt)* weighing fully 20 dareikens.

This inscription (translated by Ceresko 1980) provides unexpected support for our proposal that the true monarchic crown was crafted in gold, and greatly strengthens the case for the singular reading. Here, as in verse 11, we have placed the word "other" in brackets to assist the reader of the English text. Verse 14 resumes the language of divine imperatives to the prophet begun in verses 10–12a. It also links the crowning of Joshua with the ultimate crowning of a Davidide.

as a reminder. The deposition of the crown of royalty—that is, the second crown—in the Temple of Yahweh *lĕzikkārôn* "as a reminder" is an action meant to assuage the concerns of those committed to the monarchist tradition and needing to be reassured of the continuing validity of the inviolable Davidic covenant. The word *zikkārôn* involves remembering and has the nuance of a sign evoking remembrance. The word often occurs with *ʾôt* ("sign") and denotes an object that is intended to remind the community of God's favorable consideration of the Davidic promise (Eising 1978:62–82).

The grammatical construction, with the verb "to be" (here, "it will be") plus *l* ("for" or "as"), may seem awkward, but analogous combinations are found in several places in the Pentateuch (Num 10:10; Exod 30:16) along with the phrase "before Yahweh." Both those instances occur in sacral contexts, the former referring to the two silver trumpets used for the calling of the assembly, the latter referring to the atonement money of the children of Israel. Num 31:54 although lacking the verb "to be" is also apposite in that it refers to the gold of the captains of the thousands and of the hundreds being placed before Yahweh as a "reminder" or "memorial" to the children of Israel. It is significant that in each of these four occurrences, either silver or gold plays a role as does a deposition within the temple or its equivalent, the Tent of Meeting. Zech 6:14, in a manner similar to the other three texts, concludes a command "to take," begun in verse 10 and continued in verse 11, and brings the action to conclusion with the placing of the second crown in the Temple of Yahweh. The prophetic action in Zechariah has precedents in Israelite life which evidently would be understood by and have meaning for the witnesses the prophet had assembled to observe his deeds. This last action represents a vital and culminating event in the overall Crowning scene, for it puts the crowning of Joshua, reported in verse 12, in a perspective which includes a Davidic figure.

Helem, Tobiah, Jedaiah. See NOTES to verse 10. Helem is to be identified with Heldai of verse 10; note that Syriac reads "Heldai." These men together are carefully chosen representatives of several factions of exiled Yahwists.

Hen. This name intrudes into the place occupied in verse 10 by Josiah. The versions were obviously bothered by this intrusion and provide diverse resolutions. The LXX is similar to verse 10 but translates "Hen" as "favor." Syriac has Heldai, Tobiah, Jedaiah as in verse 10 but adds Josiah. The Vulgate has Helem, Tobiah, Jedaiah and Hen. The Hebrew as it stands can be explained in several ways: 1. Josiah of verse 10 had an alternative name, which is used here. 2. Only Josiah's house is actually mentioned in verse 10; perhaps Josiah himself was not the witness and instead a brother named Hen was part of the group assembled by Zechariah. 3. Josiah is intended but is called "Hen" in an honorific way. 4. "Hen" is not a name at all but rather a designation for "favor" or "grace." 5. The name is a hypocoristicon of a name like *ḥănayâ,* which is a well-known priestly name in postexilic times and would fit with the idea that Josiah belonged to a priestly family (cf. last NOTE to 6:10). 6. The Hebrew has "to" *(l)* before "Hen," as it does before the names of the other three men. This may not be a preposition but rather part of a word *lḥn,* which is an Aramaic term for a temple or court steward (Demsky 1981:101). If so, it has been used here as a title for Josiah because of his association with cultic apparel. The family name of Zephaniah is in fact associated with such an office in Second Temple times (so Mishnah Sheqalim 5.1 and Yoma 3.10–11).

None of these explanations is entirely satisfactory. We can only conclude that Josiah or someone of his family is designated by "Hen." Still, the reason for the shift from "Josiah" is obscure, if "Hen" is indeed original in the MT. Note that many English versions (e.g., RSV, NEB) follow the Syriac and read "Josiah," while others (NJPS, AV) retain the enigmatic "Hen."

15. *Those who are distant.* Both the identity of "those distant" *(rĕḥôqîm)* and the integrity of the entire verse are a matter of scholarly disagreement. As to the former concern, it is nearly impossible to determine with certainty whether the statement here pertains to the exiled Judeans and/or to other non-Yahwist groups (Elliger 1975:131). Had the author of the statement intended the "nations," that is, non-Yahwists, to be included, we would expect him to have included the word *gôyîm* as in 2:15 (RSV 2:11) and 8:23. The thematic similarity of verse 15a to verses 12b–13 supports the view that "those who are distant" are probably non-Yehudite Yahwists, perhaps as represented by Heldai and Tobiah, rather than people of other nations. More specifically, the term probably indicates Yahwists who are still in exile but who will participate in a future rebuilding of the temple, not the present temple project, which was by the time of this oracle near completion and which was a Yehudite project, supported in part by Persian remission of a portion of the taxes collected in the subprovince of Yehud (see COMMENT to Hag 1:1–15a).

The language of the first half of this verse has a universalizing tone, especially because of its similarity to that of 2:13 and 15 (RSV 2:9 and 11), which would have appealed to Yahwists everywhere. Yet in this context, which deals with various elements of the Yahwist community, the expression "those who are distant" along with the second statement of verse 15 ("Thus you will know that Yahweh of Hosts has sent me to you") would not appear to constitute an appeal addressed to all mankind (Mitchell 1912:193). Furthermore, the Deuteronomistic tone of the third statement of verse 15 ("This will be so when you truly listen to the voice of Yahweh your God"), while lofty and homiletical in tone and style is anything but universalistic; rather, it focuses upon the corporate responsibilities of Israel. The supposition that the nations might participate in the temple rebuilding project stems from the identification made by some exegetes between the temple of Joshua and Zerubbabel (520–515 B.C.E.) on the one hand and the eschatological tone of the vision of Haggai (2:6–7) and the oracle in Zech 6:12b–13 on the other. However, verse 15 resumes the style and intent of verses 9–12a and for this reason a universalistic meaning for "those who are distant" is unlikely but cannot be ruled out.

Verse 15 as a whole is widely regarded to be the work of a redactor and secondary to the Crowning section (6:9–15). Mitchell (1912:192) in fact places it with the Zerubbabel insertion of 4:8–10a, and most commentators simply regard it as a kind of editorial comment to the whole of the vision cycle (Elliger 1975:131). Other, far more radical proposals rearrange the wording at the end of chapter 6 in a variety of ways and shift the order of the verses or parts thereof (see Petitjean 1969:300–3). The MT, however, is to be preferred above other possible arrangements. Since verse 15 concludes The Crowning passage, its tone would naturally reflect both the particular concerns of The Crowning section as a whole (vv 9–15) and the broader temple ideology of the oracle enclosed within it. The ambiguity of "those who are distant" for this reason suits the literary position of the verse it introduces. Because the entire verse ties in with 6:12b–13, the statement would have to stem from a rather early stage in the redactional process if it did not in fact represent a summation by the prophet himself.

work on the Temple of Yahweh. Although the verb *bnh* ("to build") and its object ("Temple of Yahweh") are the same as the twice repeated phrase of verses 12 and 13, the verb in this case is followed by the preposition *b* ("on"). The subjects of the verb are portrayed as acting upon the temple in a subtly different way from the Davidide above: they contribute to the temple work whereas the Shoot directly builds the temple. As the dynastic figure responsible for the work, he is credited with having constructed it all by himself. For the future time of this intended activity, see our NOTES to "build the Temple of Yahweh," verse 12. The language here echoes that of the oracle of verses 12b–13 and involves the audience of the oracle's framework, thus integrating the two parts of this Crowning section.

Thus you will know . . . to you. The language is formulaic and closely resembles the statements in 2:13,15 (RSV 2:9,11); 4:9 and also in Hag 1:12, where there is similarity in content but not an exact correspondence of stylized language (see NOTES above). The refrain is characteristic of the nonvisionary, oracular portions of the Book of Zechariah. In its resemblance to the language of preexilic apostolic prophecy, it serves to provide authority to the oracular materials assembled. The idea that the prophet has been sent by Yahweh characterizes all the parallel citations and is one of the distinguishing features of biblical prophecy.

when you truly listen to the voice of Yahweh your God. In this summary statement one hears the Deuteronomic charge, at the introduction of the blessings/curses section of the end of the Book of Deuteronomy (28:1), to the Israelites to obey Yahweh and his commandments. Various other pentateuchal passages (e.g., Exod 15:26; Deut 11:13; Lev 26:14) contain similar statements if not identical phraseology. The use in Zechariah of this language, however, shifts the covenant orientation of the pentateuchal examples. In the Pentateuch the notion of listening to or obeying God or his voice is the stated condition upon which the prosperity and well-being of the Israelites depends. The clauses are conditional: "if you obey . . ." In Zechariah, the future situation of a Yahwistic temple in association with a Davidic dynast is the anticipated result of obedience to Yahweh. That is, the Davidic covenant is to be renewed, with the temple signifying dynastic legitimacy, and then, a step removed in comparison with pentateuchal portrayal of the Mosaic covenant, prosperity presumably will prevail in the land.

The similarity of this verse—the present clause and also the previous one—to the language of Hag 1:12 is of special interest. There too the pentateuchal covenant language is used in the context of temple building. The idea that obedience to Yahweh's voice ultimately involves prosperity is implicit in the overall message of Haggai; and Haggai indeed invokes (2:5) the memory of the Sinai covenant. Haggai however, unlike Zechariah, does not explicitly address the problem of monarchic participation in temple building. He appears to expect Zerubbabel to be counted fully as a Davidide, whereas Zechariah treats that idea as a possibility to be fulfilled in the more distant future.

COMMENT

These seven verses constitute the final and, in many ways, the most important of a series of nonvisionary portions of Part Two of First Zechariah. In addition, The Crowning passage is the third in a grouping of oracular sections which relate directly to the administrative reshaping of the restoration community (see also COMMENT to 4:6b–10a, the Zerubbabel insertion, and to 3:8–10, the Supplementary Oracle). In these passages the Davidic governor must cooperate with the high priest, whose expanded powers now impinge upon areas traditionally viewed as part of the civil realm of authority. Furthermore, The Crowning scene completes the prophet's statements regarding the place of the refounded Jerusalem temple in the life of the community in Yehud and also in the diaspora.

It is no accident that The Crowning passage begins with an oracular formula that is identical to the one in the oracular insertion of 4:8 and nearly identical to the oracular introductions in chapter 8 (vv 1 and 18) as well as to the superscription to the First Vision (1:7). The positioning of the formula in these particular places in First Zechariah serves to highlight the beginning and end of Part Two, and to join Part Two to the conclusion of the whole work, Part Three. The superscription to Part One (1:1) also fits into this pattern although with a slight variation in tense and only the inclusion of the prophet's name distinguishing it from the other occurrences. Such correspondences give a sense of the overall unity of Zechariah 1–8 and suggest direct involvement of the prophet or one of his disciples in the editorial process which appears to have been completed before the rededication of the temple in 515 B.C.E.

Although many commentators have doubted the integrity of this passage, our exegesis has discovered both its soundness and also its subtlety, a feature which apparently led the critics astray. No Interpreting Angel is utilized, as in the visions, in order to explain the meaning of the oracular discourse. The text eloquently affirms in its description of symbolic actions and items what has already been implied or stated in the preceding visions and oracles: that the high priest Joshua and not a king will be crowned for the present and that the royal scion, the Shoot, may only one day in the future assume full powers and "bear royal majesty and sit upon his throne and rule" (v 13). What was perhaps less explicit in the Zerubbabel insertion (4:6b–7) is now carefully and directly presented: the high priest has assumed a more central role in the life of the community.

The divine command to Zechariah to take the silver and gold which is being brought by Heldai, Tobiah, and Jedaiah, and perhaps also by the enigmatic Hen of verse 14, in order to prepare crowns signals the commencement of the prophetic action from which the entire scene unfolds. The language describing that action is very difficult and somewhat elliptical, but nonetheless may be understood in terms of late Hebrew syntax without recourse to wholesale emendation (see NOTES). The list of participants in the scenario, which also includes Josiah ben-Zephaniah, reveals a logic and coherence not easily accessible to the modern reader. It suggests the prophet's keen understanding of the demography of Jewish life on the eve of the completion of the Jerusalem temple and demonstrates his profound concern for the welfare and involvement of many diverse elements of the postexilic community, both within and outside Yehud.

The Edict of Cyrus in 538 B.C.E., which allowed the exiles to leave Babylon and return to their homeland to settle and rebuild the Temple of Yahweh, surely was accompanied by a sense of hope and promise. The optimistic view of the potential of the first return under Sheshbazzar is reflected in Deutero-Isaiah (44:28; 45:1). Yet the initial response of the exiles to the twofold enterprise of return and of rebuilding was evidently rather limited. The precise details regarding Sheshbazzar's failed leadership and a concomitant lack of popular support (see Introduction) are not available; it is only at the period of around 520 B.C.E. when Zerubbabel was governor that the social dynamics at work in the postexilic community can be discerned. Through the inspired preaching of Haggai and Zechariah as well as the effective leadership of Zerubbabel and Joshua, those who returned to Jerusalem responded at long last to the call to rebuild the destroyed Temple of Yahweh (Ezra 6:14). Because of the immediacy of the seventy-year prophecy, which predicted that

Judah's exile was to last such a span (see NOTE to Zech 1:12 and cf. Zech 7:3; see also Ackroyd 1958:23–27 and Jer 25:11–12 and 29:10), and also as a result of the new administrative policies which accompanied Darius I's accession to the throne in 522 B.C.E. (Cook 1983:77–90), it was the second return that ultimately decided the fate and character of the Yehudite community. Many more exiles returned to Yehud for the first time under Zerubbabel's leadership. Many of those who remained in Babylon to live far away from their historic homeland achieved a good measure of success, some of them being assimilated into their environment and others holding to their Yahwistic heritage, as witness the onomasticon of the Babylonian Jews (Zadok 1979: *passim*).

In the final oracular scene the prophet addresses himself to this set of complex circumstances and social realities. His choice of witnesses may be meant to reach all factions of the fragmented community of Yahwists still worshipping Yahweh and recognizing the historic significance of the "Holy Land." Heldai appears to be a representative of the community of exiles remaining in Babylon and a delegate to the putative ceremony of crowning which is the subject of the prophetic action (see NOTE to "Heldai," 6:10). By naming Heldai first in the delegation, the prophet may be sending an important signal to all who would listen: that even the diaspora community is to be regarded as present at the epochal event of rebuilding the Jerusalem temple, which is conceded in the present passage and officially initiated by the ceremony of refoundation of chapters 3 and 4 (3:8–10; 4:6b–10a).

Heldai is joined in observing the symbolic actions of the prophet by Tobiah and Jedaiah, apparently returned from Babylon. The phrase "who have come from Babylon" certainly applies to these three individuals and probably to Josiah as well. The absence of patronymics in reference to Heldai, Tobiah, and Jedaiah is a telling feature, suggesting that they represent families well known in their time. Both names are attested in the postexilic corpus of biblical literature, and the Tobiads in particular figure preeminently in nonbiblical sources (see Mazar 1957 and chart in NOTE to "and from Tobiah and from Jedaiah," 6:10). The inclusion of the Tobiads among the delegates to the crowning thus suggests that some members of this rather large and influential family did in fact return to their family estates in Gilead during the reign of Darius I. The example of the Tobiad return indicates that some returnees did not settle within the small confines of Yehud proper but rather within the larger historic area of *'ereṣ yiśrā'ēl,* "the land of Israel." The makeup of the delegation therefore constitutes a carefully chosen set, and each individual represents a group of Yahwists that has a special relationship with the territory of Yehud and to the Temple of Yahweh being rebuilt there. Whether or not such individuals came for an actual or symbolic crowning, their inclusion by Zechariah in his account of such an event apparently reveals the prophet's awareness of the geographical diversity that characterized the Yahwist community in his day.

The fourth individual, mentioned in verse 10, is one Josiah ben-Zephaniah. Despite the use of the patronymic, his precise identity remains somewhat conjectural. Josiah was perhaps a descendant, probably the great-grandson, of the priest Zephaniah who was carried off into exile and executed at Riblah in Hamath. The very fact that his parentage is included indicates that he belongs to a family, a priestly family, for which lineage was especially significant. Furthermore, the importance of the actions to be performed in his house make it likely that Josiah was more than an average citizen, that he held an official position. As Zephaniah's direct descendant, he would be second priest, and it would make sense for a ceremony involving the chief priest to take place in his house.

What is it that the delegation brings to the house of Josiah? Silver and gold are specified, and the context for these gifts is clear: they are brought by delegates from the diverse factions within and without Yehud for the specific purpose of the preparation of *two* crowns. But more than this, providing silver and gold represents the fiscal and ideological support of those factions in the enterprise of reestablishing the temple. Such a practice of freewill giving was known from preexilic times (2 Kgs 12) and apparently accompanied the first attempts under Cyrus to rebuild the temple (Ezra 1:4–6). Ezra 2:69 might then refer to the continuation of this practice in the days of Cyrus (but see NOTE to "silver and gold" in 6:11) as is certainly the case here.

If The Crowning scene as a whole may be taken as the final statement of the prophet on the subject of the new administration of Yehud in the restoration era and as a complement to his previous utterances on the subject, then the MT plural "crowns" of 6:11 poses no inherent difficulties. Indeed, the present context demands the plural in anticipation of the crowning of Joshua (v 11b) and the placement of the second crown in the Temple of Yahweh (v 14) as a reminder that the crown of royalty will be borne by a Davidide only at some future time. Nonetheless, generations of scholars have preferred the singular and have understood it to refer to the unnamed Zerubbabel, whose name they suggest has been intentionally excised from the text (see NOTE to "crowns"), though a minority of scholars have taken exception to such a view. In addition to philological reasons for accepting the plural, the probability that "silver and gold" were used separately to make two distinct crowns, a silver one and golden one, supports the originality of the Hebrew text.

Whether or not there was an actual ceremony of crowning cannot be ascertained. It is perhaps more important to focus upon the reasons why Joshua's purported crowning would be so central to the oracular conclusion of Part Two. Already in chapter 3, the terminology of Joshua's priestly headgear may be identified with a subtle shift that corresponds to his assumption of greater authority in the postexilic administration. A new term, ṣānîp, "turban," is substituted there for the more familiar miṣnepet, "headpiece" of the priestly texts of the Pentateuch. The former term is clearly associated with royal authority (Isa 62:3) as is the present term *ʿăṭārâ,* "crown" (vv 11 and 14). There is no question that the chief priest's attire included a crown or headpiece in former times. The point is that here the new terminology signifies the increased judicial powers the high priest will exercise by virtue of Persian imperial policies, which allowed for semiautonomy but no monarchy. However strong the royal associations of the new terms are, Joshua's crown is only one of a pair; and it is the symbolic placement of the second crown which is intended to accommodate traditional attachments to the monarchic model of governance.

To a large extent those who would emend the text in verse 11 to the singular and understand Zerubbabel as the intended recipient of the crown presuppose that Zerubbabel represents the sudden end of the Davidic line with respect to its leadership role. However, the marriage or close association of Elnathan, Zerubbabel's successor as governor (Avigad 1976a:30–36), with Shelomith, the daughter of Zerubbabel as his *ʾamah* (1 Chron 3:19), seems to indicate a continuing participation of a Davidide in public office (E. Meyers 1985), although it is clear that by the fifth century the governorship had been taken away from the House of David entirely. Furthermore, there is no evidence for supposing that Zerubbabel himself did not continue on as governor for a time, presumably for some years after Zechariah had concluded his prophetic career and while Joshua was still high priest. The notion that Zerubbabel disappeared because of a hypothetical, abortive attempt to reestablish the monarchy is supposedly reflected in a secondary textual correction. This emendation removes his name in order to bring prophecy closer in line with reality. Since that reality is purely conjectural, the emendation required to accommodate it is not one that we can accept. It is more likely that Zerubbabel is no longer mentioned in the text because of the success of the prophet Zechariah in resolving the monarchic issue, by allowing for a Davidic governor to stand as the symbol, but not the reality, of an ultimate or eschatological enthronement of a Davidic king.

Zechariah's accomplishment in emphasizing the future, eschatological role of a Davidide and supporting a government led by a priestly officer is reflected in the diminishing importance of the Davidic house in times to come. Despite the possible role of Shelomith, Zerubbabel is clearly the last direct descendant of David to exercise political authority of any kind so far as we can tell. The Davidic line apparently continued, because the lists in 1 Chronicles 3 give the genealogy of the royal house of Judah well past the time of Zerubbabel. There must have been heirs presumptive available to claim royal authority should the circumstances ever warrant such action. Yet after Zerubbabel and his son-in-law(?) Elnathan, it seems that no one with either direct or collateral Davidic lineage served as governor. By the fifth century, the governorship has clearly been removed from the House of David. In all of Ezra 7–10 and Nehemiah nothing more is mentioned about either the restoration of a monarchy or even the appointment of a Davidide to the governorship. The idea of a Davidide appears to operate entirely on an eschatological level. King David and his house were remembered chiefly in terms of messianic hopes and expectations after the time of Zechariah.

The shift to the eschatological Shoot in verse 12 serves to reassure the community of two important details: 1) that the high priest's authority, while greatly increased, nonetheless has its limitations; and 2) that a future Davidide will surely be installed as monarch and will himself renew or rebuild the Temple of Yahweh. Hence the prophet's audience is told once more that the present internal reorganization of Yehud is not permanent and that the long vision included both national autonomy and royal leadership. As an interim measure, the ascendancy of the priesthood could surely be supported by everyone in the interests of self-preservation, peace, and accommodation to Persian domination. The indefiniteness of the language in verse 12 contrasts with the stronger and more specific language of 3:8: "I am indeed bringing my servant the Shoot." Perhaps the actual presence and participation of Zerubbabel in the ceremony of refoundation evokes the more exact frame of reference in chapter 3. The present text, "Behold, there is a man—Shoot is his name—," is vague and would deflate any monarchist feelings that might have been stimulated by the fact that Zerubbabel had participated in the ceremony of refoundation. The omission of Zerubbabel's name is thus quite intentional; the appearance of the term "Shoot" following the oracular introduction "Thus said Yahweh of Hosts" and within the oracular statement itself lends strength to the notion of its originality. The editor of this passage in *BHS* would restore the definite article *he*, which might have been lost through haplography, to "a man" in order to read "Behold the man whose name is *Ṣemaḥ*," but there is no versional support for such a change nor would it affect the meaning.

The continuation of verse 12 has also puzzled commentators because of its reiteration of the theme of rebuilding the temple by a Davidide, here and again at the beginning of verse 13. But the eschatological context here is quite certain, compared to the direct reference to the present temple-building project in the Oracular Insertion of chapter 4; the duplication serves to emphasize the role of the future Davidide. In addition, the wordplay in "from his place he will shoot up," represents a commentary on Jeremiah 33:17, where the continuity of the Davidic line is assured. The ancient audience, unlike the modern reader, would not have been bothered by the seemingly anomalous situation in which the building of a temple by a Davidide was promised at the very time when the Second Temple was being completed without a king or builder. The mention of monarchic temple building merely accedes to the ancient Near Eastern requirement that a dynastic state have a temple-palace seat of government. Since the present oracle places the fulfillment of the dynastic hope in a future time, the temple must be (re)built at that time too.

While the royal involvement in temple building is given a future orientation in verses 12–13, the text does not answer the question of just how far in the future that might be. The language about building the temple could still apply to the present project. Zechariah is clearly less sanguine than Haggai, who expected that a new Davidic kingdom would emerge from the collapse of Persian rule (Hag 2:21–23). He is somewhat more obscure in his language, and perhaps he even thinks that the new Judah might somehow be part of the Persian Empire. Zechariah is also influenced by the seventy-year prophecy, and while the temple is almost finished it has not yet been dedicated. Zerubbabel has had his hand in its refoundation; Zechariah could well have hoped that the Shoot would yet be allowed to participate in the dedication and ascend the royal throne. The combined Book of Haggai-Zechariah 1–8 was put together in anticipation of that event. The monarchic dimension never did materialize, and the lack of specificity in Zechariah's mention of the Shoot allowed his words to retain their significance for a distant rather than a near future. Zechariah is talking about present work as the beginning of the realization of dreams and hopes, of a future promise growing out of the current efforts of his fellow Yahwists.

Verse 13 provides additional information about the role of the future Davidic ruler. The expression "to bear royal majesty" draws upon imagery found in both Hebrew and Mesopotamian literature and affords the Davidic scion both legitimacy and authority. But the following expression, "to sit upon his throne and rule," reveals even more closely the hopes which the prophet and his audience attached to the future Davidic monarchy. At that time the king will again resume responsibility for meting out earthly justice. Since the oracular statement is contiguous with verse 13b regarding the priest's future role in concert with the rule of a monarch, we must look to the word "rule" (mšl) in order to ascertain the nature of cooperation that is to mark their relationship.

"To rule" or "have dominion over" appears to be used only for the Davidic kings whose rule extended beyond the borders of Judah, and also to express Yahweh's rule over all kingdoms. This supranational meaning of "to rule" indicates that Zechariah is reserving for the future monarch the prerogative of administering justice beyond the confines of Yehudite territory, and in this respect the Shoot is to be distinguished from the priest whose responsibilities pertain only to the more limited community of Yehud within its territorial boundaries. The eschatological dimension of the Shoot's responsibility is therefore expressed in the universalizing language that one associates with such a time. Zechariah 6:12–13 in this way echoes the Isaianic depiction of the ideal future king whose domain will extend outward beyond the confines of Judahite territory to the nations (11:9–10; cf. Ps 72; etc.). However, that this impulse toward universalism is tempered with reference to priestly rule reflects the reality of the postexilic situation, in which Joshua has some authority over judicial and civil as well as religious affairs. The word "throne" is utilized for priest as it is for king, in recognition of the high priest's continuing importance. The ideal future for Zechariah thus incorporates both aspects of Israel's judicial heritage; king and priest together will rule in perfect harmony. The dyarchic pattern of leadership that is later reflected in the Dead Sea community at Qumran is hereby elevated to a position of legitimacy in Zechariah as a consequence of postexilic events and circumstances. The new hierocratic emphasis, which endorsed a role for the high priest that was to remain a distinctive feature of Second Temple Judaism, has become grafted onto the old monarchist tradition. This process represents an innovative if not ingenious accommodation to social, political, and religious realities of the restoration era, while at the same time it must have drawn upon ancient, premonarchic antecedents. It was not necessarily intended to serve as a model for all subsequent generations. However, it did facilitate a very different transition and apparently served for a time as a model acceptable to the many diverse elements in the emerging Jewish community (E. Meyers 1985). It succeeded in doing so because the dyarchic structure was always present in Israel's traditions and political and religious institutions. There were variations at different periods, with wide swings in the degree and proportion of power and authority held by the civil and ecclesiastical authorities. Clearly during most of the monarchic period, the greater weight of power and authority lay with the kingship. Yet there had always been, since the wilderness period, a chief priest in Israel's history. The postexilic period sees the balance shifting in his direction.

As we have explained in the NOTES, either the slight adjustment of the consonantal MT to singular "crown" (*ʿăṭeret*) in verse 14, or the reading of MT *ʿăṭārōt* as an old Phoenician singular, is necessitated by both the text (e.g., singular verb *tihyeh*, "will be") and the context, the latter being the distinction between the present crowning of Joshua and the eschatological crowning of the Shoot. The deposition of the second crown in the Temple of Yahweh is to serve as a tangible reminder to all who hoped that the present era would enable a Davidide to assume full monarchic power that such a time is yet to come. Placing the crown in the temple concludes the command "to take" (v 10), completes the action, and is reminiscent of several pentateuchal passages that have a sacral context. The significance of the memorial is underscored in the repetition of the names of the delegates first mentioned in verse 10 and mentioned again in verse 14 framing the material in between.

The concluding verse of The Crowning passage is also the final verse of Part Two of First Zechariah (Zech 1–8). As such it does double duty, and as might be expected, several proposals have been made to explain its rather ambiguous position in this oracular section. The first statement (v 15a), with its universalizing tone, bears a thematic similarity to verses 12b–13. The third clause (v 15c), however, has a Deuteronomistic cast in its focus upon the corporate responsibilities of Israel. In a way, nothing could be more characteristic of Zechariah than the mixing of these two elements. Some commentators sensing the special character of these verses understandably have proposed that the entire verse was appended to this final oracular section at a late stage in the redaction process. In our view, since this process is completed under the supervision of Zechariah or one of his disciples, it would stem from the time when the visionary portion of the book, Part Two of First Zechariah, assumed its final shape, sometime between 518 and 515 B.C.E.

The Crowning passage allows the major segment of Zechariah 1–8 to end on a note of hope and with a call to obedience (cf. COMMENT to Part One, 1:1–6). Zechariah concludes his presentation to the Yehudites of his day by again espousing a doctrine of support for the status quo, but with the understanding that such support represents only an interim position. He is an advocate of both priest and king, and knows that at some future time a monarch will rule alongside the high priest. He has justified the current state of affairs because of his appraisal of the true extent of Achaemenid power and might.

The Crowning scene demonstrates Zechariah's ingenuity in formulating an alternative way of looking at contemporary events and perceiving in them a creative opportunity for religious and theological response. This prophetic contribution helps mark the restoration era as one of the most innovative periods in Israelite and Judean history. Although rooted in the historical present, Zechariah's views are also linked to the eschatological future when the present order will give way to another. Within this inclusive temporal scope, all principals are afforded significant roles that find historic precedent within the tradition. Moreover, within that scheme all segments of Jewish life both inside and outside the holy land are involved in Jerusalem's fortunes.

The careful balance between monarchic and premonarchic tradition that Zechariah achieves is comparable to that found in the Primary History (Freedman 1983), which is also a product of the sixth century. The Genesis through Kings corpus presents a viable nonmonarchic structure as the original pattern of Israelite life, under the aegis of Israel's greatest prophet and leader Moses, with the assistance of his brother, the chief priest Aaron. As viewed from the sixth century, the Exodus and Wanderings play a central and formative role in the tradition. But David and the monarchy are hardly ignored, and the description of the monarchic period with its glorious successes and tragic failures rounds out the story as it had unfolded by the mid-sixth century. For Zechariah, the restoration meant a return to a nonmonarchic structure but with the hope and expectation that the classic kingdom would also be reestablished.

Whether or not there was an actual crowning in Jerusalem cannot be established. But for Zechariah and for those whom he addressed, the scenario of 6:9–15 touched upon issues that required resolution. The Hebrew text, more or less as received, represents the articulate voice of a prophet wrestling with those issues. Zechariah offered a realistic way of living under the circumstances. The organization of community life that he espoused made it possible for his contemporaries to retain the distinctive characteristics of traditional Yahwism and to develop them further. Second Temple Judaism was to emerge from this process. Furthermore, in the late sixth century B.C.E., under very difficult conditions, Zechariah offered the hope of a glorious future, which provided comfort to the souls of the people and enabled them to remain in readiness to achieve consummation of their efforts and aspirations.

Part Three

ZECH 7–8

ADDRESS TO
THE DELEGATION FROM BETHEL,
AND CONCLUDING ORACLES

12. ADDRESS TO
THE DELEGATION FROM BETHEL:
INTRODUCTION
(7:1–6)

7 ¹ Then in the fourth year of King Darius (the word of Yahweh came to Zechariah) on the fourth [day] of the ninth month, in Kislev, ² Bethel sent Sar-ezer, and Regem-melech and his men, to entreat the favor of Yahweh, ³ to speak to the priests of the House of Yahweh of Hosts and to the prophets:

"Should I weep in the fifth month, restricting myself as I have done all these years?"

⁴ Then the word of Yahweh of Hosts came to me: ⁵ "Speak to all the people of the land and to the priests:

When you fasted and lamented in the fifth [month] and in the seventh, these seventy years, was it really for me that you fasted? ⁶ For when you eat and when you drink, are you not eating and drinking for yourselves?"

NOTES

7:1. *in the fourth year . . . on the fourth [day] of the ninth month, in Kislev.* This is the third and final chronological heading in Zechariah (cf. NOTES to Zech 1:1 and 1:7). The Julian calendar equivalent is December 7, 518 B.C.E. Approximately two years have elapsed since the time of Zechariah's first utterances in the winter of 520, when the prophet Haggai was concluding his brief ministry (see NOTES to Hag 2:10 and 2:20), the last date for Haggai being December 18, 520. The activity referred to in the ensuing verses, the visit of the delegation from Bethel, presumably comes less than a year after the ceremony of temple refoundation alluded to in the prophetic vision of chapter 3. Although the reason for the visit seems to be to clarify the fast of the fifth month and hence the authority of Jerusalem (see below, v 3), the text of Zech 8:19 also mentions a fast to be observed in the tenth month, one that would be imminent and possibly involve an element of concern that would influence the delegation to come at this date to Zechariah for prophetic counsel.

Although the timing of this mission may have something to do with the sacral calendar, as the content of the delegation's query seems to indicate, the chronological information may well have significance that supersedes the simple meaning of the question posed. We have discussed at several points above, as in our Notes and Comment to Zechariah 3, the mechanisms by which Darius achieved control over the vast territories conquered for the most part by his predecessors, especially Cyrus. Darius's major achievements lay in the attention he gave to the administration of the various geographic regions and ethnic communities that were part of the Persian Empire. As Cook (1983) and the historians of ancient Persia who preceded him have pointed out, Darius chose to work through existing and responsible bodies within the system of satrapies and provinces that he organized or reorganized. In order to establish social order in these subunits of the empire, he promoted the use of existing legitimate institutions wherever appropriate. We have records of this practice for Egypt, and we infer this for Yehud on the basis of the intrinsic connection between temple building, priestly authority, and traditional sources for dealing with the regulation of daily life.

Darius's interest in semiautonomy for satraps and provinces is obvious, again with respect to Egypt, in his order for the codification of Egyptian laws that had existed up to the time of Cambyses. These laws included not only royal decrees and decisions but also religious practices and hitherto unwritten customary procedures (Olmstead 1948:142). Indeed, Diodorus (I 95) considered Darius one of the great law-givers for Egypt. Darius's treatment of Egypt with respect to its legal system may have culminated in a personal visit by the emperor sometime late in 518, although Cook (1983:60–61) disputes such a possibility. Whether or not he traveled to Egypt in the winter of 518–517, there can be no doubt that this was the time when he dispatched instructions in writing to the Egyptians concerning his policies with respect to their internal self-rule by traditional Egyptian law. At some point prior to December 30, 518, Darius wrote to Aryandes, his satrap in Egypt, about the standardization of Egyptian law (Olmstead 1948:142).

This kind of activity, near the end of 518 B.C.E., or in the second half of Darius's fourth regnal year, may be directly related to the appearance of the final two chapters of First Zechariah (Zech 1–8) and the related compilation of Haggai and all of First Zechariah. Two possibilities must be entertained. First, the known Egyptian policy of Darius might have been paralleled by a similar policy toward Yehud, which possessed a traditional native body of legal materials that could be utilized in the establishment of peace and order in the provincial subunit. In such a case Yehud, too, at the end of 518, would have had the opportunity of establishing self-rule. The second possibility is that although Darius might not have issued orders directly to Yehud at this time, information about his communication to Egypt would have been known in Yehud and would have stirred the expectation or hope that a similar policy would be instituted in Jerusalem. In either case the result would have been the same. The authority of traditional law was about to be mandated, and those in the position of transmitting and codifying that law were to be entrusted with its enforcement. Local social harmony would thereby be effected, contributing to the ultimate stability of the empire.

Such a development would be exactly the sort of situation which would have created in the cities of Judah, those formerly under the aegis of Jerusalem during the monarchy, the need for those cities to submit again to the rule of Jerusalem, which itself was subject to the Persian authorities. The delegation from Bethel, the major city (see below, Notes to Bethel, 7:2, and to "cities around it," 7:7) of the northern or Benjamin district of Judah/Yehud, had acceded to the authority of Jerusalem, which now rested in the hands of the "priests of the House of Yahweh" and also the prophets. Zechariah seized upon the occasion to respond to the delegation and then to give utterance to a series of oracles which further legitimized legal or covenant authority and connected it with the temple restoration project being completed at that time.

A further observation about the date in 7:1 can be made. The "ninth month" evokes memory of a preexilic event that took place in the ninth month of the fourth year of Jehoiakim's reign, or 605 (Jer 36:1). At that time, as the result of Nebuchadnezzar's march toward Egypt and conquest of Ashkelon (Bright 1981:326–27, n. 47), Jeremiah was aroused to prophesy in public. For reasons unclear to us, he could not do so in person and instead dictated his words so that his scribe Baruch could later deliver them to the intended audience in the temple. Jeremiah's language with reference to the fast of the ninth month (36:9) and the situation in 604 are not unlike Zechariah's language and the situation of December 518. Both involve a fast, the hearing of prophetic words (cf. 8:9 and NOTE to "from the mouths of the prophets"), and the attention of an eastern ruler (Nebuchadnezzar; Darius) toward his westernmost territories. Can this be mere coincidence?

Finally, we note that this date formula replicates only that of Hag 1:1 in the fact that it begins with the regnal year of the Persian monarch rather than with the month and day. An apparent additional instance of this, Hag 2:1, must be excluded because the year there precedes the month and day only because it occurs at the end of chapter 1 and does double duty for the dates of 1:15 and 2:1 (cf. last NOTE to Hag 1:15). Furthermore, in Zech 7:1 the day is given before the month, a situation reversing that of Hag 1:1 where the day follows the month. The first date in Haggai and the final one in Zechariah correspond in their structure, both initiating with the regnal year and containing a chiastic arrangement of the month and day. This situation sets the tone for Part Three, the final part of First Zechariah, which not only recapitulates some of the themes that occur earlier in Zechariah, but also expands upon or refers to, in language and in content, the material contained in Haggai. Chapters 7 and 8 of Zechariah therefore appear to be a conclusion to a Haggai-Zechariah composite work in which there is balance between the first unit (Haggai's two chapters) and the last (Zech 7 and 8). The intervening two sections—the oracular introduction of Zech 1:1–6 and the visions with oracles of Zech 1:7–6:15—are marked with chronological headings in which the regnal year follows the other calendrical data.

Since the heading provides the latest date in the Books of Haggai and First Zechariah, it is perhaps helpful to remind the reader that December 7, 518, falls by anyone's reckoning a full two, and more probably three, years before the rededication of the fully restored Second Temple on March 10, 515, or possibly 516 if the biblical headings count the accession year as year one (see Ezra 6:15). As we have stated above at several points, the absence of any reference to the ceremony of rededication makes it most plausible that the final editing of both Haggai and Zechariah 1–8 took place between December 7, 518, and March 10, 515, possibly in preparation for activities associated with the rededication.

(the word of Yahweh came). This formula, identical to the ones in Zech 1:1 and 1:7 minus the patronymic (see NOTE to 1:1; cf. below 7:8), interrupts the chronological heading. A similar oracular formula, announcing the transmission of a divine message, occurs in verse 4 and in 8:1 and 8:18, with the word "Hosts" appended to Yahweh in

two of those instances. Many commentators since Mitchell (1912:195) have taken this formula in 7:1 to be an interpolation. Indeed, the secondary nature of it is so apparent that we have added parentheses to indicate the break in the narrative heading. By so doing, we do not intend to suggest that its insertion is later than 515. Rather, since it corresponds to the formulas introducing Parts One (1:1) and Two (1:7), we suggest that the final editor at some time between 518 and 515 felt constrained to include the formula in the opening heading of Part Three, even if he then had to separate the day of the month from the regnal year of Darius. The inclusion of the oracular formula in verse 1 provides not only continuity with Parts One and Two of the Book of Zechariah but also offers legitimacy and additional clarity to the beginning of a section in which the prophet is to receive God's word. Comparison with Hag 1:1 shows that the proper place of the oracular formula would be after the date formula, and it is not clear what has caused the dislocation in this verse, with the text as it stands being in error.

2. *Bethel.* A place name that may be identified with an important city of the northern kingdom, the site of the syncretistic cult of the Kingdom of Israel in the time of Jeroboam I (1 Kgs 12:29), and with the district of Mizpah in the northern section of the province of Yehud in Persian times (see Map 3). Originally it was in the territory of Benjamin (Josh 18:13,22). Although several of the versions (Greek, Syriac, and Targum) take Bethel to be the accusative of direction, the context makes it quite clear that Bethel is the subject of the verb "sent." Another proposal, which we reject, makes Bethel the first element of a compound name, Bethel-Sar-ezer (see following NOTE on "Sar-ezer").

Bethel is situated some twelve miles north of Jerusalem. There is some disagreement as to what the correct number of districts in Yehud is and where their sites should be. We have followed Stern in this (1982:247–49) and refer the reader to the fairly complicated arguments of Kallai (1960:82–94) and Aharoni (1979:418), who differ on many specific points. The following information regarding the place names and the lists of returnees and their families is found in the Books of Ezra and Nehemiah: Ezra 2:21–35; Neh 3:1–22; 7:25–38; 11:25–35; 12:28–29 (Stern 1982:287; 1984:84).

The site of Bethel was first excavated by W. F. Albright in 1934 and later by J. L. Kelso in 1954, 1957, and 1960. Although there is some disagreement about the time of the destruction of the site, G. E. Wright, P. Lapp, and Stern argue convincingly that it took place in the fifth century B.C.E. Whether Bethel's demise should be dated to ca. 480, during the time of the Babylonian uprising, or slightly later, ca. 460, to the time of the Egyptian revolt, is still not clear (Stern 1982:31, 254). In any event, there seems little reason to doubt the existence of the site during the period under consideration. Indeed, Bethel probably occupied a prominent position among the cities of Benjamin that had come under the aegis of Jerusalem during the late preexilic period (cf. our NOTE to "cities around it" in 7:7). This fact may underlie the role Bethel plays in this passage. Apparently a substantial number of exiles from Bethel and Ai, some 223, returned from the Babylonian exile (Ezra 2:28). These individuals undoubtedly constituted a significant group that would be disposed to accept the reemerging power and authority of the Jerusalem temple establishment.

To be sure, Bethel is situated in the northern corner of the province of Yehud very close to Samaria, but there is no reason to conclude as some scholars have (e.g., Baldwin 1972:141) that the city fell under the influence of the province of Samaria in either religious or administrative matters. The mere fact that a delegation is sent to consult with "priests" and "prophets" (see NOTE in v 3 below) in Jerusalem suggests the degree to which Bethel and its population recognized the burgeoning power of the Jerusalem authorities.

Sar-ezer. Wellhausen was probably the first modern scholar to propose that Sar-ezer was only the second element of a compound name, the first element of which was the West Semitic theophoric Bethel (1898:186). This theophoric is well attested in neo-Babylonian and late Babylonian sources, and it is also attested in the Elephantine papyri. Hyatt was among the first to update the corpus of such Bethel names (1937). However, the simple name Sar-ezer, one of the sons of Sennacherib, occurs in 2 Kgs 19:37 and Isa 37:38, which also list his brother Adram-melech. The compound name Nergal-sar-ezer is attested in Jer 39:3. Hyatt's suggestion, which is followed by many contemporary scholars (e.g., Baldwin 1972:142; Thomas 1956:1082; Ackroyd 1968:206), that one Bit-ili-shar-uṣur, possibly a Babylonian official, is the same person as the putative individual in our Zechariah text must be rejected. Aside from linguistic considerations, the major reason for opposing such a view is that the individuals in the delegation appear, on the most simple reading of the text, to be Yahwists who mourn the temple's destruction and whose purpose is "to entreat the favor of Yahweh" (see NOTE below). As for the East Semitic character of the simple name Sar-ezer, we are in full agreement. If Sar-ezer represents an abbreviated, hypocoristic name, it is quite possible that the theophoric element had been intentionally dropped by Sar-ezer who would seem to be a Babylonian exile who has returned to Yehud. Mitchell (1912:196) long ago put forward such an interpretation. That Sar-ezer had special standing within the community is indicated by the fact that he has been sent as part of an official delegation.

Regem-melech. The second member of the delegation is also an individual of high standing in the community who apparently has authority over the men (or retinue) who accompany him. The name itself suggests that he is second in command though the secondary literature is replete with fanciful theories as to his possible identity. There are several examples of compound names in the Hebrew Bible with the element "melech" which means "king"—e.g., Nathan-melech (2 Kgs 23:11) or Ebed-melech (Jer 38:7), and the simple name Regem occurs in 1 Chron 2:47. The Syriac version, apparently under the influence of Jer 39:3 and 13, transcribes Rab-mag, which in Assyrian indicates a high royal official of some sort. At Ugarit the expression Regem-melech seems to refer to the king's spokesman (Gordon 1965:1010). There is no reason to conclude, however, as Ackroyd does, that Rab-mag (= Regem-melech) should be "thought of as a high royal official, no doubt a Jew (and conceivably a successor to Zerubbabel)" (1968:209).

It is impossible to decide with any degree of certainty whether Regem-melech was a returnee or a Palestinian. That he too had a position of leadership is clear from the context. The assertion that the meaning of his name suggests that he has a royal association, however, simply cannot be substantiated with any data. We have argued above (see NOTES to "Zerubbabel" and "governor" in Hag 1:1) that the royal line of the house of David was preserved through the institution of governors, a fairly complete list of which is now available. Regem-melech, whether born in Babylonia or

Palestine, has come with the delegation with a good deal of authority and recognition but not with a royal pedigree.

entreat the favor. The Hebrew phrase *lĕḥallôt ʾet-pānîm* (literally, "to mollify the face") occurs sixteen times in the Piel in the Hebrew Bible. The relationship of the verb *ḥlh* in this idiom to the Qal verb meaning "to be weak, sick" is uncertain. Most likely a separate root, otherwise unattested in Hebrew, is involved and has been integrated by affinity into the root *ḥlh* (Seybold 1980:407; Ap-Thomas 1956:239). Despite the difficulties in understanding the concrete meaning that would have been part of the original verb, the formulaic use of the expression can be well established. Most of the occurrences have Yahweh as the object and refer to a ceremonial appearance made before Yahweh. Such an appearance is invariably linked to the idea that an official human entreaty can persuade God to respond to the petitioner in some way, by changing his anger to favor (e.g., Exod 32:11; Jer 26:19) or by ensuring his assistance in the first instance (as in 1 Sam 13:12). Although "entreat the favor" is not a technical cultic term, a cultic act is apparently involved. In the passage in 1 Samuel 13, the mention of a burnt offering is juxtaposed with the account of Saul's entreaty to God in the face of a confrontation with the Philistines. The idiom belongs to the religious language of the laity (Seybold 1980:409).

The most noteworthy feature of the entreaty ceremony in Zechariah concerns the identity of the initiators of the ceremony. The subjects of this verbal phrase as it appears in preexilic literature are political or royal figures: Moses, Saul, Jehoahaz, Hezekiah, Manasseh, and Jeroboam (via a prophetic representative). Furthermore, all of these figures appear as subordinates to Yahweh, whose power over them is implicit in the very fact of their supplication. These two features of the idiom's usage allow us to make several observations about its meaning in Zechariah (here at 7:2; cf. 8:21–22). The delegation from Bethel recognizes the authority of Yahweh. It also presumably accepts the legitimacy of the personnel attached to Yahweh's sanctuary, the priests and prophets of verse 3. In short, the administrative restructuring of Yehud set forth by the temple visions in Part Two of Zechariah has been accepted not only in Jerusalem but also in the other cities of the subprovince (see NOTE to "the high priest" in Zech 3:1).

While these aspects of the formulaic use of "entreat the favor of Yahweh" seem clear, the matter of the relationship of the purpose of the delegation's entreaty to the purpose of entreaties recorded for the premonarchic period is less clear. There is no hint in this verse or in the two subsequent occurrences in Zechariah (8:21,22) that the officials are acting as a result of some calamity. Indeed, the ceremonial context of the phrase appears to be paramount and not directly related to the business that ensues. Officials have simply gained an audience with the supreme authority.

3. *priests . . . prophets.* Both prophet and priest in ancient Israel served to communicate Yahweh's will. The Bethel delegation, in seeking a ruling from Yahweh as sovereign, addresses itself in this case to both kinds of conveyers of God's word. This convergence of prophetic and priestly roles with respect to a single inquiry diverges from the information about such roles in preexilic sources. Normally it is either the prophet(s) (e.g., 1 Kgs 22:6ff.) or the priests (e.g., Judg 18:5; 1 Sam 22:10ff.) who are consulted. However, this appears to be a unique instance in which an official query is posed simultaneously to both prophet and priest. This consultation perhaps represents a new stage in the development of the traditional functions of these two kinds of

officials (see below our analysis of the question posed, v 3, and the nature of the response, vv 5–6). The enhanced status and enlarged responsibilities of the priesthood, as revealed in the prophetic vision in Zech 3:1–10, coincide with the diminution of prophetic activity in the postmonarchic world of the restoration. Prophecy is being absorbed by the temple domain where, historically in the ancient Near East and to a certain extent in Israel, it had always had its rightful place (cf. Blenkinsopp 1983:53–60, 251–55, and the literature cited).

House of Yahweh of Hosts. The usual term for temple, "House of Yahweh" (cf. Hag 1:2 and NOTE), is expanded here by the addition of "Hosts," a word that is a significant part of the vocabulary of postexilic prophecy (cf. NOTES to Hag 1:2; Zech 1:3). This expanded phrase is found in Hag 1:14, perhaps as an editorial supplement, and not again in the Haggai-Zechariah 1–8 work until this usage and a subsequent one in 8:9. Its appearance in the first section of Haggai and in the last section of Zechariah may be considered part of the conscious framing which brings these two prophetic works together into a single, continuous work.

"Should I . . . years?" From the point of view of form, this question put to both priests and prophets is of the sort that would be addressed to priests for an oracular response. Priestly divination characteristically responded to binary questions—that is, questions that could be answered "yes" or "no." Through the use of lots, perhaps the Urim and Thummim, decisions affecting an individual or a group could be made. As Huffmon has pointed out (1983:355–59), such procedures did not provide chance results. The situations posed for oracular comment really could tolerate only one answer. The divinatory process operated not to offer a true decision but rather to legitimize a course of action that was in fact already a predetermined choice. The function of divination was therefore an important one: it allowed critical matters of policy to be given divine sanction. The client and the public he represented would thereby be provided with the necessary assurance that the action in question was proper.

The biblical texts describing such oracular procedures characteristically deal with issues of major importance, particularly decisions about military strategy. Danger is often a component of the actions for which divination provides sanction. In the present instance, the question posed to priests and prophets does not appear to have such a quality. We can deal with this fact in one of two ways. First, it is possible that the biblical examples of this procedure have been included in the narratives of Joshua through Kings precisely because they represented difficult political situations, and that many other, and more mundane, issues were resolved by oracular consultation but have not been preserved in the biblical record. Second, the question posed by the Bethel delegation may in fact represent a more critical problem than its seemingly specific cultic formulation suggests.

The second alternative must receive serious consideration. Just as Haggai used priestly oracles as vehicles for prophetic undergirding of the temple restoration efforts, Zechariah would be expected to employ an oracular situation for equally weighty decisions. However, we would contend that it is the oracular situation itself (unlike that of Hag 2:12), rather than the content of the oracle, in which non-Jerusalemites seek advice from Jerusalem authorities, that constitutes a matter of major political importance. The question deals with an action that signifies continued loyalty to Yahweh after the termination of political independence in Judah. Now, with the rebuilding of the temple, the inhabitants of Jerusalem itself are obviously to come under the aegis of the temple establishment which formed the infrastructure of local governance under Persian domination. But how were non-Jerusalemites to respond to this development? The Bethel delegation represents the cities around Jerusalem (cf. 7:7) which, along with the settlements of the Negev and the Shephelah, composed the latest preexilic kingdom. The official character of the delegation, implied by the use of the idiom "entreat the favor of Yahweh" (cf. NOTE, 7:2), makes it clear that a highly significant political-religious question is at stake (cf. NOTES to "peoples," 8:20). Finally, the ensuing response (vv 5–6) is addressed to a wider public and a direct "yes" (the foregone response) is not ever articulated; both actions place the question within the pattern of oracular divination that addresses critical public problems.

Should I weep. The Hebrew root *bkh* denotes crying in general. It can also, as in this instance in which it is related to fasting and lamenting (cf. 7:5), describe a formalized collective response to an impending or existing public distress (Hamp 1975:119). Since the delegation is an official one, and since the oracular question deals with a sensitive political problem on formal grounds, formalized public weeping is no doubt the meaning of the word here. While the delegation consisted of a party of at least several men, one individual—probably the first-mentioned Sar-ezer—actually framed the oracular query. Speaking in the first person, he nonetheless represents the group he leads as well as the community that dispatched him. The response he evokes is addressed to a large audience and the verbs are in the plural.

the fifth month. An official lament had evidently been instituted in response to the trauma of the destruction of the temple, the palace, and the city of Jerusalem. According to 2 Kgs 25:8, this calamitous event took place on the seventh day of the fifth month in the nineteenth year of Nebuchadnezzar's reign. Since the superscription in 7:1 provides a date in November of 518, the question concerns a mourning ritual which had already been performed for nearly seventy years. The next possible observation of that ritual would be less than a year away and would be the seventieth year. The temple is nearly functional again in Jerusalem; should its existence be recognized, so precluding commemorative fasts, in the cities of Yehud as well? The theme of the fifth month is echoed in the answer to the query in verse 5, where an additional fast day is mentioned, and also in the eschatological oracle of 8:19, where two more fast days are included. That this fast serves as the *raison d'être* for the Bethelite mission, and is mentioned twice again, probably arises from the fact that already in the sixth century B.C.E. it had achieved its place as one of the most important fast days in Jewish tradition (cf. NOTES to 7:5 and 8:19), second only to the Day of Atonement which was probably celebrated in some form already in First Temple times (cf. Haran 1980:291–92).

restricting myself. The Niphal of the root *nzr* has a cultic connotation, particularly as it is used in the Nazirite vows in Numbers 6:2–6. Its use in association with mourning rites here is problematic. Does it refer to an unspecified dietary aspect of Sar-ezer's mourning? Does it mean an abstinence annually at the fifth month? Or does it refer to an ongoing practice? The infinitive absolute of *nzr* appears to do double duty. It makes weeping a kind of setting apart or distinctive behavior that is practiced in the fifth month; it also indicates that certain special observations have been carried out consistently since the destruction. Nazirite behavior entails a variety of restrictions, but the context here apparently makes the use of the verb *nzr* a reference to dietary restrictions. In verse 5, fasting is linked with lamenting; in verse 6, eating and drinking are at issue. The act of mourning, which includes abstaining from food or drink, has been practiced in the fifth month by the delegation and those they represent in the years since the destruction.

all these years. This is an obvious allusion to the imminent completion of the temple, which has lain destroyed for so long, and to the termination of the seventy-year prophecy proclaimed by Jeremiah (25:11–12 and 29:10) and recapitulated by Zechariah in 1:12 (see NOTE to "these seventy years") and in 7:5. The nonspecific language of this verse is clarified in the amplification of verse 5. The point at issue for the delegation, however, is whether or not their behavior might be changed now that the temple is about to be rededicated and now that the Jerusalem establishment in its nonmonarchical form has reasserted its authority.

4. *Then the word of Yahweh of Hosts came to me:.* This standard statement is a sign of the message transmission phase of prophetic activity and precedes the delivery of the oracle itself, which is often (although not in this instance) introduced by a further authoritative formula, "Thus said/spoke Yahweh (of Hosts)." See our discussion at Hag 1:2.

5. *all the people of the land.* Yahweh's word comes to Zechariah with the command that he speak not simply to the delegation from Bethel but also to the "people of the land." This phrase, as we have indicated in our NOTE to Hag 2:4, refers to citizenry, especially in light of the way Haggai uses it in establishing the legitimacy of the temple work. Insofar as the Bethel contingent is a delegation, meant to convey some response back to the wider public represented by "Bethel," this oracular address to "all the people of the land" rather than to Sar-ezer alone is not out of place. The question really concerns the issue of whether the phrase is meant to indicate the citizenry of Yehud as a whole, and not simply that of Bethel. We would prefer the former option, for two reasons. First, the phrase is paired with "priests," who represent the internal leadership of Yehud in the postexilic period and thus the natural counterpoint to a general designation for citizenry. It is not simply because the ensuing oracle has cultic content that the priests also need to be apprised. A matter of national policy is at issue, and both leaders and the people are the proper objects of the oracular address. Second, the retrospection that follows the oracle specifically mentions all the territory of Yehud beyond Jerusalem. In combination with that inclusive geographical language, the audience of verse 5 is likely to be similarly diverse and all-inclusive.

priests. As we have noted above, the priests here are national leaders of Yehud, the complement to the citizenry which the phrase "all the people of the land" denotes. We find no basis for identifying "priests" as corrupt Bethel functionaries, schismatic Samaritans (cf. Mason 1979a:65; Ackroyd 1968:206–8), or enemies of Yehud (see Ezra 4:1). While the query of verse 3 is addressed to both priests and prophets, it is a priestly question in form. Yet the response is not a priestly response; it is not the foregone "yes" or "no" one would expect. The response is a prophetic one, introducing a profound message that transcends cultic detail. Therefore the priests have been relegated to audience; they are not conveyers of this kind of oracular response.

fasted and lamented. The combination of words meaning fasting and weeping or lamenting is also known to us from the story of the death of David's first son, by

Uriah's wife Bathsheba. In the story of David and his son (2 Sam 12:21,22), the fasting and weeping *(bkh)* were carried out while the child was still alive and in the hope that God would take pity on the child because of David's action. David used fasting and weeping as a praying practice or as an intercessory measure, in order to save the child's life and so to achieve the avoidance of mourning. In contrast, in this case the interrelated actions of fasting and weeping clearly come in response to loss. They were observed as fast days in remembrance of the destruction of the temple (2 Kgs 25:8–9; Jer 52:12ff.) in the fifth month, and of the assassination in the seventh month of Gedaliah whom Nebuchadnezzar had appointed governor over Judah after the fall of Jerusalem (2 Kgs 25:25; Jer 41:1ff.). The combination of the second-person plural *ṣwm* ("fast") plus the infinitive absolute of *spd* ("lament") effectively conveys the interrelatedness of these actions and their intensity. The two terms together also provide an absolute contrast with the eating and drinking of verse 6 (see NOTE below to "eat . . . drink"). Just as eating and drinking together convey the intensified meaning of full meal or satiety, so too does the pairing of fasting and lamenting convey the profound quality of deep mourning.

in the fifth [month]. As indicated above, this is a reference to the fast commemorating the destruction of Jerusalem and its temple in 587 or 586 in the month of Ab. According to 2 Kgs 25:8, the actual day is recorded as being the seventh, while in Jer 52:12 it is mentioned as being the tenth. The absence of the actual word for month poses no problem here and is also not utilized in the elaboration of this oracle in Zech 8:19. In the three headings in the Book of Zechariah, however, the word for month is used (1:1,7; 7:1) as it is in the Book of Haggai (1:1,15; 2:1,20). It is interesting that it is omitted in the two internal oracular portions of Haggai where the chronological information is presented in a slightly abbreviated way. The shortened form may well be the result of the final editorial process.

in the seventh. This probably refers to a fast held in memory of the murder of Gedaliah, the governor installed by the Babylonians in Jerusalem (2 Kgs 25:25; Jer 41:1–3). Gedaliah, the scion of a prominent Jerusalem family, was assassinated along with his companions by Judean nationalists who evidently felt that in accepting the governorship he was collaborating with the enemy. Although the biblical text specifies the seventh month (October), the year is not supplied. It is not clear whether only two months or several years and two months had elapsed since the destruction of Jerusalem in the fifth month. Although it might seem that a longer period of time would be needed to account for the activities undertaken under the rule of Gedaliah, it is also possible to argue that the assassination took place before he had a chance to consolidate his power and eliminate his opponents. Whenever it had occurred, the fast held to mark this event, the termination of even a semblance of Judean self-rule until the Persians came upon the scene many decades later, persists in Jewish tradition as does the fifth-month fast. The latter, commemorating the destruction of Jerusalem, is a full fast; and the former, known as the Fast of Gedaliah, is a half fast.

these seventy years. This is an explicit reference to the near completion of the years between the destruction of Jerusalem and the present passage (587–518). If we reckon from 587 to 518, then the oracle can be dated to the seventieth year itself, which is significant since it shows that the actual dedication of the restored temple as a historical event is correctly dated in Ezra at least two years later (Ezra 6:14–16). Ezra cites the sixth year of Darius, 516, as the time of the completion of the temple and its dedication. That date postdates the expected restoration of the temple by two years and therefore must be considered one of two possible dates for the rededication. Taking 586 instead for the destruction of Jerusalem, we arrive at the more familiar date of 515 B.C.E. See above NOTES to "all these years" in verse 3 and to "these seventy years" in Zech 1:12.

was it really for me that you fasted? The second-person plural *ṣamtûnî* has had the pronominal suffix added, a rather infrequent occurrence in the Hebrew Bible (cf. Num 20:5 and 21:5). Just as unusual, however, would be the phenomenon of an intransitive verb *(ṣwm)* seemingly becoming transitive as a consequence of the modification of its original meaning, so *GKC* § 117x. This would be the reason why the verb "fast" has had to absorb an accusative suffix. Literally the text reads: "did you fast at all for me, even for me?" However, the suffix can be described as dative, substituting for the normal or expected prepositional phrase. The use of the dative suffix is quite common in poetry and also in the case of elevated prose, such as the oracular prophetic utterance of this verse. This elevated discourse or prose-poetry is the sort of context in which the force of the preposition would be present but not the preposition itself.

6. *eat . . . drink.* Although the word "to eat" is found far more frequently than the word "to drink" in the Hebrew Bible, both are common terms. The appearance of the two verbs together, as in other Semitic languages, intensifies whatever meanings are appropriate to the particular context. "Ate" and "drank" together imply a full meal, or satiety (e.g., Gen 25:34). The most basic meaning, of course, is the consumption of food and drink in order to sustain life. That aspect is clearly present in this text, since the benefits to the individuals are pointed out in the oracle. However, eating and drinking are also, in this context, contrasted with fasting and mourning. Thus a connotation of celebration, or of festal meals, is perhaps also present as part of the range of meanings that "eat" and "drink" provide in combination. Since the oracle containing those words is addressed specifically to priests along with the "people of the land," it would not be out of place to posit a reference to cultic meals, or to the partaking of sacrificial portions.

COMMENT

The third part of Zechariah 1–8 begins, as do Haggai and the first two parts, with a chronological heading specifying the regnal year of Darius as well as the month and the day. As in Haggai 1:2, this information is arranged with the year as the first item, giving the reader or listener who has been following these postexilic prophets from Haggai through the first six chapters of Zechariah a sense that a prophetic work is being concluded. And indeed, as we have discussed in some detail above, Zechariah 7–8, as might be expected of the concluding unit in a Hebrew work, does correspond in many ways with the two chapters of Haggai.

These concluding chapters of the Haggai-Zechariah 1–8 corpus have their own introductory passage, which lays out for the audience the time setting, the place, the cast of characters, and the situation that is the stimulus for the three subunits of prophetic utterances that make up the rest of Part Three. We shall consider each of these features in turn.

Unlike the eight other chronological markers of Haggai-Zechariah 1–8, 7:1 presents us with a date in the fourth, and not in the second, year of Darius. The events and the associated oracles that constitute Haggai and Zechariah 1–6 are clustered at the end of 520 B.C.E. and the beginning of 519. This section is attributed to a time nearly two years later than the last date provided, namely February 519, which appears in the superscription (1:7) to the visions, or Part Two, of Zechariah. Zechariah 7–8 in this way stands apart. The prophet's world is not the same, nearly two years later, as it was in 520 with respect to both Persian policy and Yehudite activity. The content of Zechariah 7–8 reflects this shift.

What can be said about the world of 518 that differentiates it from 520, at least as far as the inhabitants of Yehud are concerned? The reader can review the information we have provided in our first NOTE to 7:1 about the chronological heading. December 7, 518, coincides with the time in which Darius had issued orders for the Egyptians to codify their traditional legal heritage and use that body of material to govern and adjudicate internal Egyptian affairs. No direct evidence exists for an equivalent mandate to have been issued to Yehud at this time. But we have postulated that because of the proximity of Yehud to Egypt as well as because of the prior attention given to both Egypt and Yehud (among others) with respect to the revitalization of temples, Yehud at this time was also under some pressure to order the legal underpinnings of its community life.

Temple building, as we have asserted in our discussion of various parts of Haggai and Zechariah 1–6, was a critical beginning step, initiated through Persian policy, in the establishment of Yehudite self-governance within the imperial structure. It provided a physical setting and legitimization for indigenous leaders—i.e., priests—who would attend to local internal affairs in cooperation with the Persian-appointed governor, who would handle relations with the empire, mainly by providing the requisite tribute. All of Haggai reverberates with the efforts made in 520 to begin the restoration of the temple. Zechariah picks up that theme in his set of visions and oracles and adds to it his program for the leadership associated with the temple in this postmonarchic era. The priesthood emerges as the key to Yehudite governance, although Zechariah wisely and skillfully retains the strong monarchic component that normally accompanied temple building and that was the dominant feature of Yehud's political heritage.

The events and prophecies of 520–519 dealt with temple and priesthood, yet one other element essential for Yehudite stability was lacking: an authoritative legal system that could resolve community problems and dispel contention among individuals in their everyday affairs. With temple construction well under way under the direction of the high priest Joshua and his cohorts, the end of 518 saw the matter of governing procedures, not personnel, brought to the fore, probably by Persian policy, either through the example of orders to Egypt or perhaps even directly to Yehud through documents or messages not known to us. Concern for justice and references to Yahweh's words and the Torah are recurrent features of Zechariah 7–8 and support our view that the authorization of traditional law (covenant and prophecy) was the event that stimulated Part Three of First Zechariah.

Reference to Persian policy and its effect on Yehud does not exhaust the significance of the year 518 for Part Three. As the response itself (7:5b–6) to the oracular question indicates, 518 marked the imminent termination of the seventy-year period. That symbolic time span, which already figures in the prophecies of Zechariah (1:12), represented a fixed term of divine punishment after which restoration could occur. Although it is not a literal number, the near completion of the span and process it represented was obviously a factor in the positive response by Yehud in 520 to the task of temple restoration. And it would have been a further impetus in the reestablishment of other aspects of preexilic life as Darius went forward with his imperial reorganization in 518.

The significance of the time setting requires considerable effort to comprehend. Not so for the place. There is movement of people, a delegation from Bethel, toward Jerusalem. Jerusalem is not specified by name, at least not until the rhetorical question (7:7) which initiates the second subunit. Yet because the delegation leaves Bethel and then entreats Yahweh through the priests of God's house, or temple, as well as the prophets, can any setting other than Jerusalem be possible? Although the oracular question is posed by the delegation in Jerusalem in the vicinity of the partially restored temple, the fact that the people involved are non-Jerusalemites has the powerful effect, immediately upon the appearance of the toponym Bethel at the beginning of 7:2, of widening the scope of Part Three. Jerusalem's authority is being recognized, as the idiom "entreat the favor" suggests, by the larger community of Yehud. Bethel is the city that represents that larger community perhaps because of its leading role among the cities of Judah in the late preexilic era. Although other cities of Judah play a role in Part Two of First Zechariah, they do so only in a future or eschatological setting; here the area beyond Jerusalem figures in the business of the prophet's own day. The focal point of Jerusalem and the temple is thereby expanded. Ultimately Zechariah, in the last subunit (Judah and the Nations: Three Oracles), will expand the circle of those who acknowledge Yahweh in Jerusalem even further, to its full global extent.

The Introduction to Part Three provides us with a full cast of characters. Darius presides in the background, through the inclusion of his regnal year in the date formula. Zechariah too is named in the insertion of the message transmission formula. Thereupon two individuals from Bethel are listed. Their names are fraught with exegetical difficulties, which we have examined in our NOTES. We have concluded that the text gives us two personal names, Sarezer and Regem-melech. The former individual may well have been, like one or more of the persons mentioned in Zechariah 6:10 and 14, a returned exile because he bore (like Zerubbabel himself) a Babylonian name.

In addition to the four individuals noted by name in 7:1–2, three groups of people appear in the Introduction. First, the priests attached to the temple appear as the ones to whom the Bethel delegation directs its query and also the ones to whom the oracular response is given. Although the temple itself would not yet have been fully restored, it is clear that its priesthood is active. Probably the altar was functional and the sacrificial cult was partially in effect; the priests no doubt were involved in overseeing the temple work as well as in generally administering the province. Next the text informs us that the delegation from Bethel addresses its queries to the prophets as well as the priests. Surely Zechariah is one of them and other prophetic figures are also present, but it is unlikely that Haggai is there. His whereabouts at that time are unknown, and he probably never uttered another prophecy after the potentially inflammatory oracle of Haggai 2:22–23 in the second year of Darius (cf. NOTES to Hag 2:10). Whoever the "prophets" were that the delegation addressed, Zechariah is the one who utters the oracular response to the inquiry. Finally "all the people of the land" are mentioned. The exact meaning of this designation is problematic; it evidently has shifting meanings throughout the long history of its usage in ancient Israel. We tend to place it closer to its prevailing preexilic meaning of citizenry rather than to its later postexilic meaning of simple folk. Although "Bethel" has asked a question, the answer is directed to everyone: general population plus leadership, as represented by "all the people of the land" plus "priests."

The situation portrayed in the Introduction to Part Three involves an oracular question submitted to those who are qualified to provide an oracular response and then the delivery of such a response. We learn several things from this scenario. First and foremost, the acknowledgment by non-Jerusalemites of Jerusalem's authority is established, as we have already indicated. The way is thereby paved for the recurrent emphasis on justice in the subunits that follow, as well as for the ultimate inclusion of all nations among those who acknowledge the supremacy of Jerusalem. We also become aware that descendants of the Judeans conquered in 587 have maintained for nearly seventy years their identification with the nation-state of Judah that had existed for several hundred years in southern Palestine. They have practiced regular mourning rites "all these years." The observance of not one fast day per year (7:3), but rather of at least two (7:5) if not four (8:19), obviously signifies the pervasive and persistent influence of the destruction on its survivors. The cessation of Judean independence clearly held a prominent place in the collective consciousness of the inhabitants of Bethel and probably of other former Judean cities. Therefore the restoration of at least some of the institutions (temple; priesthood) that had characterized the preexilic polity provoked the issue of whether or not to continue to mourn the loss of the monarchic state.

That the delegation addresses both prophets and priests with its oracular question also deserves comment. Our NOTES explore this matter, and we only reiterate here our suggestion that the mention of the two groups, where we would expect to see one or the other, reflects shifting configurations of prophetic vis-à-vis priestly functions in the postmonarchic world. The priesthood is in an ascendant position, taking over as it does in the late sixth century some of the political-juridical responsibilities that the palace bureaucracy had held during dynastic rule. Yet the response is evidently a prophetic one: the yes or no form that would characterize an answer to an oracular question as posed to priests does not materialize; the priests themselves become audience to the oracle. The entire audience for the oracle is far more inclusive than the delegation members or the specific community they represent, and the answer does not really offer a direct response to the query but rather uses the query to launch a broader or more profound message. These features of the prophetic response in Zechariah set it apart from a somewhat analogous query in Haggai 2:12–14, where the priests provide their perfunctory yes-no replies and then, as a separate step, the prophet appends his oracular interpretation.

How then are we to understand Zechariah's oracular response of 7:5b–6? It is provocative in nature by the very form in which it is cast—viz., a pair of rhetorical questions. It also does not directly answer the question. What it does is draw attention to the function of fasting on the one hand and feasting on the other hand in the lives of those who observe such occasions. The "eating and drinking" are communal festal meals and are not individual family banquets in this context. Together, the mourning and the celebratory behavior constitute all manner of public rites which provided continuity, after the destruction, with the formal national life that had terminated in 587. In other words, national identity without an accompanying political structure was sustained through the observance of these occasions, all of which have historical content.

This meaning of the oracular response is not obvious, and the result of our analysis remains somewhat tenuous. However, we did follow certain clues. We took seriously the matter of the audience addressed by 7:5b–6 as well as the content of the message itself. The audience, we repeat, is larger than the Bethel delegation; it consists of the general population and its leaders. Therefore the "you" and "yourselves" (second person plural) in the language of the oracle have this inclusive audience as their antecedent. The questions are not directed to individuals, nor is any individual, spiritual effect of mourning or celebrating at issue. The feasting and fasting would have been ongoing activities on the part of all the descendants of the Judeans. Cultural continuity with the preexilic state persisted during the seventy years in which a formal political structure was absent.

The prophetic answer redirects the question. It is not a matter of should you or shouldn't you fast. Rather the issue is one of recognizing what that fasting and its complement, the feasting, have accomplished in the seventy years. At this critical moment, with local authority and quasi-autonomy being reestablished, and with the seventy years of destruction nearly at an end, the emphasis on awareness of continuity with the preexilic state offers support and encouragement to those for whom self-rule without the revival of a Davidic monarchy might be difficult to conceptualize and accept. The prophet thus reminds them that they have been behaving in certain public ways, to their own benefit in sustaining community identity, even without dynastic rule or temple focus. The people had inaugurated fasts in response to certain events. Yahweh had not commanded the people to fast nor would he tell them to stop fasting: God was not the beneficiary of such acts (see Friedman 1983:5–12).

13. ADDRESS TO THE DELEGATION FROM BETHEL: FURTHER RETROSPECTION ON DIVINE JUSTICE
(7:7–14)

[7] Are these not the words which Yahweh proclaimed through the earlier prophets, when Jerusalem was inhabited and secure along with its cities around it, and when the Negev and the Shephelah were inhabited? [8] (The word of Yahweh came to Zechariah:) [9] Thus spoke Yahweh of Hosts:

Judge with true justice and act with love and compassion toward one another. [10] Do not oppress the widow and the orphan, the sojourner and the poor; and do not devise evil in your hearts against one another.

[11] But they refused to give heed; and they set a defiant shoulder. Their ears they dulled from hearing; [12] and they made their hearts stony lest they hear the Torah and the words which Yahweh of Hosts sent by his spirit through the earlier prophets. Then great wrath came from Yahweh of Hosts. [13] Thus it was when he proclaimed but they did not listen.

So they will call out and I will not listen—said Yahweh of Hosts. [14] I have strewn them among all the nations which they have not known. The land was left wasted behind them, with no one moving about. Thus they made a desirable land into a wasteland.

NOTES

7. *Are these . . . ?* The language of this verse is highly reminiscent of the oracular material of Part One of First Zechariah and also of the oracular sections of the visions of Part Two. In particular, this reference to the preexilic prophets picks up upon the language of 1:4–6. The tone of that retrospective oracle is established to a certain extent by the probing statements of 1:5–6, in which a series of rhetorical questions are put to the prophet's audience. This retrospective section of Part Three (7:7–14) connects with the interrogatives of the conclusion (1:6) of the retrospective oracle of Part One by opening with a rhetorical question of its own. The form of this section, in addition to the specific word choice, thus links it with chapter 1. In the previous

instance (1:4–6), the rhetorical queries follow the quoted words of the preexilic prophets; here the query precedes them.

words. As we have noted above (NOTE to Zech 1:1), the substantive "word" *(dābār)* is a term for prophecy; when linked with Yahweh, it represents divine revelation. The reference to the "words" in association with the "earlier prophets" duplicates the pairing of "words" and "earlier prophets" in 1:6. However, in this instance "words" is not accompanied by "statutes," in contrast with the language of 1:6. The omission here is elliptical, since the actual oracle of verses 9–10 obviously presents divine commandments which could be classified as "statutes." The combination "words and statutes" of 1:6 may in fact be a hendiadys, with statutes constituting the specific aspect of the divine revelation indicated by "words" (cf. NOTE to "words and statutes," Zech 1:6).

The noun "words" is in the nominative, yet is preceded by the particle *ʾet,* which usually introduces a direct object. This feature is probably a characteristic of Late Biblical Hebrew (Polzin 1976:32–37).

proclaimed. Of the many verbs which take "words" as the object, "proclaim" is used infrequently. The root *qrʾ* means "read" as well as "proclaim." Hence, the hint of God's word as concretized in the covenant or in some other fixed (written) form following its oral transmission by the prophet is provided. Jer 36:6–8 refers to an occasion on which Baruch reads Yahweh's words from a scroll that Jeremiah has dictated, and 2 Kgs 23:2 describes Josiah's public reading of Yahweh's words. For a full discussion of this verb in prophetic contexts, see our NOTE to 1:14, where the imperative of *qrʾ* introduces the three oracles which conclude the first vision, and also the discussion in the NOTES to "proclaimed" and "they will call out" in 7:13 below.

earlier prophets. These are preexilic prophets, as in Zech 1:4 (see NOTE; also cf. 1:6), in the oracle of Part One of First Zechariah. The theme of recalling traditional prophetic pronouncements and the people's response—or lack of response—is the central feature of this third part of Zechariah. Zechariah reviews past oracles delivered by the prophets, relates the results, considers the present situation, and looks toward the future. Each step of the way, prophetic utterance is invoked: earlier prophets (here and in 7:12), present prophets (8:9), and the prophet Zechariah's own oracular conclusion (8:18ff.).

Jerusalem was inhabited. The oracular language of 2:8 (RSV 2:4; cf. NOTES to that verse) is reflected in this statement, although the correspondence is not exact. The oracle included in the third vision describes a future Jerusalem: "Jerusalem and its villages will be inhabited." Here, the past Jerusalem is similarly depicted: an inhabited city, not a desolate one as was the case during much of the exilic period. The context of the future Jerusalem is "its villages," unwalled settlements able to survive peacefully in the eschatological age. Here the context is described differently, as befits the past historical setting; see the following two NOTES.

secure. Although Zechariah does not elsewhere use this word *(šēlēwâ),* its meaning here clearly lies at the "security" end of the range of meanings it exhibits. While "ease" or "prosperity" would not be inappropriate, the relationship of this verse to 2:8–9 (RSV 2:4–5) mandates the choice we have made. In 2:9 (RSV 2:5), Jerusalem will become populous and Yahweh will protect it ("wall of fire"); in 7:7, Jerusalem was populous and secure, presumably because of its own walls and the network of walled cities associated with it. Note the contrast between unwalled villages of 2:8 (RSV 2:4) and cities (= walled settlements) of this passage. Consider also the use of this word in parallel with another word for security *(bṭḥ)* in a passage describing an unfortified nation, in Jer 49:31.

cities around it. The mention of cities, which are fortified settlements in ancient Palestine, in association with Jerusalem gives this phrase a decidedly political, territorial cast. Jerusalem and its hinterland, with respect to the satellite communities comprising the urban-rural continuum typical of Palestinian cities, would be indicated by "Jerusalem and its daughters" or "Jerusalem and its villages *(ḥāṣērîm)*." Only in one other place are cities mentioned as subsidiaries of another city (Josh 10:39, with respect to Debir), and there are textual problems with that occurrence (see the discussion in Frick 1977:56–57). Because "around it," in reference to Jerusalem, is coupled with "cities of Judah" in earlier prophetic sources (e.g., Jer 17:26), the "Jerusalem . . . with its cities around it" of this verse appears to be a designation for the urban settlements that composed preexilic Judah. "Judah" is not specified in this instance, perhaps because the prophet is accommodating the situation of his own day when Judah no longer exists. The picture here therefore is not of a city or city-state with its supporting villages, but rather of a capital city of a larger political entity including many cities, each with its secondary settlements, all acknowledging the administrative authority of Jerusalem. The picture is completed by the conclusion of this verse, which refers to the rest of the territory, less populous than areas in which cities dominated the geographic and demographic landscape, controlled by Judah in the preexilic period.

One cannot be certain that Zechariah had access to accurate information about the size or shape of Judah in the early sixth century. However, his use of Jerusalem and her cities, and then "Negev" and "Shephelah," reflects a region similar to that recorded in Neh 11:25–36, which is understood to depict the early sixth century and which records sites in three areas: in Benjamin, in the northern Negev, and in the Shephelah bordering Philistia (Aharoni and Avi-Yonah 1968: map 165). Since many of the cities in the Neh 11 list were not part of the Persian province of Yehud, the particular distribution of settlements recorded there may well reflect the late preexilic period (Aharoni 1979:91, 409–11; but cf. Stern 1982:245–46), as this passage in Zechariah specifies, or the period of Babylonian rule.

The Benjaminite cities are for the most part larger and exhibit far closer proximity to Jerusalem than do the settlements of the south and west. If such a threefold division of early sixth-century Judah is accurate, then Zechariah's terminology fits well, with "Jerusalem . . . along with its cities around it" denoting the more populous and urbanized Benjamin component. An interesting feature of the Benjaminite list in Neh 11:31–36 is that Bethel receives distinctive treatment. It is the only one of the fourteen cities of Benjamin which is said to have "villages." Apparently it was larger than the other cities of Benjamin or otherwise enjoyed the status of having secondary settlements. The fact that Bethel is the city sending a delegation to Jerusalem makes good sense. Bethel has a special place among Jerusalem's cities in the late preexilic period or during the time of Babylonian rule, which would have carried over into the early restoration (cf. NOTE to "Bethel" in v 2 above).

Bethel had been the leading shrine of the northern kingdom for centuries, and its importance clearly carries over into the period following the destruction of the northern kingdom in 722. The rivalry between Jerusalem and Bethel had been intense. It is no accident that the one serious example in the Primary History of the insertion of a prophecy after the fact concerns the prophetic denunciation of Bethel and the prediction that Josiah would one day destroy the place (1 Kgs 13:1–3; cf. 2 Kgs 23:15–20). Feelings in Judah against Bethel were strong. However, once its idolatrous high place had been destroyed by Josiah in 622 (or 628; cf. 2 Chron 34:3b–7) Bethel never again became a rival center. The success of Josiah's actions is reflected in this and the previous sections of Zechariah: the delegation from Bethel acknowledges the supremacy of the Jerusalem temple and priesthood.

Negev . . . Shephelah. As we have described above, settlements in the northern Negev and in the area of the Shephelah adjacent to Philistia apparently constituted, along with Benjamin, the extent of Judah on the eve of the destruction. Incomplete as it may be, archaeological evidence reveals early sixth-century strata for sites such as Lachish (cf. Neh 11:30) in the Shephelah and Beersheba (Neh 11:27) in the Negev. Note that this short list in Zechariah can be compared with the list of Jer 17:26, except that "hill country" is here omitted; cf. also the change in the designation of Jerusalem.

8. *(The word of Yahweh came to Zechariah:).* This is virtually the same formula that appears above in verse 1 and occurs often in Zechariah in nearly identical form, with "of Hosts" added after Yahweh. The first two occurrences are in Zech 1:1 and 1:7 and contain the prophet's patronymic. The intrusive and parenthetical nature of this clause in verse 8, as in verse 1 (cf. NOTE above to "the word of Yahweh . . ." in 7:1), supports the view that Part Three is a collection of oracular materials appended to the visions of Zechariah to complete the book. The two rather intrusive occurrences here in chapter 7 provide evidence of the final editorial process in which the three parts of First Zechariah were arranged. The formulaic language in Part Three echoes that of Parts One and Two and tends to bind the whole of First Zechariah together and also to connect First Zechariah with Haggai.

The appearance of this formula here introduces, as it does in 8:1 and 18 with Yahweh of Hosts, a separate section within the larger cluster of oracular material. In 8:1 the formula precedes the seven oracles we have entitled "Zion and Judah Restored"; in 8:18 it comes before the three oracles called "Judah and the Nations." In this passage the four precepts of 8:9–10 constitute the oracular material announced by the formula.

9. *Thus spoke Yahweh of Hosts:.* This is the fourteenth of a total of twenty-four occurrences of this formula, five of which are in Haggai and nineteen of which are in Zechariah 1–8. In every instance it appears either in oracular material or in material that can be said to be the work of an editor. Its appearance here within the Retrospection on Divine Justice serves to demarcate oracular statements that were probably part of the original utterances of the prophet. The remainder of the material in chapters 7 and 8 is undoubtedly part of a larger body of oracular sayings uttered by the prophet or a disciple and now, before publication in 515, deemed worthy of inclusion in the composite work.

The last ten occurrences of the formula are found in chapter 8 (8:2,3,4, 6,7,9,14,19,20,23), where they seem to introduce a diverse collection of oracular sayings that are appended as a conclusion to the work as a whole. As Mullen (1980) has pointed out, this formula suggests that the content of these oracles was probably originally delivered orally and introduced by the words of the formula itself (cf. NOTES to Hag 1:1 and Zech 1:3).

Judge with true justice. This is the first of two positive precepts enunciated in verse 9. The importance of carrying out this command is conveyed by the prophet as he places it first among four. It helps to demonstrate the centrality of the teaching of justice in ancient Israel. Also, with the negative formulation of a similar idea at the end of verse 10 it provides a framework for this set of four stipulations. Although the root *špt* ("to judge") can have a narrow legal and judicial connotation, its use here in the cognate verb and noun conveys the idea of the general social justice and harmony that derive from proper action between individuals. Such behavior is at the heart of the idea of covenant justice and is a theme that is repeated in almost the same way in 8:16. Here the precept concludes with *mišpaṭ ʾĕmet* ("true justice"); there it concludes with *mišpaṭ šālôm* ("complete justice"; cf. the expression *tôrat ʾĕmet,* "true Torah," in Mal 2:6). The two sets of precepts would appear to be even closer from a literary point of view: both have four commands, the first two of which are positive and the second two of which are negative.

The Hebrew text of "Judge with true justice" omits the preposition "with." This is another example (cf. NOTE to "was it really for me that you fasted?" 7:5) of a dative construction, in which the nouns are in an adverbial or dative relationship with the verb rather than an accusative one. The normal usage with the preposition included is superseded here, in the context of elevated, oracular prose, by an archaic or poetic construction in which the preposition is not used.

with love and compassion. The linkage between "love" *(ḥesed)* and "compassion" *(raḥămîm)* is not at all unusual; it is found, e.g., in Ps 77:9–10 (RSV 77:8–9); 103:4; Jer 16:5; and Hos 2:21 (RSV 2:19). *Ḥesed* is also often paired with such words as *ʾĕmet* ("truth"), as in Gen 24:27; Ps 25:10; 40:11,12 (RSV 40:10–11); and *ʾĕmûnâ* ("faith"), Ps 89:25 (RSV 89:24); 98:3. The effect in Zechariah is to express the idea of the total love of which compassion is a part. "Love" and "compassion" together form a hendiadys: compassionate love. The carrying out of "true justice" is to be complemented by acting with compassionate love toward one's fellow human beings, "toward one another." The order of this precept with respect to the preceding one is reminiscent of Micah 6:8, where "doing justly" comes before "loving mercy" *(ʾahăbat ḥesed)* and of Deut 10:18, where "justice" comes before "love." This love, with respect to the four oppressed groups listed in the next verse, can be equated with charitable acts; note that in Deut 10:18 the matter of loving the sojourner is given specific content: "giving food and clothing to him." Acting with compassionate love—i.e., charity—is equivalent to the behavior stipulated in negative form in the next, or third, command. The charitable attitude toward the four groups in verse 10 is also called for in the gleaning and tithing laws of the Pentateuch (Deut 14:28–29; 24:19–22; Lev 19:9–10; 23:22).

one another. This phrase is identical in Hebrew to the expression rendered "one another" in the next verse, except that in this verse the indicator particle *ʾt* precedes "another" and in verse 10 it is omitted.

10. *Do not oppress.* Heb. *ʿšq* can also mean "deprive, wrong." Since most biblical usages of this verb involve economic oppression, it could be rendered as "deprive," but that would be too weak a term. The economic overtones of the verb appear either as failure to pay what is owed to a hired (and poor) worker (e.g., Lev 19:13; Deut 24:14)

or as taking away the meager resources of the weaker groups in society (as in Hos 12:8 [RSV 12:7]; Lev 5:23 [RSV 6:4]; Ezek 22:29). The latter situation, involving theft and lying, might be termed extortion; indeed the verb "to extort" *(gzl)* is often found parallel to *ʿšq*. Clearly *ʿšq* can encompass severe economic constraints for its victims, who either fail to receive wages or, worse, are cheated out of what they already possess. Such individuals obviously also need the love (charity) indicated in the previous precept.

the widow and the orphan. The third in the series of four commands, and the first of two negative ones, this pair presents two of the weaker components of society who might easily be taken advantage of in economic matters. The prophet has altered a familiar pair, "orphan and widow," and reversed the order to "widow and orphan," *ʾalmānāh wĕyātôm.* The present order occurs elsewhere only in Exod 22:21 (RSV 22:22). The image evoked draws upon pentateuchal language (e.g., Deut 10:18; 14:29; 16:11,14; 24:17,19,20,21; 26:12,13) as well as that of the earlier prophets (Isa 1:17,23; 9:16 [RSV 9:17]; 10:2; Jer 49:11; Ezek 22:7), demonstrating an innovative oracular style which draws upon familiar material. The inclusion of these two groups of people stems from the fact that both were often if not always lacking in property and therefore in status and income as well. They needed special consideration in economic and also legal matters. This set of four precepts deals with both such needs.

The pair, "widow and orphan," in reverse order not only is common in the Bible but also appears in Ugaritic literature (so Dahood 1970:103, 342, 450, who cites *UT,* 127:48–50; *UT,* 2 Aqht v:7–8). In these two texts, the word order varies, *ytm . . . almnt* in one and *almnt . . . ytm* in the other. We also note, on the basis of the Ugaritic material, that the judgment or protection of the widow and orphan is a royal function carried out by King Danʿel. In preexilic Israelite society, which this passage recalls, the king too was the ultimate source of judicial authority (cf. NOTES to 3:6 and to "twenty cubits . . ." in 5:2), a situation no longer possible in Zechariah's day.

the sojourner and the poor. The second pair, *gēr wĕʿānî,* is unusual in several respects. First, "poor" is normally paired with some other word for poor or needy, such as *ʾebyôn* in Jer 22:16; Ezek 16:49; 18:12. In the only instances in which "sojourner" and "poor" are paired, they appear in reverse order (Lev 19:10 and 23:22). The word *gēr,* moreover, is frequently joined to the pair "orphan and widow" (cf. Exod 22:20–21 [RSV 22:21–22]; Deut 24:17; 27:19; Jer 7:6; 22:3), which appears in the opposite order ("widow and orphan,") in this verse. The introduction of an additional word, "poor," in this context and sequence would thus seem to be significant.

The addition of "poor" can be interpreted in various ways. Providing for the disenfranchised is one of the basic social tenets of the Hebrew Bible. It is a persistent message of the prophetic corpus, and it receives due attention in pentateuchal law. The inclusion of the "poor" among the disenfranchised groups, although not directly in any listing of them, is given special and eloquent justification in Deut 15:7–11. Clearly by the late preexilic period, the growing social stratification in Judah and the disruption of community life because of Babylonian incursions warranted the inclusion of the "poor" in groupings of social categories to which special attention was directed. That Zechariah, in referring to the words of preexilic prophecy, includes "poor" may mean that he is combining Deuteronomic and prophetic emphasis. Note that Ezekiel (22:29) at one point combines "poor" and "needy" with "sojourner," omitting only "widow" from his listing.

The association of "poor" with "sojourner" *(gēr)* along with "orphan" and "widow" can be further elucidated by consideration of *gēr*. In the Hebrew Bible, the "sojourner" occupied a position between the foreigner and the native. Living as he did among people who were not his kin, both his livelihood and his safety depended upon the formal and informal attitudes of the society in which he dwelt (so the discussion by Kellerman 1975:443–49). The "sojourner" was a specially protected inhabitant, a person who as a rule owned no property in the area in which he resided. By the late monarchic period, if Deuteronomic law is a reliable indicator, the *gēr* had become, by and large, a day laborer or hired hand. Deut 24:14 forbids the oppression of a hired laborer, who is poor and needy, whether he is a Judean citizen ("one of your brothers") on the one hand or a sojourner *(gēr)* living in Judean territory on the other hand. The late preexilic period saw an increase of *gērîm*, since emigrants and fugitives from the northern kingdom were considered sojourners in Judah (cf. 2 Chron 15:9; 30:25). Like the widow and the orphan, sojourners were in a tenuous position, economically speaking, and needed special consideration. Practically synonymous with "poor," *gēr* represents non-Judeans who were financially depressed, and "poor" would thus designate those Judeans who were struggling to make ends meet. The context here involves not only the economic problems that beset the sojourners and the poor as well as the other two groups (widows and orphans); protection from disadvantage in the legal system is also at issue (see the next NOTE and also "Judge with true justice" in the previous verse), along with the need for charitable action toward those who lack normal means of subsistence. Deuteronomy, the reader will recall, legislates that the "sojourner" (along with the "orphan" and the "widow," Deut 24:17 and 27:19) is to receive special assistance in the carrying out of justice.

do not devise evil in your hearts. A second negative command, balancing the initial precept in this set in its concern for justice, concludes verse 10. This clause closely parallels 8:17, where it is linked to the taking of false oaths. This oracle thus ends as it began, with a focus on the full justice, or social harmony, that must exist for all according to God's word.

one another. This is the same phrase, except for the omission of the indicative particle, as "one another" in the previous verse.

11. *refused to give heed.* The verb *m'n* is followed by *l,* "to," plus the infinitive in nearly all of its biblical occurrences. The largest group of usages concerns the refusal of an individual or group to obey Yahweh's word. Among the prophets, Jeremiah in particular expresses with this word his dismay over Israel's failure to keep God's covenant. Jer 11:10, for example, has a retrospective tone not unlike the present passage: the Judeans and Jerusalemites had returned to *their* forefathers' sins and had "refused to hear my words." Zechariah is unique, however, in coupling "refuse" with "heed." He uses the verb to introduce a series of four phrases, all of which describe the failure of the people to do Yahweh's will, as established in the covenant and as enjoined by the prophets. All four verbs are graphic in their depiction of Israelite defiance. This first one *(qšb)* is a verb of hearing.

set a defiant shoulder. This phrase continues the physical imagery of Israel's disobedience and introduces the nuance of rebelliousness, in that "defiant" is from *srr,* meaning "to be rebellious, stubborn." The participle of that verb is used with "heart" in Jer 5:23, *lēb sôrēr*, a usage which is part of the general vocabulary of this verse. The entire phrase is replicated in Neh 9:29, where it is part of another retrospective on Israelite disobedience and is coupled with "stiffened the neck" as a way of emphasizing human disobedience.

Their ears they dulled from hearing. Although somewhat awkward in English, the phrase in Hebrew makes its impact through the Hiphil of the verb *kbd*. Both in the Qal and Hiphil, *kbd* is used with parts of the body to indicate that the normal functioning of those parts ("eyes," Gen 48:10; "ears," Isa 6:10 and 59:1; "heart," Exod 8:11,28 [RSV 8:15,32]; 9:7,34; 10:1) has been impaired. The ears, for example, are made heavy and therefore insensible, incapable of hearing God's word. This third clause of verse 11 elaborates the first clause of the verse.

12. *they made their hearts stony.* We should not be surprised to find "heart" the final phrase in this series. The imagery drawn from parts of the body is aptly completed with the notion of a stubborn or "stony" heart. The first and third phrases present aural insensitivity and hence lack of adherence to divine will; the second one depicts an external part of the body—the shoulder—and the fourth one an internal part of the body—the heart as inner seat of emotions, passions, and will. The figurative use of shoulders in the Blessing of Moses is interesting in this respect: Yahweh dwells between the shoulders of Benjamin, presumably in his heart (Deut 33:12). Could the presence of Bethel as representative of Benjaminites have caused the prophet to have selected this particular combination of physical images?

Normally, the concept of strong-hearted involves the ordinary word for "stone," *'eben* (e.g., Ezek 11:19). The use of *šāmîr*, a word of dubious origin, is unusual. Insofar as Zechariah 7–8 shares the vocabulary of Ezekiel 3, the occurrence of this word for an extremely hard stone there (3:9) perhaps has influenced Zechariah's choice. Ezekiel uses *šāmîr* in reference to "forehead," but his usage comes fast upon discussion of a "hard forehead and a stubborn heart."

the Torah . . . words. In tandem, these terms apparently represent two categories of authoritative revelation. While the individual usage of *tôrâ* is not unusual, when coupled with *dĕbārîm* the compound expression becomes unique. The pairing of "Torah" and "words" suggests both a connection to past usage and the invention of a new idiom which may very well have a technical connotation. The reference to the earlier prophets which immediately follows demonstrates Zechariah's cognizance of his ties to an inherited and inspired prophetic past (cf. Zech 1:4; 7:3,7). The word *dābār*, however, as suggested by the text in Hag 2:5, can also convey a sense of covenantal loyalty that is not fully rendered by "Torah." However, the occurrence of "the words" after "the Torah" leads us to believe that "the Torah" is to be more strictly and narrowly understood as specific "words" which were previously uttered, as, for example, in the reference to "the words" of Haggai and Zechariah in 8:9 (see following NOTE). It would seem noteworthy of speculation, therefore, that "words" refers to the working canon of prophecy which would have existed in Zechariah's day. Similarly, it is also possible that "the Torah" refers to the Pentateuch, plus perhaps a portion of the Primary History (Gen–Kgs).

by his spirit. As in Neh 9:30, the description of preexilic disobedience is coupled with information about what the people disregarded. Although Zechariah refers to both

"Torah" and prophecy, Nehemiah picks up only on the latter. In both cases, the prophetic word is said to have been sent by Yahweh's spirit. Similarly, Joel's eschatological vision of prophecy is proclaimed in terms of the pouring out of Yahweh's spirit (Joel 3:1–2 [RSV 2:28–29]; see Num 24:2 and 2 Sam 23:2 for further examples). Prophecy as divine revelation is expressed in these passages by the association of God's spirit with the prophetic utterance. Compare the somewhat different use of *rûaḥ* for God's "spirit," his active presence, in the oracular insertion to the lampstand vision (Zech 4:6) and in the Seventh (chariot) Vision (6:8). Haggai (2:5) similarly uses "spirit" to indicate God's potent presence (see our NOTES).

through the earlier prophets. The third of Zechariah's references to preexilic prophecy; cf. NOTES to 1:4 and 7:7. In this instance, the prophets are the object of the verb "send," which is part of the vocabulary depicting prophets as divine messengers (cf. Zech 1:10; 2:12,13,15 [RSV 2:8,9,11]).

great wrath. God's covenant anger was vented against the preexilic community; that is, the destruction of Jerusalem, the temple, and Judah resulted from the refusal of the Judeans to obey God's word as expressed in the covenant and as affirmed by the prophets. Parts One and Two of First Zechariah both refer (1:2 and 1:15) to great divine anger *(qeṣep),* and hence it is not surprising to find it here in Part Three with its similar retrospective treatment of disobedience followed by exile.

came from. Literally, "was from," as in the formulas introducing prophetic speech (cf. NOTE to Zech 1:1, "the word of Yahweh came to").

13. *proclaimed.* The retrospective on divine justice—i.e., on Yahweh's response to the people's disobedience—is framed by the use of "proclaim," here and in verse 7 above, in reference to the message of the preexilic prophets. The verb *qr'* evidently has a meaning verging on the technical when it introduces or signifies oracular material. That it may refer to a written text which is to be read aloud (see our discussion in the first NOTE to Zech 1:14) would suit the present context, insofar as the proclaimed words are those uttered seventy and more years before Zechariah's prophecy. The likelihood that they would have been committed to written form in the interim, if they weren't already written down immediately at the time of utterance, is great.

they did not listen. If the single word "proclaimed" represents the oracular statement of verses 9–10—that is, the essence of God's preexilic message—then this simple statement, expressed in one word plus the negative in Hebrew *(wĕlō' šāmĕ'û),* conveys the response of the people. The sequence of four descriptions of denial and refusal in verses 11 and 12, most of which are expressed in terms concerning the hearing process, are summarized aptly and succinctly by "they did not listen." We have rendered the verb *šm'* as "listen," which goes somewhat further than the mere act of audition; but we point out that the same root underlies our translation of "hearing" in verse 11 and "hear" in verse 12. Similarly, the verb *šm'* appears a fourth time in this section at the end of this verse. This statement ("they did not listen") terminates the narrative of 7:7–13, which included the oracle of verses 9–10, reflecting back on the preexilic period.

So they will call out. The root *qr',* "proclaims" or "call out," recurs here, along with *šm',* "listen" or "hear." Just as *qr'* in verses 7 and 13a framed the retrospective narrative dealing with the preexilic situation, so *qr',* together with the root *šm'* that ended the narrative, appears once more to introduce the attached oracle of verses 13b–14 and to relate it to the preceding section.

This time *qr'* is in the third person plural ("they"), as was the previous verb ("they did not listen"). The series of four verbs in verse 13 thus has a chiastic structure, with the first and fourth verbs referring to Yahweh and the second and third ones describing the people's response. This arrangement helps move the time period forward. Verses 7–13a dealt with the period up to and including the destruction; and the next section will be a set of seven oracles dealing with restoration. But what about the interim? What about the "seventy years" of exile when, to the exiles, it seemed as if Yahweh's presence was removed and *he* did not hear?

We have included this statement and the following one with the oracle of verse 14. Together, they introduce God's description of his wrathful deeds in bringing about the exile and of the ensuing desolation. Since the fact of exile is inextricably linked with preexilic disobedience, the oracle describing exile is verbally linked with the retrospective on the preexilic period by the repetition of the two verbs, *qr'* and *šm'*. In addition to linking the two time periods, they provide great irony. The chiastic structure of the verbs, appearing in English as the pronouns, makes the people now the ones who cry out and Yahweh the one who does not listen.

I will not listen. As we have explained in the preceding NOTE, the verbs *šm'* ("listen") and *qr'* ("call"), repeat the verbs of the concluding statement (v 13a) of the retrospective and so connect that section with the following brief oracle of verses 13b–14 referring to the conditions of exile. The first-person singular of this verb clearly refers to Yahweh. Both "listen" and "call out" of verse 13b are in the imperfect tense, in contrast with the perfect of the two verbs of verse 13a. The shift to the prophet's contemporary world, the last stages of the exilic period, is thereby effected and provides further justification for including the second set of verbs with the oracle of verse 14. There is no cause to change these verbs to the past, as do the RSV and other English versions. Nor is there any reason to alter the pronouns of either the first (cf. Syriac) or fourth verbs. The "he" of 13a is part of the narrative describing God's deeds; the "I" of 13b is part of the oracular statement quoting God.

14. *I have strewn them.* The use of this root, *s'r* in the Piel, is singular in the Hebrew Bible, and its occurrence as a verb in general is quite rare. The verb signifies storm or rage; see, for example, the Qal usages in Hab 3:14, Jon 1:4, and Isa 54:11. A paraphrase would be "I have hurled them about with a storm," and the imagery is that of a violent tornado or hurricane which can hurl people or houses great distances. The lone Niphal attestation, in 2 Kgs 6:11, denotes the personal rage or turmoil of the Syrian king. Perhaps our English translation does not sufficiently convey the strong sense of rage or tempestuousness, but we have intentionally sought to keep the English similar to Zech 2:2,4 (RSV 1:19,21) where the Piel of *zrh*, "to scatter," is used to describe the dispersion of Judah, Israel, and Jerusalem in the vision of the four horns. In both cases the force of the action is dramatic and severe.

among all the nations. Literally "upon" or "against" (*'al*) the nations. The preposition *'al*, regularly used after *s'r*, contributes to the intensity or ferocity of the verbal idea. That is, God's punishment of his people is a direct consequence of his "great wrath" (see above, v 12). Israel was willy-nilly exiled to "the nations," to unfamiliar surroundings. The reference to "the nations" therefore points directly to the Babylonian exile and anticipates the negative implication of that status as specified in the following clause, "which they have not known." Although Zechariah most probably had in mind the Babylonian diaspora, the force of the verse is inclusive and hence could well refer to the Egyptian diaspora or to that of any other area.

land was left wasted. The harsh effects of the destruction of the territory of Judah are expressed in the language of the rest of verse 14. The Hebrew root *šmm,* or possibly *nšm,* maintains the level of severity in the tone of the oracle and conjures up the image of the land being so desolate that none could move about. Desolation of the land is concomitant with destruction and exile. Thus the retrospection finally closes with the awful description of the result of disobedience to Yahweh. The result is twofold: exile from the land, and the destruction and wasting of a land that once flowed with milk and honey (Exod 3:8; Lev 20:24). While there may be some literary hyperbole here, the Babylonian conquest no doubt had severe consequences for the land. Not only were great portions of it plundered by foreign troops, but also much of it was left uncultivated. When some of the exiles returned, they found the land wasted and unproductive; initially, the harvests would have been meager. Such indeed was the economic setting which Haggai interpreted to be the direct result of the "desolation" of the temple (see, e.g., NOTE to "desolate" in Hag 1:4).

with no one moving about. Literally "without anyone crossing (traversing) or anyone returning." This could refer to a) the depopulation that the exile involved; b) the reduction of productive activity brought about by the loss of population as well as by the military devastation of arable lands; and c) the absence of travelers owing to general insecurity resulting from the destruction of the Judean military and the fortified cities that served as way stations for the road system. In any case the picture is the absence of people crossing back and forth.

a desirable land . . . wasteland. The people's responsibility for the sad plight of the land is reiterated with the reminder that Judah was once literally "a desirable, attractive land," *ḥemdâ* (cf. NOTE to "riches" in Hag 2:7), but is now a "wasteland," with the latter word derived from the same root *(nāšammâ,* or *lĕšammâ,* also to be translated "left wasted").

COMMENT

Zechariah's strong awareness of his prophetic predecessors and their role takes the form of a second retrospection (cf. 1:3-6). He opens in 7:7 with a rhetorical question about the words of preexilic prophets. Note that his initial retrospection in Part One concluded with a similar rhetorical question. Not only is Zechariah asserting once more, through recollection, the validity of the earlier spokesmen of Yahweh, but also, in taking up this message in precisely the way that he ended the analogous one in 1:6, he provides evidence that the Book of First Zechariah (1-8) has been consciously constructed so that the oracular materials in the concluding section of Zechariah 1-8 contain this retrospective inclusio with the opening section. Part Three of Zechariah does double duty; it contains correspondences with Part One and so frames First Zechariah; and it also echoes aspects of the themes and the language of Haggai, thereby forming an envelope around the compendious work Haggai-First

Zechariah (see Introduction). We have no reason to doubt the involvement of Zechariah himself, or at the least a close contemporary and follower, in producing this arrangement; cf. the discussion of authorship in our Introduction.

The retrospection itself commences with reference to the "words" that Yahweh "proclaimed." It concludes in verse 13a with the repeated use of the verb "proclaim." The material contained in verses 7–13a constitutes a section somewhat distinct from verses 13b–14. The latter passage is clearly attached to 7–13a, in that the two clauses of verse 13 are relational and contrasting. But verse 13b moves from the preexilic past to the prophet's day as does verse 14, with the result that 13b–14 together serve as a thematic bridge between the retrospection and the following collection of seven oracles in the next subunit.

The words "proclaim" and "words," as we have explained in the NOTES, may well be technical terms reflecting the existence of a written form of the prophetic corpus: Zechariah's habitual quotation of materials from, as well as his reference to (Zech 1:2–6; 7:12) earlier prophets, and also his direct and indirect allusions to the words of his contemporary Haggai (e.g., 8:9) provide evidence of the availability of those materials in written form and of the authority they held for Zechariah. That Zechariah uses or expands his own utterances of two years before may further indicate that such materials already occurred in written form. If Zechariah reveals familiarity with the growing corpus of prophetic literature, in verses 9 and 10 and also in 8:16–17, he also shows his knowledge of pentateuchal materials. Twice he formulates a set of four seminal precepts that indicate a knowledge of Torah as a book or group of books authoritative for community practice and belief. These two segments of the Bible, Torah and Prophets such as they existed in his day, constituted the very core of his cultural and religious heritage. Both his oracles and his visions drew upon those sources as he directed his attention toward the national and international issues of his own day.

Yahweh's words were known to Israel through those men who prophesied prior to the time when Judah and Jerusalem were destroyed. Zechariah's geographical specificity reflects well the configurations of Judah during the waning days of the monarchy in the early sixth century. In those earlier times the capital city Jerusalem was secure along with the other cities of Judah and the territories to the south and west. Such security, the prophet avers, would have lasted but for the people's stubborn refusal to obey God's words. It is against such a historical backdrop that Zechariah introduces, with the familiar formula "Thus spoke Yahweh of Hosts" of oracular transmission, his listing in verses 9 and 10 of four precepts (cf. 8:16–17).

Although verses 9 and 10 are cast as part of the message of preexilic prophets, the style is hardly that of oracular prophecy and so signals another aspect among the many that distinguish Zechariah from both his contemporaries and his predecessors. In utilizing phrases that exhibit a pentateuchal if not Deuteronomic cast, he introduces an idiosyncratic form of prophetic expression, one that makes creative use of the evolving corpus of ancient Hebrew scripture. He has formed a unit of discourse in which a positive statement begins a series of four commands and is balanced by the concluding statement that is formulated in the negative but is roughly synonymous with the first imperative. The initial positive command is followed by another one, and the concluding negative one is preceded by a negative one. The negative injunctions are chiastic counterparts of the two positive ones. True justice finds its negative counterpart in the beginning of verse 10a; love and compassion have their negative in verse 10b. Dividing the two verses of the prophetic discourse, we may observe the following patterns:

	positive		negative
verse 9a	true justice	10a	don't deprive
9b	love and compassion	10b	don't devise evil

A strikingly similar sequence occurs in 8:16–17:

	positive		negative
verse 16a	truth	17a	don't devise evil
16b	complete justice	17b	don't perjure

The subtle variation in content and language between these two similar oracular passages reflects the changes in societal conditions that occurred between ca. 600 B.C.E., which is the context for 7:9–10, and 518 when the present oracle was composed. Zechariah's retrospective into the preexilic period reveals a stratified society. The prophets of the monarchy had called upon their countrymen to treat the disadvantaged elements fairly. Verse 10a identifies those groups: widows, orphans, sojourners, and the poor (see NOTES), all of whom are in evidence in Deuteronomy. None of these is listed in the parallel passage in 8:16–17. The absence of these groups and of the concomitant call for love (= charity) in chapter 8 suggests that economic conditions had improved in the restoration but perhaps that the social stratification of preexilic times had dissipated as a result of the destruction of Judah and of her exile (see below). Zechariah's use of exhortations to the preexilic kingdom is evidence of his characteristic sermonic and midrashic style, which is perhaps even more in evidence in 8:16–17.

Recollection of Judah's disobedient behavior follows immediately upon the citation of Yahweh's words attributed to preexilic prophets. In the final verses (7:11–14) of this subunit of Zechariah 7–8, a string of idioms betrays the prophet's strong negative assessments ("defiant shoulder," "ears . . . dulled from hearing," "hearts stony") of the preexilic situation. Judah's stubborn resistance was to "the Torah" and to the words of Yahweh proclaimed "through the earlier prophets." As we have already noted, this defiance reflects the authority of prophetic and pentateuchal materials—that is, of an evolving corpus eventually to be known as the canon of Scripture.

The inevitable result of the Judeans' disobedience was that God would not listen when they called out. Destruction could not be averted, nor could dispersion and the wasting of the land. Judah's trials and tribulations become the object lesson of Zechariah's retrospection on divine justice. But the retrospection is not only an oblique plea by the prophet for his contemporaries to be obedient but also is a compelling rehearsal of God's great power and unbending will with respect to his dealing with his people, for ill and equally for good. The retrospection leads directly to two sets of positive oracles which are future-oriented. It helps convince Zechariah's audience that the wonderful condition offered in those oracles can be realized, as part of God's justice, just as were the traumatic consequences of God's justice in the past.

The language of 7:12b–14 provides the prophetic emphasis on God's punitive response to Judean disobedience. "Wrath" and the idea of the scattering ("strewn") of the people serve also to connect this section of Part III with the language of Part I (for "wrath," see 1:2 and for "scattering" see 2:2–4 [RSV 1:19–21]). Having been dispersed and spoiled, the experiences that will allow for Israel's redemption have been established (cf. Zech 3:2, "Is this not a brand plucked from the fire?"). The stage has been set for the return of Yahweh to Israel and thus of Israel to a secure existence in its land. The oracles which follow are predicated upon the facts about Judah's history and about God's actions reviewed by Zechariah in this retrospection.

14. ZION AND JUDAH RESTORED: SEVEN ORACLES
(8:1–17)

8 ¹ Then the word of Yahweh of Hosts came:

² Thus spoke Yahweh of Hosts,
   I have shown for Zion great zeal
   With great fury I am zealous for her.
³ Thus spoke Yahweh,
   I have returned to Zion;
   I will dwell in the midst of Jerusalem.
   Jerusalem will be called the City of Truth,
      the Mountain of Yahweh of Hosts, the Mountain
         of Holiness.
⁴ Thus spoke Yahweh of Hosts,

Old men and old women will again sit in the open places of Jerusalem, each with a staff in his hand because of great age.
⁵ The open places of the city will be filled with boys and girls playing in its open places.

⁶ Thus spoke Yahweh of Hosts,

Though it will seem difficult to the remnant of this people in those days, should it also seem difficult to me?—Oracle of Yahweh of Hosts.

⁷ Thus spoke Yahweh of Hosts,

I will deliver my people from eastern lands and from western lands. ⁸ I will bring them in, and they will dwell in Jerusalem. They will be my people and I will be their God, in truth and in righteousness.

⁹ Thus spoke Yahweh of Hosts,

May your hands be strong, you who in these days hear these words from the mouths of the prophets, on the day when the House of Yahweh of Hosts was refounded, the Temple to be rebuilt. ¹⁰ For before those days, the earnings of a man were nil, and the earnings of an animal were nothing. For him who went out and came in, there was no peace from the foe; for I had set every man, each one against the other.

¹¹ But now, unlike the earlier times, I will belong to the remnant of this people—Oracle of Yahweh of Hosts.

¹² For there will be a prosperous sowing:

the vine will yield its fruit,

the earth will yield its produce,

and the heavens will yield their dew.

Thus will I cause the remnant of this people to possess all these things. ¹³ Just as you were a curse among the nations, O house of Judah and O house of Israel, so I will save you that you may be a blessing. Do not fear; may your hands be strong.

¹⁴ For thus spoke Yahweh of Hosts,

Just as I decided to afflict you when your ancestors angered me —said Yahweh of Hosts—and I did not relent, ¹⁵ so have I again decided, in these days, to do good to Jerusalem and to the house of Judah. Do not fear. ¹⁶ These are the things that you shall do: speak truth, only truth, to one another; judge with complete justice[a] in your gates. ¹⁷ Do not devise evil in your hearts, each man against

---

[a] The word "truth" (ʾĕmet) is repeated in MT but omitted in most of the versions.

the other; do not love a false oath; for all these are what I detest—
Oracle of Yahweh.

NOTES

8:1. *Then the word of Yahweh of Hosts came:*. A slight variation on the transmission
formula that appears in 7:1,4,8, this clause introduces the first part of chapter 8, which
is composed of seven oracles. A nearly identical statement (8:18) opens the concluding
part of chapter 8, a set of three oracles (8:19–23). Together these formulas, which also
appear in 7:1 and 8 (see NOTES there) provide a clear structure for Part Three of First
Zechariah. We have followed this structure in our subheadings, except for 7:4, which
also contains this formula but apparently for contextual and not for structural purposes. In every instance, the formula serves to introduce a discrete oracular unit. Here
in 8:1 and 18 and above at 7:1 and 8, these formulas introduce sections which actually
are large clusters of oracular materials rather than single units such as we have in
7:4–6.

2. *Thus spoke Yahweh of Hosts.* This pronouncement formula introduces each of the
ten oracles in the two parts of chapter 8. In every case except verse 3, God is referred
to as "Yahweh of Hosts"; in verse 3 (cf. NOTE there) the word "Hosts" is omitted. This
omission occurs elsewhere in Zechariah only in 1:16 and not in Haggai. The sequence
of the transmission formulas of verses 1 and 18 and the pronouncement formulas for
each oracle lends a sense of unity to the whole. It also indicates the diverse nature of
individual prophetic utterances. Whereas previous oracular portions of Zechariah have
been selected and inserted with reference to corresponding visionary materials, as is the
case with Zech 1:14–17 (see NOTES and COMMENT), the material in chapter 8 has been
selected and organized with reference to the whole of First Zechariah and also to the
composite work of Hag-Zech 1–8. That the Book of Haggai is involved in an integrated
structuring of the combined works is suggested, for example, by the fact that the
formula at 7:1 which opens Part Three of Zechariah incorporates the date heading and
superscription of the composite work in reverse order to Hag 1:1. Insofar as this is a
deliberate reversal (cf. NOTE to 7:1), it shows that the selection of formulas was not a
casual matter, but rather a purposeful and artful achievement (see discussion in COM-
MENT to Zech 7–8).

I have shown . . . for her. The first of seven oracles is poetic in structure. It consists
of a symmetrical bicolon, chiastically arranged, with balance in stress and syllable:

verb + indirect object	(6)	direct object, with adjective (5)	11 syllables
direct object, with adjective	(6)	verb + indirect object (4)	10 syllables

Parallelism appears only in the two central elements: the verb of the first colon is
repeated in the second, and the indirect object is likewise repeated, with a pronoun
substituted for the noun "Zion." The rather stilted and repetitive form of the oracle is
perhaps the result of its relationship to Zech 1:14b. It expands the first line of the
oracle included in the First Vision, except that it focuses upon Zion alone. The normal
pairing of Zion and Jerusalem comes only in the second oracle, in 8:3. The first two
oracles together, however, contain a balance in the use of this pair: Zion is mentioned

twice, and then Jerusalem too appears twice. "Zion" in verse 2 initiates the pairing, which follows the normal order—i.e., Zion first and then Jerusalem. This order contrasts with that of 1:14, where Jerusalem appears first. That reversal, however, can probably be explained as part of an envelope with the "Zion . . . Jerusalem" pair at the end of chapter 1 (1:17; cf. NOTES to 1:14,17).

The root *qn*², "passion, ardor, zeal," appears three times in this verse: twice as a verb and once as a substantive, in the form of a cognate accusative, in the first clause. This repetition serves to emphasize Yahweh's intense and absolute commitment to Israel. Yahweh's passionate attachment to his people provides the linkage from the account of his destruction and exile of the people in the preceding retrospective to the description of his present restoration of the people and the anticipation of the future benefits of that restoration. It would be inconceivable for the horrors of exile and desolation to be reversed were Yahweh not so utterly devoted to his people. Only in the light of that zeal does the prospect of full restoration gain credibility. Although the concept of Yahweh's ardor *(qn²)* in punitive response to disobedience is well established in the Bible for the preexilic period (cf. Exod 20:5; 34:14), the positive aspects of God's affective nature and behavior are associated with this root only in exilic or postexilic passages (only in Ezek 39:25 and Joel 2:18 in addition to Zech 1:14 and this verse). That Zechariah repeated the root three times in this verse perhaps signifies that his audience had to be convinced that the sting and pain of the destruction had not yet been overcome in a psychological sense. Precisely because this is the first of seven oracles dealing with the present and future, the positive nuance of *qn²* seems assured. Only in Israel's past, as recounted in the retrospective of 7:7–13, would Yahweh's punitive ardor be appropriate. Similarly, 1:14b above denotes the present-day, positive ardor of Yahweh. However, as in 1:15 above, the passionate attachment to Zion has a negative concomitant.

"Great wrath" *(qṣp gdwl)* in 1:15 and "great fury" *(ḥmh gdwlh)* in 8:2 balance Yahweh's overwhelming zeal for Zion (and Jerusalem). We assume that in this verse, on analogy with 1:15, the "fury" is directed against the nations that have maintained the desolation of Zion. Admittedly, 8:2 is elliptical; and many translators and commentators have understood that all the words of passion have been negative, referring to God's punishment of his people. However, to reiterate, because of this oracle's position at the outset of this present- and future-oriented series and because of its explicit connection with 1:14–15, positive connotations of zeal outweigh the negative ones. Yet we would not go so far as does the NJPS, which understands *ḥmh* solely in terms of an intensification of "zealous" in the second clause; that noun is too consistently associated with destructive anger and wrath. Again, the connection of the passage with 1:14–15 would seem to preclude such an understanding. For another instance of *ḥmh* referring to God's fury directed to the wicked so as to restore the fortunes of his people, see Jer 30:23.

3. *Thus spoke Yahweh.* The slight variation in the proclamation formula, which here lacks the expected "of Hosts" after "Yahweh," as does Zech 1:16, is striking. Its omission in 1:16 has caused at least one ancient version, the Syriac, to add it; in this verse numerous Greek manuscripts supply "of Hosts," a term that is a prominent feature of the vocabulary of Haggai and First Zechariah (cf. NOTE to "Yahweh of Hosts," Hag 1:2). Despite the tendency of the versions to add "of Hosts," its original

omission seems preferable and intentional. In fact, there are an impressive number of examples in the Hebrew Bible of deliberate deviation from a pattern (e.g., "I will send/ kindle a fire" in Amos 1–2).

Its absence here reflects the way in which the content of the second oracle echoes that of the oracle in 1:16. First, both oracles begin with the statement "I have returned to X" (X = Jerusalem in 1:16 and Zion in 8:3). Second, both oracles mention Jerusalem twice. Third, both oracles deal with the temple, explicitly in 1:16 ("my house") and metaphorically in 8:3 ("Mountain of Holiness"; cf. last NOTE to this verse). The strong thematic and stylistic correspondence of the two oracles has, in our opinion, caused the formula of 8:3 to leave out "of Hosts" because the formula introducing the 1:16 oracle has omitted it. The author or redactor of chapter 8 is intentionally echoing earlier oracular material and draws attention to the thematic continuity by employing the same shortened form of a familiar phrase, even though that shortened form is otherwise unusual for Zechariah.

The anterior question which this arrangement poses is the reason for the omission of "of Hosts" in 1:16, if we assume that the formation of the set of oracles of which that verse is a part preceded the formation of the set of seven oracles in chapter 8. That question can only be answered by investigating its absence from 1:16, as we do in our first NOTE to that verse. To recapitulate briefly, we remind the reader that 1:16 is the second of a set of three oracles which together complete the First Vision; they reiterate themes introduced in the vision itself and also provide a bridge to succeeding materials. The second oracle, the one that concerns us here, is outstanding in that it is the first place in Zechariah which refers explicitly to the rebuilding of the temple (cf. our COMMENT to 1:14–17). Rather than being a stylistic variant, the introduction to the second of these three oracles varies the expected introductory formula for the direct purpose of alerting the audience to the special character of that oracle. Because temple restoration is the central issue underlying, directly or indirectly, all of Zechariah's visions (Part Two of First Zechariah) if not all of Zechariah's prophecies, the initial specific reference to that issue should indeed be signified in some way. Thus in 8:3, as in 1:16, the importance of the temple, referred to here for the first time in the oracular sequence, is underscored. Yahweh in the temple is Yahweh of Hosts according to the language of these two postexilic prophets, Haggai and Zechariah.

The second oracle (8:3) which is introduced by this abbreviated formula appears set off as poetry in our translation. In truth, its poetic character has been somewhat diminished by the appearance of prosodic elements, such as the repeated use of the definite article. Nonetheless, the two bicola of the oracle have several features we would describe as poetic. The first bicolon is fairly well balanced, with respect to themes and stress. However, the juxtaposition of Zion and Jerusalem, influenced no doubt by the oracular appendix to the First Vision in 1:14–17, has broken up an even count in syllables. In such an instance the author has favored thematic integrity over poetic balance and style: he inserts Jerusalem in the second clause ("I will dwell in the midst of Jerusalem"), upsetting a balance of syllables, which could otherwise have been achieved by using a pronoun referring to Zion, as in 8:2 ("for her"). Perhaps the introduction of the multisyllabic word Jerusalem was more important than syllabic balance (see NOTES below to "Zion" and "Jerusalem"). In contrast, the second bicolon is more balanced. It lacks a second verbal element; "will be called" does double duty for both halves of the bicolon. The ellipsis thus created means that the line is somewhat balanced in terms of stress and syllable count.

The oracle as a whole is bracketed on either side (8:3 and 4) by formulas that establish the extent of the oracular unit. The internal integrating factor is certainly the repetition of words and images of Jerusalem and its holy mountain. The effect is achieved through a mixing of prosaic features and poetic devices. No other oracle is quite so hybrid; but then, as shown by its exceptional introductory formula, no other oracle is quite so relevant to Zechariah's central concern.

I have returned. See NOTE to 1:16 where the same expression occurs. The use of the perfect tense indicates that Yahweh's return has already begun, an action which in the eyes of the prophet has profound implications for Israel and for all mankind.

to Zion. Here Zion precedes Jerusalem in the bicolon, as might be expected. The usual pairing of these two terms has the more common word (Jerusalem) falling in final position. In the oracular additions to the First Vision in 1:14–17, a section to which this oracle exhibits striking correspondence, this pattern is altered. Jerusalem/Zion opens those oracles in 1:14 and the reverse order, Zion/Jerusalem, closes them in 1:17. "Jerusalem" is clearly the point of focus in that section as it occurs two additional times in the intervening verses (see NOTE to "Jerusalem and Zion" in 1:14).

The word "Zion" occurs several times in Zechariah but not at all in Haggai. In Zechariah it appears only in the oracular sections (1:14,17; 2:11,14 [RSV 2:7,10]; 8:23; also twice in chapter 9, Deutero-Zechariah). Its absence from Haggai probably underscores the more developed view of Zion after the temple refoundation ceremony. Its absence from the visions does not appear to be significant: the visions themselves concern the temple and so represent Zion, which at least in this oracle is equated with the temple mount (cf. NOTE below to "Mountain of Yahweh" in this verse).

I will dwell in the midst of Jerusalem. We have discussed above the use of *škn* ("dwell") language in Zech 2:14 and 15 (RSV 2:10–11; see NOTES above). Its usage here similarly draws upon temple terminology. If Yahweh has returned to Zion, he then dwells in his holy habitation which is within, or "in the midst of," Jerusalem. Jerusalem as a whole becomes the symbol of all that accompanies sacred space, including the authority of the temple's administrative institutions (cf. 7:9). Neither "dwell" nor "Jerusalem" occurs in the Book of Haggai.

the City of Truth. This is a unique expression in the Hebrew Bible, and even in English it arrests the attention of the reader. The effect here is to link the oracular unit of 7:9, which begins its listing of four precepts with the command to "carry out true justice" *(mišpaṭ ʾĕmet)* with the second oracle of chapter 8 by means of the repetition of the word *ʾĕmet.* This unusual epithet for Jerusalem, *ʿîr hāʾĕmet,* "the City of Truth," conveys the importance of the holy city for the process of establishing justice in society. The word "truth" appears only in Part Three of First Zechariah (7:9; 8:3,8,16²,19) and nowhere in Haggai. It has a Levitical context in Mal 2:6 *(tôrat ʾĕmet).* Its use by Zechariah perhaps draws upon Isa 1:21, where Jerusalem is designated "a faithful city full of justice in which righteousness has dwelt." In the final oracle of the first set of oracles of chapter 8, Zechariah provides additional details regarding the precepts humans should follow and specifies the ethical principles to be carried out (v 16). In other words, God's presence has been restored to Jerusalem so that the ideals of justice inherent in Torah and prophecy might be realized. The sermonic quality of this and much of the succeeding material provides a fitting conclusion to the book as a whole, which culminates eloquently in the universalistic oracles of verses 20–23. Mason has recently (1982) commented on the heuristic character of this material, and von Rad long ago noted its Levitical and sermonic character.

The phrase "City of Truth" balances the next phrase, "Mountain of Yahweh" and so signifies that Jerusalem is the City of the True (God), meaning the faithful and loyal God. As the mountain is the mountain of Yahweh, so the city is the City of Yahweh. As an expression of its essence or character after Yahweh's presence has been reestablished there, this designation of Jerusalem is analogous to the symbolic title given to Jerusalem at the end of Ezekiel. Ezek 48:35 states that Jerusalem will be called "Yahweh Is There" upon completion of the temple and Yahweh's concomitant return. These epithets attached to Jerusalem establish its identity.

Mountain of Yahweh. This is the fourth term referring to a place in the two lines that constitute the third oracle. "Zion" appears first in the first colon of the first bicolon. Then Jerusalem comes at the end of the first bicolon and again near the beginning of the second. "Zion" and "Jerusalem" are syntactically parallel in the first bicolon of this oracle. "Jerusalem" and "Mountain of Yahweh" likewise exhibit syntactic parallelism in the second bicolon. The position of "Jerusalem" in the second and third of the four half-lines creates a chiastic structure. In this way, "Zion" is related to "Mountain of Yahweh" so as to imply identity in this passage between temple mount and the term Zion.

The close connection between sanctuary and mountain already established by Zechariah (see 4:7, NOTES, and Talmon 1978:444) is here extended to Zion. Zech 8:3 brings together temple, mountain, and Zion as does Joel 4:17 (RSV 3:17) and Isa 2:2–3. Ps 48:2–3 (RSV 48:1–2) also equates the holy mountain and Zion with Mt. Zaphon, a connection which by this point has surely been cut loose from its literal geographic and mythological context. The centrality of the temple rebuilding in Zechariah's visions contributes to the association of Zion with temple, as we have already suggested in our NOTE to "Jerusalem and Zion" in 1:14. Jerusalem and Zion together, here and in 1:14–17, convey the combined religio-political centrality of the city. The "City of Truth" (see above) and the "Mountain of Holiness" (see following) have become inextricably linked.

Mountain of Holiness. This phrase concludes the second oracle by contributing a new epithet to the vocabulary associated with Jerusalem's temple mount. The inclusion of the definite article, *har haqqōdeš,* makes this expression analogous to the one coined in 2:16, "the Holy Land," *'ădmat haqqōdeš.* For consistency in this verse, where the definite article is found with "the City of Truth" and "the Mountain of Yahweh of Hosts," we have translated the text "the Mountain of Holiness" instead of "the Holy Mountain."

Petitjean has suggested (1969:148ff.) that the term "the Holy Land" in 2:16 (RSV 2:12) is equivalent to "the Mountain of Holiness." As we have indicated in the NOTE to 2:16 (RSV 2:12), such a suggestion does not help in either case. The context of 2:16 (RSV 2:12) is much too broad and the specific nuance here far too specific to allow these expressions to be interchangeable. However, to be fair to Petitjean, the notion of sacred space does underlie the language here in 8:3 and should be noted.

4. *Thus spoke Yahweh of Hosts.* This formula introduces the third oracle of this set of seven. See the initial NOTES to 8:2,3 for discussion of the use of this formula.

Old men and old women. The older generation of this verse, taken with the younger generation ("boys and girls") of the next verse, constitute a merism signaling the full repopulation of Jerusalem. The future will thus reverse the situation brought about by the events of the early sixth century, namely exile and destruction. Lam 2:21 contains a merism, similar to that of 2:2–5, which depicts the great loss of life at the time of the destruction: "on the ground, on the streets, lie the youth and the elderly . . . you have slain them in the day of your anger." Likewise, Lam 2:10 presents a slightly different merism: "old men" and "young women" sit in silent mourning. Together, these passages in Lamentations remind us that the destruction caused widespread death and made mourners of all the survivors. The third oracle, then, presents a situation that reverses both those features of the past.

Zechariah, however, differs from Lamentations in his construction of the merism, in which old and young might stand for all the population. Lamentations uses "elder" or "old one," *zkn* in the masculine, and does not pair it with the feminine. Similarly, "youth" are represented in Lamentations by a single word *(na'ar)* and not by "boys and girls" as in the next verse. Why does Zechariah use pairs of gender words when such usage is not called for by his purposes of reversing the picture of destruction as expressed in Lamentations? The addition of the feminine equivalent, here and in verse 5, as well as the supplementary information about "staff" and "age" in this verse (see NOTES), indicate that this passage involves more than simple merism.

The mention of old men *and* old women, along with the suggestion of the physical infirmity of aging, perhaps adds a socioeconomic nuance. The labor value of humans is, after all, established according to sex as well as age (Lev 27:7; cf. C. Meyers 1983:583–86). This passage shows both men and women *not* at work. In an agrarian society, such a situation could only represent, whether in a city or on a farm, the existence of a healthy and stable economy whereby the senior citizens are relieved of the necessity of contributing substantially to subsistence tasks. In other words, the phrase "old men and old women" is not only part of the stylized pairing of old and young but also contributes specifically to the prophetic depiction of the future. Older people will be released from the demands of productive labor and will have the leisure to gather in a public place.

Open places. Hebrew *rĕḥōbôt* is found here and twice in the next verse. It denotes a broad or open area in a city, often near the city gate (cf. 2 Chron 32:6 and also Lam 5:14, which connects old men with the city gate). The Palestinian city in biblical times was highly congested, with many dwellings and other buildings crowded into a walled enclosure of relatively small size. The nature of a city, rising as a tell upon the ruins of previous settlements, meant that urban growth could not normally be matched by an expansion of the city limits. Even sites that exhibit some signs of city planning show very little provision for open spaces within the confines of the city walls. The few places that would have existed would surely have taken on great social significance, as a meeting place and as a place where children could run about. The open places near city gates also served as official administrative and judicial function (cf. last NOTE to 8:16).

The image in these two verses of people sitting or playing in such "open places" reverses the imagery of destruction and exile, as found in Lamentations, which frequently mentions "streets" *(ḥûṣôt)*, a word often linked with "open places," the two together being public outdoor space in a city (cf. Jer 9:20 [RSV 9:21]; Amos 5:16). Actually, the Hebrew word *ḥûṣôt* is not a precise term for street. No such word exists to denote a clearly bounded strip of land intended for the passage of people or animals within a city. The growth of Palestinian cities usually did not take such needs into account in any systematic way (Frick 1977:85) Rather than being conceptualized as continuous pathways, "streets" were considered outside spaces between houses. Since houses were not ordinarily organized in a regular pattern, the streets were usually a confusing maze of narrow passages. Furthermore, those passages could be very unpleasant insofar as they often served as refuse dumps for the adjacent domestic areas. The description of the destruction of Jerusalem in Lamentations refers repeatedly to streets: to bodies strewn in the "streets" (as in the verse, 2:21; quoted above); to children faint with hunger in the streets (2:11–12,19); to formerly revered citizens, prophets or priests, wandering blind and defiled in the streets (4:13–14). The imagery in Zechariah of "open places" presents a striking contrast with that of Lamentations, in terms of the spatial distinction between "open place" and "street" in the topography of a Palestinian city and also in terms of the distinction between the death associated with "streets" and the life activities associated with "open places." The threefold repetition of "open places" intensifies the contrast. It conveys the impression of many open spaces, which is a condition not normally found in Palestinian sites and which thus may give an idealistic if not an eschatological cast to this oracle.

staff . . . great age. The addition of this phrase contributes toward the delineation of the elderly who are introduced at the outset of this verse. This information is somewhat unexpected; it seems unnecessary, just as the gender distinction for the elderly seems gratuitous. We have suggested above that the separate mention of old men and old women, like the mention of boys and girls in verse 5, is meant to carry the imagery of old and young beyond their function in forming a merism. Old people as such (both male and female), leaning for support on staffs because of their advanced years, are the antithesis of able-bodied workers. Their leisure to sit in social gatherings in public places indicates that the normal constraints of the Palestinian economy, which required at least some contributive labor both from the very old and the very young, have been removed.

5. *open places . . . open places.* This verse begins and ends with the same word *(rĕḥōbôt)*. See our NOTE above to "open places" in verse 4 for a full explication of the term and of its role in this oracle.

will be filled. The Niphal of *mlʾ*, with "open places" as subject and with "boys and girls" in adverbial relationship to it, reverses the arrangement of the previous verse, where "old men and old women" is the compound subject and "in the open places" stands in adverbial relationship to the verb. The nearly chiastic structure of the two verses together, with the human figures as close as possible to the beginning and the end of the oracle, lends to those human figures the merismatic function we have noted above (NOTE to "old men and old women," 8:4).

playing. Children are not working. Although youngsters old enough to run about on their own would normally be required to contribute to some extent to the labor needs of the family, even in an urban setting, these children can play. These children are alive and well, in contrast with the picture of dead or malnourished children of Lamentations mentioned above (NOTE to "old men and old women," 8:4). They are free enough of tasks to be able to play, meaning that the economy is strong.

6. *Thus spoke Yahweh of Hosts.* The fourth oracle begins with this familiar formula; cf. NOTES to verses 2 and 3 above.

it will seem difficult. The Niphal imperfect of *pl'* often expresses the idea of wonderment, literally "it is amazing." Yet a sense of being "difficult" can also be conveyed by this verb, as for example in Gen 18:14 and Jer 32:27. The use of the imperfect tense places the time of action for this oracle in an eschatological future and enables the prophet to close the oracle with a rhetorical and ironic question. For many of the returned Yehudites of the prophet's audience, the beatific vision of the preceding oracle must have seemed amazing if not highly unlikely, given the difficult circumstances of the restoration period.

remnant of this people. This expression, *šĕʾērît hāʿām,* occurs three times in the Book of Haggai (1:12,14; 2:2) and is normally thought to be the language of the compiler (see NOTE to "rest of the People" in Hag 1:12). It occurs also in verses 11 and 12 below. In Haggai the expression is devoid of theological meaning. In the present context, however, and in verses 11 and 12 below, it seems justified to translate "remnant" and to allow for a narrower or more technical meaning such as we find in Isa 46:3, Ezra 9:14 and many other places (see *BDB* 194). Those of Yehud who will survive the trials of the present era will truly constitute a special group within society. This group or "remnant" will enjoy once more its special relationship with Yahweh. The designation therefore, unlike its use in Haggai, has a more specialized meaning which derives its theological coloring from the overall context.

in those days. A familiar expression which designates future, eschatological time— i.e., the end of time when the historical process will reach fulfillment, as in Haggai 2:23 (see NOTE to "in that day"). It is used in Zechariah in this way a number of times (2:15 [RSV 2:11]; 3:10; 6:10; 8:10,23), and in every single instance appears in an oracular context. It also occurs regularly in Deutero-Zechariah.

should it also seem difficult. The Niphal imperfect of *pl'* is repeated (see NOTE above) and made interrogative by the initial *gam* ("also") which lacks the interrogative *he,* possibly due to haplography. The irony of the question cannot escape anyone's attention. Mitchell (1912:209) has pointed out that the purposeful omission of the interrogative lends to the clause it introduces an element of incredulity, sarcasm, or irony as in 1 Sam 21:15–16 (RSV 21:14–15); 22:7; Hab 2:19; Job 2:10; 11:3; 37:18; 38:18; 40:30 (RSV 41:6); Lam 3:38. Obviously, for Yahweh, the task could not be very difficult; hence the disbelief of the people constitutes a radical questioning of Yahweh's power. The unusual, emphatic arrangement of the Hebrew sentence has led to much discussion of this point.

to me. Literally "in my eyes" which comes as the second element in the Hebrew sentence.

7. *Thus spoke Yahweh of Hosts.* This oracular formula introduces the fifth oracle of chapter 8; cf. NOTES above to verses 2 and 3.

I will deliver. The use of the participle plus *hinĕnî* is similar to previous instances in which *hinĕnî* with the participle occurs in Zechariah (2:13,14 [RSV 2:9–10]; 3:8,9). Here it lends an eschatological cast to this oracle. The Hiphil of the verb *yšʿ,* which is also used below in verse 13, is very powerful, having the meaning of "deliver" or "save." It sets the tone of this oracle, which constitutes the climax of the central three oracles in this series of seven, all of which have an eschatological focus. In addition, it anticipates the eschatological conclusion of the set of three oracles at the end of this chapter (vv 19–23), and of this third part of First Zechariah.

from eastern lands and from western lands. Literally "from the land of the east (rising) and from land of the setting (entering) of the sun." Together the two form a merism which express a totality. Although "east" can be identified with Babylonia and the waves of returnees who had already begun to leave their mark on Yehud, it is difficult to understand "west" in a literal way. Perhaps the prophet was aware of an Egyptian diaspora, but there is no historical indication that people returned from there in the restoration period. Indeed, the unique use of *bw'* plus *šemeš* in a directional sense as opposed to a temporal sense—i.e., as the sun sets (as in Exod 22:25 [RSV 22:26]; Deut 16:6; 23:12 [RSV 23:11]; Josh 8:29; etc.), suggests that this phrase transcends both the historical present and the literal understanding of two directions. Cf. our NOTES to "northland" and "southland" in Zech 6:6 for a discussion of the use of directions. Note that in Mal 1:11 *mizrāḥ* is used in construct with *šemeš* to indicate "east," and in Amos 8:12 *mizrāḥ* has a simple directional sense.

The use of directional words, a pair intended to represent the entire diaspora, corresponds to and goes beyond the use of "land of the north" in 2:10 (RSV 2:6). Other elements of the language of this oracle draw upon, yet change the oracular addendum of 2:10–17 (RSV 2:6–13).

8. *I will bring them in.* Parallel and analogous to "I will rescue" in verse 7, the Hiphil of *bw'* vividly underscores the role of Yahweh in causing his people to be brought to the holy city. The equivalent form without *waw*-consecutive occurs in the well-known oracular verse in 3:8 announcing God's bringing of his servant, the Shoot. Note that the first use of "dwell" in reference to Yahweh in 2:15 (RSV 2:11; cf. next NOTE) is preceded by *bw'* in verse 14 (RSV v 10) and used in the Qal to signify Yahweh's coming.

they will dwell in Jerusalem. This is the only occurrence of *škn* ("dwell") in Hag-Zech 7–8 where it does not refer to God's "dwelling." In the oracles of 2:10–17 (RSV 2:6–13), *škn* twice occurs in reference to Yahweh: "I am coming to/I will dwell in your midst" (2:14,15 [RSV 2:10,11]). By shifting to the fact of the people's return to Jerusalem and their "dwelling" in the holy city, the prophet integrates the eschatological reality of God's return to Zion with the people's return. In the concluding oracles of verses 20–23, all the peoples and nations will participate in the return to Jerusalem, but here only Yahweh's people, Israel, is specified.

they will be my people and I will be their God. Those who have returned and those who will return are to be joined to Yahweh in renewal of the covenant. Again Zechariah's language echoes that of 2:10–17 (RSV 2:6–13), "they will be a people to me," 2:15 (RSV 2:11; cf. NOTE). Here, however, the full statement—expressing both the people's role and God's role—of covenant is found. The eschatological context means that the new covenant will not be like the old one (Jer 31:31–32). Rather, it will be like the new one when God's Torah will be placed among the people so that it touches their hearts, and "I will be their God" and "they will be my people" (Jer 31:33). The language of Jeremiah is identical to that of Zechariah and is reminiscent of other formulations of the covenant election formula (e.g., Exod 19:5; 29:45; Lev 26:12). The inclusion of such language here provides greater veracity to the eschatological hope and claim and also places Zechariah squarely within the stream of pentateuchal and prophetic thought.

in truth and in righteousness. Once again the prophet has used two familiar words, which would seem to be quite common in a pair, together in a covenantal context. In fact the only exact parallel is 1 Kgs 3:6, where God appears to Solomon in a dream and refers to David's exemplary behavior. In Isa 48:1 the two words occur with the negative; and they appear together in Jer 4:2, though not as a pair. Zechariah's application to God of a phrase used elsewhere only in reference to David suggests an emphasis on theocracy compatible with the postexilic situation.

9. *Thus spoke Yahweh of Hosts.* Formulaic introduction marking the presentation of the sixth oracle; cf. first NOTE to 8:2.

May your hands be strong. The imperfect of the verb *ḥzq* ("be strong") is used with jussive force to intensify the encouragement. This oracle, here and in verse 10 following, echoes the language and sentiments of Haggai. In 2:4, Haggai three times exhorts his audience to "be strong." Haggai's threefold use of *ḥzq* occurs because he separates his audience into three components (cf. NOTES to Hag 2:4): Zerubbabel, the governor of Yehud; Joshua, the high priest; and "all you people of the land." Presumably Zechariah's audience here corresponds to the third group in Haggai's set of exhortations. The "people of the land," or citizenry, have already been addressed in 7:5 in an oracle which introduces all the material of chapter 7–8. It is difficult to know whether Zechariah's omission of the name of the leaders is deliberate and significant. We might speculate that, in the two years since Haggai's oracle, the administrative structure of the restoration community had taken the shape advocated by Haggai, and by Zechariah in the temple visions. Consequently the leadership was functioning by this time and did not require the special encouragement provided by this oracle.

The exact repetition in verse 13 of these words of encouragement ("may your hands be strong") brings this, the longest in the set of seven oracles, to a close. Together, as framing devices, the repeated clauses establish the tone of this oracle, which expresses the strong conviction that the temple rebuilding will be a turning point, that it signifies a new and prosperous existence for the postexilic community. Zechariah, like Haggai, provides words of encouragement to assure the people that their efforts will not be in vain.

in these days. Zechariah is apparently referring to the present moment, the time at which he is delivering this oracle.

from the mouths of the prophets. The Hebrew phrase *mippî hanĕbî'îm* occurs only here in Haggai-Zechariah. Elsewhere in biblical usage, except in Ezek 3:17 = 33:7, which may be only an apparent and not an actual exception, the use of "from the mouth of" along with "prophet" or the prophet's name is an idiom (which usually also includes the verb "to write") meaning "dictate." Actually, it is only for Jeremiah that such a process is recorded. In 36:4,6,17,18,27,32, and in 45:1, Jeremiah orders his prophecies recorded on a scroll or a book. Jer 36:4, for example, informs us that Jeremiah summoned Baruch; and Baruch "wrote from the mouth of Jeremiah [i.e., at the dictation of Jeremiah], on a scroll, all the words of Yahweh which he had spoken to him." The circumstances accompanying Jeremiah's description of this process include the use of the verb "to call, proclaim" *(qr')* in reference to Baruch's subsequent assignment to proclaim, or read, the words that he had recorded. Furthermore, the occasion for Baruch's task of reading aloud, three times in succession, from the scroll he had prepared at Jeremiah's dictation was a fast day proclaimed in the fifth year of Jehoiakim, "in the ninth month" (36:9). That fast, in November 604, was occasioned by the advance of the Babylonian army to Philistia, a move that upset the balance of power in the world and caused great consternation in Judah (Bright 1965: lxviii, 179–83).

The information contained in Jeremiah is striking, for several reasons, in connection with this third part of First Zechariah. First, we have already noted that the use of "proclaim" (cf. NOTE to 7:7) may have a technical nuance arising from a written form of the prophecies so introduced. Second, the context for Part Three involves the gathering of representatives from outside Jerusalem along with Jerusalemite priests and prophets, a situation similar to that of Jer 36. The assembled group in Jeremiah's day "hears" the prophetic oracles as recited by Baruch, an event paralleled by the designation of the audience in this verse as "you . . . who hear." Finally, the ninth month date, marking a crucial journey of Darius or of his minions to Egypt to establish internal Egyptian rule of law (cf. NOTE to 7:1), is strangely reminiscent of the ninth-month date in Jeremiah, the occasion of a previous highly significant—for opposite reasons—journey of a Mesopotamian monarch toward Egypt.

The phrase "from the mouths of the prophets" thus signifies here, as in the rather similar situation in 604, the written words of a previous prophet. As in Jeremiah, there is a relatively short time lag between the utterance of the words and the moment of their being read aloud. In Jeremiah, the dictation takes place sometime in Jehoiakim's fourth year, and the reading occurs toward the end of the following year. Less than two years have elapsed. Zechariah here is referring to the words of Haggai that were uttered "on the day when the House of Yahweh of Hosts was refounded" (cf. following NOTE), a date almost exactly two years earlier. In other words, Zechariah's statement here can be rephrased: "May your hands be strong, you who today hear the prophecies dictated by Haggai at the time when the temple restoration work was begun." Haggai's prophecies, according to the meaning of this verse in Zechariah, had been set down in written form close to if not at the same time as the occasion during which they were proclaimed.

The use of the plural "prophets," even though Haggai alone would fit the circumstances specified in the following verse, can be explained in several possible ways. First, Haggai may have been only one of several prophets who were active during the momentous days of temple restoration. Indeed, Zechariah himself could be included in that group. Second, Zechariah frequently refers to "earlier prophets" (e.g., 1:4,6; 7:7), and the plural here may have been influenced by such usage.

the day . . . refounded . . . rebuilt. The terminology recalls Haggai's words of the twenty-fourth day of the ninth month of the second year of Darius (December 18, 520), the time when temple restoration commenced. That date was obviously a momentous one. Haggai mentions it three times directly (2:10,18,20) and twice indirectly (2:15,18), and he transmits two revelations from Yahweh on that day (2:20, "the word of Yahweh came a second time . . ."). The language of Hag 2:18 in particular corresponds with this verse insofar as they both mention a day of refounding of the "Temple of Yahweh."

Zechariah's language, however, is more inclusive than that of Haggai in his reference to temple restoration. The terms for founding *(ysd)* and for (re)building *(bnh* "build," in the Niphal) are brought together for the first and only time in this verse. Hag 1:2 anticipates the time of rebuilding; and near the end of Haggai (2:18) the day of refounding *(ysd)* is emphasized. In the visionary section of Zechariah, the founding *(ysd)* of the temple is expressed (4:9). Zechariah's visions also include, with the Qal of *bnh,* references to future temple building (6:12,13,15). But only in this third part of First Zechariah do the two words referring to temple restoration come together. A kind of balance is thus achieved: the building terminology from the beginning and the end of Haggai and from the middle (Oracular Insertion) of the central (Fourth) vision of Zechariah merge in this concluding section of Zechariah.

House of Yahweh . . . Temple. Just as the two verbs found in Haggai and in Zechariah in reference to the temple restoration activity are brought together in this verse, so too are the two terms denoting the temple. "House of Yahweh" as the general term (cf. Hag 1:2 and NOTE to "House of Yahweh") for temple and *hêkāl* (see Hag 2:15 and last NOTE to that verse) as an alternative designation are found together in this verse for the only time in the Haggai-First Zechariah corpus.

10. *before those days.* That is, before the time when temple restoration commenced; cf. preceding NOTES to verse 9.

earnings of a man . . . an animal. The language, especially in the appearance of the word *śēkar,* "earnings," is reminiscent of Haggai 1:6 (cf. NOTES to "hired hand"). The combination of man and animal is reflective of Haggai's use of "mankind and beast" (cf. NOTES to Hag 1:11). This pair is also found in Zech 2:8 (RSV 2:4). Although our translation varies, the Hebrew words for "man/mankind/people" *('dm)* and "beast/animal" *(bhmh)* are the same in all three instances.

him who went out and came in. This phrase apparently designates a traveler, one who is moving to and fro; the going and coming constitute (cf. Gen 8:7) a merism denoting movement. Free movement or travel is normally associated with military security (see Josh 6:1; 1 Kgs 15:17). The matter of economic prosperity is typically coupled with that of political security, as in the blessings of Deuteronomy (Deut 28:2–8) which influenced Haggai with respect to agricultural or economic matters. The ability of people to plant seeds and harvest crops in peace also required, of course, freedom from the threat of interference from an adversary, whether an external enemy or a contentious neighbor. Deut 28:6 specifies that latter dimension of blessing. "Blessed are you in your coming in and blessed are you in your going out." Zechariah echoes that theme, in its negative sense and in reverse order.

no peace from the foe. The lack of peace so recalled contrasts with the full peace that follows once temple work has been inaugurated. The succeeding verses (8:12,16,19) repeat *šālôm* ("prosperous," "peace," "complete") three times in its several nuances. The inability of people to move about, as we have indicated in the previous NOTE, can stem from military threats or from internal social disharmony. The latter seems to be the case here; cf. following NOTE.

each one against the other. The economic woes of the early years of the restoration were accompanied by problems of law and order. The Persians had recently instituted the policy of local autonomy (cf. NOTE to 7:1, *inter alia)* in their constituent provinces or subprovinces. Yehud was in the throes of responding to that policy by creating mechanisms of self-rule to replace the old monarchic forms of the preexilic period. Temple restoration was, symbolically but also pragmatically, part of the (re)establishment of priestly responsibility for day-to-day matters of social order. Zechariah's visions, especially the prophetic vision of chapter 3 with its treatment of the high priesthood (cf. NOTES and COMMENT), reflect the ancient notion in the Near East that the building of a temple and the establishment of justice and social harmony as well as prosperity were inextricably interrelated. The picture of economic straits in the early years of the restoration (538–520) is necessarily accompanied by a recollection of interpersonal tensions. The Persians, in stimulating the Yehudites to restore their temple, were simultaneously promulgating the authority of a priestly institution which possessed and hence could implement traditional law.

Zechariah in this third part, in the recapitulation of themes from Haggai which focus upon the economic benefits of temple building, adds the concern demonstrated earlier in Zechariah for accompanying administrative restructuring. He produces a conclusion which combines the two dimensions of the enterprise: prosperity and order. In vocabulary and in theme, this oracle brings together the material in Haggai with that of Zechariah 1–6.

11. *But now.* The adversative *waw* introduces a critical time shift in this rather long oracle (vv 9–13). Although it began in verse 9 with reference to the prophet's own day, in verse 10 the sequence shifted back to the days before the work on the temple had recommenced. This "now" thus emphatically brings back the prophet's present time.

unlike the earlier times. Literally, "former days." Again, as in verse 10, the unhappy situation of the early postexilic era is contrasted with the optimism inherent in present times. In this case, the negative aspect of earlier times is indicated only by implication and not by direct statement. In that earlier period, just as hard social and economic times were in evidence, so too was Yahweh distanced from his people in both a literal and metaphoric sense. Those earlier times were the days prior to the recommencement of work on the temple—i.e., prior to December 18, 520. The general period of exile, when Israel was separated from God, could also be implied insofar as the "seventy years" consciousness has been introduced in Part Three of First Zechariah (cf. NOTE to 7:5).

I will belong to. The Hebrew has no verb; the first-person pronoun plus *l,* "to," indicates that those represented by the following substantive will "possess" God. As in verse 8 above, adoption-covenant language asserts the belief that God will be reunited with his people. This concept complements the image of God's dwelling again in Jerusalem, the restored covenant relationship being a concomitant of the restored temple. Just as Haggai emphasizes the building project itself, Zechariah once more focuses on the attendant structuring of life in Yehud through a revalidated covenant.

remnant of this people. This is the second of three occurrences in Zechariah (cf. NOTES to "remnant of this people" above in v 6 and "rest of the people" in Hag 1:12) where the phrase apparently connotes both the returnees from Babylon and also the entire community which will reestablish its true relationship with Yahweh. Presumably not all elements of Yehudite society embraced the new theocratic scheme as Hanson has so forcefully argued (1975). The exclusive nature of Yahweh's "remnant," however, is not clear at all, and it is best to understand that term in the most inclusive way.

12. *prosperous sowing.* Literally "sowing (or seed) of peace," *zeraʿ haššālôm.* This is a

unique expression in the Bible though similar in syntax to Zech 6:13 "peaceful counsel," literally "counsel of peace" (see NOTE). *BHS,* following a host of commentators,
suggests that the text is corrupt and should be emended to "I will sow prosperity,"
'ezrē'ā šālôm. We find this unnecessary; cf. Mitchell (1912:214).

The Hebrew word "peace" *(šālôm)* occurs four times in these oracles of chapter 8
(vv 10, 12, 16, 19; cf. Hag 2:9 and Zech 6:13). Its agricultural nuance in this verse
seems clear from the next three clauses, which expand the notion of agricultural plenty.
Zechariah here reflects the concern found in Haggai, in both their negative (1:11) and
positive (2:19) formulations. For Haggai, "peace" and prosperity are linked with the
process of temple building, a concept common in the ancient Near Eastern world (see
NOTES to Hag 2:19). Here a "prosperous sowing," a good harvest that will result from
agricultural labors, is assured by Yahweh as a result of the reestablishment of the
covenant relationship between Yahweh and his people which accompanies the temple
restoration.

the vine will yield its fruit. Symbolic of all agricultural products that will produce
fruit is the vine, which in Hag 2:19 follows directly after the word for seed; cf. the
listing in Hag 1:11. In Hag 2:19 a series of additional fruits follows "vine": date,
pomegranate, and olive. Those products are not repeated here. Rather, Zechariah has
taken the first item in Haggai's list and has used it to represent all that follow.

the earth will yield its produce, and the heavens will yield their dew. A nearly identical
pair of clauses appears in Hag 1:10, in the negative and in the opposite order, in
reference to past conditions: the heavens withheld the dew so that the earth limited its
yield. In the Haggai passage, a partitive *mem* attached to "dew" (see NOTES to 1:10)
expresses the reduction in productivity, a situation Zechariah portrays as being
changed. The reversing of the order of the two clauses perhaps symbolizes the reversing of fortunes that comes with God's active involvement: the natural prior existence of
dew is no longer at stake. More likely, the change in order is part of the overall
tendency of Zech 7–8 to form correspondences, not only with Zech 1:1–6, but also with
Haggai. These latter correspondences serve to make Hag 1–2 and Zech 7–8 frame the
first six chapters of Zechariah. The reversing of the "heavens" and "earth" statements
creates a chiasm, with the God-related "heavens" in the opening (Hag 1:10) and closing (Zech 8:12) positions. This pair of statements is part of the final explicit mention by
Zechariah of the agricultural themes prominent in Haggai, so the intentional variation
of the order comes at an appropriate place.

will I cause . . . to possess. The Hiphil of *nḥl,* literally "to cause to inherit," anticipates the result of covenant loyalty—namely, possession of all the heretofore mentioned features of agricultural plenty. "The remnant" which will possess all of this may
be the community as returned from exile and those who have accepted the administration of Yehud under Persian auspices and semiautonomous home rule. But a wider
intention for "remnant" may be suggested by the language of the next verse.

13. *Just as you were a curse among the nations.* This concluding verse of the sixth
oracle continues the covenant language of the preceding verse. Judah had been regarded as a curse among the nations (Jer 24:9; 25:18; 29:22) because it had been cast off
by Yahweh, according to covenant stipulation. The full recitation of the blessings and
curses of the covenant are found in Deuteronomy 28 (cf. NOTE to "no peace . . ."

above in v 10). By drawing attention first to the people's past plight, destruction and exile, the prophet is able to highlight the opposite condition, that of blessing.

O house of Judah and O house of Israel. Though many would like to remove this apostrophic address, the context easily justifies it. The first half of this verse (13) is retrospective and hence it must be understood as reflecting those earlier conditions at the beginning of the exilic period. Since it looks to the future in the use of the imperfect of *yšʿ* (literally "so I will save"), it also serves as a kind of inclusive explanation of the meaning of "remnant"—i.e., "the remnant" will draw upon the two previous tribal groupings when it comes to possess the land. The order of Judah/Israel is the same as that in Ezekiel (37:15–22) as opposed to that of Jeremiah (e.g., 5:11; 11:10,17). This is to be expected with the center of all restoration activities focused upon Jerusalem and the temple. Yet the inclusion of "house of Israel," a term referring to the northern tribes from the time of Rehoboam and later, seems to diminish a single-minded focus on a restoration of the southern tribes (cf. 1 Kgs 12:21).

may be a blessing. At the least, the restored community of Yehud will serve as a "blessing" to the nations. This felicitous state anticipates the universalistic tone of the conclusion of First Zechariah in verses 20–23 below. It also summarizes the combined agrarian sufficiency and societal harmony of the covenant blessings alluded to in this oracle. This statement, insofar as it balances the "curse" of the beginning of this verse, can also be understood to include therefore the "House of Israel" as well as the "House of Judah" in its proclamation of blessing. The intervening apostrophic mention of both units of all Israel goes with the "you" of both clauses of the first sentence of verse 13. The language of Zechariah in this passage is indeed inclusive.

Do not fear. This expression also concludes the following oracle in verse 15 and occurs in a similar position in Hag 2:5. The negative command preceding the exhortation to be strong forms a powerful statement of encouragement.

may your hands be strong. These concluding words are identical to those which open the oracle in verse 9. Together they form an envelope to demarcate this longest single oracle of Part Three. The repetition of key words and of expressions such as this one is characteristic of Hebrew literature. Cf. for example Hag 2:15,18,19 "reflect" *(śym lb).* Cf. also NOTE on this expression above in verse 9.

14. *For thus spoke Yahweh of Hosts.* The familiar formulaic pattern introduces the seventh and last oracle of this set. Cf. NOTE to 8:2 above. The addition of *kî,* "for," at the beginning is to be expected since the oracle concludes a series. The three oracles of the succeeding verses, 18–23, are introduced as a unit with the more inclusive formula "Then the word of Yahweh came to me" (see NOTE to 8:1) followed by repetition of the formula used repeatedly in the series of seven.

Just as. With these initial words the prophet provides the structure for an antithetical compound statement, as in verse 13.

decided to afflict. The use of *zmm* plus a complementary infinitive occurs here and in the following verse as well as in Zech 1:6. The reference here is to the destruction of Jerusalem and the end of Judean independence, just as it was at the beginning of First Zechariah (1:6). There the disobedient people (as well as the earlier prophets) are expressly mentioned (see NOTES), as they are also in verses 11–14 above. The repetition of this word in chapter 8 is one of many ways in which the opening of Zechariah is linked with the conclusion.

when your ancestors angered me. The addition of the *b*-preformative to the infinitive absolute *haqṣîp* enables the author of the oracle to indicate the time sequence. The provocation of the ancestors, literally "fathers," was obviously their failure in preexilic times to heed the words of the earlier prophets as in Zech 1:4–6 and 7:11–12.

I did not relent. A Niphal perfect of *nḥm* ("relent"; often translated "repent") expresses the fact that God was not moved to soften his position vis-à-vis the earlier generation. Compare the Piel usage of the same root in Zech 1:17 (see NOTE to "comfort" in Zech 1:17).

15. *so have I again decided.* Although the Greek and Syriac add a connective, the absence here of *waw* is intentional and creates rather elegant Hebrew, *šabtî zāmamtî,* with *šwb* forming a periphrasis for "again" (so *GKC* § 120g). The repetition of *zmm,* which occurs in verse 14 above, contributes to the contrast between this clause and the previous one.

in these days. The specification of the time is integral to this verse, which spells out the good Yahweh will do to the restoration community. The same phrase is used above in verse 9. Indeed, attention to time and sequence is a salient feature of the seven oracles of chapter 8. Note these time indicators: in verse 6, "in those days"; "in these days" in verse 9; verse 10, "before those days"; verse 11, "in earlier times"; "in these days" here in verse 15.

to do good. The Hiphil infinitive of *ṭwb* expresses the exact opposite of "to afflict" in verse 14, where the verb is the Hiphil infinitive form of *rʿʿ,* "to cause evil or bad."

to Jerusalem and to the house of Judah. In this oracle God's good intention for the present restoration is made clear. The fate of the Judeans and of Jerusalem are one and the same. Not only does this accord well with the reality that the province of Yehud was not much more than Jerusalem and environs, but also by pairing the two it emphasizes the centrality of Jerusalem in the postexilic theological scheme. Further, the restoration is conceived of as a reconstitution of the community as it existed in its latest preexilic form. Whether or not Judah's destiny is to be tied to a broader-based community that would include northerners is difficult to say. Verse 13 above is inclusive in that way as an ideal statement, whereas this verse is apparently more attuned to the reality of Persian policy as well as to the general disintegration of northern tribal integrity in the centuries since the fall of Samaria. In any case, the intent here is to equate Judah's destiny with the improved status of Jerusalem, which has been achieved as a result of the temple rebuilding and the administrative reorganization within the structure of the Persian Empire.

Do not fear. The repetition of this phrase, which also occurs in the last sentence of verse 13 (see NOTE), links these last two oracles, or at least the last part of the rather long sixth oracle, with the first part of the seventh. Surely those two oracular subunits (v 13 of oracle 6 and vv 14–15 of oracle 7) have a common theme. Moreover, they both use the "Just . . . so" *(kaʾăšer . . . kēn)* particles to establish contrast. These make the last two verses of the set of seven oracles seem quite distinct, sharing none of the thematic or stylistic characteristics of the last two oracles. Verses 16 and 17 are in fact rather independent of the oracles and can be viewed as a concluding statement to all the seven oracles of 8:1–15.

16. *these are the things that you shall do.* The beginning of this verse is unique though we find close parallels in Exod 19:6 and 35:1, in the well-known opening of

Deuteronomy (1:1), and twice in prophecy (Isa 42:16 and Jer 30:4). It is the addition of "you shall do" that distinguishes this expression from its parallels. The injunctions that follow can be compared to the listing in chapter 7:9–10 (see NOTES above), though the order here is different. Both consist of four commands, two positive ones followed by two negative ones. The heading or introductory sentence for these commands in 8:16 is more in keeping with the nature of the succeeding material than is the oracular introduction to 7:9, "Thus spoke Yahweh of Hosts." Although the content of the two passages is similar, it is the distinctive character of the heading in 8:16 which renders the stipulation of 8:16–17 distinctive. Clearly the prophet or the redactor of the oracles intended to imitate pentateuchal language and draw attention to what he believed to be the epitome of covenantal law.

However, it is difficult to say precisely what the prophet or redactor is imitating, because each of the pentateuchal passages cited can be considered relevant to the restoration community. Exod 19:6 calls upon Israel to be a nation of priests; 35:1 commences to list the Sabbath as the first of many things which Moses commands; and Deut 1:1 places the whole of Deuteronomy in the form of an address given by Moses. Pentateuchal law as a whole may have influenced Zechariah's language here.

The legal and communal focus of the commands and precepts which follow in Zechariah reveal their centrality in the life of the postexilic Yehudite community. This is understandable in view of Darius's policy of encouraging local lawmakers to codify traditional legal materials as well as royal directives (see above NOTE to "in the fourth year . . ." in 7:1). There can be no doubt about Darius's motives in all this: the establishment of social order and peace within his territories.

speak truth, only truth, to one another. Of the four requirements enumerated here, this is the only one which finds no analogue in the corresponding section in 7:9–10. Yet, as obvious a formulation as it may seem, the expression as stated is original to Zechariah even though it builds upon a large corpus of biblical sayings that extol the virtues of speaking truthfully (e.g., 1 Kgs 22:16; Jer 23:28; Prov 22:21). This attribute, perhaps more than any other, undergirds the fabric of a stable society. The occurrences of the word *ʾĕmet* ("truth") in association with the word *mišpāṭ* ("judgment"), as in Ezek 18:8,9 or Zech 7:9, or Ps 19:10 (RSV 19:9), indicate that "truth" was viewed as not just a personal attribute but rather a quality which should pervade the entire social order and judicial system. Jerusalem is undoubtedly called "City of Truth" (see above NOTE to 8:3) for this reason. The meaning of this positive call for truth is reiterated in the negative formulation of the fourth precept, against perjury, in verse 17 (see NOTE).

The repetition of *ʾĕmet* ("truth") in this phrase (literally, "speak truth to one another, truth") has caused many of the ancient versions (Greek, Latin, Syriac) to omit the second "truth." It is possible that the second occurrence is a dittography, or it may be a gloss influenced by 7:9, which has *mišpāṭ ʾĕmet*, "complete truth." The "complete justice," *mišpāṭ šālôm* of the following clause of this verse may also have contributed to the confusion. Most translators have chosen to delete the second "truth." However, the repetition of "truth" in the MT could be understood as a reinforcement of the first occurrence, as in Deut 16:20 where *ṣedeq* ("justice") appears twice for emphasis. The NJPS also retains the second "truth" but connects it with the following clause and translates "render true and perfect justice."

judge with complete justice. This is the second of the set of four stipulations dealing with social order. In the list of stipulations in 7:9, the similar command to carry out justice appears first. Here in the 8:16–17 stipulation, *šālôm* is coupled with "justice." This combination of *šālôm* with another noun occurs also in 6:13 (see NOTE to "counsel of peace") and 8:12 (see NOTE to "prosperous sowing"). Zechariah seems to have a penchant for such phrases, with *mišpāṭ šālôm* here lending a sense of the proverbial even though this particular pairing is unique to Zechariah. The word *šālôm*, often translated "peace," comes from the root *šlm* and can mean "to be complete or sound," hence the noun "welfare." Used in conjunction with *mišpaṭ*, usually rendered "judgment" in English, it conveys the ultimate purpose of executing judgment—i.e., carrying out justice so as to achieve social harmony or peace.

in your gates. Gates were prominent features in the layout of Palestinian cities. Although the dominant function of the city gates was for defense, a wide space or open plaza sometimes existed on its inner side, serving as a gathering place for the urban dwellers (cf. "open places" of 8:4–5) and for civic assemblies (Neh 8:1; 2 Chron 32:6). Commercial transactions may also have been effected there (Neh 3:1,3). The designation "gates of righteousness" in Ps 118:19 is probably derived from the fact that lawsuits and legal proceedings were also conducted at the city gate (e.g., Deut 21:19; 22:24; Ruth 3:11; 4:1,10,11). So important was the gate area to Palestinian urban life that the word "gate" occasionally means "city," through synecdoche, with this critical area representing the whole of the city (Frick 1977:44–45).

Campbell, in his Anchor Bible commentary on Ruth (1975:124, 151–52) argues that, because of the association of the city gate with public assembly and judicial functions, *šaʿar* should sometimes be translated "assembly" rather than "gate." In Ruth 3:11 "gate of my people" actually designates the legal body of the town or city which is charged with the responsibility of caring for the poor, the homeless, the sojourner—i.e., meting out "complete justice" as well as adjudicating specific instances of wrongdoing. Zechariah thus reflects the vocabulary of judicial practice in his formulation of this injunction. "In your gates" (= assembly) expands the similar notion, "carry out true justice," of 7:9.

Do not devise evil in your hearts. This third command is identical to the one in 7:10, where it is listed fourth among the precepts to be followed. The reordering here does not appear to have special significance beyond stylistic variation, although it does allow the following negative admonition about truthfulness to be in final position, so balancing the initial directive about speaking truth.

This third command is the only one repeated in exactly the same form as it had in chapter 7. It must have been regarded as important to warrant such verbatim repetition. Perhaps its twofold appearance in chapters 7–8 reflects strong sectarian tensions that disrupted the unity of the restoration community, as some scholars contend (notably Hanson 1975); cf. NOTE to 7:10. However, it is simpler to understand any social tension underlying the need to repeat this command as deriving from the fact that an authoritative legal structure had not been established in the postexilic community until Darius's concerns for his empire led him to legitimize indigenous legal traditions early in his reign. Clarifying the use of legal precedents and recognizing the mechanisms for judicial functioning, both under Darius's rule, would have removed the societal tension that would naturally have existed in the absence of such arrangements.

do not love a false oath. The introduction of a precept not in the 7:8–9 list brings this second catalogue to a close. The concept expressed here in the negative is itself not new, appearing as it does in the Decalogue and in other important pentateuchal passages (Deut 5:20; Exod 23:7; Deut 19:16ff.). The prophet, by so concluding this unit, emphasizes the judicial honesty that must prevail in the new administrative scheme— viz., the Persian-supported self-rule by Yehudites, carried out by local officials and courts operating through the restored temple and its administrative structure. This scheme could not succeed if perjurious behavior impeded the establishment of the justice essential for societal stability.

The last of the four precepts echoes, albeit in negative formulation, the first. "Truth" is the essential prerequisite for the "complete justice" in verse 16, and the lack of truth —i.e., perjury or "false oath"—is the opposite condition. Compare Isa 59:14–15, where the removal of truth "in the public open places" (= courts) is equated with the absence of justice. These two clauses, "speak truth to one another" and "do not love a false oath," frame this set of four apodictic statements that proclaim the qualities of human behavior essential for a just and stable society.

all these are what I detest. "All these" must refer to the previous two negative commands, which in their neglect would represent a detestable situation. They share the quality that divisiveness and disharmony would obtain in their absence. The planning (and doing?) of evil surely disrupts social order, which cannot be restored if perjury impedes the pursuit of justice under the law of Yahweh. The two conditions together would undermine the scheme worked out with the Persians and supported, directly or indirectly, by both Haggai and Zechariah. The monarchic rule of the tenth to sixth centuries was to be replaced by the dyarchic rule of a governor and high priest, with the latter charged with responsibility for internal stability.

COMMENT

The appearance of the formula "the word of Yahweh of Hosts came" to indicate the transmission of a message from God is, as we explain at various points in the NOTES (to 7:1,8; 8:1,18), a major criterion for identifying this section as well as the concluding one (8:18–23) as distinct subunits of Part Three of First Zechariah. The specific oracles that constitute the message are then introduced by another formula, "Thus spoke Yahweh of Hosts," which occurs seven times, all in precisely that form except 8:3, which lacks "of Hosts" (see our first NOTE to 8:3) and apparently is a deliberate deviation from the norm. The repetition of this formula signifies seven individual oracles which we have numbered as follows:

8:2	Oracle 1
8:3	Oracle 2
8:4–5	Oracle 3
8:6	Oracle 4
8:7–8	Oracle 5

8:9–13	Oracle 6
8:14–15	Oracle 7
8:16–17	Coda

The seven oracles are concluded with a distinct coda, verses 16–17, which are very similar to 7:9–10; ostensibly they are part of the seventh oracle but in reality are an appendage to it.

While they constitute a set of seven, the individual oracles exhibit rather different literary and thematic features. For example, some (Oracles 1, 2, 6) exhibit strong poetic flavor, and others are entirely prosaic. The first five oracles are relatively short, consisting of one or two verses each. The last two, if one includes the coda with Oracle 7, are four or five verses in length. In general, however, they express strong prophetic awareness of past history and previous prophecy.

As a subunit, the seven oracles follow the retrospective concerning the failure of the preexilic community to heed God's word and the terrible destruction that resulted. Chapter 8 makes a transition from that past situation in its first two oracles, which emphasize God's eternal love for Zion (v 2) and perpetual "presence" (škn) in Jerusalem (v 3), thereby establishing the commitment of Yahweh to the present generation. The language of both these oracles contains familiar biblical words and phrases but introduces subtle changes, such as in the Zion/Jerusalem pairing, that we explored in the NOTES. New terminology also appears: Jerusalem is called "the City of Truth." Oracles 1 and 2 also exhibit affinities with the oracular material of Part Two of Zechariah 1–8. Oracle 1 recalls the addendum to the First Vision (1:14–17); Oracle 2 reflects 1:16 and the Oracular Insertion of 2:14–15. Together they state Zechariah's awareness of and emphasis upon certain central themes of Israel's past as they affect the expectations of the present generation.

The third oracle extends the time perspective into the future. It does this through merism, specifying the old and young (= everyone). As everyone had suffered in the events of the early sixth century, so everyone will achieve peace and prosperity in the future. The images of little children at play and of elders at rest provide contrast with the death and destruction of the Babylonian conquest. They also epitomize a healthy society, wherein people live to a ripe old age and children are free to amuse themselves, neither group being absorbed by economic necessity in the work of a struggling community. The future orientation and the idealistic picture of Jerusalem anticipate the three eschatological oracles of the end of Part Three (8:18–23), where the happy state of Jerusalem is extended to all the world.

If the beatific vision of the third oracle strains the imagination of Zechariah's contemporaries, who were faced with hard work, struggle, and uncertainty, Oracle 4 (v 6) offers encouragement in the form of a reaffirmation of God's power. It accomplishes this in a way that is typical of Zechariah—i.e., in the form of a rhetorical question (cf. 1:5,6; 7:5,6,7). The frequent use of such questions is in fact a stylistic feature of the oracular portions of Zechariah. Here the questions call attention to the indisputable fact of Yahweh's might, which can produce the most "difficult" and unexpected of changes.

The final three oracles expand in greater detail the working out of God's promised deliverance: the return from diaspora lands to Jerusalem (Oracle 5, vv 7–8), the promise of election and of temple blessing (Oracle 6, vv 9–13), and the restoration of Judah and Jerusalem (Oracle 7, vv 14–15). Together they form a rather comprehensive presentation of the features pertinent to the restoration of Zion and Judah. Only the place of the gentile nations does not appear in this scheme, but the final set of oracles (8:19–23) addresses that subject.

Oracle 5, which has affinities of language and content to 2:10–17, especially verses 10 and 14–15, has an eschatological focus. At first glance, since it deals with the return of exiles, that focus appears out of place. Many of the exiled Judeans have already returned by Zechariah's time. However, the language of the oracle—e.g., "eastern . . . western"—is meant to signify a totality. The present restoration is hardly complete, and only the future will bring full deliverance of Yahweh's people from the entire diaspora. These people will "dwell" in Jerusalem, in contrast to the other nations and peoples of the world who will only come to Jerusalem to acknowledge Yahweh's rule (8:22,23).

The sixth oracle in this group is the longest; it is also the most complex from a literary perspective. Bounded by the encouragement of "may your hands be strong" (8:9 and 13) and reminiscent of Haggai 2:4ff., it spans three time frames: past, present, future. This remarkable historical perspective, which includes specific reference to a previous event as well as prophetic activity in relationship to that event, makes Oracle 6 the premier example of the tendency toward inner biblical exegesis that surfaces periodically in Haggai-Zechariah 1–8.

Zechariah's consciousness of earlier prophetic activity culminates in this oracle, which draws heavily upon his familiarity with Haggai's work and words. His direct use of the prophecies of his colleague should not surprise us. Their ministries overlapped in the final months of 520 B.C.E., and the prophecies of both exhibit an acute awareness of the importance of temple restoration. Haggai was the one who concentrated on the temple project and who spelled out the material benefits that would accompany the rebuilt sanctuary and God's renewed presence in it. Zechariah uses Haggai's words and perhaps even a written text of his colleague's prophecies (see NOTES) in order to recall ideas and articulate concerns common to both. As elsewhere in Zechariah, the reference to and reshaping of the words of earlier prophets constitute the midrashic and homiletical activity that is one of the hallmarks of Part Three of First Zechariah. The existence of this feature contributes to our view that

Haggai-Zechariah 1-8 is a composite work, given its final shape in 518 B.C.E. or shortly thereafter in preparation for the rededication of the temple.

Although Zechariah, particularly in this oracle, relies heavily upon Haggai's language and interests, he goes far beyond an endorsement of his colleague's promotion of temple work and emphasis on the economic factors. This oracle concentrates upon the restoration of the temple and of felicity to Yehud, but elsewhere the concomitant restructuring of sociopolitical leadership and the establishment of social justice emerge as issues that are equally vital for the restoration community. Both in the visions and in the oracles, Zechariah provides divine sanction for the reshaping of national identity and the establishment of legal authority.

Oracle 6 also contains, in verse 13, covenant language that alludes to the blessings and curses of Leviticus and Deuteronomy. Zechariah's use of pentateuchal materials along with prophetic ones strengthens the authority of his message and supports the future vision. The "just as . . . so" formulation again links past events with present-future expectations. It also, along with the repetition of "Do not fear," connects the end of the oracle with the material of the seventh oracle (vv 14-15).

The third subunit of Part Three is concluded in Oracle 7 with a further statement of hope and optimism. If the preceding oracles have an eschatological character, this one sees the future age as beginning in the present. God is already dealing favorably with Jerusalem and the house of Judah "in these days." Again, the forcefulness of the prophet's expectations of good derives from his appreciation of God's past action, albeit for evil.

The seventh oracle completes a group which highlights past, present, and future conditions of community existence as functions of the relationship of Yahweh to his people. The concluding verses of this subunit of seven oracles, however, depart from that pattern; they are imperatives, urging the Yehudites to establish justice. Not only by content are verses 16 and 17 set off from the oracles, but also the placement of "do not fear" at the end of verse 15 terminates the seventh oracle and leaves the following two verses as a discrete passage. We have labeled this passage a "coda"—i.e., a concluding section or postscript that is formally distinct from the main portion of this subunit, Zion and Judah Restored: Seven Oracles. Although it stands formally and thematically apart from the seven oracles, it provides an essential complement. It establishes the fact that God's beneficent action on behalf of his community is predicated not only on his love and passion for them but also upon their adherence to covenant law.

The four commands of the coda express, as we have argued in the NOTES, Zechariah's role in sanctioning Yehudite acceptance of the authority of its traditional legal materials. As a group of four, these precepts are analogous in part to those of 7:9-10. However, the previous set of commands included reference to disenfranchised groups, as is appropriate to its retrospective preexilic setting. This group deals with Zechariah's day, in which socioeconomic disparity was a less compelling issue than was the establishment of sociolegal order. The Persians not only supported temple restoration in many of their provinces, but also encouraged the codification and legitimization of laws. Zechariah urges his countrymen to accept the authority of those laws, carried out through priestly rather than monarchic rule. Justice must prevail for social harmony to be restored in accordance with God's plan.

The four precepts, headed by the Deuteronomistic-sounding introduction "These are the things that you shall do" (cf. Deut 1:1), thus interject the factor of human morality and ethical behavior into the eschatological hope of the oracles. This combination secures Zechariah's place in the mainstream of classical prophecy. His sermonic tone and midrashic tendencies may distinguish his work from that of older prophets, but his concerns for truth and justice are the same as those of Israel's greatest prophetic figures. The seven oracles and the coda together bear the concluding stamp "oracle of Yahweh" (nĕʾum-Yhwh) and reveal the ministry of a prophet sensitively attuned to the present of his day, as it has been shaped by the past and contains the seeds of the future. The future lies simultaneously in God's hands and in the people's responsibility for obeying God's word. The final group of oracles will further enhance Zechariah's position in the matrix of Hebrew prophecy by placing this depiction of Yahweh's people in a universalistic context.

15. JUDAH AND THE NATIONS:
THREE ORACLES
(8:18–23)

18 Then the word of Yahweh of Hosts came to me:
19 Thus spoke Yahweh of Hosts,

The fast of the fourth [month], the fast of the fifth [month], the fast of the seventh [month], and the fast of the tenth [month] will become for the house of Judah [times] for joy and for gladness, and for happy festivals. Therefore love truth and peace.
20 Thus spoke Yahweh of Hosts,

Peoples and leaders of many cities will yet come; 21 the leaders of one will go to another, saying, "We will surely go to entreat the favor of Yahweh and to seek Yahweh of Hosts. I too am going."

²² Many peoples and mighty nations will come to seek Yahweh of Hosts in Jerusalem and to entreat the favor of Yahweh.

²³ Thus spoke Yahweh of Hosts,

In those days ten men from nations of all tongues will take hold, they will take hold of a Yehudite by the hem, saying, "Let us go with you, for we have heard that God is with you."

NOTES

18. *Then the word of Yahweh of Hosts came to me:.* This formula introduces the last section of Zechariah and therefore of the combined Haggai-Zechariah 1–8 work. With minor variations, it is the same as the statements that introduce the major units and subunits of Zechariah (cf. 1:1,7; 7:1,4,8; 8:1 and NOTES to those verses). In this case, a series of three oracles, each with its own formulaic introduction, follows.

Unlike most of the previous appearances of this formula, it is cast here in the first person. It concludes with "to me" rather than the expected "to Zechariah" of the narrative framework, as in 1:1,7 and 7:1,8. Only 7:4, which also introduces an oracular statement about fasting, is also in the first person, with 8:1 lacking a prepositional phrase identifying the person through whom God's message was being conveyed. This variation in the usage of the first and third person bears upon the question of the editing and compiling of Haggai-Zechariah 1–8. It allows for the possibility that Zechariah himself was involved, if these first-person formulas represent the prophet's direct reporting of God's words. The shift to the third person, i.e., the actual name of the prophet, could conceivably represent Zechariah's accommodation to the more formal pattern of section headings when he arranged all his prophecies for ongoing public use (cf. Schneider 1979:125). We might reconstruct it in this way: Zechariah ends the work with his signature so to speak, with a first-person attribution. Similarity of content dictates a similar formula at 7:4. Otherwise, he accedes to the convention of earlier prophetic works by referring to himself in the third person in the message transmission formula that heads the major sections of Zechariah 1–8.

19. *Thus spoke Yahweh of Hosts.* The formula associated with the delivery of the prophetic message initiates the first of this set of three oracles. See our discussion in the NOTES to 7:9; 8:2,3.

fast of the fourth [month]. This fast, if all the fasts enumerated here are to be associated with the fall of Jerusalem and the events leading up to that trauma, would have commemorated the time when the Judean leadership fled Jerusalem (2 Kgs 25:3–7; Jer 39:2–7; 52:6–11). After a siege of eighteen months at the end of Zedekiah's reign, the famine within the city had reached such desperate stages that a "breach was made in the city" through which the king and his army escaped. They headed southeast, through the Judean desert toward the Arabah, but were apprehended by the Babylonians near Jericho. Zedekiah himself was spared, although his eyes were put out, but all his sons and the princes of Judah—that is, all potential successors to the throne—were put to death. A fast of the fourth month, therefore, would have commemorated the end of this branch of the Judean royal family as well as the ending of the siege of

Jerusalem. However, Zedekiah's nephew Jehoiachin was already in exile in Babylon at this point so that the slaughter of Zedekiah's family did not mean the end of dynastic figures but rather the termination of the political existence of the Davidic monarchy in July of 587.

fast of the fifth [month]. The actual destruction of Jerusalem took place the following month in August, when Nebuzaradan entered Jerusalem, burning the palace, temple, and all the houses, and tearing down the walls (2 Kgs 25:8ff.; Jer 52:12ff.). This fast day was ostensibly the occasion for the Bethel delegation to come to Jerusalem. The introduction to the third part of First Zechariah describes that mission and specifies the fifth month; see our discussion in the NOTES to 7:3 and 7:5. The fourth-month fast marked the end of Davidic rule; this fifth-month fast recalled the end of the capital city and the institutions of monarchy: temple (priesthood), palace (bureaucracy), walls (military), houses (citizenry). The fast of the fifth month, known in Jewish tradition more specifically as the fast of the Ninth of Ab, became the premier fast in Judaism. In discussing Tisha b'Ab, it is not clear why the ninth day becomes the fast day, although it may have something to do with a discrepancy in the biblical sources recording the destruction. It is listed in second place here, apparently, because the ordering is a chronological one.

fast of the seventh [month]. The fast of Gedaliah, like that of the fifth month, is mentioned in the introductory section (7:1–6) of chapters 7–8. See NOTE to "in the seventh," 7:5.

fast of the tenth [month]. The siege of Jerusalem began on the tenth day of the tenth month in the ninth year of Zedekiah's reign (2 Kgs 25:1; Jer 39:1). A fast had evidently been observed to mark that moment, the beginning of the end of Judean independence and the rule of Davidides. This fourth fast completes the listing of fast days in this passage. All four fasts are related to events connected with the demise of Judah. Other fast days were sporadically or regularly observed—to mourn for the dead (1 Sam 31:13); to seek God's help (Judg 20:26); to pray for rain (Mishnah Ta'anit 1–3); to commemorate other tragedies (Jer 36:6)—by individuals or by the public as a whole. The listing of these four particular days dealing with the termination of Judean self-rule presents a dramatic contrast with the situation in 518 in which self-rule in Yehud is being reestablished.

house of Judah. This specification of Judah, as in 8:15 (cf. NOTE), differs from the inclusive language of 8:13 (cf. NOTE), where "house of Israel" is also mentioned. The appropriateness of Judah alone here can be related to the listing of the four fasts, all of which commemorate events in Judean history. Since those fasts do not deal only with the loss of the temple, which theoretically could be an occasion that might have been marked by Israelites as well, those observing the fasts would have been those who were part of the political kingdom of Judah in the early sixth century. Evidently Bethel, though originally part of the northern kingdom, had been brought under Jerusalem's authority at some time following the destruction of Israel in 722. In the late seventh century, Josiah destroyed the sanctuary still in use at Bethel and surely thereafter exercised sovereignty over that area. He and his successors would have kept a close watch over Bethel to make sure it would not ever again become a rival to Jerusalem; see our discussion of "Bethel" (in NOTE to 7:2) and of the geographical terms (in NOTES to 7:7) which effectively delineate the extent of Judah in the late preexilic period. Despite the use of Judah alone, as necessitated by the context in this verse, there is no reason to suspect that Zechariah would omit former northerners from the universal vision of these three oracles. Northerners had been assimilated into many non-Palestinian cities and would thereby be automatically included in the universalistic language of verses 20, 22, and 23.

joy and . . . gladness. Just as "month" is omitted in the designation of the fast days above, time words do not appear before this pair or before the complementary phrase that follows. The mourning and fasting referred to in the first part of this verse are contrasted with opposite behavior, as expressed in these two words. A similar transposition of emotions is presented in Jer 31:13, which follows a verse (31:12) proclaiming the agrarian prosperity anticipated in the return to Zion. The opposite transposition, the change from festivals to fasts, is noted in Amos 8:10.

happy festivals. Literally, "good assemblies." The noun *mōʿădîm* can be used as a general term for all kinds of Israelite festive occasions, those held weekly and monthly as well as the annual celebrations (cf. Hos 2:13 and Andersen and Freedman 1980:250). It refers to the assembling of celebrants at appointed or regular times (see Num 29:39) rather than to spontaneous or occasional celebrations. The point is that all such gatherings are now to have positive connotations, not negative or sorrowful ones; that is, they are to be festivals and not fasts. The imagery of joyful celebration at special times is a complement to the picture of the natural behavior of old and young in everyday life presented in 8:4–5 (cf. NOTES).

truth and peace. This pair perhaps summarizes the detailed series of exhortations in verses 16–17 above (see NOTES). "Truth" appears here in the last of six occurrences in Part Three of Zechariah (its only occurrences in Haggai-Zechariah 1–8), and "peace" likewise makes its final and sixth appearance in this verse. It is in this passage and in 8:3 (see above NOTE to "City of Truth") that *ʾĕmet* is found with the definite article and here only that *šālôm* occurs with it. In all three instances the nouns take on an independent and abstract quality. Elsewhere, they are found without the definite article, in construct or with prepositions, and so have adjectival or adverbial force (Zech 7:9; 8:3,8,16; Hag 2:9; Zech 6:13; 8:10,12,16; see appropriate NOTES to those passages). The shift to a more abstract or independent force for these words suits the eschatological context of the oracles that follow. Their appearance in this oracle provides a bridge from the summation (vv 16–17) of the previous set of oracles (8:1–17) to the universal scope of the end of Zechariah. Truth and peace have been established, allowing for all festivals in Judah now to be celebrations. That situation is the necessary prelude to the global recognition of Yahweh which is to ensue.

20. *Thus spoke Yahweh of Hosts.* Formulaic introduction to the second of three concluding oracles in First Zechariah (see NOTES to 7:9; 8:2,3).

Peoples. The plural *ʿammîm* occurs in Haggai-Zechariah 1–8 only here and in verse 22 below. Elsewhere in this corpus, "people" in the singular refers to one component or other of the Yehudites—e.g., "this people," "all the people," "remnant/rest of the people," "people of the land." The question arises as to the population indicated by Zechariah's use of the plural in this eschatological vision. Many commentators, undoubtedly influenced by the use of "peoples" together with "nations" *(gôyîm)* in the next verse, as well as by the inclusive "nations of all tongues" in verse 23 (cf. NOTE), have assumed that "peoples" here is equivalent to "nations" and represents foreign political entities. While the equation of "peoples" and "nations" is conceivable, we propose that they are not synonymous terms in this passage.

The scholarly literature on "peoples" and "nations" is rather extensive, because of the frequent occurrence of the two terms in the Hebrew Bible as well as because of the variation in the meanings they exhibit. Nonetheless, it is generally accepted that "people" tends to be used as a social and cultural term with implications of consanguinity, whereas "nation" exhibits features of political or territorial affiliation. These distinctions, however, are hardly complete or fully consistent (see the summary provided by Clements 1975).

Because ʿam, and not gôy, tends to be applied to Israel or parts thereof, the appearance here of ʿammîm should be given consideration as a designation for Israelites in the broadest sense. Some cultural identification of non-Yehudite groups, Samaritans and others living north, south, or east of the territory of Yehud, must have persisted into the postexilic period. Linguistic affinity if nothing else would have given such peoples a feeling of connection with the inhabitants of Yehud. Especially since "nations" are specified below (verse 23) in terms of their lack of a language common to that of the Yehudites, "peoples" in this context can logically represent groups culturally akin to those of Yehud. Support can be found in Amos's oracles for the possibility that Zechariah conceptualized a group of "peoples" connected to Israel/Judah more closely than were the great foreign nations of Egypt and in Mesopotamia. Amos deals primarily with a group of eight nations, including Judah and Israel, that occupy the territory between Egypt and Assyria. This group is treated as though they all had a connection with Yahweh at one time or were dealt with by Yahweh in some direct way (cf. especially Amos 9:7). In other words, Zechariah may have been following Amos in his designation of "peoples" as a group distinguished from "nations" in terms of their relationship to Israel/Judah.

Not only does the examination of "peoples" in relationship to "nations" in these oracles allow for such a meaning, but also the general sensitivity displayed by Zechariah to groups of people with varying relationships to Jerusalem and its institutions helps to justify it. We remind the reader of the careful attention to the distinct factions, with respect to the community of exiles of Babylon, that are apparently represented in The Crowning episode of 6:9–15 (see NOTES to 6:10 and 14 and COMMENT to the whole section). Moreover, in the structure of the visions as a whole, Zechariah moves his audience from a global purview toward the central point, the temple in the central vision (chapter 4), and back out to a whole-world setting (see Introduction). Zechariah's work exhibits consciousness of the progression from Jerusalem outward of that city's role and destiny.

It should not surprise us, therefore, to find an analogous movement in Part Three of First Zechariah. This section is initiated (7:1–6) by a focus on the relationship of Yehudites not resident in Jerusalem to the new authority now associated with Jerusalem institutions. The set of seven oracles (8:1–17) is dominated by the prophetic concern to include that population in the Yehudite administration, a subunit of the Persian Empire, based in Jerusalem. In this last set of oracles the prophet's message is gradually extended outward, ultimately achieving, as do the visions albeit for a radically different purpose, a universal perspective. In such a progression the culturally aligned but politically undefined "peoples" precede the larger world of all "nations," those both culturally and politically distinct from Yehud. Eventually they are linked in verse 22.

leaders of many cities. If "peoples" (preceding NOTE) designates populations of the Levant culturally akin to the Yehudites, this associated phrase gives that term the political coloring that eventually allows it to stand next to the more political word "nations" in verse 22. Similarly, we might interject, "tongues" lends to "nations" in verse 23 a cultural component that enables that other term to be paired with "peoples."

Usually rendered "inhabitants of many cities" (RSV, NJPS, etc.), this phrase is more likely a technical, political designation for the "rulers" of a city or of a larger territorial entity. Gottwald (1979:512–34) has carefully and in great detail provided evidence for, among the more than a thousand occurrences of *yšb* ("to dwell, inhabitant") in the Hebrew Bible, a small but significant set of usages of that verb in which it denotes leadership. Usually in participial form, as in this instance, *yšb* represents the ellipsis of an idiom, "sitting on (the throne of) X" which is the same as saying "ruling X." The participle thus signifies a "ruler/leader," one who holds an office and exercises the authority of that office (cf. NOTES to "associates who rule" 3:8, where Joshua's colleagues are so described). The term is used idiomatically in reference to community leaders, and is usually found in the plural, as a collective for the "authorities" of a place. Of the sixty or so times that *yšb* has this particular idiomatic meaning, it designates local Canaanite officials, including Israelite ones, in the majority of its occurrences. To state it in a slightly different way, whenever "rulers/leaders" refers to non-Israelite authorities, it almost always is used for other Palestinian officials (usually ones who come into conflict with the Israelites).

"Leaders of many cities," in light of the foregoing, contributes a political dimension to the pair of terms formed by coupling this phrase with the preceding cultural word "peoples." The strong association of *yōšĕbîm,* "leaders" in its political nuance, with the rulers of Palestinian political entities lends support to our contention that "peoples" here refers to groups having some cultural affinity with the Yehudites. Surely Palestinians, east or west of the Jordan—Samaritans, Edomites, Sidonians, Tyrians, Syrians, Philistines, and others—would constitute related groups. If archaeology is able to measure cultural affinity, it has surely provided evidence that Israel/Judah and then Yehud remained part of Levantine material culture throughout their history and did not adopt, except superficially, the material culture of Egypt or of the Mesopotamian states even when dominated politically by those empires.

The "cities" of this phrase, we might add, probably reflects the prevailing form of local political organization, whereby urban centers dominated the relatively small ecological units that made up the Palestinian landscape. Cities were part of a larger rural-urban system in which the city or walled settlement itself actually represented a much larger territory and population—i.e., its hinterland—than that contained within the city walls.

yet. Two Hebrew words, *ʿōd ʾăšer,* underlie this single English adverb; or rather, "yet" translates *ʿod* but doesn't actually represent the second term, *ʾăšer.* As a time indicator (cf. NOTE to "in those days," verse 23 below, and also *inter alia* our NOTE to "in these days" in 8:15 above), *ʿod* alone would be sufficient. The juxtaposition with the relative *ʾăšer* ("which, that") is difficult. The Vulgate sensed the difficulty, or else had a different text, and reads *ʿod* as *ʿad,* "until." Modern English translations have not been able to express the *ʾăšer* in English syntax. If the relative is retained, the following clause would normally be a subject and not an object clause (so Mitchell 1912:217). The intrusion of the verb before the subject in this clause is awkward but not impossible, and so the excision of *ʾăšer* is not mandatory. Perhaps *ʿôd* together with *ʾăšer* forms a compound temporal expression akin to *kaʾăšer*, "when." Note that below in verse 23, the relative *ʾăšer* again appears before the verb, "take hold" (see NOTE).

come. The verb "to come," *bwʾ*, appears twice in these verses, here and again at the beginning of verse 22. In addition, the verb "to go" *(hlk)* is repeated five times: three times in verse 21, once in verse 22, and once more in verse 23. Together they provide a strong sense of movement. Furthermore, the sevenfold repetition of motion verbs may indicate totality, since the number seven can function in that symbolic way in Semitic literature. "Will come" of verse 20 thus introduces a group of verbs that depict the total flow of nations to Jerusalem, or the universal recognition of Yahweh.

21. *leaders*. Without the prepositional phrase "of the cities" as in verse 20 and without the associated "peoples," "leaders" by itself stands for all that is represented by the full subject of the preceding sentence. We translate "leaders" rather than "inhabitants," for reasons set forth in the NOTE to "leaders of many cities" in 8:20.

entreat the favor. Zechariah's use of this idiom connects this oracle with the introduction to Part Three, where the same idiom is found (see 7:2 and NOTE to "entreat the favor"). As we pointed out above, this is political language, used almost always with political leaders as the subject and with Yahweh as the object. The supreme authority of Yahweh is conveyed. Here the circle of those recognizing Jerusalem's supremacy is extended from the Yehudites outside Jerusalem (i.e., the Bethelites and company) to the related Palestinian groups, as we have indicated in our NOTES to "peoples" and "leaders of many cities," 8:20.

seek. The common verb *bqš*, when used in cultic contexts such as this verse, involves activities associated with prayer or request (e.g., Exod 33:7). Sometimes "Yahweh," or "the name of Yahweh," or "the word of Yahweh" is the object of such action; in other places it is the more anthropomorphic "face/presence of Yahweh" that appears as the object of *bqš*. However, the specific cultic activity in seeking Yahweh or his face is nowhere specified. The latter is more descriptive and may be the original or oldest usage, deriving as it probably does from royal contexts in which supplicants come "to seek the face of the king"—i.e., to gain the king's attention and favor (Wagner 1975: 236–39). As such, it is closely related to the idiom "to entreat Yahweh," literally "entreat the face of Yahweh," which accompanies "seek" here and in the next verse, and which occurs in the introduction of Part Three of First Zechariah (cf. NOTE to "entreat," 7:2). Together, these terms in the cultic sphere apparently indicate the desire for an oracle, or a divine decision, on some matter brought before God by a supplicant. Yahweh thereby becomes the ultimate authority for an individual who is seeking guidance and legitimation for something he is about to do in his own life or, more likely at least as far as "entreat" is concerned, in the community he represents.

"Seek" and "entreat" here and in the next verse extend the community of those who recognize Yahweh's authority. First in 7:2, Yehudites not resident in Jerusalem acknowledge Yahweh's will, as mediated through priest and prophet. Now the leaders of peoples surrounding Yehud accede to Yahweh's supremacy. And finally in verse 22 all the other nations join in this recognition of Yahweh's global existence and power. This progression is reviewed in our first NOTE to verse 22 below.

Note that "seek" follows "entreat" in this verse, and that the reverse order appears in the next verse. The resulting chiasm links the two verses and makes the combined subjects of these verbs into an inclusive set. That the order of terms can be changed indicates that if a technical procedure was once associated with each of the terms, whereby one would have to precede the other, such a procedure is no longer operant. Or, the two terms may not refer to technical cultic acts related to divination but rather to the general notion of appearing before the deity in order to initiate some cultic act which will secure the desired message from or approval of the deity.

I too am going. The curious change of number from the first person plural to the first person singular is probably occasioned by the fact that the "rulers" are said to have expressed individually, "one . . . to another," their determination to go to Yahweh's presence. Like "go up" *('lh)* and "come" *(bw'),* the verb *hlk* ("go") can be used in a technical sense to refer to a visit to a sanctuary (e.g., 1 Kgs 3:4; Isa 30:29). Even though neither Jerusalem nor the temple is specified, the idiom "entreat the favor of Yahweh" establishes the cultic context. Indeed, the repetition of this idiom along with a parallel one ("to seek Yahweh") in the next verse includes the mention of Jerusalem. The verb *hlk* is the first word and also almost the last word in verse 21. As such the movement toward the destination of Jerusalem is underscored. The eschatological picture of peoples—or many nations—"going" to the "mountain of Yahweh" is shared with Isa 2:2–3 and Mic 4:1–2 (cf. NOTES to "Mountain of Yahweh of Hosts" and "Mountain of Holiness" in Zech 8:3).

22. *many peoples and mighty nations.* In our NOTE above to "peoples" (8:20), we explored possible nuances for "peoples" and concluded that "peoples" and "nations" here are not synonymous but rather complementary. We can look at Jerusalem and Yehud as the center of several concentric geographic circles. Actually, Jerusalem would be at the center, and Yehud would be the first circle. "Peoples" then would constitute the next circle, moving outward, in that it refers to neighboring groups with some cultural affinity to Yehud. Because it is linked with "leaders," a political coloration accompanies its essentially cultural meaning. Finally, the other "nations" of the world would be the outermost circle.

"Nations," from the perspective of the Palestinian, would probably designate the larger political entities of the ancient world, the nation-states or empires that had periodically arisen in Mesopotamia, Anatolia, and Egypt. The word for nations, *gôyīm* as we have explained in our NOTE to "peoples" in verse 20, usually has a decidedly political connotation, as it does indeed here. But a cultural dimension is also present because of the identification of the nations in the next verse (cf. NOTE to "nations of all tongues," v 23). The adjectives in this pair, "great" and "mighty," *rabbīm* and *'āṣûmîm,* are somewhat interchangeable, each meaning "great" or "mighty" as well as "many" or "numerous" (cf. Exod 1:9; Mic 4:3). Both are regularly found, along with *gādôl,* "great," as adjectives describing both "people" and "nation."

seek . . . entreat. The order here reverses that of the preceding verse; see our discussion of these terms in NOTES to "entreat the favor" in 7:2 and 8:21 and to "seek" in 8:21. "Entreat the favor" in second position in this verse creates a chiasm with the preceding verse and so joins the two verses. Furthermore, its terminal placement in this verse, the second to the last verse of Part Three of First Zechariah, corresponds to its appearance (without "seek") in the second verse (7:2) of this major section of Zechariah's work. An overall framework for Part Three is so provided.

23. *thus spoke Yahweh of Hosts.* This is the final occurrence of this oracular formula (cf. NOTES to 7:9; 8:2,3). A variant occurs in Deutero-Zechariah (11:4), and the same formula occurs once in Malachi (1:4).

in those days. The eschatological meaning of this standard expression applies to this last oracle and also to the previous one (vv 20–22), which likewise concerns the "nations." It is less clear that it can also be applied to the first oracle (v 19), which may refer to the prophet's present as well as to the eschatological future. The plural form, unlike the singular—as in Hag 2:23 (see NOTE to "on that day")—leaves the future time unspecified. All occurrences of the plural form in First Zechariah occur in chapter 8 (i.e., Zech 8:6,9,10,11,15). It is likely that the highly favorable picture of the future depicted in 8:18–23 as well as in the longer presentation in 8:2–23 emerges from the positive mood in Yehud in the period just prior to the rededication of the Second Temple—i.e., 518–515 B.C.E. Statements (direct or indirect) pertaining to the restoration of the Davidic monarchy are not present in Part Three of First Zechariah. Apparently, for the author and/or compiler of these final oracles, the new status quo under Achaemenid sovereignty is sufficient cause for optimism.

ten men. The symbolic character of the number "ten" has long been recognized (Farbridge 1970:140ff.). Its special place among all numbers no doubt derives from the convenience of using two hands for calculations, a decimal system of numeration being universal. The most basic use of ten is to denote a round or complete number (Pope 1962:565), which is its purpose here and in many other places in the Bible (e.g., Gen 24:10; Lev 26:26; Num 14:22; Josh 22:14; Isa 6:13; Jer 41:8). It may also function as a special sacred number because it is the sum of two other significant numbers, three and seven. For example, the institution of tithing in Israel—giving one tenth to the Lord— is intended to show how all that a person possesses belongs to God. In the present context "ten men" surely represents all mankind other than Israel (Yehud).

The symbolic nature of ten in this context is evident from the way in which these ten gentiles are related to a single Yehudite. The prophet is not talking about a single Yehudite any more than he is talking about ten foreign individuals. Rather, he is dealing with a ratio of ten to one. For every ten foreigners there will be one Yehudite for the former to attach himself to, the general idea being that the many will seek out the few in order to go to Yahweh. Not only do the "ten" say "Let us go" in the first person plural, but also the pronoun used with the preposition "with" in the statement made by the foreigners is plural. "With you" refers to more than one person, that is, to more than one Yehudite. Together, ten foreigners for every Yehudite, they proceed toward Yahweh.

nations of all tongues. Literally "tongues of the nations," *lĕšōnôt haggôyīm.* This is the only occurrence of this expression in the Hebrew Bible though these two words occur together, but not in construct, in Isa 66:18 to denote the totality of the non-Israelite world: "The time has come to gather all the nations *(kōl haggôyīm)* and tongues *(lĕšōnôt);* they will come and behold my glory." The meaning of *lāšōn* as "tongue" or "language" is assured here; it is parallel to *gôy* ("nation") a number of times (Gen 10:5,20,31 and to *ʿam* "people"; see Neh 13:24; Est 1:22; 3:12; 8:9). Hence, the construct form here surely denotes those foreign nations outside Israel/Yehud that speak other languages. Insofar as language is a cultural phenomenon, this expression adds a nonpolitical dimension to the inherently political connotation of "nation" (*gôy*, cf. NOTE to "peoples," 8:20). For the meaning of "nation" see our NOTES to Hag 2:7, and to "many peoples and mighty nations" above in verse 22.

This concluding oracular section (vv 18–23) has progressively included in its eschatology the Jerusalemites, the Yehudites, the neighboring groups, and now the more distant foreign nations. Such an ever-broadening circle of people to be accounted for as part of Yahweh's redemptive scheme makes Zechariah one of the most universalistic of all the prophets.

will take hold. The relative *'ăšer* is as awkward here before the Hiphil verb *yaḥazîqû* as it is before "will . . . come" in verse 20 above. In both cases the relative appears in the Hebrew directly following a time indicator, "yet" in verse 20 and "in those days" here. We would argue for the retention of *'ăšer* ("yet") in both cases despite the unusual word order.

The forceful verb "to take hold," (*ḥzq* in the Hiphil) graphically portrays the way in which the foreign nations will come to Yahweh—that is, by accompanying the Yehudites. The verb appears twice in this verse, first here as an imperfect and in the following clauses as a perfect with a *waw* consecutive. The repetition highlights the importance of the act described, namely, the taking hold of the hem of a garment. It may also help to explain the presence of the *'ăšer* in this complex syntactical situation. We have indicated this difficulty in our translation by adding a dash between the two "take holds" in the English.

they will take hold . . . by the hem. This repetition of the verb brings the object of the verb into the picture. As recent studies have shown (see McCarter 1980:208) *heḥĕzîq bakkānāp,* "seize the hem, take hold of the garment," depicts the act of supplication, submission or importuning (AKK *sissikta ṣabātu;* Aram. *'ḥz bknp).* The most famous example for ancient Israel is recorded in 1 Sam 15:27, where Saul is reported to have grasped the robe of Samuel, who was about to walk away, in a final plea for mercy. In addition, "to spread a garment" (or "wing"), as in Ruth 2:12, and 3:9, was an expression of a pledge of marriage (Campbell 1975:123). The taking hold of the hem of a Yehudite's robe by *ten* men of foreign nations of all tongues conjures up a picture of rapprochement, submission, and loyalty. A well-known gesture of the ancient world therefore vividly suggests the eschatological prospect that all the nations will come to Jerusalem to accept the one God, and that they will recognize Yehudite primacy by performing that action.

We refer the reader to the use by Haggai of *knp* ("corner") in a rather different context but one which likewise signifies the special role of the edge of a garment, be it "hem" or "corner." See NOTE to "corner," Hag 2:12. Perhaps this is another instance where the vocabulary of Part Three of First Zechariah corresponds to that of Haggai.

Yehudite. The word *yĕhûdî,* "Yehudite," specifies, in terms appropriate to the postexilic period, the role of God's people in the universal acknowledgment of Yahweh. Even in an eschatological perspective a "Yehudite" is a citizen of Yehud who has accepted the new reality of postexilic Israel: its new administrative structure, its restored temple, and Yahweh's sovereign presence. By taking hold of the garment, the non-Yehudite signifies his willingness to accept the supremacy of the God of Israel. This beatific vision involves no cataclysmic reversal of the current situation; rather, the future will emerge from the present order. "Yehudite" is singular, but it has a collective sense, since the preposition of the following phrase, "with you," has a plural object.

Let us go with you. The cohortative first person plural of *hlk* ("to go") plus *ʿm* ("with") presents the purpose for which the nations take hold of a Yehudite: their intention to go to Jerusalem and acknowledge Yahweh's dominion. The prophet has retained the biblical idea of Jerusalem's centrality in the cosmos, for even the non-Yehudite must go there according to his imagery. On God's "Holy Land" (cf. NOTES to Zech 2:15–16) will the new era commence. This locative principle is one of the hallmarks of Hebrew literature, both biblical and postbiblical. In this cohortative utterance, nations desire to embrace Yahweh not only together with the Yehudites but also on the terrestrial location of Yehud/Jerusalem (cf. Zech 6:15, which is addressed to Yahwists). These notions are articulated in a similar way in the oracular additions to Zechariah chapter 2, especially verses 15 and 16.

The object of the preposition "with" is "you" plural, as it is also in the final words of this verse. Since the antecedent is "Yehudite," it is clear that the single Yehudite is really a symbolic person and that the prophet is dealing with a ratio of ten to one. See NOTE above to "ten men."

God is with you. The use of *ʾelōhîm,* "god," at the very conclusion of the Book of First Zechariah is climactic. It is used only three times in Haggai (1:12², 14), all cases possibly attributable to the compiler, and three times in Zechariah (6:15; 8:8,23), in contrast with the ubiquitous appearance of "Yahweh" (about 125 times). In the last chapter especially, "Yahweh of Hosts" punctuates almost rhythmically the succession of oracles. The term *ʾelōhîm* as the generic word for God is used in this universal context because it is an all-embracing designation. "Yahweh," which occurs nearly seven thousand times in the Bible, as opposed to the approximately twenty-five hundred usages of *ʾelōhîm,* is the name of the God of Israel, whereas *ʾelōhîm,* especially when preceded by the definite article (e.g., Deut 4:35,39; 2 Sam 7:22; 1 Kgs 8:23) expresses the notion of incomparability (Ringgren 1974:282). In this final utterance of the prophet, *ʾelōhîm* lends literary style and grace to the last oracle and adds the universality of the image.

COMMENT

The concluding section of the third part of Zechariah 1–8, and indeed of the Haggai-Zechariah 1–8 composite, is marked by the final appearance in this corpus of the formulaic announcement of the transmission of a message from Yahweh to the prophet. The first of the three oracular statements in this section refers directly to the first section of Zechariah 7–8, the Introduction of 7:1–6. Its history of fast days revives the question put by the delegation from Bethel in 7:3 as well as the prophetic response of 7:5b–6. In addition to the mention of fast days, the language of 8:21–23 picks up on that used in the Introduction by using the same word ("to entreat") to describe official or formal movement to Jerusalem. These features clearly link 8:18–23 with 7:1–6, and Part Three of Zechariah is provided with a literary framework that denotes an integrity to chapters 7 and 8 as a unit.

We have discussed above in the Introduction the ways in which the last two chapters of Zechariah 1–8 are related to Haggai 1–2 in the construction of a composite work. As part of that formation, the concluding section of Zechariah 7–8 provides several additional correspondences to Haggai upon which we have not yet commented. The second clause of verse 23, which repeats the verb of verse 22 and then introduces its object, contains two words which echo elements of Haggai.

First, the verb "take hold" is the Hiphil of *ḥzq*, which appears in the Qal in Haggai 2:4, where it is used to encourage Zerubbabel, Joshua, and "all the people of the land" to "be strong" in their task at hand, the restoration of the temple. Similarly, Zechariah uses it in 8:9 to refer to that situation of 520 and also in 8:13 to indicate Judean-Israelite revitalization of the land. Our English rendering "take hold" (= "grasp") does not reveal the connection between the Qal and Hiphil usages, and in fact the semantic link is not entirely clear. Nonetheless, the repetition of this root would be obvious to the Hebrew-speaking audience and might further connect Haggai with the end of Zechariah while also providing contrast between the hoped-for strength of Yehudites in Haggai and the foreign subjects of the same verb of Zechariah 8. At the end, and in the future, the nations perform an act which acknowledges a flow of power outward from the Yehudite individuals of whose garments they take hold.

In somewhat analogous fashion, the word "garment" *(knp)* repeats and transposes a motif found in Haggai. Haggai 2:10–19 presents a priestly ruling and provides a prophetic explanation. The passage utilizes "corner" *(knp)* as an element in the question posed to the priests. There it refers to the part of a garment that touches some foodstuff, or, probably, a corpse, which might thereby convey sanctity or defilement. The use of *knp* comes in the question there; here at the end of Zechariah 7–8 it comes in the prophetic answer. There it concerned the Yehudites and the meaning of their efforts; here it involves the international community. There it was rooted in a technical cultic point; here it conveys the role of God's people in bringing all people to Yahweh. The same word, in a dramatically different context, represents the way in which Haggai-Zechariah 1–8 as a whole concerns both the particular and the universal.

The expansion of prophetic interest to the worldwide community is replicated in the sequence of people involved in the three oracles of 8:19–23. The question about fasting in the Introduction of 7:1–6 served to demonstrate that by 518 B.C.E. Yehudites outside Jerusalem acknowledged Yahweh as their God and the institutions of Jerusalem as the means for the establishment of his theocratic rule over his people. This concluding section develops that theme.

Its three eschatological oracles widen the scope of those who acknowledge Yahweh so that Haggai-Zechariah 1–8 concludes with a vision of all the world going to Jerusalem, an act which symbolizes recognition of Yahweh's supremacy.

The first oracle recapitulates the fasting theme by referring to four fast days and thereby augmenting the mention of the one (fifth month) and then the two (fifth and seventh month) fasts in the Introduction of 7:1–6. The group of four, all dealing with fasts that commemorate one aspect or another of Jerusalem's demise early in the sixth century, establishes the wider community of all those descendants of the preexilic state of Judah. Not just Jerusalem, and not simply Bethelites, but the entire "house of Judah" will become part of the festal atmosphere. Societal order and prosperity will entail happiness for all. The future vision involves a transformation. World events in the past evoked fasting, but in the future world events will bring about joyous feasts.

The inclusiveness of Zechariah's optimistic view becomes fully apparent in the following two oracles. There appears to be a progression in verse 20 through 23:

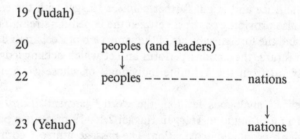

```
19 (Judah)


20                    peoples (and leaders)
                             ↓
22                    peoples – – – – – – – – – – nations



                                                      ↓
23 (Yehud)                                         nations
```

We have suggested in our Notes that "peoples" may in this passage refer to the groups around Yehud which bore some cultural and linguistic resemblance to the Yehudites. "Nations" then would be the broadest possible term, designating political-cultural entities from far beyond the Palestinian setting of Yehud. The most inclusive perspective is that of verse 23, where "ten" and "all tongues" combine with "nations" to symbolize global participation in the acknowledgment of Jerusalem as the legitimate terrestrial seat and symbol of Yahweh's universal rule.

Zechariah's vision of the future is fully inclusive, as is Haggai's (2:7), and at the same time it is rooted in the particularity of the geographic and sociopolitical epicenter of Yahwism. The territorial orientation is provided by the direct mention of Jerusalem (v 22) and by the allusion to temple festivals (v 19). In addition, the choice of verbs in verses 20–23 reinforces the centrality of Jerusalem in this scheme.

Two sets of verbs accomplish this task. First, the verbs "to come" *(bw')* and "to go" *(hlk)* appear repeatedly—seven times, to be exact. The repetition in itself creates a sense of movement, with the sevenfold appearance of these verbs intensifying the movement and perhaps also signifying the totality of the flow toward Jerusalem. The selection and positioning of these action verbs in the last two oracles underscore the full global acknowledgment of the centrality of Jerusalem. In addition, the combination in verses 21 and 22 of "entreat" *(ḥlh)* and "seek" *(bqš),* two words that are part of the vocabulary of political and cultic recognition of authority, provides graphic depiction of individuals appearing in supplication at court. Rather than a royal palace and a human king, the temple or earthly residence of God and the deity are the objects of the international gathering to Jerusalem. The coming/going has its counterpart and completion in the entreating/seeking that is the purpose of that flow.

Not only does Jerusalem play an integral role in the involvement of all people and nations in Yahweh's rule, but also Yahweh's people are to be a distinct part of the eschatological inclusiveness. The final verse of Haggai-Zechariah 1–8, which represents the pinnacle of Zechariah's global scope, includes the personal and the particular. The tiny Yehudite community, symbolized by the single Yehudite of verse 23, provides the historic and functional contact between the future worldwide membership in Yahweh's domain and the past-present relationship of Yahweh with a tiny portion of the population of the world. The rest of the people in the world will eventually find their way to Yahweh through those who already stand in relationship to God.

INDEX OF AUTHORS
INCLUDING MODERN TRANSLATIONS*

Ackroyd, lxii, lxviii, lxix, 19, 23, 34, 49, 51, 52, 57, 58, 63, 66, 117, 118, 122, 164, 173, 191, 194, 208, 212, 286, 291, 302, 303, 330, 337, 353, 362, 368, 383, 387
AH, 235
Aharoni, Y., 382, 397
Aharoni, Y. and M. Avi-Yonah, 397
Ahlstrom, G. W., 22, 318
AID, 63
Albright, W. F., 11, 13, 78, 181, 204, 382
Alt, A., 14, 15
Alter, R., 57
Amiran, D. H. K., 29
Amsler, S., 19, 36, 63, 167, 180, 198, 205, 338
Andersen, F., 24, 51, 63
Anderson and Freedman, lxii, 5, 7, 61, 91, 116, 122, 170, 202, 258, 356, 435
ANEP, 305
ANET, 235, 319, 320
Ap-Thomas, 384
AV, 51, 364
Avigad, N., 9, 12, 13, 15, 154, 182, 370

Baldwin, J., 19, 57, 120, 151, 176, 180, 200, 208, 212, 215, 254, 352, 362, 382, 383
Barker, M., 97, 297, 298
Barrick, W. B., 110

BDB, 20, 59, 60, 62, 110, 113, 139, 140, 141, 142, 190, 195, 196, 248, 257, 258, 306, 354, 417
Begrich, J., 55
Bentzen, A., 204
Berakhot, T. B., 187
Bertman, S., 56
Beuken, W., lxvii, lxix, 94, 97, 191, 196, 215, 361
Bewer, J. A., 65, 211
BH³, lxi, lxii, 97, 330
BHS, lxi, lxv, 49, 61, 63, 67, 92, 190, 297, 326, 330, 337, 346, 371, 423
Blenkinsopp, J., 385
Bratsiotis, N. P., 171
Brenner, A., 112, 321, 322
Brichto, 283, 284
Bright, J., 9, 10, 11, 16, 78, 202, 303, 381, 420
Brockington, L. H., 9, 10
Broshi, M., 156

CAD, 190, 191, 234
Camp, C., 301
Campbell, E. F., 427, 441
Caquot, A., 187
Carroll, R. P., 52
Cazelles, H., 167
Ceresko, A. R., 350, 363
Chary, T., 164
Chiat, M. J., 254

* This and subsequent indexes were prepared with the kind assistance of Stephen Goranson, graduate student at Duke, and John Jorgensen, editorial assistant at ASOR Publications, Durham, N.C.

Childs, B. S., 331
Christiansen, D. L., 18
Clements, R. E., 436
Clifford, R. J., 162, 169, 245, 320
Cohen, G., 170
Coogan, M. D., 343
Cook, J. M., 4, 14, 20, 37, 72, 102, 147, 181, 185, 194, 203, 232, 278, 279, 317, 318, 324, 368, 380
Cooke, G., 183
Cowley, A. E., 198
Cross, F. M., Jr., 13, 15, 16, 65, 118, 168, 182, 193, 211, 345, 353
Cross, F. M., Jr. and D. N. Freedman, 170
Cross, F. M., Jr. and R. J. Saley, 283

Dahood, M., 124, 245, 252, 306, 400
Davies, W. D., 170
Demsky, A., 364
Dever, W., 303
Diodorus, 102, 380
Donner, H. R. and W. Rollig, 154, 202, 210, 350, 363
Driver, G. R., 122
Dumbrell, W. J., 74

Edelstein, G., 154
Eichrodt, W., 352
Eising, G., 363
Eissfeldt, O., lxvi
Eitan, I., 122
Elliger, K., 23, 122, 157, 166, 171, 330, 364, 365
Ellis, R., 81, 210, 245, 246, 247, 248, 249, 251, 253, 270, 272, 304

Fairbridge, M., 440
Falkenstein, A. and W. von Soden, 208
Feliks, J., 27, 31, 33, 111, 238, 306
Fensham, F. C., 117
Fisher, L. R., 55
Forbes, R. J., 300, 304
Frick, F., 154, 155, 397, 416, 427
Freedman, D. N., 9, 11, 16, 57, 116, 200, 245, 278, 374
Freedman, D. N. and M. P. O'Connor, 281, 305, 306
Friedman, R. E., 394
Frymer-Kensky, T., 285

Gadd, C. J., 168
Galling, 233
Gaster, T. H., 184
Gelston, A., 63
Gerber, P. L., 348
Gerstenberger, G., 162
GKC, 20, 28, 52, 245, 249, 252, 298, 308, 337, 344, 353, 358, 386, 425
Goodenough, E. R., 233
Gooding, D. W., 229
Gordon, C., 191, 383
Gottwald, N. K., 198, 437
Gutmann, J., 291

Halpern, B., lxix, 51, 195, 211, 223, 246, 259, 270, 296
Hamp, V., 386
Hanson, P. D., lxix, lxx, 51, 58, 66, 68, 97, 114, 157, 185, 422, 427
Haran, M., 21, 29, 188, 192, 195, 231, 386
Hareuveni, N., 61, 111, 113
Hensley, L. V., 16, 102
Herodotus, 147
Hill, A., lxii, 26
Hoftijzer, J., lxii
Horayoth, T. B., 193
Huffmon, H., 385
Hurowitz, A., 21, 64, 250, 270
Hurvitz, A., 184, 323
Hyatt, J. P., 383

James, F., 68
Janzen, W., 162
Japhet, S., 15
Jepsen, A., 185
Josephus, 182
Junker, H., 9

Kallai, Z., 382
Kapelrud, A. S., 250
KAT, 24, 63
Kaufmann, Y., 34, 57, 141, 157, 188, 202, 212, 223, 352
Keder-Kopfstein, B., 348
Keel, O., 136
Kellerman, D., 401
Kelso, J. L., 9, 382
Kingsbury, E. C., 183
Koch, K., 24, 57
Köhler, A., 10

Kuhrt, A., xxx, 137, 147, 165
Kutsch, E., 258

Lacocque, A., 157
Lane, E., 190
Lapp, P. W., 342, 382
Le Bas, E. E., 246
Levine, B., 79, 188
Liedke, G., 195
Lindblom, J., 180
Lipiński, E., 117, 208, 212, 246, 270, 323, 358
Liver, J., 230
Loud, G., 135
Luciani, F., 26
Lundquist, J. M., 21, 22, 65, 73, 206, 211, 213, 244, 245, 318
LXX, lxv, lxvi, 10, 11, 18, 49, 60, 110, 112, 123, 142, 164, 180, 181, 190, 196, 209, 234, 248, 249, 253, 257, 258, 278, 297, 308, 326, 337, 340, 341, 343, 346, 349, 357, 360, 361, 364

McCarter, P., 441
McConville, G., 28
McCown, C. C., 342
McEvenue, S. E., 15
McHardy, W., 112, 321, 325
Malamat, A., 117
Marenof, S., 296, 298, 301, 308
Marti, K., 330, 350
Mason, R., lxvii, 34, 36, 58, 93, 97, 122, 154, 176, 195, 196, 215, 303, 331, 387, 414
May, H. G., 57
Mazar, B., 341, 342, 368
Mettinger, T. N. D., 18, 54
Meyers, C., 21, 60, 71, 72, 75, 191, 202, 230, 231, 233, 235, 254, 280, 415
Meyers, E. and J. Strange, 170
Meyers, E. M., 12, 55, 78, 170, 271, 370, 373
Milgrom, J., 55, 57, 346
Miller, P. D., Jr., 135
Mitchell, H., 8, 9, 10, 19, 23, 61, 92, 97, 109, 117, 153, 164, 165, 176, 199, 215, 250, 286, 296, 298, 343, 344, 350, 365, 382, 383, 417, 423, 438
Möhlenbrink, K., 233, 237
Mowinckel, S., 202
MT, lxv, lxvi, lxviii, 19, 28, 31, 51, 60,

61, 110, 112, 140, 164, 190, 191, 209, 215, 234, 235, 236, 241, 286, 297, 298, 308, 309, 320, 321, 325, 326, 343, 346, 349, 350, 352, 360, 361, 363, 364, 365, 369, 370
Mullen, E. T., 7, 182, 398
Muraoka, T., 25
Myers, J., 49, 72, 345

NEB 22, 24, 28, 51, 59, 63, 110, 164, 183, 228, 249, 257, 286, 300, 337, 364, 426, 437
Neusner, J., 79
Niditch, S., 136, 139, 141, 142
NJPS, 22, 24, 51, 59, 63, 110, 142, 164, 165, 183, 228, 249, 257, 286, 300, 337, 364, 411, 426, 437
North, R., 155, 233, 236, 239
Noth, M., 116
Nowack, W., 296, 330
NT, 325

Oded, B., 137, 138
Olmstead, A. T., 380
Oppenheim, A. L., 111, 184, 191
Oppenheimer, A., 50
Orlinsky, H. M., 109
Ottosson, M., 113, 323

Parker, R. A. and Dubberstein, W. A., 4
Peshitta, 179
Petersen, D. L., lxviii, lxx, 39, 58, 59, 65, 181, 246, 250, 270
Petitjean, A., lxix, 97, 124, 163, 164, 172, 199, 200, 202, 204, 211, 212, 242, 246, 249, 250, 253, 270, 340, 357, 358, 365, 414
Plöger, J. G., 171
Polzin, R., 337, 396
Pope, M., 304, 306, 440
Porten, B., 230
Porter, P., 136, 139
Preuss, H. D., 201

Rad, G. von, 168
Rainey, A., 14
Rignell, L., lxix, 228, 352, 362
Ringgren, H., 45, 442
Roberts, J. J. M., 120
Robinson, H. W., 182

Rothstein, J. W., 223
Rudolph, W., lxix, 10, 19, 57, 63, 97, 110, 153, 164, 165, 170, 184, 196, 199, 212, 215, 228, 249, 253, 286, 303, 330, 337, 344

Sarna, N., 319
Scharbert, J., 283
Schmidt, W. H., 118
Schneider, D. A., 90, 433
Scott, R. B. Y., 61, 164, 296, 299
Seebass, H., 70
Sellers, O., 299
Sellin, E., 163, 164
Seybold, K., lxix, 69, 384
Smith, M., 15, 233
Speiser, E. A., 57
Sperber, D., 233
Steck, O. H., 19, 28
Stern, E., 13, 15, 182, 210, 211, 236, 237, 382, 397

Talmon, S., 9, 10, 11, 13, 15, 55, 57, 161, 414
Thomas, D. W., 57, 117, 151, 190, 383
Thompson, J. A., 113
Tidwell, N. L. A., 180, 182, 183, 190

Toombs, L., 69
Townsend, T. N., 57
Tufnell, O., 69

Uffenheimer, B., lxix, lxx, 202
UT, 400

Van der Woude, A. S., 97
Vaux, R. de, 10, 55, 57, 68, 78, 180, 181, 191, 193, 204, 258

Wagner, N. E., 438
Warmuth, G., 359
Weiser, A., 184
Wellhausen, J., 350, 383
Wevers, J. W., 317
Whitelam, K., 194, 280, 285, 359
Widengren, G., 13, 15
Wiklander, B., 116
Wright, G. E., 172, 182, 183, 382

Yadin, Y., 13, 113, 317
Yoma, 193

Zadok, R., 341, 342, 368
Zobel, H. J., 162
Zohary, M., 27, 65

INDEX OF SUBJECTS

Aaron, 74, 189, 193, 335, 374
Abraham, 130
Accuser, 183–85, 217
agriculture, 25, 29, 32–33, 41, 61, 64, 74, 97, 156
Ahab, 113–14
Ahimaaz, 152
Ahura Mazda, 317–18
Alexander the Great, 272
altar, 24, 29
Anat, 135
angels, lvi, 35, 102, 110, 114–16, 118, 120, 126, 128–30, 132, 152–53, 159, 183, 188–89, 194
archive, Murashu, 8
articles, 20, 31
Assyria, 121–22, 312

Babylon, 117, 142–43, 145, 163–64, 308, 312
Babylonians, 49
beasts, 156
Bethel, 382, 386, 387, 391, 397–98
bowl, 234–35, 238, 239–40, 254, 265
bronze, 320
bullae, 9, 13, 15

Cambyses, xxx, xxxv, 147
cavalry, 115
cedar, 28, 36
chariots, 67, 114, 127, 317, 318, 327, 333, 334
chiastic arrangement, 6, 152, 381
chronology, 4–6, 16–17, 36–37, 49, 55,

59, 63, 76, 81–82, 89–91, 98, 100, 108, 125, 379, 386, 388, 433–34
City of Truth, 413–14
city-state, Canaanite, 155
cleansing, 188
coins, 182
Commonwealth, Second, xli
compassion, 125, 399
copper, 320
council, 7
Council, Divine, 7, 35
Court, Heavenly, 7, 182
court, royal, 7
covenant, 45, 52
Covenant Code, 285
crown, 348–54, 362
crowning, 125, 177, 373, 374
cult, foreign, xli, 37
cult, Jewish, xxviii, xxix, 29, 384, 385
curse, 278, 283–84
Cyrus, xxviii, xxx, xxxv, xxxvii, 37, 117, 122

Daniel, 5
Darius I, xxxvi, xxxviii, xxxix, 5, 20, 37, 44, 49, 72, 102, 115–16, 122, 133–34, 147, 278, 287, 380
date formula, 38–39
Davidic house, 13
Davidic line, 13, 202
Davidic scion, 39, 73, 201–3, 206, 337
Davidide, xxxvi, xxxvii, 9, 13, 39–40, 68–69, 116, 183, 201, 232, 250, 276, 366, 369, 371, 373
David, 12

defilement, 56–58, 79
desolation, 32, 43, 405
Deuteronomy, 45–46, 150
dew, 31–32
diaspora, xxvii
dittography, 67
Divine Council, 115
drought, 32, 41
dual, 34

earth, 31–32, 115, 323–24, 328, 333
Eber Nahara, xxxvi, 14
economy, 21, 25–27, 41, 42, 54, 61, 73–
   74, 76, 80, 97, 160, 348
Edict of Cyrus, xxix, 63, 136, 166, 367
Edomites, xxvii, xxviii
Egypt, 115, 380, 390
Ehyeh, 156
El, 135
elderly, 416
Eleazar, 193
Eli, 185
Elnathan, xxxvii, 12–13
ephah, 295–300, 301, 302, 305, 307, 313
eschatology, 6, 15, 17, 52–54, 58, 66,
   68, 71, 82, 111, 157, 187, 226, 330–
   31, 344, 348, 353
evil deeds, 97, 99, 103–4, 122
Evil-Merodach, 5, 16
exile, Babylonian, xxviii, 17–18, 40
eye, 166, 208–9
eyes, 274
eyes of the king, 128
Ezekiel, xxviii, 183
Ezra, xxxii

fasting, 388–89
fertility, 66
festivals, 435
fig, 64, 212
fire, 157, 187, 218
formula, date, lviii–ix, lx
formulaic, introduction, lxi, 7
foundation, 63–64
four, 127, 135–36, 139, 143, 317, 319

Gabriel, 110
Gad, 8
gates, 427
glory, 18, 28, 50, 53–54, 157, 165
glory of the Temple, 72–75

gods, Near Eastern, 191, 217, 303, 305
gold, 43, 54, 72, 75, 231–32, 234, 256–
   57, 263, 274, 338, 339, 346–48, 357
governor, 9, 12–13, 15, 19, 39, 66, 82,
   182, 206, 271, 370, 390
grain, 33, 60, 61, 65, 80

Habakkuk, 8
Haggai, lxvii, 8–9
hamlet. See village
Hananiah, 12
haplography, 33, 325
Hasmoneans, 104
heavens, 31–33
Heldai, 340
Helem, 364
Hen, 364
Herod, 12
holiness, 57–58, 78–79, 188
Holy Land, 170–71
homoearcton, 325
homoeoteleuton, 33
horns, 135–37, 139–43, 148, 312
horse, 110–15, 127, 129, 320–21, 325–
   26, 333, 334
horsemen, 128–30
household, 30
hymns of Gudea, 65

Iddo, 92
impurity, 189–90
infinitive, 19–20, 26–27
inheritance, 169
iniquity, 189, 193, 211, 218, 298
inscription, Behistun, xxxvi
intermarriage, 301–2, 313, 341
Isaiah, xxviii
Israel, 138

Jedaiah, 339, 340–41, 364
Jehoiachin, xxxvi, 5, 16, 120
Jehosaphat, 78
Jehozadak, 16
Jeremiah, 8, 38
Jerusalem, 71, 75–76, 96–97, 116, 118,
   120–21, 124, 134, 138, 150–52, 154–
   55, 157, 171, 185, 187–88, 385–86,
   392, 396–97, 412, 418, 425
Joshua, xxxvi, xxxvii, 16–17, 39–40, 49,
   185, 187, 189–90, 192–93, 196, 205,
   207–8, 213, 218–20, 229, 351

Josiah, 50, 344, 345, 346, 369
Jubilee, 237
Judah, xxx, xxxii, xl, 14–15, 17, 21, 51, 72, 117, 131, 138, 145, 385–86, 390, 397, 434
Judahites, xxvii, 57, 441
Judeans, xxvii

kernos, 237
kingdoms, foreign, 67

Lachish letters, 341
lamp, 229–38, 254, 262–65, 273–76
land, 170–71, 284, 298
language, formulaic, 40
languages, 440
Law, 101
lead, 300, 303–4
lead-stone, 303–4
lineage, Davidic, 12
lineage, Joshua, 16
lord, 259
love, 399

Malachi, 8, 183
marriage, 10, 13
measuring, 158–59, 161
measuring-cord, 149–50, 153, 158
measuring rod, 151
Megiddo ivories, 135
menorah. See Lamp
Meshullam, 12
messenger. See Angels
Messiah, xxix
metalworkers. See Smiths
Michael, 110
monarchic period, 19, 373
monarchy, Davidic, xl, 17, 21–22, 42, 51, 73–74, 103, 122, 155, 220, 226–27, 356–60, 374
monarchy, Persian, 5
monarchy, restoration, xxxix, 206–7
Moses, 35, 74, 96, 130, 194, 207, 335, 374
mountain, 270, 319–20
myrtle, 110–11, 114–15, 126
mystics, 113
mythological, 7
mythology, Canaanite, 65, 91, 155, 171, 217, 315, 320

names, Babylonian, 10
names, Yahwistic, 16
Nathan, 8
nations, 143, 165, 168, 175, 404, 439, 440
Nazarite, 386–87
Nebuchadnezzar, xxvii, xxx, 16
Negev, 398
Nehemiah, xxxii
New Year, 108
New Year of Trees, 113
northland, 324–25, 328, 330, 335

Obadiah, 37
offerings, 62–63
official, 154, 160
oil, 33, 236, 258, 264, 276
olive, 64–65, 74, 233, 238, 240, 254, 258, 264
onomasticon, 8, 340
open places, 415–16
orphan, 400
ostrich, 113

palace, 22
Pashhur, 17
peace, 423, 435
Pedaiah, 10
Pentateuch, 16, 52, 78
Persia, xxviii, xxx, xxxviii, 6, 35, 101–2, 114–15, 122, 130–31, 136, 146–49, 312
Peshitta, 89
platform, 245–46
Poetry–Prose Relation, lxi–lxv
pomegranate, 64–65
poor, 400–1
population, 156, 160
portent, 199
prayer, 31, 81
premier stone, 246–48, 272
priest, 7, 200
priest, chief, 16–17, 180, 189, 220–21
priest, high, 17, 19, 50, 180–81, 197, 198, 221
priesthood, 42, 55, 69, 77–80, 182, 185–86, 194–96, 198, 201, 217, 220, 229, 335–36, 374, 384, 387
Primary History, 16, 18
prophecy, 58
prophets, 17, 44–46, 94–95, 101, 104,

130, 197, 200–1, 384, 396, 403, 419–20
prosperity, 65–66, 134, 211–12
purity, 190

redaction, 15, 39, 100
Regem-melech, 383, 392
religion, Canaanite, 168–69
remnant, 417
repentance, 96
restoration, 33, 49–50, 96, 100, 118, 123, 173, 224, 339
Return, First, xxx, xxxii, 11
Return, Second, xxxi, 11
revocalization, lxv

sacrifice, 21, 29, 55–58
Samaria, 14–15, 382–83
Samaritans, xxvii, xxviii, xxxii, xxxiii, xxxv, 57
Sar-ezer, 383, 386, 392
Satan, 115
satrapies, xxx, 13–14, 37, 73, 380
scripture, 101
scroll, flying, 277–83, 286, 287–88, 290–92
seal, 69
seer, 109
Seraiah, 16, 72, 345
seven, xlvi, 68, 225, 229, 235–36, 243, 254, 273–74
seventy, 117–18
Shabbatai, 8
Shealtiel, 10
Shelomith, 12–13
Shephelah, 398
Shiloh, 186–87
Shinar. See Babylon
Shoot, 202, 212, 224, 226, 266, 352, 355, 356, 357, 371, 373
signet. See Seal
signs. See Portent
silver, 43, 53, 72, 75, 338, 339, 346, 348, 354
sin, 97, 104
smiths, 138–39, 139–43, 148, 312
sorrel, 111–13
southland, 324–25, 328
spirit, 35, 50, 52, 74–75, 243–44, 329–30, 402
stamps, jar, 182

statutes, 95
stone, 205–11, 224–25
stork, 306–7, 314
Sheshbazzar, xxx, xxxii, 11
Succoth, 24
sun-god, 319–20
sycamore, 27
symmetry, 60
synagogue, xxviii

tabernacle, 168, 175, 189, 195–96
talent. See Weight
Tattenai, xxxii
tax, 40
temple, 18, 20, 42, 50, 59, 71–72, 123, 160, 186, 193, 195, 280–81, 307, 308–9, 385, 414, 421, 425
temple, dedication of, xxxvii, xliii, xxxix, 193
temple, rebuilding of, xxxviii, xxxix, xl, 6, 19–22, 28, 35, 41, 46, 51, 59, 151, 171, 217, 356, 357, 365, 420–21
Temple, Second, 54
Temple, Symbol of, xxxix
temples, Near Eastern, 37, 246, 270, 271, 296–97, 308
theocracy, 74, 83
thief, 284–87
throne, 67, 361, 372–73
tin-stone, 253–54
tithes, 60
Tobiah, 339, 340–41, 342–43, 364
Torah, 7, 282–83, 292, 402–3
tree, 233, 255, 263, 275–76
tribute, 42, 53–54, 73, 168
truth, 426, 435
turban, 190–92, 205, 369
Tyre, 117

Ugarit, 66
Ugaritic poetry, 135
Ujahorresne, xxx, xxxvi
uncleanliness. See Defilement
universality, 176

Vestment Scene, 17
village, 154–55, 156, 397
vine, 64–65, 212
Visions, liv–lvi

walls, 155, 160–61

warrior king, 82
wasteland. *See* Desolation
weight, 299–300
widow, 400
will of God, 43–54
winds, 164, 173, 306, 322–23, 334
wine, 33, 60
wings, 306
wives, foreign. *See* Intermarriage
word, prophetic, 7
word of Yahweh, 18
Worship, Synagogue, xxviii
wrath of Yahweh, 403, 411

Yahweh, 7, 19, 34–35, 44–45, 67, 122, 127–28, 145, 163, 188–89, 372, 418, 442, 445
Yahweh, blessing of, 75–76, 80, 97
Yahweh, Council of, 7

Yahweh, House of, 21–23, 73
Yahweh, promise of, 99
Yahweh, Word of, 23, 91, 95–96, 118–19, 242, 249–50
Yahweh of Hosts, 18–19, 29, 36, 51, 91, 131, 412
Yehud. *See* Judah
Yehudites. *See* Judahites
youth, 415

zeal, 411
Zechariah, 8, 91–92, 222
Zedekiah, 17
Zephaniah, 345
Zerubbabel, xxxiii, xxxv, xxxvii, xxxix, 9–13, 17, 39–40, 49, 67, 73, 82, 203–4, 242–43
Zion, 120, 164, 169, 244, 413

INDEX OF HEBREW WORDS

ʾ unvocalized

ʾb, 95
ʾdm, 326, 421
ʾhyh, 156
ʾwryw, 182
ʾḥry, 325
ʾḥry hym, 325
ʾḥt, 52
ʾyš, 141
ʾyšwn, 166
ʾl, lxv, 33, 49, 61, 62, 325
ʾllh, 241
ʾlt, 283
ʾm, 194
ʾmṣ, 326
ʾmr, 328
ʾnky, 156
ʾšr, lxii, 29, 33, 324
ʾrṣ, 31, 212, 323, 324, 325
ʾt, lxii, 62, 179, 343, 399
ʾt (syntagmemes), lxii

ʾ vocalized

ʾāb, 29, 97
ʾābōt, 111
ʾādām, 155
ʾădāmâ, 171
ʾadmat haqqōdeš, 170, 171, 176, 414
ʾadōn, 241, 259, 261
ʾadōnay, 240
ʾadōnî, 240, 257
ʾahăbāh, 399
ʾaḥar, 164
ăḥôr, 325

ʾal, 4
ʾālâ, 283, 284, 285
ʾalmānāh, 400
ʾamah, 12, 13, 14, 271, 370
ʾămānâ, 112
ʾāmar, 17, 93, 94, 118, 122, 329, 355
ʾāmōs, 112
ʾamoṣ, 322
ʾămuṣṣîm, 112, 321, 322, 326
ʾānâ, 150
ʾănî, 155, 156
ʾăšer, 164, 256, 345, 346, 425, 437, 438, 441
ʾat / ʾattâ, 23, 358
ʾeben, 249, 304, 401
ʾeben habbĕdîl, 253
ʾeben hārōʾšâ, 246, 270
ʾeben pinnâ, 248
ʾebyôn, 400
ʾehyeh, 155, 156, 157
ʾēl, 10
ʾel, 7, 8, 60, 62, 91, 156, 165, 175, 319, 329
ʾēlleh, 139, 209
ʾĕlōhîm, 63, 442
ʾĕmet, 399, 409, 413, 426, 435
ʾĕmûnâ, 399
ʾên, 141, 142
ʾēn, 26, 62
ʾêpâ, 295, 296, 297
ʾereṣ, 32, 115, 171, 284, 290, 298, 322, 323, 325, 328, 332
ʾereṣ yhwh, 170
ʾereṣ yiśrāʾēl, 368
ʾeš, 155, 187

ʾet, 61, 62, 97, 142, 195, 328, 337, 338, 339, 340, 346
ʾētîm, 142
ʾim, 194
ʾîš, 55, 285, 355
ʾîšôn, 166
ʾiššâ, 302, 305
ʾohel moʿed, 231
ʾôt, 199, 363
ʾûlām, 235, 280, 281, 285, 286

b unvocalized

b, 34, 62, 186, 212, 286, 306, 323, 324, 328, 343, 344, 354, 365
bʾ, 167
bbl, 10
bbt, 166
bdl, 253
bhmh, 421
bwʾ, 20, 36, 61, 168, 224, 343, 353, 418, 438, 444
bwz, 252
bzh, 252
bḥr, 70, 124
bṭḥ, 397
byd, lxv
byt, 29, 30
bkh, 386, 388
bn, 339
bnh, 22, 23, 357, 365, 421
*bnh, 251
*bṣʿ, 251
bqš, 55, 326, 327, 445
bryt, 52
bt, 166, 296

b vocalized

bābâ, 166
bābel, 164, 345
bayit, 21, 63, 195, 307, 308, 356
bānāh, 358
bārād, 62
bāśār, 171
bat, 164, 166
bath, 296
bĕgādîm, 192
bĕhēmâ, 155
bĕyad, 7, 78, 257
bēn, 258
bĕrît, 283

bĕtôk, 155
bôʾ, 3, 19, 20, 60, 62, 140, 343, 345, 346, 358

g unvocalized

gbwl, 170
gdwl, 411
gwlh, 399
gzl, 400
gll, 278, 324
gnb, 284
gʿr, 186, 187

g vocalized

gābîaʿ, 231, 235, 238
gādôl, 181, 439
gam, 194, 417
gannōb, 284
gĕbûl, 170
gēr, 400, 401
gôlâ, 339, 345, 348
goy, 142, 143, 175, 364, 435, 436, 439, 440, 441
gullâ, 231, 234, 235, 238, 239, 254, 255, 256, 265
gullāh, 234

d unvocalized

dbr, 7, 329
dyn, 195
drk, 24

d vocalized

dābār, 51, 91, 101, 118, 329, 396, 402
dĕbar, 91, 242
dĕbar-yhwh, 91
dĕbîr, 280, 281
derek, 24, 25
dîn, 195

h unvocalized

h-interrogative, 417
h-directional, 150
h, lxii, 31, 34, 344, 371, 397, 413, 417, 419, 440
hyh, 156
hlk, 115, 294, 326, 327, 439, 442, 444
hmmh, 241, 298
hnnh, 298

hnh, 29, 179
hpk, 66

h vocalized

hādār, 358
hāyâ, 3, 7, 29, 48, 60, 91, 156, 175, 349, 362, 373
hālak, 196
halakah, 55, 56, 70
hāmēš, 60
hallāz, 153
has, 171
har haqqōdeš, 170, 414
harbê, 25
hêkāl, lx, 59, 60, 231, 280, 296, 356, 421
hēm / hēmmâ, 4, 122, 199, 256
hinĕnî, 167, 417
hinnēh, 109, 179, 224, 294, 317, 355
hôd, 358, 359
hôy, 162, 173
hûʾ / hîʾ, 29, 212, 344, 358, 359

w unvocalized

w, 142, 143, 163, 339, 343, 344, 358, 359, 400, 403, 418, 422, 425, 441

z unvocalized

zʾt, 301
zh, 29
zhb, 256
zyt, 238, 256
zkn, 415
zmm, 424, 425
zʿm, 116, 121
zʿq, 328
zr, 25, 122
zrh, 137, 143, 168, 404

z vocalized

zāhāb, 234
zayit, 238, 256
zākar, 337
zāmām, 425
zārāh, 143
zāraʿ, 122, 422, 423
zeh, 59, 286
zĕkaryâ, 91
zĕkaryāhû, 91

zeraʿ, 9
zerūʿăbĕbābel, 10
zikkārôn, 347, 363, 364

ḥ unvocalized

ḥgg, 8
ḥgyh, 8
ḥzq, 50, 418, 441
ḥyl, 244
ḥlh, 384, 445
ḥlṣ, 190
ḥmh, 411
ḥnn, 249
ḥsd, 306
ḥrb, 24, 29, 32
ḥrd, 141, 142

ḥ vocalized

ḥag, 8
ḥāggā, 8
ḥaggay, 8
ḥādad, 142
ḥāzaq, 441
ḥālāh, 384
ḥamātî, 330
ḥămūdōt, 47, 53
ḥănayâ, 364
ḥārad, 141, 142
ḥārāšîm, 139
ḥārēb, 24, 32
ḥasîdâ, 306
ḥāsōp, 60
ḥāṣēr, 195
ḥāṣēr happĕnîmît, 280
ḥebel, 149, 150
ḥēleq, 169, 176
ḥemdâ, 405
ḥemdat, 47
ḥēn, 249, 271
ḥesed, 399
ḥōdeš, 89
ḥoma, 155
ḥōreb, 24, 32
ḥôtām, 69
ḥûṣ, 416

ṭ unvocalized

ṭwb, 425

ṭ vocalized

ṭāhôr, 191, 234
ṭāmē', 188
ṭerem, 58, 59
ṭôb, 124

y unvocalized

ybl, 237
ygy', 32, 33
ydh, 142, 143
yhwh, 10, 17, 62, 122, 153, 183, 209,
    356, 432
ym, 324
ysd, 22, 23, 63, 64, 421
*ysd, 251
y'n, 30
ypy, 166
ypyp, 166
ys', 152, 294, 306, 311, 318, 324, 327,
    329
yṣb, 323
yṣq, 236
yšb, 198, 199, 359, 437
yš', 417, 424
yšr, 245

y vocalized

yād, 57, 62
yayin, 33
yāsad, 63, 251
ya'an, 29
yārâ, 78
yārāh, 142
yāšab, 155
yātôm, 400
yĕḥizqiyyâ, 182
yĕhôṣādāq, 16
yĕhôšûa', 16
yĕhûdâ, xxx, 13
yĕhûdî, 441
yērāqôn, 62
yĕrēša, 246
yĕrûšālēm, 155
yeqeb, 60
yēšuâ', 16
yishar, 258
yiṣhār, 33, 58
yôm, 212, 252, 344

k unvocalized

k, 425, 438
kbd, 28, 402
khn hgdwl, 180, 181
kwn, 308, 309
khd, 141
kl, 4, 33, 47, 49, 323, 324
kl', 31
klh, 287
*klh, 251
kns, 164
knp, 56, 441, 443
kpy, 141
kpym, 32, 33, 34
krr, 299

k vocalized

kābēd, 28
kābôd, 18, 50, 53, 54, 155, 157, 164,
    165
kālâ, 251
kammeh, 286
kĕmô, 286
kānāp, 441
kēn, 425
kesep, 347
kĕpî, 140
ki, 164, 174, 424
kikkār, 299, 300
kisse', 361
koh, 17, 122
kōhēn hagādôl, 17, 180
kōhēn hārō'š, 17, 180
kol, 62, 171, 346, 440

l unvocalized

l, 23, 29, 122, 156, 175, 245, 249, 252,
    285, 286, 298, 363, 384, 401, 422
l', 156
lb, 424
lbš, 190
lḥn, 364
lpny, 182
lqḥ, 337, 338, 346, 348, 349, 353

l vocalized

laylâ, 109, 110
lākēn, 122, 124
lāšôn, 440

lāqaḥ, 337
lĕ, 122
lēb, 346, 402
lĕpî, 140
lĕšammâ, 405
lipnê, 208
lō', 403

m unvocalized

m, 10, 58 59, 60, 110, 155, 256, 286,
    298, 337, 338, 339, 340, 345, 346,
    419, 423
m'n, 401
mh, 241
mwš, 211
ml', 416
mlk, 360
mmlkwt, 67
m't, 29
mrkbwt, 327
mšl, 359, 360, 372

m vocalized

mâ, 29, 48, 60, 150
maggal, 278
maḥalāṣôt, 190
mākôn, 308, 309
mal'āk, 35, 182, 183
mal'āk haddōbēr bî, 114
malā'kût, 35
malkût, 358
mas'ōt, 337
ma'aśēh, 57, 62
māqôm, 24, 55
mârāšâ, 246
māšîaḥ, 258
mattĕnōt, 337
mĕgîllâ, 277, 278
mekes, 347
mĕlā'ka, 35
mĕnôrâ, 230, 240, 255
mĕ'at, 52
mĕ'ôn, 171
mĕṣillâ, 110
merkabâ, 67, 317
mibbên, 319
middâ, 123, 149, 150
miṭṭāl, 31
min, 10, 31, 59, 339
miśtakkêr, 26

mîšōr, 245
miṣwâ, 101
miṣlâ, 110
miṣnepet, 191, 351, 396
miqdāš, 189
mirša'at, 303
mišpaṭ, 399, 413, 426
mô'ēd, 435
môpēt, 199, 200
môṣā', 319
mōšeh, 78
musaqot, 209, 257
mûṣeqet, 236, 237

n unvocalized

n'm, 153
ng', 166
ngd, 353
nwh, 170
nḥm, 123, 124, 425
nwḥ, 329
nzr, 386
nḥl, 169, 176, 423
nṭh, 123
nqh, 286
nś', 179, 300, 306, 307, 358
nšm, 405
ntn, 7, 208, 353

n vocalized

nā', 198
nādab, 346
naḥălâ, 150
nākâ, 62
nāsag, 96, 97
nāsa', 163
na'ar, 9, 153, 154, 415
nāśā', 143
našammâ, 405
nāśîm, 302, 305
nātan, 358
nĕ'ûm, 62, 432
nĕwēh-ṣedeq, 170
nēzer, 191, 350, 351
nĕḥošet, 320
nĕśî'îm, 347
nēr, 209

s unvocalized

s'r, 404

spr, 283
srr, 401

s *vocalized*

sābîb, 155
sāgûr, 234
sārar, 402
sēper, 278
sĕpûnîm, 23

ʿ *unvocalized*

ʿ*br*, 190
ʿ*d*, 64
ʿ*wd*, 194
ʿ*wn*, 297
ʿ*wr*, 35, 171, 228
ʿ*zn*, 179, 297, 298
ʿ*trh*, 350, 351
ʿ*l*, 4, 30, 32, 186, 323, 354
ʿ*lh*, 11, 439
ʿ*m*, 442
ʿ*m yhwdh*, 51
ʿ*md*, 110, 182, 186, 259
ʿ*nh*, 57, 328
ʿ*s*, 238
ʿ*śq*, 399, 400

ʿ *vocalized*

ʿ*ad*, 48, 437
ʿ*ad-mātay*, 116
ʿ*āwōn*, 189, 205, 211
ʿ*ăwōn*, 297
ʿ*āzar*, 228
ʿ*ăṭārâ*, 349, 350, 351, 354, 370
ʿ*ăṭeret*, 192, 336, 349, 351, 362, 363, 373
ʿ*ayin*, 166, 208, 209, 297
ʿ*al*, 165, 239, 256, 259, 308, 309, 351, 404
ʿ*al-kēn*, 30
ʿ*ām*, 34, 175, 417, 435, 436, 440
ʿ*am hāʾāreṣ*, 50, 51
ʿ*āmad*, 275
ʿ*aṣûmîm*, 439
ʿ*āśâ*, 51, 140
ʿ*arĕmōt*, 48, 60
ʿ*attā*, 19
ʿ*ebed*, 13, 355
ʿ*ēdâ*, 194
ʿ*ēlâ*, 58, 59
ʿ*ēynî*, 162

ʿ*ēynô*, 162
ʿ*ênāyim*, 208, 209
ʿ*ēṣ*, 111, 238
ʿ*eṣâ*, 118, 362
ʿ*eśrîm*, 60
ʿ*et*, 19, 20, 384,
ʿ*îr*, 154, 413
ʿ*ōd* / ʿ*ôd*, 48, 52, 64, 1.., ...,
ʿ*ōperet*, 300

p *unvocalized*

pwṣ, 124
phḥ, 14
pḥt yhwdh, 14
plʾ, 417
prś, 163
ptḥ, 209, 210

p *vocalized*

pānâ, 28
pānîm, 280, 384
peh, 419
pĕrāzôt, 154, 155
pittûaḥ, 209
pûrâ, 60

ṣ *unvocalized*

ṣdq, 202
ṣwh, 7
ṣwl, 110
ṣwm, 388, 389
ṣwq, 237
ṣl, 110
ṣll, 110
ṣmḥ, 202, 203
ṣmt, 142
ṣntrwt, 256

ṣ *vocalized*

ṣaddîq, 355
ṣāmaḥ, 202, 355
ṣānîp, 191, 192, 351, 354, 369
ṣantĕrôt, 257
ṣāpôn, 324, 328
ṣĕbāʾôt, 18
ṣedāqâ, 355
ṣedeq, 426
ṣēl, 110
ṣemaḥ, 202, 224, 229, 355, 371

˒2
, 397
˒or, 257
˒ṣ, 191, 205
ṣô˒îm, 187
ṣôr, 342
ṣûm, 389
ṣûr, 304

q unvocalized

qwh, 123
qdš, 170
qṣp, 121, 411
qn˒, 120, 411
qr˒, 32, 94, 118, 119, 152, 396, 403, 404, 419
qrb, 58
qšb, 401

q vocalized

qāw, 108, 123
qāṭon, 252
qāṣap, 425
qeṣep, 121, 403
qeren, 142, 143
qōdeš, 176

r unvocalized

rᵃ, 425
rbh, 29
r˒h, 109, 138, 179, 317
r˒š, 246
rḥm, 116, 123
rwḥ, 329
rwṣ, 152
ryq, 256, 257
rkb, 110
r˒š, 52, 53, 66, 331
rnn, 167
rṣ, 30

r vocalized

rā˒â, 109
rabbîm, 439
raḥămîm, 116
rāṣâ, 28
rā˓â, 122
rāša˓, 303
rehob, 415, 416

rĕḥôqîm, 364
rewaḥ, 306
rē˓a, 285
rîq, 256
riš˒â, 302, 303
rob, 155
rōkbîm, 67
rûaḥ, 35, 52, 244, 306, 323, 330, 403
rûḥôt, 323, 330

ś unvocalized

śym, 191, 353, 354, 424
śṭm, 183, 184
śṭn, 183, 184, 186

ś vocalized

śārîm, 347
śāṭān, 182, 183, 184, 186
śēkar, 421
śērēpâ, 187
śēruqqîm, 112
śîm, 58, 191

š unvocalized

š˒l, 10, 55
š˒ryt, 49
šbly, 256
šb˓, 286
šwb, 93, 94, 95, 96, 97, 123, 168, 228, 229, 277, 425
šḥr, 326
škn, 168, 169, 175, 176, 413, 418, 429
šlḥ, 62, 156, 165
šlk, 35, 303
šll, 166
šm˓, 34, 198, 353, 403
šmym, 31, 33
šmm, 405
šny, 256
špr, 237
špṭ, 399

š vocalized

ša˒anān, 121
šābā˓, 284
šabbāt, 340
šabbātay, 8, 340
šākar, 26

šālôm, 55, 362, 399, 421, 422, 423, 426, 427, 435
šāmaʿ, 403
šāmar, 195
šāmîr, 402
šāqar, 284, 286
šebâʿ, 209
šĕʾaltîʾēl, 9
šĕʾērît, 34, 417
šĕʾiltîw, 10
šĕhōrîm, 112
šĕlāmîm, 55, 56
šĕlēwâ, 396
šēm, 18, 284, 286, 355
šemen, 33, 258
šeqer, 286

šibbōlet, 238, 255
šibʿâ, 209
šidāpôn, 62
šub, 155, 317, 425
šûṭ, 254

t vocalized

têmān, 328
tĕʿûdâ, 200
tĕrûmâ, 346, 347
tĕrûʿâ, 249, 271
tĕšûʾâ, 248, 271
tipʾeret, 351
tîrôš, 33
tôrâ, 55, 81, 118, 200, 399, 402, 413

INDEX OF OTHER LANGUAGES

Akkadian

a-ptu, 296
a-pu, 296
êkallu, 59
ellu, 191
gabuāti hûrasi, 235
gabūtu, 235
ḥalāṣu, 190
ha-si-in, 248
kalû, 65, 247, 249, 271
libittu maḥritu, 248, 270
lu, 245
maḥru, 248
māšu, 211
paḥatu, 13
rakabu, 110
šamnâ ḥalṣa, 190
zērbābili, 9
zeru, 9

Arabic

afta, 296
ʾašpar, 113
ghazura, 122
la, 245

Aramaic

mahlĕkîn, 196

ʾḥz bknp, 441

peḥâ, 11, 13, 15, 17, 19, 74, 194, 206, 243, 251, 353
pḥwʾ, 14
ṣlh, 110
šabbātay, 8, 340
yĕhûd, xxx, 13

Phoenician

bn ṣdq, 202
bōd ʿăstart, 202
ytnmlk, 202
ʿāṭārōt, 362, 363, 373
ʿaṭrt, 363
šmʿbʿl, 363

Sumerian

ê-gal, 59
E-pa, 296
temen, 246

Ugaritic

almnt, 400
iqnim, 191
ṭhr, 191
ytm, 400
zhr, 191

INDEX OF SCRIPTURAL REFERENCES

OLD TESTAMENT

Genesis

3:6	303
3:8	115
5:12	117
8:7	421
10:5	440
10:10	308
10:20	440
10:31	440
11:2	308
11:26	117
13:10	299
13:11	299
14:1	308
14:9	308
16:3	13
18:2	135
18:14	417
18:15	57
19:1	110
19:21	66
21:10	13
21:12	13
21:13	13
22:16	51
24:12	240
24:19	440
24:27	399
25:34	252, 389
26:18	228
27:39	31
27:41	184
28	lxix

(Genesis)

28:18	236
29:5	57
31:10	321
31:12	321
32:25	110
37:10	343
40:20–21	141
41	255
42:35	256
44:18b	50
46:16	8
48:10	402
49:23	184
50:15	184

Exodus

1:9	439
3–4	167
3:2–4	157
3:5	170, 171
3:8	405
3:13–15	35
3:14	156
4:21	199
6:7	45
7:3	199
8:11	402
8:28	402
9:7	402
9:34	402
9:35	7
10:1	402

(Exodus)

11:3	181
12:4	140
12:49	55
13:21	157
14:13	323
14:25	318
15:1	67
15:4	318
15:4–8	303
15:5	304
15:10	303, 304
15:13	170
15:17	169, 170
15:26	366
18:13–14	197
18:20	194
19:5	418
19:6	79, 425, 426
19:18	141
20:5	120, 411
20:8	337
22:6–10	285
22:6–12	220
22:10	280
22:20–21	400
22:25	418
23:7	428
24:10	191
24:16	54
24:17	54
25:2	338, 346
25:3	348

(*Exodus*)
25:8–9   lvi
25:18–22   305
25:31–40   230
25:37–38   231
26:2   289
26:8   289
26:35   230
27:20   231, 256
28:9   210
28:9–12   205, 225
28:11   210
28:17–21   205, 225
28:21   210
28:30   280
28:36   210
28:36–37   348–49
28:36–38   189, 205, 225
29   189, 193
29:5–7   192
29:6   189, 191, 351
29:7   258
29:43   54
29:44–46   168
29:45   418
30:16   363
30:27   230
32:11   384
32:23–33:3   189
32:32–33   283
32:36–38   189
33:7   438
34:9   169, 176
34:14   120, 411
34:28   52
35:1   425, 426
35:4   346
35:22   346
37:14–24   230
37:22–23   231
38:29   300
39:6   210
39:14   210
39:27   230
39:30   189, 210
40:4   230
40:13   351
40:15   351

(*Exodus*)
40:24   230
40:25   230
40:35   54
40:43   54
48:35   414

Leviticus
2:6   236
4:3   351
4:5   351
4:16   351
5:23   400
6:15   351
7:7   55
7:15–16   55
7:31–34   346
7:34   338
8   193
8:7–9   192
8:9   191, 351
8:35   195
9:6   54
9:23   54
10:10–20   78
13:5   298
13:37   298
13:55   298
14:43   164
14:48   20
18:30   195
19:2   79
19:9–10   399
19:10   400
19:13   399
20:24   405
21:10   180, 351
21:12   351
23:22   399, 400
23:40   111
24:1–4   230
24:2   231
25:8–12   237
26   65
26:6   141
26:12   45, 418
26:14   366
26:26   440
26:33   137
27:7   415
27:7–24   237

Numbers
1:2   141
1:49   141
1:53   195
3:7   195
3:8   195
3:9   358
3:31   230
4:9   230
5:11–31   220, 285
6:2–6   386
7   347
8:2–3   230
8:16   358
10:10   363
11:7   298
14:22   440
14:42–44   35
15:16   55
15:29   55
16:28–29   167
18:1   189
18:5   195
18:23   189
19:11–13   56
20:26–28   193
22:22   183
22:32   183
26:2   141
27:20   359
28:26   346
29:39   435
31:37–42   347
31:49   141
31:51–54   347
31:54   363
35:25   181
35:28   181
35:32   181

Deuteronomy
1:1   426, 432
1:34   121
3:5   154
3:10   246
4:34   199
4:35   442
4:39   442
4:43   246
5:9   120
5:12   337

(*Deuteronomy*)

5:20   428
7:19   199
8:18–20   302
9:4   302
10:18   399, 400
10:21   252
11:1   195
11:12   209, 212
11:13   366
12:17   258
14:23   258
14:28–29   399
14:29   57, 400
15:1–2   237
15:7–11   400
15:12–14   237
16:6   418
16:11   400
16:14   400
16:15   57
16:20   426
17:9–10   195
18:4   258
19:16   428
21:19   427
22:12   56
22:24   427
23:12   418
23:14   187
24:14   399, 401
24:17   400, 401
24:19   57
24:19–21   400
24:19–22   399
25:5   10
26:8   199
26:12–13   400
26:15   171, 172
26:17   45
27:19   400, 401
28   65, 101, 423
28:1   365
28:2–8   421
28:12   57
28:15   95, 96
28:22   61
28:26   141
28:33   320
29   283
29:9–20   283

(*Deuteronomy*)

29:19–28   120
29:22   66
30:1–10   99
30:9   57
31:26   337
32:8–9   45, 169
32:9   150
32:10   166
32:36   195
32:43   170
33:12   402
33:17   135
34:11   199

Joshua

3:11   259
3:13   259
6:1   421
7   280
7:21   308
8:29   418
10:39   397
11:5   36
11:6   318
13:9   246
13:16   246
15:19   234
18:1   207
18:13   382
18:15   325
18:22   382
20:6   181
22:14   440
24:1   323

Judges

1:15   234
3:11   115
3:19   259
4:10   328
4:13   328
4:15   318
5:12   171
6–8   35
6:12   35
6:13   35
6:16   35
6:17   35
6:37   32
6:39   32

(*Judges*)

6:40   32
8:3   330
8:12   141
8:18b   50
9:5   208
9:8–9   238
9:8–15   351
9:13   26
14:4   360
15:11   360
17:1–4   349
18:15   384
20:6   169
20:26   434
21:24   327

1 Samuel

1:9   361
1:19   207
1:20   10
2:27–33   185
2:36   299
3:3   231
4:1   91
4:4   305
4:12–13   343
4:13   361
4:18   361
8:11   318
9:6   20
9:9   109
9:16   351
10:1   236, 258, 351
10:24   70
12:7   323
12:16   323
13:12   384
14   280
14:15   141
15:16   109
15:17   351
15:27   441
16:1   351
16:7   298
16:21–22   182
18:17   12
20:41   325
21:15–16   417
22:7   417

(*1 Samuel*)

22:10	384
24:6	56
24:7	56
24:12	56
29:4	184

2 Samuel

1:10	351
3:4	8
3:18	68
5:8	257
6:2	305
6:21	70
7:22	442
8:10	348
12:21–22	388
12:30	351
14:17	91
16:18	70
17:6	51
18:19–32	152
19:23	184
21:20	236
22:3	135
22:11	279, 305
32:2	403
38:8–39	340

1 Kings

2:41–42	343
3–11	230
3:4	439
3:5–14	lvi
3:6	419
4	76
4:7	12
5–7	72
5:5	212
5:18	184
6:2	289
6:3	280
6:5	60
6:9	23, 251, 271
6:14	251, 271
6:17	60
6:23–26	281
6:23–28	305
6:29	210, 234
6:32	234
6:35	234

(*1 Kings*)

6:36	280
6:37–38	251, 271
7	231
7:1	251, 271
7:27–43	309
7:41	234
7:49	230
8	81
8:6–7	281
8:9	52, 281
8:23	442
8:29	209
8:31	285
8:35	31
8:44	124
8:48	124
9:14	300
10	76
10:9	359
10:27	27
11:1–8	301
11:14	184
11:25	184
12:21	424
12:29	382
13:1–3	398
13:1–5	199
13:30	162
15:5	91
15:13	303
15:17	421
17:1	91
20	113
20:14	154
20:20	114
21:1	59
21:8	69
22	159
22:6	384
22:11	136
22:16	426
22:19	259
22:19–22	191
22:21	52

2 Kings

2:11	319
2:12	319
4:10	230
4:32–33	343

(*2 Kings*)

6:11	404
6:17	319
8:26	303
9:1	258
9:2	343
9:3	258
10:21	343
11:12	351
12	369
12:3–17	347
12:5	73
14:21	51
18:27	187
18:31	212
18:32	258
19:18	57
19:21	252
19:28–31	121
19:37	383
20:8	199
21:24	51
22–23	lxviii
22:4	180
22:8	180, 278, 290
22:12	17
22:15	62
23:2	396
23:4	180, 303
23:6	303
23:7	303
23:11	319, 383
23:15–20	398
24:8	11
24:13	50, 72
24:14–15	345
24:15–16	339
24:15–17	11
24:17	10
25	231, 291
25:1	434
25:3–7	433
25:4	110
25:8	386, 434
25:8–9	388
25:12	41
25:15	231
25:16	235
25:18	180, 344, 345

(2 Kings)
25:18–21   187
25:25   388
25:27–30   16

Isaiah
1:17   400
1:21   413
1:23   400
2:1–4   53
2:2   76
2:2–3   245, 414,
    439
3:13   195
3:23   192
4:2   203, 224
4:4   188
5   258
5:10   25
6   165
6:1   109
6:1–11   191
6:2–4   54
6:5–7   188
6:8   35
6:10   402
6:11   116
6:13   440
8:1–4   338
8:1–20   199, 200
8:2   92
8:20   338
9:6   359
9:16   400
10:2   400
11:1   203
11:10   203
11:11   308
11:15   167
13:12   348
13:17   35
13:22   59
14:5   360
16:5   359
17:5   255
18:4   31
19:16   167
19:17   8, 362
20:2–6   199
22:2   248
28:6   197

(Isaiah)
28:16   246
30:29   439
32:18   121
33:20   121
37:33   165
37:38   383
40:1–2   124
40:1-11   191
40:10   360
41:19   111
42:1   70
42:16   426
44:12   139
44:28   xxix, 103,
    147, 324, 367
45:1   xxix, 103,
    147, 324, 367
46:3   417
48:1   419
48:20   163
49:16   34
51:9   171
52:9   124
54:11   404
55:13   111
56:3–8   169
56:6   169
56:7   169
59:1   402
59:14–15   428
60   161
62:3   192, 351,
    363, 370
63:3   60
66:2   141
66:5   141
66:13   124
66:15   318
66:18   440

Jeremiah
1:1–2   7
1:2–3   5
1:6   153
1:7   165
1:11–12   109
3:17   161
3:18   163, 324
4:2   419
5:5   181

(Jeremiah)
5:11   424
5:23   402
6:1   324
6:22   163, 324
7   284
7:3   94
7:5   94
7:6   400
7:18   303
8:7   306
9:20   416
11:6   119
11:8   94
11:10   401, 424
11:16   238
11:17   424
12:5   113
13:18   351
15:4   94
15:7   137
16:5   399
17:25   318
17:25–27   156
17:26   397, 398
18:1–11   338
18:19   338
19:15   154
21:1   17, 344
21:12   195
22:1–2   17
22:3   400
22:4   318
22:16   195
22:18   165
22:24   69
23:5   202, 203,
    224, 355
23:8   163, 324
23:21   152
24:9   423
25:4–5   95
25:11–12   6, 20,
    38, 117, 368, 387
25:18   423
25:33   67
26   lxviii
26:6   187
26:9   24
26:19   384
28:9   167

(*Jeremiah*)

29:1	339
29:10	6, 20, 38, 117, 368, 387
29:22	423
29:25	344
29:27	187
29:29	344
30:4	426
30:10	141
30:23	411
31:8	201
31:12	258
31:12–13	435
31:23	170, 245
31:31–33	418
31:33	169
31:38–40	161
31:39	123
32:14	278, 337
32:27	417
32:30	57
32:38	169
32:42	201
33:10	24
33:12	24
33:14–17	359
33:15	202, 203, 224
33:15–17	355
33:17	356, 371
33:18	356
35:15	95
36	lxviii, 278, 420
36:1	381
36:2	278
36:4	278, 419
36:6	278, 419, 434
36:6–8	396
36:8	119
36:9	381, 420
36:10	119
36:14	278
36:17–18	419
36:23	278
36:27	419
36:29	20
36:32	419
37–41	lxviii

(*Jeremiah*)

37:2	7
37:3	344
37:7	62
38:7	383
39:1	434
39:2–7	433
39:3	383
39:10	343
39:13	383
40:1	164
41:1–3	388
41:4–8	xxviii
41:8	440
41:16	164
44:17	303
44:19	303
44:25	303
45:1	419
46:19	164
46:20	343
48:11	339
48:18	164
49:3	339
49:11	400
49:20	362
49:31	397
49:36	164
50:5	169
50:8	163
50:9–16	165
50:14	142
50:26	60
50:28	163
50:45	362
51:1	35
51:6	163
51:11	35
51:26	248
51:45	163
51:46	360
52:6–11	433
52:7	110
52:12	5, 182, 183, 388, 434
52:15–16	343
52:24	180, 344
52:31	5, 141

Ezekiel

1–3	305
1:1	109, 339
1:1–2	5
1:4	298
1:7	298, 320
1:16	298
1:22	298
1:27	298
1:28	54
2:9	278
3:1–3	278
3:9	402
3:11	339
3:15	339
3:17	419
4:1	208
5:1–3	112
5:2	137
5:10	137
5:12	137
5:13	330
6:8	137
7:6–7	343
8:1	5, 197
8:2	298
8:4	54
9:3	54
10:3	195
10:4	54
10:5	195
10:9	298
10:18	54
10:19	54
11:15–25	343
11:19	402
11:22–23	54
12:3–15	199
12:4	339
14:1	197
16:6	358
16:49	400
16:59	252
17:16–19	252
18:8–9	426
18:12	400
20:1	197
21:31	351
21:36	139
22:29	400
23:43	20

(*Ezekiel*)
24:1   5
24:5   337
24:15–24   199
30:9   141
33:7   419
33:11   95
33:33   343
34:1–14   33
34:5   124
34:23   68
36:17   303
36:24–27   188
36:24–31   99
37:5   201
37:9   164
37:15–22   424
37:24   68
37:24–28   168
38:11   154
39:25   411
39:28–29   79
40–42   151
40–48   lxx
40:1   5
40:2   325
40:3   183, 320
40:6–7   289
40:20   325
40:44   325
40:45   195
41:1   60
42:10   325
42:16–19   325
43:2   54
43:4–5   54
43:11   72
44:4   54
44:14–18   195
44:17–19   193
45:1   151, 289
47:15   325
48   289
48:9   151, 289
48:15   152
48:35   414

Hosea
1:1   91
1:9   156
2:10   258

(*Hosea*)
2:13   435
2:18   67
2:21   399
2:24   258
3:1   124
3:3   61
4   284
8:7   202
9:3   170
12:8   400
13:15   54

Joel
1:1   91
2:4   112
2:11   51
2:17   281
2:18   411
3:1–2   403
4:13   278
4:17   120, 414

Amos
1:2   120
2:15   113
4:6   61
4:9   61, 62
4:10   61
4:11   61, 66, 67
5:16   416
6:1   122
6:14   51
7   181
7–8   180
7:17   188
8:1–2   109
8:10   435
8:12   418
9:1   109
9:7   436
9:11   67

Jonah
1:1   91
1:4   404
3:1   91
3:2   119
3:4   66
3:7   328

Micah
1:1   91
1:11   418
4:1–2   439
4:1–4   53
4:3   439
4:4   141, 212, 213
4:8   167
4:10   167
4:13   259
6:8   399
7:3   34

Nahum
2:10   54
2:12   141
3:1   66
3:2   318

Habakkuk
2:3   343
2:19   417
3:3   67

Zephaniah
1:1   7, 91
1:7   171, 172
1:10   167
3:13   141
3:14   167

Haggai
1:1   xxiv, xxxii,
    xxxv, xxxvi, xliv,
    lx, lxvi, lxvii, 49,
    65, 66, 67, 72, 78,
    91, 108, 109, 125,
    163, 180, 242,
    243, 271, 289,
    340, 353, 381,
    382, 383, 388,
    399, 410, 423
1:1–4   59
1:1–10   xlvi
1:1–11   xlvi, 115,
    206
1:1–15   xlvi, 3–46
1:1–15a   364
1:2   lxv, 54, 59,
    64, 65, 81, 91, 93,
    206, 355, 385,

(*Haggai*)
387, 389, 411,
421
1:3   lxvii, 242
1:3–11   xxxv, lxvii
1:4   lxvii, 59, 123,
203, 405
1:5   58, 99
1:5–7   24
1:5–9   58, 59
1:5–10   lxv
1:6   xlvii, 61, 213,
232, 337, 421
1:6–9   82
1:6–11   61
1:7   58, 99
1:8   58, 63
1:8–9   xlvii
1:9   lxv, 24, 59,
61, 75, 206, 307,
356
1:9–11   232
1:9b–11   xlvii
1:10   423
1:11   258, 421
1:12   xxiv, lxvi,
lxvii, 71, 96, 165,
180, 243, 365,
366, 417, 422,
442
1:12–13   xxxviii
1:12–14   lxvii,
lxviii
1:12–15   xlvi
1:12–2:10   lxv
1:13   51, 62, 114,
119, 163, 183
1:13a   lxvi, lxvii
1:14   lxvi, lxvii,
49, 71, 180, 243,
385, 417, 442
1:15   xliv, xlvi,
lxvi, lxvii, 49, 63,
108, 123, 381,
388, 421
1:15a   49
1:15b   49
1:15b–2:23   46
2   xlviii
2:1   xliv, lxv, xlvi,
lxvi, lxvii, 7, 23,

(*Haggai*)
36, 37, 108, 242,
381, 388
2:1–2   lxvii, lxviii
2:1–9   xlvi
2:1–23   xlvi, 47–
84
2:2   lxvii, 9, 13,
17, 19, 34, 119,
180, 243, 417,
443
2:3   22, 157, 343,
344
2:3–5   lxviii
2:4   lxviii, 17, 19,
34, 180, 243, 387,
419, 430
2:5   19, 244, 330,
366, 402, 403,
424
2:6   331
2:6–7   365
2:6–9   232, 360
2:7   lxv, 28, 35,
157, 405, 441,
444
2:7–8   168, 175
2:7–9   167
2:9   lxv, 22, 99,
157, 423, 435
2:10   xliv, lxvi,
lxvii, lxviii, 7, 23,
36, 98, 103, 108,
123, 125, 193,
194, 242, 278,
379, 420
2:10–14   xxxix,
45, 338
2:10–18   xliv
2:10–19   xlvi, lxvi,
41, 190, 196, 351,
443
2:10–20   90
2:11   200
2:11–14a   lxviii
2:12   385, 441
2:12–14   393
2:12–23   lxv
2:13a   lxvi
2:14   lxv, 19, 34
2:14a   lxvi

(*Haggai*)
2:15   22, 23, 24,
100, 356, 420,
424
2:15–17   232
2:15–18   24
2:15–19   27, 36,
193
2:16   lxv, 25, 26,
31
2:16a   lxv
2:17   lxv
2:18   xliv, lxviii,
22, 23, 24, 89,
100, 108, 123,
213, 251, 296,
420, 421, 424
2:18–19   xlviii
2:19   lxv, 25, 32,
33, 134, 171, 206,
212, 213, 226,
238, 256, 284,
423
2:20   xliv, xlvi,
lxvi, lxvii, 89, 98,
108, 125, 171,
242, 379, 388,
420
2:20–21a   lxviii
2:20–23   xxxvi,
xxxix, xlvi, lxv,
15, 17, 103
2:21   lxv, 13, 243,
331
2:21–23   39, 202,
372
2:22   318
2:22–23   360, 392
2:23   9, 169, 203,
210, 224, 232,
243, 417, 440

Zechariah
1   322, 332
1:1   xliv, xlvi,
lviii, 6, 63, 108,
109, 125, 172,
217, 242, 281,
355, 366, 376,
381, 382, 388,
396, 398, 433

(*Zechariah*)

1:1–4   164
1:1–6   xl, xlviii, l,
lviii, 76, 89–104,
132, 145, 175,
242, 265, 374,
381, 423
1:2   403, 408
1:2–6   406
1:3   122, 123, 309,
355, 385
1:3–6   405
1:4   117, 119, 355,
402, 403, 420
1:4–6   395, 396,
425
1:5   430
1:6   xlix, 19, 52,
131, 396, 420,
424, 430
1:7   xliv, lviii, 89,
90, 91, 98, 168,
172, 177, 217,
355, 366, 379,
381, 382, 388,
390, 398, 433
1:7–17   107–134
1:7–6:15   xlviii, l,
lviii, lix, 96, 98,
100, 104, 125,
381
1:8   67, 102, 136,
152, 183, 229,
317, 326, 332
1:8–11   317
1:8–13   191
1:9   lvii, 240, 322,
332, 333
1:10   323, 327,
403
1:10–11   332
1:11   183, 274,
323, 324
1:12   lix, 6, 20,
23, 138, 183, 368,
387, 389, 391
1:13   152, 399
1:14   32, 93, 94,
223, 355, 396,
403, 411
1:14b   410

(*Zechariah*)

1:14–15   136
1:14–17   176, 178,
410, 412, 413,
414, 429
1:15   92, 403, 411
1:16   lxvi, 19, 95,
96, 145, 150, 187,
309, 410, 411,
412, 413
1:17   lix, 70, 93,
145, 171, 186,
187, 355, 411,
425
2:1   109, 149, 179,
277, 317, 350
2:1–4   xxx, 53,
135–49, 166, 174
2:2   xlix, 163,
173, 240, 404
2:2–4   408
2:2–5   415
2:3   179, 350
2:4   xlix, 121,
163, 166, 173,
174, 187, 204,
404
2:5   109, 135, 179,
317
2:5–9   242, 288
2:6   214, 289
2:8   9, 33, 164,
173, 288, 289,
421
2:8–9   119, 120,
178, 396
2:8b–9   132, 158,
288
2:9   54, 180
2:10   127, 136,
307, 322, 324
2:10–11   150, 187
2:10–17   lvii, 120,
132, 134, 150,
158, 161–78, 180,
222, 242, 265,
418, 430
2:11   413
2:12   lxvi, 54, 93,
180, 355, 402,
414

(*Zechariah*)

2:12–13   35
2:13   228, 251,
364, 365, 403,
417
2:14   xlix, 19, 33,
228, 309, 413,
417
2:14–15   429
2:14–17   lxv
2:15   212, 251,
315, 364, 365,
403, 413, 417
2:15–16   53, 134,
442
2:16   70, 124, 150,
186, 188, 211,
314, 414
3   xl, 7, 17, 74,
79, 120, 132, 172,
175, 177, 201,
229, 246, 254,
259, 260, 266,
267, 268, 275,
290, 323, 345,
351, 369, 371,
380, 422
3:1   xxxvii, lv, 17,
36, 39, 93, 109,
110, 111, 115,
119, 138, 151,
250, 260, 266,
278, 323, 384
3:1–7   liv, lv, 151
3:1–10   16, 50,
178–227, 239,
276, 351, 385
3:2   70, 124, 171,
408
3:4   297, 308
3:5   351, 354
3:6   400
3:7   17, 93, 266,
281, 292, 355,
359
3:8   17, 69, 232,
239, 352, 355,
371, 417, 418,
437
3:8–10   lvii, 49,
59, 69, 132, 177,

(*Zechariah*)
242, 265, 266,
267, 268, 270,
366, 368
3:8–11   250
3:9   59, 69, 128,
185, 205, 234,
236, 253, 254,
266, 269, 284,
297, 320, 348,
350, 417
3:10   284, 285,
417
3:10–12   270
4   xl, 9, 67, 125,
175, 177, 191,
206, 209, 215,
216, 222, 224,
227, 277, 290,
318, 353
4:1   109, 135, 317,
328, 329
4:1–14   227–277
4:2   lxvi, 109,
209, 238, 295,
317
4:2–3   350
4:4   322, 333
4:5   307
4:6   9, 52, 197,
204, 403
4:6b   225, 330
4:6b–7   367
4:6b–9   166
4:6b–10   59, 223,
356
4:6b–10a   xxxix,
lvii, 6, 13, 15, 39,
49, 69, 132, 177,
204, 216, 222,
224, 337, 366,
368
4:7   9, 59, 66,
123, 124, 125,
194, 205, 206,
221, 223, 224,
309, 319, 320,
348, 414
4:7–8   100
4:7–10   22, 64, 81
4:8   337, 355, 366

(*Zechariah*)
4:8–10a   365
4:9   lxvi, 9, 167,
365, 421
4:10   9, 59, 128,
205, 224, 304,
348
4:10a   223
4:10b   185, 223
4:12   256, 362
5:1   36, 109, 135,
195, 228, 232,
281, 317
5:1–2   220
5:1–4   232, 277–
293
5:2   195, 295, 361,
400
5:2b   290
5:2–3   359
5:3   288, 298, 333
5:3–4   289
5:4   132, 158, 288
5:5   109, 135, 152,
297, 317
5:5–11   293–316
5:6   152, 320, 329,
333
5:7   350
5:9   152, 317, 350
5:11   329
6   111, 227, 267,
321, 322, 324
6:1   67, 109, 110,
114, 135, 136,
152, 228, 277,
350
6:1–8   191, 316–
36
6:2   111
6:2–3   112, 326
6:3   321
6:4   240, 333
6:5   136, 152, 164,
168, 175, 259,
261, 274, 290,
324, 328, 350
6:6   111, 152, 163,
418
6:6–7   112
6:7   114, 152, 324

(*Zechariah*)
6:8   53, 66, 113,
125, 152, 163,
244, 403
6:9   91, 242, 250
6:9–15   xli, lvii,
15, 23, 50, 77,
125, 132, 144,
147, 172, 177,
178, 216, 222,
226, 244, 250,
265, 266, 270,
336–75, 436
6:10   212, 392,
417, 427
6:11   lxvi, 17, 54,
180, 192
6:11–13   16
6:11–14   17
6:12   23, 93, 202,
203, 224, 354,
421
6:12–13   232, 235,
271, 372
6:12–15   267
6:13   67, 421, 423,
427, 435
6:14   lxvi, 203,
250, 347, 392
6:15   45, 125, 167,
212, 421, 442
7   442
7–8   xli, lix, lx,
lxi, 6, 39, 50, 52,
265, 419, 423
7:1   xliv, xlvi, lx,
6, 20, 36, 55, 89,
91, 93, 95, 98,
100, 102, 108,
109, 125, 172,
177, 194, 201,
242, 268, 279,
290, 355, 356,
398, 410, 420,
421, 426, 428,
433
7:1–6   lxi, 53,
147, 379–94, 434,
436, 444
7:1–7   443
7:1–8:23   lviii

(*Zechariah*)
7:2   434, 438, 439,
  440
7:3   xli, 55, 77,
  117, 286, 368,
  402, 434
7:4   xlv, 91, 242,
  410, 433
7:4–6   410
7:5   lix, 6, 20, 23,
  117, 419, 422,
  434
7:5–7   430
7:7   xli, lix, lxi,
  52, 94, 100, 117,
  119, 154, 156,
  223, 402, 420,
  434
7:7–13   411
7:7–14   lxi, 93,
  395–408
7:8   91, 242, 410,
  433
7:8–9   428
7:9   93, 355, 413,
  426, 427, 433,
  435, 440
7:9–10   426, 429,
  431
7:11–12   425
7:12   xli, 52, 92,
  94, 100, 406
7:12b–14   lxi
8   122, 337, 366,
  398
8:1   xlv, 91, 242,
  250, 329, 355,
  381, 398, 433
8:1–17   lxi, 408–
  32, 435, 436
8:2   lix, 93, 120,
  124, 433
8:2–3   440
8:2–23   440
8:3   lxi, 19, 55,
  93, 120, 122, 168,
  170, 171, 245,
  433, 435, 439
8:4   93
8:4–5   435
8:6   34, 93

(*Zechariah*)
8:6–15   440
8:8   lx, 442
8:9   22, 23, 50,
  60, 93, 381, 385,
  396, 406
8:9–10   398
8:9–12   lx, 90
8:9–13   41
8:10   33, 212, 289,
  417, 435
8:11   34
8:12   34, 212, 213,
  226, 284, 423,
  435
8:13   50, 52, 65,
  434
8:14   xlix, 92, 93
8:15   xlix, 124,
  434, 437
8:16   399, 435
8:16–17   406, 407
8:17   212, 401
8:18   91, 242, 250,
  329, 381, 396,
  398, 410
8:18–23   lxi, 57,
  68, 428, 429,
  432–45
8:19   93, 379, 386,
  388, 392, 413,
  421, 423
8:19–23   410, 418,
  430
8:20   93, 168, 197,
  386
8:21–22   384
8:22   168
8:22–23   lx, 50,
  53, 175, 212, 213,
  331
8:23   xli, 56, 93,
  364, 413, 417,
  442
9   lxii, 413
9–14   6
9:9   355
9:10–14   67
10–14   lxii
11:4   440
11:9–10   372

(*Zechariah*)
13:2   67
13:7   124
14:4   67

Malachi
1:1   7, 35
1:4   117, 302, 440
2:3   187
2:6   399, 413
2:7   55
3:2   187
3:7   93, 99
3:10   256
3:11   187
3:14   195
3:15   302
3:16   212
3:19   302

Psalms
5:6–8   209
6:4   116
11:4   209
17:8   166
18:3   135
18:11   279, 305,
  306
19   319
19:7   319
19:10   426
21:4   349
21:6   358
21:9   186
22:29   360
24:3   245
24:8–10   54
25:10   399
26:8   54, 171
33:6   51
33:11   362
34:16   209
38:21   184
40:8   278
40:11   399
40:12   399
45:4   358
47:3   323
47:8   323
48:2–3   245, 414
52   239

(*Psalms*)

52:10	234
55:4	184
59:14	360
66:7	209
68:6	172
71:13	184
71:19	252
72	372
74:3	248
74:6	20, 210
74:10	116
75:5–6	136
75:7	319
77:9–10	399
78:43	199
78:54	170
78:55	150
78:59–61	187
78:67–68	187
78:68	124
78:70	68, 124
78:70–71	70
80:5	116
82:2	116
82:8	169
84:3	167
89:13–14	186
89:18	136
89:21	258
89:25	399
89:40	351
90:13	116
92	239
92:13–14	234
94:3	116
96:6	358
97:5	259
98:3	399
98:4	167
98:8	167
102:15–16	54
103:4	399
103:20	51
104:1	358
104:3	306
104:17	306
105:2	360
105:11	150
105:27	199
106:21	252

(*Psalms*)

106:41	360
109:6	184, 186
110:4–5	360
118:19	427
118:22	248
122:5	197
125:1–2	120
126:6	20, 343
132:18	351
135:9	199
141:6	257
145:5	358
148:8	51
148:14	136

Job

1–2	183
1:6	323
1:6–12	191
1:16	64
1:17	64
1:18	64
2:1	323
2:1–7	191
2:2	115
2:10	417
5:9	252
11:3	417
11:19	141
15:23	257
16:9	184
19:24	304
24:24	255
29:14	192
30:21	184
30:22	284
31:36	350
36:29	248
37:18	417
38:5	123
38:6	248
38:18	417
39:7	248
39:13–18	113
40:10	358
40:30	417
42:7	164

Proverbs

5:16	124
6:30	252
11:12	252
16:32	330
17:8	249
19:21	362
22:21	426
29:11	330

Ruth

2:2	255
2:5–6	154
2:12	441
3:7	60
3:8	141
3:9	441
3:11	427
4:1	427
4:10	427
4:11	427

Canticles

3:11	351
7:2	57
7:3	60

Ecclesiastes

4:1	228
4:7	228
4:15	196
9:4	245
12:6	234

Lamentations

2:6	187
2:11–12	416
2:19	416
2:20	187
2:21	416
3:38	417
3:53	142
4:13–14	416

Esther

1:22	440
2:6	339
3:12	440
8:9	440
9:4	181

Daniel
5:4   348
7–8   136
8:16   110
9   97
9:2   118
9:21   110
10:6   298
10:13   110
11:7   356
11:8   54
11:10   20, 343
11:13   20
11:21   358
12:1   110

Ezra
1:1   35, 147
1:1–4   xxix
1:2–4   102
1:4–6   347, 369
1:5   35
1:5–11   54
1:7   231
1:7–8   11
1:8   11, 14
1:8–11   xxx
1:11   11
2:1–58   41
2:2   11
2:21–35   382
2:36   16, 341
2:59   xxviii
2:60   341
2:63   15
2:68–69   347
2:69   369
3–5   12
3:2   16
3:2–3   24
3:2–6   29
3:3   12, 15, 309
3:6–11   64
3:7   28
3:8   16
3:10   271
3:10–12   249
3:12   232
3:12–13   49
3:15   xxviii
4:1   387

(*Ezra*)
4:4   51
4:7–10   102
4:11–22   102
4:12–16   xxxvii
4:17   xxxii
4:23   102
5–6   44
5:1   xxxii, xxxv,
    xxxviii, 8, 96, 103
5:2   16
5:11   250, 251,
    271
5:13–16   231
5:14   11, 14
5:15   xxxv
5:15–16   11
5:16   12
6:1–5   xxix
6:4   28
6:7   15
6:8   xxxvii, 40
6:10   xxxvii
6:14   xxxv, xxxvii,
    xxxviii, xliii, 8,
    96, 103, 367
6:14–16   388
6:15   98, 118
7–10   370
7:1–6   345
7:5   180
7:7   6
7:14   13
8:33   182
9   97
9:14   417
10   301
10:3   362
10:18   301
10:18–22   341

Nehemiah
2:1   6
2:10   341, 342
2:19   341
3:1   427
3:1–22   382
3:3   427
3:7   361
4:16   110
4:22   110

(*Nehemiah*)
5:14   14
5:15   13, 15
6:6   157
7:7   11, 16
7:25–38   382
7:39   16, 341
7:65   341
8:1   427
8:3   119
8:8   119
8:15   110
9   97
9:10   51
9:29   402
9:30   402
10:30   283
10:38   258
11   397
11:10   341
11:25–26   397
11:25–35   382
11:27   398
11:30   398
11:31–36   397
12:1   11
12:6–7   341
12:19   341
12:21   341
12:26   13, 14
12:28–29   382
13:23–27   301
13:24   440

1 Chronicles
2:47   383
3   370
3:17–19   xxxii, 69
3:18   11
3:19   12, 370
5:26   35
5:40–41   16, 187
6:14–15   345
6:19   10
7:1   245
9:10   341
11:7   356
11:10–41   340
16:18   150
16:27   358
18:10   348

(*1 Chronicles*)
20:2   351
20:6   236
21:1   183, 184
22:1–6   208
26:14–16   325
27:15   340
27:28   27
29:7   300
29:12   360
29:25   358

2 Chronicles
2:6   210
4:7   230
4:16   320

(*2 Chronicles*)
4:20   230
6:6   124
6:34   124
6:38   124
7:21   245
8:3   124
8:16   251, 271
11:13   323
13:11   230
15:9   401
16:9   254
17:9   78
19:8–11   78
21:16   35
22:2–3   303

(*2 Chronicles*)
23:11   351
24:7   303
24:12   139
25:8   20
30:7   94
30:25   401
31:2–20   258
31:3   258
32:6   415, 427
32:16   68
32:24   199
34:3b–7   398
36:21   118
36:22   35
36:22–23   xxix

NEW TESTAMENT

Matthew
1:12   10

Luke
3:27   10

Revelation
6:2–8   321
21:13   325

APOCRYPHA AND PSEUDEPIGRAPHA

1 Esdras
5:5–6   16
6:4   23

1 Maccabees
1:21   233
1:54   233
4:38   233

Testament of Judah
21:2   362

Testament of Levi
8:8–9   259

Qumranic Literature
1 Q M
14:10   187

1 Q Sa
2:11–14   362

RABBINIC LITERATURE

Mishna Sheqalim
5.1   364

Mishna Ta'anit
1–3   434

Mishna Yoma
3.10–11   364

T.B. Berakhot
51a   187

T.B. Horayoth
12a   193

T.B. Yoma
52b   193